# LOGY

# An Introduction

## Second Edition

## and Others

**Holt, Rinehart and Winston**
New York   Chicago   San Francisco
Dallas   Montreal   Toronto

Acquiring Editor   Patrick Powers
Developmental Editor   Rosalind Sackoff
Managing Editor   Jeanette Ninas Johnson
Senior Project Editor   Ruth Stark
Art Director   Robert Kopelman
Cover   Robert Barancik
Designer   Ron Farber
Photo Researcher   Linda Gutiérrez
Production Manager   Annette Mayeski

Library of Congress Cataloging in Publication Data

Main entry under title:

Sociology: an introduction.

  Includes bibliographical references and index.
  1. Sociology.  I.  McGee, Reece Jerome.
HM51.S66337 1980        301        79−17812
ISBN O−03−043891−8

CREDITS (continued on p. 581)
We wish to thank the following artists, photographers, and
publishers for permission to reproduce their work:

p. 2, Charles Gatewood

Chapter 1
p. 7, Napoleon Chagnon; p. 9 (left), Charles Harbutt,
Magnum; p. 9 (right), Hiroji Kubota, Magnum; p. 16, The
Bettmann Archive.

# Preface

As anyone knows who has had to face the choice of what introductory sociology text to adopt for his or her own classes, there are a great variety of books on the market. Some texts that might be suitable for presenting sociology as a scientific discipline may not do at all for emphasizing its significance in the liberal arts. Some texts are deliberately designed to be used in conjunction with assigned readings in the professional journals or popular literature; others attempt to integrate materials from these sources within their pages. Some are carefully "written down" for students with limited academic backgrounds or with reading problems; other choose to avoid the inevitable trivialization of abstract concepts and technical materials that necessarily accompanies that entirely legitimate goal.

I feel it necessary to inform the potential user of the nature and purpose of this work. As an aid in the selection process, the paragraphs immediately below describe my perceptions of this text and attempt to estimate the degree to which my intentions in constructing the book have been accomplished. Further discussion describes the ancilliary works developed to accompany the book and various ways of using the book itself.

## THE NATURE AND PURPOSE OF THIS TEXT

Every year almost one million students take at least one semester of introductory sociology. Many of these "college kids" are over thirty years of age, a significant fraction are nonwhite, and a much larger proportion than ever before are female. This will probably be the only course in sociology most of them will ever take. The institutions in which they are exposed to sociology for the first time are as various as the students: universities and four-year colleges; community colleges and technical-vocational schools, medical schools and military extension courses. The authors of this work and I have attempted to produce a text with the maximum possible utility for this immensely diverse audience. We have tried to survey the field of sociology for people who are unlikely ever to have another concentrated exposure to it. Guiding us in our work have been two over-arching objectives: (1) to adequately and accurately depict what sociologists have learned about human social behavior and how they went about learning it, and (2) to present this information in such ways that the reader may find it relevant and useful in his or her own life, purposes, goals, and understanding of the world. The book may thus be summarily described as "comprehensive, integrated, and eclectic."

## Comprehensiveness

I call the book "comprehensive," and we think it is. We have tried to present all of the major analytic concepts of the field of general sociology in their appropriate substantive and theoretical contexts and in such ways that students may recognize their utility in everyday understanding. Most of the research and illustrative material is drawn from American life and society because most of the readers will be American, but we have tried to integrate sufficient cross-cultural material to highlight, contrast, and emphasize that other lifeways are also possible, workable, and morally acceptable. Each chapter is written by an author who is not only an academic expert on its subject matter, but who also is or has had extensive experience as an undergraduate instructor in that subject matter. I think, then, that few users will find fault with the intellectual quality and coverage of the book. (In this respect, in fact, I proudly believe that this text is the best of its kind on the market.) We have not, of course, covered *everything*, and no introductory book can. While a number of decision rules operated in the selection of subject matter, the overriding one was, "Is this topic fundamental to an introduction to sociology for general education?" Many texts now on the market, for example, have separate chapters on sex roles and/or sexuality. My decision in this instance was that while these topics are inarguably significant in introductory sociology, they are not the essence of the subject, and so we treat them in context throughout the work rather than devoting separate chapter status to them. (The teacher interested in sex roles will find considerable coverage of that topic in appropriate locations in several chapters.) But if comprehensiveness is important to you, I invite you to compare this work with others. I extend the invitation with confidence.

## Integration

Judging from my own experience and from text evaluations provided by generations of introductory students, lack of integration is a very common failing in introductory texts, and so the authors and I have worked very hard to insure that this work will not have that problem. There seem to be two different categories of phenomena included under this general label: conceptual integration and theoretical integration. Surprisingly enough, my own analyses of various books over the years shows faults in one to be as common as those in the other. Basic terms, such as status, role, socialization, and social control are frequently defined one way at some point in a work and then used in other ways, either before or after the formal definition. Similarly, while having a formal chapter or chapter segment devoted to classical and contemporary theory is common in introductory texts, few of them make any serious attempt at consistent theoretical integration. Research materials are presented as "subject matter" in topically appropriate places with little or no explanation for the student of their theoretical grounding. I believe that you will not find these problems in this work.

## Eclectic Quality

Because the book is intended for a very general audience, we have tried to present and utilize the different positions or schools of thought constituting what have come to be called the "conflict" and "consensus" categories of sociological theory accurately and consistently. We make no special brief for any one of them but have instead attempted to *utilize* them analytically in the intellectual areas where they may be most fruitful. For example, the chapters on social differentiation and minorities are flavored, although not overwhelmed by, the conflict perspective, whereas the institutional chapters are basically, although not exclusively, functional in orientation. And since the student reader will have been introduced to the perspectives from the beginning and is informed what is going on in any particular analysis, we think that the meaning and epistemological utility of this approach will be apparent.

## HOW THE BOOK WAS DEVELOPED

The first edition of this text, published in 1977, was developed from a content analysis of the major texts of the preceding decade on the rationale that the popularity of those works indicated what sociology teachers wanted to find in textbooks. The authors for that work were chosen for their subject specialties and for being "teachers with a rage to teach." At the time the first edition was published, I was pleased with the quality I felt we had been able to attain but under no illusion that improvement was not possible. On the basis of user review and reaction, we have reorganized some of the book, done extensive rewriting in a number of chapters, and produced several entirely new chapters by authors new to the book. And all relevant statistics have, of course, been brought up to the latest possible date.

The major changes we have made for this edition can be summarized as follows: integration of the introductory and theory chapters; removal of the methods chapter to the end of the book where those who do not wish to address this topic may skip it without logical gap in reading assignments; collapse of the three chapters on social organization into two under new authorship; major or complete reworking of the chapters on theory, minorities, urbanism, the family, education, politics, and collective behavior. All of the remaining chapters have been reworked, some of them strenuously. In every chapter we have tried to pay serious attention to the problem of reading level, but I have been unwilling to sacrifice sociological accuracy for simplicity. Inevitably then, one or two of the more technical or abstract chapters such as demography or social organization may prove somewhat more difficult than others.

## THE ANCILLARY MATERIALS

Your attention should be called to the three ancillary publications designed to accompany the text, even if you do not normally use such things in your teaching. They are the *Instructor's Guide*, the *Student Study Guide*, and the *Test Bank*, all prepared by Professor Joseph Rogers of New Mexico State University at Las Cruces. If you are an experienced evaluator of introductory texts, you may have a skepticism about ancilliary materials, test banks in particular. I think you will be pleased by what you see here; they are among the very best available. Professor Rogers is a brilliant and dedicated undergraduate instructor and his expertise is reflected in these materials. Suggestions for alternative uses are contained in each. Needless to say, I have carefully scanned each one of them and indeed, use them myself.

## THE ORGANIZATION OF THE BOOK AND ALTERNATIVE USES FOR IT

The book is constructed around five parts and the chapters are written to be read in sequence. We are entirely aware, however, that the organization preferred by an instructor will depend upon the school calendar, student abilities, the interests of the instructor and so forth. Consequently, I want to suggest two possible ways to use *Sociology: An Introduction*.

The first is consecutive assignment of chapters either doubling up or omitting some so as to fit reading assignments to the length of the term. Chapters are mostly 30 to 40 pages in length and not overly difficult, so in most instances the assignment of two chapters for a week's work should not be onerous for students. The most difficult chapters for the typical student will probably be seven on social differentiation, nine and ten on cities and population, and nineteen on methods. These might best be assigned alone. Instructors wanting to devote less attention to social institutions might well double-up on some of those assignments, or decide to drop one or more on the valid assumption that the basic concepts and understandings undergird all of them. If this is an option, two possibilities present themselves: dropping family and religion because education, economics, and politics are less frequently treated elsewhere in the text, or dropping one or more of the latter three because family and religion touch so closely upon the lives of most students.

A second organizational strategy is to teach the chapters on methods, deviance, social interaction, and social organization out of sequence. Although the logic of ordering in the text is from micro to macro analyses, these chapters can be treated at several different points in a course, and other good texts sequence them differently. In my opinion, one place to take up sociological methodology would be after Chapter 2, and deviance could be assigned after either Chapter 4 or 6. A word of warning is in order about such reordering, however. Because we tried very hard to make the book conceptually integrated, you will find that concepts once defined—always upon the first occasion of their technical usage—are used in a consistent manner, and chapters later in the book presume previous definition. Thus terms such as role and status are used in the deviance chapter without specific definition because they have been defined in Chapters 5 and 6. The instructor can work around this easily. Each chapter has glossary terms in bold-face type within the text with the definition in a box on the upper righthand corner of the double-page spread on which the term is first used. Every term in the running glossary is also printed in bold face in the index for easy reference by the student. If you choose to assign a chapter out of order, it is a simple matter to identify the key concepts that have not been defined in the materials your students have already read, and define them for the class when making the assignment.

One final word about chapter ordering. Collective Behavior and Social Movements are frequently regarded as unessential for introductory sociology, and Social Change can also be used as a "floating" chapter, i.e., subject to reordering. The Social Change chapter also serves as a summary of the dominating themes of modern life treated throughout the text. Thus, there is considerable flexibility possible in chapter ordering. It would probably be unwise, however, to reorder the various parts of the book. The work *is* developmental and the parts presume mastery of previous material. I am doubtful that Part IV, for instance, could be successfully assigned before Parts II or III, and the presumption that students have read Part I informs the rest of the entire work.

## Acknowledgements

Primary acknowledgement for assistance in the development of this work must go, of course, to the dedicated professionals who authored it. There is little monetary reward and less academic glory from this kind of authorship; it must—and obviously was—a labor of love and dedication to the teaching craft. I am also deeply grateful to Rosalind Sackoff of Holt, Rinehart and Winston for hard and scrupulous work in the development and preparation of the manuscript. A good editor is a hard taskmaster, a devoted friend, and of value beyond imagining to an author. Roz qualifies.

I also wish to acknowledge the contribution to this edition of the nine sociologists who wrote for the first edition but who are not formally represented here. Some portion of the work of each remains and their contribution needs to be recognized:

J. Kenneth Benson, University of Missouri, Columbia
   (Chapters 5 and 7 of the first edition)

Helen Rose Fuchs Ebaugh, University of Houston
   (Chapter 6 of the first edition)

Kathleen V. Friedman, University of North Carolina, Chapel Hill
   (Chapter 15 of the first edition)

R. Kelly Hancock, Portland State University
   (Chapter 18 of the first edition)

Patrick S. Mazzeo, Central Oregon Community College
   (Chapter 9 of the first edition with David T. Wellman)

Sharon McPherron, St. Louis Community College at Florissant Valley
   (Chapter 10 of the first edition)

Joseph E. Ribal, El Camino College
   (Chapter 12 of the first edition)

Michael N. Ryan, Niagara County Community College
   (Chapter 13 of the first edition)

David T. Wellman, University of Oregon
   (Chapter 9 of the first ediction, with Patrick S. Mazzeo)

My thanks additionally go to the sociologists named below who reviewed either or both the first edition text and the second edition manuscript. I also extend thanks to users of the first edition who took time to write me or discuss the book with Holt representatives. Without this kind of critical feedback from the profession, informed revision is impossible.

DAVID ARNOLD—SONOMA STATE UNIVERSITY, ROHNERT, CALIFORNIA
PAUL B. BREZINA—COUNTY COLLEGE OF MORRIS, P.O. DOVER, NEW JERSEY
HOWARD DAUDISTEL—THE UNIVERSITY OF TEXAS AT EL PASO, EL PASO, TEXAS

WILLIAM GARRETT—ST. MICHAEL'S COLLEGE, WINOOSKI, VERMONT

BENJAMIN HARRISON—VALDOSTA STATE COLLEGE, VALDOSTA, GEORGIA

DON LANDON—SOUTHWEST MISSOURI STATE UNIVERSITY, SPRINGFIELD, MISSOURI

HUGH LENA—PROVIDENCE COLLEGE, RHODE ISLAND

GILBERT MERKX—UNIVERSITY OF NEW MEXICO, ALBUQUERQUE, NEW MEXICO

BORIS MIKOLJI—ROCHESTER INSTITUTE OF TECHNOLOGY, ROCHESTER, NEW YORK

VIRGINIA McKEEFERY—REYNOLDS—SOUTHERN ILLINOIS UNIVERSITY AT CARBONDALE, ILLINOIS

EDGAR G. NESMAN—UNIVERSITY OF SOUTH FLORIDA, TAMPA, FLORIDA

JOSEPH ROGERS—NEW MEXICO STATE UNIVERSITY, LAS CRUCES, NEW MEXICO

PAUL TSCHETTER—EAST CAROLINA UNIVERSITY, GREENVILLE, NORTH CAROLINA

FREDERICH WENZ—UNIVERSITY OF SOUTH CAROLINA AT SPARTANSBURG, SOUTH CAROLINA

THOMAS YACOVONE—LOS ANGELES VALLEY COLLEGE, VAN NUYS, CALIFORNIA

MARY YAGER—WICHITA STATE UNIVERSITY, WICHITA, KANSAS

Finally, my sincere thanks to the authors and organizations who gave permission for the reproduction of copyrighted material. The credit lines for these are placed in the credits section starting on the copyright page and continued on p. 581.

REECE McGEE
Purdue University
West Lafayette, Indiana
January 1980

# Contents: Overview

# Contents

# ONE
## The Field of Sociology

# TWO

# The Organizing Concepts of Sociological Analysis

# THREE

## Elements
## of Social
## Structure

xvii

# FOUR

## Social Institutions

# SOCIOLOGY
## An Introduction

CONTRIBUTING AUTHORS

SOCIO

REECE McGEE

PURDUE UNIVERSITY

# FIVE
## Collective Behavior and Social Change

# ONE
## The Field of Sociology

This book is divided into five major parts with a final chapter on social research methods. This first part consists of two chapters about the field of sociology itself, what it is and why it has the particular nature it does. Later parts explore its content or subject matter and the conclusions sociologists have reached about that content.

Chapter 1 is about the *nature* of sociology and the types of thought it utilizes: what kind of a discipline it is in a general sense, the underlying assumptions and rationale of sociological thinking and how it differs from its great bugaboo, common sense. We end the chapter with a discussion of the origins of the field in order to see the historical roots of the great questions that undergird it, direct its activity, and determine its character.

Chapter 2, called "Asking Sociological Questions," carries on the final discussion in Chapter 1, picking up the great questions with which sociology originated and exploring the ways in which those questions, and various attempts to answer them, were elaborated during the last century and the present one. It is, in a sense, an intellectual roadmap tracing sociology's journey of growth from its origins to its present-day condition and concerns. Here we explore the three classical views of social reality developed during the nineteenth century and how we use them in this, the last quarter of the twentieth century. The logic of this form of presentation is essentially developmental or historical: in order to understand where we are today and why we are there, it is necessary to know where we came from and by what routes. Only then can we usefully explore the terrain where we now find ourselves.

# Chapter 1
# Introduction to Sociological Thinking

## A LETTER TO THE STUDENT

Welcome to your first course in sociology. We believe you will find it an enjoyable and useful experience. The other authors of this book and I have done everything we can to be sure you will. Give it a chance, and you will find that our field — which fascinates us — provides powerful intellectual tools with which to understand yourself and the world of which we are all a part.

If you are like most students I've taught, before you take a particular course or read a particular textbook, you want to have some idea of its utility for you, some belief that it will do you some good in some way. Looking at this book and the course it accompanies, you might well ask: What is the value of sociology to me? What can it do for me, especially if I am taking only this one course and perhaps will read only this one book? Why should I bother with it and why, if it is required by my college or university, should I be forced to spend time on it?

These are perfectly reasonable questions, and they can be answered in several ways. The answer I like best is that a general understanding of sociological principles can help us better understand and control our own lives. To see why this is so, however, you may have to take on faith for a while the idea that social phenomena are "real" and do influence each of us a great deal. Because our society is so strongly individualistic this may at first be a little difficult to grasp, or even seem misguided. In many ways we are all brought up to believe that questions about human behavior are best answered by examining the characteristics of individuals. Our culture (see Chapter 3) is strongly psychologistic; it looks to individuals for explanations of behavior. For example, how do you explain murder? Study murderers, obviously.

But much human behavior *cannot* be adequately explained by reference to the individual characteristics of particular social actors. We may understand why Byron Witsqueak Cadwallader committed suicide by examining the poor fellow's biography and psychology. (He was the runt of his family, was improperly toilet trained, had athlete's foot and dandruff; his children hated him, his wife ran off with an itinerant balloonist, and the day he killed himself, his own dog had bitten him.) But facts like these cannot explain variations in suicide rates among different cities or neighborhoods, or among different racial, ethnic, religious, and occupational groups (psychiatrists take their own lives much more frequently than chiropodists). And they cannot explain such matters as the influence of the calendar, economic conditions, or *social mobility* on suicide. (More people kill themselves on holidays than on workdays, there are more suicides in a booming economy than in normal economic periods, and suicide is more frequent among those who have newly "made it" than among the perpetually poor.) Further, it is simply impossible to explain or interpret the characteristics and behavior of human *groups* on an individualistic or psychologistic basis. (Why do all modern armies organize their combat forces into units of approximately the same sizes?) So one reason for studying sociology is simply that it attempts to organize our understandings of a whole world of phenomena that have great impact on us, but with which most of us are unfamiliar except through personal experience.

And the reason that such a study is useful is that until we understand some aspect of our world, (such as how germs transmit disease), we are at the mercy of it. Ignorance usually is not bliss, and learning something about social behavior and its impact upon our individual selves gives us the opportunity to react with or against it. Thus sociology offers the possibility of greater control over our own lives. Knowledge in this sense contributes to personal freedom.

## THE PURPOSE OF THIS BOOK

The underlying purpose of this book might be expressed as "How to live more effectively in a complex, highly organized, bureaucratized, mass society." Unless you know something about that society and how it works, you will be as much at the mercy of your ignorance as a person who has no knowledge of germs. (If you are of European extraction, your ancestors once believed they could avoid the plague by saying the rosary and breathing through a nosegay of fresh flowers—and the plague killed them by the millions.) The more you understand the social system of which you are a part, the more control you will be able to exert over those features of it that affect you. In each of the chapters that follow, we will examine an important aspect of how human social systems work, how to understand them, and how individuals behave in them. This is knowledge that, while abstract and analytical, is highly useful in your own life, when properly applied.

The object of the book is to tell you some things about the ways in which the social world works. You may then deal with it more effectively. You need not always be at the mercy of bureaucracy or racism or a political machine any more than you need be at the mercy of germs. But in order to deal with them effectively and *freely*, you must know what they are and how they function. The biblical injunction "You shall know the truth, and the truth shall make you free" (John 8:32) is no less true in modern context than it was when it was written. Only by understanding society and how it operates can we free ourselves from bondage *to* society. That is a goal worth striving for.

But this book and the course in which it is used should not be looked to for final answers about the truth of things. Their purpose is to give you a perspective, a way of looking at and understanding the complexities, ambiguities, inconsistencies, and paradoxes of the world around you, and to offer you ways of dealing with it and living in it more successfully than you otherwise might. If, before you read the book, you think that sociology is a lot of rubbish, remember that the notion that there are tiny, invisible animals in the water we drink might seem like rubbish to an illiterate, too—but those little animals can kill nonetheless. Just because something seems to go against common sense, that is, to contradict the popular understanding of things, does not prove that it is incorrect. Much common sense is so-called because it is exactly that—common. Not necessarily correct, just popular. We will return to this.

These are some of the reasons we believe that sociology is worth knowing something about, and some of the things you can do with it if you wish. But what is it? The answer to that question, of course, is what this whole book is about, but we can start out here, in this chapter, with some general outlines of what we're going to show you.

## WHAT IS SOCIOLOGY?

Oddly, this can be a troubling question for a sociologist to answer. Even people who are thoroughly familiar with the subject sometimes have trouble explaining it to others because the field is broad, in some respects ambiguous, occasionally vague, and it overlaps considerably with some other disciplines, such as psychology and anthropology. A useful attempt at an answer, however, could start with a few things that sociology *isn't*, but with which it is often confused. Sociology isn't social work, socialism, or "working with people" in some unspecified way. (Neither is it, by the way, sinful, sexy, or silly, although the newspapers sometimes talk about it that way.) It *is* a certain kind of study of human behavior, specifically human *social* behavior, the things we do and are, not as biological organisms, but as members of those ancient and universal human organizations called "societies."

Sociology is sometimes particularly difficult for American college students to grasp because, as we said, its subject matter and means of exploring it run contrary to the American grain, to some very deep values and understandings in the American way of looking at the world. Americans are taught from birth to understand human behavior in terms of specific individuals and their unique characteristics; but sociology's basic assumption is that much of what we do and are can only be explained by reference to things outside of and beyond the individual, many of them (such as suicide rates) over which individuals exercise no control and which have little or nothing to do with personality characteristics. Such things are social phenomena and may be understood only at the social, not at the individual, level.

Sociologists sometimes put this another way, saying that social phenomena are **emergent,** which means "appearing as a result of organization and unpredictable from knowledge of the properties of component parts." To use a simple chemical example, what we experience as "wetness" is a property of the compound we call water, not of the chemicals hydrogen and oxygen that make it up. We could know everything there was to know about hydrogen and oxygen as separate and unique elements without being able to predict that, when combined in the proper two-to-one ratio, they result in a compound that would have "wetness" as an emergent property. (Not all liquids do.)

A social example of the same phenomenon is a classroom demonstration I have used in my introductory sociology course for years: On the first day of the semester, I offer to give five dollars to any male student in the room who is not wearing trousers. In more than twenty years of making that offer on eight different campuses, I have had to pay off only once, to some dude

**psychologistic:** characteristic of psychology or psychological explanation; looking to individuals or individual characteristics for explanations for social behavior; explaining social phenomena by reference to the qualities of individuals.

**social mobility:** movement of persons from one social group or position to another.

**emergent:** pertaining to a quality or condition emerging as a consequence of organization and unpredictable from knowledge of components.

from a bagpipe band who was present in kilts. What accounts for this remarkable uniformity in male student attire? Could we predict it from specific knowledge of individual students and their personalities, biographies, and so forth? Hardly, because it is not a matter of individual behavior at all. The explanation, of course, is the emergent social phenomenon called custom or tradition, a phenomenon present in American society before you and I were born and one

If you are an American male, you wear trousers to a dinner party. These Indians of Brazil wear paint. You may select your trousers for style, and the paint designs are individualized, but it does not occur to anyone to wear anything else. Custom is rarely questioned.

which will exist after we are both dead. This observation about the nature of much social behavior leads us to the first and simplest answer to the question "What is sociology?"

### Sociology Is the Study of Human Groups and Their Influence on Individual Behavior

Human groups are emergent social phenomena. They have qualities, properties, or characteristics of their own, different and unpredictable from the qualities or characteristics of the people who make them up. If you knew nothing about the kind of group we call a school "class," you would be unable to predict the classroom behavior of other people in your sociology course even if you knew everything about them personally. But if you know that a given number of anonymous strangers are to be members of your class, you will be able to predict much of their classroom behavior with high accuracy from your acquired experience in previous classes. Further, similar groups have similar properties. All lecture classes, like all football teams, are more alike than they are different, phenomena again unknowable from information about the personal characteristics of their members. The human social group, thus, is a subject matter with properties of its own and worthy of study in its own right.

Perhaps more important, however, is the fact that group membership has great influence on individual behavior. Even artificially created laboratory groups of strangers can have powerful impact on their members. An indication is another exercise I often use in my own classes. I ask students to write down in one minute as many answers as they can think of to the question "Who are you?" The answers are then collected and tabulated. Now this is a simple question, but it has profound depths. It may be the most intimate question we can ever be asked, it probes to the bottom of that peculiar and unique phenomenon, the human self. "Who are you?" asks us to place ourselves in the universe, to give a kind of moral and metaphysical accounting. It is not an easy question. But when student answers to that question are analyzed, invariably over 90 percent of the responses are worded in terms of group membership; and of the remainder, when proper names are discarded, almost all will be erroneous responses to the question "Who?"

What this simple exercise shows is that who we are is a unit in a social network. "I am a student, sister, Black, husband, daughter, American, Democrat, Catholic," and so on and on. Each one is a statement of what sociologists call role or status membership in a social group or category. Who we are is *what* we are, and it is defined by the social contexts in which we exist. Probably no more profound evidence for the significance of group membership could ever be suggested, and this is a good reason for learning something about sociology all by itself.

### Sociology Is the Study of Social Order and Social Change

A second answer to the question "What is sociology?" is that it is the study of social order and social change. (It is really the same answer as the first, as is the third, below, but they are at different levels of theoretical complexity.) When Auguste Comte (the French philosopher who invented sociology about two hundred years ago) defined it, he called it the study of "social statics and social dynamics," and meant pretty much the same thing as we do now by "order and change." It is important to realize that when sociologists talk about social order, they don't mean at all what was meant by the political catch phrase "law and order." That was a code phrase for strict and repressive law enforcement under the Nixon administration. What sociologists mean by "order" is the consistent pattern and regularity of social life. (The universality of trouser-wearing among American males, noted above, is a simple example of one such pattern or regularity.)

Social order is the product of the great web of social relationships in which each of our lives is embedded. This is called "the process of social organization," and we will discuss it in Chapters 5 and 6. The fact that our lives are socially organized produces the pattern and regularity visible in our behavior and is, in fact, all that makes survival possible. This is so because not only are our individual lives patterned and orderly, but so are all of our lives collectively. Not only can you see regularity in your own behavior from day to day, you can also see it in the behavior of the others all around you. This permits you to understand them and know what to expect from them, and vice versa. And this, in turn, makes it possible for people to live and work together.

Orderliness makes social life possible. Would you dare cross this intersection if you had no idea what other people there were going to do?

and of how much regularity there is in everyday behavior.

Now you may regard this as a farfetched example. Who would want to risk a life on such a dumb bet? In fact, we all do, all the time. Every time you take your car onto the highway, you are betting your life that the drivers in the oncoming lane will remain there while going past you, that there will be no oncoming car in your lane as you round the curve or climb the hill. Every time you go out in public you bet your life that you will not be killed by a maniac. And we are able to survive, individually and as a society, because most of the time the bets we make on the regularity of the behavior of others are won. We have only to look at world situations like that in Northern Ireland or the Middle East to see what happens to social life when people are unable to count on not being assaulted at random or by fanatics. Social order, the pattern and regularity of social behavior, is the basis of human and societal survival.

But, as you know from your own experience, few things in life remain unchanged for very long, and the phenomenon of change is just as prevalent in all society as it is in life immediately around you. So in addition to having a

To make this more clear, let's make a bet. You and I will take a plane to an American city which is strange to both of us. When we deplane at the airport, we'll go to the nearest telephone book and check the yellow pages under the restaurant heading. We'll select something that sounds like a beanery, a cheap eating place likely to have a counter and stools. We'll go there in a cab and, when we arrive, I'll take a seat at the counter that has an occupied stool next to it. I'll order a plain hamburger and, when I get it, I'll turn to the person next to me and ask him or her to pass me the ketchup. AND I WILL BET YOU A THOUSAND DOLLARS TO YOUR ONE THAT HE OR SHE WILL GIVE IT TO ME! We'll have to stipulate that the person must be English-speaking, but aside from that, it doesn't matter who or what the stranger is—old or young, black or white, rich or poor, male or female. Would you take that bet and expect to win?

Almost certainly you wouldn't, because you know that the odds against winning are astronomical, far greater than the thousand to one I offered you. In fact, if I made it sufficiently worth your while, you might even be willing to bet your life that I *would* get the ketchup. Say that I offer you a million in cash against your life. If I get the ketchup, you get the million; if I don't , you lose your head. Many readers might be willing to risk that bet because the possible reward is so large and the risk of losing so small. But how can we be so sure? Because we are aware of the social order in our own society

When we cannot count on regularity in the behavior of others, normal social life is impossible—Northern Ireland yesterday.

preoccupation with social order and regularity, the sociologist is also compelled to confront social change. We do not, in truth, know as much about social change as we do about social order, in part because it is more difficult to study for two different, but related, reasons. The first of these is that historically, sociology grew within the tradition of the natural sciences and adopted the scientific method as its mode of inquiry. Scientific investigation requires recurrent and orderly phenomena to study; the unique (onetime) or capricious event is not amenable to scientific analysis. It doesn't hold still long enough, nor can it be predicted to occur in such a way that the scientist can be on hand to watch it. Thus sociologists have learned a great deal more about social order and regularity than they have about change. Things that recur in predictable ways are much easier to study than things that are altering before your eyes.

The second reason that we know less about change than about order is that social change takes a long time to occur and often takes place on a scale so large that it is difficult even to see properly the outlines of the phenomenon to be studied. There is no doubt, for example, that industrialization has had a profound impact on the world and has left immense change in its wake. (It is a change process in itself.) But it is taking place over so long a span of years—centuries—and reaches into so many aspects of human life so deeply, that no one investigator could ever hope to study more than some tiny aspect of it, and no one lifetime of research would be enough to begin to see it as a whole.

A number of the chapters of this book will deal with specific social changes of importance in contemporary society, and Chapter 18 discusses social change as a phenomenon in itself. For the reasons discussed above, however, as you read the book, you will find that more attention is paid to social order than to change. As we implied above, this is not because change is less important, but simply because we know less about it.

### Sociology Is the Search for Social Causation

A third answer to the question "What is sociology?" has already been suggested by the foregoing discussion: Sociology is the search for the social causes of things, the ways in which social phenomena influence human behavior. That is the purpose of the discipline; that's what it's *for*. The fact that sociology frames its explanations in terms of social causes of, or influences on, behavior is what makes it unique. If we answered questions about behavior in terms of human chemistry or biology or psychology, we'd be playing a different ball game, one already preempted by another team.

But why bother to play this one? Because, as we have said, social phenomena are worthy of study in their own right, and simple curiosity is a good reason to look into things. More important, social phenomena are as "real" as cats and chemicals and chromosomes and have important influences on us whether we know and acknowledge them or not. What we don't know *can* hurt us, and what we *do* know is always there to offer us potential help, if we can find ways of using it to do so.

Well, then, sociology is the study of human groups and their influence on human behavior. That in turn means the study of social order and social change because the very existence of a group implies the existence of social order. It must be ordered to *be* a group. One of the most profound effects groups have is the production of order or regularity in behavior. But few behaviors are completely fixed or patterned, so change is always possible and frequently occurring. This way of looking at things is an expression of a socially causal explanation. We look for social components of behavior because we expect them to exist.

In order to carry out this study, and in the process of doing it for the century in which the field has been in existence as a distinct discipline, sociologists have developed a set of *concepts* (ideas, intellectual tools) and *theoretical perspectives* (specific ways of looking at and comprehending their subject). Such concepts and perspectives are the way of understanding human society that *is* the field called sociology. Regard them as a set of rules for analyzing things or as a lens of a particular shape that shows what the world would look like if you chose to view it through that glass. If you elect to understand human behaviors in terms of ideas like culture, socialization, social role, group, institution and so forth, then you are using the tools of sociology and your understanding will be a sociological one. (These are all defined and discussed in the next few chapters.)

This is not the only possible way of looking at

the world, of course. There are also the natural sciences, which use a different set of intellectual tools and study a different subject matter. And there are the other social sciences. Many of the latter have more or less the same subject matter as sociology, but they study it from different perspectives and with different conceptual tools. Thus there is a division of intellectual labor in the general study of human behavior, and sociology's place in it is clear. It is not the only human science, or the oldest; but it has interests and perspectives that, in general, the others do not share, and that is its claim to existence as a discipline.

## SOCIOLOGY AND COMMON SENSE

The legitimacy of the sociological claim is persistently challenged, however, by the claim of "common sense." From the newspaper, the political rostrum, and even sometimes the pulpit, comes the criticism that sociology is "merely an elaboration of the obvious," that its sometimes pretentious language "just says in complicated ways what everyone already knows," and that sociological research is largely devoted to proving expensively "what anyone with any sense could have figured out alone." (Members of Congress with an interest in budget cutting love to find federally funded research projects with elaborate titles and then explain that what the research is "really" about is something very simple and intuitively obvious—at least to sensible people like their constituents.)

There are probably a number of reasons why the challenge of common sense is directed at sociology so much more frequently (or so it seems to sociologists) than it is at other academic disciplines. One is that sociologists, unlike anthropologists, historically have tended to study their own societies more than they have those of other peoples. Thus, because sociologists study phenomena that other members of their own society have some familiarity with, their findings often appear obvious, although they might not have been before the fact.

We read with relish anthropological descriptions of weird practices in the daily life of the Cannibal Islanders, but we do not stop to think that if such reports were read to the islanders themselves, the conclusions would often be "just common sense" *to them.* Similarly, psychology is popularly understood to be about

"the unconscious" and "why we *really* do things even if we don't know it." It is not expected to be as familiar as the home, workplace, and church, which are often the subjects of sociology. People do not expect to have special knowledge of a subject like physics because they consider it esoteric, although they have lived with and by it every day of their lives. But because they are familiar with the objects the sociologist studies, they feel they already have a special knowledge of them and resent any sociological claim that they do not. (In the same way students who are members of racial or ethnic minorities sometimes regard themselves as experts on race or ethnic relations. It would be more accurate to say that they may be expert in the experience of minority group membership.)

Another reason sociology experiences the criticism of common sense is that people often fail to distinguish between things they have a general awareness of and things they know and understand *precisely.* But knowing that something is generally so and knowing *why* it is so and to what exact degree and in what exact ways and under what circumstances it is so, are not the same things. Establishing such precise knowledge about "what everybody knows" is one of the tasks of sociology.

Finally, there is the fact that common sense is frequently wrong. Consider the following propositions, which many Americans, at least, might consider "just common sense":

1. Since people tend to avoid unpleasant experiences, one way to deter them from particular actions is to punish them when they commit them. The greater the punishment, the greater the deterrent effect—at least as regards capital punishment for the crime of murder.
2. When black people move into a formerly all-white residential neighborhood, property values decline.
3. Most American Roman Catholic priests support the Church's ban on contraception.
4. Reading or seeing pornographic materials increases the likelihood of committing sex offenses.
5. The civilian suicide rate in time of war is higher than in time of peace.
6. The welfare rosters are filled with able-bodied people who would rather loaf than work.

Each of these statements would undoubtedly be perceived as true by many Americans, and each might also be regarded by many as "obvious" or "just common sense." According to the sociological evidence, however, all of them are false. In each case, in fact, the evidence *contradicts* the statements: Not only are they untrue, the truth is just the opposite of what is claimed.

This is not to deny that the criticism of common sense is sometimes valid. Sociologists, like other people, occasionally say things in public that they would have been wiser to keep to themselves or to check out more thoroughly before announcing them. Like other people, sociologists sometimes dress up simple thought in complicated language. And one of the tasks of the discipline is to explore conventional wisdom, some of which, unlike the examples above, turns out to be correct. In such cases, the sociologist has examined the obvious; but one cannot know, as we have seen, unless one tries. We suspect that when you are finished with this book, you will know a great deal about human society, and your own society, and perhaps yourself, that you did not know before.

We think you will find sociology to be a powerful intellectual tool that will enable you better to understand yourself and the world of which you are a part. What was your nature at birth? How did your family and other social conditions and institutions shape your personality? What are your expectations regarding education, religion, marriage, occupation, and the life style you hope ultimately to achieve, and where did such expectations come from? Has your social class origin affected them? To what degree is it reasonable to expect that you will be able to fulfill your hopes within our society as it now exists? And how might that society be changed in order to increase your chances? The more you understand the social system of which you are a part, the greater the likelihood that you can achieve your personal goals. Similarly, if you can come to understand your society more clearly and find you do not approve of some of its social arrangements and conditions, the better position you will be in to cooperate with others to modify them.

Join us in the task of examining our social structure and culture, the human personality and the socialization process, and the distribution of wealth, power, and prestige in our society. What is happening to marriage in the United States? What proportions of our population will eventually marry, divorce, remarry, find satisfaction in marriage? What social conditions affect marital satisfaction, and what are the characteristics of the marriages that endure or fail? These are the kinds of questions sociologists research and attempt to answer.

Similarly, we will examine the structure and social functions of religion, education, politics, and the economy and try to understand how these institutions are interrelated and how they influence peoples' behavior. If you master the concepts, perspectives, and descriptive information offered you here, you should understand yourself and others as you never have before. We hope that you will use this knowledge to benefit yourself and our society.

Before getting into the actual subject matter of sociology, I'd like to say a final word about how the other authors of this book and I hope you will approach your reading of it. Every author represented here is or has been an undergraduate teacher of the subject matter he or she has written about. I myself am sometimes called a "professional teacher of introductory sociology." I asked many of the authors to contribute to the book because they had reputations as teachers with a rage to teach. We should, then, know what we're talking about. We have enjoyed working on the book and we hope that you will enjoy reading it. Beyond that, we hope you will profit from it. We do not expect that you will agree with everything we say here, but we urge you, when you don't, at least to stop and think about the matter. In the long run, that's what a first book in sociology is meant to do: to give you the chance to think about your life and your society in a new way, rather than just taking them for granted in the ways you have been taught to accept them. Good luck and best wishes.

## ASKING SOCIOLOGICAL QUESTIONS*

Preceding pages have introduced you to the beginnings of a sociological way of looking at the world. Before you can have a complete grasp of that, however, to understand fully what sociology is all about, you need to know something about *how* sociologists ask the kinds of questions they do, and *why* they choose those kinds of questions to ask. The first is a matter of what is technically called **epistemolo-**

*This section is based on material prepared by Robert M. Pankin, author of Chapter 2.

**gy,** the branch of philosophy concerned with the process of knowing and how we know what we think we know. The second is a matter of history, because where we are now—the kinds of questions we ask—is a consequence of where we came from. *Here* is always related to *there.* And the reason that the questions themselves are important, of course, is that the questions you ask determine the answers you get. Questions about elephants do not normally receive answers concerning porcupines. Any body of knowledge, then, begins with questions.

## The Origins of Sociological Questions

Questions do not come from out of the blue; they come from somewhere; they have a reason for being asked. The question *we* start with, therefore, is "How do sociologists begin to ask questions?" Where are they "coming from?"

Part of where sociologists "come from" has to do with how they—or anyone else—grew up and were reared or socialized (see Chapter 4). As children, we ask endlessly the "how" and "why" questions that begin to give us information about the world we live in. The answers we are given to our first questions give us the basis for others, and those answers lead to still other questions. "Why can't I play outside?" "Because it is raining." "Why is it raining?" "Because nature makes it rain sometimes." "What is nature?"—and so forth. Through a process of this kind, we accumulate information, and as we gather more and more information, we begin to know what questions—and answers—are relevant to particular situations. We organize a basis, a framework, for asking yet further questions.

By the time we are grown, we have all developed a large number of such frameworks for organizing information and seeking more. Such frameworks are sometimes called perspectives or points of view. In science and the other intellectual endeavors they may be called theories or schools of thought. In sociology they may be called models, positions, or paradigms. Whatever label is used, the purpose is the same: To provide a means for asking organized questions in order to accumulate information systematically. Sometimes we use one framework or perspective to ask questions about very different things; sometimes we ask questions about the same thing from a number of differ-

**epistemology:** the branch of philosophy concerned with the process of knowing and the nature of knowledge. The fundamental epistemological question is "How do we know *that* we know *what* we know?"

ent points of view, in order to get different perspectives on it.

Sociologists' questions typically come out of a perspective or theoretical framework that has been learned through a long career of study, or, perhaps more typically, out of several of them. (You are about to be introduced to the major ones in this book.) Thus an investigator might choose several different perspectives to ask questions about different things, a question from one perspective about crime, from another about health care, and from yet a third about the economic system. Another sociologist might elect to stay within only one perspective and to understand crime, health, and economics all from that single point of view.

Part of the reason that sociological questions are asked in the way they are has to do with the history of the discipline as well as the personal history and inclinations of the particular investigator. Sociology was born in the nineteenth century and was aimed from the beginning at asking and trying to answer some of the questions raised by the political and industrial revolutions of that tumultous epoch. That is a fascinating topic in itself, but for our purposes we must restrict our concern to how the issues of that period have carried over into the way in which sociological questions are asked today.

One way in which the nineteenth-century issues to which sociology was originally addressed have carried over into modern times is in the form of major concerns or value orientations that underlie specific perspectives or theoretical frameworks in the field. Some of the writers who contributed to early sociological development, for example, saw their age as a time of social disorder or even chaos; they were concerned with the conditions necessary for social order or its reestablishment. Others viewed the turmoil and change of the time as offering enhanced opportunities for individual freedom and self-expression which they believed people could handle in a rational and positive way. Thus the conditions of personal freedom became their intellectual focus. Still others, responding to the brutal exploitation of workers in the early industrial era, became concerned with justice and equality and the conditions under which these are obtained or denied. These concerns still underlie the major theoretical perspectives in modern sociology, although they are often unstated in particular pieces of work within a given theoretical tradition.

The original nineteenth-century concerns of the field are also revealed (again, often without specific expression) in the *basic assumptions* that underlie its principal perspectives.

### Basic Assumptions and Intellectual Questions

We said earlier that a theoretical framework or perspective is a means of asking organized questions for the purpose of accumulating systematic information. Such sets of questions must have a starting point, some basis or grounding or taken-for-granted information that is accepted as true and from which further questions may be asked. This is likely to be a set of basic assumptions.

Assumptions are starting points. The best are so simple they are open to controversy. For example, if we are interested in human behavior, it is possible to assume that our behavior is based on some kind of fundamental human nature and that human nature has some general character, such as good or bad, selfish or altruistic, cooperative or competitive, and so forth. Now if we were to stop at this point, as common sense often does, we would merely have created the opportunity for a debate that could never be ended because no evidence can ever be produced that would permit us to resolve the issue conclusively. But the purpose of assumptions in intellectual investigation is to provoke questions about the world which, in turn, focus our attention on the evidence that may provide answers. An assumption, in other words, is never tested as such, but it makes us ask questions whose answers may be used to explore the topic for which the assumption provides a platform or grounding.

### Basic Assumptions in Sociology

The logic of the sociological perspective requires that the questioner make at least one assumption from each of four fundamental topics or categories of information about the world. These are (1) the nature of human nature, (2) the nature of society, (3) the purpose of sociological inquiry, and (4) the appropriate sociological method or means of investigation. Any sociological theory, perspective, position, or framework will have at least one basic and unquestioned assumption from each of these categories as a starting point for asking its questions.

**The Nature of Human Nature** What are people like? Are we basically good, bad, rational, irrational, passive, aggressive, or an infinity of other things? The assumptions we make in this area are absolutely fundamental to any inquiry, because they limit so clearly the kinds of questions we will want to ask or discard and because they color our understanding of the evidence we acquire as answers to our questions. If we assume that human nature is fundamentally selfish, for example, and then observe someone acting altruistically, we are compelled to ask why, or under what conditions, an individual would behave in ways apparently contrary to basic human nature. But the character of our original assumption would lead us to *interpret* any evidence we gathered as indicating that people act altruistically out of selfish motives; they do, indeed, act generously sometimes, but only when it is in their self-interest to do so.

**The Nature of Society** For sociologists, this is a most important category. One perspective in the field, for example, assumes that the whole of a society is different from, and greater than, the totality of the characteristics of the individuals who are members of that society, that is, society is an emergent phenomenon. Another assumes that the whole of a society or a group is merely the sum of those who make it up. This is called **reductionism.** A third ignores this issue and assumes that society consists in essence of the social relationships between individuals and groups, while another starts with the assumption that a society is basically a symbol system.

The assumption about the nature of society is important because it gives us some of the most direct questions we can ask. If, for instance, we adopt the assumption that society is more than the sum of its parts, we will be inclined to ask questions about whole societies as entities in themselves. On the other hand, if we assume that a society is merely the sum of its individual members, we will ask questions about individuals in order to determine what society is like. The assumption about the nature of society is one that attracts the attention of most sociologists.

**The Purpose of Sociology** The last two categories of assumptions have to do with the professional concerns of sociologists, with their understanding of the discipline and its meaning. Assumptions typical of the third category are that the purpose of sociology is (1) to assist in the establishment of a modern moral order, (2) merely to provide knowledge for whatever use it may have, or (3) to provide knowledge that individuals may use to change their social system if they are dissatisfied with the conditions in which they find themselves. These assumptions have the function of justifying the sociological endeavor. They answer the question "Why should one spend time asking sociological questions?" Since different sociologists make different assumptions about why they are doing what they do, there is a fair amount of controversy in the field concerning questions raised by assumptions in this category.

**The Appropriate Sociological Method** Assumptions from this category are concerned with how social life is best or most usefully studied. Chapter 19 is specifically devoted to this question. In a sense, only one of two possible assumptions needs to be selected here, and the choice is obviously influenced by the assumption(s) adopted from category 3, since the appropriate method is clearly a function of the purpose or object of study. One assumption is that the scientific method is the appropriate one for sociological investigation. This is likely to be adopted by those who believe that the purpose of sociology is the production of knowledge for its own sake, for whatever use to which it may be put. It is likely to be justified by the belief that only the scientific method is capable of producing *reliable information*. (See Chapter 19 for a discussion of the concept of reliability.) The other assumption is that social life may or should be studied by any method that produces *understanding*, and this is likely to be chosen by those who believe that the study of sociology should have some direct and immediate relevance to the social conditions in which people live.

**reductionism:** the philosophical or theoretical attempt to "reduce" a phenomenon to its simplest constituent parts or terms. A thoroughly reductionist explanation of human behavior, for example, would probably be framed in terms of cell chemistry.

## Two Approaches to Sociological Reasoning

Two important issues surface in asking sociological questions or, indeed, any question about the nature of the world. The first is *the nature of reality*. How do we *know* if something is real? When sociologists deal with basic assumptions about the nature of society, they are probing the nature of social reality. What is ultimately *real*—whole societies, individuals, or relationships among people? Directly or indirectly, sociological thinking is likely to focus on one of these three as the starting point for observation.

A second problem confronting the sociologist is, *Where does knowledge come from?* Is it derived from previous knowledge and ideas, or is it generated by our behavior? This is an important issue, because if knowledge is derived from previous knowledge, we would be led to the study of subjective phenomena—ideas—in order to understand behavior. On the other hand, if we believe that knowledge is the result of behavior, of acting, we would be led to study behavior itself and tend to ignore subjective matters. The relation of these issues to the problem of appropriate method is plain. A focus on the subjective—on knowledge and ideas themselves—would suggest that any means of deriving an understanding of others is an appropriate sociological method. A focus on the objective—on behavior and action—would suggest science as the more appropriate methodology.

## CONTEMPORARY SOCIOLOGICAL INQUIRY AND THE HISTORY OF SOCIOLOGY

All of these issues and concerns are highlighted in the history of the development of sociology. The present state of that discipline, of course, is directly related to its past. Sociology was invented and developed into a distinct discipline in the nineteenth century, and the people responsible for that invention and development shaped the ideas we have been discussing in ways that still characterize the endeavor. We will see in Chapter 2, for example, that Emile Durkheim (1858–1917), the great French sociologist, was concerned with the problem of social order and believed that human nature needed to be controlled by some external force. He thought that society was greater than the sum of its individual members, that the purpose of sociology was the construction of a new moral order to replace the feudal order overthrown by the Industrial Revolution, and that the scientific method was the appropriate means for obtaining the information to do this. Karl Marx (1818–1883), on the contrary, was concerned with social justice and equality. He assumed that human nature was basically good, that society was different from the sum of its members, and that the purpose of social inquiry was the promotion of social change. Marx called his own methods scientific, but other thinkers in the same tradition have often argued for other approaches.

The classical sociological thinkers of the nineteenth century will be discussed in detail in Chapter 2. They were all Europeans who, through their concerns with the major social questions of their times, established the basis for and defined the interests of the discipline. Their work was rooted in certain assumptions, and these led their reasoning in specific directions. Their questions about the nature of human nature and society were so significant that they had profound influence on the thought of their time. They continue to dominate social theory today, although most of the specific conclusions they arrived at have been superseded by later developments. But contemporary theoretical perspectives, most of which are American, have to a great degree expanded upon and elaborated the work of the classical thinkers.

### The Beginnings: Saint-Simon and Comte

Most sociology texts call Auguste Comte (1798–1857) the inventor or founder of sociology.[1] Emile Durkheim, Comte's most famous follower, however, gave that credit to Claude

Auguste Comte

Claude Henri de Saint-Simon

Henri de Saint-Simon (1760–1825), whom Comte served as secretary for a number of years. Saint-Simon was an artillery officer with the American forces during the War of Independence and was an enthusiastic supporter of the French Revolution during which he renounced his aristocratic title and made a fortune in land speculation. After the Revolution, he began to habituate the intellectual circles of Paris, where he became interested in science and eventually in the problem of the construction of a new, post-Revolutionary society which would have a rational basis. His vision was a multinational Europe somewhat similar to the contemporary Common Market.

Comte became Saint-Simon's secretary in 1817 while still a student at the Ecole Polytechnique. He was deeply influenced by his master's scientific interests and political enthusiasms. The association between the two lasted for seven years during the early portion of which Saint-Simon even put his own name on some of Comte's writings which were so revolutionary as to be potentially dangerous to the younger man. The master and his apprentice were a brilliant team, but they quarreled in 1824 over the authorship of some articles and broke off the relationship. Saint-Simon died a year later, distraught over the estrangement from his brilliant pupil.

One of Comte's first interests, no doubt encouraged by his association with Saint-Simon, was in the history of science. He thought scientific development has an evolutionary trend, commencing with mathematics as the basic discipline and culminating in sociology, the "queen" of all scientific endeavor. Comte coined the name *sociology* and also the name **positivism,** for the philosophical position that asserts that the world must be explained by means of observable facts rather than metaphysical conceptions such as divine action. For

> **positivism:** the eighteenth century philosophy basic to science which holds that the events of the world are explicable by reference to observable or discoverable facts and laws and that unobservable phenomena, such as God and free will, should not be used as explanatory variables.

this reason he might be called the first true social scientist. Comte believed in the perfectability of human nature and that society, if properly organized, would be rational and moral and thus create the conditions for that perfection. He saw the planning of such a society as sociology's purpose and the scientific study of society on the natural science model as its appropriate method. In his concern for such matters, he laid the groundwork for the more truly *sociological* thinkers who were to follow him. Modern sociologists do not study Comte and, indeed, many of his ideas seem foolish today. (It is sometimes remarked that while he talked about science all the time, he never practiced it himself, his work being much more of the cast today called "armchair theorizing.")

The contemporary utility of the work of Comte and his distinguished master, Saint-Simon, is not significant, however. Their important influences were upon those who immediately followed them and upon the directions the new field of study they invented were to take during its formative years. They met head-on the fundamental assumptions discussed above and fixed the sociological focus permanently upon them. The richness and utility of their insight in doing this are demonstrated by the immense power and influence of the sociologists whose works are discussed in Chapter 2, the classical social theorists of the ninteenth century, Karl Marx, Emile Durkheim, and Max Weber.

## SUMMARY

The chapter opened by responding to the question, "Of what value is the study of sociology?" It was suggested that an understanding of sociological principles can give us greater control over our own lives. This is so because social phenomena are quite real and have significant influence on us even though the individualistic, psychologistic character of American culture tends to ignore their existence.

We then turned to the question "What is sociology?" We saw that the simplest answer is that it is the study of human groups and their influences on individual behavior. But such study necessarily involves the study of social order and social change, which, in turn, leads us to the most comprehensive answer to the question: Sociology is the search for the social causation of human behavior. This attempt to discover the social causes of behavior is the field's reason for existing, its intellectual justification. No other discipline has that particular mandate.

This suggests, then, that sociology is best understood as a form of inquiry, a means of asking particular kinds of questions about the world. That means, in turn, that it is likely to produce particular kinds of answers because, in a way, every question we ask dictates the answers it may have. Thus the nature of sociological questions, the basic assumptions on which or from which they are asked, and the means of seeking answers to them, in a sense *are* the discipline of sociology.

Upon examination, sociological questions were seen to derive from four categories of basic assumptions dealing with the nature of human nature, the nature of society, the purpose of the field of sociology, and the appropriate sociological method. Assumptions from within these categories, modified by the approaches to knowledge dictated by beliefs about the nature of reality and the source of knowledge, produce sociological frameworks of explanation or theoretical perspectives.

Sociology was invented by Saint-Simon and Comte in the early part of the nineteenth century. Their ideas and definitions of the field, modified by the classical thinkers of the latter part of the century, Marx, Durkheim, and Weber, still define the major outlines of sociological inquiry today.

## SUGGESTED READINGS

BERGER, PETER L. *Invitation to Sociology.* Garden City, N.Y.: Anchor, 1963. This brief paperback has become a classic expression of the humanistic position in sociology. Immensely popular with students from the time of first publication, it remains in wide use and is often a book the student keeps after completing the first course in the field.

COLE, STEPHEN. *The Sociological Method,* 2d ed. Chicago: Rand-McNally, 1976. This is a brief introduction to the field of sociology approaching it from the perspective of doing sociological research, concentrating on sociological methodology as the means of investigating the field.

CUZZORT, RAY P., AND EDITH W. KING. *Humanity and Modern Sociological Thought,* 2d ed. New York: Holt, Rinehart and Winston, 1976. An introduction to the sociological way of thinking through review of major theorists and their work, this book was very popular in its first edition and is more comprehensive in its second. Another kind of humanistic perspective.

HAMMOND, PHILLIP E., ed., *Sociologists at Work: Essays on the Craft of Social Research.* Garden City, N.Y.: Anchor, 1967. This is a collection of essays by major sociological researchers describing the ways in which specific classic researches were conducted, the intellectual problems encountered in a particular work, and so forth; the worker telling how he or she actually did the work. One of the few published pieces of sociology that lets the reader see "behind the scenes" of social research.

INKLES, ALEX. *What Is Sociology? An Introduction to the Discipline and Profession.* Englewood Cliffs, N.J.: Prentice-Hall, Foundations of Modern Sociology Series, 1964. A very brief review of the major intellectual tools of the discipline of sociology and what sociologists do with them. An excellent summary overview.

MCGEE, REECE. *Points of Departure,* 2d ed. Hinsdale, Ill.: Dryden, 1975. This simply written "core text" explores the six or seven principal concepts of sociological analysis showing how sociologists use them to understand the social world. Oriented to the epistemology of positivist functionalism.

# Chapter 2
# Visions of
# Social Life

Sociology was born in the nineteenth century, asking and attempting to answer the profound questions raised by the political and industrial revolutions of that turbulent time. European social institutions had been deeply shaken and much was in ferment. Monarchies established for centuries were toppled by revolution; customs and relationships unchanged since the Middle Ages were being altered or discarded. New social classes had been created by the new industrial order, and the power and prestige of aristocratic groups, unchallenged since the Dark Ages, were altered or discarded by maturing mercantile and industrial interests. Scientific modes of thought undercut religious certainties previously unquestioned and, as millions left the land and made their way to the growing cities to staff the factories, old ways died, new political forms appeared, familial relationships altered, legal and educational ideas changed, and to many life appeared uncertain and turmoil was the rule.

To these circumstances social observers had differing reactions. Some, concerned with what appeared to be a need for the reestablishment of social order, believed that human nature needed to be controlled. Others wanted to increase individual freedom still further, believing that people could handle it in a rational way. Others, worried about the injustice and inequality apparent all about them, raised questions about these issues; rich and poor, for example, were treated very differently by the courts. Why? Questions and assumptions of these kinds remain in the background of modern sociology even though they may not be specifically articulated in every research.

While Saint-Simon and Comte are considered the founders of sociology as a systematic discipline (see Chapter 1), sociologists today usually turn to three other thinkers for the origins of their basic questions—Karl Marx, Emile Durkheim, and Max Weber. The problem of the dominance of the many by the few led Marx to questions of social justice and equality. The problem of social and moral *heterogeneity* led Durkheim to the question of social order. The increasing purposefulness of social life and the growing individual freedom led Weber to focus on the nature of rationality and the role of the individual. Each of these thinkers are concerned with all of these issues, and others as well, but each tended to emphasize different problems. These differences in emphasis led them to ask different questions and, from those questions, to develop different intellectual frameworks or theories.

## THREE CLASSICAL VIEWS OF SOCIAL REALITY

### Karl Marx

Karl Marx's lasting contribution to sociology is to be found in the unusual and incisive questions he was able to ask. Like all great social thinkers, he recognized a fundamental paradox. People claimed to be honest and to believe in social justice, but everywhere injustice and poverty were normal occurrences. Marx reasoned that if most people were good (and he thought they were), then something external to the individual must be making things go wrong. That something, in his view, was the organization of society, the way in which things were arranged. He wanted to study social relationships carefully and critically in order to change them. Marx's assumptions came from his recognition of the fundamental social paradox: people are good, society is composed of social relationships, social organization should be altered, and we must study society carefully and critically in order to alter them.

**The Nature of Human Nature**   Like most socialists then and now, Marx assumed that human nature was good and that people could live together cooperatively. But why don't people live that way? Marx reasoned that human beings now live in an unnatural competitive or conflictual relationship. The natural relationship between a worker and work is that the product of labor is returned to the laborer; the farmer plants and also harvests; the cobbler makes the shoe and sells it for himself. Under capitalism, however, workers do not keep what they produce. Deductions are made for the profit and property investment of the capitalist who employs them. This produces an unnatural relationship between the worker and the product. Somebody besides the worker gets part of the result. One effect of altering the natural human state of cooperation Marx called **alienation.** This concept led him to question the role of private property in social life.

**The Nature of Society**   For Marx, society consisted of the relationships between people and between social groupings. Since he thought that human nature was essentially good and that a crucial distinction existed between individual behavior and social structures, he located the causes of social problems in the social environment rather than in individual evil or inadequacy. To solve the social problem, one would have to bring about a fundamental change in the social environment; to change the social environment, one would have to analyze it thoroughly; and according to Marx, *no society can be analyzed without understanding the structure and organization of the basic relationships of its central institution.* The central institution in a society is the one whose ideas, values, norms, and social relationships most directly influence human survival. That institution might be the family, the political order, the military, education, the economy, or religion.

Marx had no doubt that the economy was the dominant institution in Western society. He argued that an unnatural social relationship permeated that institution, dominating the whole society, and causing alienation. This unnatural social relationship is *the contract,* a short-term specific relationship based on the exchange of one promise for another. A contract treats people as if they were objects instead of human beings and thus formalizes human relationships. All this Marx saw as undermining the natural, spontaneous, cooperative relations between human beings.

But how did things get this way? Through the process of **dialectical change.** In any social situation, the existence of one force (the *thesis*) tends to produce a counterforce (the *antithesis*). The conflict between the thesis and the antithesis produces a third element, the *synthesis,* which resolves the original contradiction (see Figure 2.1). An example can be found in race relations in the United States during the decades of the 50s and 60s. The Black Protest Movement marched to the slogan, "Freedom Now!" to which the segregationist resistance answered, "Never!" Out of the clash of these two opposing forces and ideologies has come the gradual process of racial integration now characterizing American society.

Another example is Marx's theory of social class. The owner and the worker in a capitalist system are thesis and antithesis, and a synthesis should arise from their struggle. For Marx, history operated through this sort of dialectical change. He felt that a worker's revolution would result in a communist state (the synthesis).

**The Purpose and Method of Sociology**

Marx was concerned with the future. He felt that social change was inevitable, but he reasoned that it would be foolish to start a revolution only to put power in the hands of different people, or to begin to change society without having some idea of why the old structure worked so imperfectly. It would be too easy to make the same mistakes again. Thus he advocated studying the present system in order to gather the data to change it. He even prepared a questionnaire for the French Socialist Party to help them gather data about conditions in France.

Marx called himself a scientist and used scientific method to analyze social life. To get the facts needed for changing the world, he systematically gathered economic data from all parts of the globe, derived ideas, and constructed hypotheses to ask questions of this data. He remained skeptical about all ideas, and looked for

**heterogeneity:** the condition in which members of a given population or category do not share many characteristics.

**alienation:** the condition of being estranged, separated, disunited, unreconciled. The concept of alienation is important in sociological theory. It was originally introduced by Marx, who saw industrial workers as "alienated from" their work by separation of labor from product. It is now often used in five different, although related, ways to refer to a sense or condition of powerlessness, meaninglessness, normlessness, isolation, or self-estrangement.

**dialectical change:** the idea that change occurs as a consequence of the opposition of inconsistent or conflicting elements. The existence of one element, the thesis, tends to produce an opposing element, a counterforce called the antithesis. The conflict between them is resolved through the creation of a third, unifying element, the synthesis. An example may be seen in American race relations in the past generation. The black protest slogan "Freedom now!" was responded to with the segregationist slogan "Never!" Out of that clash came the civil rights program of gradual integration.

FIGURE 2.1   **The process of dialectical change**

**The general model**

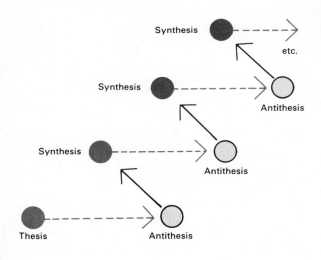

**Marx's example**

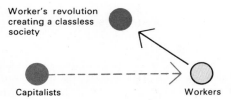

concrete objective evidence rather than confirmation of preconceived ideas. What Marx meant by science was a systematic study from a critical point of view.

**The Productive System and Social Class**

For Marx, Western industrial society works through its economic productive system. There are two types of production—production for use and production for exchange. Each of these has different implications. Things can be used for human purposes or they can be exchanged to create wealth. Those who control the exchange process through ownership are in an economically dominant position. Those who do not control the process become dependent on those who do. Ownership of, and access to, the means of production determine social standing and social power.

Exchange in and of itself is not productive. Reward, however, accrues to those who participate in exchange relationships. The worker is

### KARL MARX (1818–1883)[1]

Karl Marx was born in Trier in the Mosell district of Germany. He was one of nine children, four of whom died young. While Marx was raised as a Christian, there were several rabbis on both sides of his family. Marx's father was not a particularly religious man and had a worldly orientation toward life. The turning point in the religous life of the family came in 1815 when Henrich Marx converted to Christianity in order to keep his job. The children were baptized in 1824 and Karl's mother, Henriette, was baptized in 1825.

The young Marx gave no signs that he was to make a revolutionary impact on the world. Karl was described as "a good average student" and he had an early interest in poetry. Significantly,

however, his future father-in-law, Baron von Westphalen, introduced Marx to St. Simon's writing. Karl was secretly engaged to Jenny von Westphalen in the summer of 1836 and they married, finally, in 1843.

Marx began his university career with the intention of following his father into law. It didn't take him long, however, to turn to philosophy. He eventually wrote a doctoral thesis about Greek philosophy after Aristotle. Marx's thesis was accepted at the University of Jena in 1841. All the work on the thesis was done in Berlin, but it was the custom of the time for any faculty that found a thesis acceptable to grant the degree. A major influence on Marx were the Hegelian philosophers of the Berlin faculty.

One of Marx's first jobs after finishing his degree was as editor of the *Rheinische Zeitung (Rhenish Gazette)*. In that paper he defended liberal ideas of the time and criticized the German Communists. This paper was banned by the government in 1843. Marx believed the banning was largely due to his articles about poverty among the wine growers in his home district, Mosell.

After the *Rhenish Gazette* was banned, Marx left Germany and settled in Paris. He became the editor of the *German-French Journal*. During this period he got to know Fredrich Engles. Marx had originally met Engles in Cologne in 1842 but their relationship was cool. Engles was a member of a group of early communists that Marx had rejected. As a result of an article that Engles published in the *German-French Journal*, Marx saw that they were now in agreement. They began to correspond and one of the most fruitful collaborations in history began in 1844. An important early product of that collaboration we now know as the *Economic and Philosophical Manuscripts of 1844*.

*The Economic and Philosophical Manuscripts*

---

paid at a fixed rate (by the piece, by the hour, or by salary), but the person who participates in exchange relationships is free to charge what the market will bear even though that person may not have produced anything at all. The person who produces the product has little if anything to say about what it will sell for. One could produce the best product in the world, but if it could not be sold there would be no reward whatsoever. Of course, the maker could keep the product, but in an age of industrial specialization (where people make only one

thing or a small part of one thing) this would be self-defeating. How many pairs of shoes can a shoemaker wear? The system of production for exchange supports the system of capitalist economics. This led Marx to his classic analysis of social class.

There are two social classes, the *property-owning* **bourgeoisie,** on the one hand, and the *propertyless* **proletariat,** on the other. The bourgeoisie own the means of production while the proletariat own nothing. It is in the interest of property owners to get as much as they can out

*of 1844* are fundamentally a criticism of private property. Through this work Marx became, for the first time, favorable to socialism and communism. He began to transform the communist ideas of his day.

Because of pressure about ex-patriot radicals from the German government, Marx was expelled by the French in 1845. He gave up his Prussian citizenship and for the rest of his life was a man without a country. Marx settled in Brussels until 1848. He wanted to return to Germany but could not because the Prussian government had issued a warrant for his arrest. While in Belgium he was banned from writing on current political affairs. Once again the German government applied pressure and Marx was expelled from Brussels. He then returned to Paris at the invitation of a new French government.

Marx went to Cologne later in 1848 in the midst of the worker's rebellions. During the unsuccessful revolt, the government suspended all democratic institutions and the four editors of the *New Rhenish Gazette* left the country. The paper revived with Marx as editor, but in the summer of 1849 Marx was again expelled from the country because of his support of the workers. He went to London where he lived for the rest of his life.

In 1850 Marx received the privilege of doing research in the library of the British Museum. Mythology holds that Marx spent 12 to 15 years buried in the library doing his research for the famous *Capital*. As with most myths this is only partially true. Marx suffered a variety of illnesses and was unable to work for months at a time. He was very poor and could not afford proper medical care. He also needed to earn a living. He became the London correspondent for the *New York Daily Tribune* in October of 1851. By 1854, however, his articles began to appear anonymously because of their controversial content.

The story of Karl Marx's family is tragic. They were very poor until 1869. Because of ill health brought on by the family's poverty, three of Marx's children died when they were very young. The family constantly had to struggle, and Marx himself was ill for most of his lifetime. He was too proud to ask for money from friends, even Engles. Occasionally, Engles would offer a small amount of money and a few bottles of wine, which Marx always accepted under protest. Even after the publication of *Capital* in 1867, things did not improve. Finally, in 1869 Engles sold his textile business and set up an annuity for Marx out of the proceeds. Marx died from pleurisy in early 1883. Engles took the many pages of Marx's notebooks and published much of the work we know as *Capital* after Marx's death.

Karl Marx's biography is interesting because we can draw some inferences from it about the circumstances which allow significant social questions to be asked. Marx led a marginal life; he was not a part of "normal" society, nor was he a complete outsider. He was a Christian with a Jewish cultural heritage who became an atheist, a well-trained academic philosopher who never held an academic position and spent his life studying economics and founding revolutionary organizations. Until he finished college he was comfortable financially, but for most of his adult life he was poor. He was a man without a country in an age of nationalism. Given this unique position it should not surprise us that Marx could ask the penetrating questions that were so unusual in his time and still produce fruitful intellectual debate. Marx was able to transcend his personal circumstances and recognize that it was human society which produced marginality, poverty, and injustice: private troubles are often the consequence of public issues.

of a worker's labor. The more production, the more the property owner makes, while the workers get no reward for greater production. Marx thought this was the result of the dialectical process. The owners came to capitalism with the unfair advantage of their inherited mantle of feudal power. Their ancestors had owned land while the workers' ancestors had been serfs. Because of their longstanding power, the capitalists took over the machinery of the newly developing industrial society and molded it to fit the economic system.

## Emile Durkheim

Like Marx, Emile Durkheim recognized a fundamental paradox. As people came to live and work closer together in cities and factories, they seemed to think differently and even behave differently from one another. At the same time, however, there was a great deal of behavioral regularity. Durkheim reasoned that although people thought they were different, collectively they were very much alike. Even the feeling of individuality was so universal that there had to

Charlie Chaplin in *Modern Times* portrayed the alienation of the industrial worker. Spending his working life turning one bolt clockwise and one counter-clockwise on a machine part he does not understand, Charlie becomes robotic himself, just as Marx prophesied.

be something else behind it. Durkheim thus assumed that human beings were passive, that society was more than just the sum of its parts, that sociology should try to discover what held society together and what produced order so that a new morality could be developed, and that the best way to do this was by using science.

**The Nature of Human Nature** Durkheim discusses the nature of human nature by raising the question, "What is a social fact?" *Social facts are ways of acting, thinking, and feeling that are to some extent common to a number of people.* Social facts are external to individuals, things such as customs, laws, and the general rules or norms of behavior (see Chapter 3). Social facts are more than behavioral guides, they have coercive power. We do not choose to conform with the prevailing social mode; we simply do not realize that there is a choice.

For example, drivers obediently stop at red lights even at 3:00 A.M. because they are afraid of the consequences of going right on through. Our behavior is, thus, socially coerced, and Durkheim concluded that human nature is therefore essentially passive. Individuals are products of society, not the creators of society.

**The Nature of Society** Durkheim's consideration of social facts led him to his major con-

cern with social order, which he was certain could be found even in the seemingly chaotic society he was observing. "Why," he asked, "is there social order?" His answer was that people are morally and psychologically dependent on society. They survive only through interaction with others. Without help, no infant could live. Without cooperation, no adult could live long. People are born into a social group that already exists, with more or less set ways of doing things. This social order precedes all human life; it tells us how to go about surviving; it is the precondition of individual life.

Durkheim felt that the social order was based on a fairly concrete moral order, a code of right and wrong in which some things are required and other things are prohibited. The moral order produces social facts that limit behavior and make society possible. Any particular social order and its associated social facts are dependent on their particular moral order. A moral order, therefore, defines a particular kind of society.

**The Purpose and Method of Sociology** In observing the social change going on around him, Durkheim thought that the chaos he discerned was caused by the lack of an appropriate moral order for the conditions newly brought about by the industrial and nationalist revolutions. He reasoned that a new moral order was necessary in order to produce social order under these circumstances. He felt that it was sociology's task to help discover the principles of social change and social order, and that social theory would then be able to dictate social practice and develop the new moral order.

How should sociologists go about developing this new moral order? This was the same question that Saint-Simon had asked, and Durkheim was impressed with Saint-Simon's work. Saint-Simon was one of the first to argue that morality could be developed scientifically and, like him, Durkheim said that the proper method for sociology was the scientific method.

Durkheim's study of suicide is often held up as a model of scientific research in sociology.* In his book, *Suicide,* he compared data from different countries, different religions, different periods of history, different times of the day

*This section is based on material prepared by S. Dale McLemore, the author of Chapter 19.

**EMILE DURKHEIM (1858–1917)[2]**

Durkheim was born in Lorraine, France, in 1858. His father was a rabbi and his background may have influenced Durkheim as concern with morality stayed with him throughout his illustrious career. Durkheim entered one of the best schools in France, the *École Normale Supérieure,* in 1879. He was unhappy with his teachers, for the most part, except for two philosophers at the university. These men led Durkheim into later political activity in establishing a "rationalist, progressive, liberal or (in the non-Marxist sense) socialist . . . political victory in the third republic. . . ."[3] This political activity came to a head during the later 1890s. Durkheim worked with the political left in the struggle against the Catholic royalists.

Durkheim taught in three different high schools between 1885 and 1886 and received a scholarship to go to Germany to study philosophy and the social sciences. At that time he read Marx but was not impressed. On returning from Germany Durkheim took a position at the University of Bordeaux remaining there until 1902 when he realized his life's ambition, an appointment to the Sorbonne.

Politically, Durkheim was interested in socialism and even began an historical survey of socialist thought. He disagreed with most socialists, however, arguing that the question was not one of social class but rather that the social problems they addressed were a general phenomenon common to whole societies. In 1896 Durkheim founded the *Aneé Sociologie,* edited it, and contributed many articles each year.

Emile Durkheim led a distinguished if uneventful life. Yet he too experienced marginality. He was Jewish in a society dominated by Catholics. Such outsider status may have contributed to his interest in anomie and the conditions of social bonding. Durkheim's successful academic and social life may also account for some of the questions he raised. He wanted to insure that a "normal" social order would continue, and we may speculate that this interest was an outgrowth of his secure position in that social order at a time when many French Jews were insecure. (Durkheim was active in the Dreyfus case.) Instead of asking questions about poverty, like Marx, Durkheim asked questions about the overall direction of society. As a comparative base he used non-Western societies instead of the different segments of Western society. Western society was a whole in his opinion and he did not see national divisions as causal, but was able to raise significant questions about European social order by contrasting it with ancient and preliterate societies.

and year, and so on.[4] There were variations *within* religions as well as *between* religions, and between married and unmarried people, and the like. Durkheim concluded that suicide was a *social* phenomenon; it was not caused by individual distress (such as alcoholism or mental illness) or by environmental factors, such as climate, geographical location, or the season of the year. Different social environments exert different amounts of pressure on individuals

thus promoting certain kinds of behavior and inhibiting others. Protestants, for example, are freer of the control of the church than are Catholics; but one of the prices Protestants pay for that increased freedom is an increased probability of suicide. Similarly, when political or economic crises decrease the unity or cohesion of a society, individuals are under less pressure from society's rules and are more likely to commit suicide. In short, the more an individual is integrated

Societies characterized by *organic solidarity* (top) are based on difference; those characterized by *mechanical solidarity* (bottom) are based on sameness.

examining *the way the essential tasks in a society are divided up and assigned to people.* Sociologists call this the **division of labor.** Task assignment is always made on the basis of social categories and includes a division by age and sex (men's work, women's work, or children's work). Societies in which the division of labor is very involved are called complex societies.

Societies originate in moral order, Durkheim said, and they remain stable because of social solidarity. Solidarity is an integrative device, something we might call social glue. It holds people together and bonds them to the moral order. Solidarity is a product of the collective consciousness, the set of beliefs, feelings, and sentiments held by most people in a single society. These beliefs together form a religious, moral, and intellectual system that spreads through the whole society.

Durkheim studied different societies at different periods of time in order to look at different collective consciousnesses. He gathered together anthropological information and combined that with his own observations of Europe. He discovered two distinctive types of collective consciousness. In one type, common religious beliefs and practices tended to dominate all social life. This type of collective consciousness, found in nonindustrial societies, had a form of social organization Durkheim called **mechanical solidarity;** that is, everything in these societies could be depended upon to operate in rigid traditional fashion.

Durkheim noted that the collective consciousness of Europe in the latter half of the nineteenth century had become increasingly nonreligious and more oriented to the here and now. It was more purposeful or rational. Most important, supreme value was no longer attached to society or the interests of the whole group. Individuals and subparts of society were becoming more important. Societies distinguished by this kind of collective consciousness, Durkheim said, had **organic solidarity.** The characteristics of the two types of social solidarity are shown in Table 2.1.

In nonindustrial societies, with mechanical solidarity, people are bonded to each other and to the group by their similarities. Individuals all have the same tasks, the same values, and the same expectations. Tradition is the guiding force. In industrial societies, with organic solidarity, people are bonded together because of their differences. They depend on each other

into intimate social groups, the lower is the probability that he or she will commit suicide.

Durkheim's premise that social facts are things, makes it possible for sociologists to get outside of what they are looking at—just as the chemist is outside of the test tube—and thus study social life scientifically (see Chapter 19).

**The Division of Labor** Durkheim reached his conclusions about the new moral order by

TABLE 2.1    Characteristics of Durkheim's Types
              of Social Solidarity

*Mechanical*

Found in simple, preliterate societies
Moral and social similarity
Great conformity to tradition
Individual difference and variation restricted
Most property communally owned
Religion in the form of cult and daily ritual
Individual thought and conduct controlled by
    community opinion
Widely extended kinship network
Interpersonal relations based on loyalty and trust
"Sacred" orientation: life ordered by religious values
Sentiment or feeling as a major value
Repressive, or punitive, law

*Organic*

Found in complex, industrial societies
Moral and social diversity
Essentially traditionless
Individual difference and variation encouraged
Most property privately owned
Religion formally institutionalized, as in churches
Little community control over individual thought and
    conduct
Nuclear family (parents and children as principal kin)
Interpersonal relations based on contracts
"Secular" orientation: life ordered by worldly values
Rationalism as a major value
Restitutive, or restorative, law

**bourgeoise:**   Marx's term for property owners or, more generally, the upper or dominant class.

**proletariat:**   Marx's term for nonproperty-owning workers or, more generally, the lower or subordinant class.

**division of labor:**   the way in which the work and other activities and functions of a society are allocated to its members for performance, typically according to social categories. The simplest and most universal division of labor is by age and sex; the more complicated forms are represented by the social-occupational structures of the industrial society. The term includes social function or performance as well as occupation. In Britain, for example, some pursuits or activities are associated exclusively with the aristocracy. An American contrast is the ugly phrase, "nigger work."

**mechanical** and **organic solidarity:**   Durkheim's terms for the two varieties of social organization he believed were polar opposites in human society. Mechanical solidarity is social organization based on "sameness" or similarity of persons, values, and activities. It characterizes tribal societies. It is "mechanical" in that the members of such societies are alike, like mass-produced machine parts, and the basis of their social order is similarity. Organic solidarity is based on reciprocal, interdependent difference, like that between the organs of the body. It characterizes industrial societies. It is "organic," in that the members of such societies, although very different in values and attitudes, are dependent upon each other for the smooth functioning of the community.

**anomie:**   a condition of normlessness, being without values, that results from the weakening or dissolution of the social ties between people; a state in which social facts have lost their coercive power over individuals.

for things that they cannot do for themselves: the farmer needs the mechanic, the mechanic needs the doctor, and so forth. In societies with organic solidarity, Durkheim observed, there is a greater possibility of some of the social glue coming unstuck. The absence of bonding, he called **anomie,** *a state in which social facts have lost their coercive power and people do not know which rules to follow.*

### Max Weber

Like Marx and Durkheim, Max Weber noted a paradox in the social life of the late nineteenth century. Although people seemed to go about their lives reasonably and purposefully, their behavior did not always lead to the best solutions to their problems. Because he focused on individuals, Weber assumed that society was equal to the sum of the individuals involved. The purpose of sociology was to discover how society worked, but sociology had no separate goals of its own. The proper method of sociology was science, since this permitted detached observation of social life.

**The Kinds of Social Action**   Weber's scholarship was more concerned with individuals

**MAX WEBER (1864–1920)**[5]

Max Weber and Karl Marx came from similar backgrounds. Weber's father was an attorney and Max was born in the small town of Erfurt, Thuringia, Germany. When he was five, the Webers moved to the suburb of Berlin in which many of Germany's noted academics and intellectuals lived. Weber's mother was an educated and intelligent woman who had many humanitarian concerns. She faced one of the contradictions of educated women then as now in subordinating herself to care for her busy politician husband and her six children.

The relationship between Weber's parents deteriorated throughout his childhood and early manhood. This seemed to trouble him greatly and at the age of 31 he had a showdown with his father. He insisted that his mother be allowed to visit him without the father being present. This led to a bitter battle won by Max, Jr., and he never spoke to his father again. The senior Weber died a few months later.

The difficulties of his parents and the argument with his father may have contributed to Weber's well-known mental illness. While he was one of the best known educators of his time in Germany, he was rarely able to work full time at an academic job. He was hospitalized at one point and a good deal of his life was spent traveling to escape the pressure of work. When he did work, Weber had frequent bouts of insomnia and conditions bordering on nervous breakdowns.

From the age of four Weber preferred books to sports and the other activities of young boys. However, in college he changed, becoming an enthusiastic member of a Prussian dueling society, in due course receiving the required

than that of either Marx or Durkheim. **Social action,** for Weber, is *behavior undertaken by one person while taking into account another person.* It is best understood in terms of ends and means—goals and how you achieve them—and on the basis of whether rationality is present or absent. Weber thought that this approach would enable sociologists to distinguish between societies that used the four different types of social action—rational action, evaluative action, affective action, and neutral or traditional action.

In *rational action*, a person deliberately selects first a goal and then the most efficient means of achieving that goal. To do this, the person must consider all the consequences of all possible behavior and calculate the costs of the goal in relation to its worth. Decision making of this kind is called rational behavior or rational action. A society where most members make decisions in this way can be called a rational or rationalistic society.

In *evaluative action*, the goal is chosen not through deliberate consideration but rather because it is highly desired or valued in the culture for its own sake. The means for achieving the goal may be subject to rational calculation, however. In modern America, for example, personal financial security is a widely shared goal. It is generally considered good in and of itself, and most people aspire to it without much thought. But there are alternative means for achieving this goal—a long period of education, inheritance, hard work, saving, or holding up a bank. Most people do use their reasoning powers to choose among the alternative means.

The third type of action is called *affective action*. Its goals are not rationally chosen at all. The end desired is simply emotional satisfaction. The way to achieve it is through sponta-

facial scar and a commission in the Prussian army. His new found *machismo* became so strong that it disgusted his mother and when he returned home she greeted him with a slap.

Weber traveled to the United States to deliver a lecture at the World's Fair of 1904. While here, he traveled extensively and this experience may have contributed to some of his later ideas.

The key focus of Weber's experience of America was upon the role of bureaucracy in a democracy. He saw that "machine politics" were indispensable in modern "mass democracy" unless a "leaderless democracy" and a confusion of tongues were to prevail. Machine politics, however, mean the management of politics by professionals, by the disciplined party organization and its streamlined propaganda. Such democracy may also bring to the helm the Caesarist people's tribune (an elected defender to protect the rights of the people from the upper class) whether in the role of the strong president or the city manager. And the whole process tends toward increasing rational efficiency and therewith bureaucratic machines: party, municipal, federal.[6]

After his return to Germany, Weber was active in establishing a sociological society. When World War I began he wanted to lead his company into battle, but since he was 50 years old he was not permitted to do so. Instead, he was put in charge of nine hospitals in the Heidelberg area. Here Weber experienced bureaucracy from the inside. After the war he went to Vienna for a summer term where he gave his first university lectures in 19 years. These lectures became events which not only students but professors, state officials, and politicians attended. He was offered a permanent position in Vienna but declined. He accepted a position in Munich a year later but shortly thereafter died of pneumonia in June, 1920.

Weber, like Marx, and to some degree Durkheim, also presents an image of marginality. He was a troubled individual who spent a large portion of his adult life suffering from mental illness. Of all the great classical sociologists, Weber was most concerned with the individual, which we speculate may have been the result of trying to understand his own situation. He was a famous academic who had few chances to participate in academic life. When he did, he had a conflict with his students concerning his nationalist viewpoint. He tended toward a very masculine, almost "macho," view of the world, but supported the appointment of the first woman to a government post. This type of contradiction runs throughout Weber's work and is most apparent in his attempt to weld an individualistically oriented theory to studies of whole civilizations.

neous reactions in a given situation. People follow their emotional instincts and "do their own thing."

*Traditional action* means behaving in ways that are customary just because they are customary. Decisions are unnecessary because the behavior is required, or seems to be. Reason is not employed at all, though the person may believe in the rationality of the behavior. Indeed, habitual behavior may seem to be the only behavior possible. A person behaves without question as tradition dictates, for example, shaking hands when we are introduced, using "Dear" to start letters (even angry ones), and eating three meals a day.

**The Nature of Society**   Weber regarded society as equal to the sum of its individual members and social actions as the building blocks for societies. Social actions multiplied become social relations, in which, among several people, the action of each takes into account, and is oriented to, the behavior of all the others. When we find whole societies where social relations are similar, we can classify them according to the type of social relations we observe. If the social actions and the resulting social relations are characterized as rational, then we would characterize that society as rational.

Weber observed that some parties to social relationships seem to be able to get what they want more easily than others. This led him to formulate his concept of power. **Power** is *the ability to influence social organization and get people to do things, even against their will.* Weber identified three types of legitimate power or **authority**—charismatic, traditional, and rational-legal. *Charismatic authority* is an almost magical quality possessed by, or attributed to, an individual—personal magnetism, the ability

Can we doubt that what is operating here is rational-legal rather than charismatic or traditional authority?

to attract groups or individuals and sway them. Jesus, Hitler, and John F. Kennedy are all examples of the charismatic leader.

*Traditional authority* is perceived as always being wielded by the occupants of certain social positions. Kings were obeyed as long as they followed the traditions of their societies. When they neglected traditional duties or abused traditional rights, their power was deemed illegitimate and they were overthrown.

*The rational-legal authority* of modern industrial nations is legitimated by accepted rules. This is because the most important components of modern societies are organizations; that is, social groups that are goal-directed and have rules that are the means for achieving their goals. When an organization is highly developed, the rules deal with everything and it is said to be complex and highly bureaucratized (see Chapter 6). Weber's theory of bureaucracy remains the basis for most modern work in the field of complex organizations.

**The Purpose and Method of Sociology**
Weber wrote extensively about the methods of sociology late in his career, when, in the political atmosphere of Germany before World War I, political and religious discrimination often made it impossible to get an academic job. The well-known sociologists Michels and Simmel had difficulty securing academic posts because they were non-Marxist socialists and Jewish. Against this background, then, Weber advocated academic freedom. He argued that sociology should propose no political goals nor should it have such goals imposed upon it. For Weber, the purpose of sociology was to provide information about society with which others might accomplish goals of their own choosing.

To maintain the neutrality he felt was necessary for sociology, Weber concluded that the only proper method was the scientific method. But he realized that this was difficult in sociology, because much of the subject matter concerned values which were internal to the individual and could not be directly observed. To make it possible to take an internal perspective, Weber invented what he called the **verstehen** technique, in which the investigator uses insight and empathy to determine the values and motives in a social relation. Once values and motives have been identified, the researcher can treat them objectively and scientifically. Thus Weber enabled subjective values to be treated objectively (see Chapter 19 for further discussion of related problems).

**Social Class**　Weber attempted to refine and develop Marx's notions of social class.[7] He argued that social class, besides being related to property ownership or ownership of the means of production, was also connected to power, wealth, and social honor or prestige.

Wealth usually buys power and social honor, even if the source of the wealth is not legitimate. Wealth may also be seen as the ability to acquire things and experiences. Property ownership, wages, and welfare payments are important sources of wealth that allow (or limit) consumption. The positively privileged have enough to buy what they want when they want it. The negatively privileged have low access to wealth and have limited opportunity to acquire goods, education, travel, and costly kinds of recreation. They lack skills and training. Most people fall into a middle group with some skills or training or both. This includes professionals, government officials, people in the crafts, and skilled workers.

The two classifications of wealth—power and the ability to consume—overlap. Together they make up what Weber called social class. On the basis of relative wealth, people express power relations with each other. This is also the primary mechanism for the overall determination of prestige (see Chapter 7).

## CONTEMPORARY VIEWS OF SOCIAL REALITY

Contemporary views of social reality are for the most part extensions and elaborations of the classical positions outlined above. Structural functionalism flows from Durkheim's ideas, modern radical sociology and some types of conflict theory are derived from Marx, and phenomenology is part of the German tradition exemplified by Weber. Symbolic interaction stems from American pragmatic philosophy and has elements that are derived from, and compatible with, all three classical positions.

### Structural Functionalism

Structural functional theory, often called functionalism, has dominated sociology and the other social sciences for the past fifty years. It is

**social action:** action that takes others into account; behavior reflecting the needs, demands, or presence of others. Weber distinguishes four types: (1) rational, (2) evaluative, (3) affective, and (4) traditional (See **action**)

**power:** the capacity of an individual or group to exercise his, her, or its will despite resistance; the capacity to "get one's way."

**authority:** legitimated power. Weber distinguished three types: charismatic, traditional, and rational-legal.

**verstehen:** a German word usually translated as "understanding," it was used by Max Weber as the name for a sociological technique of empathetic identification with another for the purpose of observation on the grounds that one must understand the other's motives and meanings in order to comprehend his or her behavior.

the logical extension of Durkheim's thinking. Like Durkheim, the functionalists see individuals as fulfilling the requirements for society's survival and perpetuation. They view human nature as plastic, readily molded by society into any useful form. Society is similar to an organism, a system of action and interaction among its members, balanced, bounded, and interrelated. Society works through the coordination and interdependence of all the elements in the system with each other, which in turn is made possible by the general agreement in the society about important values and norms.

TABLE 2.2   **Assumptions of the Three Great Classical Thinkers**

| Assumption | Marx | Durkheim | Weber |
|---|---|---|---|
| Nature of human nature | People are good, cooperative | People are passive | People are capable of being rational |
| Nature of society | Composed of social relationships | Society is different from the sum of its parts | The sum of individuals equals the whole |
| Purpose of sociology | To change society | To discover proper morality | To analyze society in order to understand it; but sociology should be neutral |
| Proper method | Emphasized science from critical perspective | Science | Science |

**The Individual and Society** Functional theorists see human beings responding to the requirements of their societies. People find their place within the social order and tend to stay in that place. They may change, but only in the manner prescribed by the society. Thus society is the active agent in history, and human beings are passive responders. To a large degree, individuals are overwhelmed by the pressures their societies place on them to conform to social expectations, and they reflect such pressures most of the time. Even if they assert their own wills to act differently, their individuality itself is likely to conform to societal definitions of what is possible and permitted.

**The Concept of a Social System** One of the crucial concepts of functionalism is that society is a system. That is to say, first of all, it is balanced. Any upsetting forces are subject to the basic stability of other parts of the system. Second, as a system, society has boundaries. You can discriminate between the items that are in the system and those that are outside it. To keep the system balanced, its boundaries must be maintained, or only slowly altered. Third, all the parts or elements in the social system are related to each other. If one element changes, all the other elements will have to change as well. Each part is interrelated with, and dependent upon, every other part.

**The Concept of Function** *A* **function** *is some event positively influencing the system of which it is a part. It is determined by the system and simultaneously helps determine the nature of the system.* For example, what happens in our society when two people get married? Their behavior changes. They stop acting like single people or an engaged couple and begin to act married. People begin to treat them differently (they are permitted to sleep in the same bed while visiting their parents). They begin to see themselves as a couple rather than as single individuals. They act in the interests of a new family rather than in their own individual interests as before. In our society we strongly believe that people of opposite sexes who want to live together should get married. Marriage is thus behavior that is determined by the social system, and it in turn helps determine the nature of the system. It functions to perpetuate the system.

All parts of every system are either functional or dysfunctional. Most parts are **functional:** *they perform a positive service by helping to maintain the system or its balanced state.* **Dysfunctional** *elements are either useless (in which case they tend to be discarded or disappear) or have negative effects.* The human heart, for example, is clearly functional for the body and all of the subsystems within it. But a heart defect is dysfunctional; it not only does not contribute, it detracts or even endangers.

Many people regard crime as dysfunctional for the society, dangerous and damaging at the least, threatening collapse at the worst. Durkheim, the first functionalist, saw crime as having positive functions, strengthening the moral order by calling attention to the importance of the laws violated and by forcing us sometimes to define the laws more precisely.

Functionalists also distinguish between manifest and latent functions, because the social usefulness of some things is not always obvious. A **manifest function** can be *directly associated with the purpose for which it is intended.* A **latent function** is *the social purpose served unconsciously, unknowingly by those who perform the act in question.* The familiar ceremony of playing the national anthem before a public sports event, for example, may appear to have political meaning. It seems to be intended as a reminder of the rewards of living in the United States, designed, perhaps to fuel our patriotism. A sociologist might view it, however, as a latently religious ritual in the civil religion that many Americans share regardless of their church membership (see Chapter 13).

Society works because all of its elements are in constant interaction with their own environments, and, in ways both latent and manifest, interact to support the general welfare of the social system as a whole. Things that serve no useful purpose tend to be discarded or to find new, positive, functions. The few elements that endanger the system or throw it out of balance are actively resisted. The system may also shift its structure so that a new balance is struck, thus removing the threat of a dysfunctional element. For example, when a new invention disrupts the established way of doing things, the system usually either rejects it or adjusts to it, incorporating it into the culture.

Table 2.3 shows some ways in which functionalists have applied these ideas to under-

TABLE 2.3  Some Social Institutions and
Their Functions

| Social institution | Functions performed |
|---|---|
| The economic system | Production and distribution of necessary goods and services |
| The education system | Socialization of the young to cultural values, transmission of basic information and skills, ''keeping the kids off the streets'' |
| The family | Procreation and rearing of children, basic socialization, sexual regulation and satisfaction, transmission of social status |
| The law | Maintenance of internal order in the society, formal enactment of the moral order, control of deviants |
| The military | Protection from external threat, exploitive aggression |
| The political system | Organization of power, legitimation of authority, routinization of collective decision making for the general welfare |
| The religious system | Worship of one or more deities, interpreting the unknown, development and support of a moral order |

In the functionalist view, social institutions perform social functions for the perpetuation of the society itself and are developed by society to accomplish that purpose.

**function:** the positive service performed by some element of a system in maintaining the system's balance, boundaries, or interrelationships; a positive or favorable consequence of, or purpose for, an act, event, or object.

**functional:** operating to maintain a social system or its balanced state.

**dysfunctional:** operating to threaten the maintenance of a social system or its balanced state.

**manifest function:** the purpose or end for which an act, event or object is intended.

**latent function:** an unintended (and perhaps unknown) consequence of an act, event, or object.

**social institution:** a persistent, normative pattern for the ways in which groups and associations interrelate to carry out common activities; a way of doing things so common and normative as to have become mandatory. Social institutions are typically understood to address their activities to functions that must be performed in order for a society to endure, e.g., food-gathering and distribution, mating, etc.

standing **social institutions.** The social institutions are conventional ways of getting important things done in a society. When the customary means of accomplishing such things become so conventional that they are regarded as the only way, they are said to have become institutionalized (see Chapter 6).

**The Purpose and Method of Sociology**
Most modern functionalists believe that sociology's purpose is to discover social laws and let others apply them. Some, however, have moved into policy making and in so doing, perhaps they are going back to Durkheim's idea of creating a new morality.[8]

Critics of functionalism, however, argue that its hidden purpose is to support the status quo. Functionalists assume that society as a system tends to maintain itself; they ask questions about how society remains stable rather than about how society changes. When problems arise, functionalists tend to seek ways to bring things back to ''normal'' rather than suggesting change.

Functionalists attempt to use scientific method, but since many of their definitions are circular (for example, they define function as something that is determined by the system while helping to determine the system), there is little in them that can be measured. The concepts of functionalism are usually expressed in terms of relationships, and the elements are difficult to isolate. If functionalists are to develop more scientific credibility, they will have to construct other methods to measure their concepts.

## Conflict Theory

Very few theorists have regarded conflict as the basis for all human social arrangements. The two most influential modern proponents of **conflict theory,** Ralf Dahrendorf and Lewis Coser, do not go that far, although their work has helped direct the attention of sociologists to the nature and functions of conflict in modern society. Both have focused on the integrative nature of conflict. They believe that somehow conflict helps hold society together, but they do not assume it is the basis of social life.

For conflict theorists, human nature is largely passive; the many are dominated by the few. Since rewards and resources are scarce, people inevitably become competitive, even if they don't want to. The nature of society is a balance of opposed or conflicting groups or associations. The mechanism that keeps society going is conflict between organized groups over the rewards available within the social system. Because it is rarely possible for one group to dominate another permanently, a kind of dynamic stability is created by the continuing contest.

**Power and Authority** Since they believe that the nature of most human beings is to follow and that only a few lead, power is a crucial concept for conflict theorists. Power is the probability that an actor can carry out his or her will despite resistance. Authority is legitimated power. It is always associated with social positions and is a common and necessary feature of social life. Conflict theory assumes that people must either dominate or be dominated and that direction and leadership are necessary in social affairs.

**The Role of Associations** According to Dahrendorf, conflict and authority take place primarily in associations; conflict between individuals is socially unimportant. An association is a social group with an authority structure. It is composed of two quasi-groups, holders and nonholders of power. When these quasi-groups recognize their separate interests, they become interest groups, or classes, and the probability of conflict in the society becomes higher.

Conflict tends to produce a balance of forces which eventually produces stability in the system. Change takes place through change in the authority system. Since we always have conflict in society, and yet society remains relatively stable, then logically conflict must contribute to order and stability.

**The Role of Conflict** The basic mechanism that makes society work is social conflict, a struggle over values and scarce resources like status, power, and property. Conflict attempts to neutralize, injure, or eliminate rivals. It is usually seen as a conscious social process, taking place between organized groups.

Some of the outcomes of social conflict are described by Coser's theory, and have been expressed in a series of formal and abstract propositions such as the following:[9]

1. The more unlimited the goals of the opposing parties in a conflict, the more prolonged the conflict will be. When goals are unlimited, the participants feel most threatened; thus it is harder to secure unconditional surrender from an enemy than a negotiated armistice.
2. Conflict is less prolonged if people think the total attainment of their goals will involve a cost greater than that required for a limited victory. The reason for this is that when victory is at hand, opponents are tempted to settle for what they have rather than make further sacrifices for ends that may not be attainable.
3. The more intense the conflict, the more clear-cut the boundaries of the respective parties. Under the pressure of severe conflict, fence straddling is not permitted. People make strong efforts to draw away from and distinguish themselves from the enemy. For example, some American schools stopped teaching German during World War I.
4. The more intense the conflict, the greater the solidarity within conflicting groups. This is in part a function of the "with us or against us" mentality and in part a result of the ideological simplification that occurs under pressure; fine points and qualifications become obscure. As people withdraw from any identification with the enemy, they draw more closely together and identify more closely with each other.[10]

Conflict theorists treat sociology in much the same way as the functionalists. They feel that the purpose of sociology is analytic. Once goals have been prescribed by others, sociologists can use scientific methods to determine the best way to reach those goals.

## Symbolic Interactionism

**Symbolic interactionism** was introduced through the lectures of George Herbert Mead at the University of Chicago in the 1930s.[11] Although it is usually regarded as a microtheory (small-scale theory) designed to explain socialization (see Chapter 4), some interactionists treat it as a total theory of society. In their view, human beings are active and communicative. Society is an extremely complex network of actions and interactions between individuals, all of them organized and powered (motivated) by group membership, with its inherent roles and demands. Society continues to function because people are *socialized* (trained) to meet role expectations from the time of birth and because the interdependency of individuals makes them rely on each other for necessary services and rewards.

**Symbols and Meaning** Mead begins with the assumption that human beings, like other animals, are incessantly active. They constantly make **gestures**—movements or sounds—that are reacted to by others. But only human beings turn gestures into symbols, marks, or acts that come to stand for something, to have symbolic meaning (see Chapter 3). Symbols become significant when they have the same or similar meaning for the person receiving them as they do for the person making them. Meaning is

**conflict theory:** the theoretical position that views social conflict as a principal means through which human groups interact and as the basis for social structure; the notion that structure is the negotiated outcome of conflict and that, as a consequence, social change results from conflict.

**symbolic interaction theory:** the theoretical position that views social interaction between individuals, ordered by their symbolically defined, reciprocal expectations for each other's behavior, as the basis for social life.

**gesture:** a motion or sound that becomes associated with some meaning through repeated experience of the association, as when we learn when it is proper to say "ouch" (a meaningless sound), or that a hand is waved in greeting or farewell.

shared and social. It is learned through interaction with others. Human beings possess the capacity for thought, which is a consequence of language. Human nature is thus an entirely social phenomenon, the product of symbolic social interaction with others.

Conflict theorists see confrontations like this one involving gay activists as the raw material of social structure and change.

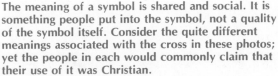

The meaning of a symbol is shared and social. It is something people put into the symbol, not a quality of the symbol itself. Consider the quite different meanings associated with the cross in these photos; yet the people in each would commonly claim that their use of it was Christian.

**Expectations and Behavior**   Society is the sum total of the symbolic social relations its members have with one another. It is composed of groups and the relationships between groups. Behavior within groups and intergroup relations are ordered by expectations created by both significant (individual or personal) others and generalized others (see Chapter 4). Through interaction, people learn to reflect on their own behavior, and come to have certain expectations about it and the behavior of others. They also learn that others have similar expectations for themselves. The patterns of relations between people and their groups constitute the structure of society. Society is a collection of reciprocal expectations and expectation-fulfilling behavior.

**Roles and Interaction**   Society works because human beings are capable of language. The most important product of this is self-consciousness. As language skills develop, the human child learns first the meanings of words and the attitudes associated with them by those who use the words. Later the child learns the expectations people have for his or her behavior, and in time learns to have similar expectations for others. Sets of these expectations that are associated with the behavior of particular persons are called roles. Thus, through interaction with Mommy and Daddy, the child learns what to expect of them and what behavior they expect in return. Mommy and Daddy, of course, behave the way they do because they are acting out a social role, a "part" in a "play" called "the family" which they, in turn, learned when they were growing up.

The generalized roles that people learn to play (father, mother, Catholic, plumber, and so forth) exist in the culture of any society at a particular time and define how one ought to act in particular roles. Growing up in a family, children learn not only how to act toward other family members, but also how the family and its members relate to other groups such as the church, the government, and the school. Mommy and Daddy may grumble as they prepare their tax forms, but they acknowledge that they ought to pay taxes, and the child learns something about the relation of the citizen to the state.

Symbolic interactionism sprang from American thought in the latter half of the nineteenth and beginning of the twentieth century, a period characterized by populism or popular democracy. While it is difficult to find statements of its goals, it does seem to favor the establishment of popular democracies where individuals may express their individuality. Symbolic interactionists often take the part of the underdog.[12]

Regarding methodology, symbolic interactionists argue that science may not be sufficient for sociological investigation. They want to be part of the ongoing research, not detached from it. Thus they use participant observation and other methods of becoming part of a social investigation (see Chapter 19).

## Phenomenology and Ethnomethodology

**Phenomenology** and its subdivision, ethnomethodology, find their roots in the work of the German philosopher Edmund Husserl as interpreted by Alfred Schutz. It is closely related to Weber's work, but it draws some ideas from symbolic interactionism as well.

Phenomenologists say that people create a context that allows them to think they share a social order. Thus they create society and define it. Sociology's purpose is to discover how people create social order and society. Phenomenologists try to look at these processes from the inside—the point of view of the actor—by temporarily changing people's perceptions of reality.

**The Nature of Human Nature** Phenomenologists see human nature as creative. In their influential book, *The Social Construction of Reality,* Peter Berger and Thomas Luckmann argue that reality is created by people as they go about their everyday tasks.[13] For example, in some households there is a rule that glasses are always washed first and pots

**phenomenonology:** the theoretical position stressing the subjective nature of the human experience of "reality," the individual basis of the human activities that constitute society, and a tendency to focus on how people voluntarily construct their lives in everyday encounters.

last. The rule probably developed from the recognition that dirty water leaves glasses streaked. The rule defines a small corner of reality, brings order to a small segment of social life, and has become so accepted that no one ever thinks to question it.

**The Nature of Society** Phenomenologists see society as created by individuals interacting in their everyday lives. Society and social reality exist only because people create them and agree on the definition of what they have created. Society does not exist except as human beings subjectively imagine it. That is, normal everyday acts become habitualized and then

Role playing: We learn our behaviors and expectations from others.

institutionalized as they are passed on to the next generation. Society becomes a set of institutions defined by interacting people who accept the order they have created.

For phenomenologists, the purpose of sociology is to find out how people create an orderly social world and maintain social order. The goal of research is to examine interaction situations to find out how people create their own social order. Like Weber, the phenomenologists try to get a view of the situation from the inside — from the point of view of the people doing the acting.

A branch of phenomenology that has recently made a strong impact is **ethnomethodology.** This is an attempt to invent a new sociological method. The basic technique of ethnomethodology is to interrupt or disturb the routine flow of social life and contrast what happened before the surprise interruption with what happens afterwards. A classic ethnomethodological experiment, for example, is to pause at the table of a stranger in a restaurant and take a sip from his water glass. The "rules" for "normal" behavior are often exposed by the reaction this receives.

### Modern Radical Sociology

Modern radical sociology has many variations but they all share a common heritage in the work of Karl Marx. This type of social analysis came to the forefront during the latter half of the 1960s. Students of that era were dissatisfied with mainstream sociological thinking because they felt it had failed to deal adequately with the civil rights movement and the war in Vietnam. The radicals argued that since sociology professed itself to be concerned with human beings, it should take a position against United States involvement in the war. Mainstream sociologists tended to take the position that sociology should remain neutral.

**The Nature of Human Nature** Radicals assume that people are good and can live cooperatively. They ask why people so often act uncooperatively. Their explanation focuses on the relationships people have with the rest of society. C. Wright Mills and Hans Gerth, drawing on the work of Marx, Weber, and Mead argued that human character structure is built from roles that people take in association with dominant social institutions and the class system.[14] For example, people explain their behavior by referring to something socially acceptable. We are motivated to act because justification for the behavior existed beforehand. Acceptable justification is culturally defined (see Chapter 3) and that definition is in its turn produced by the institutions such as the economy that dominate the society.

In modern society, competition prevails and is supported by power in social relationships. That is, some people come to dominate other people. Radicals reason that these relationships are unnatural, thus most people are alienated. The problem is to discover how these relationships continue to exist and expose their operation. For example, people become part of "the mass" and have less and less to say about decisions that affect their lives. People are spoken to by the mass media and have little chance to answer back.

**The Nature of Society** The strength of modern radical sociology lies in its analysis of total societies, focusing on the development of the institution of capitalism. In his book, *The Modern World System*, Immanuel Wallerstein documents the historical conditions that led to the rise of the market system and its configurations of social classes.[15]

Radicals want to know who holds power and how it is exercised. They make power a matter for sociological inquiry rather than accepting the existence of power as a *fait accompli.* C. Wright Mills, in *The Power Elite*, argues that a very small number of people control American society by running the organizations that make up the government, the military, and the corporations.[16] So powerful are the international corporations, in fact, that one could argue that the people who run them run the world. Many of these corporations have budgets and incomes larger than those of many countries (see Chapter 15).

The issue of social power leads directly to the issue of social class. Radical sociologists have recently attempted to bring together the work of Marx and Weber by showing how Weber's work can be seen as an extension of Marx's.[17] Weber's categories of power, prestige, and wealth are seen as springing from the nature of the economic institution.

**Purpose and Method** For radical sociologists the purpose of sociology is to understand social life in order to change it. Many radical sociologists spend their lives engaged in social activism, such as political demonstrations and community work. Others labor to expose the ideological biases of other theoretical perspectives.[18] Radical sociolgists freely admit to having an ideological bias, but sociologists who take other positions usually claim neutrality. Radicals try to show that all ways of asking questions and methods of inquiry are inevitably biased because they are always products of specific social and historical conditions.

Another major tendency in modern radical sociology has been to criticize the standard scientific techniques. Jürgen Habermas and other leaders of the Frankfurt School argue that standard science is not the only way to understand society.[19] According to Habermas, we

**ethnomethodology:** a subschool or variant of the phenomenological position concentrating on the social or individual construction of everyday behavior and often employing the disruption of such behavior as a way of exposing its underlying relationale or assumptions.

must construct a society that enables people to have rational discourse, and use it to guide the flow of history. This means that if people could discuss the significant issues of their time without economic or political pressure being brought to bear, it would be possible to develop more humane conditions for human life. Special interests would no longer play a significant role, and the interest of the whole would predominate.

## SUMMARY

All sociological theories are based on assumptions concerning (1) the nature of human nature, (2) the nature of society, (3) the purpose of sociology, and (4) the proper method of study. In general, the differences between the classical and contemporary views of social reality flow out of divergences in these assumptions (see Table 2.4).

The three great classical theorists in sociology were all Europeans of the last century, Karl Marx, Emile Durkheim, and Max Weber. For Karl Marx, people are basically good, so poverty and social injustice must be the products of society and the way it is organized. Since the economic institution is dominant in the Western world, the root of social evil is capitalism, the principal Western economic system. Capitalistic society is based on production, of which there are two kinds: production for human use and production for exchange. The first is natural, but the second is unnatural and exploitive. Production for exchange has divided society into two social classes, the proletariat and bourgeoisie. There is a natural conflict between them, and because of the dominance of the bourgeoisie, the proletariat are alienated from the products of their labor and from themselves; they are exploited for the profit of others. When the proletariat recognize their common

condition, they will revolt, destroy the capitalist system, and create a communist workers' state.

For Emile Durkheim, human beings are passive and are coerced by social facts. Society is to be understood primarily in terms of its moral order, the source of social facts. Society works through individual cooperation through the division of labor, which, in turn, produces social cohesion or solidarity, the force that binds individuals to each other and society. There are two kinds of social solidarity: mechanical solidarity, as represented in simple or preliterate societies, and organic solidarity, as seen in industrial societies. These produce two different forms of the division of labor and different legal-moral systems. Mechanical solidarity is found in social systems based on similarity, where the moral order is universally shared by everyone and forces all members of the society to behave in similar ways. Organic solidarity produces societies based on differences among individuals, where social order is based on mutual interdependence.

Max Weber found the distinguishing characteristic of Western society to be its rationality. This led him to concentrate on social action. For Weber, people are rational beings who act to accomplish their ends. But while the individual seems rational and his or

TABLE 2.4  Assumptions of Classical and Contemporary Views of Social Reality

| Theorist or theory | Nature of human nature | Nature of society | Purpose of sociology | Proper method |
|---|---|---|---|---|
| **Classical Theorists** | | | | |
| Marx | Good, cooperative, decent | Determined by the nature of the dominant institution; in capitalism, the economic system | Analyze society in order to change it. | Science from critical perspective |
| Durkeim | Passive, morally neutral, controlled by "social facts" | Preeminent, an active agent, controlling individual behavior | Develop new moral order | Science |
| Weber | Rational, choice-making | Varying; determined by the type of social action that is historically typical | Analysis | Science |
| **Contemporary Theories** | | | | |
| Functionalism | Reactive, responsive to social requirements | A balanced, bounded system with all parts interrelated | Analysis, some policy formation | Science |
| Conflict Theory | Mostly subordinate, subject to domination by leaders | A dynamic balance of competing or conflicting groups or associations attempting to secure their own ends | Analysis | Science |
| Symbolic interactionism | Social, active, communicative | Interaction networks of groups and individuals | Develop popular democracy | Science using internal perspective |
| Phenomenology | Reality-creating | Buildup of institutions coming from habits | Analysis | Science using interruption of everyday life and internal perspective. |
| Radical sociology | Good, cooperative | Social relations built into structures. In Western world economic institution dominant. | Analyze society in order to change it. | Science, critique of science and any method which will provide social analysis and synthesis. |

her behavior always has meaning for her or him, it need not always be objectively logical. Societies may be essentially rational or nonrational, depending on the kinds of social actions that predominate in them. The four possible types of society are: (1) rational, (2) evaluative, (3) affective, and (4) traditional. Society works through these kinds of social action, in which people accommodate their own behavior to their understanding of the behavior of others.

Contemporary sociological perspectives are largely extensions and elaborations of these classical views. There are five major schools, or positions, in today's sociology. In structural functionalism, human beings are essentially reactive, responsive to the requirements their societies impose upon them. Society is a system, or composed of various systems, whose purpose is self-perpetuation. Social systems have three basic characteristics: (1) balance, (2) boundaries, and (3) interrelationships or interdependence. Society works through consensus resulting from interdependence and the requirement of balance. Thus whatever is functional for the perpetuation of any social system is likely to endure. Whatever is dysfunctional is likely to be extinguished or disappear.

In conflict theory society is seen as a series of trade-offs and people as essentially rational. Conflict theory assumes that people are unwilling to give up values and must be forced to do so by threat or violence. Social structure is a reflection of power, so society is a kind of dynamic equilibrium among competing groups. The normal relation of person to person, then, is one of dominance and subordination. But since individual conflict is rarely productive, people form associations to secure their interests. Society works through the conflict of various types of associations (group with group, nation with nation). Instead of being pathological, conflict serves the positive function of maintaining a balance between competing groups.

Symbolic interactionism views human beings as social, active, and communicative. Society consists of the interactions that take place between people as individuals and between groups of people. Group life creates sets of expectations for other people's behavior, and the fulfillment of such expectations is what makes social life possible. Society works because people cooperate in acting out role expectations that are learned through infant socialization to the general culture and, later, through socialization to specific group rules, customs, and expectations.

Phenomenology sees human beings as creatures of habit. Habits are built into institutions, and the institutions combine to form societies. Society works because people need the rules that come out of successful ways of doing things. The rules are needed so we know where to go next. The best way to find out about these things is to interrupt the flow of everyday life.

Radical sociology accepts human beings as good and having the ability to live together cooperatively. People come together in social relations and these relationships, taken together, form the structure of society. Society works through people's attachment to the central institution; the economic institution.

You will be meeting these views, throughout the book.

None is "right" and none is "wrong." They are views, perspectives, ways of looking at things, frameworks used for asking questions. Any of them can provide a reasonable explanation of the way the social world works, but each calls our attention to different aspects of it, emphasizing some things and ignoring others. That is the purpose of theory.

## SUGGESTED READINGS

BLUMER, HERBERT. "Symbolic Interaction." in James M. Henslin, ed., *Down to Earth Sociology*. New York: Free Press, 1972, pp. 96–100. This article provides a brief and very readable summary of symbolic interaction theory. It covers the essential concepts and shows how they are related to each other.

ETZIONI, AMITAI. "From Zion to Diaspora." *Society* 15(4) May/June 1978, pp. 92–101. A self-portrait of a major modern social theorist. He describes how his ideas were influenced by his childhood experi-

ences and how he is applying social theory to social policy.

HOOVER, KENNETH. *The Elements of Scientific Thinking.* New York: St. Martin's, 1976. A comprehensive and not too difficult review of basic terms and concepts.

MERTON, ROBERT K. *Social Theory and Social Structure,* 2d ed. New York: Free Press, 1968. The classic statement of the functional position in sociology by the acknowledged dean of American functionalists.

The book is not easy reading for many beginning students but accessible to the better prepared.

MILLS, C. WRIGHT. "The Structure of Power in American Society," in C. Wright Mills *Power Politics and People*. New York: Ballantine, 1963, pp. 23–38. The most influential modern radical sociologist describes a new and different type of social structure that has emerged in the United States. This article summarizes Mills' analysis of the power and class structure.

REX, JOHN. "Threatening Theories." *Society* **15**(3), March/April 1978, pp. 46–49. From a Weberian point of view Rex considers some of the problems of modern social theory.

# TWO
# The Organizing Concepts of Sociological Analysis

In the next four chapters, we take up the fundamental concepts with which the field of sociology organizes its understanding of the world, the basic tools with which the sociologist understands things *sociologically*. The use of these ideas, as explained in the chapters, is what makes a given description or explanation of something *sociological* instead of psychological or economic or chemical. Any sociologist finds these tools required again and again, in the same way that any carpenter, no matter how sophisticated his collection of power tools, still reaches again and again for hammer, screwdriver, and ruler.

Chapter 3 discusses the concepts of *culture* and *society*, perhaps the most basic and irreducible of all sociological ideas. Chapter 4 deals with *socialization*, the process through which the human *self* is created by the society into which it is born and which, once developed, it will forever mirror. Although we think of ourselves as unique individuals, born the way we are now, we will find here that in fact we are products—constructions —of social interaction; and when the interactions change, so do we.

Chapter 5 explores the nature of another fundamental concept: *interaction* itself. In addition to describing the nature, meaning, and significance of interaction in human social behavior, the chapter also treats more formally and analytically the central concept of *role*, which is first introduced in Chapter 4.

Chapter 6 summarizes the sociological concept "par excellence": *social organization*. The theme stresses that it is organization that makes human society, and therefore individual survival, possible. The process of organization is basic to everything human: language, group behavior, society; it is the foundation upon which all human behavior rests. Treating organization as both process and structure, the chapter describes its nature, the fundamental processes that produce it, the types of organizations in which we live, and the critical organizational trends of our time.

# Chapter 3
# The Meaning
of Culture
and Society

"Consider Balinese trance. The Balinese fall into extreme dissociated states in which they perform all sorts of spectacular activities — biting off the heads of living chickens, stabbing themselves with daggers, throwing themselves wildly about, speaking with tongues, performing miraculous feats of equilibration, mimicking sexual intercourse, eating feces, and so on — rather more easily and much more suddenly than most of us fall asleep. Trance states are a crucial part of every ceremony. In some, fifty or sixty people may fall, one after the other ("like a string of firecrackers going off," as one observer puts it), emerging anywhere from five minutes to several hours later, totally unaware of what they have been doing and convinced, despite the amnesia, that they have had the most extraordinary and deeply satisfying experience a man can have. What does one learn about human nature from this sort of thing and from the thousand similarly peculiar things anthropologists discover, investigate, and describe? That the Balinese are peculiar sorts of beings, South Sea Martians? That they are just the same as we at base, but with some peculiar, but really incidental, customs we do not happen to have gone in for? That they are innately gifted or even instinctively driven in certain directions rather than others? Or that human nature does not exist and men are pure and simply what their culture makes them?"[1]

What, indeed, are we to make of the Balinese behavior described by Clifford Geertz in the passage above? To each of the questions posed at the end of the passage we might answer "well, yes and no." Let's explore those questions in a little more detail.

Balinese trance behavior is so alien to the values and life experiences of Americans that we might be compelled to conclude that yes, so bizarre is this behavior the Balinese might as well be "South Seas Martians," beings from

48

another world. But by any scientific measure—social, biological, or physical—or humanistic intuition the Balinese are as fully human and as much citizens of this planet as we are. Yes, it *is* the customs of the Balinese that make them so different from us. They grow up as members of Balinese society and learn Balinese culture—which, obviously, is quite different from our own, at least in some areas. But no, the customs that differentiate the Balinese from Americans are not merely incidental pecularities—tacked on like so much window dressing—but provide them with a set of expectations about and interpretations of the world through which they express their humanness, as we express ours through *our* customs. Yes, to some of us the Balinese may seem blessed with a gift for living a life more unrestrained than the ones we lead. But no, there's nothing innate or instinctive in the particular things the Balinese do while in a trance. They have simply *learned* how to behave like Balinese, just as we learn to behave like Americans. And finally, but most importantly: Yes, people are largely products of their cultures, and to learn one culture or another is the very essence of human nature.

The Balinese think and behave differently than we do because they grow up in Balinese society and participate in Balinese culture, and Balinese culture and society are different from our own. But simply to say that the Balinese (or Navajo, or French, or Bushman—or any of the hundreds of other cultures and societies) do what they do because they have learned to be Balinese (or Navajo, etc.), or that Balinese culture is different from ours, is, while accurate, quite superficial. Balinese trance behavior is only a *part*—an element— of Balinese culture, interrelated with other parts of Balinese culture. And to approach anything near an understanding of Balinese trance behavior, we must first know

The Meaning of Culture

The Nature of Culture
Culture Is a System
Culture Is Diverse
Culture Is Shared
Culture Is Learned
Culture Is Based on Symbols
Uses of the Term *Culture*

The Meaning of Society
The Size of Society
Interaction and Societal Organization
Culture and Society

Summary

Suggested Readings

49

something about the entirety of Balinese culture.

While it is not the intention of this chapter to acquaint you with Balinese culture, a familiarity with the concepts of culture and society should provide you with a context for viewing—and understanding—ideas and behaviors that differ from the American pattern that we consider normal.

A culture is an integrated whole in which, in general, all major elements are more or less synchronized with all the others and all are more or less logically consistent with one another. Individual members of a society are in one sense prisoners of their culture—they have learned it as they grew up, and know of no other way to behave. This chapter explores the concepts of culture and society as social scientists in general, and sociologists and anthropologists in particular, understand and use them.

## THE MEANING OF CULTURE

Culture is a basic concept in both sociology and anthropology. In popular use, the term *culture* refers to the "finer things in life": good taste, refinement, achievement in and appreciation of the fine arts, music, and literature. Thus, in everyday English we speak of a person who eats the proper foods at the proper places with the proper utensils and using the proper manners as a cultured individual. This cultured person reads the best of books, sees the best plays, listens to the best music, and enjoys the best art. In these examples, *culture* is applied to individuals, but in popular usage, the term may also be used to refer to groups—peoples, nations. Thus we refer to a nation that has achieved refinement and distinction in art, for instance, as being a nation of *high culture*.

In sociological usage, however, the term *culture* is much more inclusive than in the examples given above. The simplest and most general way to define culture in its sociological

sense is to say that it refers to anything that human beings do that does not have a biological basis, all human phenomena that are not the products of biological inheritance. Thus the sociological concept of culture includes not only behavior that is refined and proper, but *all* learned behavior; not only learning to place a high value on a painting or a piece of music, but learning to place *any* value on *anything;* not only learning to use the correct eating utensils with correct manners, but learning how and when and why to make and use *any* tools.

In the sociological sense, then, **culture** *includes any piece or pattern of behavior, any attitude, value, or belief, any skill that human beings learn as members of a human group, plus the manufacture or use of any material item that is derived from these human abilities.* In the sociological sense, a hamburger, paint-stained bluejeans, and saying "Hi Toots" with a smirk are as much a part of culture as are duck *a l' orange,* a tuxedo, or kissing a woman's hand. The songs of a preliterate tribe in the highlands of New Guinea are no less traits of culture than Bach's *B-Minor Mass,* nor is the design scratched on a piece of wood by an Australian aborigine any less an

This, too, is part of American culture.

example of culture than the paintings of Vincent Van Gogh. These are simple, but important and elusive, points. The sociological interpretation of the concept of culture treats all human products and learned abilities equally. No distinctions are made between them on the basis of taste and refinement, · nor are judgments made about their quality. Sociology places all such phenomena in the same general category, the category of culture.

## THE NATURE OF CULTURE

So far we have defined culture as everything that human beings learn to do, think, use, and make. But simply to define culture so broadly and let it go at that would be a disservice to your understanding of the nature of culture, its content, and its powerful influence on human thought and behavior.

Sir Edward B. Tylor, an English scholar of the last century, is considered to be not only the founder of anthropology, but an influential figure in the development of sociology as well. In his book *Primitive Culture* (1871), Tylor defined culture as "that complex whole which includes knowledge, belief, art, morals, law, custom, and any other capabilities and habits acquired by man as a member of society."[2] Tylor's definition, the first view of the concept of culture in its modern, social scientific sense, is still generally accepted and used in the social sciences as a base upon which to elaborate.

Tylor viewed culture as a totality, composed of various parts, and learned through the agency of society. Later definitions emphasize other aspects of culture. One frequently cited definition is that offered by Kluckhohn and Kelly, who see culture as all "historically created designs for living, explicit and implicit, rational, irrational, and nonrational, which may exist at any given time as potential guides for the behavior of men."[3] This view stresses that humans learn culture from the past, like a set of rules or guides for behaving. Kluckhohn and Kelly also point out that some cultural guidelines are consciously stated and some are hidden; and that some are of obvious utility ("rational"), some are not, and for still others, usefulness is not a consideration.

If you consider the definitions of culture just

> **culture:** anything human beings do that does not have a biological basis. More technically, any piece or pattern of behavior, attitude, value, belief, or skill, that people learn as members of human groups, plus the manipulation of any material item derived from these abilities.

discussed, you will see that, while they all refer to the same thing, each focuses upon different aspects of our understanding of what culture is. In the sections that follow we will discuss the details of that understanding.

### Culture Is a System

Culture is an entity composed of many different parts—a "complex whole," as Tylor called it. These parts are integrated, put together in such a way that each part is related to all the other parts. A change in one part of the system will alter the relationships between parts and cause reverberations in the system as a whole. Consequently, viewing only one, or a few, of the parts of a cultural system in isolation will be an inadequate approach to an understanding of the system as a whole.

But just what are the parts of a cultural system? The rings on your fingers and the shoes on your feet are parts of a cultural system. So are the Empire State Building and a skateboard. Thus *things*—material items—are parts of a cultural system. Other parts of a cultural system are *norms,* the rules and guidelines for regulating interaction to be discussed later in this chapter. The norms that characterize a culture are a reflection of its ideas about the nature of things and the value it places on particular ways of behaving. Rules for greeting and leave-taking, business deals and baseball games, getting married and running for mayor, are all parts of a cultural system. Ideas, attitudes, values, and beliefs—which are reflected in norms—are themselves parts of a cultural system. Using the color red to represent courage or the color white for purity; viewing time, space, matter, and the nature of reality in particular ways; considering roses beautiful and dandelions a nuisance; what is considered appropriate to say or do to one's sister or employer are also components of a cultural system.

The parts of a cultural system may be classified in categories. One approach to classification is *analytic*. It takes an entire cultural system—an integrated and patterned whole—and attempts to break it down into smaller constituent units. The smallest meaningful unit of culture is called a *trait*, an example of which would be the ring on your finger. A ring is obviously a small unit, but consider the ways in which this single item fits into a larger pattern. To begin to understand a ring, we would have to know about the technology of making it. To understand that technology fully, we would have to know about the economic patterns of the culture in which the ring was produced. To reach a more complete understanding of the ring, we would want to know the relative values of the materials from which the ring is made and what determines those values. We would also want to know something about the relationships symbolized by particular rings. Some rings symbolize marriage while others indicate graduation from a particular university or membership in a certain organization. But then we would have to know more about marriage, universities, and organizations. Where do we draw the line?

Although breaking culture down into its traits is useful, most sociologists are more interested in looking at components of culture larger than traits. This approach, called *synthetic*, is more concerned with investigating how traits are built up into broad patterns than in tearing culture down into tiny bits. Related traits can be put together at a higher level to form *trait complexes*. Using this viewpoint, a ring can be seen as an item of jewelry related to bracelets, necklaces, earrings, and other items of personal adornment. Such trait complexes can be put together to form still broader categories, called *configurations*, which form the overall patterns, the distinctive flavor, of a particular culture. A common practice is to view culture as made up of two large and interrelated configurations or *components*: material culture and nonmaterial culture, each of which will be discussed in turn (see Figure 3.1).

**Material Culture**   That component of culture to which objects—physical traits—belong is **material culture.** This category includes anything that human beings use or make. The inventory of these material traits is large in any culture, and in contemporary industrial cultures, it is enormous. No one has ever bothered to compile an exhaustive inventory of the material traits of a culture, nor would such an inventory be necessary, for we can derive these traits from their definition. A gold wedding ring is quite obviously a material trait of culture: It has a physical existence and is of human manufacture and use. Less obvious, perhaps, is the fact that a bunch of flowers presented to someone on St. Valentine's Day is also a material culture trait. It is true that flowers have an existence independent of culture, but the human *use* of flowers identifies them as a part of culture.

Birthday cakes and the ingredients from which they are made are both elements of material culture.

FIGURE 3.1   **The components of culture.**

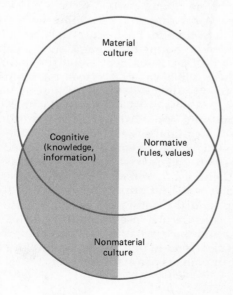

**Nonmaterial Culture** These examples bring us to a very important, but somewhat elusive, point. While wedding rings and Valentine bouquets have a material existence (they are physical things that can be seen, touched, etc.), there are aspects of their existence that are *nonmaterial*. That is, material traits are always associated with ideas concerning their use. Wedding rings and Valentine bouquets symbolize attitudes, values, and beliefs that characterize our culture, and there are *rules* for their appropriate use in certain kinds of interpersonal relationships.

Whereas elements in the *material* component of culture have a physical existence, those elements that belong to the *nonmaterial* component of culture do not. Such elements as rules for appropriate behavior (norms), attitudes, values, and beliefs all fall into the realm of **nonmaterial culture.** It is convenient to break down this nonmaterial component of culture into two subcategories: *normative* culture and *cognitive* culture.

**Normative Culture** Normative culture is that subdivision of nonmaterial culture that consists of norms. **Norms** are rules for behaving, standard ways of doing things, blueprints for expectations about behavior. Norms are both *prescriptive* and *proscriptive;* that is, they tell us the things that we should do as well as the things that we shouldn't. There are norms in any society that cover all areas of behavior, except the unique or the very trivial; and sociologists recognize different varieties of norms.

William G. Sumner, an early American sociologist, identified two such varieties of norms which he called *folkways* and *mores,* in his book *Folkways* (1906).[4] The difference between these two types of norms is not in their content. They both apply to many of the same areas of behavior, and both types are largely survivals from an earlier time. The important distinction between them lies in the degree to which a member of a society feels compelled to conform to them, the intensity of feeling associated with adherence to them, and the strength of the reaction to their violation.

**Folkways,** synonymous with customs, are the norms that specify the way that things are usually done. Adherence to folkways leaves some room for eccentric but harmless behavior. Violations of folkways usually provoke only mild

**material culture:** physical or material objects, things, made or used in the natural state by humans.

**nonmaterial culture:** the normative and cognitive aspects of culture: laws, customs, habits, ways of doing things plus ideas, attitudes, values, and beliefs.

**norms:** cultural rules and guidelines for regulating interaction and using and doing things.

**folkways:** norms specifying the ways things are usually done; customs.

feelings or raised eyebrows. Most folkways have been handed down to us from the past, and their beginnings and original functions have been blurred by time. For example, the custom that a gentleman walking with a lady keeps between her and the street seems to have originated in medieval Europe, where it was the habit to throw garbage and the contents of chamber pots into the streets from overhanging second-story windows. As a culture changes, folkways change with it: Old ones are discarded and new ones are added.

Codes of dress and rules of etiquette are common examples of folkways. To take an example from our own society, imagine a semiformal, "sit-down" dinner party. This is a common, well-defined situation in American middle-class culture. There are certain expectations about how a guest at such a gathering is supposed to act. Let's say that a male guest slurps his soup and mashes up his peas and eats them with his knife. He would certainly be violating folkways of American middle-class culture regarding table manners. His oafish behavior would be considered impolite or crude and some of the other guests might feel embarrassment for him, but there probably wouldn't be a strong reaction to his violation of these norms. Nor is it likely that the crude guest would be punished for his indiscretions, although the host and hostess might not invite him to another dinner party.

But consider behavior of a more serious nature on the part of the guest at our hypothetical dinner party. Suppose he began to use foul and abusive language to the host during dinner or even went so far as to fondle the breasts of the hostess. These outrageous behaviors would violate norms more serious than those classified as folkways. The guest would be guilty of breaching **mores**—norms embedded in what members of a society consider to be morality.

Mores, like folkways, come to us from the past and change with time; but unlike folkways, mores involve rather clear-cut distinctions between right and wrong, and are associated with values that a society holds dear. Adherence to these norms is considered essential to the smooth functioning of the society. Violations of mores provoke relatively intense feelings and strong reactions. Punishment, ranging from avoidance and ridicule to death, is often handed out for the violation of mores. The dinner guest in the example above would no doubt be told to leave and never come back. It is even possible that he would be struck by the host or one of the other guests, and thrown bodily from the house. Such are the reactions violations of mores provoke.

Moving along a continuum of intensity of feelings and compulsion to comply to norms, we come to another, rather special type, called **taboos,** a word that comes to us from Polynesia through anthropology. The culture of any society contains some norms that are considered so basic that to violate them would be to weaken the moral integrity of the society. A violation generates feelings of the utmost intensity, from dumbfounded shock to rage. Thus restrictions, taboos, are attached to these norms. An example of a taboo in our culture is having sexual relations with "blood" relatives or with corpses. Sometimes the violation of a tabooed norm is so abhorrent, so unthinkable, that no specific punishment exists. Thus, although cannibalism is a tabooed act in our culture, some states have no laws on the books to deal with it as a crime.

The mention of the lack of legal sanctions for the violation of certain tabooed norms leads us to a discussion of **laws,** another type of norm. Like the other kinds of norms, they regulate social behavior; but they are unlike them in some important respects. First of all, we usually know where laws come from. They are norms that are formally enacted by legislative bodies, for specific purposes, to regulate particular forms of behavior. Punishment for the violation of various laws is also clearly stated. The punishment is conceived as fitting the crime or civil offense and is carried out by a branch of society (a judicial system) that is superordinate to the individual members of the society.

The intensity of feeling connected to laws varies with the nature of the law. Thus overtime parking and a chain saw massacre, while both violations of law, are poles apart in the responses they provoke. All contemporary industrial societies have laws, of course, consisting of an elaborate code of written statutes administered by a large number of specialists (policemen, attorneys, judges, etc.). But laws don't have to be written down. In some preliterate societies, norms that are recognizable as laws exist, specific norms for which specific punishments are meted out. The laws are not written, obviously, in societies that have no writing systems, but they are nonetheless present in oral form.

It is not difficult to see the differences between laws and other types of norms, but it should be pointed out that these other types of norms are sometimes codified into laws. Thus the outrageous behavior of our dinner guest toward his hostess might violate not only some of society's mores, but some of its laws as well. His actions might constitute assault, and the host might feel compelled to call the police to arrest his unruly guest. Figure 3.2 illustrates certain relationships between various sorts of norms and the adherence to them. Note that the boundaries between folkways, mores, and taboos are not always definite, that these three types of norms lie along a continuum. These hazy boundaries may also vary among different subgroups within a society.

**Explicit and Implicit Norms** Some norms within a culture are explicit, out in the open; everyone in the culture is able to formulate the rule. We all know that to murder someone is a

FIGURE 3.2  Types of norms

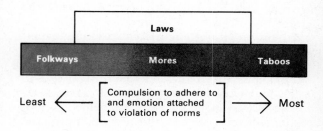

**Implicit norms.** This young man is carrying a *borsette,* a small clutch bag or pocketbook. The custom is common in Italy, but few American men would be caught dead with one. Why? Because in our culture there is an implicit norm that equates male use of purses with homosexuality. (It is acceptable, however, for a man to sling an old army musette bag over his shoulder — that's macho.)

**mores:** morals; norms making clear-cut distinctions between right and wrong, the violation of which produces strong feelings in and reactions from others.

**taboos:** norms so basic that violation is considered to threaten the moral integrity of the society. For Americans, cannibalism is an example.

**laws:** norms formally enacted by specific bodies and enforced by special agencies of the society with specific punishments attached to violation.

crime, a violation of a legal norm; and we all know that it is considered immoral to walk around in public with no clothes on. Explicit norms are learned through formal means, as when parents tell their children, "Don't talk with your mouth full," or, "Nice boys and girls don't hit each other."

Other norms are implicit; they lie beneath the surface and are not easily stated. Who has ever told us explicitly to cover the body of a dead person? Yet who would doubt that this is proper behavior in the treatment of a corpse? Other examples of implicit norms include the rules governing the use of one's body in face-to-face interaction. A recent study demonstrated that people from different cultures use their bodies differently when conversing with each other and, furthermore, that there is almost no normal and explicit means of transmitting these rules.[5] They are just "picked up," probably through imitation of others. When Arab men converse with each other, for example, they usually do so at closer distances, in louder voices, with more direct facing toward each other, and with more touching and direct eye contact than do American men. Implicit norms are less subject to conscious control and verbal statement than explicit ones. They are, in short, rules that you know without knowing that you know them.

**Real and Ideal Norm Behavior** Finally, a distinction must be made between real and ideal behavior in relation to norms. A norm is a rule, explicit or implicit, a statement about the ways in which people in a particular culture should or should not behave. Following a norm rigidly is ideal behavior, absolute conformity to the norm. But, as we all know, norms are constantly being violated, and the degree to which norms are followed (or not followed) in fact is real behavior.

Every society has some slippage, some leeway, between real and ideal behavior, and no norm is always followed to the letter by everyone. These small deviations from norms are tolerated, even expected, but there are limits to the deviation. Perhaps we all secretly admire the adventuresome and independent person who believes that rules are made to be broken, but every society, while tolerating some eccentricity, has limits of toleration for nonadherence to norms. Too great a gap between ideal and real behavior is considered disruptive in any society.

But where do norms come from? What is their source? Why does a society have certain norms and not others? Why does one society have one set of rules and another society a strikingly different set? The answers to these questions are to be found in the aspect of nonmaterial culture that sociologists call cognitive.

**Cognitive Culture** *Cognitive culture* consists of the "mental" aspects of a cultural system: ideas (ways of thinking), attitudes (feelings about something), values (standards of desirability, the "rightness" or "wrongness" of something), and beliefs (what is supposed to be true). These cognitive elements of culture provide members of a society with a framework for viewing the world and a means of constructing and understanding reality. They consist of the thoughts that give a society its distinctiveness. Every society has a conception of the way things are or should be, notions about what is right or wrong, good and bad. These cognitive elements provide the background for the expression of norms. Normative culture consists of the rules for appropriate behavior, but cognitive culture is the *source* of these rules, the matrix in which they are embedded. The cognitive elements of culture cover all aspects of human life and can be as simple as an opinion about what pair of socks look best with what shirt, as unexamined as the attitudes one sex has about the other, or as complex and serious as a set of beliefs concerning the fate of a human soul after death or, indeed, if such a thing as the human soul even exists.

If, as we suggested earlier, it would be fruitless to attempt an inventory of all the material elements of a culture, it would be impossible to list all the cognitive elements, so pervasive are they and so difficult to tap. People in any society grow up learning to value and believe in certain things and certain ways of behaving. So ingrained have these ideas, attitudes, values, and beliefs become that adults are generally not conscious of them, although they behave in accordance with them. We can, however, isolate certain major themes or motifs that permeate a particular culture.

In United States society, for example, there are certain values and standards of judgment that are familiar to all of us. The major values that characterize American society have been discussed by the sociologist Robin Williams. They include the high positive value Americans place on the worth of the individual and on achievement and success through hard work, efficiency, and practicality.[6] These values are reflected in, and reinforced by, popular media (films, novels, television programs, songs, etc.), and in everyday conversation. We Americans admire someone who rises from humble beginnings to a position of prominence through hard work and individual effort. On the other hand, we hold in low esteem persons who are poor due to what we interpret as laziness or lack of effort. We also place a high value on getting the job done with a maximum of efficiency. The fact that the assembly line system of production and the interchangeability of machine parts was first developed in the United States is due to more than chance. Americans also put a high value on the integrity of the individual personality and see each person as different and worthy of respect. We think poorly of someone who uses or manipulates another person for some reason.

A large number of our most important laws have as part of their function the protection of our personal freedom and our physical and social integrity. For example, a person cannot even voluntarily be sold as a slave, imprisonment for debt is illegal, as are libel and slander, improper search and seizure, cruel and unusual punishment, and so on. Perhaps the most striking instance of the lengths to which our laws go in the attempt to protect the individual is found in the definition of suicide as a crime. Free individuals in our society are not free to take their own lives because of the axiomatic value that we place on individual life.

These values (and others) mirror the world view of American culture, the assumptions we make about the nature of reality, what is expected of us, and what we expect from other people. Other cultures, however, have different assumptions about reality, as Carlos Castaneda has brilliantly pointed out in his series of books about Don Juan, a Yaqui Indian sorcerer whose view of time, space, matter, and causality—a "separate reality"—is quite different from the dominant Western one.[7] Those who comment on Castaneda's accounts of Don Juan by saying, "Did he really *believe* all those things?" or "Are those things that Don Juan does really *real?*" have missed the point of the books (and, incidentally, of much of anthropology as well). Castaneda vividly "translated" Don Juan's cognitive culture into terms understandable, if not acceptable, to ours.

Systems of symbols, of which language is the most obvious, play a prominent role in cognitive culture. The human capacity to manipulate symbols will be discussed later in this chapter and again in Chapter 4.

### Culture is Diverse

Some recognizable universals apply to all cultures. All cultures have norms that regulate sexual relations between their members. All cultures assign economic activities to individuals on the basis of age, sex, skill, and other basic criteria. All cultures have norms that govern the exchange of goods and services. All cultures have some sort of technology with which their members exploit the resources of the physical environment. But even more striking than the many characteristics that are common across all cultures is the diversity—the flustering range of differences—among them.

While culture is common to all human societies, every society has a unique culture, a design for living that, viewed as a total pattern, is different from that of all other cultures. Some cultures forbid marriage between certain kinds of cousins, other cultures insist on it; some cultures assign important economic activities to men, other cultures assign these roles to women. In some cultures, individuals who display bizarre behavior are regarded as mentally ill; in others, such individuals are considered specially gifted. Members of some cultures share goods equally. Members of others buy cheap and sell dear. Members of some cultures make their living with bows and arrows, members of other cultures use internal combustion engines; and on and on, in a bewildering and almost endless series of differences.

**Cultural Relativity** The documentation of the diversity of culture has given rise to a very important view in the social sciences, that of **cultural relativity.** This notion sees each culture as a unique adjustment to a particular set of circumstances and suggests that to understand and appreciate the structure and content of a particular culture, you must understand its particular circumstances. To take a simple example, you cannot compare the value of using a clay pot to hold water in one culture to that of using a metal pitcher to hold water in another culture merely by comparing these utensils and

**cultural relativity:** the social-scientific perspective or understanding that since every culture represents an adjustment to a unique set of circumstances, one cannot judge one culture from the perspective of, or with the standards of, another, particularly in matters of morality.

assigning comparative values to them. You must also consider their appropriateness within their total cultural context.

The principle of cultural relativity can be seen as both a philosophy and a methodological base in the social sciences. From a philosophical point of view, the sociologist sees values themselves as products of culture. The values of a particular culture reflect the interests of that culture. Given the great range of cultural diversity and the differences in behavior and "morality" between cultures a cultural relativist would argue against judging the behavior of one by the standards of another. Since each set of standards is specific to its own culture, there is no foundation upon which to base an absolute judgment. In the social sciences, cultural relativity dictates that social and cultural phenomena are perceived and described with sci-

Cultural relativity: Would an Eskimo person understand this cartoon?

Sidney Harris/Saturday Evening Post.

*"Nobody likes to fall, Rocco—but this is ruining our image."*

entific detachment.[8] That is, scientific objectivity is the goal in collecting data in the social sciences, and scientific methodology requires that the observer rise above the values of his or her own culture in order to describe objectively another culture and to avoid assigning any absolute value to practices that may be "immoral" or "foolish" or "impractical" in the observer's own culture.

The concept of cultural relativity is particularly important when we consider activities in another society that violate the moral standards of our own. For example, nineteenth-century American missionaries were shocked by the Polynesian female custom of going bare-breasted and insisted that "native" women cover themselves in "Mother Hubbard" dresses. This caused endless confusion among the natives, who did not share the American fascination with the female mammary organ. It also appalled the missionaries that young people were permitted, even encouraged, to engage in sexual relations before marriage, because the Americans did not understand that Polynesian marriage rules were the reverse of our own: In the United States, marriage is the appropriate occasion for pregnancy; among the Polynesians, pregnancy was the appropriate occasion for marriage. Note that either system effectively produces and regulates the two social-organizational essentials in question: the arrangement of mating for the young and the production and assignment of offspring.

**Ethnocentrism** The other side of the coin of cultural relativity is **ethnocentrism,** viewing other cultures from the point of view of one's own. For the lay person, ethnocentrism can lead to faulty conclusions about other cultures. For the social scientist, it can undermine objectivity and invalidate description and analysis.

Ethnocentrism is common around the world and could be, in fact, one of the cultural universals. This is easy to understand, for people who are part of a particular culture necessarily come to view the normative or cognitive aspects of that culture as "good," or "right," or "moral." They may use these norms and ideas as yardsticks against which to measure other cultures. Ethnocentrism probably even serves some positive functions. It promotes solidarity and cohesion within a society, a feeling of "us" against "them." But as industrial technology has improved the means of communication and transportation, more cultures have come in contact with each other than ever before, and the positive value of ethnocentrism has sharply diminished. With cultural diversity more obvious now than it has ever been, tolerance for that diversity is increasingly necessary.

## Culture Is Shared

Although cultural diversity is great, all "normal" human beings, in one sense, share culture; that is, everyone is a participant in that uniquely human phenomenon called culture. But, since not everyone in the world shares the *same* culture, culture is shared in another sense as well, at the level of particular cultures. Not that all members of a particular society know everything everybody else in the society knows, for no single individual ever embodies all the intricate details of his culture; but all members of a particular society, having a particular culture, share a "core" culture, a basic set of common expectations toward social life. Even in a complex, heterogeneous society such as our own, with its numerous subgroups and regional differences, there are numerous commonalities. Included in the core of American culture, for example, are the attitudes toward achievement and freedom discussed earlier. The commonalities are even greater, of course, in the simpler, smaller, and more homogeneous societies of the world.

But one should not conclude that everyone, even in small societies, sees the world in exactly the same way or holds exactly the same convictions. An incident which occurred among the Gururumba, a small, preliterate society in the highlands of New Guinea, should make the point sufficiently clear. Philip L. Newman describes a Gururumba belief concerning "lightning balls," stones having great magical power. When lightning strikes a tree and disappears into the ground, the Gururumba dig deep holes near the tree in search of the "lightning balls" formed by the electrical discharge. Newman writes:

I was sitting on the edge of one of these holes one day when a man named DaBore came along and sat down beside me. He asked the men in the hole what they were doing, and after they explained, he turned to me and said, "There are no lightning balls." He then got up and walked away. The men in the hole laughed at my surprise and assured me that as long as they had known DaBore he had never believed lightning balls could be found. As far as could be discovered, this was the only part of the supernatural belief system he did not believe in. He had no rationale for his disbelief, nor did it stem from trying one out and finding it did not work. Like other men he had a spirit house in his garden, and attributed his various illnesses and misfortunes to ghosts, sorcerers, and witches. There was nothing in his life history or his position in society that would help explain it; he just did not believe in them.[9]

**The Cumulative Nature of Culture** *Social heritage* is a phrase applied to culture to emphasize its cumulative nature. Kluckhohn and Kelly referred to the cumulative aspects of culture when they termed it "historically created designs for living."[10] The point here is that the culture shared by an individual with other individuals in the same society is the product of centuries—or millennia—of gradual accumulation and transmission, from generation to generation, of knowledge and techniques. In a way, then, every culture is a repository for everything that ever went before it. Not that all the objects ever invented or all the ideas ever formulated are present or used in a culture; but the knowledge of them is there.

Thus, the Egyptians don't build pyramids anymore, but they know about them (and could construct one if they had reason to do so). Nor does any industrial society find the stone and bone tools of its cultural predecessors useful technology in the machine age, but museum cases full of these implements attest to our awareness of them and few readers would be unable to make a serviceable—if not expert—stone projectile point. Very few things are ever lost from the storehouse or memory of a culture, they are just replaced by new things. But even in spite of replacement of most elements, a surprising number of cultural traits have a remarkable persistence. Most Boy Scouts know how to produce fire with a bow-drill, an invention of great antiquity.

The cumulative nature of culture provides us with ready-made solutions to such universal human problems as getting food, building shelter, and generally keeping body and soul together. The use of fire for cooking and warmth, for example, doesn't have to be rediscovered by each new generation; it is already there—as a part of culture—waiting to be used. The discovery of countless solutions to human problems of survival raises the point that culture is an *adaptive mechanism*.

**ethnocentrism:** judging another people, culture, custom, or value from the perspective of one's own; lack of cultural relativity.

**Culture Is an Adaptive Mechanism** *Adaptation* is the process whereby an animal species adjusts to its physical environment in order to meet the requirements of survival. Nonhuman species adapt through physical means that are products of biological evolution: predators must have the physical equipment for hunting (claws, sharp teeth) if they are to survive; prey, on the other hand, must be equipped with the means to escape (speed, a highly developed sense of hearing). These increase their chances of survival. Humans have evolved physically, of course, and continue to do so, but in human populations, adaptation to the physical environment is not accomplished primarily through physical means. At the raw, physical level, we humans are a pretty unimpressive species. If left to purely physical resources, it is highly unlikely that we could compete with other animals. We are not very large, or very fast, or very powerful compared to other animals. As a species, however, we are very bright. Our high level of intelligence gives us the capacity for culture, and we are almost totally dependent upon culture to adapt to our physical environments. Culture makes us able to extend ourselves: We can keep warm in cold climates without fur or thick blubber by using such culturally derived mechanisms as clothing and shelter; we can hunt gazelles (which are far swifter than we are) and overcome elephants (by far our physical superiors); and we can outdistance even the most inspired of seagulls without the aid of wings on our bodies, through our technology. Culture helps us come to terms with, and adapt to, our physical—and social—environment so that we may pursue our basic needs in a relatively efficient manner.

*Culture Is Learned*

Culture is a phenomenon that is over and above biology, and it is not transmitted genetically. This means that human beings acquire culture through learning. All "normal" babies everywhere are born, in regard to culture, like blank sheets of paper. What gets written on this blank paper depends on where and when the baby is

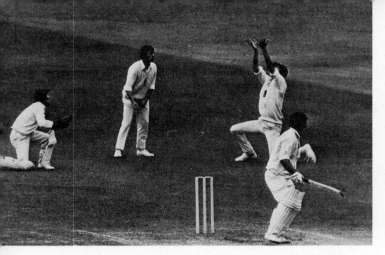

"What's going on here?" If you were British, you'd know.

born. It depends, in other words, on what *culture* the baby is born into. Not that our metaphorical blank paper doesn't have some biological underpinnings. Every newborn baby is the product of millions of years of biological evolution during which humans became human; that is to say, they developed the ability to be bearers of culture. This capacity for culture is, to be sure, genetically transmitted as part of the organism, but *culture itself must be learned*. This means that an Eskimo child is not born with a natural inclination to speak the Eskimo language nor an urge to hunt seals and chew animal skins into the suppleness necessary to make clothing. Eskimos do these things simply by learning to be Eskimo. If we were to take an Eskimo baby and put it in the care of an American family living in Los Angeles, the child would grow up speaking English, playing baseball, eating hamburgers, and doing all the other things that Americans do, because those things are a part of American culture, which is different from Eskimo culture, as both of these cultures, in turn, are different from all others. To reiterate, humans are born with an innate capacity for culture, but what culture they learn is dependent upon what culture they grow up in.

Humans owe their humanness, and their capacity for culture, to their enormous abilities to learn. Think of it: Children are born knowing nothing of culture, but by the time they reach maturity they have learned to manipulate a complex system of symbols—language—with remarkable facility; they have learned to appreciate the past and ponder the future; they have learned where souls go when the body dies, how to drive automobiles or ride horses, how to make love, how the world came into being, how

to differentiate mother's brother from father's brother, what to cherish, and what to fear. All cultures contain such elements and pass them along to their new members. What is remarkable about learning a culture is not that it takes so long—and childhood constitutes a relatively long period of time in any culture—but that such a complex system gets learned at all. Look into your own mind for evidence of these complexities. If you are familiar with the game of baseball, pause for a moment to consider the complicated set of rules that govern the game. An appreciation of the complexity of the rules you carry around inside your head can be obtained by explaining the game to an Englishman who has never seen it played. While you're at it, have your English friend explain cricket to *you*.

Culture is learned behavior, but is there no behavior that is *non*cultural, that is, genetically transmitted? Yes, there is. There are certain reflexes, such as sneezing, which are involuntary responses to certain stimuli, such as dust in the air. Some convincing research demonstrates that some aspects of the expression of basic emotions, such as fear and sorrow are *panhuman*, that is, common to all humans.[11] Humans also have some biological needs, or *drives*. The need for food and drink, the drives of hunger and thirst, and the need for reproduction, (sexual drive), are basic prerequisites for life. But culture is a mediator for these universal biological traits, a filter for their expression. Culture tells us that a sneeze is an expulsion of demons from the body (as in Medieval Europe) or a sign of virility (as in Japan); culture tells us in which situations to feel sorrow or fear; culture teaches us to eat with chopsticks, forks, or our hands; from culture we learn when and where to eat, with whom, and, to a surprising extent, *what* (termites or roast chicken). Sexual drives are biological, but with whom we can or cannot have sexual relations, and under what circumstances, are culturally mediated.

**Learning in Nonhuman Species** Humans possess culture and culture is learned. Other animals do not have culture, as we shall see, but that does not mean that other animals don't learn. Any trainer of dogs or horses will be quick to point that out. But dogs and horses are trained by humans, not by other dogs and horses, while humans learn culture from other humans. But wait, you say. Are there not animals that learn from members of their own species? Yes, the songs of some species of birds are learned, as is the hunting behavior of some predators. And there are some even more striking examples, more germane to our discussion of culture and learning. Consider the example of a group of monkeys on a small island in Japan. In the early 1950s researchers started leaving food—sweet potatoes—on the beach near the water. At first, the monkeys rubbed the sand off the sweet potatoes before they ate them, until one day a young female dipped her potato in the water to clean it. Within a few years, about 90 percent of the monkey population were cleaning their potatoes by dipping them into the water.[12] This was clearly an example of a new idea that spread throughout the group, but could it be considered an example of culture? Keep that question in mind until we come to the next section, which will be concerned with the learning skills of other nonhuman primates.

**Feral or "Wild" People** For the moment, let's refer to the part of Tylor's definition of culture that stated that we acquire culture as members of society. This is an obvious, but extremely important point. The reciprocal of learning a culture is teaching a culture, and a culture is taught by the members already present in the society into which a child is born. Children thus grow up learning the behavior and values that their society teaches them are correct.

But what would happen if, for some reason, a child grew up in the absence of human company? Stories of children who were raised by animals run through the folklore of the world, dating at least from the time of Romulus and Remus (the legendary founders of Rome) who, as the story has it, were suckled by a she-wolf, to that of Victor, the "Wild Boy of Aveyron," who was found running through the woods of France in the nineteenth century and with whom you may be familiar from Francois Truffaut's film *The Wild Child*. Victor was found in the forest—naked, dirty, and covered with scars—and was taken in by Dr. Itard, a French physician. Dr. Itard worked with the boy in an effort to teach him language, but all his attempts failed. It appeared that Victor was incapable of learning. Finally, the boy ran away.[13]

Truffaut's movie *The Wild Child*. **People reared in isolation cannot become fully human.**

Itard's failure to teach Victor the rudiments of culture may have been attributable to two causes: First, Victor may have been mentally deficient. In some parts of the world, retarded children were commonly abandoned in the wilderness. The few who survived may have been the sources of the stories about children "running with animals," and Victor may have been such a child. Second, there may be a critical period in human development beyond which learning a culture is impossible. Victor may have been beyond this stage, and thus had a greatly diminished capacity for acquiring culture. Whatever the case, the fact remains that there must be someone there to teach a culture, as it cannot simply be picked out of the air.

Perhaps the essential questions to ask in seeking to understand the nature of humanity and culture are questions regarding neither culture nor biology. It's not so simple as that, although the complexities are beyond the scope of this chapter. It is probable that the essential nature of humanity is the result of the interaction of culture *and* biology. Clifford Geertz, an anthropologist, maintains that humans are not merely biological beings who later have a cultural layer superimposed over their basic nature. The cultural, social, and psychological aspects of humanity are not applied in neat layers, to be stripped off, one by one, to reveal the real self. Geertz argues persuasively that all humans are products of their unique and various cultures, and that these unique and various cultures cannot be torn away without tearing away the meaning of humanity itself, leaving totally unworkable brutes. Thus, Geertz concludes that "one of the most significant facts about us may finally be that we all begin with the natural equipment to live a thousand kinds of life but end in having lived only one."[14] We humans have, in other words, only one crack at culture.

### Culture Is Based on Symbols

What makes us so different from other animals is that we have culture, and culture is not based so much on quantitative differences between human beings and animals — on the fact that we learn so much more than the other animals — as it is on qualitative differences — on the fact that culture is something different in kind. Descartes, the seventeenth-century philosopher, put these differences this way in his *Discourse on Method:* "Not only that the brutes have less reason than man, but that they have none at all." What makes us different from all other animals is our ability to use symbols, and symbols are the basis of culture.

**The Meaning of Symbols**   A **symbol** is something that represents, stands for, or refers to, something else. Thus, in our culture, the word *table* is a verbal symbol that refers to an object on which we eat our meals; it also refers to the class of objects to which any particular table belongs. Similarly, in our culture the color white stands for purity; a flashing red light at an intersection stands for "stop"; and a wave of the hand stands for "hello" or "goodbye." The anthropologist Leslie White defines the ability to symbolize as being able "freely and arbitrarily to originate, determine, and bestow meaning upon things and events in the external world, and the ability to comprehend such meanings."[15] Such meanings cannot be perceived with the senses — that is, instinctively — but must be *learned*.

Let's examine White's notion of the symbol by using language, the most obvious — but certainly not the only — example of the human ability to symbolize. First, symbols are arbitrary. That is, we invent them or designate them as we need them; they do not exist in the nature of the object referred to; there is no necessary

connection between a symbol and what it represents. Thus when we call an object a *table*, we have learned to do so; there is nothing inherent in the object to tell us that it should be called *table*. There is no *tableness* connected to the object. This is demonstrated by the fact that in Spanish the object is called *mesa*, and in other languages it has other names. The relationship, then, between a referent (in this case, a table) and what we call it is arbitrary, and it is human beings who arbitrarily bestow the meaning on the symbol.

The second point White raises is that symbols cannot be interpreted through one's senses. For instance, there's nothing in the word *table* that would enable Spanish speakers to interpret its meaning with their senses. We call the object *table* only because that is what English speakers have "agreed" to call it. If you wanted to call the object *mandingo* (or anything else), you certainly would be free to do so, but to have *mandingo* become accepted you must have everyone in your speech community agree on that as a choice. This might be difficult because, after all, the word *table* seems to have caught on. To use a less concrete example, there is nothing inherent in the color white to tell us that it should be a symbol for purity, as it is in our culture. In other cultures, white is symbolic of other things — mourning, for example, in China.

**Symboling in Animals**   When a dog responds to the command *Roll over* or a horse to *Whoa!* it is not, as a careful look at White's definition will reveal, engaging in symboling behavior, but is acting in accordance with what White calls a *sign*. The dog has established a connection between the combination of sounds that make up the command *Roll over* and the desired piece of behavior, but has not bestowed the meaning on the combination of sounds. But do nonhuman animals have *no* capacities to engage in symboling behavior? A look at some attempts to teach animals such behavior will shed some light on this question.

In the 1930s W. N. and L. Kellogg, husband and wife psychologists, "adopted" an infant chimpanzee the same age as their own child, and raised the two babies together.[16] Careful attention was paid to giving the two infants the same stimuli. They developed at about the same rate and in the same ways until the Kellogg child began to acquire language, at which time the cognitive development of the human child greatly outstripped that of the chimp. Long and careful attention was devoted to teaching the chimp to speak, but the results were disappointing. The chimp was finally able to retain the use of a very few simple English words, but the experiment was deemed a failure.

In the 1940s a similar experiment was undertaken by K. J. and C. Hayes, another husband-wife team of psychologists.[17] The results were about the same, and it appeared that the gap between humans and chimpanzees, one of the most intelligent of nonhuman animals, was

**symbol:** something representing or "standing for" something else by arbitrary human invention and agreement. Symbolizing *ability* is the capacity freely and arbitrarily to bestow meaning on things.

enormous and unbridgeable. The Hayeses concluded that chimpanzees lacked the neural equipment to "comprehend and generate" language. This conclusion was commonly held as recently as 1965, when a popular book on primates published a picture of Vicki (the Hayes's chimp) which bore the following caption: "Although chimpanzees have the necessary equip-

---

## GORILLA "TALKS" SAME LANGUAGE AS DEAF PERSON

Washington — Koko is making gorilla history.

She is not only the world's first "talking" gorilla, she is the world's first gorilla that lies to avoid punishment, extorts bribes for good behavior, declares her love for a gorilla doll and her fear of anything that looks like an alligator, plays practical jokes and behaves like a backseat driver when she's a passenger in a car.

Koko "talks" in the gestural sign language of the deaf and occasionally also communicates with the help of a special computerized typewriter connected to a voice synthesizer. She has a working vocabulary of 375 signs.

She understands the spoken word as well as sign language and has demonstrated an amazing ability to understand abstract concepts like "good" and "bad" and to create sentences and distinguish between past and future events.

For the last six years Koko has been the subject of a research project at Stanford University, Palo Alto, Calif. Her trainer, companion and "surrogate mother" is Francine "Penny" Patterson, a 31-year-old doctoral candidate in developmental psychology.

Patterson taught sign language by "molding" Koko's hands into the proper shape representing an activity or object. She would do this by taking Koko's hands in hers, a process that at first resulted in a few gorilla bites. But Koko caught on and, for the first 1½ years, acquired a new sign every month. Patterson says she thinks Koko — now 7 — has

great potential for learning. "I see all the rudimentary abilities (in Koko) that we have. I haven't seen anything missing yet," she said. "(Charles) Darwin wouldn't have been surprised." Koko may someday even learn to read, she said.

Koko's vocabulary includes such diverse terms as airplane, belly button, lollipop, friend and stethoscope.

She has designated some words as insults which she uses in anger or to joke with one of her young trainers. She calls people who are unmannerly "birds" and "nuts." Once, in a fit of pique, she strung together a series of insult words and called Patterson, "Penny toilet dirty devil."

Like humans, she exploits the language by lying. Once, when Patterson's back was turned, Koko removed a chopstick from a drawer and tried to poke it through a window screen. When Patterson confronted the gorilla about this "bad" behavior, Koko feigned innocence, pretended to smoke the chopstick like a cigarette, and said in sign language, "Smoke mouth," meaning "I was smoking."

Koko has a well-developed sense of humor and kids her human companions sometimes by saying the opposite of what is expected of her. She once insisted to one of her trainers that a white towel was red, saying "red, Red, RED" with increasing emphasis. Finally, with a wide grin, she held up a tiny speck of red lint clinging to the towel.

From article by Barbara O'Reilley. Lafayette *Journal and Courier.* Oct. 30, 1978, p. B—9. By permission of Gannett News Service, Washington, D.C.

ment of jaw, tongue and larynx, their brains do not permit them to say more than a few simple words."[18]

Pause for a moment and consider the faulty logic that led to that conclusion. Using this reasoning, we would also have to conclude that deaf-mutes lack the ability to symbolize because they cannot speak, and such is simply not the case. Keep in mind that language is only one of the systems of human communication in which the ability to symbolize is expressed, and complex systems of symbols are used by people who lack speech. These systems are not based on sound, of course, but they are no less *symbolic* than language. Consider, for example, musical notation, or computer languages. It should also be pointed out that although chimpanzees have the same vocal organs as humans, there are anatomical differences that make it impossible for chimps to duplicate most sounds of human speech.

Alan and Beatrice Gardner, yet another husband-wife team of psychologists, saw the Hayes' films of Vicki, and noticed that she gestured constantly and consistently during her attempts to speak. This gave them an idea that developed into one of the most careful, creative, and exciting experiments of its kind.[19] In 1966 the Gardners took a female infant chimpanzee, which they named Washoe, isolated her for six years from the other members of her species, put her into an "enriched" environment, and attempted to teach her a system of symbols based on the gestures of the American Sign Language (ASL) widely used in this country by the deaf. The Gardners and their assistants learned ASL and used this system of communication exclusively with Washoe. Great care was taken not to use spoken language around the chimp. Washoe made steady progress in learning ASL symbols, and at the end of ten months of training she used her first combinations of symbols ("gimme sweet" and "come open"). At this time Washoe was a little less than two years old, "which is about the age that human infants begin to form two-word combinations." By the time Washoe was about four years old she was using 245 different combinations involving three or more symbols, and at about age six, her official vocabulary was 160 words.

There is substantial evidence that Washoe was using the ASL gestures not just as signs but as symbols. She demonstrated that she could generalize the gesture for a particular member of a class to other members of that class. For example, she would signal "dog" in the presence of a live dog, as well as to pictures of dogs. She was able to put gestures together spontaneously to generate rudimentary sentences. When, for example, an experimenter put a doll in Washoe's drinking cup, she responded by symboling "baby in my drink."

In 1971 Washoe accompanied Roger Fouts, one of the Gardner's graduate students, to the Institute of Primate Studies at the University of Oklahoma, where she spent most of her time on an island in a lake with other chimpanzees who were also being taught ASL. The chimps communicated with people on the shore with ASL. One day while Washoe was on the island, she noticed that her human companions on shore were drinking iced tea. She then began excitedly and repeatedly to symbol, "Roger ride come gimme sweet eat please hurry you come please gimme sweet you hurry you come ride Washoe fruit drink hurry hurry fruit drink please." Not the most literary arrangement of words, you'll agree, but the point could not be mistaken. Lucy, one of the older chimps at the Institute, has demonstrated the same capabilities for the spontaneous generation of combinations of gestures. On one occasion, for instance, she tasted a radish, spat it out, and referred to it as "cry hurt food," and "cry" or "hurt" from then

Chimpanzee Washoe using American sign language to name objects: in this case, the word "sweet" for a lollipop.

on. After having tasted watermelon, she called it "candy drink," "drink," or "drink fruit." Lucy also swears: she calls her leash "dirty leash," and a local tomcat, "dirty cat."[20]

Washoe, Lucy, and the other chimps at the University of Oklahoma by no means represent the only research dealing with the capacity of nonhuman primates to manipulate symbols. For example, in similar experiment, David Premack of the University of California at Santa Barbara has taught a chimpanzee named Sarah to communicate by arranging differently shaped plastic tokens in different orders.[21] The tokens represent objects, actions, and "grammatical operations," and Sarah has shown herself capable of knowing (and stating) the difference between the tokens and what they represent. She is also capable of making a conditional (if . . ., then . . .) statement.

The chimps at the University of Oklahoma not only communicate with humans in ASL, but they have also begun to use ASL with each other. The significance of this fact is striking and leads one to ask, "Are chimpanzees capable of symboling behavior?" A rush of enthusiasm for these experiments could lead one to shout, "Of course!" but a careful comparison of human symboling abilities and what Washoe, Lucy, Sarah, and the rest are actually doing is in order first. As part of their capacity to engage in the use of symbols, humans display *productivity;* that is, we can generate new combinations of symbol units, putting basic symbols (words) into new arrangements to make new symbols. The chimpanzee experiments have demonstrated that chimps are capable of productivity—remember Lucy's "cry hurt food" and "candy drink." Human symbol systems also have the characteristic of *displacement,* that is, using symbols in the absence of their referents. This means that we can talk about things that are not present, and discuss the past and the future, as well as the here and now. Chimps show some rudimentary capacity for displacement, referring to objects in their absence. Another important component of human symbol systems is, of course *arbitrariness.* The chimpanzee experiments have demonstrated that they have the ability to use gestures that are not obviously connected to their referents.

So, in the light of this evidence, couldn't we say without reservation that chimpanzees share the human capacity for engaging in symboling behavior? A strict interpretation of Leslie White's definition of "symboling" would preclude our defining chimpanzees as symboling animals, because they themselves do not bestow the meanings to the gestures; they have learned something that they would not have learned without the intervention of human beings. If, however, Washoe and the other chimps started to teach ASL to other chimps independent of human influence (and this is the research plan of the Institute of Primate Studies at the University of Oklahoma, by the way), we would have to grant them another step on the road to culture. And why not? Would it be threatening to our concept of ourselves as unique creatures, alone capable of bearing culture? It probably would, for humans seem to put a high value on the notion that we are not only quantitatively different from other animals, but also qualitatively unique. There is no doubt that chimpanzees are far more capable of culturelike behavior than was earlier thought possible, but as yet our concept of ourselves is not seriously threatened. As research in animal communication progresses, however, that threat becomes more imminent.

## Uses of the Term Culture

The term *culture* is used in two different ways in the sociological literature. First, it is used in an abstract, general sense to refer to that universal human phenomenon, common to all humankind, at all times and in all places.

Second, the term is used to refer to culture as it is manifested by a particular human group having a particular pattern of ideas, behavior, and material artifacts (manufactured items) that characterize that group and distinguish it from other such groups. In this sense, the term refers to *a* culture, as used in the phrases "in our culture . . .," "Japanese culture," or "the culture of the Maori of New Zealand."

**Subcultures and Countercultures** *Culture* is also used in compound terms to denote subunits of a particular culture, the most common of which is **subculture.** All members of a large, complex culture, such as ours, share the same life style to a large extent, but within that large culture are smaller groups that have interests, outlooks, values, and behaviors somewhat different from those of the culture at large. These

Actor Telly Savalas has helped to popularize Greek ethnic subculture in the United States.

smaller groups, called *subcultures*, derive their distinctive differences from such bases as occupation, ethnic affiliation, geographic region, socioeconomic status, age, and sex. We speak of American culture as being a distinctive whole, but within that totality we can speak of a physicians' or truckdrivers' subculture, Afro-American or Polish-American subculture, Southern California or Appalachian subcultures, teenage or retired people's subcultures, men's or women's subcultures, and so on.

To put these subcultural differences in concrete terms, an Irish-American lawyer in New England, a Japanese-American student from Los Angeles, and a German-American farmer in the Midwest are all members of American culture and would be expected to share certain similarities. But based on regional, ethnic, and occupational subcultural differences, each would also be somewhat different from the others. All would speak English, but with slightly different dialects; they might share a love for hamburgers and baseball, but each might have favorite foods and recreational activities unheard of by the others; each might like American music, but in forms the others might find distasteful; and so on. (See boxed material.)

Subcultural differences are strikingly obvious in complex, industrial cultures, but even small, preliterate cultures are not completely homogeneous and undifferentiated. Even in these cultures there are differences in outlook, interests, and behaviors based on age and sex, and within these, we can usually identify three basic subcultures, men's, women's, and children's.

When the ideas and behavior patterns of a subculture conflict with those of the majority of a culture and when members of the subculture actively, and sometimes violently, oppose the dominant ideas and behaviors, the subculture is usually called a *counterculture*. Probably the best-known example of a counterculture is that of the student activists and hippies of the late 1960s, the group of young people whose modes of dress and grooming, behavior patterns, and political ideologies ran counter to those accepted by Americans as a whole.

## THE MEANING OF SOCIETY

Like culture, society is a basic concept in sociological thinking. You probably have the idea that a society is a group of people, and, indeed, the word is used in that sense in sociology; but it implies more than the mere physical existence of a group of people. In defining society in sociological terms, two aspects of the group are especially important: (1) the social organization that regulates interaction between members of the group and (2) the size of the group.

To constitute a society, the members of a group must be interrelated by a pattern of social organization (see Chapter 6). But without further qualification, this definition could be applied to several different kinds of groups for example, a community, a political party, or a branch of the military.

Another important dimension of a definition of society, necessary to distinguish it from other collections of interacting individuals, is the *size* of the group. Sociologists view society as the largest socially organized group distinguishable from other such groups. Combining the two aspects of the term, we can define **society** as the *largest distinguishable unit of interacting individuals who share a pattern of social organization that regulates the interactions between them.*

We should also note here that the term *society*, like *culture*, is used in two ways in sociology. First, it is used in an abstract, general sense to refer to the concept itself, as in the statement, "sociology is the study of *society*." Second, sociologists use the term to refer to a *particular* society, a specific group of interacting individuals with a specific set of organizational patterns for regulating interaction, as when we refer to "contemporary Japanese *society*," or "the *society* of thirteenth-century England." The first usage refers to the concept itself, while the second designates a particular manifestation of the concept.

## The Size of Society

Just how large is a society? In sociological usage, the size of a society is not specified by the *number* of people who belong to such a group—a society may have many members or very few. Instead, "size" refers to the level of

**subculture:** a group within a larger culture whose members share interests, outlooks, values, and behavior somewhat different from those of the culture at large. Subcultures are typically racial, religious, ethnic, occupational, and so forth.

**society:** the largest or most inclusive politically autonomous unit of human social organization, in which membership is normally acquired by birth and characterized by shared social organizational patterns.

---

### THE VICE LORDS

R. Lincoln Keiser, an anthropologist, studied a gang of Black youths (the "Vice Lords") who lived in a ghetto of Chicago. Although Keiser and the Vice Lords were all members of American society and shared the same generalized American culture, there existed *subcultural* differences between Keiser (a "middle-class" White) and the Vice Lords ("lower-class" Blacks). The passage below, from Keiser's book *The Vice Lords,* makes clear some subtle subcultural differences in certain norms for interaction.

. . . to an extent, I was always an outsider—even to my close friends. The history of Black-White hatred separated us. They, as well as I, felt the need to constantly verbalize that we were friends *in spite* of the racism that exists between Blacks and Whites. Cultural differences also underlined our separateness. I dressed in casual clothes—Levi's and a sport shirt—but these were different from the clothes worn by Vice Lords; I was not conversant in street slang; and I did not act properly in certain social situations. This last factor was especially important. For example, one evening I was in a bar with Sonny. We were standing together talking when three attractive girls walked by. Sonny shook his head slowly and said, "Foxes! Stone Foxes!" (A "fox" is an attractive girl. A "Stone fox" is an extremely attractive girl.) I laughed and raised my hand to slap him on the shoulder. In the ghetto there is a particular way people express agreement. This is what I have called "hand slapping" in *The Vice Lords* and Blacks generally call it "slapping fine." This custom has now begun to diffuse to

Whites but at the time, it was not generally known outside the ghetto. If A says something felt by B to be worth emphasizing, B will raise his hand. A will then put out his hand palm up, and B will slap it. Now when I raised my hand to slap Sonny on the shoulder, I was initiating an action that was both very similar, if not identical, to the beginning moves of a hand-slapping episode, and it occurred in a context that was grammatical for such an episode. Therefore, without thinking, Sonny put out his hand palm up. However, as soon as he did so he realized that I was White, and did not customarily emphasize agreement in this manner. At the same time, I knew about hand slapping, and understood what Sonny was doing. For an instant we were staring at each other—Sonny with his hand out, but making motions to drop it, and me with my hand raised in the air. Sonny did not know whether to drop his hand or not, and I did not know if I should slap his hand or his shoulder. I decided to slap his hand at the same time he decided to put it down. We both laughed with embarrassment and shook our heads. But the ease of the moment had been lost, and the Black-White gulf that separated us was brought sharply into focus. Anthropologists often have experiences like this in their work with alien cultures, but in this case the incident had extra significance because of the history of Black-White relations in the United States. It emphasized that we were from two different cultures, but it also emphasized that we were from two groups of people who had a long history of hatred and suppression between them.

From R. Lincoln Keiser, *The Vice Lords: Warriors of the Streets,* 1979, pp. 89–90. New York: Holt, Rinehart and Winston.

organizational inclusiveness and distinctiveness involved.

Some sociologists would define society as the largest group to which an individual feels a sense of belonging, as distinct from other such groups. While such a qualification might be valid, it would be very difficult to determine. A more useful criterion would be cast in terms of autonomy and thus would be used to define society as the largest autonomous (independent) group, distinct from other such units, to which an individual belongs. Frequently the autonomy involved is political, and in such cases the term *society* may be used synonymously with *nation-state*. For example, California and Pennsylvania are certainly political units, with well-defined boundaries and distinctiveness, but they wouldn't qualify as politically autonomous because they belong to a higher order political entity which *is* autonomous — the United States — which *does* qualify as a society.

Societies, then, may be very large. Societies can also be quite small. A self-sufficient and politically autonomous band of preliterate hunters and gatherers, numbering as few as 25 members, also fits our definition of a society. So keep in mind that the actual number of members composing a society is an unimportant component of the definition of *society*. What *is* important is political autonomy, distinctiveness from other such groups, and the presence of social organization patterns among the members that others groups do not share.

## Interaction and Societal Organization

**Social Interaction** is an interpersonal relationship that is directed to or takes into account another person or other persons, a process that takes place *between* individuals. Through interaction, individuals exchange information, come into conflict or cooperate, and in general deal with each other. An interaction can be an exchange of pleasantries or a threat; as trivial as asking the attendant at the service station to "fill it up" or as crucial as a peace conference between leaders of warring nations. People in a society "share a pattern of social organization that regulates the interactions between these individuals."[22] This complex social organization involves a set of rules (the "norms" discussed earlier in this chapter) that provide

expectations for individuals who enter into interactions with others and act as guidelines to insure that interactions proceed smoothly. Such patterns of social organization are essential in any society to prevent chaos, to insure the integration of the individuals who are members of that society, and to maintain the "social order."

Societies, as you already know, can be quite large. The United States is a society with over 200 million individual members, and the chances that everyone in the United States will interact with everyone else are nil. But the point is that the *rules* are there, more or less shared by everyone in the society, to provide guidelines for interaction with *any other* member of the society. Thus, you may never order an ice cream cone in Cleveland, but it you ever have the opportunity, you'll know how to do it. Or, if you are a business executive who has never left your native California, you will know what to expect if you ever have to transact business in New York. On the other hand, if you were to go to Mexico or Japan to close a deal, you would be unwise to make any assumptions about members of those societies sharing your set of rules for interaction (see boxed material). The fact that such rules are shared among the members of a society and that each society's rules vary to a greater or lesser degree from the rules of other societies are important criteria for distinguishing one society from another.

The patterns of social organization that regulate the interrelationships between members of a society are extremely important — indeed, indispensable — for the cohesion of the society. Yet, as important and as pervasive as they are for the fabric of human social life, they are only a part of the complex whole, the totality, that is culture.

## Culture and Society

Sometimes the terms *culture* and *society* are used interchangeably in the sociological literature, as synonyms that refer to the same thing. This is very confusing, and sloppy besides, because the concepts the terms label have distinctive, even obvious, differences. Culture, as it has been defined and used in this chapter, is the *totality* of human learned phenomena, while society refers to only a *part* of that totality. Contained within the concept of culture are *all* the ways in which human beings learn to view the world, to behave, and to make and do things. The concept of society concerns only those ways of thinking, doing, and acting within the organizational patterns that constitute the rules for interacting. To call a human group

**social interaction:** an interpersonal relationship in which the participants take account of or respond to one another, act toward or with reference to one another or others. Interpersonal social action.

## HOW CLOSE IS CLOSE?

An analysis of the handling of space during conversations shows the following: A U.S. male brought up in the Northeast stands 18 to 20 inches away when talking face to face to a man he does not know very well; talking to a woman under similar circumstances, he increases the distance about four inches. A distance of only 8 to 13 inches between males is considered either very aggressive or indicative of a closeness of a type we do not ordinarily want to think about. Yet in many parts of Latin America and the Middle East distances which are almost sexual in connotation are the only ones at which people can talk comfortably. In Cuba, for instance, there is nothing suggestive in a man's talking to an educated woman at a distance of 13 inches. If you are a Latin American, talking to a North American at the distance he insists on maintaining is like trying to talk across a room.

To get a more vivid idea of this problem of the comfortable distance, try starting a conversation with a person eight or 10 feet away or one separated from you by a wide obstruction in a store or other public place. Any normally encultured person can't help trying to close up the space, even to the extent of climbing over benches or walking around tables to arrive within comfortable distance. U.S. businessmen working in Latin America try to prevent people from getting uncomfortably close by barricading themselves behind desks, typewriters or the like, but their Latin American office visitors will often climb up on desks or over chairs and put up with loss of dignity in order to establish a spatial context in which interaction can take place for them.

The interesting thing is that neither party is specifically aware of what is wrong when the distance is not right. They merely have vague feelings of discomfort or anxiety. As the Latin American approaches and the North American backs away, both parties take offense without knowing why. When a North American, hav-

ing had the problem pointed out to him, permits the Latin American to get close enough, he will immediately notice that the latter seems much more at ease.

My own studies of space and time have engendered considerable cooperation and interest on the part of friends and colleagues. One case recently reported to me had to do with a group of seven-year-olds in a crowded Sunday-school classroom. The children kept fighting. Without knowing quite what was involved, the teacher had them moved to a larger room. The fighting stopped. It is interesting to speculate as to what would have happened had the children been moved to a smaller room.

The embarrassment about intimacy in space applies also to the matter of addressing people by name. Finding the proper distance in the use of names is even more difficult than in space, because the rules for first-naming are unbelievably complex. As a rule we tend to stay on the "mister" level too long with Latins and some others, but very often we swing into first naming too quickly, which amounts to talking down to them. Whereas in the U.S. we use Mr. with the surname, in Latin America the first and last names are used together and senor (Sr.) is a title. Thus when one says, "My name is Sr. So-and-So," it is interpreted to mean, "I am the Honorable, His Excellency So-and-So." It is no wonder that when we stand away, barricade ourselves behind our desks (usually a reflection of status) and call ourselves mister, our friends to the south wonder about our so-called "good neighbor" policy and think of us as either high-hat or unbelievably rude. Fortunately most North Americans learn some of these things after living in Latin America for a while, but the aversion to being touched and to touching sometimes persists after 15 or more years of residence and even under such conditions as intermarriage.

From Edward T. Hall, "The Anthropology of Manners." *Scientific American*, April 1955, pp. 4–5.

a culture implies that we are referring to the total and distinctive way of life of that group. Calling the same group of people a society implies reference to the social organization patterns of that group of people which, strictly speaking, are only a *part* of their culture.

The contrast between culture and society raises some other problems, too. Conceptually, culture *contains* society. But sometimes, as a result of historical accident or military conquest, a politically autonomous unit, that is, a society such as the United States, the Soviet Union, Canada, or India, will contain within it other, smaller groups that are, in fact, societies as well. Some American Indian groups, such as the Hopi of Arizona, clearly qualify. Technically speaking, however, the Hopi are *not* politically autonomous, yet they have quite a different set of social organizational patterns from the norm for the United States at large. Although such distinctive groups as the Hopi are becoming rarer and rarer in today's world, this definitional ambiguity will exist until such groups have adjusted to the norms of the larger political unit within which they are contained. The important thing to remember is that societies have cultures and that it is the culture a society possesses that provides its rules for interaction, the norms or patterns of behavior and organization that make one people distinctive from another.

## SUMMARY

This chapter has introduced you to culture and society, two of the most basic concepts in contemporary sociology. We have defined *culture* in two senses: First, we have said that it is that universal and uniquely human phenomenon consisting of patterns of thinking and believing, doing and behaving, making and using that all human beings learn in growing up as members of a human society. Second, we have discussed culture in the sense of *a culture*, the distinctive life style that characterizes a particular society and that serves as a basis for the social-organizational patterns that distinguish one society from another.

In discussing culture, we noted that it has five basic characteristics. First, culture is a *system,* a whole made up of interrelated parts, the two major components of which are *material* and *nonmaterial.* Material culture is composed of things: tools, weapons, toys and so forth. Nonmaterial culture is composed of elements which don't have a physical existence and is subdivided into *cognitive* and *normative* culture. Cognitive culture is composed of *knowledge:* the way in which a particular tool is used to produce an artifact, for example. Normative culture is composed of *rules, values,* and *attitudes* and the like, the do-and-don't judgments we imposed on ideas and things. Important elements of normative culture are: *folkways,* or customs; *mores* (important norms that can be thought of as almost the same as morals); and *taboos,* a special kind of norm whose violation is considered unthinkable, obscene, or reprehensible in the extreme. *Laws* are another kind of norm. They are primarily distinguishable from the others by the fact that they are formally enacted, that punishments for violations are clearly stated, and that they are enforced by special agencies of society. Norms may also be explicit or implicit, "real" or "ideal."

A second major element of culture is its *diversity.* So various are human cultures that, in order to understand them, we must practice *cultural relativity,* the habit of viewing them on their own terms rather than ours. Failure to do this creates the familiar, and sometimes misleading, phenomenon called *ethnocentrism,* the habit of judging others from the perspective of our own normative system.

Third, culture is shared, both among different societies and among generations. Thus culture is *cumulative,* and it can act as an *adaptive mechanism,* enabling the people of one time or place to adjust to their problems by using solutions worked out at other times and in other places.

Fourth, culture is learned. Human beings are born with a genetic capacity for culture, but the culture itself—its content—must be learned by each individual. In general, only human beings seem to be capable of doing this. Other animals can learn, of course, but only human beings seem to be capable of spontaneously generating cultural elements themselves. Certain quite intelligent nonhuman species, chimpanzees in particular, have been taught elements of human culture (specific symbol systems, for example), but they do not seem capable either of generating them themselves or of transmitting them to others.

Finally, culture is based on *symbols,* and it is only through the use of symbols that human beings can learn it. According to recent research, chimpanzees are capable of greater symbol-using capacity than previously believed and thus capable of more "culturelike" behavior. But no animal species has ever developed a culture of its own, and none seems capable of transmitting culturally acquired learning.

In discussing society, we noted that, like *culture,* the term *society* is used in two senses: In an abstract, general sense, society refers to the organizational patterns that regulate

interaction in the largest distinguishable unit of interacting people, as in "the study of society." In a specific sense, the term refers to the organizational patterns that characterize *a* society, a specific group of people sharing a particular set of organizational patterns.

Finally, keep in mind that culture and society are concepts—constructs of the human mind. They are abstractions, not things having a physical existence. No sociologist has ever seen (or felt, touched, heard, or smelled) culture or society, any more than a physicist has ever seen energy or a psychologist has seen thought. Culture and society serve as principles for the pursuit of sociological knowledge, conceptual frameworks that guide sociologists in their research.

## SUGGESTED READINGS

BENEDICT, RUTH. *Patterns of Culture.* Boston: Houghton Mifflin, 1934. A beautifully written book (available in several paperback editions) that has had a great impact in the introduction of the concept of culture to the general public. Benedict compares the "patterns," or configurations, of various cultures and demonstrates how they differ. Now somewhat out of date, the book still is valuable and interesting reading for the student.

CASTANEDA, CARLOS. *The Teachings of Don Juan: A Yaqui Way of Knowledge.* Berkely and Los Angeles: University of California Press, 1968; *A Separate Reality: Further Conversations with Don Juan.* New York: Simon & Schuster, 1971; *Journey to Ixtlan.* New York: Simon & Schuster, 1972; *Tales of Power.* New York: Simon & Schuster, 1974; *The Second Ring of Power.* New York: Simon & Schuster, 1977. In this fascinating series of books (all available in paperback), an anthropologist describes his apprenticeship to a Yaqui Indian sorcerer in the Sonoran desert of Mexico and the different "reality" he learns to apprehend as a result. Probably no better examples of the cultural construction of reality exist, since many of the experiences reported appear flatly contrary to American understandings of how the world works (disembodied flight, being in two places at the same time, and so on). Castaneda's work has been called brilliant by many but some have accused him of being a perpetrator of a hoax, and the reader should be aware of the controversial nature of Castaneda's work. For a critical review of Castaneda's books, see Richard de Mille's *Castaneda's Journey: The Power and the Allegory* (Santa Barbara, Calif.: Capra Press, 1976).

GEERTZ, CLIFFORD. *The Interpretation of Cutures.* New York: Basic 1973. This collection of Geertz's essays may be a little heavy going for the beginning student of social science but well worth the effort. Particularly recommended is "The Impact of the Concept of Culture on the Concept of Man" in which Geertz argues brilliantly for the view of culture as a set of mental "blueprints" or "programs" that provide an idea of what to expect in life and what to believe in, and upon which humans are totally dependent.

HALL, EDWARD T. *The Silent Language.* Greenwich, Conn.: Fawcett, 1959; *The Hidden Deminsion.* New York: Doubleday, 1966. These books (both available in paperback) explore in detail how culture is learned and how different cultural components affect behavior and the perception of reality. Concentrating particularly on differential cultural understandings of time and space, these books explain how such learning structures mentality.

LINDEN, EUGENE. *Apes, Men and Language.* Baltimore: Penguin, 1976. This fascinating and highly readable paperback documents the recent research dealing with teaching chimpanzees to manipulate symbol systems. Linden raises and discusses many issues relevant to the concept of culture and the ability to symbol as being a uniquely human trait.

MEAD, MARGARET. *Sex and Temperament in Three Primitive Socities.* New York: Morrow, 1935. This book, by the most famous anthropologist of this century, is a pioneering work and, although somewhat dated, is still considered a classic and valuable piece of social science research (available in several paperback editions). The book points out the influence of culture (as contrasted to biology) on sex roles. Mead demonstrates that the concepts of "maleness" and "femaleness" differ from culture to culture, and that the ideas of what males and females are and how they are expected to behave is determined in large part by culture.

# Chapter 4
# Socialization: Society and Self

"My God, how could human beings do a thing like this?" Grayson Kirk, president of Columbia University, upon first view of his office following the ouster of student protestors in 1968.

"The great sociological question is not how it could be that human beings could do a thing like this, but how it is that human beings do this sort of thing so rarely." Sociologist Erving Goffman, responding to Kirk's reaction in Goffman's book, *Relations in Public,* 1971.

Kirk reacted as many people would, with shock that "human beings" would break into and defile his office. He had assumed that other people shared his respect for his office and its contents. Goffman, on the other hand, points to the problematic nature of people behaving like "human beings"—which in this case meant sharing Kirk's values, norms, and ways of understanding and reacting to situations.

Chapter 3 suggested that the culture we grow up in has much to do with the kind of people we become. In this chapter, we shift our attention from the cultural approach to human behavior to focus on the individual. Within the limits of our particular culture, how do we come to be what we are? How does the child become a unique person or "self?" This general question can be divided into a series of specific questions: What is the nature of human nature? What role does biology play in behavior? What is the significance of learning? How does learning occur? What is the relationship between culture and personality? How is human interaction related to behavior? How is a self-concept formed? Is *socialization* completed in childhood, or is it a lifelong process? And, finally, what is the relationship between socialization and social control—behaving in culturally accepted or approved ways?

# THE MEANING OF SELF

Each of us has a conception of who we are, a complex bundle of perceptions, feelings, and beliefs about ourselves. It includes definitions of ourselves based upon our roles and social position. Jane may be among many other things, a helpful, friendly, athletic person sometimes careless, but usually competent, at her tasks. She also is — and thinks of herself as — a wife, a mother, and a physical therapist.

Such definitions are learned through interaction with other people. As children, and later as adults, we observe and behave and react to the behavior and communications directed to us. We are dependent upon others for knowledge of how to act and how to think about ourselves. As an active participant in this process, analyzing, interpreting, and organizing the messages of others, we not only learn social roles, but form a conception of the self in terms of such characteristics as goodness, competence, bravery, strength, talent, and cleverness, or the reverse. Self-esteem is thus shaped by our own interpretations of others' responses.

This understanding of self is related to the concept of personality. Although some psychologists define personality in terms of "behavior patterns,"[1] most view it as composed of dispositions — traits or tendencies — that lie behind behavior.[2] *Personality* may be seen as a fixed entity, an organized set of characteristics, formed in childhood relatively unchanging over time, that differentiate one individual from others. The *self*, in contrast, focuses attention on a perceiving, interpreting, reacting entity, continually shaping and modifying itself through interaction with others, not only a social product, but a participant in an ongoing social process. This view meshes well with much recent work in social psychology.

73

In numerous experiments, behavior has been made to vary markedly depending upon the situation defined by the experimenter. How can we explain the fact that such behaviors as independence or conformity, helping or hurting, striving to achieve, or resigning oneself to failure vary with the kind of situation people are placed in?[3] Of course, there are individual differences, but they cannot explain the extraordinary shifts in behavior that sometimes occur. A view that sees the person not only as someone with an identity and a past, but also as someone involved with others in an ongoing situation, has obvious advantages for our understanding of human behavior. It is this view of the person that the term *self* is intended to convey.

## THE BIOLOGICAL BASIS OF HUMAN DEVELOPMENT

The preceeding discussion indicates the significance of the concept of *self* in sociology. But human beings are not disembodied spirits. Genetic make-up, inherited characteristics, hormones, and the brain—in short, biology—is also involved in the self.

### Biological Determinism

The view of humanity that sees behavior as the result of biology is called **biological determinism.** During the past century or so several primarily biological approaches have been proposed. We will consider three. The first two, *social Darwinism* and *instinct theory,* ignored social and cultural variables altogether. Today both are rejected by social scientists. The third is *sociobiology,* a new and controversial field that recognizes the relevance of social variables, as a supplement to a biological explanation of human behavior.

**Social Darwinism** In the last part of the nineteenth century, many people believed that a person's behavior and position in society were due solely to biological inheritance. This form of biological determinism was based on a misinterpretation of Charles Darwin's important work concerning the physical evolution of living species. Darwin found evidence that those members of a species best suited biologically to survive in their environment are most likely to live long enough to produce offspring. As a result, those physical characteristics best adapted to the way a species fits into its ecological niche become more common over many generations, while less suitable characteristics tend to disappear.

Darwin's work was widely believed to apply to human society. It was easy for the wealthy and powerful to believe that their positions were due to natural superiority. The upper classes in the industrial countries used Social Darwinism to justify the low wages of their own working classes and the colonization of less developed parts of the world. Today Social Darwinism is discredited. Biological evolution takes far too long to explain existing social inequities. Moreover, physical survival and social success are not related. The rich are not necessarily physically superior to the poor. A discussion of social inequality and its causes—which are social rather than biological—will follow in Chapter 7.

**Instinct Theory** As the term is used biologically, an **instinct** is an unchangeable, complex behavior that is genetically transmitted from parent to offspring. Instinctive behavior can neither be learned nor unlearned. It is biologically programmed into the physical make-up of the creature. A bird builds a nest and cares for its young because it is programmed to do so. Human beings, however, have no instinct for building cribs or taking care of children; they must *learn* to be parents.

When we say, "He caught the ball instinctively," or, "She instinctively shifted into high gear," we are actually referring to behavior that occurs immediately and unthinkingly because it is so well learned. For an instinct to explain behavior, the behavior would have to occur among all normal members of the species, and among humans there are no such readily predictable complex behaviors. Yet the appeal of biological explanations persists. Recently a field called sociobiology has gained attention. It is thus far the most sophisticated attempt to link complex behavior to the biological nature of human beings.

**Sociobiology** Edward O. Wilson, a major figure in this field, argues that in the process of evolution, humans have developed traits, or at least strong predispositions, that determine much of their behavior.[4] People whose behaviors best contribute to survival pass on genetic tendencies for that behavior. Among such survival behaviors are the formation of dominance hierarchies (inequalities in power), religious practices, and female concern with child care. Aggression, selfishness, and xenophobia (fear of strangers) are included, as are cooperation, altruism, and self-sacrifice. Sociobiologists do not claim that people are aware of the biological cause of their actions, but they do argue that feelings, emotions, and tendencies to act in certain ways are the result of genetic characteristics. They acknowledge that environment—social as well as physical—plays a role in behavior. The interaction between genes and environment is such that individuals will be produced who behave adaptively. By this they do not mean that a particular individual will necessarily live longer, but that the biological tendencies for perpetuating one's genetic make-up will be enhanced. *The genes for adaptive behavior* will recur with increasing frequency with each new generation.

The fact that there are some universal social patterns in human societies is consistent with the sociobiological view. But some system of family or kinship ties, some sort of economic organization to provide and distribute material needs and wants, some form of religious belief and practice, and some inequality in the distribution of power and prestige, may also be the result of cultural evolution alone. We simply do not know.

> **socialization:** the process, beginning at birth, through which one eventually adopts as one's own the norms, values, and beliefs of one's culture, and the roles appropriate to one's social position.
>
> **personality:** a relatively enduring set of largely learned predispositions to behave in certain ways; the complex set of feelings, thoughts, and behaviors that are characteristic of an individual and set him or her apart from others.
>
> **self:** the perceptions, feelings, and beliefs one has about one's own identity, personality, and biography, including definitions of one's self based on one's social roles and position and the responses of others.
>
> **biological determinism:** the view that behavior is the consequence of biological structure and inheritance. Often expressed in instinct theory, the idea that bad (disapproved) behavior is the result of "bad genes," that males and females are innately different in aptitudes and attitudes, and so on.
>
> **instinct:** a complex, unchangeable, genetically transmitted behavior. Among animals, nest building and direction finding are common examples. No instinctive behavior among human beings has ever been shown to exist, although the belief that people have instincts (for example, for self-preservation) remains popular.

**Instincts do not determine human behavior . . . nor Snoopy's either, apparently.**

© 1964 United Feature Syndicate, Inc.

Sociobiology may be free of the ethnocentrism, racism, and classism of the Social Darwinists, but much that is of great concern to students of human behavior cannot be adequately explained within its framework, such as major cultural differences, differences between individuals in the same culture, and major shifts within a relatively short period of time in how people in a culture behave. Since any meaningful genetic change in human groups takes hundreds, probably thousands of years, sociobiology cannot explain such widespread shifts in behavior as the major changes in birth rates during this century in the United States (see Chapter 10).

In his most recent work[5] Wilson often refers to tendencies, predispositions, or capacities to behave in certain ways, thus avoiding the problem of variability and change. But if people behave in ways contrary to their genetic tendencies, the result is an hypothesis that cannot be scientifically tested. For example, Wilson believes that there is a genetic reason for women, rather than men, to concern themselves with child care. Are the numerous women in many societies who leave their children in the care of others acting against their genetic makeup? In the absence of biological evidence of specific genetic material that predisposes to one kind of behavior or another we cannot answer such questions. If we are to understand ourselves fully, the biological and social sciences must make contact. But at this stage in knowledge, sociobiology appears to provide few useful guideposts for explaining human behavior.

**Human Nature** Social scientists recognize that biology affects people in two major ways. First, physical characteristics are important *because of the way they are viewed* within a particular culture. Physical differences influence how people are likely to respond to one another and the opportunities they are likely to find for socially valued achievement. Skills highly valued in one society, such as physical strength, may be of little importance in another. Moreover, standards vary—what is beautiful in one culture may be ugly in another.

Second, the physical characteristics shared by members of our species are relevant to behavior. The ability to walk erect, to grasp and manipulate objects, and to perceive depth, are among the advantages common to the species.

Language is a resource of the greatest significance, the basis of human culture. Through language, the learned system of complex symbols that sets human life apart from that of other species, day-to-day interaction is transformed, and a vast storehouse of human experience and knowledge can be transmitted from one generation to the next.

Upon examining other behaviors often thought to be a part of human nature, we find that there simply are no complex forms of behavior common to all people. The things that *are* universal are some biological capabilities, drives, and reflexes. *Human behaviors* are responses to *present situations* based on *past learning;* they are not the result of characteristics common to all human beings. Whether we are lazy or ambitious, selfish or sharing, hurtful or helpful is not due to human nature, but to how we have learned to behave and react to specific situations.

### Inherited Characteristics

Inherited characteristics, then, do not *determine* behavior, but such characteristics do exist, and some of them have considerable social importance within a culture. In Western cultures, three—intelligence, race, and sex—deserve our attention. These characteristics can open opportunities for, or set limits on, what a person can become, in ways that are socially defined.

**Intelligence** Intelligence refers to the capacity for certain mental achievements, but there are considerable problems in defining and measuring these abilities. One dictionary defines intelligence as the capacity for understanding; psychology texts are likely to speak of it as the ability to solve certain kinds of problems. Many social scientists reject the idea that intelligence is nothing more nor less than what intelligence tests measure. Most are paper-and-pencil tests in which high scores depend heavily upon learned symbol systems—language and mathematics. Furthermore, any test score reflects motivation and the learned skills of test taking.

Researchers generally agree that (1) there are biologically based differences in intelligence among people; (2) these differences are heritable—that is, the parents' genetic qualities can affect those of the child; and (3) I.Q. test scores can reflect these genetic differences to some degree. But there is little agreement about the extent to which intelligence, of the kinds measured by the tests, is inherited. One researcher estimates that as little as 50 percent of individual differences in I.Q. scores is the result of heredity. Another places the estimate at 80 percent.[6] Whatever the true figure, it is clear that the test scores reflect much that is *not* inherited.

Serious consequences can follow a child's being labeled as "bright" or "dull" on the basis of I.Q. testing. As we shall see, both the child and others come to think and respond in terms of the label. Besides the harm done to individual children, cultural and social-class bias in the tests tends to perpetuate social class, ethnic and racial differences from one generation to the next. Whatever their real abilities, middle-class children have certain socially learned advantages over lower-class children in obtaining high scores and consequently moving through the school system toward middle-class careers.

**Race** Biologically speaking, **race** refers to a population in which certain genetic characteristics appear with greater frequency than they do in other populations. Despite many efforts to prove the contrary, there is no accepted scientific evidence that any of the biological differences on which racial classifications are based are responsible in themselves for differences in behavior. Moreover, there are enormous variations in behavior *within* any race. The most likely sources of differences associated with race are cultural and social-class differences, and these are often due to racism and the expectations and opportunities associated with it. These will be discussed in Chapter 8.

Historically, the relation between racial differences and intelligence has aroused the most interest. Many English-speaking whites believe that white people are the intellectual superiors of nonwhites. This idea was first questioned scientifically after World War I, which saw the first large-scale I.Q. testing of more or less normal adult populations—American draftees of all races. Although the results at first appeared to validate the belief in white superiority in intelligence (white draftees, on average, scored higher than blacks), more refined analysis showed that this difference could be accounted for by differences in social background and education. Indeed, black soldiers from the

**race:** biologically, Mendelian (interbreeding) populations that differ in the incidence (frequency) of some genetic variants in their gene pools. More simply, a population in which certain genetic characteristics appear with greater frequency than they do among other populations. Popular conceptions of race often mistakenly assume that learned cultural or subcultural differences that may be associated with physical appearance are caused by genetic characteristics.

northeastern states averaged *higher* I.Q. scores than white soldiers from the deep South.[7] Almost all further research has produced similar results, and most social scientists have concluded that purely racial differences in intelligence do not exist.

The controversy was recently revived by a psychologist, Arthur Jensen, and an engineer, William Shockley. They argue that, since whites consistently average fifteen points higher on intelligence tests than blacks, this must be due to genetic differences. Jensen and Shockley maintain that if social factors accounted for the differences, they would not remain consistent over time.[8] It is true that such differences exist, but Jensen and Shockley cannot explain the fact that the range of scores within the races is the same—some blacks score as high as any whites, and some whites score as low as any blacks. This suggests that something other than race is responsible for the average difference, and the results of almost every competent study suggest that this something is social experience.

Unfortunately there is no conclusive way to test the hypothesis that racially based differences exist. If all children grew up in the same environment, we could attribute to heredity whatever I.Q. differences appeared. In a racist society, the question cannot be finally answered. A *non*racist society would not ask the question in the first place.

**Sex** What is typically male and what female? What part does biology play in defining and maintaining these differences? A male, Americans commonly believe, should be independent, self-reliant, assertive, achieving, analytical, decisive, and strong. On the negative side, he may be somewhat lacking in sensitivity to others, compassion, emotional expressiveness, and helpfulness. The image of a woman is

Males are, typically, more aggressive than females, but most *behavior* is learned.

almost the exact opposite. The dominant independent male characteristics are replaced by passive, dependent ones. The negative traits are somewhat offset by maternal characteristics that extend to a general concern for the well-being of others. A good male is good because of what he does; a good female is good because of what she does for others.

These sterotypes are commonly held by both men and women, and seem to be supported by history. There are few women warriors, government leaders, executives, philosophers, and scientists. But what do we know about the roles of biology and experience in shaping these results? Within a culture, it is very difficult to separate these effects because boys and girls are thought of as different and treated differently from the moment of birth. However, we do have some studies that can help us with this difficult question.

Recently, Eleanor Maccoby and Carol Jacklin reviewed over 2,000 books and articles concerning sex differences in motivation, abilities, and behavior.[9] They found convincing evidence for only four sex-related differences. One of these—that boys are typically more physically aggressive than girls—appears very early, usually before the age of three. But for the others—that girls have greater verbal ability than boys, while boys excel in visual and spacial ability and in mathematics—the differences do not appear until age eleven or older. This does not prove that these differences are learned rather than inborn, but given the social expectations

for boys and girls, this is a reasonable conclusion.

Those who argue that learning is of greater importance than biology in sex-related differences in behavior often cite the pioneering work of the anthropologist Margaret Mead.[10] During the 1930s, she studied three separate cultures in New Guinea. In one culture, the Arapesh, both men and women were gentle and unaggressive. Parents cooperated in caring for their children, with greater emphasis on affection than on discipline. In contrast, among the Mundugumor, men and women were equally competitive and aggressive. Neither parent was especially affectionate with the children. Both sexes were harsh, suspicious of others, and aggressive. Finally, the Tchambuli people reversed our traditional ideas as to what is normal for males and females. Women did most of the work related to the physical survival of the group, while the men spent much of their time performing ceremonies. The women were generally practical, while the men were inclined to gossip and fuss over their appearance. Tchambuli women were believed to be stronger emotionally and more highly sexed than their men.

Yet despite such cultural variations in what is typically male or female, it is true that in most societies men traditionally occupy the positions of power and prestige. Is this natural and inevitable? As we have seen, sociobiologists believe that it is. However, in cultures with varying environments and varying economic and technological ways of coping with those environments, there are variations in sex-related differences in power and prestige. The crucial factor seems to be control over scarce and valued goods and services.

In the economically simplest societies, in which both sexes spend much of their time gathering food, male dominance is often minimal. When physical strength and mobility (as in hunting or warfare) become important to the society's welfare, bearing and nursing many children characterizes the adult life of women, and male dominance is the result. About three hundred years ago, lowered infant mortality, lengthened life expectancy, and increased industrialization combined to transform some societies. Today, in industrial societies, physical strength is no longer of overriding social significance, and women can expect to have few children and live into their seventies. These societies may now be in a position to choose to dismantle the sex-role differences that are traditional in their cultures. Or are the things we think of as typically male and female so rooted in our biological natures that significant change is impossible? Let us look at some intriguing evidence on biology and sex-linked behaviors from our own society.

The obvious physical differences between the sexes are associated with genetic and hormonal differences. But in the rare cases where gender identity at birth is unclear or mislabeled, the social definition of sex is usually decisive in determining the child's self-concept and behavior. A child thought of as a boy becomes "masculine"; one seen as a girl becomes "feminine."[11] This can best be illustrated by an extreme case involving identical male twins.[12] One accidently lost his penis during circumcision. The parents decided to have the injured child surgically reconstructed as a girl. Following the surgery, the parents began to treat the twins differently—different clothes and hair styles were accompanied by different behavior toward the children. The twins remain genetically identical, yet at last report, in late childhood, they behaved very much like a traditional little boy and girl.

Whatever the biological bases of sex differences, societies do not just let nature take its course. Considerable effort, often unconscious, is devoted to ensuring that male infants become men and female infants become women. We will examine this important aspect of socialization later in this chapter. But first we must undertake a more general discussion of the social transformation of the infant into a person.

## SOCIAL THEORIES OF HUMAN DEVELOPMENT

Although it is important to recognize the biological basis for human behavior, biology can rarely be said to explain it entirely. We must look to cultural, group, and individual experiences and influences. Three of the social sciences have contributed to our understanding of the human self and human behavior. Psychology, Anthropology, and Sociology all view the individual as someone who becomes a person through interactions with other people. We shall note the contributions of our sister disciplines, but focus primarily upon the contributions of the sociological perspective.

### Personality and Behavior: The Psychological Perspective

Psychology's major contributions lie in three traditions: the psychoanalytic, the behavioristic, and the cognitive-developmental. They differ in the extent to which they focus upon the social experiences of the child, but they all acknowledge the importance of these experiences and their unique contributions help us understand the developing person.

**Psychoanalytic Theory** Sigmund Freud (1856–1939) was the founder of psychoanalysis. Although some aspects of his work are open to criticism, it is impossible to overstate Freud's impact on social science. Freud began publishing in a world in which most people believed that people are born with a "still, small voice"—a conscience. If people, however young, behaved badly, they deserved to be punished because their behavior was a matter of choice. Punishment was not a way to change behavior, but a retribution for intentional bad behavior. Freud contradicted these beliefs with his revolutionary idea that people are affected

**Many sex differences are learned.**

Look Magazine, April 9, 1963. Reprinted by permission of Chon Day.

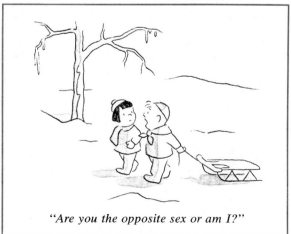

*"Are you the opposite sex or am I?"*

by unconscious mental states and that the conscious self is developed through social experience.

According to Freud, personality emerges as the child passes through a series of stages. These stages correspond to biological stages, but their outcome is the result of other people's behavior. Depending upon what parents — especially mothers — do, children develop normally or they may become *fixated* at a certain stage. Thus, stopped at the *oral stage,* an overindulged or excessively frustrated infant may become an alcoholic or seek emotional sustenance through overeating as an adult. Or the child whose toilet training is too early and severe may remain an "anal" personality, greedy and stingy. In Freudian theory, an especially important stage occurs between three and six, when the child

desires to become the sole object of affection of the parent of the opposite sex and is jealous and resentful of the same-sex parent. This *Oedipal* phase reaches a healthy resolution if the child represses that hostility toward, and identifies with, the same-sex parent.

Some of Freud's specific hypotheses have not been validated by later studies. For example, specific parental actions involving feeding, weaning, and toilet training seem to have no effect on adult life.[13] But the importance of childhood experiences, the significance of others — especially parents — in socialization, and the existence of an unconscious part of the mind, remain important Freudian insights. Perhaps Freud's most significant contribution is his theory of the human self.

Freud saw the person as engaged in a strug-

TABLE 4.1  **Social Theories of Personality Development**

| Theory | Principal concepts | Central ideas, propositions | People |
|---|---|---|---|
| Psychoanalytic | Unconscious<br>Developmental stages<br>id, superego, ego | Adult behavior is a consequence of responses learned as a child and/or frustration of psychosexual development | Freud |
| Behaviorism | Operant conditioning<br>Positive and negative reinforcement | Behavior is determined by conditioning, mainly in the form of the rewards and punishments that follow particular behaviors | Watson, Skinner, Homans |
| Cognitive developmental | Physical maturation<br>Moral and cognitive development | The stage of physical maturation determines the kinds of learning that can occur | Piaget |
| Culture and personality | Culture creates personality | Personality results from culturally determined experiences | Benedict, Kardiner, Reisman |
| Symbolic interactionism | Interaction<br>Significant symbol<br>Self-consciousness<br>Role playing<br>Play stage and game stage<br>Self-concept<br>   Generalized other<br>   Looking-glass self<br>   Pygmalion effect<br>Socialization | Self-concept is learned from interaction with others<br>Interaction takes place through symbols, particularly language<br>Meaning is social<br>Roles are the products of socialization | Mead<br><br><br>Cooley |
| Dramaturgical | Performance<br>Face<br>Team<br>Impression management | Behavior is centered around efforts to preserve face — the definitions of ourselves we establish in interaction with others<br>The self is defined for one's self and others through role performances | Goffman |

gle between biological urges and selfish wants on the one hand, and societal pressures on the other. In Freudian terms this is a battle between the *id,* present at birth, and the *superego,* acquired through interaction with parents. In the normal child, the struggle is mediated by a third part of the self, the *ego,* the conscious self, which seeks a balance between personal desires and the need for acceptance from other members of society. While social scientists often criticize specific Freudian concepts, they generally share Freud's view of the person as a creature whose healthy development depends on human interactions that mediate among physical drives, cultural ideals, and social needs.

**Behaviorism**   Unlike psychoanalysis, behaviorism, which originated in the 1920s, claims that human behavior is best studied without measuring states of mind. Only the environment and behavior or activity itself are relevant. Behaviorism is based on the assumption that people are the results of their experiences and that one is what one does. The key concepts in a basic behavioristic approach involve two kinds of *conditioning:* classical and operant.

**Conditioning**   Some of the earliest work in behaviorism—the first and famous experiments on **classical conditioning**—was done by the Russian physiologist Ivan Pavlov (1849–1936). *Classical conditioning* means training an organism to exhibit an involuntary response when presented with a stimulus that would not normally invoke the response. In Pavlov's best known experiments, he conditioned dogs to salivate at the ring of a bell. A hungry dog (or person) will salivate involuntarily when food (a natural stimulus) is placed before it. This is an *unconditioned response.* Pavlov rang a bell (another stimulus) when he gave food to the dogs. This "conditioned" the dogs to associate the sound of the bell with the presence of food. After many such experiences, the dogs would salivate at the sound of the bell alone, in the absence of food. This was a *conditioned response.* It is psychologically significant because salivation is an involuntary action, a reflex over which an organism has no conscious control.

The second major form of behavioral conditioning is **operant conditioning,** a form of learning in which *reinforcers* change the frequency of

**classical conditioning:** the psychological learning procedure that trains or "conditions" an organism to exhibit an involuntary response, such as salivation upon the presentation of a stimulus such as a ringing bell, that would not normally evoke the response.

**operant conditioning:**   modifying behavior through positive or negative experiences that follow selected behaviors. Behavior that is rewarded tends to be repeated, that which is punished tends not to recur.

a behavior. *Operant conditioning* occurs when a creature does something and almost immediately experiences reinforcement in the form of pleasure or pain. Pleasure is a positive reinforcer; pain, a negative one. As the process is repeated, a positively reinforced behavior becomes more frequent, and a negatively reinforced behavior becomes less frequent. Operant conditioning may be most familiar in connection with learning experiments utilizing rats. In maze learning, for example, the rat may be given an electric shock when it makes an incorrect turn in the maze and a food pellet when it finds its way to the end of the maze.

The most important behaviorist figure today

Ivan Pavlov observing a classical conditioning experiment.

is B. F. Skinner. Extending the common observation that people avoid pain and seek pleasure, Skinner believes that "Behavior is shaped and maintained by its consequences."[14] The concept of the self is unnecessary and even misleading, since it suggests that we look inside the person for an understanding of behavior. For behaviorists, all we *can* know about people — and all we *need* to know — is their behavior (what they do and say). Actions followed by positive, pleasurable reinforcements tend to be repeated in the same situations, and actions negatively reinforced, or punished, tend not to recur. The consequences of present actions determine future ones. Thus motives, values, beliefs, attitudes, and interpretations are merely ways of thinking about behavior. The *causes* of behavior lie outside of the person in the environment.

Skinner's experimental work in operant conditioning is of unquestioned importance; but his efforts to convince the public, as well as the scientific community, that human societies and human lives can be vastly improved by conditioning people along socially desirable lines have met with considerable resistance.

There is clear evidence that conditioning does work. Behavior can be changed by controlling the reinforcements, positive and negative, that follow actions. Clinics devoted to helping people stop such behaviors as smoking, drinking and overeating produce successes and also failures. Skinner would attribute the failures to the clinic's limited control over its patients' reinforcements but this leads to ethical and value questions: Who has the right to control others' behavior and to what ends? Since conditioning is most effective if the conditioners have virtually total control over the experiences of those to be conditioned, the moral issues involved in attempting complete control, and the practical problems of achieving it, are major ones.

A further problem with the environmental determinism of behaviorism is that human beings do not simply feel pleasure and pain; we also interpret our experiences. Most of the conditioning studies have been done with nonhuman species, rats and pigeons, for example. Thus the behaviorists need not concern themselves with the subjective nature of a self that analyzes, interprets, and judges behavior and experience; they pay scant attention to symbolic, rather than physical, rewards and punishments.

**Exchange Theory** Some sociologists have attempted to fill this major gap in behaviorist theory. George Homans is one. His *exchange theory* includes the concepts of reward and punishment, along with some basic ideas from economics. But while Homans pays considerable attention to social and symbolic reinforcements, he has been no more able than the psychological behaviorists to specify how situations and experiences are interpreted and symbols assigned meaning. Will my smile be properly interpreted, and if so, what meaning and importance will that have for you? It may be true, as Homans suggests, that an interaction continues as long, but only as long, as the positives exceed the negatives for all concerned. But the subjective nature of human values and of human interpretations of how well our values are being served have so far blocked efforts to specify how the rewards and punishments we communicate to each other affect how we act. Why, for example, do some people spend years with someone who is constantly hurting them? To say that they are masochists — people who enjoy pain — is merely to add another label. Yet exchange theory may be a valuable starting point for exploring human behavior, and it will be discussed more fully in Chapter 5.

**Cognitive-Developmental Theory** The third major psychological approach contrasts sharply with behaviorist theory by focusing upon thought processes and reasoning. Cognitive-developmental theory shares with psychoanalysis the view that human development proceeds in stages set off by biological transitions. The most important figure in this field is the Swiss psychologist Jean Piaget, who accumulated evidence that cognitive and moral development proceeds in stages determined by the child's intellectual capacity, which, itself, can develop no faster than the child's physical maturation. Briefly, very small children, those in the *sensory-motor stage* (birth to two years), observe and explore. They cannot understand their society's rules no matter how diligently they are taught. In the *preoperational stage* (two to seven years), they acquire language and learn

*"Well, I'm 26. I guess I'm through
with all my stages."*

Reprinted by permission of Universal Press Syndicate.

to manipulate symbols. Now they can learn the rules, but they perceive them merely as something not to be questioned—though not always obeyed. Finally, in the *concrete* and *formal operational stages*, they can develop the full capacity to reason and imagine. They understand the spirit as well as the letter of the law. They learn the meaning—and the arbitrariness—of rules.

One of Piaget's important contributions is the idea that moral judgments, as well as intellectual abilities, require specific levels of maturation. For example, if you ask a child, "Who did the worse thing, a child who deliberately smashed a glass or a child who, in trying to be helpful, accidently broke a whole tray of glasses." A five-year-old will usually answer, "The child who broke the most glasses." Most ten-year-olds will assert that the deliberate destruction of one glass is the more serious offense.

To summarize the major contributions of the psychological perspectives: psychoanalytic thinking offers insights into the developing self, coping with the clash between individual wants and cultural commands; behaviorism demonstrates the importance of positive and negative social experiences; and the cognitive-developmental approach describes the growth and development of reasoning. Now we will shift to a broader level of analysis. Anthropology contains ideas and information about the relationship between culture and the individual.

## Culture and Personality: The Anthropological Perspective

The relationship between culture and personality first became a focus of systematic study during the 1920s. Abram Kardiner is prominent among those who have tried to specify how culture both shapes personality and reflects the dominant personality characteristics of its members. Kardiner, a psychoanalyst greatly influenced by Freud, begins with the assumption that early childhood experience is crucial in personality development. If this experience is similar for most children within a culture, a common personality type should result. Kardiner called the customary ways of thinking about and behaving toward children the society's *primary institutions*. A *basic personality structure* results from the influence of the primary institutions. Social institutions apart from the family and childrearing are called *secondary institutions*. These both express and require the type of personality furnished by the primary institutions. Thus, the circle is complete: culture determines personality and personality determines culture.

During the 1940s a number of anthropologists began to study the relationship between cultural differences and personality in various European and Asian nations. This work is often referred to as studies of *national character*. Ruth Benedict, who believed that understanding the cultures of other nations could contribute both to victory in World War II and to a better world order thereafter, made a study of Japanese national character, *The Chrysanthemum and the Sword*, which was remarkably lacking in ethnocentrism. Her discussion of the role of hierarchy, the significance of indebtedness, and the importance of honor in traditional Japanese society introduced Western readers to a world greatly different from their own, but no less worthy of respect. History, cross-cultural comparisons with similar and very different cultures, literature, and films are all seen as relevant. The acquisition of a special kind of personality is not emphasized. A child learns cultural values and practices, but does not thereby become fundamentally different from the child of any other culture.

Another study of culture and personality is that of David Riesman, a sociologist, who examined social change in the United States in terms of shifts in *social character.* In *The Lonely Crowd* (1950), he is primarily concerned with the problem of social control. How does society get at least the minimal conformity to norms necessary for its survival? Riesman believes this is accomplished through three distinct personality types, one of which has been dominant at each stage of our history.

The first is the *tradition-directed* person. Such people accept the legitimacy of existing norms because they have no knowledge of alternative social rules. In societies where the tradition-directed character prevails, most people share the traditional belief, conformity to conventional ways is usually unquestioned, and there are few incentives to change. Tradition-directed personalities are typical of small, isolated societies with simple technologies.

During the period of early industrialization, a new character type emerges: the *inner-directed.* This kind of person learns certain norms and values early in life and tries to follow them no matter what others may say or do. Because an industrializing society undergoes rapid social change, the consistency in norms characteristic of tradition-directed societies disappears. People who face challenges from others concerning their ways and beliefs must rely upon strong inner direction to guide them.

Finally, in an economically developed country, social change accelerates. Most people learn to adapt by changing their beliefs and behavior in response to the changing expectations of those around them. The *other-directed* character becomes the dominant type.

Riesman's work is more concerned with how people respond to economic and social conditions than with the relationship between culture and personality. How close is that relationship? The absence of convincing evidence for a link between specific cultural practices and particular personality structures, the variability of behavior within cultures, and the speed with which behavior can change in response to environmental or social change, all suggest that the relationship between culture and personaltiy is neither close nor precise. Given the complexity of cultures, the variety of human interactions within a culture, and the part our perceptions of our encounters plays in our definition of ourselves, it would be surprising if there were clear-cut relationships between characteristics of a culture on the one hand, and personality traits on the other. Perhaps the difficulty lies in our concept of personality.

### The Sociological Perspective: Symbolic Interactionism

The approach that focuses upon the person as a self, evolving through individual perceptions of social experience, is called symbolic interactionism, the dominant approach within sociology. It shares with psychology and anthropology the assumption that socialization is basic in human development. It is distinguished from them by its special concern with (1) interaction, (2) the importance of symbols, especially language, in that interaction, and (3) the individual's interpretation of the messages received from others.

**Socialization**   There are two dimensions to socialization. The first, and most basic, occurs

The first and most basic stage of socialization transforms the infant into a person. The human being is created through hundreds of experiences like this.

in childhood. It involves transformation from totally egocentric infants, whose behaviors are dominated by biological urges, into persons capable of taking the perspective of others. We thus develop a self-concept and become able to anticipate, evaluate, and consciously experience our own behavior. In the process we also develop an understanding of the expectations, desires, and feelings of others. We learn to relate to other people.

The second dimension of socialization is related to the first. It begins in childhood and continues throughout life. We learn what is expected of members of a particular culture, and also what behaviors are appropriate to various situations — both our own roles, present or anticipated, and the roles of relevant others. How is this dramatic transformation possible? Part of the answer lies in the nature of human interaction, and a most significant feature of this interaction is language.

**Socialization and Language** Throughout our discussion of the place of language in socialization, we shall rely heavily upon the work of George Herbert Mead (1863–1931), the founder, as we saw in Chapter 2, of symbolic interactionism.

In infancy, before we acquire language, we communicate by what Mead calls a "conversation of gestures." This form of communication is shared with many other species. Gestures are signs that communicate, for example, where food may be found, or the persence of danger. But gestures are limited in kind and complexity. In contrast, symbolic communication permits a great variety of information to be transmitted in a great variety of ways. Moreover, because symbols stand for something, they have meaning apart from themselves. They open up a complex world of meanings that requires interpretation. The transition from the conversation of gestures to interaction through "significant symbols," to use Mead's term, sets humans apart from members of other species. How does the developing child make this transition?

## SOCIALIZATION IN CHILDHOOD

In the early stages of socialization, through interaction with others, children acquire symbols and meanings, begin to apply them to them-

> **internalization:** to make an external value, idea, concept, etc., a part of one's own self structure; to adopt as one's own something originating outside of the self.

selves, play roles, and develop a self-concept. In the typical experiences of the great majority of children, others interact with the child and thus become the agents of his or her socialization. Language acquisition is crucial to this process.

### Stages of Early Socialization

According to George Herbert Mead's interactionist theory, an infant does not learn language all at once.[15] At first, words appear as gestures or signs — sounds attached to certain events or objects: The sound *Ma-ma* is associated with the mother's face. Later, children begin to acquire the meanings of words and, just as important, the norms and values that society attaches to the things they stand for. As children mature, they begin to talk to themselves, thus practicing the same meanings and values that others have been unconsciously teaching them. In short, they learn to use and understand symbols. Mead has described three significant stages of early socialization, the stage of developing self-consciousness, the play stage, and the game stage.

**The Stage of Developing Self-consciousness** This stage, apparent in most children by the age of two, is the product of language learning and the social interactions that necessarily accompany it. To illustrate: A child approaches the television set and reaches out to twirl the dial. Suddenly, he slaps himself on the wrist and says, "No-no, bad boy, mustn't touch!" The act of reaching for the dial has stimulated in him the same response that his action had previously elicited from someone else. By reacting to himself as others react to him, the boy demonstrates that he has internalized the role of someone else; he has become conscious of himself in the same way that others are conscious of him.

**Internalization** is a key aspect of socialization. It is also the most basic and effective form of social control. *Internalization* means that a person has taken on the values and behavior or ideas of someone else, as his or her own. The person need not always conform to these standards or ways of behaving, but they have become at least a part of the way this person feels about things. Fortunately, what we internalize does not forever limit us to a precise set of ways of thinking and acting, but internalized values and general conduct rules form a basic part of the self. This enables us to want to do what **significant others** want us to do. The process of internalization also results in awareness of ourselves. We become *self-conscious*—not in the sense of being uncomfortable with ourselves, but rather in the literal sense that we can evaluate our own feelings and behavior.

The self can be viewed as consisting of two parts, subject and object, or actor and role. The subjective aspect of self is the actor, the "I" that initiates, plans, and experiences. The objective aspect of self is the part played by the actor, the "me" that others observe acting out the initiatives of the actor. The "me" consists of a number of roles or parts (for example, student, son or daughter, sister or brother, Catholic or Methodist), while the "I" thinks about these roles and acts them out.

**The Play Stage**   In the play stage, Mead's second major growth stage, verbal ability increases, and play takes on increasingly organized forms. At the age of three, a little girl having a tea party with her dolls may vary her voice range from high squeaks to low growls in order to play all the roles her activity requires. She may even stand behind each doll as she plays its part. A year later, she will probably conduct the entire scene from one spot and in one voice having reached a level of verbal organization where she can manipulate the various roles imaginatively, without physical action.

Here it is useful to define more precisely the concept of **role.** In all societies there are groupings, such as the family, whose social organization is standardized by conventionalized behaviors. These standardized behaviors are called positions, and the way in which people enact a given position is called a role. No two people play the same role in exactly the same way, but guidelines exist, called norms, that bring a general consistency to most role playing. For example, the position *mother* is associated with some general expectations of how a mother ought to behave. Each woman does not invent the behaviors appropriate to mother-

hood all by herself. These ideas are formed and maintained through interaction with others. Human groups differ somewhat in how they define the motherhood role. Some are strict, some are permissive. Even in a particular group, however, variation in role behavior occurs, and no two mothers are identical. Still, most people have a fairly clear idea of the kinds of behaviors that generally accompany the position "mother." This is because we have learned the norms of our culture or subculture.

How does this learning take place? It begins even before a child can talk. Experiencing mother's efforts to keep us fed and clean and warm, we learn both the role of baby and, reciprocally, the role of mother. Role learning is closely linked with language learning. As children learn language, they also learn the norms that shape roles. In the tea party example, the little girl is likely to enact the role of mother. She behaves according to the norms she has learned for mother behavior. Acting out the mother role, she treats her dolls as children— who had better behave as she has been made to! The child thus demonstrates not only knowledge of the mother role she may one day assume, but also that of the child role, which is of greater immediate importance.

When children play, they are not simply having fun. They are also involved in the crucial process of learning how to play roles. Some of the make-believe role playing is direct preparation for roles the child will take on later in life. An example is the general role of "adult responsible for a child" enacted through such specific roles as father, mother, or teacher. In this especially important type of role playing, the child identifies with particular adults and gradually internalizes their values and standards. Other role playing is not directly applicable to immediate or future positions. Most children will never find themselves in the positions of princess or astronaut, yet this type of role playing is also vital to the child's learning. In trying out such idealized roles, the child is practicing the role of respected adult of the appropriate sex, although some mothers today would prefer that their daughters play at chairing a board meeting rather than at being saved from a dragon!

Practicing "being" someone else is also central to the process of learning to view one's self from the perspective of others. Children learn who they *are* by "being" someone they are not.

They try out different roles, seeing how it might be to play a specific role or to feel a particular emotion. Whatever the chosen role, it is organized by norms the child has learned in "real" life. However unreal the make-believe may appear, the child is actually engaged in the serious business of learning how to be a member of society.

All the roles in children's play are those of **particular others**—a firefighter, a detective, a storekeeper. Models for these roles come from television, storybooks, and daily life. They are always concrete, that is, the child imaginatively imitates some specific person, character, or occupational role as seen from his or her own viewpoint. Role playing is fluid, subject only to the limitations of the child's own understanding of the role. Playmates do not determine the character of the role played. A child can define the role of cowgirl, for example, without reference to the way another child acts the role of Indian. The play requires only transitory agreements between the children as to the general outlines of their behavior.

**significant other:** a person to whom one must respond, or take cognizance of, as a consequence of the importance of his or her relationship to self.

**role:** an interrelated set of expectations and actions that is an integral part of a social position in some group or organization, or organizational process.

**particular other:** one's understanding of the roles associated with specific other persons or social positions: mother, police officer, cowboy, ballerina, sister.

**The Game Stage** When the child becomes about eight, the third and final stage of childhood socialization appears. This level Mead called the *game stage*. It is manifested by the ability to demonstrate the mental and verbal organization demanded by and incorporated in games.

In play, roles are free, fluid, and independent of each other; children can do and be what they

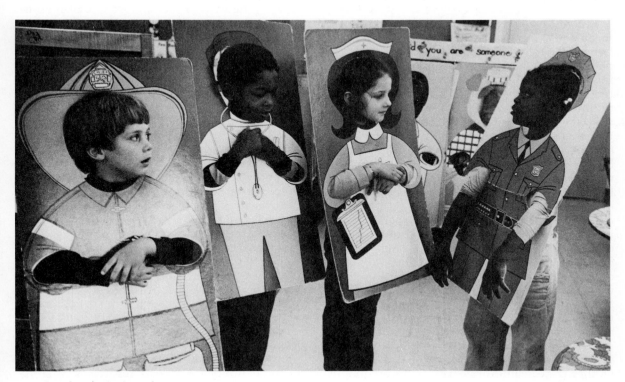

Learning the particular other.

wish, and other players can adjust their behavior accordingly. In games, however, the roles are related to each other by rules (explicit norms) that define what the roles are and how they are to be played. The rules also define the object of the game, the limits placed on the players, the ground on which the game is to be played, and so on. In free play, the action *is* the play; in a very profound sense, however, rules *are* the game. In play, the meaning of the role is what one does with it. In games the meaning of the role is defined by the rules. In fact, *the meaning of one role lies solely in its relation to the other roles; it has no meaning outside that relation.* In perhaps the most simple and universal of all games, hide-and-seek, for example, there are only two roles—hider and seeker—although more than one person can take either role and any number can play. But there is no meaning in hiding if no one seeks, or in seeking if no one hides. A sociological definition might put it that play is characterized by role playing, while games are characterized by position-enactment, since the rules are, in effect, the social norms of the game.

Game playing indicates a new stage of development because the player must know the roles of all the other players and adjust his or her behavior to theirs. When a football quarterback is deciding what play to call, he must take into consideration not only what might work but also how every person on the field has been performing, the ground position, score, time, down, weather, and so on. He must know the role not of *particular others* but of a *general other:* he must assess all his expectations *simultaneously,* as a response to the total situation. In addition, he must act within the limits permitted by the rules: A pass-defense problem cannot be solved by shooting the defender.

The significance of games for social development lies in their duplication of the individual's experiences in the community. Most people organize their behavior around their expectations of **generalized others,** that is, around their understanding of norms and positions and how the society expects them to behave. Society becomes a part of us because of our learned understanding of its expectations (norms), which we internalize as part of ourselves. We get this understanding through language, and we integrate it into ourselves by internalizing the values and expectations that constitute the

normative system and social organization of our society. This in turn makes role playing and normative behavior possible. Another important consequence of this socialization process is the development of a self-concept.

## Self-concept

Charles Horton Cooley (1864–1929) is often regarded as the cofounder, with Mead, of symbolic interactionism. His principal contribution is an examination of the **self-concept**—how one sees and evaluates one's self. The notion of self-concept is important because it calls attention to the fact that what we think of ourselves often determines how we behave; people who do not believe they can swim do not often go off the high board.

**The Looking-Glass Self**  Cooley coined the phrase **looking-glass self** to refer to the origins and nature of self-concepts. The looking-glass self has three elements: (1) our imagination or image of how we appear or present ourselves to others, (2) an imagination or image of the other's judgment of that appearance or presentation, and (3) some self-feeling about that judgment, such as pride or shame that another sees us in that way. Thus, we accumulate a set of beliefs and evaluations about ourselves, and about whom and what we are and what that means in our society. This is our *self-concept.*

**Self-Concept Is Learned**  Cooley's widely accepted understanding of how the looking-glass self operates implies, of course, that we learn our self-concepts from and in interaction with others. In the same way that we find out literally what we look like by inspecting our reflections in a mirror, we find out figuratively how we appear to others by inspecting their reactions to us. How do we know that we are clever or dull, good-looking or plain, or even male or female? Only because all of our lives, in one way or another, others have told us so. Or, to put it within the looking-glass self framework, because we have interpreted their reactions to us as telling us so. Not all people are equally important to us, of course. The reactions of significant others are most important, but every person's self-image begins with and remains influenced by the responses of some other people.

An essential quality of the self-concept is that it is subjective. It goes on in our heads and is based on our interpretation of the reactions of others, which are frequently ambiguous. This means that the self-concept is vulnerable to error. First, we may misinterpret the reactions of the other, assigning them meanings the other did not intend. Second, the responses of all others to us are not entirely consistent, so that we receive mixed messages in the course of interacting with a number of people. Finally, of course, our own behavior is not entirely consistent either, so that varying responses from others are sometimes an accurate reflection of varying behavior on our own part, although we may not be aware of it.

**The Pygmalion Effect** These facts about the nature of self-concept make possible two kinds of **self-fulfilling prophecies**—forecasts that create the conditions for their own fulfillment. The first kind we bring on ourselves, and the second others impose on us. The first is a commonplace to psychiatrists (because it is often the basis for maladaptive behavior), while the second has become familiar to sociologists and educators under the name **Pygmalion effect.**

In the first instance, the things we expect to happen are brought about by our expectation of them. If we really believe that other people are unfriendly and manipulative, we are likely to find many who will treat us that way. Our own expectations will cause us to behave in ways that produce the responses we expect from others.

**generalized other:** a person's perception of the expectations for him or her shared by others in the community. When someone says, "What would people think if I did such a thing?" the people they are thinking about are their generalized other.

**self-concept:** how one sees and evaluates one's self; one's self image.

**looking-glass self:** a term coined by Charles Horton Cooley to describe the processes through which the self-concept is formed. It has three stages: (1) an idea of how we "appear" to another, (2) an idea of the other's judgment of that "appearance," and (3) some self-feeling, such as pride or shame, about the imagined judgment.

**self-fulfilling prophecy:** a forecast or expectation whose existence creates the conditions for its own fulfillment.

**Pygmalion effect:** a type of self-fulfilling prophecy in which people conform to the expectations that others hold for them regardless of their true characters or abilities, as when school children believed by their teachers to be dull act dull.

The Pygmalion effect works in a similar way: the expectations that others hold for us may produce confirming behavior. You may be familiar with the Greek myth in which the sculptor Pygmalion falls in love with his statue and

Copyright, 1971, G. B. Trudeau. Distributed by Universal Press Syndicate.

Pygmalion effect.

miraculously brings it to life. In George Bernard Shaw's play *Pygmalion* and the musical *My Fair Lady,* based on it, a young ignorant, awkward, cockney girl, is remade into an English society lady by a speech teacher with high expectations for her. Despite her background, she alters her behavior to conform to his expectations, becoming something quite different from anything she or anyone else would have believed possible.

The Pygmalion effect also works in the other direction: people may learn to be stupid, crazy, or "bad" to conform to others' expectations for them. Children considered dull by their teacher often act so as to confirm the teacher's expectations. This, of course, causes the teacher to continue to treat them as if they were dull and so the process is circular, or self-confirming.

### Significant Others in the Child's Socialization

For most children, interaction with others forms a major part of their waking experience. Before we discuss the various agents of socialization and note which of these are apt to be most important, we shall consider the consequences of a childhood deprived of normal social interaction.

**Effects of Isolation**   Because young children are dependent upon at least some contact with at least one adult for their very survival, total isolation and survival do not occur. There are, however, two kinds of evidence for the effects of extreme isolation—experimental studies with animals and case studies of human children who have been deprived of normal contact with people. Both kinds of studies confirm that social interaction is necessary for normal development. The best known studies of nonhuman primates are those of the psychologist Harry Harlow. In a famous study, Harlow separated infant rhesus monkeys from their mothers and all other monkeys. The infants were given a dummy "mother," equipped with a bottle for feeding. When put with other monkeys as adults, they were unsocial, behaved bizarrely, and were not able to mate. The few female monkeys impregnated by normal males did not mother their offspring, and their rejection sometimes took the form of physical attacks on their infants.[16]

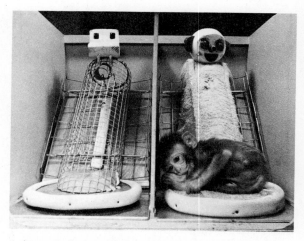

Infant monkeys isolated from their real mothers prefer a soft surrogate mother, but do not develop normally.

The evidence for human beings often comes from the discovery and study of children kept in isolation. One such child was a girl named Anna, who had been largely deprived of human interaction until she was discovered by authorities at the age of about six. Anna lacked the characteristics we consider human. She could not talk or walk properly and was almost entirely helpless. She was afraid of people and reacted wildly. She never fully recovered despite efforts to help her.[17] Feral children, such as the boy Victor discussed in Chapter 3, are probably also the result of severe social deprivation. Fortunately, the great majority of children have ample human contact and interaction. The people most significant in the child's early years are referred to as **agents of socialization.**

**Agents of Socialization**   For most people, the family is the most important socialization agent. In some societies this means that a large number of people will be involved in the process, while in highly industrialized societies the family often includes only one or both parents and their dependent children. Parents, or people playing the parent role, are most important to the child's socialization. Most of a child's early interaction is with these people. Since there is evidence that children tend to imitate most those who have power or control over things they want,[18] it is especially likely that the parents will be taken as models to be imitated. Siblings also play a part in socialization, especially older ones, as we would expect if the less powerful tend to imitate the more powerful.[19] Outside the family, the major influences on the child are the school and the **peer group**—a primary group whose members are similar in age and usually of the same sex.

The most powerful socializing agents are those on whom the child is most dependent, emotionally as well as physically, and those with whom there is the greatest amount of face-to-face interaction. Cooley calls such interaction *primary* because it is crucial in the individual's personal and social development. Typically it occurs in primary groups. A **primary group** is a small group, like the family or a play group, where interactions between members are frequent and emotionally close. Most of our emotional needs—like needs for affection and approval—are met within the bounds of primary groups.

In modern societies, however, socialization also occurs through exposure to the mass media—books, magazines, newspapers, radio, films, and television. In our society, the most important mass medium is television. At least 95 percent of homes in the United States have television, and in the typical home, a set is on about six hours a day. In 1971, the U. S. Surgeon General's Scientific Advisory Committee on Television and Social Behavior concluded that television does have an impact on children, and that both aggressive and prosocial behavior is to some degree related to the kinds of programs children watch.[20] Most of the studies the committee cited concerned aggression, and they concluded that violent programs encourage aggressive behavior in at least some children. We do not know the full extent to which television influences children's ideas, but since the average high school student has passed more time watching television than attending school, it would be surprising if television had no effect.

To summarize and illustrate the major ideas and concepts of childhood socialization, we will now look at a key aspect of role learning—learning how to be a "real" boy or girl. Even in this period of change in how the sexes view themselves and each other, no role distinction is more basic, or has such far-reaching consequences for every aspect of a person's life, than one's definition of self as female or male.

**agent of socialization:** a person, group, or organization providing socialization experiences for individuals: family, school, peer group, fraternity, boot camp.

**peer group:** a primary group composed of members who are social equals, often of similar age and the same sex. It is probably the most important socializing agent aside from the family.

**primary group:** a small group, such as a family or play group, in which interaction among members is frequent, most often face-to-face, and characterized by a high degree of openness and intimacy.

## Socialization and Sex

Biological differences provide a basis for differential social development, but they do not fully explain it. What can the social theories of human development contribute to an understanding of the experiences and their consequences that begin when the newborn is pronounced a boy or a girl?

**Sex-Role Socialization**  In all known human groups, typical differences exist between the

The electronic agent of socialization: By the time these children are 18, they will have watched thousands of hours of television, spending more time with it, perhaps, than with their parents.

sexes in work performed and in beliefs about what is "naturally" male and female. The specifics vary from one culture to another, but males usually hold positions socially defined as dominant and most important. Every child is born into a culture characterized by centuries-old expectations that define the natures of men and women. The child's first significant interactions are with adults who have learned the sex roles deemed culturally appropriate for themselves and for people of the opposite sex.

All social theorists agree that the child's parents or parent substitutes are of major importance. Psychoanalytic theory contributes the concept of *identification:*—the child learns to be a boy or a girl through establishing that he or she is essentially the same as an adult of the same sex, usually a parent. Similarly, the symbolic interactionists view significant others as instrumental in the child's internalizing a definition of sex as part of a self-concept. Are these significant others always people of the same sex, as the Freudian view of identification im-

Identification plays a major role in sex role socialization.

plies? No. To learn what it is to be a girl, for example, one must also learn what it is to be a boy. Moreover, one learns to be a girl from one's father as well as from one's mother, since fathers usually behave differently toward daughters than toward sons.

From the behaviorist and social learning perspectives, certain behaviors are differentially reinforced depending upon whether the child is male or female. To predict a parent's reaction to a child winning a fight with the neighborhood bully, or being called the sweetest child at a birthday party, it is useful to know the child's sex. Little boys learn how little girls are supposed to behave, and they also learn that it is best for them to avoid some of these behaviors. It is not necessary, however, for a child to try a certain behavior and be punished for it to learn to avoid that behavior—as a strict behaviorist view would suggest. Children learn that whole categories of behaviors are best striven for or avoided, because of their sex, without having to try out each one.

The cognitive-developmental approach is relevant here. Lawrence Kohlberg, elaborating on the work of Piaget, asserts that, as their mental development progresses, children form a conception of themselves as male or female, realize that this characteristic is basic and does not change, and desire to fully become what they are. Once the child defines herself as female, for example, she is prepared to learn a whole general category of female behaviors by identifying with and imitating females.

The symbolic interaction perspective views the individual as forming a male or female self-concept through interaction with others. It goes beyond other social theories in holding that the meaning of this interaction for the person lies in interpreting, judging, and anticipating the symbols that make up that interaction. In this process, the child is subject to Pygmalion effects, as he or she responds to others' sex-linked expectations. A child recognizes its own sex-identity, and develops an increasingly complex conception of a male or female self through organizing information about sex roles from every aspect of experience. While face-to-face interaction is of primary importance—for it is here that the child gets direct feedback or reinforcement from people—other experiences play a supplementary part. In all societies, toys and stories carry sex-related information. In our own culture these are supplemented by books, magazines, films, and probably most important, television.

But what of human sexuality? Are sexual behavior, and the experiences and attitudes related to it, so closely tied to one's biological nature as to make this aspect of life inevitably and basically different for men and women? If man is by nature the hunter, the assertive pleasure seeker, and woman the passive home-maker in search of love and security, does this imply that a woman's sexual nature is basically different from a man's? Can she function in a society in which one's sex is not related automatically to one's life experiences? Can women be happy in a society with equivalent expectations for men and women as lovers, parents, workers, and citizens? Can men be comfortable with such an arrangement?

**Sexuality** The scientific study of sexual behavior, which began with Alfred Kinsey,[21] has exploded many myths. The physiological experience of orgasm, for example, is much the same for men and women. Women, however, can experience repeated orgasms within a very short span of time, while men cannot.[22] These data contradict the Victorian view that women cannot—and should not—enjoy sex. Moreover, modern means of contraception now make it possible for woman to have an active sex life with one or many partners without the consequence of pregnancy.

Yet the great majority of men and women continue to behave differently and to think differently about sex. For example, although premarital intercourse has been on the rise in the United States, most sexually experienced unmarried women still have only one partner, most often the man they eventually marry. Men more often have several partners before marriage, have more sexual experience of all types, and tend to view sexual experience differently from women. Men and women are likely to agree that sex without love is all right for a man but not for a woman. Most women continue to link sex with love, while many men associate sex primarily with pleasure. Studies of other cultures suggest, however, that both sexes can enjoy and experience sex on an equal basis. Of course, if societies are to survive, they must devise workable rules to regulate sexual behavior because sex is a powerful drive with

**total institution:** an organization in which some people ("inmates") are confined and subject to the control of a staff whose authority extends into every aspect of the inmate's life. The purpose of such places is to resocialize inmates into new, and presumably "better," selves.

obvious implications for reproduction and for relationships among people, such as love, jealousy, hatred. Yet with our modern understanding of the physiology of sex and the biology of reproduction suggests there is no *biological* basis for differentiating the sexual lives of men and women, and most of the evidence shows that culture, experienced primarily through social interactions—rather than biology—will be the decisive factor.

The major task of childhood, then, is to learn the culturally approved ways of interacting with others and the social roles necessary for interaction to occur. Through this learning process the person develops a self-concept. But after the formative years, are the ways of behaving and thinking established for life? Or does socialization continue in adult life?

## ADULT SOCIALIZATION AND RESOCIALIZATION

As long as a person continues to interact with others, self-concept and behavior are open to change. Transformations in how we think of ourselves and how we behave are relatively infrequent in adult life, but they do occur. Especially in places called **total institutions** the person, no longer a child, is subject to significant change. Changes in social position, such as socially defined age roles, can also result in shifts in self-concept and behavior. We will begin an examination of the person as someone continuously defining the self throughout life with a discussion of the dramaturgical approach.

### The Dramaturgical Approach

Erving Goffman, a sociologist in the tradition of Mead and Cooley, is the leading figure in the dramaturgical approach.[23] Like other symbolic interactionists, Goffman is concerned with role

According to Erving Goffman, these young people may be performers in more ways than they know.

playing in face-to-face interaction, but he adds a new dimension to their work.

For Goffman, a person's behavior is a *performance*, presented before particular others (the *audience*) in a particular setting (out *front* or *back* stage). When one first establishes a role in an interaction, one takes on a *face*, a competent lawyer, for example, or a devoted spouse. From this point on, the individual is motivated to maintain this face in all subsequent interactions before that particular audience. Impression management becomes a major concern, though usually an unconscious one. To fail at this task, and be *out of face*, is to experience shame and the loss of self-esteem. Tactics for preserving face are therefore vital and numerous.

It is important for an audience to determine whether a performer is genuine or a phony, but impressions are often difficult to verify, and once we accept a performer at face value, our own faces are involved in maintaining the definitions. In Goffman's view the self put forward is not so much valid or false as it is accepted or disclaimed. The forces for acceptance are

strong. Our performances, however received, are our *selves*.

Goffman uses the term *face-work* to describe behavior intended to preserve one's image. The audience can usually be counted upon for help. Missteps or potential embarrassments are overlooked or laughed off. People are expected to try to save the feelings and faces of others present. To do otherwise is to be heartless or hostile.

From Goffman's perspective, the usual goals of interaction—task accomplishment, receiving information, expressing one's beliefs—are really secondary, since maintaining face is a condition of interaction. Unless we protect each other's presentation of self, action is either broken off or sidetracked. The payoff for cooperation is order and predictability. To put it another way, everyone's vested interest in maintaining the performer's face and the ongoing definition of reality results in social organization.

Goffman describes a *front region*—where performances take place—and a *back region*—where preparations are made and performances may be dropped. Common back regions include kitchens, bathrooms, and bedrooms. It is not that behavior in back regions expresses one's "real" self, however, so much as a different self. Backstage behavior is often informal and relaxed, irritable or indifferent, while courtesy and warmth are characteristic of front performances. Backstage is reserved for members of one's own *team*, those who normally cooperate in performances before audiences. Teams are characterized by mutual dependence, familiarity, and shared secrets. Team members do not have to love one another, only work together. Occasionally a performer will break off cooperation with a teammate before an audience. When a performance becomes highly inept or inappropriate in the eyes of a teammate a serious disruption can follow—marital fights before acquaintances are an obvious example.

Protection from performance disruption lies in such things as the loyalty and discipline of teammates (waiting until the guest has departed before raising the roof); control over others' access to front and back regions (locks on doors); and the tendency of the audience to help the performers (knocking before entering, joking about or ignoring missteps).

*Out-of-character communication* also occurs and, when well managed, does not disrupt. One example involves criticizing one audience to another. This is especially common among people, such as salespeople, whose roles involve putting out more than they receive. The patience and politeness required in the role are balanced by the hostile remarks that follow the customer's departure. For Goffman, this tendency to run down those to whose faces one must strive to be polite is not human nature, but an effort to keep up the morale of team members. Salespeople, social workers, teachers, psychiatrists, and others need the reassurance that failures like the loss of a sale or the suicide of a patient are due to the inadequacies of their clients and not to a weakness in their own role performance. In another form of out-of-character communication, *team collusion*, signals and hints are passed among teammates that are not meant to be noticed by the audience. The classic kick under the table is one of many ways teammates try to help along each other's performances.

Communications out of character are important in Goffman's analysis as evidence that performances are not fully spontaneous and that various realities exist for a person. Thus, the self is composed of a variety of often inconsistent performances, and the potential for shifts is always present. The most common reason for such a shift in self-definition is a change in role and audience. The adolescent who is happy-go-lucky to friends may present an entirely different face to parents. We all have many potential ways of being, and these can be inconsistent or unrelated. To ourselves these changes and inconsistencies are usually not apparent. We are involved in the ongoing performance, and because we believe our performances, we feel true to ourselves.

Goffman's work is filled with insights on human interaction. A perspective that can integrate consistency and change in behavior and anchor these in observable interactions has much to offer, but he shares the limitations of behaviorism, seeing overt behavior as the sole definer of the self. His use of theatrical terminology is not simply a helpful analogy. The self exists only as a series of more or less coherent and successful performances. One *is* one's role performances. "A correctly staged and performed scene leads the audience to impute a self to a performed character, but this imputation—this self—is a product of a scene that comes off, and is not a cause of it."[24] The inner self as a *real* self—built out of past performances and interpretations of others' reactions—is absent. We shall turn again to Goffman's work as we consider the major changes in self that can occur in total institutions.

### Resocialization in Total Institutions

Socialization and change are a life-long process. As we shall see, the life cycle offers new roles and the loss or discard of some old ways of being, but in general, the sense of self endures without a decisive break. Sometimes, however, there is an experience of radical change. Often this is brought about in a *total institution* where the experience of an infant and young child can be approximated. In such contexts, all outside ties are curtailed or severed, and the person exists in a situation controlled by others. Goffman provides us with an analysis of such places.[25]

Total institutions, such as boarding schools, prisons, military academies, seminaries, and mental hospitals,—whether recruitment is vol-

Resocialization in total institutions produces a new Self.

untary or coerced — share a dedication to remaking people. Sometimes they make them more socially desirable; sometimes, although unintentionally, they make them more deviant. A total institution strives for complete control over the lives of its inmates. Access to outsiders and to reminders of one's past are restricted.

First, the new recruits are stripped of their past. This involves taking away personal possessions and altering appearance. Haircuts and uniforms are common. A new name or a number may be assigned. The stripping off of the old self is accompanied by various forms of abasement, such as beatings or shock therapy. There are usually rituals of submission to the staff. One may not question orders; one must do as one is told when one is told. Going to the bathroom, eating, getting a drink of water, writing a letter, smoking a cigarette all become privileges.

The total institutions that function best share the following characteristics: Entrance is voluntary. Once the self-abasement has proceeded satisfactorily, the resocialization begins, including training in the new role and strong positive reinforcement for doing well. At the end of the long road of self-abasement and submission lies a new and superior person — a Jesuit priest, perhaps, or a U.S. marine.

When the total institution deals with the involuntary, and worse yet, the already stigmatized (as, for example, criminals or the mentally ill), and when the resources of the institution are not directed toward socialization into a new self, the outcome for the person and the society is often less desirable. The inmate is frequently stripped of socially approved characteristics, such as a sense of worth and initiative, and thus becomes more fully labeled as deviant. Within total institutions, inmate subcultures flourish and contribute to resocialization. Where people are held against their wishes, the inmate subculture is often a reaction to the coercive control of the staff. Socialization occurs, but often in the form of increased commitment to a deviant role.

### The Case of the Blind

The loss of sight is an unusual example of an adult experience that can result in profound resocialization without confinement in a total institution. Being blind is such a major physical characteristic that one would expect that behavior commonly found among the blind would be due to the physical nature of the disability, but Robert Scott's work, *The Making of Blind Men*, presents compelling evidence that human interaction, not the biological characteristic in itself, shapes the self-definitions and behavior.[26] Scott shows that blindness is a learned social role.

Adults who lose their eyesight face a serious assault on their self-concept. Of course, the loss of sight is a handicap. Things that were previously easy become arduous or even impossible. But the self-concept and behavior typical of blind people are not inevitable, but rather the product of a socialization process in which the behavior of others plays a key role.

The first factor in this process is the sterotypic view of the blind as helpless, dependent, docile, sad, and serious. To be free of this negative self, the sightless person must find or create significant others who also reject this stereotype.

A second factor, one that increases the difficulty of overcoming the first, lies in the nature of human interaction. The blind must depend upon the assistance of the sighted—in many ways at first and, even for the highly rehabilitated, in some ways, sometimes. The blind person is socially dependent. Unless there is some wealth, skill, or talent that can balance the social debt incurred in interaction with the sighted, the blind must take an inferior role. Here exchange theory, presented in more detail in Chapter 5, is relevant: When reciprocity in rewards and costs breaks down between people interacting, the relationship, if maintained at all, becomes one of superior to inferior. The situation is ripe for a self-fulfilling prophecy in which the blind person becomes dependent, docile, and grateful.

While organizations designed to help the blind are thought of as havens from such negative or demeaning interactions, this is often not the case. They do provide services and personnel accustomed to dealing with the blind, but Scott's study documents how the common result is to accelerate socialization into dependence and lowered self-concept. This is particularly so in organizations adopting an *accommodative approach,* where a special environment designed to "help" the blind helps them into a helpless, inferior, grateful role. Scott describes the cafeteria in one such organization as providing pre-cut-up food and only spoons for utensils.

But isn't this what the blind need? Perhaps not. Scott points to the programs for blind veterans. Here the emphasis is on putting the person back into society as a functioning equal. Those who turn out to need a long-term special environment are rare: When family, friends, and employer are there and cooperate with—not just help—the outcome can be a person who has lost vision, but not self-esteem or competence.

## Socialization and the Life Cycle

The socialization experiences of people confined within total institutions or adapting to a major physical change are limited to a relative few. Socialization accompanying changes in age status is common to us all. In addition to the distinctions made in traditional societies among children, mature adults, and the aged, modern societies often include the stage of adolescence. Adolescents are physically mature and

**rites of passage:** formal, customary rituals marking transition from one social status to another. Weddings and graduation ceremonies are examples.

are expected to behave more responsibly than children, but they are not granted the privileges (and obligations) of adults.

Adult roles in societies with simple economies and technologies are often physically difficult, but usually not otherwise demanding. In complex, industrial societies, many adult roles require skill and complex decision making. Within a culture, socialization to different adult roles also may vary in difficulty. The socialization in becoming a priest or military officer, for example, is more intensive and demanding than the socialization for most other roles in our society. For most people in most societies, however, the disadvantages of adult statuses are more than offset by their power and prestige.

Although old age everywhere brings physical decline, it is far more pleasant in some societies than in others. In many traditional societies, the old are honored for their wisdom; but in rapidly changing societies, old people are often regarded as out of date rather than wise. Their economic usefulness is deliberately reduced through retirement, and they are segregated from the rest of society in retirement communities or old-age homes. Many of the elderly resist socialization to the role society has defined for them as useless, old-fashioned, and meddlesome people. Many others, powerless to do anything about their fate, face the task of adjusting more or less gracefully.

Effective socialization requires not only knowing what is expected of one at each stage in life, but also knowing when one has arrived at that stage. Modern societies are less helpful than traditional ones. Traditional societies mark important transitions in the life cycle with **rites of passage.** Following a public ceremony, the person has a new self-identity and a status that is recognized by other members of the community. In modern societies, confirmations or bar mitzvahs, marriages, graduations, and funerals remain as relatively weak vestiges of the old definitive rites.

Socialization to old age is difficult — and sometimes painful — in American society.

## SOCIALIZATION AND SOCIAL CONTROL

Through socialization we learn behaviors, attitudes, and beliefs appropriate for our age, sex, social status, and role in the economy of the culture. In the process of interacting with others, we create a concept of ourselves in the minds of others; and through impressions of their reactions, we form a concept of ourselves. We become a person. Others can usually rely upon us to behave like ourselves consistently in certain situations. We can think about ourselves and approve or disapprove of our actions, depending upon how they mesh with what we have come to expect of ourselves.

Through socialization, one internalizes the norms and values appropriate for one's status in a particular society, the rules for proper conduct. This means that one will punish one's self for misbehavior through guilt whether or not punishment is forthcoming from others. The

social control exercised by people over their own actions, is an essential ingredient in maintaining a social order.

Yet no society relies completely upon internalized values and rules. Other forms of social control are always present. If you do not do what is right, other people will punish you through harsh looks or words, isolation, or assaults on your property or body. Socialization is said to have succeeded when an internalized expectation of guilt at rule-breaking as well as concern for the possible disapproval or punishments of others motivates behavior. This is especially appropriate for a society such as ours, in which rules, roles, and audiences are subject to rapid change, and in which diverse subcultures provide alternate and sometimes inconsistent standards. The truly socialized person interacts with others, responding to their behavior and seeking favorable responses from them. These others are a part of one's anticipated future as well as one's past, and they exist most powerfully of all in the present.

We will see in Chapter 16 how critically important the process of socialization is to social control. No society could exist for long if most of its members conformed to its norms only through fear of punishment and felt free to violate them any time it appeared that punishment would not ensue. The rule or custom we do not wish to violate is far more efficiently enforced than that which others must impose on us, and the essence of the social bond that holds all societies together is voluntary compliance or conformity with norms. Social control, in fact, is one of the two principle functions that socialization accomplishes. The other, of course, is the production of self. This issue will appear again in the following chapters on social organization as well as Chapter 16 on deviance.

## SUMMARY

In this chapter we looked at the process through which a child becomes a person aware of his or her *self* and a member of society. Biological maturation alone cannot explain how an infant is transformed into an adult whose behavior is consistent with the values and norms relevant to the person's social position in a particular culture. While biological determinism in the form of social Darwinism and instinct theory is now discredited, links between biology and behavior are found in sociobiology, a field that acknowledges that culture and learning affect human behavior, although its central hypothesis is that many adaptive behaviors are linked to genetic characteristics. Other sociologists point to the diversity of human behavior and the speed with which it can change. Our species is distinguished by a unique combination of biological characteristics, most significant of which is the capacity for language. Biological capabilities shared by all physically normal people cannot explain all of human behavior.

To further explore the significance of biology we looked at inherited differences among people. We considered the effects of intelligence, race, and sex on behavior and concluded that the relationships that exist are the consequences of culture, not biology. Human behaviors are not biologically caused; they are responses to present situations based on past learning.

Freud was among the pioneers who established the view that the person is shaped by experiences with others. The behaviorists' experiments linked behavioral change to positive and negative experiences. The cognitive-developmental approach provides a useful bridge between biology and society by studying the stages of mental maturation that make possible increasingly complex ways of incorporating social experience.

Anthropology gives us the concept of national character. The kind of person one is rewarded for becoming varies somewhat among modern industrial states as well as among the more isolated traditional ones. David Riesman believes that in the United States today the dominant character type is the other-directed, which has replaced the earlier tradition-directed and inner-directed personalities.

The relationship between human interaction and behavior is the focus of the symbolic interactionist perspective. Interaction is fundamental to normal human development. George Herbert Mead, the founder of this perspective, described three key stages in childhood socialization—the stage of developing self-consciousness; the play stage; and the game stage. Through the development of language and role playing children come to view their own selves from the perspective of others. They learn to anticipate, evaluate, and consciously experience their own behavior while developing an understanding of the expectations, desires, and feelings of others. Children become persons capable of relating to, responding to, and interpreting and evaluating themselves through their relations with,

**social control:** the social forces, formal and informal, internal and external, that constrain us to behave in socially acceptable ways, including "conscience," the expectations and pressures of others, and our dependence upon them, rules, laws, the police, and so forth. It may be *functional*, resulting from task specialization, or *normative*, resulting from shared values.

responses to, and interpretations and evaluations of others. In this process they also learn what is expected of them in a general way by others in the culture and what they can generally expect of them, thus developing what Mead calls a generalized other.

Through socialization one forms a self-concept—a view and evaluation of one's self. Cooley, the cofounder of symbolic interactionism, has described this in terms of a looking-glass self. We see ourselves as we believe others see us. This makes possible the Pygmalion effect, one kind of self-fulfilling prophecy: people act as they are expected to by others, living up (or down) to the expectations others have for them.

Interaction with other people is crucial for normal human development. This is supported by evidence concerning the consequences of isolation. Fortunately, most children can interact with a number of people. Usually one or both parents are the most significant agents in a child's socialization. Socialization is of great importance in determining a person's sexual identity. Available evidence strongly suggests that the patterns of thinking and behaving that commonly differentiate men from women in a particular culture are also learned.

Adult experience is a continuation of the processes experienced in childhood. Through social interaction, the person maintains and modifies the self developed as a child. The dramaturgical approach, originated by Erving Goffman, is centered around the proposition that we strive to maintain the images of ourselves we have established before various audiences. For most of us, the changes that occur in adult life are not radical. Continuity with the past is maintained as we move through the stages of the life cycle. For some, however, extreme basic change can occur when a person is confined in a total institution, or if a severe physical affliction is suffered, such as loss of sight.

Socialization is crucial to social control. Through socialization we internalize certain values and rules that we break only on pain of self-punishment. Moreover, knowing the rules, and being motivated to avoid breaking them by the possible disapproval or punishment of others, is the consequence of socialization.

## SUGGESTED READINGS

GOFFMAN, ERVING. *Presentation of Self in Everyday Life.* Garden City, N. Y.: Doubleday, 1959. This major work in the dramaturgical approach is rich in observations of everyday interaction. Although intended primarily for an audience of sociologists, it is filled with examples everyone can recognize from daily experience.

HALEY, ALEX. *The Autobiography of Malcolm X.* New York: Grove, 1964. The widely acclaimed author of *Roots* describes the black Muslim leader's struggle to establish a definition of self for American blacks, free of sterotypes of white racism.

KELLER, HELEN. *The Story of My Life.* Garden City, N. Y.: Doubleday, 1954. In 1904 Helen Keller graduated with honors from Radcliffe College. What makes this —and her subsequent achievements—so truly remarkable is the fact that before she was two years old, Helen Keller became both blind and deaf. Her story is moving evidence of the crucial significance for becoming a person of loving contact leading to communication through language.

MEAD, MARGARET. *Coming of Age in Samoa.* New York: Morrow, 1928. The late anthropologist Margaret Mead's first book is also in her words, "the first piece of work by a serious professional anthropologist written for the educated layman . . . ." It remains a readable classic. The question, "Are the problems and anxieties associated with adolescence in the industrial societies of the West the result of biology or culture?" is answered through her observations of the Samoan girls and women with whom she lived. Culture is the significant factor.

RIESMAN, DAVID, REUEL DENNEY, AND NATHAN GLAZER. *The Lonely Crowd.* New Haven, Conn.: Yale University Press, 1950. This study of American national character is chiefly authored by a noted sociologist, who employs ideas and information from psychology, anthropology, and history, as well as sociology, to define characteristics shared by most people in the United States. Riesman sees the dominant personality type as shifting through history from tradition-directed, to inner-directed, and finally to the contemporary, other-directed.

SHEEHY, GAIL. *Passages.* New York: Dutton, 1974. This widely read work by a journalist is concerned with significant transitions in life experienced by many American men and women. Sheehy's book describes how each stage in adult life is affected by socially defined circumstances and expectations.

SKINNER, B. F. *Walden Two.* New York: Macmillian, 1948. The behaviorist psychologist's fictional account of a utopian, or ideal, community. Members of this group follow the principles of reinforcement learning to shape the behavior of their children in ways that are socially productive and individually satisfying, and to maintain these kinds of behaviors among adults.

# Chapter 5
# Social
# Interaction

We have already come upon the concept of *social organization* a number of times. It means, of course, the process and structure through which social behavior becomes recurrent, patterned, and stable. In Chapter 3, for example, we discussed norms and how they act as guides for our behavior, but we did not ask how norms come about or why people follow them. Similarly, in Chapter 4 we discussed role learning in the child, but not the nature and functions of roles themselves. In this chapter and the next one, we will consider the phenomenon of social organization more directly and in detail. We will be trying to understand how social patterns come into being and work, rather than what effects they may have upon individuals. Our focus in this chapter is on the social organization of society from the perspective of the individual, how you and I perform as actors in the drama called society or social life. In Chapter 6 we will consider the nature and structure of the drama itself.

A micro-analytical or individual approach to social organization must begin with social interaction. This means, of course, an interpersonal relationship in which the participants take account of, or respond to, one another in some way, recognize the existence of each other, and do something about it themselves. They may alter their own behavior, or emit a particular symbol or gesture, for example. Interaction is always interpersonal. It takes place *between* two or more people and it involves them in acting toward, or with reference to, the other or others.

The idea of social interaction is fundamental to sociology because it is the medium through which all social behavior takes place. It is the smallest unit to which specifically social behavior can be reduced, the least common denominator of human social activity. Anything more basic takes place subjectively, within the individual, and is psychological or social-psychological rather than purely social (which means *interpersonal* by definition). Thus interaction is of central importance in understanding human behavior. Beginning with the process of self-development, it includes the very thing that makes us human, and the means through which we fulfill our personal needs and life goals.

The section following focuses on two questions: Why is social interaction important, and what has it to do with the development of self? The answers to those questions indicate the central place of the concept in sociology and the significance of the phenomenon in personal life. With that as background, the chapter turns to an examination of interaction itself.

## THE SIGNIFICANCE OF SOCIAL INTERACTION

### Interaction and Development of Self

You will recall from Chapter 4 that sociologists conceive the self as something that develops in us as a direct consequence of our interactions with others. It is a social product. We learn to be who and what we are by taking the role of another person, internalizing the expectations of that person, imitating the roles we see other people playing, and so forth. These activities commence when we begin to acquire language, and they continue throughout our lives. The significance of social interaction for the development of the self is thus readily apparent.

In addition to being the mechanism or process through which the human self is actually constructed, interaction is also central to the fulfillment of personal needs of various kinds. Abraham Maslow, a famous psychologist of personality, sees such needs as making up a hierarchy of types or categories.[1] The needs that are basic to survival itself must be met before any other, according to Maslow. These are our physiological needs, such as those for food and water. Next in importance to each of us are the needs for safety and a sense of security. When these two levels of need have been satisfactorily met, we are free to seek satisfaction for the needs for love and belonging. Adequate fulfillment of these needs frees us further to try to meet the need for self-esteem (a positive self-concept or image), and beyond this, the need for self-actualization. This Maslow describes as the need to stretch our abilities and talents, to become whatever we are capable of becoming.

Maslow's hierarchial ordering reflects the relative potency of the various needs. We must satisfy the more important ones before we may attempt to fulfill the less important. The order in the listing also reflects the chronological order in which such needs develop in the maturing human being. It is important to note that all of the needs Maslow describes must usually be satisfied or fulfilled through interaction with others. Few of us raise our own food, for example, weave our own blankets, or heat our dwellings with fuel we have procured ourselves. We are dependent upon interaction with other people to secure the things that are critical for physiological well-being. Similarly, the feeling of being loved and belonging somewhere clearly can occur only in interaction with others. At the high end of the scale, Maslow's studies of the kind of people he calls *self-actualizing* show that interaction with others is essential to that relatively rare condition.

Everyone has goals that he or she wishes to attain in life. These may be articulated (things we know we want to have or do or be) or they may be unexpressed (sensed only as vague yearnings or longings). Social interaction is crucial in realizing, or sometimes even in recognizing, such goals because of our dependence upon other people in attaining them. In order to get, do, and be what we want to have, do, or be, we must learn, bargain, cooperate, and exchange with others. (Want to be a lawyer? Consider all the people with whom you will have to interact in order to make that possible.)

We can see from this brief discussion that social interaction is absolutely basic to us *as individuals*. Through interaction we construct our selves, fulfill our essential needs, and attain our life goals.

### Interaction and Social Organization

In addition to being essential to us on an individual level, interaction is crucial to us as social beings. It is the basis of organized social life, fundamental to the group, the community, the society.

As we saw in Chapter 3, *organized social life*—the norms, expectations, customs, relationships, and ways of doing things that constitute a culture or a society—is often described as a pattern, something fixed and set. This is a useful notion and could be called a *structural* view of social life. It may be more accurate, however, to see it as dynamic, as a *process* that never ceases. Social life, in other words, is constantly created and recreated through the interactions we have with other people. The family and its functions are a familiar example. As we will see in Chapter 11, a family is more than just a group of people who live together. It is a particular set of relationships among those people including affection, child-care, nurturance, and many others. Certainly in the conventional family roles, patterns may easily be discerned: Fathers have standard behaviors and responsibilities in most families, but for the family to endure, those acts and relationships must be reenacted constantly. *Father* and *Mother* are more than descriptions of biological relationships. They are sets of doings and beings that constantly construct and reconstruct the parts of which the family is made.

Further, as this example suggests, organized social life emerges from social interactions when they become patterned and recurrent. A group of people of different ages and sexes walking together on a street may or may not be a family. We cannot tell from looking at them. But if we were to watch them from afar for a day or two, we would become quite certain about the matter. As behavior between people becomes fixed over time, whether by habit, custom, cultural norm, or law, it also becomes *organized* by mutually understood, reciprocal expectations. Social organization is born in interpersonal interaction. We will explore this process and its implications for social life in greater detail in Chapter 6.

## THE PROCESS OF SOCIAL INTERACTION

Social interaction, then, is of enormous significance, both in the development of self and in social organization. We need to understand first of all the concepts with which sociologists analyze interaction. Next we must consider the basic dimensions along which it takes place, the major forms of interaction, and some specific interaction situations. Later, we will examine the idea of social roles, the patterns we follow as we interact in social life.

### Concepts for Understanding Interaction

Four major ideas are used in the analysis of social interaction, those of the actor, action, interaction, and relationship. Each, of course, has a common meaning and we have already used them more than once without specific definition because the special sociological meanings attached to them are sufficiently close to the common ones. At this point, however, we will begin to use the words in particular ways for the analysis of social interaction, and so we must define them.

**Actor**  A social **actor** may be a person, a group, or even an organization, in interaction with others. In groups and organizations, of course, individual people actually do whatever it is that is done, but they do so for, and as rep-

**social organization:**  the complex, dynamic process by which social interactions and relationships become recurrent, patterned, and stable; the process that brings order and meaning into social life created as actors establish relationships that become patterned over time.

**actor:**  a person, group, or organization in interaction with other persons, groups, or organizations.

**action** (social):  the activity performed by a social actor. Social action is always a response to another actor or an attempt to secure such a response. It becomes interaction when the response occurs.

resentatives of the group or organization in question, some or all the members of which are seen as acting in concert, as a unit. Thus when a sociologist wants to study some organizational activity like decision making, that activity is the point of focus, not the individuals who make the decisions.

**Action**  A social **action** is an action done by a social actor. As used by sociologists, the word always means *social action* — activity oriented to others or taking others into account. This, in turn, means action based in *shared meaning,* not something individuals do for and by themselves. Social action is always either a response to another actor or an attempt to secure such a response. Other persons need not be immediately present for an activity oriented to them to be called social, however. We write letters to people far away who will not receive them for

**Organized social life** *emerges from* **social interactions.**

some time, or we make decisions about our own behavior in the present by referring to standards of conduct that our parents taught us long ago.

**Interaction** Interaction is defined as interpersonal social action. It is action that affects the recipient in some way, usually resulting in—and usually intended by the actor to result in—a reaction back to him or her. If the original actor then reacts to the other's reaction, an ongoing social process has been initiated.

**Relationship** Another characteristic of all social interaction except the most fleeting is **relationship.** Any time an interaction among a particular set of actors endures through time, three things may be expected to happen to all concerned: (1) Each will in some way become dependent upon the others, requiring their continued reaction as a condition of their own behavior. (2) Each will develop expectations about the future actions of others based on past actions. (3) Each will identify with the others and with the relationship between them that the interaction has established.

These phenomena are illustrated by a remark once made by a perceptive sociologist named Ivan Belknap. "If you truly want to put someone in your debt," Belknap observed, "let him do you a favor. The bigger the favor, the more he will owe you." The truth behind this apparently paradoxical statement stems from the relational characteristic of social interaction. A person's willingness to do you a favor implies recognition of some kind of relationship with you. If the favor is a big one, it implies a close or important relationship. Once having done the favor and thus having affirmed the relationship, the individual cannot later repudiate it. The benefactor is thus bound to the relationship that the favor implies. So think twice before you give alms to a street beggar who habituates a standard location. If you have given today, what reason can you offer for not giving tomorrow?

### Basic Dimensions of Interaction

Social interaction may be conceived as taking place in three dimensions, each a polar-opposite pair. These are transitory-recurrent, instru-

Exchange.

mental-expressive, and formal-informal. They are categories that sociologists impose on events, of course, not the actual events observed. They serve to clarify our understanding of the significance and complexity of this basic phenomenon of social life.

**Transitory interaction** is the one-time exchange or, at the most, a very short series of actions and reactions. **Recurrent interaction,** as the name implies, is ongoing through time and involves long-range relationships. We engage in hundreds of both kinds every day, waving casually at neighbors simply to acknowledge the relationship with them, and interacting with family members and coworkers in dozens of different ways that have been fixed for years.

**Instrumental interaction** is so called because it is used as an instrument or tool for doing or getting something else; the interaction itself is just a means to an end. Telling a taxi driver where you want to go would be an example. **Expressive interaction,** on the other hand, is action that is engaged in for its own sake, for the pleasure of interacting. Most sexual interaction is expressive, as is "shooting the bull" with a friend, playing intermural sports, keeping your roommate company on a trip to the coin laundry, and so forth.

The formal-informal dimension of interaction is self-explanatory. **Formal interactions** are guided by well-defined, often written, norms. The actors in them are likely to be more concerned with what the other actors do than with who they are. **Informal interactions,** on the contrary, are less structured by established norms, giving actors more room for creativity and self-expression.

## THE STRUCTURE OF SOCIAL INTERACTION

Thus far we have been concerned largely with interaction as a process, the ways in which interpersonal behavior is acted out. Interaction also has a structure, however; it occurs in patterned forms. Let us turn our attention to some of these now.

### Major Forms of Interaction

Interaction generally takes one of four major forms, or to be dominated by one with admixtures of one or more of the others. These are

**relationship** (social): an interaction among a particular set of actors that endures through time.

**transitory interaction:** the one-time or very brief exchange carried out for a trivial practical purpose, to smooth a temporary relationship of great brevity or to support temporarily an enduring one.

**recurrent interaction:** interaction ongoing in time that maintains long-term social relationships.

**instrumental interaction:** interaction undertaken as a means to some other end or goal.

**expressive interaction:** interaction engaged in for its own sake and without further goals.

**formal interaction:** interaction guided by well-defined, often written, norms. Usually essentially impersonal in nature.

**informal interaction:** interaction guided by spontaneous innovation and creativity, unstructured by formal norms. Usually rather personal in nature.

**exchange** (social): the form of interaction motivated by the returns or rewards it is expected to bring from others.

exchange, power, conflict, and cooperation.

**Exchange** George C. Homans, an outstanding American sociologist, defined **exchange interactions** as "an exchange of activity, tangible or intangible, and more or less rewarding or costly, between two or more persons."[2] Following this lead, Peter Blau, another major sociologist, notes that it refers to " . . . voluntary actions of individuals that are motivated by the returns [which the exchanges] are expected to bring and typically do in fact bring from others."[3] Implicit in these statements are several assumptions about the role of exchange in social interaction. We can summarize them as follows: (1) Actors seek to interact with others who can satisfy their needs or facilitate the attainment of their desired goals. (2) All actions entail costs to the actor, such as time, energy, or resources expended. (3) Actors generally seek to keep the costs of their actions proportional to the outcomes or benefits they expect from them. (4) When choosing among alternative courses of action, the actor tends to select those that are most economical in terms of costs and benefits. (5) An actor will terminate a course of action the cost of which consistently exceeds its benefits.[4]

The basic principle that governs exchange interactions seems to be that an individual who supplies rewarding services to another person obligates the other. To discharge this obligation, the second person must return benefits to the first in some way. The need to reciprocate for benefits received in order to continue receiving them serves as a self-starting mechanism for social interaction. Social exchange differs in a number of important ways from economic exchange, despite the apparent similarities. Among the most important of these is that a social exchange creates *unspecified* obligations. It involves favors that create diffuse obligations for the future, not precisely specified ones. The nature of the return cannot be bargained about; it must be left to the discretion of the one who will make it.

Further, social exchange engenders feelings of personal obligation, gratitude, and trust; purely economic exchange does not. The terms of an economic transaction are clear, formal, and stated in writing. We are not grateful to the banker who makes us a car loan. A variety of conditions affect the social exchange process: the stage of development and the nature of the relationship between the exchange partners; the benefits to be derived and the costs incurred for both; and the social context in which the exchange takes place. The profits from a specific exchange relationship diminish as the number of exchanges increases. The person who is happy to help push your car out of a snowbank once will become less gracious if you continue to put it there.[5]

In one way, what these observations call attention to is the fact that self-seeking and instrumental manipulation may play a greater role in social life than most of us like to admit. A teacher should be happy to assist his or her students simply because that is part of the job of a teacher, and students should feel free to ask questions for the same reason; answering them is part of the teacher's job. But in fact the student is likely to grease the wheels of the interaction by showing deference to the teacher's sta-

tus, and the teacher is more likely to be helpful when appropriate deference is offered.

**Power**    The second major form of social interaction is power or the exertion of power. Social **power** can be defined as the ability to affect or alter social life, social actions, social order, or culture in some way.[6] It is the ability to shape the processes of social organization through time, even against resistance. Power is a *relational* phenomenon, not a psychological one. It exists in social relationships, not in individuals, although certainly some individuals have unique qualities that maximize the probability that they will be able to exert power in interactions with others. Power may be exerted by groups and organizations as well as by individuals. In fact, organizations are likely to be far more effective at exerting power than individuals because of their greater resources and more efficient use of them.

Social power in all of its forms—force, authority, dominance, attraction—is both a cause and a consequence of social interaction and social organization. This will be discussed in greater detail in Chapter 6, but for the moment, we can draw certain general conclusions about its nature and exertion. Social organization enables people to accomplish things collectively that they could not do separately. (Could you build a skyscraper or suspension bridge by yourself?) Power is inseparably linked with social interdependence; it exists and can be exerted only so long as social organization is maintained. It can be exercised toward any social object and in any social dimension (upward,

Power.

downward, or laterally in an organization, system, or relationship), and once some power has been generated in some way, it can be used to create more in an expanding cycle.

Power tends to be unevenly distributed among the members of groups and organizations. This is because group members vary in their control over the sources of wealth, in the occupancy of positions of authority, in control over the flow of resources or information, in individual qualities such as intelligence, energy, or education, in proximity to others in even more powerful positions, and so forth.

**Conflict** Conflict interactions have long been a matter of interest to sociologists. **Conflict** (social) can be defined as action intended to destroy, injure, thwart, or control another party. A conflict relationship is one in which the par-

> **power** (social): the capacity of an individual or group to shape the process of social organization, to exercise his, her, or its will despite resistance.
>
> **conflict** (social): the form of interaction intended to destroy, injure, control, or thwart another party and arising from conditions of scarcity or incompatible or mutually exclusive goals.
>
> **cooperation:** the form of interaction that involves collaborative effort to attain a common goal. It may be spontaneous or directed, voluntary or involuntary, contractual or traditional, and large or small in scale.

Conflict.

ties can gain only at one another's expense. As in the cases of exchange and power interactions, certain principles define the essential nature of such interactions.

Conflict requires at least two parties; it is not something that can be engaged in alone. It arises from *position scarcity*, (competition for status), *resource scarcity*, or mutually exclusive or incompatible values. Conflict is a form of interaction and cannot exist without interaction; conflict actions and counteractions are mutually interdependent; there can be no conflict without opposition. Conflict interactions involve attempts to gain control of scarce resources or positions, or to influence behavior in specific directions. Thus conflict always is concerned with attempts to acquire or exercise power. Contrary to popular understanding, conflict interactions do not represent a breakdown in regulated conduct. Like other social relationships, conflicts are conducted according to social rules. What is involved is a shift in the norms and expectations governing a specific set of interactions from one variety (exchange, for example) to another. The labor union that goes on strike when bargaining fails is an example.[7]

**Cooperation** The fourth structural form that interaction takes is **cooperation.** Robert A. Nisbet, a leading American sociologist, defines it as "joint or collaborative behavior toward some goal in which there is common interest."[8] Cooperative interactions may be spontaneous or directed, voluntary or involuntary, contractual or traditional, large or small.

*Spontaneous cooperative interaction* is the oldest, most natural, and most common of the four. It is situational (that is, undirected by tradition or command) and is found whenever people associate with any closeness or duration. While it usually occurs in small face-to-face groups, it may be found everywhere, even in the largest and most impersonal of bureaucracies.

*Directed cooperative interaction* is the outstanding characteristic of organizations. It is planned in advance and requires leadership to be effective. It is found everywhere in modern societies.

*Contractual cooperative interaction,* like the directed form, is planned. It involves a set of mutual decisions, usually documented in a contract and enforceable by legal sanction. *Mutuality* is what distinguishes the two. The bureaucratic official cooperates as directed from above or loses his job. The parties to a contract enter into it voluntarily. In modern societies a significant proportion of cooperative interactions are contractual in nature.

*Traditional cooperative interaction* is built into the customs and mores of a culture. Nisbet describes the joint family of India, the Chinese clan, and the village community of medieval Europe as prime examples. In the medieval village, for instance, planting, cultivating, and harvesting the crops was handled cooperatively following ancient traditions. It would have been unthinkable for one individual to refuse to assist another. Modern American examples of cooperative interaction may be found in almost any neighborhood in such phenomena as informal organizations for baby-sitting and car pooling. Most such interactions are probably essentially spontaneous, at least at the outset; but if they endure over time, some contractual understandings are likely to emerge as well.

### Interaction Situations

We have thus far discussed the significance of social interaction, the principal concepts the sociologist uses in understanding it, the basic dimensions along which it takes place, and the principal forms in which it occurs. But interaction does not proceed in a vacuum; it always has a structural context. That context is the social situation.

A **social situation** is a complex setting involving at least two actors interacting in a variety of ways. They may be enacting established roles as we shall see, but they need not be. A casual conversation between strangers at a bus stop also takes place in a social situation.

Social situations can be grasped as a whole and are worthy of analysis in their own right. We are all familiar with certain regularly recurring situations in which two or more persons join in carrying out some kind of activity: the family dinner table, the classroom, the office staff meeting, the supermarket checkout counter. The kinds of events and interactions that occur in each of these situations are sufficiently regular and predictable to permit us to conceive of them as distinctive occasions. Crowd behavior at a football game and the interaction between clerks and customers in a department store are highly patterned and predictable. We could go to hundreds of games in different locations, or observe hundreds of people buying, say, gloves, and yet be able to anticipate with considerable accuracy what would occur in each instance. Nor would we generally have any difficulty distinguishing a football crowd from the congregants at a mass revival meeting in the same stadium, or a department store transaction from, say, a used car purchase.

Part of our ability to make such distinctions comes from shared cultural definitions and expectations for specific situations. We all know what to expect in each circumstance because we have all been exposed to a common culture. A person from a different culture who did not share our expectations might have difficulty understanding the classifications we make of similar events which seem so natural to us. It is possible, for example, that a Central American Indian might mistake the football game for a religious ritual. This appears preposterous to us, but is understandable in someone who does not share our cultural definitions, especially in view of the fact that football games often open with a religious invocation and a quasi-religious flag-raising ceremony. To further complicate matters, prehistoric Meso-Americans apparently engaged in what we now call ball games for ritualistic purposes.

A sociologist analyzing a social situation tries not to take such generally understood events for granted. Rather the sociologist attempts to see how situations are enacted, how they direct the behavior of the people involved, how they become recurrent, and how they fit into larger social contexts. Two topics of particular importance in such an analysis are situational definitions and situational contingencies.

**Situational Definitions**  As we have suggested, social situations are not simply objective sets of events. Occurrences that might appear similar to an uninitiated observer may have subjective meanings that make them very different to the participants: The flag ceremony before a football game may look something like a religious ritual, but few Americans perceive it as such. These subjective features are crucial to understanding the events involved in a situation. **Situational definitions,** then, are the normative side of any interaction; what people think and understand and believe about what they are .doing *is* the reality of the situation for them.

Situational definitions also consist in part of roles, which we will discuss more extensively in the next section. In a general way, we antici-

> **social situation:** a complex social setting involving at least two actors interacting in a variety of ways.
>
> **situational definitions:** the subjective meanings situations have for the actors in them, what the situation means *to them*, including roles to be played, relevant norms, and probable courses of action.

pate the roles we will have to play in a given situation, and we prepare ourselves to respond to the roles others will play. We also anticipate that others will respond to us in a certain way because of the roles they will assign to us. Such subjective definitions also include generalized expectations that go beyond the roles of participants. These apply to the situation as a whole; norms concerning decorum, mood, and demeanor are involved. A religious ritual is a solemn occasion, for example, and participants approach it with that in mind.

Situational definitions also include anticipated courses of action, sequences in which we expect a given situation to develop. We expect roles to be carried out in predictable sequences and to be geared to each other in predictable ways. We expect to know the order in which the events will take place. Sometimes the rules governing the order of events are formalized and thus can be predicted exactly, like the procedures governing courtroom behavior in a trial. But even in cases where the rules are informal, generally understood norms about sequencing are likely to develop to specify both general and particular courses of action. *Doing the dozens*, for instance, is a patterned interaction sequence common to informal groups of young, black males in urban communities. In a relatively standardized pattern insults are exchanged in an escalating sequence until one player loses the game by "blowing his cool" or failing to come up with an adequate response. The rules of this game are not written down, but they are so widely understood that an individual may readily transfer his or her skills from one informal group to another.

**Situational Contingencies**  **Situational contingencies** are the flexible side of an interaction situation. Regardless of the actors' definitions of a situation and the expectations associated with them, the situation itself im-

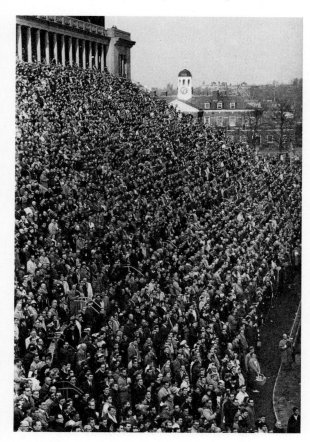

Pledging allegiance at a football game. What are these people really doing?

## THE TERM PAPER MILLS GRIND AGAIN

In the early 1970s, students at Harvard and the University of Michigan were discovered turning in identical papers purchased from the term paper mills. The resulting publicity drove the mills underground, but not out. . . . The firms usually do business through the mail, making contact with potential customers by advertising in campus newspapers and on student union bulletin boards and by passing out business cards as exam time approaches. Their ads also appear in National Lampoon and other magazines popular with students. . . .

Many of the companies conspicuously stamp FOR RESEARCH ONLY on their papers, or have students sign a declaration on the order form stating that the paper "will be used for research purposes only." Educational Research in Chicago has gone so far as to copyright its material. Insists Archie Jaudon of College Research Services in Austin, Texas: "A student buys a copy of a paper for research purposes. He knows he is not supposed to use it verbatim. We expect the student to read and redo the paper. Time is so much a factor at a university—students have to wait weeks for a book at the library. We can help them avoid that."

College officials are unimpressed with this argument. . . . Students caught turning in

purchased papers are typically put on probation or expelled, say college administrators. . . .

A situational contingency: Students often feel overworked or that assignments are irrelevant; but grades have a lot to do with what happens after graduation; the paper mill fills the gap.

poses limits on the participants and provides them with opportunities and channels for action. Responses are contingent, or dependent, on the limits, opportunities, and channels present in the situation. These features are called situational contingencies.

Situational contingencies frequently enter into explanations of behavior. It has often been argued, for example, that criminal activity depends partly on the inclinations of the individual, but also partly on the opportunities available. If a person wants money and legitimate work is not available, he or she may turn to illegitimate activity. The desire for money combines with the contingency (unavailability of work) to produce an illegal act. In other situations where work *is* available, the same motivation may produce social success. Some analysts have developed a theory of delinquency by extending this type of reasoning. (See Chapter 16.)

For a more comprehensive illustration, we can look to Michel Crozier's study of a French manufacturing plant.[9] Crozier found that the maintenance department, which was responsible for repair of machinery, was remarkably powerful in the affairs of the plant. Its power was based on a situational contingency. The rules of the plant had become so restrictive and elaborate that no department could take any action that might seriously affect any other department. Even superior officials had little influence on lower ranking department heads because the rules were so constraining. Thus there was little uncertainty in the organization; the rules spelled everything out and left nothing to chance—nothing except mechanical breakdowns. When the machinery failed, everything stopped until repairs were made by the maintenance workers.

This contingency—the unexpected and unpredictable mechanical breakdown—gave the maintenance department a special power over the other departments. Because the maintenance workers could carry out repairs rapidly or slowly, as suited them, they had the power to delay or expedite the work of other departments when breakdowns occurred. Theirs was the one department with power to control the one contingency in the system, and they used this power to defend themselves and extract benefits from others. The headwaiter who accepts tips from customers who wish to be seated without waiting is in a similar position. He controls access to desired rewards as a contingency of his position in the situation.

Any situation may be analyzed partially as a set of contingencies similar to these. The sociologist looks for the contingencies affecting the choices people make and the outcomes of those choices. Any course of events may be explained in part by reference to the total set of contingencies operating in the situation.

## SOCIAL ROLES

We have thus far considered as major topics the significance of social interaction for individual and collective life, and the nature and structure of interaction itself. A final subject for this chapter is another fundamental structural conception, the *social role*. Our discussion will describe the basic concepts through which roles are analyzed and understood, how roles are enacted, and the tensions, conflicts, and troubles people have with the enactment of their multiple roles.

### Basic Role Concepts

**Roles and Positions**   A social role is an interrelated set of expectations and actions that is an integral part of a position in a social organization or organizational process.[10] Roles are pat-

> **situational contingencies:** the limits and opportunities objectively present in a social situation, regardless of the subjective understandings of the actors.
>
> **social position:** social role as conceived statically, as a location in a social structure (President of . . .) or a pattern of socially ordered behavior ("old maid").

terns of action and interaction that people enact whenever they engage in any collective activity or, when alone, when they act as directed by or for such activity. A role, then, is an intersection, or point of convergence, between individual action and some kind of organized or organizational praticipation. It is the point at which the process of social organization takes place. (See Chapter 6.)

For a social role to exist in the first place, there must be some degree of social organization present in the situation. Roles cannot exist apart from patterns of social order and culture. Roles are, in effect, the smallest unit of social organization. Individuals enact roles and thus are involved in social ordering, but they are not themselves *units* of social organization.

A role is dynamic; it is what people do in response to the expectations of others, whether those expectations are internalized (so that the role behavior is self-starting in the individual) or externalized, as in a job description or a set of regulations for how to perform some business transaction.

Roles can also be viewed from a static perspective, however, as locations within a social structure or pattern of socially ordered behavior. When this perspective is adopted, the role is called a **social position**. Positions are likely, in fact, to consist of a related set of roles that their incumbents are expected to enact, and—maintaining the static perspective—they can be said to "exist" even when they are vacant, when there is no incumbent around to enact them.

For example, your sociology teacher occupies a position called *professor* in an organization called a *college* or *university* but if you were to spend a week following the professor around, you would not see the position. What you would observe instead would be your teacher's personal enactment of the set of roles that constitute the position *professor:* teaching classes, doing research, having student conferences, attending committee meetings, etc. The roles in the list would be, respectively, those of teacher, scholar, advisor, committee member. In each of these sets of activities, your professor would be enacting his or her own personal understanding of what was required in the particular situation to fulfill the obligations and expectations of that role. And in each instance the role enactment would be manifesting and constructing the pattern of collective activity that is the social position of professor in the organization called a college or university. The particular roles are thus the intersections between an individual and an organization. Social organization is constructed or manifested or made real by individuals enacting role behavior.

**Role Expectations**   A **role expectation** is a person's subjective understanding of how to enact a particular role, that is, how other people expect him or her to act. The term is also applied to the expectations one has for the behavior of others in *their* role enactments. There are three kinds of role expectation—normative, situational, and personal.[11] Normative role expectations are cultural and subcultural. They tell us how we *should* enact a given role if it is to be properly performed. Situational role expectations are those that are imposed on one by others in a specific social situation, and which one holds for them, as a consequence of the situation in question. They relate *to* the situation, for example, lowering one's voice in church. Personal role expectations are those one holds for one's own role enactment, for the style and quality of performance one expects of oneself. Any role, no matter how clearly specified by normative and situational expectations, still leaves room for individual creativity and style of enactment. In fact, it may be that the greater the specificity of role enactment required, the more important style becomes. What is the difference in performance between a great musician and a merely very good one?

**Role Acquisition**   We acquire the many roles we enact throughout our lives in one of two ways, by *ascription* or by *achievement*. **Ascribed roles,** often called *statuses* in one of the several ways in which sociologists use that word, are assigned to people by others on the basis of socially significant personal characteristics. Age and sex are the most important and universal of these, but, depending on the society in question, such factors as race, religion, family lineage, occupation, socioeconomic status, region of birth, and others may also be used. It is usually very difficult for us to escape or alter an ascribed role because it is something that others do to us and there is little an individual can do to change the behavior of others. Similarly, it is usually impossible for us to acquire an ascribed role if we do not possess the necessary characteristics. No matter how well educated and mature you may be, you will not be permitted to vote in an American election unless you are at least 18 years old.

**Achieved roles** are acquired by individuals on the basis of demonstrated capability or performance. Such roles have socially prescribed requirements, and the individual must demonstrate possession of them before others will permit the role to be adopted. Sometimes the criteria for achieving a given role are precisely defined, as those for election to public office or certification to practice medicine. More often, however, the specification is vague. What exactly are the criteria for being a "jock" in high school?

In contemporary industrial societies, most roles are achieved (educational, occupational, political, and so forth), but historically the most important roles have usually been ascribed. The historic shift from ascriptive roles to achieved roles probably could not take place within the framework of traditional societies and may be part of the reason for some of the turmoil that characterizes many emerging societies today. A society that stresses achievement places upon its members and organizations great demands for technical competence, education, social sophistication, and emotional maturity.

**Role Repertoires**   A person typically plays a large number of different roles simultaneously. A male student, for example, may be a husband, father, son, student, employee, voter, parishioner, fisherman, and amateur race driver, to name only a few. His wife might be a wife, mother, office manager, voter, parishioner, and part-time judo instructor. The term **role repertoire** refers to the total catalogue of social roles enacted by an individual at any given period in his or her life. The roles in the repertoire are held together by being enacted by the same individual.

People may maintain a degree of consistency among their multiple roles by enacting each role in a way that makes it consistent with the other roles in the repertoire. A considerate mother is apt to be a considerate wife, a mean father is likely to be a mean husband. But different roles are enacted in different settings, and not all of the roles in a repertoire are enacted simultaneously. The problem that Dagwood Bumstead and his friend Herb Woodley have with their gambler roles is their attempt to enact them in their home neighborhood, during daytime hours, when their wives expect them to be enacting more household-centered roles from their repertoires.

### Enacting Social Roles

Our discussion has concentrated on the basic concepts with which sociologists analyze and understand social roles. We now turn our attention to the ways roles are actually carried out in our behavior.

**Role Enactment**   How do we fulfill role expectations? Why do we behave as we are expected to? Two broad answers may be given to these questions. One emphasizes the processes of socialization, the other stresses social control. Through socialization, as we saw in Chapter 4, we learn what is expected and we internalize these expectations. Then we conform to role expectations by doing what we ourselves agree is right or appropriate. The socialization process is partly explicit and focused, as in elementary school or a scout troop; but socialization also occurs in more subtle ways. Just by existing in a setting, we tend to absorb the perspectives and assumptions held by the other people there. These form a taken-for-granted background to all our actions. Such generally understood expectations need not be taught explicitly. In fact, in many cases, efforts to teach them in a formal way would probably be ineffective. Nonetheless such generalized expectations play an important part in controlling behavior.

Role enactment is also governed by the ongoing processes of social control. Involved here are a variety of sanctions that others may invoke. Such sanctions reward behavior that

**role expectation:**   an individual's subjective understanding of how to enact a given role or how others ought to enact theirs.

**ascribed role:**   a role assigned to people by others on the basis of social characteristics such as age, sex, or race.

**achieved role:**   a role acquired by an individual on the basis of demonstrated capability or performance, such as occupational or recreational roles.

**role repertoire:**   the total catalogue of social roles enacted by the individual at any given time of life.

conforms with role expectations and punish behavior that violates them. A great deal of the research on roles concerns the effects of different kinds of sanctions. For example, are monetary sanctions more effective than symbolic ones like prestige, honor, or affection? Among symbolic sanctions, which are most effective, and for whom? In recent years, for instance, the Army, Navy, and Air Force have emphasized educational and vocational opportunities in their campaigns to attract volunteers. The U.S. Marine Corps, by contrast, has used subtle

Parts in the role repertoire.

combat and masculinity themes, with the low-key elitist admission that the Corps is "looking for a few good men." The sociologist might wonder whether these two different promotions produced two different kinds of recruits for the various organizations.

But role enactment is more than a matter of rigidly conforming to expectations rooted in the culture, the situation, and ourselves. It is also a process in which the individual creates and alters the expectations of others to suit the circumstance. Anyone who has ever been on the stage or around the theater is familiar with this phenomenon. The script for a play makes explicit statements of the characters' lines, and gives some stage directions as well. But it is the actors and the director who, in the last analysis, truly create the characters. If you have ever seen the same play performed by two different companies, or the same character enacted by two different actors, you have been exposed to the creative aspect of even highly specified role enactment. (Compare Charles Robeson's Othello with Lawrence Olivier's, or Olivier's movie Hamlet with Richard Chamberlin's TV version.)

As Ralph Turner points out, roles exist in varying degrees of concreteness and consistency.[12] In enacting them, we create and modify them as well as merely bringing them to light. Further, every role is a way of relating to the roles of others in the situation, so that a change in one reflects the actor's changed assessment or perception of the role of the other. The actor is not the occupant of a position for which there is a neat set of rules, but a person who must act from the perspective supplied in part by relationships to others. This idea of role enactment shifts the emphasis away from the simple process of repeating a prescribed role to one of devising a performance on the basis of what we

impute to others what we understand them to be meaning and intending and expecting.

**Role Partners and Role Sets** Role partners are other persons with whom one enacts one's own role: coworkers, friends, acquaintances, casual passersby. As Turner points out, every role somehow relates to some other role; one cannot enact a social role in isolation. A role may be enacted in solitude, that is, when no one else is present, but the enactment is always *relative to* others. Thus while I type these words alone in my office, I am acting in my role of teacher with relevance or orientation to you, the student reader.

This teacher-student example illustrates a special kind of role-partnership. A **role set** is a cluster of two or more roles that are reciprocal, that is, tied together in such a way that they must be enacted *in interaction with one another.* A worker need not necessarily have specific role partners in order to do some kinds of work. But a teacher must have a student to be a teacher. A teacher without students is unemployed; he or she is a *former* teacher, or has some other qualification added to the occupational label. The role *teacher* can only be enacted by an individual if other persons reciprocally enact the role *student.* Similarly, a student must have a teacher to be a student. Roles in a role set are reciprocal in that the rights of one role are the obligations of the other or others. As a teacher I have the right to examine students. As students, they have the obligation to be examined. Role sets are reciprocal too in that some coordination in time is required for their enactment. For me to be a teacher, I must teach when my students are present; one cannot teach an empty classroom.

**Roles and Self** Each of us builds up certain more or less stable personality characteristics that include as a prominent feature a self-concept or sense of identity. We all have certain relatively stable images and ideas about ourselves. These self-concepts either conflict or harmonize with the roles we are expected to fulfill. If harmony prevails, of course, there is no problem. But if conflict prevails, we must either adjust our self-concept to our roles (or vice versa) or experience a disturbing amount of tension between them. If we adjust our conception of self to the roles we enact, we minimize tension

Role partners.

and feel that carrying out role expectations is compatible with our own wishes. Role behavior then is relatively spontaneous and easy.

But if we are unable to resolve the conflict between role and self, role behavior becomes difficult. It involves a feeling of tension between what we want to do or feel comfortable doing and what we are expected to do. In extreme instances, such conflict leads to a sense of alienation from our roles, a feeling of being coerced into carrying out activities that are against our wishes, although we may be unable to identify the source of the coercion.

Tensions and conflicts of this kind occur in the relationship between role and self for all of us at various times in our lives. Most of us are able to continue to function, however, to prevent them from crippling us, because of the autonomy we enjoy in role enactment. The possibilities for style and creativity in role behavior that we have already discussed enable most

> **role partners:** persons (in roles of their own) with whom one enacts one's own roles, such as co-workers or friends.
>
> **role set:** a cluster or two or more reciprocal roles that must be enacted in relation to each other, such as teacher-student, parent-child.

people to keep the requirements of the various roles in their repertoires reasonably compatible.

### Role Strain or Conflict

It would appear from our discussion so far that role enactment usually goes quite smoothly. We learn the parts we are to play in life in various ways and, either as a result of the internalization of expectations, the search for reward, or the wish to avoid sanctions, we proceed duti-

Copyright, 1975, G. B. Trudeau. Distributed by Universal Press Syndicate.

**Adjusting self-concept to the roles we play is not always easy, but it reduces tension.**

fully to act them out. The play goes on, the society works smoothly, and if there are any tensions or difficulties involved in the role enactment, they are handled through the free play or flexibility made possible by individual style and creativity. If such an impression has been created, it is false. **Role strain** or **conflict** (the terms are often used synonymously) is endemic, a normal part of social interaction. William J. Goode defines role strain as "the felt difficulty in fulfilling role obligations."[13]

Examples of role strain are multitudinous in modern life, and the reader can undoubtedly find many in his or her own experience. Stereotypical is the plight of the educated woman who experiences simultaneous expectational pressures to be a housewife and mother and to have a career. In large part, in fact, the contemporary woman's movement is a response to this kind of strain. The good student who is asked for help on an exam by a lazy or inept classmate is equally familiar. All teachers know the strain introduced into their lives by pleasant, hardworking students who have tried their best and still deserve to be failed as judged by their academic performances. And any employer has faced the problem of the employee who has put in the required time but done nothing of value for the business with it. Parents often face the same dilemma when children's allowances are tied to chores: the chore is done, but so badly that it must be redone later.

**Sources of Role Strain**   The basic reason for role strain is simple: with respect to any given role expectation or obligation, there will always be some people who cannot conform or respond adequately because of individuality or circumstance. They simply do not have sufficient time, energy, resources, or information. Describing the sources of role strain, Goode notes that even when role demands are not difficult or disagreeable, they are required at particular times and at particular places, which means that conformity will not always be pleasurable or automatic.[14] In addition, all people take part in many different role relationships, and the requirements of some of these may be contradictory or involve conflicts of time, place, or resources. Further, role relationships typically require several activities or responses, among which there may be inconsistencies, different, but not quite contradictory, norms. Many role relationships consist of role sets that engage a person in interaction with a number of individuals. A parent of several children is a common example. Consequently, the individual may face a wide, distracting, and sometimes

© Jules Feiffer.

**Role inconsistency. Who is the better man by conventional social standards?**

conflicting set of obligations, and the total becomes overdemanding.

As may be inferred from the discussion above, there are two fundamental types of role strain—**interrole strain,** tensions existing between or as a consequence of the expectations for two or more incompatible roles, and **intrarole strain,** or **role inconsistency,** incompatible expectations for or within a single role. Interrole strain occurs when a person is expected to enact two or more incompatible roles simultaneously. The career woman/housewife tension is classic simply because so many employed women suffer from it. Intrarole strain occurs when an individual or one or more of his or her role partners hold incompatible expectations for a single role. Dagwood's card-playing mentioned earlier is an example. Intrarole strain can be entirely subjective; in such instances the person is, in fact, ambivalent, unsure in his or her own mind about how to enact a given role, and suffering from inconsistent expectations.

**The Management of Role Strain**  There is little empirical research describing the extent of role strain in modern life. When we consider the immense importance of role enactment in social interaction and the multitude of possible sources for role strain, it is apparent that few people can escape some degree of experience with it. "In fact," Olsen says, "role incompatibility, inconsistency, and incongruity should probably be considered normal" aspects of all role enactment.[15]

But if role strain is so prevalent in our lives, why are we not more aware of it? Why are we not all nervous wrecks from trying to deal with overdemanding, sometimes impossible role expectations? How is it that most people, most of the time, appear capable of carrying out their various roles without damaging incapacity? The answer is that although we all encounter numerous situations in which role strain is present, we are able to develop techniques of role strain management. Only in unfamiliar, unexpected, or critical situations do we consciously experience such problems. Following Jackson Toby's formulation,[16] Olsen describes what

> **role strain** or **conflict:**  difficulty felt or experienced by an actor in fulfilling role obligations. Role strain may be *interrole,* (between two or more roles), or *intrarole,* (incompatible expectations within a single role). Intrarole strain is sometimes called "role inconsistency" in the sociological literature.
>
> **interrole strain:**  tensions existing as a consequence of the expectations for two or more incompatible roles.
>
> **intrarole strain** or **role inconsistency:**  incompatible expectations for or within a single role.

appear to be six common ways in which role strain is handled. These are (1) *conformity* or role diversity, in which the person leads a double life, conforming to conflicting expectations by taking advantage of the fact that one is never simultaneously in contact with all of one's role partners; (2) *selection* or role sacrifice, in which the person conforms to one set of expectations and compromises, and avoids or repudiates others; (3) *compromise* or role-juggling, in which the person attempts to conform to some degree to all of the conflicting expectations and hopes all the partners will be satisfied; (4) *change* or role manipulation, in which the person alters the situation in some way so as to eliminate the role strain; (5) *stalling* or role-inactivity, in which we hope the strain is temporary, and simply postpone any action until one or more of the role partners relaxes their demands; and (6) *withdrawal* or role-escape, in which we abandon the strainful roles altogether.

These categories are pure types, of course, and in any actual situation an individual might combine several of them in various ways or find other means of handling role strain. But handle it most of us do, and usually in reasonably satisfactory ways, for as surprising and inconvenient as our social interactions sometimes are, the fact is that most of them go very smoothly and predictably. Social life would probably be impossible under any other circumstances.

## SUMMARY

This chapter, the first of two devoted to social organization, dealt with social interaction and its related components. It approached the problem of how social organization comes about or is possible from the individual's perspective, that is, how and why individual actors do the things they do that, from a collective viewpoint, comprise recurrent and patterned behavior.

We began by considering the significance of social interaction for social life in general and for self-development and the attainment of life goals, learning that it is critical in all three. We then broadened the inquiry to establish the importance of interaction for social organization itself, emphasizing that organized social life is really a process which is constantly created and recreated through social interaction.

Following this introduction, the chapter proceeded to analyze the process of interaction by describing the fundamental concepts sociologists use to understand it: actor, action, interaction, and relationship. The basic dimensions along which interaction takes place were then explored—transitory-recurrent, instrumental-expressive, formal-informal.

Later we looked at the forms in which interaction occurs—exchange, power, conflict, and cooperation. Another important aspect of the structure of interaction is the social situation in which it takes place, a complex setting involving multiple actors interacting in a variety of ways. The two major features of interaction situations to be understood were situational definitions and situational contingencies. The former are subjective, ideas held by the actors themselves; the latter are objective features of situations.

Finally we described the principal concepts the sociologist uses in understanding roles— roles and positions, role expectations, role acquisition, and role repertoires. Roles are enacted with role partners and often occur in role sets and are set in a context for the individual by the relationship between role and self. They often involve role strain as well, but this should probably be viewed as a normal condition since it appears to be present for all of us and most people develop techniques to manage role strain.

## SUGGESTED READINGS

CAPLOW, THEODORE. *How to Run Any Organization* (New York: Holt, Rinehart and Winston, 1976). A brief summary of sociological organization theory and research written for nonsociologists who need to put it into practice. For the student reader, one of the most practical applications of sociology's everyday utility.

CAPLOW, THEODORE. *Two Against One* (Englewood Cliffs, N.J.: Prentice-Hall, 1968). This unusual and simply written monograph explores the special structural and interaction characteristics of triads, three-member groups. A pleasant blend of theory and empirical research, it is a student's introduction to "social geometry," an unusual sociological approach.

GOFFMAN, ERVING. *The Presentation of Self in Everyday Life* (New York: Anchor, 1959). Highly popular with college students for years, this book introduced the dramaturgical approach to interaction analysis in sociology. Full of fascinating and unusual insights concerning daily life and interaction situations.

HUMPHRIES, LAUD. *Tearoom Trade* (Chicago: Aldine, 1970). A famous and controversial research on impersonal homosexual sexual activity in public places, centering on interaction situations and processes.

LIEBOW, ELLIOT. *Talley's Corner* (Boston: Little, Brown, 1967). Like *Street Corner Society,* a classic participant observation report, this one of unemployed black slum residents.

WHYTE, WILLIAM FOOTE. *Street Corner Society* (Chicago: University of Chicago Press, 1943). A sociological classic of participant observation, this monograph reports the daily life and interaction processes and structures of a gang of young men in an Italian slum.

# Chapter 6
# Social
# Organization

How do human beings, with so many individual idiosyncrasies, ever manage to cooperate in organized social life? How do we transform our daily interactions with other individuals into the millions of enduring groups, associations, communities, and societies that comprise the modern world? In brief, how do we create and maintain social organization out of the turmoil of everyday living? That fundamental question about the nature of organized social life was posed in the seventeenth century by the English philosopher Thomas Hobbes, who observed that social organization was what kept human life from being "solitary, poor, nasty, brutish, and short."[1] The question continues to be the principal concern of sociology today.

The essence of our answer to the Hobbesian question about organized social life is that social organization is the complex dynamic process through which our relationships with others become arranged into stable and meaningful patterns. These patterns form organizational units that have a reality of their own distinct from the reality of their individual members. The term *organization* thus refers to both a dynamic process and to the stable units, such as groups, associations, communities, and societies, that are created by that process. All organized social entities, in short, are the outcome of the process of social organization.

As an example of organization in everyday social life, imagine a city street corner. Cars speed by on one street; the light changes and they stop to allow traffic to move along the cross street. Four people stand on the sidewalk talking despite the throngs of pedestrians. A line of pickets marches back and forth in front of a store, watched by two police officers. A number of strangers stand in line to board a bus without arguing about who will be first. A crew of construction workers are renovating an old building. This may seem unremarkable, but it illustrates several different processes and forms of social organization, the focus of this chapter.

What makes stable and enduring social life possible? Let us return to our street corner. It illustrates two difficulties we encounter whenever we examine social life. The first is that we cannot directly perceive the flow of time. Our example is only a single slice of time, isolated from everything that led up to it and everything that will follow it. It tells us nothing about the other activities in which these people may be engaged. It says nothing about other events that may occur at that street corner during the rest of the day. To become fully aware of the dynamic nature of social organization through time, we must look beyond such momentary events such as those to the ongoing patterns that underly them.

The second difficulty we encounter when we examine social organization is that we cannot observe it directly the way we perceive individuals and their actions. On our street corner, we saw four people talking together, but we could not see the bonds of friendship that link them into a close-knit group. We could not observe directly the patterns of job specialization and coordination that enable the construction workers to cooperate smoothly in their work, nor the planning and experience that got the pickets onto their line or the police on their beat. The existence of social organization must be inferred from its effects on the actions of the people involved, just as the existence of gravity must be inferred from its effects on falling objects. We will begin the discussion of social organization by considering the concept, the idea itself. What do sociologists mean by the words? How does it come about? In what sense can it be understood as a reality rather than as a verbal abstraction? Following *that beginning, the chapter examines the processes through which social organization takes place, types of social organizations, and the critical organizational trends that mark our times.*

## THE NATURE OF SOCIAL ORGANIZATION

### The Concept of Social Organization

Social organization develops as interactions and relationships among individuals are repeated through time and become stable and meaningful. Social interactions and relationships are the threads of organized social life, but separate threads are not the same as a whole bolt of fabric. Countless ongoing combinations of numerous hues and textures must be woven together into ordered patterns and de-

signs to create the material of human social organization. In other words, *social organization is the process of bringing order and meaning into our shared social activities.* This occurs as ongoing relationships form stable patterns of social ordering and eventually acquire common cultural meanings.

Consider your own family. In a functioning family unit, each individual must, at least part of the time, interact with the other family members in ways that are recurrent and predictable, so that the relationships comprising the family remain stable over the years. Each person enacts a set of roles, such as income earner, cook, yard tender, or vacation planner, that mesh with the roles of the other family members in a coordinated division of labor. At times, some of the family members may conflict with one another, while at other times, one family member will exert influence over the others. All this activity is guided and regulated by norms, values, and role expectations shared by all family members.

Like the family, all social organization is an

We cannot tell from this one picture what relationship is being enacted here, but that an interaction is occurring is unquestionable. If we could observe a large number of such moments in the lives of these people, we could discover the pattern of social organization existing between them.

ongoing dynamic process. To illustrate, suppose that you are observing a man and a woman in conversation, with the man reaching out his hand to the woman. Your mind perceives a continuous series of static observations of the interaction, like the frames in a motion picture film. No one frame tells you much about the nature of the dynamic relationship being enacted by these individuals. Whatever pattern of social organization they are creating—a marriage or a sales transaction or a play production—existed as an ongoing process before you observed them, and will continue into the future. Each observation you make of this situation freezes the ongoing process into a static picture isolated in time. It cannot fully represent what is really occurring, although from a series of observations, you can construct an approximate idea of the dynamic social process that is happening.

The term *social organization* is sometimes confusing, because it refers both to ongoing processes and to established social entities. We speak of social organization as the process through which individuals create a friendship group or a political party or a business firm, and then we go on to describe each of *these* as a particular type of social organization that exists as a recognized entity with a stable structure. There is a good semantic reason for this double meaning of the term. *The entities that we call organizations are always outcomes of the ongoing process of social organization.* They are stable patterns of social ordering that result from dynamic social processes. Using the term *social organization* to refer to both process and entity should continually remind us that social reality, no matter what form it displays at any given moment, is always an ongoing creative process.

### The Emergence of Social Organization

Social organization develops as individuals interact to create patterns of social ordering that are infused with cultural meanings. All social organization consists of three components or levels of activity: *recurrent interpersonal interaction, stable patterns of social ordering,* and *shared cultural meanings.* Social organization is an emergent process because it can be imagined as flowing upward through these three levels of activity. Each successive level—interaction, ordering, meaning—grows out of the level preceding it, and is dependent on lower levels for its existence.

Social ordering emerges from the actions of individuals. It can never be completely separated from them. If the members of a group all cease to interact with one another, the group will no longer exist. Similarly, cultural ideas grow out of collective social ordering and social interaction. Those ideas become only historical memories when the social ordering that created them or the individuals who express them no longer exist. At the same time, each level of activity in the emergent process is partially autonomous; it is not identical to, nor fully determined by, any of the lower levels. A group is more than just several interacting individuals. It cannot be adequately explained with psychological concepts and processes. A culture is more than just a symbolic reflection of social ordering. It cannot be understood solely in terms of its social setting. Each level of activity emerges from a lower level but transcends it to become a new level of reality.

The process of social organization encompasses all three levels of activity, but its core lies in the level of social ordering. Sociologists are therefore especially concerned with the processes and forms of social ordering, such as how groups set goals, or how the size of an organization affects its authority structure. At the same time, they must also take into account both social interaction and cultural ideas, since these other levels of activity directly affect social ordering. Social organization always involves the merging of interaction, ordering, and culture into a unified whole. In a family, for example, the separate individuals merge their actions and interactions into ordered patterns of activity such as providing a home, purchasing necessary goods, performing household chores, bringing up children, and enjoying leisure activities. At the same time, they also develop a common set of family values, rules, rituals, and other shared cultural ideas, such as doing well in school, being on time for meals, locking up at night, and watching the late news on TV.

### The Reality of Social Organization

The organizational units, such as families, communities, or nations, that emerge through the process of social organization are real phenomena. They are not just abstractions based on generalizations about the behaviors of individuals. They are just as real as the individuals who comprise them. This fundamental fact is often difficult for beginning sociology students to grasp, since organizations cannot be seen, touched, or experienced in the same manner as individuals. Moreover, contemporary Western culture contains a strong psychological bias, not found in many Eastern and other cultures, that holds that individuals and psychological processes are more important than groups and social processes.

The fallacy of a reductionist perspective — which holds that only individuals are "real" — can be easily demonstrated, however. We do not actually see or touch individual personalities any more than we see or touch social organizations. What we directly experience when interacting with another person is a biological organism taking certain actions and emitting certain sounds. From these actions and sounds we infer the existence of a self or personality with particular characteristics. Perhaps, then, only organisms are real. But if we have studied biology, we know that a living organism is a system of interrelated organs and that these are in turn composed of individual cells, molecules, and atoms. Is true reality then only chemical or physical in nature? Modern chemistry and physics tells us that molecules and atoms are ultimately composed of energy. Energy is certainly real, and in one sense it is the essence of the entire universe. But if we accept reductionist logic we are forced to deny the reality of all other aspects of our existence beyond pure energy.

In contrast, *the emergence perspective tells us that each successive level of existence is real in the sense that it is something more than just the sum of its component parts.* Each level of existence possesses a unity and distinctive properties of its own that are not inherent in its component parts. These give it reality in its own right. The emergence process can be illustrated with a very simple example. Take the letters *n*, *o*, and *w*. They can be arranged to spell *now*, but they can also be used to spell *own* or *won*. None of these three words are inherent in the letters themselves. They emerge as the separate letters are arranged into a particular configuration whose existence and meaning lie in its pattern of ordering. A similar process occurs with social

organizations. Each organization displays a particular pattern and set of characteristics that give it emergent reality.

The properties of a social organization include its size, patterns of social ordering, decision-making arrangements, conflict management techniques, and overall cohesion. Such characteristics pertain to the organization as a distinct social entity, not to its individual members. They are qualitatively distinct from the personal characteristics of the individuals who comprise the organization. Knowing the personal characteristics of Tom, Dick, Harry, Bill, and Bob — such as how outgoing or ambitious each of them is — will not tell you anything about the basketball team they comprise — such as the duties of their various positions on the team, the play patterns the team uses, its stability under pressure, or its ability to win basketball games. If characteristics such as these are not inherent in the individual members, they must be properties of the team as a whole. And if the team or any other organization exhibits characteristics that are distinctly its own, then it is a real entity.

The reality of social organization also appears in its exteriority and constraints, as noted by Durkheim in his discussion of social facts.[2] The *exteriority* of social organization means that *a group continues to exist over time despite changes, or even a complete turnover, in its membership.* Nothing short of simultaneous unreplaced withdrawal by all the members will destroy a basketball team, a community, or a society. In fact, many organizations — of which a university is an excellent example — establish regular procedures for the separation of old members and the acquisition and training of new members. As a result of the relatively stable persistence of social organizations through time, individuals must treat them as exterior to themselves.

The *constraints* of social organization on individuals are *the ways it influences their actions.* Patterned social arrangements limit or prevent some kinds of individual behavior and provide opportunities for other kinds. If Tom, Dick, Harry, Bill, and Bob are to participate as members of the basketball team, they must abide by the established rules of the game, as well as the requirements of the sponsoring organization and the instructions of the coach. By joining the team, the members gain the opportunity to enjoy a competitive sport and test their athletic ability against other teams, but more generally, in all social organizations, the members may be punished for doing some things (such as stealing) and for not doing other things (such as failing to perform an assigned task), and are rewarded for doing some things (such as making a successful sale), and for not doing other things (such as not accepting a bribe). These social sanctions are constraint procedures used by organizations to ensure that their members contribute to the common welfare of the total organization.

In sum, social organizations exhibit unique characteristics that are distinct from those of their members, they are real entities that have discernable consequences for human life, and they possess a unity that is greater than the sum of their component parts. Social organization exists not solely in individual actions or cultural ideas, but in ordered patterns of meaningful social relationships that persist through time in a dynamic process of becoming.

## SOCIAL ORGANIZATIONAL PROCESSES

Common to all the general processes of social organization and to the social units that result from them are a number of more specific social processes than can be separately identified and analyzed. By examining four of these component processes—social ordering, power exertion, social conflict, and social cohesion—in some detail, we will gain a more thorough understanding of the major features of all social organizations.

### Social Ordering

*Social ordering develops as interactions and relationships become woven into relatively predictable patterns that persist through time.* These patterns may be as simple as the web of friendships among a group of people who enjoy doing things together, or as complex as the set of financial arrangements that comprise the stock market. The resulting regularities in social life give rise to stable social structures that constitute the core of all social organization. As a result of social ordering or structuring (sociologists often use these two terms interchangeably), individuals are able to act collectively to achieve goals that would otherwise be unob-

Can we doubt that these men know exactly what they are doing and how the activity of each must mesh with that of the others? Social ordering is essential to all human survival. It is simply readily apparent in occupations such as this.

tainable, like operating a household or putting a person on the moon. Social ordering thus magnifies the total capabilities of a population of actors, transforming it from a mere sum of individual actions into the emergent patterns and units that comprise organized social life.

Consider the following illustrations of social ordering drawn from all areas of human life: (1) Most adults live together in pairs consisting of one member of each sex, year after year, sharing countless daily activities with their partners. (2) Store clerks smoothly carry out numerous exchange transactions with multitudes of customers, most of whom are total strangers to them. (3) The members of a bridge club gather at a specified location every Monday evening at eight o'clock to engage in ritualized interactions. (4) A lecture audience remains quietly seated, rather than milling about or engaging in private conversations. (5) In most communities, stores and offices tend to be located in some areas, factories in other areas, and residences in yet another area. (6) Persons who violate legal statutes are judged and punished through established procedures, rather than by the persons whom they have directly harmed. (7) Millions of people throughout the United States participate in a nationwide social security program as a result of decisions made by a few hundred legislators.

Through empirical research, sociologists describe and explain these social patterns so that we may understand the nature of social organization. The two classic studies summarized in the following paragraphs illustrate typical sociological analyses of social ordering:

*Group Leadership* In a series of laboratory studies, Robert Bales and his colleagues created small discussion groups, gave them a task to perform, and then observed how they organized themselves to accomplish this task.[3] Observers watching from behind one-way windows kept precise counts of the number of times each group member communicated with others, the person or persons to whom each communication was directed, the length of each communication, and its content. One of the findings of this research was that two different kinds of leaders usually emerge in such groups. *Task leaders* are concerned with moving the group toward achieving its goal, while *socioemotional leaders* focus on the interpersonal relationships among the members. These two leadership roles are quite different and hence are usually performed by different people. They nicely complement each other, however, and both are vital for effective group functioning so the two leaders frequently alternate with one another. Periods of task-oriented discussion tend to be followed by periods of person-oriented interaction that resolve conflicts and promote group cohesion. Thus the group achieves its task goals and maintains itself as a viable social entity.

*Community Power Structure* The purpose of Floyd Hunter's study of Atlanta, Georgia, was to explore the way in which social power was ordered in that community.[4] He first compiled a long list of prominent people in many realms of community life, and then asked a panel of people knowledgeable about community affairs to select the most influential people, those who made crucial decisions affecting the community. A relatively small number of persons were repeatedly nominated by the panel as dominant power-wielders, while many other prominent people were described as merely symbolic figureheads or powerless socialites. The power wielders formed a relatively closed class. They interacted with each other frequently, they tended to name only each other as top influentials, and they shared a common set of beliefs about community affairs. The majority of them were businessmen, not public officials, and they exercised their power primarily through informal pressures rather than by official decision making. Their power in the community was nevertheless very real and quite extensive.

**Boundary Creation** How do social interactions and relationships come to form patterns of social ordering and thus create social organizations? One feature of this process is **boundary creation** or *setting off an identifiable pattern of social ordering from the surrounding social environment*. As boundaries are erected around a set of interactions, we can identify which relationships constitute part of that social ordering and which do not. Some social boundaries are arbitrary, such as the imaginary line running down the middle of a street that separates a city from its adjoining suburbs. In other cases, a basis for delineating social boundaries occurs naturally in interactions and relationships. For example, we can probably discover the boundaries of a small club by finding out who attends its meetings and who doesn't, and what kinds of activities are shared by those individuals.

Boundary creation.

Many social boundaries appear to be quite vague and imprecise, leaving their patterns of social ordering rather unclear. What constitute the boundaries of the typical American family? Does a family in this society consist of a married couple and their unmarried children? What about a grandparent who lives in the home, or an unmarried adult son or daughter still living with the parents, or a foster child for whom the parents have assumed responsibility? Do two unmarried adults of the opposite sex—or the same sex—who live together constitute a family? In another setting, does the membership of a church include all the persons living in its geographical area who were ever baptized in that faith, or only those persons who are currently active in the congregation?

Despite such difficulties in determining social boundaries, all patterns of social ordering are bounded in some way. The most common means of identifying boundaries include the following: (1) Geographical location in a specified area such as a neighborhood or community. (2) Interpersonal identification of members with one another. (3) Membership rosters listing the names of the members of an organization. (4) Limitations on social relationships with those defined as outsiders. (5) Demonstration of willingness and competence to perform necessary activities, from contributing money to devoting time to an organization. This list is far from complete, and several of these boundary definitions may be used in conjunction with one another. All of them nevertheless help delineate a pattern of social ordering from its surrounding environment.

**Pattern Stabilization**   A second critical feature of social ordering is **pattern stabilization,** or *ensuring that patterns of ordering remain relatively stable through time.* Although social interaction is continually being created and recreated, it requires stability and predictability through time. Because the individual members of a group often come and go, the group can remain stable only if its basic patterns of social ordering persist. How is social stability achieved in the face of such continual change? A fundamental distinction must be made between *stable* social patterns, which are necessary for social ordering, and *static* patterns, which are not necessary. A stable pattern of social ordering maintains its basic arrangements or configurations through time, even though

**boundary creation:**   the activities that set off a specific set of interactions and relationships from their surrounding social environment in such a way that specific events or activities can be clearly identified as being or not being a part of that particular arrangement.

**pattern stabilization:**   actions taken to ensure that specific patterns of social order endure over time.

activities may constantly change among its component units. In contrast, a static pattern of social ordering does not fluctuate; it merely repeats the same activities over and over. The social interactions and relationships of your community, for instance, vary considerably from day to day, yet the community as a pattern of social ordering remains relatively stable through many years. Social life is never perfectly stable, however, because disruptive tensions constantly occur in all organizations.

Paradoxically, social stability is very often achieved through constant change, not in spite of it. Static patterns may be perpetuated for some time by strongly resisting all change in a social order, as in an isolated primitive society that endures practically unaltered for hundreds of years. But if such a society suddenly encounters disruptive social forces too powerful to resist—such as economic pressures from Western societies—its inability to adjust to new conditions can seriously threaten its existence. In contrast, if a society remains open and flexible and copes with disruptive forces on a continual basis as they occur, it may retain its stability precisely because it is continually changing. The United States is considered a fairly stable society, with its two hundred years of uninterrupted democratic government, yet this society has changed extensively during that period of time. In general, the more extensively social ordering interrelates with its surrounding social environment, the more frequently it must change in many small ways if it is to remain stable through time.

*Power Exertion*

Power in social life is analogous to energy in the physical world. It pervades all social organization as both a cause and a consequence of

Eviction. Power has been exerted here.

social ordering. On the one hand, the exertion of power contributes to the creation and perpetuation of social ordering. On the other hand, people continually generate social power as they cooperate in collective endeavors. According to Amos Hawley, "Every social act is an exercise of power, every social relationship is a power equation, and every social group or system is an organization of power."[5] From this perspective, *power is the ability to shape the process of social organization, despite resistance.* Power can be *exercised* as either influence or control, but in this discussion we shall use all three terms synonomously.

Social power always exists within social relationships, and it is never a property of an isolated actor. Personal characteristics such as assertiveness can contribute to one's power in a particular situation, but the actual exercise of power can only occur as a person or an organization interacts with others. If you are chairing a committee, for instance, you may control the activities of the other members and of the committee as a whole, but that power lies in the special relationships you have with the other committee members. If you should be removed from office or leave the group, you will no long-

er wield the organized power created by the group, even though you retain the personal skills needed to conduct meetings. Similarly, organizations do not possess power in isolation, but only as they relate to other organizations.

Before either individuals or organizations can exert influence or control, they must have access to resources that can be converted into power. A **resource** *is anything that is desired or valued by others and can be used by one actor to generate power in relation to others.* Resources may be tangible, like money, land, and material goods, or intangibles, like knowledge, skills, and organizational positions. By drawing on one's resources—or threatening to do so—an actor gains the ability to exercise power. In general, the greater the resources of an actor, the more influence or control that actor can exert on others. The success of this effort also depends, however, on the power wielder's skill in converting resources into overt power, and on the recipient's ability to resist the power attempt.

One common way of resisting an exertion of power is by actively exercising counter power, which usually results in conflict. Resistance can also be expressed in more passive and nonconflicting ways, such as (1) avoiding the power situation by taking an alternative course of action, (2) being indifferent to the attempted power exertion, or (3) giving only minimal compliance. As a result of such resistance, the exercise of power is almost always a reciprocal process among the involved actors. The final outcome of any power transaction is rarely determined exclusively by any one actor, no matter how unequal the situation may appear. Moreover, since no one likes to be totally powerless in any social situation, even very weak recipients may attempt to protect their own interests by exerting some kind of power back toward the stronger actor in an effort to rebalance the relationship.

As power is exercised in social life, it usually takes the form of either force or authority.

**Force**  To exert force, you must intentionally convert your resources into overt pressures, or at least convincingly threaten to do so. That is, you must invest uncommitted resources in the relationship and be prepared to expend them if necessary to enforce your demands and overcome whatever resistance you encounter. Even if you successfully bluff the recipient into complying, your resources are committed to that power relationship for the duration of its existence and cannot simultaneously be used elsewhere. You will probably have to use part or all of these committed resources to gain your desired goals, however. Since most actors possess only a limited supply of many resources, exerting force can be a costly process, especially if you encounter stiff resistance.

**Authority**  To exercise authority, you must be granted legitimacy by others. They must give you the right to direct their activities or make binding decisions for them. Legitimacy is thus very different from force since once you have acquired legitimacy, you can draw on it to exercise authority without diminishing your resource base. The recipients will voluntarily comply with your commands because they view them as legitimate and proper. Legitimacy is sometimes given to an actor through formal procedures such as elections, but more commonly it is expressed through an informal agreement or simply voluntary compliance. Because authority is normally a more reliable form of power than is force, organizational leaders almost invariably seek to gain legitimacy and transform it into stable authority. They can hardly afford to do otherwise, since without legitimacy their ability to influence and control others is constantly in jeopardy.

**Power Utilization**  The most direct means of exercising power to attain goals is to coerce other actors to do what you want. Such coercion can be exercised through either direct force or authoritative commands. It can be a highly effective means of obtaining desired ends in particular situations, especially if it is exercised with subtlety and moderation. Two major problems with this approach, however, are that (1) sooner or later it can exhaust one's resources or destroy one's legitimacy, and (2) the recipients often resent direct compulsion and rebel against it whenever possible.

One way of avoiding the use of coercion is to make other actors dependent on you for something they need or desire. By providing critical goods or services to others, you become functionally necessary or even indispensable to them. This enables you, through the routine

> **resource:**  anything desired or valued by others which can be used to generate power over them.

performance of your roles and other social activities, to influence and control them without expending scarce resources. For example, a secretary who normally schedules appointments for a business executive exercises considerable control over the persons who want to see the executive. Another alternative to exerting coercion is to transform balanced exchange transactions into unbalanced power relationships. To accomplish this transformation, you must give others more than they give you, so that they owe you a social debt or obligation. As long as you can prevent them from rebalancing the relationship by paying their social debt, you can maintain a power advantage over them. This requires skill in utilizing your resources and conducting exchange transactions, but if carried

Authority is power that others accept as legitimate. In the United States, the highest authority is that of the Supreme Court. Here Justice Blackmun presides over a Moot Court at the Stanford Law School.

out successfully, it severely reduces the ability of others to resist your power efforts.

**Power Protection**    In addition to employing power to attain goals, individuals and organizations commonly seek to protect their resources and preserve their ability to exert influence and control. The most obvious way of doing this is to deprive other actors of their resources, thus making them unable to challenge your power, as when the leader of a religious cult requires the members to turn all their financial assets over to him. Even the most ruthless despots normally stop short of total resource monopolization, however, because the effort necessary to acquire all available resources is usually uneconomical or prohibitive. In addition, this would leave the other actors incapable of performing any useful activities (or sometimes even staying alive).

More subtle, and usually more effective, than resource expropriation is the technique of restricting the entry of others into established power structures. This can be accomplished by setting stringent requirements for membership, controlling the training or experiences needed to meet those requirements, limiting the number of subordinates delegated major responsibilities, or appointing only trusted friends or relatives to potentially powerful positions. Another way to protect power is through co-optation. If other actors pose threats that are too strong to be ignored or easily resisted, you can invite those actors to join you in a mutual endeavor. For instance, if an organizational leader is threatened by a challenger with strong backing among the members, the leader might co-opt the challenger's power by appointing him or her to chair an important committee within the established power structure. To be successful, co-optation must be carried out with considerable finesse, for the challengers must be led to believe that they stand to gain more through cooperation than opposition. At the same time, the actors doing the co-opting must be careful to keep their new partners in subordinate positions, lest they eventually acquire controlling power.

### Social Conflict

When power wielders encounter opposition to their attempts to influence or control others, social conflict often ensues. Virtually all social relationships and organizations evidence conflict at one time or another, which suggests that it is a fundamental aspect of all social organization. Conflict is a dynamic process through which individuals and organizations deal with power differences, incompatible goals, and social tensions of all kinds. By working through and resolving conflicts, social actors often strengthen their relationships and organizations, and also facilitate necessary social change.

Our commonsense notion of social conflict usually involves two or more actors seeking the same goal. Examples might be two men trying to make a date with the same woman, or several lobbyists trying to influence the enactment of a legislative proposal. Conflict can take several other forms, however. Sometimes conflicting organizations seek mutually incompatible goals, as when a labor union demands higher wages from a firm that is trying to hold down production costs. Two organizations may conflict as they seek to attract and hold members. One organization may attempt to control another organization on which it depends for vital resources. An organization may be beset by internal disputes, as when some members of a church wish to promote social change while others prefer to abide by traditional services, or when a fraternity's customary practices are inconsistent with its ideals. Some of these conflicts are located between organizations, while others occur within one organization. This distinction between interorganizational and intraorganizational conflict depends entirely on the perspective of the observer. A strike, for instance, can be described as conflict between labor and management or as conflict within the company as a whole.

In broad terms, conflict is the active expression of discord or opposition between two or more social actors. Although we often equate conflict with the disruption of social organization, it is neither identical to, nor indicative of, social disorganization. Social conflict frequently exhibits considerable patterning or ordering, especially when it is regulated by established norms as in a sports contest or a political debate. One sociologist has identified several distinct stages through which most community controversies pass as they are resolved.[6] Further, under certain conditions, conflict can increase the unification of a social organization, as we saw in Chapter 2. We shall explore that idea more extensively in the next section.

Social conflict can take many different forms, including competition (as in a sports contest), aggression (as when a political candidate attacks the reputation of his opponent), and cleavage (as when some members of a community favor a proposed new highway and others oppose it). Conflicts can also be described in more systematic terms according to where they fall along the following dimensions: (1) Is the conflict *instrumental,* that is, does it concern the means to some end, or is it *expressive,* that is, important for its own sake? If we are debating about where to go on our vacation, the conflict is instrumental, but if we are arguing in order to express anger at one another, the conflict is primarily expressive. (2) Is the conflict *regulated* by established norms and rules, or is it an *unregulated* battle in which anything goes? A courtroom trial is highly regulated by formal procedural rules, while a riot is largely unregulated. (3) Does the conflict involve *direct* interaction between the antagonists, or is it *mediated* through one or more third parties? A debate between two political candidates is a direct confrontation, whereas a dispute between a factory and an environmental group over air pollution may be largely mediated by the mass media or a professional arbitrator.

As organizations experience social conflict, they may react to it in various ways. Since some organizations view conflict as undesirable because it disrupts established practices, they may attempt to prevent or suppress it whenever possible. Other organizations remain neutral in their responses to conflict, neither encouraging nor discouraging it, but simply accepting it as it occurs. Still other organizations view conflict as desirable as long as it can be kept within limits, and attempt to use it constructively to resolve tensions and promote change. As a result of these different reactions to conflict, organizations become either rigid or flexible.

**Rigid Organizations**  An organization that attempts to suppress normal social conflict is often quite rigid in its functioning. This may enable it to survive for some time, but underlying stresses and strains will continue to impinge on the organization. Eventually the resulting organizational tensions may become uncontainable and explode in intensive or even violent conflict that can seriously disrupt or destroy the organization. Strikes, divorces, race

riots, and political revolutions are examples of disruptions in social relationships that may result from the prolonged suppression of stresses and strains.

**Flexible Organizations**  In an organization that remains flexible and encourages the expression of stresses and strains through established procedures, conflict will be a common occurrence. No single conflict will be very disruptive or extensive, since stresses and strains will be handled as they arise rather than building up over time. Conflict may be almost continuous and the organization may appear to be rather unstable, but in the long run a flexible organization is likely to remain quite stable precisely because it effectively manages rather than suppresses conflict.

If organizations are to benefit from conflict, they must develop a set of management techniques for satisfactorily resolving conflicts as they arise. Common conflict management procedures include (1) promoting open communication among the contending parties, (2) establishing rules to restrict the actions each party may take, and (3) encouraging the conflicting parties to continue working at their dispute until a mutually agreeable resolution is attained. Labor-management negotiations, as commonly practiced in many business firms, illustrate the application of such conflict resolution techniques to one form of potentially disruptive conflict. Other examples include marital counseling, community human relations commissions, and political elections. All of these procedures are means through which the contending parties in a conflict may resolve their differences in a manner that is acceptable or even beneficial to everyone involved.

### Social Cohesion

As groups, communities, associations, societies, and other social entities are created through the process of social organization, they must develop some degree of cohesion to survive or function effectively. An organization that lacks cohesion may have great difficulty handling stresses and strains and maintaining stability. As an organization becomes cohesive, its members and units become bound together so that the organization gains solidarity. A relatively cohesive organization ceases to be a mere collection of diverse activities or units,

The personnel of an airport control tower are able to
work together on the basis of *functional cohesion;*
the Women's Christian Temperance Union functions
on the basis of *normative* cohesion.

and increasingly acquires a wholeness greater
than the sum of its separate parts. It can then act
as a unified social actor. In short, **social cohesion** *is the process through which the components
of an organization become bound together into a
whole entity.* This process can occur in two different ways.

**Functional Cohesion** This form of social
solidarity is an outgrowth of task specialization
(or division of labor) among the members and
units of an organization. Most businesses, for
instance, assign specific tasks to each member
and unit. Specialization makes these actors
highly interdependent upon one another. They
must cooperate in numerous exchange transactions if the organization is to attain its goals. To
regulate and coordinate these interdependent
exchange relationships, the organization must
formulate operational rules and establish administrative procedures. As this process progresses, the members and units become increasingly bound together as a single functioning
whole.

**Normative Cohesion** This form of social
cohesion depends on the existence of shared
values among the members of an organization,
as a result of a common cultural heritage. These
values are expressed in a set of moral norms
and operational rules that specify how the organizational members and units are to act in various situations. Gradually the norms become
infused into all organization activities and are

internalized by the members through socialization. Thus, the individual members are able to
cooperate with each other and the organization
becomes a tightly unified, smoothly functioning body.

Both of these cohesive processes occur simultaneously in most organizations, from the
smallest groups to the largest societies. This is
not accidental, but a result of the fact—pointed
out long ago by Emile Durkheim—that the two
processes nicely complement each other.[7] If the
exchange transactions that promote functional
cohesion are to be maintained through time
and not degenerate into coercive exploitation,
they must be guided and regulated by rules and
norms that are derived from a set of common
values. Conversely, shared values and norms
cannot develop or be perpetuated in a social
vacuum, but are outgrowths of mutually satisfying social exchanges and collective activities.
Hence functional and normative cohesiveness
support and reinforce each other, and are really
just two aspects of a single process.

An example of this may be found in the attempt to create some kind of international organization to prevent war. To our dismay, neither
the League of Nations nor the United Nations
has proved capable of meeting that challenge.
The underlying reason for the failure of these
organizations to unify the world may be that
both have relied primarily on normative
cohesion and have largely ignored functional
cohesion. Both the League and the UN were
founded on the assumption that all participating

nations shared a common set of basic values, which were spelled out in a covenant and a charter. It is obvious that the assumption of shared values was not valid in either case. In marked contrast, the European Economic Community (the "Common Market") has achieved spectacular success in unifying the economies of its member nations. It has sought to create mutual dependence and solidarity among its members through the gradual establishment of complementary exchange relationships, not political consensus. As functional cohesion has developed in this manner, it has given rise to an expanding body of norms and values that is steadily permeating all European societies and giving Europeans a sense of normative cohesion that they have not experienced since the days of the Holy Roman Empire, if then.

At first glance, cohesion often appears to be the direct antithesis of conflict. In reality, however, the two can coexist in the same organization and can directly complement and reinforce each other. Although conflict can severely weaken an organization with little cohesion, it can greatly benefit a highly solidified organization. Cohesion enables an organization to encourage and manage conflict, and thus increase its flexibility and stability. Extensive conflict throughout an organization does not necessarily indicate lack of cohesion, nor does the absence of conflict indicate strong cohesion.

If an organization possesses only weak cohesion and lacks adequate procedures for managing conflict, it cannot tolerate recurrent or intensive disruptions without being torn apart. A football team that lacks cohesion can be immobilized by competition between first-string and second-string players for starting positions. This kind of organization must resist and suppress conflict if it is to survive and retain at least short-term stability. On the other hand, an organization that displays strong cohesion and has established procedures for effectively managing disruptions, can tolerate and even promote a considerable amount of conflict. A highly cohesive football team may be strengthened by internal competition among its members. An optimum condition for social organization is not a compromise between conflict and cohesion, but rather simultaneous development of both processes.

Social organizations throughout history have tended to suppress conflict, probably because

> **social cohesion:** the process through which component parts of an organization or organized entity are bound into a whole; almost synonymous with "social solidarity." It may be *functional*, resulting from task specialization, or *normative*, resulting from shared values.

they have lacked adequate cohesion. They have had to rely on coercion to maintain their internal social ordering, thus becoming relatively rigid and vulnerable to drastic upheavals when the underlying tensions and conflicts could no longer be contained. Examples of this kind of rigid organization would be a military dictatorship in a developing country, or George Orwell's fictitious society in *1984*. If a social organization can increase both its functional and normative cohesion and also develop effective conflict management procedures, it can expand its capacity to tolerate conflict and benefit from it. Examples of such relatively flexible organizations would be the social democracies of Scandinavia or Ernest Callenbach's fictitious society in *Ecotopia*. The outcome of such organizational maturation is greater flexibility of social ordering, continuous rather than sporadic social change, and long-term social stability.

## TYPES OF SOCIAL ORGANIZATIONS

The organizational entities that are created through the process of social organization vary tremendously in size, form, complexity, and nature. They are as diverse as small friendship groups and modern nations. In this section we shall discuss five major types of organizations. This is not a complete listing of all possible types of organizations, but it does illustrate the range of forms they can take. Prior to that, however, we must discuss the idea of populations.

### Populations

A **population** is not a social organization. Rather, it is *a category of individuals who share one or more common characteristics*. These people do not normally interact with each other or form patterns of social ordering. The existence of a population is, however, a precondition for the development of any kind of organization, so that sociologists and demographers study pop-

Groups differ along a number of dimensions.

ulation phenomena to understand how they shape organized social life.

There are endless possibilities for identifying or defining populations. We often think of populations in terms of political units such as nations or cities. Many other criteria may also be used, including age, sex, race, marital status, religion, education, occupation, income, or even hair color. Each one of these characteristics — or several of them in combination — could define a population. Examples might be senior citizens, blacks, college graduates, or redheads.

Although none of these populations of people with common characteristics constitute a social organization, they may provide bases for organizational development if the people begin to create relationships, social ordering, and a shared culture. Marxian theory, for instance,

predicted that when workers in modern societies become aware of their shared plight as pawns of complex industrial systems, they will interact to form an organized social class that can transform the entire social system. In recent years blacks and women have both created extensive social movements, as people in these populations have recognized their common interests and acted collectively to improve their positions in society.

## Groups

In common speech, the word *group* is synonymous with *social organization*. In more precise terms, however, a group is one type of social organization. A **group** *is a relatively small organization whose members identify and interact with each other in a personal manner.* The small size of most groups (often no more than 15–20 people) enables all the members to know and interact with one another as individuals, and to develop many shared values and norms. As a result, the members of a group feel strong interpersonal bonds among themselves and with the group as a whole. There are countless kinds of groups in contemporary societies, including families, friendship cliques, work crews, teenage gangs, sports teams, juries, rap groups, and committees of all sorts.

All of us are members of numerous social groups that influence or shape many of our daily activities. The family is an extremely important group in most of our lives, since bonds of love, commitment, marriage, and kinship link us closely to other family members. Even if we do not live with all the members of our family or interact with them on a daily basis, we commonly maintain these interpersonal ties through letters, telephone calls, and visits. Friendship groups are also very important for many of us, ranging from people we see almost every day at school or work, to those with whom we occasionally share activities or maintain a correspondence. Families and friendship groups are commonly described by sociologists as "primary," since their interactions are especially personal and intimate, and the interpersonal bonds are often quite strong. Other kinds of groups, such as committees or work teams, are considered secondary because there is less intimacy among the members. Categorizing groups as either primary or secondary is a convenient way of indicating the depth and inclusiveness of their social relationships.

A good example of how a group evolves is William F. Whyte's *Street Corner Society*.[8] This study dealt with the Nortons, a gang of young Italian-American men who centered their social activities on particular street corners and the adjoining barbershops, lunchrooms, poolrooms, and clubrooms. Few of the gang members had completed high school, and most of them were unemployed or had only irregular employment. The group was brought together by and built around Doc, who was respected both within the gang and by other groups in the area.

Over the course of several months the Nortons developed norms and customs that were never written down or even formally decided upon, but that every member of the group understood. For example, a corner boy was not expected to be chaste, but it was considered beneath him to marry a girl who was "no good." It was also taboo for anyone to "mess around" with somebody else's girl. Most of the time, no one in the group had much spending money, but if someone was lucky at the tables or got overtime pay at a job, he was expected to treat the rest of the gang. Selfishness and reluctance to share were frowned upon.

In the Nortons, Doc was boss. When he suggested an activity, it was understood that everyone would go along with him. Since he had good connections with other gangs as well as with the racketeers and politicians in the area, he was expected to see that diplomatic relations were maintained. If any boy got into trouble, it was Doc who interceded for him. In return, the boys were expected to look up to Doc and respect his position.

Figure 6.1 shows the social organization of the Nortons. The position of the boxes indicates the relative status of each corner boy. The lines between the boxes show how communications were apt to occur and who was most likely to influence whom in the group. Since bowling was a favorite pastime for the Nortons, there was a close connection between a boy's bowling skill and his position in the group. If a boy wanted to increase his prestige, the best way to do it was to excel in the Saturday night bowling matches. Each boy in the group knew his place and what he could and could not get away with. Ridicule and social ostracism were leveled at anyone who was "uppity" and didn't "know

**population:** a category of persons sharing at least one common characteristic and normally lacking any degree of social organization.

**group:** a relatively small organization whose members identify and interact with one another in a personal manner.

his place." Whyte even suggests that bowling scores reflected knowledge of "place" in the gang: Alec was a better bowler than Doc and consistently registered higher scores when Doc was not present; but when Alec bowled against Doc, he rarely won.

*Communities*

Although families or other groups can sometimes be relatively self-sufficient, most of them do not live in isolation. For many reasons, ranging from economic interdependence to shared cultural values, families and other groups normally join together to form communities. The community, rather than the family, becomes the social setting for most everyday economic, political, religious, educational, recreational, and similar activities. As communities become larger and more complex, other types of organizations are often established within the community to perform these various functions.

**FIGURE 6.1   The social organization of the Norton street gang**

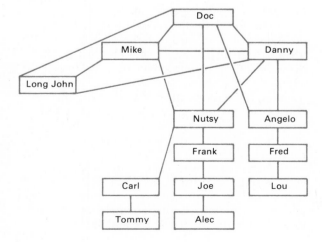

The community as a whole nevertheless remains the social setting within which most daily activities occur. Thus *a* **community** *is a type of social organization that is territorially located and provides the setting for dealing with most of the needs and problems of daily living.*

Communities vary widely in size and complexity, from Gnawbone, Indiana, to New York City. This diversity should not, however, obscure their common features of a territorial location, ordered procedures for performing daily living activities, and some kind of collective decision-making process. This sociological concept of community encompasses more than the legal term *city*, since in functional terms most communities extend beyond their legal limits to include suburbs or other surrounding areas. We frequently use other terms to designate different kinds of communities, including village, town, central city, urban area, Standard Metropolitan Statistical Area, and metropolitan region.

A major trend in all large American communities throughout the twentieth century has been suburbanization, in which families live in suburban areas or towns outside the legal central city, but commute into the city for work, shopping, and many other activities. Suburbanization is highly dependent upon adequate means of transportation in and out of the central city. Although a few railroad suburbs began to appear as early as the 1880s, the trend did not become widespread until the advent of the automobile in the 1920s. Since then, the peripheries of most urban areas have experienced two or three times as much population growth as their central cities. This mushrooming of suburbs is primarily a result of our cultural emphasis on single-family dwellings and home ownership, people's desire to escape the congestion of city life and to find adequate schools for their children, and the economic fact that the only land available at a reasonable cost for large-scale housing development is usually on the outskirts of the community. More recently, industries and businesses have also been moving to outlying areas to find inexpensive land for new buildings, to escape city taxes, and to serve the suburban population. The combined effect of suburbanization and industrial and business dispersion has often been massive urban sprawl, in which the urban metropolis incessantly spreads out over several counties and may even cross state or national boundaries.

As a result of such urban sprawl, many urban communities in the United States now face severe problems of political fragmentation. Although a metropolitan area is functionally and culturally a single community, in legal terms it may be divided into dozens of autonomous political units. These may include the legal central city, surrounding suburbs, satellite industrial cities, and specialized "authorities" for harbors, water and sewer lines, transportation, or other functions. The total urban community will then face countless problems in providing adequate housing, schools, transportation, utilities, and recreation facilities. Most of these problems can be handled only through unified community-wide programs. Yet unified action is virtually impossible when numerous separate political units, each jealous of its own autonomy, must somehow reach mutual agreement before anything can be accomplished. The result in many urban communities is virtual stagnation in which little or nothing is done to resolve pressing community problems. The recent bankruptcy crises of several large American cities illustrate the problem.

### Associations

Whereas communities encompass a wide variety of social activities, associations usually seek particular goods or perform specified activities. *An* **association** *is a social organization purposefully created to attain specific goals.* These goals may be very broad and abstract, such as healing the sick, eliminating poverty, or making a profit. They may also be quite precise and limited, such as manufacturing bicycle bearings, teaching people to type, or counseling unwed mothers.

The goals sought by associations, and hence their organizational characteristics, vary almost infinitely. Some common forms of associations include government departments and bureaus, businesses and factories, schools and colleges, churches and synagogues, labor unions and professional associations, fraternal and service bodies, hospitals and medical clinics, civic and welfare agencies, police and fire departments, and special-interest associations from antique collectors to zoology enthusiasts. One way of classifying this diverse array of associations into meaningful categories is to focus on who benefits from the attainment of their dominant goals.⁹ *Mutual-benefit associations,* such as labor unions and special-interest associations, seek to promote the particular concerns of their own members. *Business associations,* such as industries and stores, operate to provide financial and other benefits for their owners. *Service associations,* such as schools and hospitals, are established to provide various services to clients. *Commonwealth* associations, such as the federal government or public libraries, provide services to the entire public.

As these examples suggest, associations range in size from a local PTA to the General Motors Corporation. In contemporary societies, however, they are increasingly becoming not only large but also highly complex and formally organized. Many social commentators and social scientists therefore describe modern societies as dominated by giant bureaucracies, pointing out that such associations pervade virtually all areas of social life. This trend gives rise to numerous organizational and political problems that are not experienced by simpler societies. At the same time, the prevalence of

**community:** a territorially located social organization that provides the setting for dealing with most of the needs and problems of daily life.

**association:** an organization purposefully created in order to take collective, goal-oriented action.

functionally specialized associations enables us to achieve countless social goals that are beyond the means of those simpler societies.

Most complex associations have not one, but several goals that often change through time. For instance, it is often useful to distinguish between the official publicly stated goals of an association and the operative goals that actually guide its activities. One way of identifying an association's operative goals is to examine the decisions and actions of top policy makers in the association, especially decisions about the allocation of resources such as money and personnel. Such observations often reveal that operative goals are quite different from official goals. In one study of correctional centers for delinquents, for example, it was found that resources were consistently allocated to the custodial rather than to the professional treatment aspects of the centers even though the official goal was rehabilitation.¹⁰

Pressures to achieve congruence between official and operational goals, coming from both inside the association and from other associations, frequently result in goal modifications. Associations may also be forced to change their goals when the original ones are achieved. David Sills's study of The National Foundation for Infantile Paralysis illustrates this process.¹¹ The Foundation was originally established to assist polio victims by raising money through the March of Dimes, and very effectively performed this service for over twenty years. When the Salk polio vaccine was developed, however, the Foundation lost its reason for existence. Rather than disband the association, the members decided to redirect its efforts to other health problems including birth defects. The March of Dimes continues today, but with this different goal.

The goals of associations can also be altered through goal displacement. This occurs when an association is deflected from its original goals through a series of day-to-day activities that

Associations are organizations purposefully created for the attainment of specific goals.

Reprinted by permission of Newspaper Enterprise Association.

An organization's operative goals often differ somewhat from its official goals.

redefine the nature of the association. An example is the Tennessee Valley Authority (TVA), which was extensively studied by Philip Selznick.[12] The TVA was set up by Congress to build dams and generate electrical power in the Tennessee Valley by getting local people involved in planning the projects. Because of its ideological commitment to this grass-roots strategy, TVA brought into its leadership people from local communities, including members of local pressure groups who resisted the official TVA goals. By absorbing resistant elements into its policy-determining structure, a process called *co-optation*, the TVA hoped to avert threats to its stability or existence. But the organization did not anticipate the extent to which the co-opted members of its policy board would influence day-to-day decisions on immediate and pressing problems. As a result, a series of commitments were made that ultimately led to the displacement of official goals by operative ones. For example, co-opted local community leaders reversed a policy of providing a protective strip of publicly owned land around public reservoirs. Local farmers resented public ownership of prime farm acreage around the reservoirs, and the co-opted board members supported them and forced TVA officials to allow private purchase of the land.

Finally, many associations have multiple goals, some of which are incompatible with others. A prison, for instance, is supposed to incarcerate criminals so as to protect society. It is also supposed to rehabilitate its inmates. These two objectives often require incompati-ble arrangements and procedures. The authoritarian control and rigid rules designed to maintain security often generate so much hostility and resentment among the prisoners that rehabilitation becomes difficult or impossible. On the other hand, the relatively open and permissive arrangements that are most effective for rehabilitation pose severe security problems.

In sum, associations exist to attain collective goals, but the requirements of operating the association as a dynamic social organization may in time drastically alter or redefine those goals.

*Institutions*

Certain basic social needs must be met and basic problems must be solved if a society or other organization is to survive for long and function effectively. These functional requirements are not inherent in any individual members, as are the biological need for food or the psychological need for safety. Rather they are located in the social relationships that comprise an organization and link it to its natural and social environments. They must therefore be satisfied through various kinds of organization actions. Social theorists have offered different lists of these requirements, but all would include such things as (1) maintaining the population, (2) training new members, (3) providing channels of communication, (4) assigning members to roles and tasks, (5) establishing social norms and operations rules, (6) procuring necessary resources from the environment, (7) making collective decisions, (8) coordinating internal activities, (9) controlling deviant actions, and (10) defending against external threats.

Most functional requirements can be met in more than one way, through alternative courses of action. Collective decisions, for instance, can be made either autocratically by one person or democratically by all the members. Once a workable and acceptable means of fulfilling a particular requirement has been developed in a society, however, it tends to be repeated. Eventually, it becomes encrusted with convention and tradition, so that people view it as the proper way, the best way, or perhaps the only conceivable way to handle that requirement.

In all societies, networks of groups and associations tend to develop around each major functional requirement, sharing a common concern with meeting that need and developing a common set of values and norms. Sociologists refer to these networks as *social institutions.* In other words, *an institution is a persistent normative pattern of interrelated organizations that are all concerned with a particular functional requirement and hence share common activities and norms.*

In the past, the setting for most social institutions was the local community, within whose confines most groups and associations functioned. This situation has been altered, however, as associations have grown in size and scope, as rapid means of transportation and communication have linked people and organizations across broad distances, and as social problems have become increasingly interrelated. In contemporary societies, the major social institutions are society-wide systems of organizations centering on broadly defined societal requirements. For instance, we commonly speak of the major institutions in modern societies as including (1) the economy (all business, industries, stores, banks, etc.); (2) the polity (all local, state, and federal governments, political parties, etc.); (3) the family (both nuclear families and kinship networks); (4) education (all public and private schools, colleges and universities, and training programs); and (5) religion (all churches, synagogues, and religious organizations). The boundaries of these contemporary social institutions usually are not well defined, so that any particular association may participate in two or more institutions. Govern-

School as a social institution—that is, a persistent normative pattern of carrying out common activities which characterizes an entire society.

ment units, for instance, often engage in economic as well as political activities. Nevertheless, the principal characteristic of any social institution is its concern with meeting one or more basic societal requirements.

To illustrate the way in which sociologists analyze social institutions, let us briefly examine the military as a kind of institution that exists in virtually every society. In the modern Western world, the military is usually subordinate to government and hence might be included within the polity. Historically, however, the military has often operated quite independently of governments, and this condition occurs today in many developing nations. The origins of the military institution are lost in prehistory. In the simplest sense, the male hunting band may have been the first warrior group. Among hunters and gatherers even today, it is not uncommon for all adult males to share responsibility for defending the community against external marauders. The fundamental social function served by the military institution, then, is probably defensive: ensuring societal security in the face of external threats.

Once the military is organized for this purpose, however, it is an easy step to a second very common function of military organizations: maintaining internal order. Many modern armies perform police duties, or may be called upon to perform them when the normal police forces are inadequate for the maintenance of order, as in riot situations. Indeed, in some developing countries, where the army may be the only national-scale, well-organized disciplined agency in the society, it frequently performs tasks normally associated with civil government, such as road and bridge construction, irrigation and public sanitation, and even education. The significance of bureaucratic social organization, so long associated with the military, is apparent here.

War as we know it today, however, probably did not originate among people in hunting and gathering societies. Few existing primitive societies practice organized warfare. Strictly military activities probably did not begin until human societies had passed beyond the hunting and gathering stage to the gardening stage, where they could amass some surplus food and other goods. Only then would raiding for plunder become profitable. Hunters and gatherers own little property worth stealing, do not keep livestock, and have no use for human slaves. With the beginning of stable village life and the practices of cultivation and animal domestica-

Even in the most developed countries the military may be called on to perform civilian functions in unusual circumstances.

tion, however, surpluses accumulated that made raiding economically profitable and slavery useful. It may well be, then, that another major function of the military institution, societal aggrandizement at the expense of neighbors, began in this way. To some extent, it continues to the present day.

But modern wars are not really fought for the purpose of plunder, or, as a rule, even to acquire territory in any literal or permanent sense. The great Prussian theorist of war, Karl von Clausewitz, defined it as an "extension of diplomacy," by which he meant that warfare in the modern world is a political instrument and is always aimed at political ends.[13] This means, as a rule, that the military institution is an agent of the nation-state (or some organization attempting either to establish or take control of a state) and that one of its basic functions is to promote the policies of the state. In modern society, then, the military must be seen as an instrument of the government in power or of the organizations that control the state if they are not directly represented in the government.

As well as performing certain general functions common to all societies, the military institution in any society, like all other social institutions, reflects that society and its history and culture. One familiar example from American experience illustrates the point nicely. The Japanese forces in World War II were organized and equipped in ways very similar to the American forces, and their basic battle tactics were also similar. But you have only to read first-hand accounts by American fighting men to learn how alien to our mind was the psychology of the individual Japanese soldier, sailor, or airman. Americans who faced them had great respect for Japanese fighting capacity and courage, but regarded much of their behavior as crazy. The Japanese kamikaze (suicide plane) corps would have found few volunteers among American airmen, and the practice of blowing oneself up with a hand grenade in preference to capture seemed utterly incomprehensible to most Americans.

### Societies

Societies are the most inclusive and complex social organizations in today's world. Most other organizations exist within the confines of a society, all aspects of human social life are encompassed by a society, and to a large extent the way in which a society functions will influence all the patterns of social ordering and cultural ideas that comprise it. *A society is the most inclusive type of social organization, which dominates all other types of organizations it incorporates, and which possesses both functional and cultural autonomy.*

The ideas of functional and cultural autonomy require some explanation. Societies are functionally autonomous in several ways. First, most social relationships occur within the boundaries of a society, with only a few relationships involving actors from different societies. Second, societies attempt to become as self-sufficient as possible by establishing procedures for securing whatever resources they require and satisfying the needs of their members. Third, a society is the ultimate decision-making unit for its members and exercises sovereignty over all decisions concerning them. Cultural autonomy refers to the fact that all the members of a society possess a common and distinctive culture. Many specific traits of this culture may be shared with other societies, and various parts of the society may display subcultures that differ somewhat from the societal culture. Nevertheless, the common culture of the total society—and especially its basic social values and norms—forms a distinctive and unified set of ideas unique to that society.

We often think of societies as identical to nation-states, since national political boundaries commonly coincide with societies and national governments exercise political control throughout entire societies. Sometimes, however, there are wide disparities between nations and societies, as in Africa, where many nation-states were created by colonial powers without regard to native societal boundaries. In other cases, a single political unit may encompass two or more societies, as in Canada, where many French-speaking Canadians feel that Quebec constitutes a distinctive society which should have political independence. Multinational business corporations also cut across numerous societies and control financial assets that far exceed those of many national governments. And international federations, such as the European Economic Community and the Latin American Free Trade Association, may eventually unify their component societies into broader economic and political entities. Nevertheless, for the foreseeable future, societies will undoubtedly remain the dominant social and po-

**Gemeinschaft** and **Gesellschaft:**  The terms used by Töennies to describe two polar-opposite types of social organization, or societies characterized by such social organization. The *Gemeinschaft*, which can be translated as "community," "folk," "rural," or "simple," is tradition-based and the individual is bound to the group by strong, stable ties of family and community. Social relations are broad and encompassing. The *Gemeinschaft* parallels Durkheim's social organization based on mechanical solidarity. The *Gesellschaft*, which can be translated as "urban-industrial society," is based on rationality; the individual is bound to others mainly by calculation of personal advantage. Social relations are narrow and limited. The *Gesellschaft* parallels Durkheim's social organization based on organic solidarity.

litical units within which most other forms of social organization exist.

Why do patterns of social ordering and cultural ideas differ so widely among societies? For example, in some societies, social life is carried out primarily in relatively small groups (families or communities) and is governed by long-established traditions or customs. In such societies, formal organizations are relatively rare and unimportant, at least in affecting daily life. Deliberate and precise calculations of the efficiency of actions for reaching certain goals are rare in these societies. By contrast, urban industrial societies such as the United States and Canada place much importance on the precise calculation of the consequences of actions. In these societies large, complex organizations are a prominent feature.

In an effort to describe the structural features of urban-industrial societies, social scientists frequently rate societies along a scale from simple to complex, rural to urban, homogeneous to heterogeneous, undifferentiated to specialized. Examinations of societies at either end of such a continuum show numerous social and structural possibilities and serve as useful theoretical models for social change. The founder of this analytical approach was the German theorist Ferdinand Tönnies. He named the two polar types of societies **Gemeinschaft** and **Gesellschaft,** usually translated into English as *commu-*

**Gemeinschaft and Gesellschaft: Medieval food production and a modern, mass-produced chicken processing factory.**

*nity* and *society*.[14] The *Gemeinschaft* is based on what Tönnies called the natural will of human beings, where people relate to one another as total personalities within a communal context. Each person is bound strongly to the community and does not pursue private interest at its expense. Social life is governed by traditions and customs that go unchallenged. People's positions, based on family and community ties, are stable and secure, although not equal. The preliterate tribe and the medieval European agricultural village would be classic examples of the *Gemeinschaft*.

The *Gemeinschaft*, Tönnies says, is shattered by the emerging urban-industrial-capitalist order. At the core of this new social structure is the rational will of human beings. This rational will is calculative and examines all practices with a view toward efficiency in pursuing goals. The unreflective life of the *Gemeinschaft*, based on custom and community, comes under rational scrutiny. Individuals begin to pursue private interests at the expense of others and of the community's general interest, and relations among people are increasingly based on calculation of private advantage. Social relations become narrow, specific, and purposeful. These tendencies give rise eventually to a new form of society, the *Gesellschaft*, approximated by urban-industrial society.

Perhaps the most fundamental feature of the shift from *Gemeinschaft* to *Gesellschaft* is the increasing development of functional and structural specialization throughout a society. For example, as specialization progresses, economic activity may be sheared off from family relationships. The family may cease to be a significant social unit for the production of goods and services. At the same time, new organizations for economic production begin to develop. The outcome is the emergence of the economy as a separate social institution.

This transition can be seen in the roles, situations, and organizations through which economic activity is conducted in modern societies. Economic roles become separated from familial and communal roles. The entrepreneur, the worker, the banker, and others govern their activity by norms specific to their economic functions. Similarly, people regularly encounter situations of a purely economic character, where each is expected to calculate a rational course of action without regard for the expectations to which he or she responds in other settings, such as the church or family. In addition, economic organizations — manufacturing concerns, marketing companies, banks, and so on — increasingly develop according to purely economic calculations of advantage and disadvantage in the marketplace. Thus distinctively economic actions are wrenched free of traditional and customary restraints and an autonomous economic institution emerges.

A similar process occurs with respect to other social institutions. Political organizations, educational systems, legal institutions, science, and technology are all gradually freed from traditional and customary restraints. Each sphere develops distinct norms and expectations. Science, for example, progresses according to principles of discovery and verification and in relation to established bodies of knowledge distinctive to the scientific sphere. To contribute to the development of science, scientists subordinate their other social roles to the expectations that govern scientific research. Religious, familial, even nationalistic restraints are irrelevant to their performance. As specialization intensifies, science is split into numerous distinct disciplines — biology, chemistry, physics — each with independent principles of research and bodies of knowledge.

The transition to a highly specialized social structure poses significant problems for a society. Indeed, the process may entail considerable disruption and disorder. The bases of social action adequate in the past may be ill suited to the emerging order. Traditional and customary restraints are often relaxed unevenly, affecting

Functional and structural specialization: A century ago most artifacts for daily use were produced in the home, as depicted in this woodcut of a quilting party. Today almost everything we use is produced and distributed by highly specialized suppliers, as were these imported blouses in a department store.

some institutional spheres but not others. Some segments of the population are left behind as a society advances, while others are at the forefront of the process. Thus the possibility of a breakdown of social order haunts the developing society.

## CRITICAL ORGANIZATIONAL TRENDS

As we have seen, many societies and other types of social organization are continually developing toward greater specialization and interdependence. Sociologists often refer to this process as social evolution. Early sociological thinking was infused with notions of social evolution. Auguste Comte believed that all societies evolve through three cultural stages, which he called theological, metaphysical, and positive (or scientific). Herbert Spencer, the first major English sociologist, stressed the increasing complexity of industrial societies.

Tönnies saw social evolution as movement from *Gemeinschaft* to *Gesellschaft*. Emile Durkheim's thesis of the growing dominance of organic (or functional) over mechanical (or normative) solidarity in contemporary societies also expressed an evolutionary orientation. William Graham Summer, an early American sociologist, tried to apply Darwin's theory of biological evolution through natural selection and survival of the fittest to all social life. Most important of all, Karl Marx's contention that dialectical processes might ultimately sweep all humanity from feudalism through capitalism to socialism is thoroughly evolutionary in concept.

Most contemporary sociologists avoid making such sweeping generalizations about the totality of social life, focusing instead on more specific, identifiable, and analyzable trends such as specialization. Four specific evolutionary trends have contributed to the shift from *Gemeinschaft* to *Gesellschaft* and that will continue to shape our future world are: *growth, complexity, bureaucratization,* and *centralization*. They are most commonly discussed in terms of whole societies and their major institutions, but they are also found in most associations and communities as well as in many smaller groups. Depending on our personal values, we may view these trends as either desirable or undesirable, but for sociological analysis we must examine them in a neutral light as impersonal social processes. They are not predetermined or inevitable, however. Each of these trends is composed of countless specific historical events that are outcomes of human choices, actions, and values.

## Growth

Growth in the size and scale of social life is so pervasive in contemporary Western societies that it is sometimes difficult for us to realize that it is not an inevitable social trend. In fact, growth has been an unusual or unknown condition throughout most human history. The rapid rates of growth in Western societies during the past hundred years have been primarily due to industrialization. This development has produced unprecedented amounts and varieties of material resources beyond those needed for mere survival. These surplus resources have enabled populations to expand, have freed peo-

ple from agricultural work to settle in cities and pursue new activities (business, mass communications, scientific research), and have stimulated the creation and expansion of countless new forms of social organization.

Social growth in modern societies takes many different forms. Perhaps the most obvious is population expansion. The population of the United States increased 280 percent between 1900 and 1975, from 76,000,000 to 214,000,000. Another basic form of growth that affects all aspects of social life is the development of new technologies. There was a 200 percent rise in energy consumption per capita in the United States between 1900 and 1975, from approximately 40,000 kilowatt hours per year to approximately 80,000 kilowatt hours. Closely related to technology and energy consumption is economic productivity. The United States Gross

**FIGURE 6.2** **Growth of the United States on various indicators, 1900–1975.**

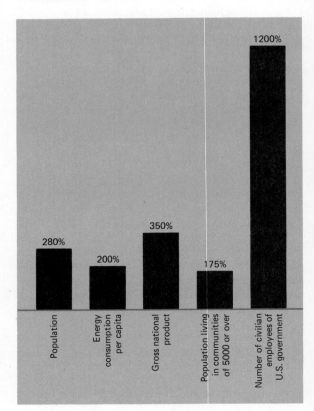

National Product per capita rose by 350 percent during that same 75-year period, from about 2000 to 7000 in 1975 dollars. Technology, energy consumption, economic productivity, and excess rural population have in turn made possible the continued growth of cities. The percentage of our population living in communities of 5000 or more jumped 175 percent during that same period from 36 percent to 63 percent. Finally, all of this growth has generated a fantastic expansion of governmental activities in an effort to keep the society operating smoothly. The number of civilians employed by the United States government increased 1200 percent between 1900 and 1975, from approximately 240,000 to nearly 3,000,000 persons.

Less easily measured, but equally important, has been the constant growth in the United States and other industrial nations of all types of social organizations. In addition to a continual expansion in the number and size of business firms, from national retail chains to General Motors and other industrial giants, this growth has pervaded the entire society. Schools and universities, labor unions, the mass media, health-care organizations, local governments, special-interest associations, urban metropolises, and many other kinds of organizations have all undergone continual growth throughout the twentieth century. This growth has occurred in the number of such organizations, in their size, and in the scope of their activities. The United States today is undoubtedly one of the most extensively organized societies the world has ever known, but even here the growth initiated by industrialization is nowhere near completion.

## Complexity

As organizations grow in size they frequently — though not inevitably — increase in internal complexity. Complex social organizations are characterized by four related features: (1) numerous component roles and subunits; (2) extensive functional specialization of those roles and subunits; (3) considerable functional interdependence among roles and subunits as a result of their specialization; and (4) numerous interwoven exchange and power linkages among the roles and subunits. In short, the patterns of social ordering that make up a complex organization are quite diverse, complicated, and interrelated. A modern university is a highly complex social organization, whereas a one-room school is not.

The key to understanding the continual expansion of complexity throughout modern associations, communities, and societies is the process of functional specialization. Instead of all organizational units performing many different activities, a separate unit is created to carry out each distinct activity, making all the units highly dependent on one another. For example, a modern industrial corporation commonly contains separate divisions for such functions as production, sales, finance, and administration. Each division is in turn composed of numerous departments, sections, branches, and other smaller units, each carrying out its own distinct activity. Each of these highly specialized components depends on all the other units in the firm to provide it with whatever resources or services it needs but does not produce itself. This means that each unit must interact on a regular basis with many other units throughout the organization. These interunit transactions usually involve some form of exchange, but they are commonly also infused with various kinds of power exertion. To maintain all of these interdependent relationships among units and to keep the entire organization operating smoothly, an extensive set of operating procedures and rules must be created and enforced. All of these features of the organization contribute to its complexity.

The transition from simple to complex forms of social organization often creates tensions and conflicts for a society that may in turn lead to serious disruptions and disorder. Patterns of social ordering that were once adequate and satisfying give way to new arrangements that displease some people, cost others their jobs, disrupt established social relationships, and threaten cherished social values. The development of modern medical care, for example, has effectively destroyed the practice of magic, reduced barbers from surgeons to haircutters, and largely eliminated the old-fashioned family doctor. Nevertheless, functional specialization frequently results in much more effective services than could ever be obtained under simpler conditions. Modern medical care saves countless lives that would have been lost a century

FIGURE 6.3   **Bureaucratization**

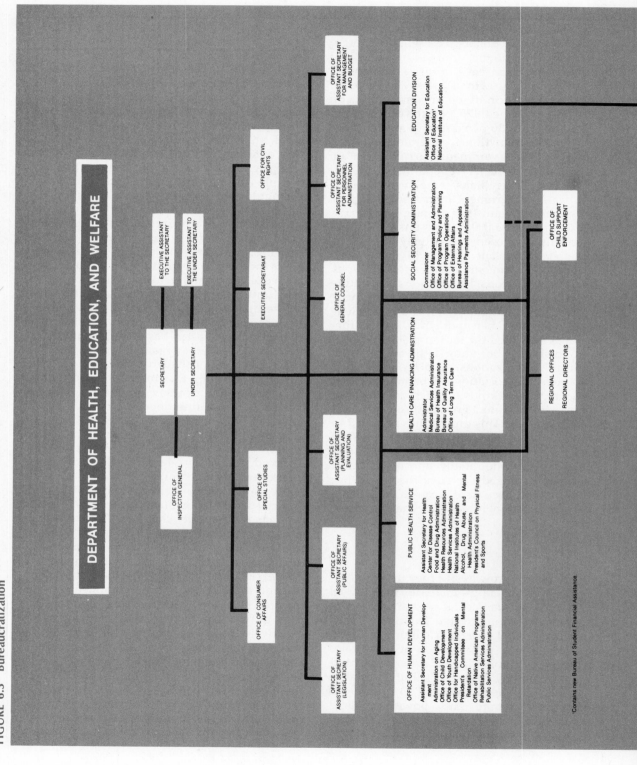

DEPARTMENT OF HEALTH, EDUCATION, AND WELFARE

SECRETARY

UNDER SECRETARY

EXECUTIVE ASSISTANT TO THE SECRETARY

EXECUTIVE ASSISTANT TO THE UNDER SECRETARY

OFFICE OF INSPECTOR GENERAL

OFFICE OF SPECIAL STUDIES

EXECUTIVE SECRETARIAT

OFFICE FOR CIVIL RIGHTS

OFFICE OF CONSUMER AFFAIRS

OFFICE OF ASSISTANT SECRETARY (LEGISLATION)

OFFICE OF ASSISTANT SECRETARY (PUBLIC AFFAIRS)

OFFICE OF ASSISTANT SECRETARY (PLANNING AND EVALUATION)

OFFICE OF GENERAL COUNSEL

OFFICE OF ASSISTANT SECRETARY FOR PERSONNEL ADMINISTRATION

OFFICE OF ASSISTANT SECRETARY FOR MANAGEMENT AND BUDGET

**OFFICE OF HUMAN DEVELOPMENT**

Assistant Secretary for Human Development
Administration on Aging
Office of Child Development
Office of Youth Development
Office for Handicapped Individuals
President's Committee on Mental Retardation
Office of Native American Programs
Rehabilitation Services Administration
Public Services Administration

**PUBLIC HEALTH SERVICE**

Assistant Secretary for Health
Center for Disease Control
Food and Drug Administration
Health Resources Administration
Health Services Administration
National Institute of Health
Alcohol, Drug Abuse, and Mental Health Administration
President's Council on Physical Fitness and Sports

**HEALTH CARE FINANCING ADMINISTRATION**

Administrator
Medical Services Administration
Bureau of Health Insurance
Bureau of Quality Assurance
Office of Long Term Care

**SOCIAL SECURITY ADMINISTRATION**

Commissioner
Office of Management and Administration
Office of Program Policy and Planning
Office of Program Operations
Office of External Affairs
Bureau of Hearings and Appeals
Assistance Payments Administration

**EDUCATION DIVISION**

Assistant Secretary for Education
Office of Education[1]
National Institute of Education

OFFICE OF CHILD SUPPORT ENFORCEMENT

REGIONAL OFFICES
REGIONAL DIRECTORS

[1]Contains new Bureau of Student Financial Assistance

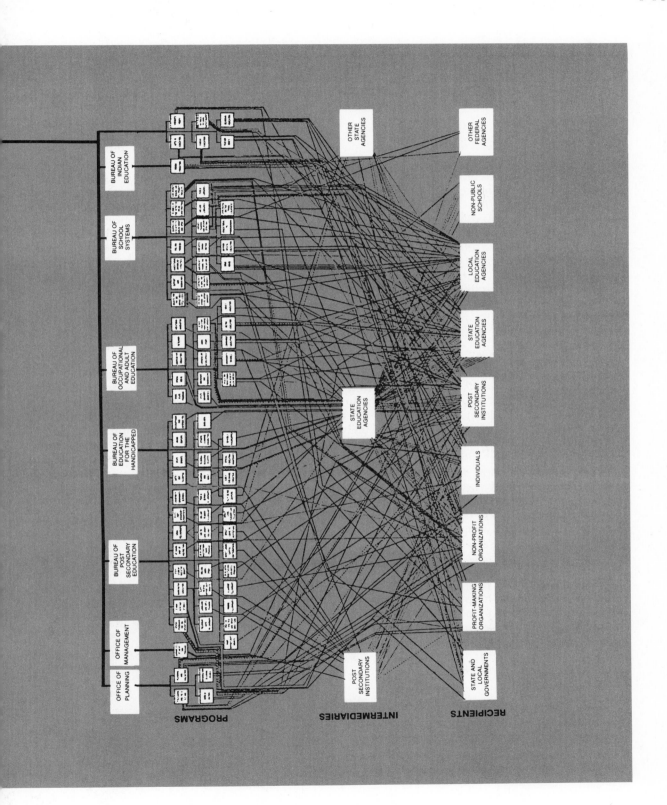

ago. In the long run, the benefits of increasing specialization usually far outweigh its short-term costs. As with growth, therefore, we have only begun to glimpse the extent to which complexity can develop in contemporary social organization.

### Bureaucratization

A distinctive feature of modern societies is the extent to which **bureaucratization** pervades organizations of all kinds, but especially goal-oriented associations. Bureaucratization is a dynamic process, not a particular kind of organization, although we often apply the term "bureaucracy" to organizations that clearly manifest this trend. In popular speech, "bureaucracy" usually implies rigidity, red tape, and general inefficiency, but in sociology the term refers to *procedures for effective goal attainment*. All kinds of operational problems may occur in bureaucratic organizations, but they are frequently the result of inadequate or misdirected bureaucratization.

As long as organizations remain relatively small and simple, there is little need for bureaucratization. Families, friendship groups, hobby clubs, and village communities can usually function fairly well without establishing formal operating procedures. Larger and more complex organizations, however, often find that such procedures are imperative if they are to attain the goals they seek. Max Weber observed that bureaucratization consists of two principle processes, (1) rationalizing social organization and (2) formalizing organizational operating procedures.[15]

**Rationalization**  In this context, rationalization does not refer to the psychological process of finding good reasons to do what one wants to do. Sociologically, **rationalization** involves such activities as *purposeful goal setting, collecting and utilizing relevant information, objective evaluation and decision making,* and *organizational planning.* In other words, a rational organization seeks to attain its goals as effectively and efficiently as possible. Instead of doing things the way they've always been done, the members of an organization ask themselves, "What do we want to accomplish through collective action, and what is the most expedient means of achieving these goals?"

**Formalization**  This process involves *establishing standardized guidelines for organizational activities so that they all contribute to the attainment of organizational goals.* These guidelines can be created in numerous ways, including the following: (1) specifying procedures and rules (either written or unwritten) for the actions and interactions of the members, (2) clearly identifying the tasks assigned to each position in the organization, (3) channeling all communications among members through prescribed routes, (4) setting uniform criteria for evaluating the performances of all members, (5) applying sanctions to members and subunits to ensure that they perform their roles and activities in the expected manner, and (6) providing consistent coordination and regulation of organizational activities. In short, formalization creates social predictability by ensuring that organizational activities are conducted in prescribed and presumably efficient ways.

Organizations vary widely in the extent to which they follow formal principles, from quite stringent formality to very lax informality. Factories are usually more formal than friendship groups, but the group may have at least some formal rules, while the factory undoubtedly contains an extensive set of informal relationships among its members. In fact, considerable research has suggested that a formal organization must contain a complementary web of in-

Formalization.

formal relationships to counterbalance the excessive formality if it is to function effectively.

Implementation of formal operating procedures and rules within an organization need not produce operational rigidity or pressures for strict behavioral conformity. If it does, it has defeated its fundamental purpose of facilitating effective goal attainment. Rules and procedures can be specified in general and flexible terms, providing broad guidelines rather than minute prescriptions for organizational activities. This approach gives individual members and subunits considerable leeway in performing their activities in the best way possible. It also keeps the organization open to necessary adjustive changes, thus preserving its stability through time. Bureaucratization can thus contribute immensely to the operational effectiveness of an organization, provided it is conducted in a flexible and sophisticated manner.

## Centralization

Large size and elaborate task specialization within organizations necessitate overall coordination and regulation for effective action. This is best done by a centralized power structure. Max Weber was convinced that the rationalization, formalization, and internal control necessary for efficient bureaucratization required a hierarchial authority structure in which positions at each level exercise legitimate authority over all lower-level positions. Over fifty years ago, Robert Michels formulated his now famous *iron law of oligarchy,* which said, ''Who says organization, says oligarchy.''[16] He argued that **oligarchy,** or *the monopolization of power by a small ruling group,* is inevitable in all organizations for several reasons, including the following: (1) Effective decision making on complex organizational matters can only be accomplished by a few leaders at any one time. (2) Incumbents of leadership positions become indispensable as they develop special skills and experience in running the organization. (3) In time, leaders acquire dominant control over organizational finances, communications, and other activities, all of which they use to strengthen their leadership roles. (4) Most ordinary members tend to be indifferent and apathetic about organizational concerns, and are quite happy to leave the problems of leadership to others.

**bureaucratization:** the special set of procedures for effective goal attainment by an organization involving rationalization of activity and formalization of organizational relationships.

**rationalization:** the process of making behavior rational through such activities as purposeful goal-setting, collection, evaluation, and utilization of relevant information, objective decision making and organizational planning.

**formalization:** the establishment of standardized guidelines for organizational activity so that all will contribute to organizational goal attainment.

**oligarchy:** the monopolization of power by a small group.

**centralization** (organizational): the convergence of social power within a relatively small set of elite positions.

**Centralization** within organizations refers to *the convergence of social power—and hence control over organizational actions—within a relatively small set of elite positions.* Centralization can occur in all kinds of organizations, although it is perhaps most evident in formal associations, large urban communities, and total societies. Highly centralized power is by definition authoritarian: it is exercised downward or outward throughout an organization from the ruling elites. These elites may be freely chosen by the rest of the members, so that centralization is not necessarily incompatible with representative democracy. They may also be selected by other elites within or outside the organization on the basis of merit or influence, or they may obtain their positions through overt coercion. Authoritarian power should not be confused with autocracy, however. Centralized authority becomes autocractic only if it is used by elites solely for their own benefit, without any concern for the welfare of the whole organization.

Centralized power within an organization frequently becomes focused within a formal ruling unit whose primary function is to govern the entire organization, making decisions for the organization and controlling organizational activities. Nevertheless, convergence of political authority in a governmental unit is only the most obvious aspect of the much broader process of centralization. Control over *economic resources* may become centralized in a few functionally dominant units within a community, a voluntary association, a business corporation, or a national economy. The use of *physical coercion* may become the special prerogative of centralized police and military units. And given modern communication technology, *the flow of information and ideas* throughout the organization may also be controlled by centralized communication media. In short, centralization can occur within all realms of society.

Until rather recently, we have tended to assume that rationalizing and formalizing organizations for effective goal attainment required power concentration. Consequently, most highly bureaucratized organizations are structured in a hierarchial pattern and operate in a centralized manner. Organizational decentralization has been seen as the antithesis of effective management. From a broader perspective, however, centralization and decentralization can be viewed as complementary processes. As random social actions become ordered into stable social organizations, it is perhaps inevitable that social power will become concentrated in a few units and roles. The process of social organization creates centralized power in place of powerless anarchy. Hence decentralization can occur only after some minimal amount of centralized power has been created. As the process of social organization progresses, however, the resources and power it generates can be increasingly distributed throughout the entire organization. The presumed benefits of power decentralization are stimulation of creativity, greater flexibility, functional efficiency, new opportunities for growth, and more effective goal attainment.

Observers of the contemporary United States have frequently noted that while the national political system and the national economy are becoming increasingly centralized, many associations and communities are experimenting with workers' councils, neighborhood councils, and similar decentralized decision-making arrangements. One explanation of this paradox may be that many kinds of smaller organizations are cohesive and stable enough to begin moving toward decentralization, whereas many society-wide institutions are not yet fully enough developed and functionally effective to permit extensive decentralization without threatening their existence. Recently, however, the federal government has begun to experiment with decentralization, in efforts such as revenue sharing with states and cities, as well as various kinds of citizen participation programs.

Michels' iron law of oligarchy may not be inescapable, but it is a serious problem for organizations that wish to preserve both political democracy and individual freedom. A fundamental question for contemporary organizations is how to provide necessary leadership and coordination, while simultaneously keeping ultimate control in the hands of their members and ensuring that their collective endeavors benefit all the participants.

## SUMMARY

To answer the fundamental Hobbesian question of how idosyncratic individual actions are transformed into ordered and relatively stable collective social life, we may say that social organization occurs throughout all aspects of social life and results in organizational units having a reality that is more than the sum of their individual members.

The process of social organization develops as individuals interact in recurrent relationships to create patterns of social ordering that are infused with shared cultural meanings. Social organization thus combines three levels of social activity—social interaction, social ordering, and shared culture—which emerge out of one another but remain highly interwoven. Organizational units such as groups, communities, associations, and societies develop out of this process of social organization as portions of it become bounded in space and time. These social units display properties that are not inherent in any of their individual members, they are exterior to these individuals, and they affect individuals' actions. Hence all social organizations are real social entities that can be studied by sociologists.

The heart of all social organization is the process of social ordering, in which interactions and relationships become interwoven into identifiable patterns that are relatively stable through time. Social ordering is an ongoing process that is constantly being created and recreated, although we often perceive and think of it in terms of static structural arrangements. All social ordering is pervaded by the exercise of social power, as individuals and organizations seek to influence or control one another's actions by exerting force or authority. The ability to exercise power in social life depends partly on the nature and extent of one's resources and skill in utilizing them, and partly on the resistance offered by the recipients of these power attempts. Power exertion is therefore normally a reciprocal interaction, although it may range from balanced exchange to grossly unbalanced coercion.

The complementary processes of conflict and cohesion also occur in all organizations to varying degrees. Social conflict is patterned interaction that can take several different forms and that frequently progresses through identifiable stages. Conflict can be highly beneficial to organizations if it is properly managed. Expression of conflict can enable an organization to cope with internal and external tensions on a continual basis as they arise, thus keeping the organization flexible and stable. In general, the more highly cohesive or unified an organization, the greater its ability to utilize conflict constructively. Organizational cohesion can be acquired through either functional specialization and interdependence among component units, or through the infusion of common norms among the members and parts of the organization. These two cohesion processes complement one another, and both are found in varying degrees in most organizations.

The transition from *Gemeinschaft* to *Gesellschaft* pervades the contemporary world. Modern industrial societies, are characterized by a number of pervasive evolutionary trends that differentiate them sharply from more traditional forms of social life. Many kinds of organizations throughout these societies are steadily growing in size, in terms of both members and activities performed. Simultaneously, many of them are becoming increasingly complex as task specialization expands and functionally specialized units are created to perform activities that were once conducted by unspecialized units such as the traditional family or village.

To cope with increasing size, specialization, and complexity, and to attain goals more effectively, modern organizations are becoming increasingly bureaucratized. They attempt to rationalize their functioning by establishing standardized procedures and rules to ensure that they operate in an efficient and effective manner. Bureaucratization frequently leads to centralization of power within a hierarchy of authority, and the trend toward power centralization can be observed in many aspects of modern societies. Although we are just beginning to experiment with power decentralization within organizations, this process appears to give organizations considerable flexibility to adjust to changing conditions, as well as increased stability through time and improved goal-attainment capabilities.

## SUGGESTED READINGS

BELL, DANIEL. "Toward a Communal Society." *Life,* May 12, 1967, pp. 112–116. Explores several current trends in contemporary societies and sketches a new kind of society that may emerge from these trends.

BENNIS, WARREN. "Beyond Bureaucracy." *Transaction,* 2, July/August 1965. Discusses some common problems of bureaucratic organizations and proposes an alternative form of social organization.

GERGSON, WALTER M. "The College Sorority as a Social System." *Sociology and Social Research,* 53, April 1969, pp. 385–394. Describes a sorority as a dynamic social organization characterized by a number of ongoing social processes.

WARRINER, CHARLES K. "Groups Are Real." *American Sociological Review,* 21, October 1956, pp. 549–554. Argues for the reality of groups and organizations, as opposed to nominalistic and interactionist perspectives on social organization.

WHYTE, WILLIAM FOOTE. "The Social Structure of the Restaurant." *The American Journal of Sociology,* 54, January 1949, pp. 302–308. Illustrates the concept of social structure as it occurs in a restaurant, and explores the ways in which this structure affects individuals' actions.

# THREE
## Elements of
## Social Structure

The four chapters that follow explore some aspects of the ways modern societies are organized, the commonalities of living and relating to each other in the Western world that determine the nature and flavor of any particular society.

Chapter 7 is about social differentiation and mobility. *Differentiation* is the process through which people invent or recognize socially significant differences between them and then put these differences into social *categories*. Age and sex differences, for example, are perceived as significant in every society in the world. *Social mobility* is movement through social space. It is virtually absent in some societies, but is pronounced in American society.

Chapter 8 is about *minority groups and relations* in heterogeneous societies, again a major feature of the American scene. The role of minorities in a society and the effects of minority status on a group's members have great significance for the people involved and the society that enfolds them.

Chapter 9 describes one of the dominating features of the modern world, *the city,* and the processes and life styles that go with it, which are called *urbanism*. Cities are social phenomena in and of themselves, independent of specific cultural or societal content, and their enlargement and increase in number is one of the overriding trends of the modern world. Chapter 10 summarizes the biosocial phenomena that represent the stage on which all human social life is played out: *population* and its effects.

These five subjects are called "elements of societal organization" or sometimes "social structure" because they are major features of the social organization of almost every society. They represent social phenomena to which every society must respond and which, in the way they occur in a given society, have a great influence on the nature and conditions of social life for individuals within it. In another sense, they are social organizational *responses* to matters that are universal.

155

# Chapter 7
# Social Differentiation and Mobility

In short, the way to wealth, if you desire it, is as plain as the way to the market. It depends chiefly on two words, industry and frugality; that is, waste neither time nor money, but make the best use of both. . . . He that gets all he can honestly and saves all he gets (necessary expenses excepted) will certainly become rich, if that Being who governs the world, to whom all should look for a blessing on their honest endeavors, doth not, in his wise providence, otherwise determine.

Benjamin Franklin,
"Advice to a Young Tradesmen,"

Negroes are still at the bottom of the economic ladder. They live within two concentric circles of segregation. One imprisons them on the basis of color, while the other confines them within a separate culture of poverty. The average Negro is born into want and deprivation. His struggle to escape his circumstances is hindered by color discrimination. He is deprived of normal education and normal social and economic opportunities. When he seeks opportunity, he is told, in effect, to lift himself by his own bootstraps, advice which does not take into account the fact that he is barefoot.

Martin Luther King, Jr.,
*Why We Can't Wait,* 1963

If all Americans are created equal, why do some people advance while others fall behind? Two famous Americans, separated by over two hundred years of American history, address the question. Benjamin Franklin was himself a successful business-man, an inventor, and a father of his country. His advice stresses the individual's responsibility for his or her own fate, barring uncontrollable misfortune. Martin Luther King, Jr. was describing a situation in which *social structure* effectively prevented some groups from achieving wealth or even a decent living in America.

How can we reconcile the two great themes in American thinking about economic advancement—the importance of individual effort and the effect of institutionalized inequalities? In a well-known children's story a little engine strives with all its might to make it up the hill, puffing, "I think I can, I think I can." After much effort, the little engine does reach the top.[1] The simple moral, "You can make it if you really try," is uncomplicated by external matters like broken railroad ties or inadequate fuel. The moral, more realistically stated, should be, "You can make it if you try, all things being equal." But all things are hardly ever equal for everyone, partly because inequalities are institutionalized in the social life of societies.

Some inequalities among human beings, of course, are inevitable. Some people are bright and some are dull; some are tall and some are short; some are physically stronger than others, and so forth, but biological differences have little to do with the social differences and opportunities evident in any modern industrial state.

## SOCIAL DIFFERENTIATION

Social inequality is built upon **social differentiation**—the distinctions that all societies everywhere (with the possible exception of a few very small preliterate groups) make among their members. All societies differentiate among their members on the basis of criteria that are socially rather than biologically based, criteria that are *assigned* social significance while intrinsically having none. On the basis of such social distinctions, rewards and opportunities—**life chances**—are often differentially distributed. (A life chance is the probability of any given social outcome: dying before you are thirty, receiving a college degree, possessing an automobile, contracting tuberculosis, being hit by a truck, making $50,000 a year.) If sex and race are socially significant in a society, being a white female will affect one's life chances in some way. Differentiation does not *necessarily* involve ranking, or the unequal distribution of social rewards—we distinguish between midwesterners and easterners, for example, without implying that one group is superior to the other—but the association between social differentiation and social inequality is often direct.

Social differentiation might be called the sociological variable par excellence, because it touches almost every facet of life. Religion and tastes in food, occupational and recreational preferences, length of life and causes of death, sexual practices and residential location, reading habits or lack of them, family size, and hundreds of other matters are all related in various ways to social differentiation. And institutionalized inequalities are built upon the social differentiation practiced by a society. As we shall see in some detail, such socially significant differences as sex, ethnicity, and the economic standing of one's family affect one's social position and life chances. Thus the study of differentiation is very important. *What happens to you in life is greatly influenced—sometimes determined—by the social differentiation practices of your society.*

Three socially significant types of differentiation are stratification, sexual differentiation, and ethnic-racial differentiation. These are certainly not the only forms of social differentiation, but they do have great impact on social life in general and on life chances in particular.

Economic position is where one stands with regard to property ownership and income. John D. Rockefeller, shown here giving a coin to a child, was the richest man in the world, but may be chiefly remembered by the public for his habit of offering dimes to the needy.

**Stratification** refers to *ranked groupings based on distinctions in economic position,* **prestige,** *and power. Economic position* is where one stands with regard to property ownership and income. It is frequently referred to as class position. *Prestige* is the status or social honor given to those who are admired and respected, for whatever reason. *Power* is the ability to influence social activities and get one's own way. Sexual differentiation refers, of course, to *the social distinctions associated with biological gender.* **Ethnicity** refers to *national, religious, and other cultural characteristics considered socially significant in a particular society; race* is a similar concept based on inherited characteristics considered socially significant. In everyday usage, the term *ethnicity* often includes racial characteristics, so we shall discuss ethnic and racial differentiation together.

These three forms of social differentiation—stratification, sexual, and ethnic-racial—are related to each other. Stratification implies ranking: one economic position is *higher* or *lower* than another; people have *more* or *less* prestige or power. Sexual and ethnic-racial differentiation do not necessarily involve ranking, except when they are linked with the stratification differentials, for example, when Anglo-Saxons have more prestige than Puerto Ricans or when men have more power than women. Sexual and ethnic-racial distinctions are often socially significant *because* they result in stratification distinctions. For example, males have more power than females *because they are males* in a social structure that supports male dominance.

## Social Differentiation and the Division of Labor

The three major forms of social differentiation are all related to the division of labor. In a complex society, roles in the division of labor become quite specialized. For example, you live in a house put together by carpenters, electricians, plumbers, and other specialists; you go to work or school via a public transportation system operated and assembled by another group of persons, or you travel in a car not of your own making. You drop your children off at a day-care center or a school where they are taught by still others. You do not grow your own grain, make your own clothing, or paint your own house. In turn, you may perform a specialized task such as cooking, writing, or driving a truck.

Stratification, gender, and ethnicity determine to some extent which role you take. Being female has traditionally prevented persons from bearing arms in war or operating a jack hammer. In certain situations, being black or Jewish or Irish Catholic has prevented many individuals from obtaining high-paying and high-status occupations. Being wealthy makes it possible for some individuals to acquire higher education and thus qualify for high-status occupations. The contacts and influence of a powerful and prestigious parent may give an individual a competitive edge in a tight job market. More subtle factors, such as parents' attitudes toward occupational achievement, may also influence the kinds of occupations children attain.

Once a role is taken in the division of labor, that in turn has an effect on an individual's economic standing, status, and power. Bank managers make more money than clerks; surgeons

**social differentiation:** the process of distinguishing among people according to socially assigned criteria, for example, wealth, birth, or occupation.

**life chances:** the probability of experiencing any given outcome in life, such as becoming a physician, marrying a movie star, or dying of tuberculosis.

**stratification:** the ways in which given societies rank their members as superior or inferior to one another along the three dimensions of class (income and property), status (prestige), and power.

**prestige:** social honor or status

**ethnicity:** national, religious, and other cultural characteristics considered socially significant in a particular society.

have higher status in the community than nurses; and business executives influence more lives than do factory workers. Which role you

FIGURE 7.1 Relationships of the three types of social differentiation to role in the division of labor

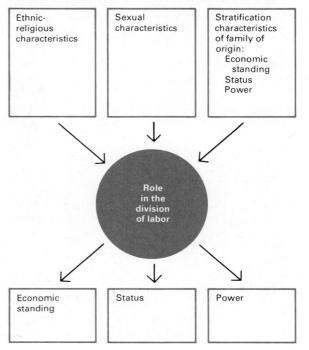

assume in the division of labor makes a difference, then, in where you will be ranked on the class, status, and power continua of a community, and that, in turn, strongly affects your other life chances. The relationships of the three major types of social differentiation to role in the division of labor are shown in Figure 7.1.

## STRATIFICATION

The principal types of stratification systems— *caste*, *estate*, and *class*—may be distinguished from each other in three ways: First, by the *dimension* (economic, status, or power) that determines other inequalities; second, by how much movement is permitted or preferred between social groupings, in other words, by how normatively *open* or *closed* they are; and third, by the extent to which positions are filled by *ascription* or *achievement*.[2]

**The Caste System**   A caste system—*the attribution of superiority and inferiority to permanent and hereditary groupings in a society*—is the most extreme form of status grouping. It is characterized by occupational specialization in which the least desirable occupations are assigned to the lowest castes. In traditional India, for example, members of the Shudra caste are confined to such occupations as craft work, farm labor, and water carrying. The Brahmins, the highest caste, are often priests and landowners. The Kshatriya, or warrior caste, are also landowners and farmers and the Vaisya, or yeoman farmers, complete the four major castes. There are hundreds of subgroups, and there are individuals who fall outside any caste group-

**Brahmins and Untouchables.**

ing, the *untouchables,* the lowest-status group of all. Their occupations are those considered most detestable, jobs associated with human and animal carnage and waste, such as cleaning latrines, washing clothes, cutting hair, sweeping floors, and butchering.

A caste system is normatively closed and relies exclusively on ascription. There is no socially acceptable way for individuals to achieve a higher social position, not even through marriage. Marriage between members of different castes is usually forbidden; when it is allowed, offspring usually take the status of the lower-caste parent. This closure of castes is reinforced by tradition and ritual. In traditional India, for example, certain types of intercaste contact rendered the higher-caste person "unclean" and in need of ritual purification. Eating and drinking with members of a lower caste was polluting, although lower castes could serve as physicians or midwives for higher castes.[3, 4]

Such extreme closure is usually built on differences considered ethnic or racial. Weber suggests that caste is an arrangement that makes it possible for different ethnic groups to live in the same community.[5]

Caste or castelike systems still appear around the world, including the Tutsi, Hutu, and Twa tribes in Ruanda, East Africa; the Japanese Burakumin, a minority group of some 3 million; and the White European colonizers of South Africa, who have established themselves as an exclusive and nonintermarrying ethnic group.[6] Similarly, blacks and whites in the United States form two distinct groups that do not usually intermarry, whites having higher status than blacks. Certainly the traditional relationships have involved extreme segregation and discrimination. Separate eating facilities, washrooms, movie houses, residential areas, and so forth have been common. The Montgomery bus boycott, described as the beginning of the black civil rights movement in the United States,[7] was a response to the 1955 arrest of Rosa Parks, who refused to give up her seat to a white passenger in the black section of a public bus.

**The Estate System**  In the **estate system,** *social position is determined by relationship to the land, by birth, and by military force.* It arose in Europe in the Middle Ages when strong, stable government disappeared and urban life declined. Society in the middle ages was essen-

> **caste system:**  a stratification system based on permanent, hereditary groupings. It is normatively closed and status is assigned by ascription.
>
> **estate system:**  the type of stratification system in which social position is based on relationship to land, birth, and military strength. There were three major estates in medieval Europe: the nobility, the clergy, and the peasantry; social position was largely ascribed, although some mobility was possible.

tially agricultural, so the new social groupings, called estates, were dependent on the land and those who controlled it.

The three medieval estates were the nobility, the clergy, and the peasants. These were social and legal groupings that had both rights and responsibilities relative to one another. In the early feudal period, the nobles were essentially warriors whose authority derived from the protection they could extend in a society in which government had broken down. They also maintained social order by acting as judges in disputes among their social subordinates. The nobles derived economic benefit from the lands they controlled, but their status or prestige was determined not so much by economic standing as by *power.* Of the three estates, the peasants ranked lowest in economic standing, social status, and power. The clergy were more difficult to categorize, because they ranged from high-ranking bishops, who were themselves nobles, to rural clergy, who were little better off than the peasants.

The estate system was relatively closed, that is, the norms allowed little movement from one grouping to another. However, some social mobility was sanctioned, so it was not a completely closed system. It relied heavily on ascription based on the estate into which one was born, that is, the social system attributed specific characteristics to, and prescribed behaviors or activities for, people on the basis of birth. Thus people who had noble blood were expected to be brave; they had to conform to a well-understood set of social conventions. Peasants, on the contrary, were defined as stupid and childlike; they were not permitted to ride horses, and could not engage in activities such as hunting with hawks. Persons of common birth were occasionally permitted to rise in social rank, chiefly in the church or the military, but the top social positions were denied them.

The contemporary **latifundia** or large agricultural holdings of Latin America form a type of social estate system. A large latifundium in Brazil or Central America, for example, would be worked by peasants kept in debt and dependence on the owner through the extension of credit. Laborers might be given a small plot of land for their personal use in return for working the land of the hacienda owner. The direct personal relationships of owners and peasants took on great significance because of the extreme dependence of the peasants. They looked to the lord for survival and security and in turn were expected to be appropriately loyal and servile. Rebellion and lack of deference were frequently punished at the whipping post.[8] Although land reform measures have been passed in several countries, the latifundium still dominates Latin American agriculture.

**The Class System**   A **class** is *a category of persons sharing a common economic situation*. In a **class system,** the chief dimension of stratification is economic; the other dimensions (social status and power) are based on economic position.

A class system is normatively open, that is, individual mobility is not improper. Of course, unrestrained mobility is only the norm and not the reality, but there is more individual social mobility in class societies than in caste or estate systems. Theoretically, a class system relies entirely on achievement to fill positions, but as ethnic-racial and sexual differentiation limit people's ability to achieve, class systems do not actually meet their norms: Mobility is limited, and ascriptive criteria like race and sex are often used along with achievement to fill occupational positions and to determine social status, class standing, and power. Table 7.1 shows how the three principal types of stratification compare as to major dimension of inequality, how open or closed they are, and the extent to which they rely on ascription or achievement.

### The Necessity of Stratification: A Functional Interpretation

The antiquity and universality of social stratification make us wonder if some form of inequality isn't a necessary fact of social life. In a classic interpretation of stratification, Kingsley Davis and Wilbert Moore argued that stratification—the distribution of unequal rewards for different social positions—is functionally necessary in a society with a complex division of labor.[9] This is because some positions are more important than others. The same positions will not be the most important in every society, because the needs and requirements of societies differ, and any one society can change over time. In some societies, the priesthood may be essential; in others, the captain of industry may occupy a vital position.

A society can insure that important positions are taken by the most capable persons by rewarding such positions highly. The most highly rewarded positions will be those most sought after, and the most able competitor will win the position. Unequal rewards are necessary to motivate qualified persons to assume important positions. In societies that rely on ascrip-

TABLE 7.1   The Main Types of Social Stratification and Their Characteristics

|  | *Major dimension of inequality* | *Normatively open or closed* | *Ascriptive or achievement-oriented* |
|---|---|---|---|
| **Caste** | Social status | Closed to individual mobility | Ascriptive |
| **Estate** | Power | Some limited mobility | Ascriptive with some achievement |
| **Class** | Economic position | Open | Achievement-oriented |

tion, unequal rewards are necessary to motivate individuals assigned to important positions to perform their duties well.

When a position is important and there are few persons qualified to fill it, a high reward will be attached to it. On the other hand, a less important position may be more highly rewarded if few people are willing and able to fulfill its requirements. Truck driving is less valued by society than, say, the practice of medicine, and most truck drivers probably make less than most doctors. But few people are willing or able to drive nitroglycerin trucks in the oil fields, so the drivers of such trucks are very well paid indeed. Generally less important positions do not compete so successfully for personnel that more important positions are not adequately filled.

The Davis and Moore interpretation has been criticized as a rationalization of present divisions of power, property, and prestige, an argument that present inequalities are justified because they are necessary to the survival of society. Some critics contend that the stratification system artificially creates a scarcity of personnel and therefore is dysfunctional. Artificial scarcity occurs when privileged groups limit entry to their position (physicians, for example), and when financial, status, and power advantages are passed on to the next generation in the form of special opportunities for the development of talent. This criticism arises from the fact that stratification includes more than just ranking and unequal rewards. Davis and Moore do largely ignore social inheritance, which creates special opportunities as well as artificial scarcity. As a matter of fact, they are not so much concerned with the passing on of position as they are with the necessity of ranking and unequal reward in a society with a complex division of labor.

Another problem is that it is impossible to demonstrate empirically what positions are functionally the most important in a society. It is also impossible to prove the necessity of unequal rewards for such positions. In addition, the functionalist theory omits many important aspects of stratification, such as job discrimination on the basis of race.

The functional theory of stratification nevertheless has an important place in the study of social differentiation. It is a rare, non-Marxist

**latifundia:** large agricultural holdings characterized by extreme dependency of the peasant on the landowner. Social rights and responsibilities are well defined.

**class (social):** a category of persons sharing similar economic positions or relatively similar amounts of property, income, or wealth, with resulting similarities in life style. In Marxian thought, a social class consists of those persons with a similar "relation to the means of production;" those connected to the economic structure in similar ways, for example, industrial workers.

**class system:** the type of stratification system where social position is based on possession of income or property, status is largely achieved, and in which considerable social mobility is possible. Many contemporary industrial nations have a class system.

attempt to explain the universality of stratification systems and is applicable to any kind of society from the simplest to the most complex. As such, it has been widely adopted by Western sociologists.

### Conflict Approaches to Stratification: Karl Marx

Another explanation of stratification originates from the conflict perspective. According to this theory, conflict arises as groups struggle for control of the state, of factories, or exclusive facilities, of anything desirable. Social inequalities are seen as the result of conflict over scarce resources. The recognition of social inequalities motivates conflict and thus threatens societal harmony. Coercion or force keeps society running as smoothly as it does, according to the conflict theorists.

**Class** Although many modern conflict approaches to stratification differ significantly from that of Karl Marx, his ideas were the inspiration for this perspective. According to Marx, individuals who share the same economic situation constitute an *objective* class, whether or not they are *conscious* of their class position. Each society must organize itself to supply basic goods and services to its members,

Conflict theorists understand stratification as the outcome of the struggle for scarce resources. The Baltimore and Ohio Railroad Strike of 1877, which was violent and bloody, would be interpreted from this perspective as a struggle for power between workers and management.

through a system of production, which also generates differences in economic position.

The system of production includes both the *forces* of production, such as technology and science, and the *relations* of production. The basic relations of production, as you will recall from Chapter 2, are that one group owns and controls the means of production and distribution while another group provides its labor. These two groups form the two major classes in most societies. The master and the slave, the feudal lord and the serf, and in the capitalistic system, the bourgeoisie and the proletariat.

Marx believed that the economic system and the class relations that sprang from it were the foundations on which other social structures were built. Class position thus accounted not only for inequalities in economic position, but also for other inequalities, especially in regard to power. Those who owned and controlled the means of production were able to control the actions of others as well. Not only did they exploit labor, but they also controlled the major institutions of the society, and their ideas influenced the philosophy, literature, and art of their period.

Marx's theory of the dynamics of social change was based on his understanding of class. The two major classes were potential political communities organized around their own economic interests. The upper or ruling class had already structured the institutions of the society to serve its economic ends. Spurred on by the disparity between their wages and the profits of the capitalists, by unemployment in times of production slowdown, and by improved means of communication, the workers would eventually see the inherent conflict of interest between themselves and the capitalists. They would, in other words, become **class conscious.** The objective class of workers would become a subjective class as well. The formation of trade unions and many small conflicts would precede a major final revolutionary struggle by the proletariat.

In Marx's theory, that revolution would lead to a classless society, the workers would assume control of the means of production. A temporary "dictatorship of the proletariat" would divest the capitalists of their control until ownership of the means of production was completely in the hands of the people. Then there would no longer be exploiters and exploited; there would be no classes, because in the new society, all the people would own as well as operate the means of production and

**Lenin proclaims the Soviet Republic.**

"the free development of each (would be) the condition for the free development of all."[10]

Proletarian consciousness of a common position and destiny did not materialize in Western industrial society for a number of reasons. Instead of becoming more simple and better defined, the class structure became more and more complex. As Marx predicted, the petite bourgeoisie, or owners of means of production such as small businesses and craft shops, decreased in number. They were absorbed, for the most part, into the mass of wage laborers. The rise of the new middle class of managers and white-collar workers and the creation of stock-held corporations radically changed the meaning of ownership and led to new complexities that blurred the Marxian distinction between bourgeoisie and proletariat. Revolutions with a Marxist theme have occurred, but not in the Western industrialized societies where Marx

> **class consciousness:** awareness of one's class position and interests in common with others of the same class.

thought the proper conditions were present. Russia, at the time of the October Revolution, was not an industrial society, nor was China in 1949.

### Dimensions of Stratification: Max Weber

You have already been introduced to some of the ideas of Max Weber, a very important theorist in stratification. He is particularly noted for carefully distinguishing the three dimensions of stratification—class, status, and power—while drawing attention to their interrelationships.

**Class** Weber's concept of class was similar to that of Marx. For both, class refers to a group of persons who share a common situation in the marketplace, but for Weber the important economic chances included not only ownership and control of the means of production or property, but also the service one could offer. Administrative or technical skills, for example, could gain high returns in the marketplace. Weber's notion of class made room for professionals, technical experts, and entrepreneurs within the framework of stratification theory. It accounted for a variety of class interests and conflicts, not just the conflict of interest between the capitalists and the proletariat that Marx had proposed.

Weber also differed from Marx in not making class position the single dominant reality promoting social change. For Weber, shared economic status does not necessarily lead to class consciousness and a political community capable of changing the society. In particular, he thought the proletariat was unlikely to achieve such organization, because of their great numbers and because they lacked the skills necessary to achieve power in the marketplace.

**Social Status: Prestige and Life Style** Weber defined **status** as *honor accorded by a community*. There are innumerable bases for the conferral of social honor: family background, ethnicity, occupation, property, education, and so on. A **status group** is a community of persons granted a certain level of prestige on the basis of the criteria operating in their larger community, for example, property, race, or religion. Members of such status groups or communities consider each other social equals and interact socially in a somewhat exclusive manner: they also pursue similar life styles that set them apart from others.[11] Weber suggested that, in a sense, class was determined by relation to the *production* of goods, while status was a matter of their *consumption.*

Status communities are distinguished from one another primarily by their styles of life, expressed through activities and consumption of goods and services. For example, a brownstone off Park Avenue in New York City has more status value than a tenement on the Lower East Side, and going to the Metropolitan Opera carries more status value than attending the Demolition Derby. Status is often indicated in work settings by differences in furniture and appurtenances, as Table 7.2 shows.

Material objects, activities, titles, and other things that convey social worth are called **status symbols.** Thorstein Veblen, in *The Theory of the Leisure Class* suggests that status is achieved through conspicuous consumption, conspicuous waste, and conspicuous leisure.[12] He discusses the creation of signs that distinguish one person from another socially, and notes that as society becomes more industrialized, accumulation of property replaces physical prowess as a sign of success. For the lower classes, this provides some incentive to work harder. For the upper classes, however, *lack* of productive activity becomes a symbol of social superiority. A life of leisure is the true mark of a lady or gentleman. Good manners, refined tastes,

**TABLE 7.2    The System of Status Symbols in a Large Corporation**

| Visible appurtenances | Top dogs | V.I.P's | Brass | No. 2s | Eager beavers | Hoi polloi |
|---|---|---|---|---|---|---|
| Brief cases | None—they ask the questions | Use backs of envelopes | Someone goes along to carry theirs | Carry their own —empty | Daily carry their own—filled with work | Too poor to own one |
| Desks, office | Custom made (to order) | Executive style (to order) | Type A "Director" | Type B "Manager" | Castoffs from no. 2s | Yellow oak—or castoffs from eager beavers |
| Tables, office | Coffee tables | End or decorative wall tables | Matching tables, type A | Matching tables, type B | Plain work table | None—lucky to have own desk |
| Carpeting | Nylon—1 inch pile | Nylon—1 inch pile | Wool-twist (with pad) | Wool-twist (without pad) | Used wool pieces—sewed | Asphalt tile |
| Plant stands | Several—filled with strange exotic plants | Several—filled with strange exotic plants | Two—repotted whenever they take a trip | One medium-sized; repotted annually during vacation | Small: replaced when plant dies | May have one in the department or bring their own from home |
| Vacuum water bottles | Silver | Silver | Chromium | Plain painted | Coke machine | Water fountains |
| Library | Private collection | Autographed or complimentary books and reports | Selected references | Impressive titles on covers | Books everywhere | Dictionary |
| Shoe shine service | Every morning at 10:00 | Every morning at 10:15 | Every day at 9:00 or 11:00 | Every other day | Once a week | Shine their own |
| Parking space | Private in front of office. | In plant garage | In company garage—if enough seniority | In company properties—somewhere | On the parking lot | Anywhere they can find a space—if they can afford a car |
| Luncheon menu | Cream cheese on whole wheat, buttermilk, and indigestion tablets | Cream of celery soup, chicken sandwich (white meat), milk | Fruit cup, spinach. lamb chop, peas, ice cream, tea | Orange juice, minute steak, French fries, salad, fruit cup, coffee | Tomato juice. chicken croquettes, mashed potatoes, peas, bread, chocolate cream pie, coffee | Clam chowder, frankfurter and beans, rolls and butter, raisin pie á la mode, two cups of coffee |

knowledge of Latin and Greek, correct spelling, dog- and horse-breeding, are all signs that one belongs to the prestigious leisure class, since laborers have neither time nor money to cultivate such knowledge or activities.

Recently conspicuous consumption of luxury items and conspicuous waste have been "out" and Americans have sought status in lower priced ways.[13] Ecology is "in" and so are bicycles; jeans and an open shirt compete with formal attire; exotic house plants and jogging are symbols of status, while pedigreed dogs, mink coats, and wall-to-wall carpeting have declined in status value (see box on next page).

W. Lloyd Warner and associates were the first to study status inequalities in American communities systematically.[14] Warner was interested in the social evaluations people made of each other. For example, in one town there were the "Fancy Crowd," those who were rated "above average, but not tops," and "people who live like pigs."[15] The criteria used in making these social evaluations included "old" family background, where people lived, taste, and manners as well as occupation, source of income, dwelling area, and house type to measure social class. These were important not in themselves, but because of what they symbolized about members of the community.

*Class and Status* For Weber, class and status were vitally linked. To a large extent class position determines style of life and style of life determines social status (see Figure 7.2), although the real life situation may not be so simple, since such factors as family background and race are often important determinants of social status as well. Especially in areas of the country where families of old wealth reside, families with the same class standing may not share the same social status. For example, families of similar wealth may differ in social status because one can trace its money back several generations, while another is newly rich.

In the long run, class position and status position coincide. That is, those who achieve an advantageous economic position are able to

FIGURE 7.2 **Relationships among class, style of life, and social status**

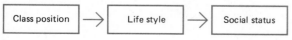

status (social): as used by Weber, the degree of prestige or social honor accorded an individual in his community or society. In sociology more generally, social position or standing.

status group or community: a group of people granted a similar level of prestige by others in the community on the basis of such characteristics as property, race, or religion, who interact with each other, regard each other as equals, and pursue a distinctive life style, setting them apart from others.

status symbol: objects or behavior representing social standing, as where possession of a Ferrari is a sign of great wealth. Status symbols tend to have value only to the degree that they are conspicuous, i.e., visible to others.

consume status items and eventually achieve a high social status in the community. On the other hand, those who lose their money eventually lose their social standing as well because they are no longer able to afford a highly valued life style. Loss of social status, like achieving it, may take several decades.

**Power** Not only are there inequalities in economic status, but there are inequalities in the ability to direct and control events and people. According to Weber, social power is expressed in political groups or parties. Parties, as he used the word, refers not only to political parties, but to pressure groups of all kinds. For example, the American Medical Association or the AFL-CIO lobbying for favorable legislation are "parties" in this sense. Weber actually saw classes, status groups, and parties as representing the power distribution in communities.[16]

*Power, Class, and Status* Weber was careful to distinguish political position from status and class, although they are all closely related. Obviously, the wealthy and those with high social status can use these advantages politically to further their own ends. A good historical example of this has been the passage and operation of vagrancy laws. The first such laws were passed in England in the fourteenth century,

## ACROSS THE NATION—THUMBNAIL GUIDE TO AMERICANS' TASTES

In a nation as big as the U.S., the earmarks of status are likely to vary from one city to another. Some people take them seriously. Others don't.

For an idea of the variation in status symbols, *U.S. News & World Report* told staff members in key cities to ask people to list some popular status symbols and some that have fallen out of favor. Their findings:

| IN | OUT | IN | OUT |
|---|---|---|---|
| **New York** | | **Chicago** | |
| Ownership of horses | Pedigreed dogs | Indoor plants | U.S. Indian jewelry |
| Season opera tickets | Color television | Owned or rented sculpture | Astrology |
| Private-club membership | European trip | Cabin cruiser (the rich) | C.B. radio |
| Persian rugs | Wall-to-wall carpeting | Renovated brownstone | Art posters |
| Ivy League degree | Winter sun tan | Mixed china and crystal | Initialed accessories |
| Corner office (executives) | Seashore cottage | Membership in private disco | Necklaces for men |
| Penthouse (the rich) | Suburban split-level | Whirlpool bath | Home sauna |
| Rolls-Royce (the rich) | Swimming pool | Harbor condominium | Transcendental |
| Bathroom telephone | Famous-designer labels | (the rich) | meditation, yoga |
| Customized van (the young) | Gas-guzzling car | Personal backgammon table | Frosted hair |
| | | Limousine with bar, color TV | Owning a Playboy |
| **Atlanta** | | (the rich) | Club key |
| Indoor plants | Unisex clothes | | |
| BMW car | Patched-elbow tweeds | **San Francisco** | |
| European trip | Trail biking | Indoor plants | Pedigreed cats and |
| Discos (the young) | Motor boat | Recreation vehicle | dogs |
| C.B. radio (working class) | Swimming pool | Discos | Swimming pool |
| Backgammon | Formal furniture | Jogging | Night clubs |
| Cheap original paintings | Mink coat | Personal wine cellar | St. Bernard dogs |
| Adidas sneakers | Men's pony-tail hairdos | Own winery (the rich) | Long hair (men and |
| Small farm | Suburban split-level | Faded jeans, imported | women) |
| Transcendental meditation | Chagall posters | (the young) | Double-knit suits |
| | | Season opera tickets | Mink coat |
| **Houston** | | Transcendental meditation | Initialed accessories |
| Custom pickup truck | Personalized, low- | and est | Costly French red |
| | number auto tags | Pottery making | wines |
| Pool and tennis court | Men's polyester leisure | | Chauffeur (the rich) |
| Personal wine cellar | suits | | |
| High-rise condominium | Night clubs | | |
| Sable coat | Cheap original paintings | | |
| Trimmed beard | Fake fur | | |
| Halston and Gucci | Prefaded Levis | | |
| apparel | Landscaped yard | | |
| Season opera tickets | Bridge | | |
| Pair of hounds | Men's pony-tail hairdos | | |
| Women's jump suits | Unisex clothes | | |

Reprinted from *U.S. News & World Report* (Feb. 14, 1977), p. 39. Copyright 1977 U.S. News & World Report, Inc.

forbidding almsgiving to beggars. The discouragement of begging insured a cheap agricultural labor supply after the plague had killed many workers. Thus political power was used to further the economic ends of the upper classes. Vagrancy laws were used in the United States by corporation heads in the first part of this century to break up sit-ins by laborers seeking unionization, and during the Civil Rights dem-

onstrations in the 1960s, vagrancy laws were used against civil rights workers.[17] There are many other instances of the use of political power by the upper classes to defend their interests. Draft laws, tax laws, zoning ordinances, criminal and civil law, all tend to protect the upper class. Although unjust, this is hardly surprising. Sociologists have documented the obvious association between power and status and class. G. William Domhoff concluded that members of the upper class hold more than their share of important decision-making positions and do in fact form a governing class. "A governing class is a social upper class which owns a disproportionate amount of the county's wealth, receives a disproportionate amount of the county's yearly income, and contributes a disproportionate number of its members to the controlling institutions and key decision-making groups of the country."[18] Domhoff showed that a governing class does control the economy, federal, state, and local government, foundations, universities, and the military.

The predominance of persons from upper-class backgrounds in government is another indication that class and power are associated. A study of the class backgrounds of 180 United States senators serving between 1947 and 1957 showed that they were recruited disproportionately from the top of the class scale.[19] More recent studies indicate a persistent pattern of upper- and upper-middle-class domination of important political positions on the national, state, and local levels.[20]

Although class, status, and political power are closely related, they are not the same. They are separate dimensions of stratification and need not be associated. For example, people can wield power in the community without having high status or much wealth. In some communities, organized crime figures are quite important and yet they do not belong to the social elite. Labor unions have become politically powerful in some cities, although their membership is largely drawn from the working class.

*The Components of a Stratification System*

**Ranking of Persons** A *category of individuals who rank close together in economic standing, status, and power* is called a **social stratum.** We usually distinguish three main social strata or classes: lower, middle, and upper, with the possibility of finer distinctions, such as lower-lower, middle-lower, upper-lower, and so on. The term *working class* refers to manual workers, sometimes called the *lower class,* although some sociologists reserve that term for laborers not steadily employed. Strictly speaking, *class* should refer only to a person's economic situa-

> **social stratum:** a single rank or level in a stratification system composed of persons of similar class, status, and power.
>
> **social inheritance:** the transmission of family social position to offspring. Social inheritance in class systems usually involves transmission of unequal social opportunity.

tion, but it often indicates both economic and status ranking, or *socioeconomic status.*

**Ranking of Occupational Positions** Occupational positions may also be ranked. The division of labor in itself does not constitute a stratification system but some occupations are more highly rewarded than others, some require or attract persons with more education, and some involve more decision making than others. Positions also differ in prestige. A Supreme Court justice or a physician is generally regarded more highly than a shoe-shiner or street-sweeper.[21] The inequalities associated with occupations may account for these differences. Highly rewarded positions tend to be highly regarded. Positions demanding scarce skills and lengthy training, like that of physician or lawyer, command more respect than positions requiring little training or skill. Those who make decisions that influence the fate of others also command high social evaluation. In addition, the *white-collar/blue-collar* prestige distinction reflects a more positive evaluation of mental than of physical labor.

**Social Inheritance** Another vital element in stratification is **social inheritance:** the transmission of social position or standing from one generation to the next. *Social position* in this sense is one's place in the stratification system, how one ranks on the stratification variables of economic standing, status, and power. If social inheritance is operating, children whose families rank high in class, status, and power are likely to rank high on these dimensions when they become adults. Likewise, offspring of families of relatively low social position tend to occupy relatively low social positions as adults. Although some people of humble origins do rise to occupy high social position in industrial

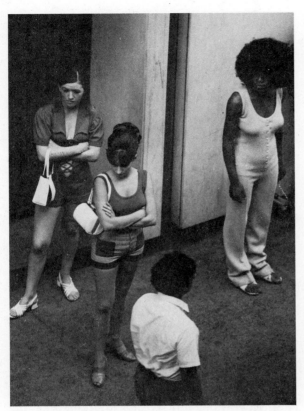

Income is not completely adequate as a measure of social position. These prostitutes may have very high incomes, but their tabooed occupation has low prestige.

ification variables. For example, occupations can be ranked according to the incomes associated with them and the educational levels of persons occupying them. Income is also associated with educational level, so that those with more education tend to have higher incomes. Let us look more closely at these relationships.

Figure 7.3 shows how the median income of full-time workers rises with the level of education attained. The median income of high school graduates is higher than that of elementary school graduates, while the median income of college graduates is higher still, although women's income at each educational level is lower than that of men. Estimates of lifetime income show that between the age of 18 and death, a male high school graduate can expect to earn $135,000 more than an elementary school graduate, and a four-year college graduate should expect to earn $279,000 more than a high school graduate.[22]

Income levels also vary by occupation. Table 7.3 shows the 1976 median earnings for men and women in various occupations. Among white-collar workers, those in professional, technical, managerial, and administrative jobs

societies, most of us occupy positions in life similar to those of our parents. Where differences do occur, they are not likely to be vast.

### Indicators of Economic and Status Position

The term *social position* or *standing,* as just noted, refers to one's place in the stratification system of society. Three variables, *education, income,* and *occupation,* are frequently used as indicators of socioeconomic status. Educational level greatly affects occupation and itself brings prestige; income is a direct but inadequate measure of class or economic standing; and occupations have prestige rankings, as we have seen, and so are an indirect measure of prestige or social status in the community.

Levels of education, occupation, and income are related to one another, as well as to the strat-

**TABLE 7.3   Median Annual Earnings of Employed Persons by Occupation, 1976**

| Occupation | Income | |
|---|---|---|
| | Men | Women |
| **White collar** | | |
| Professional, technical, and kindred workers | $16,939 | $11,072 |
| Managers and administrators, except farm | 16,647 | 9,804 |
| Sales workers | 14,586 | 6,272 |
| Clerical and kindred workers | 12,843 | 8,128 |
| **Blue collar** | | |
| Craft and kindred workers | 16,638 | 7,765 |
| Operatives | 11,688 | 6,649 |
| Laborers, except farm | 10,104 | 7,613 |
| **Other** | | |
| Service workers | 10,030 | 5,674 |
| Farmers and farm managers | 5,896 | a |
| Farm laborers and supervisors | 6,114 | a |

[a]Omitted for reason of inadequate data.

had generally higher earnings than sales and clerical workers. In blue-collar categories, craft workers received the highest incomes. Although white-collar occupations are generally more highly rewarded than blue-collar, male craft workers tend to make more money than salesmen or male clerical workers, and female sales personnel make less than female blue-collar and clerical workers.

Even within the same occupational categories, educational level makes a difference in earnings. Data on income by years of schooling support the conclusion that education pays off, no matter what the occupation. For example, the 1975 median earnings of female clerical workers with less than three years of high school was $6,784, whereas female clerical workers with one to three years of college made $7,934.[23]

Persons with more education tend to be employed in higher-paying occupations. Table 7.4 shows that among white men who have four years of high school or more, over half are in

**TABLE 7.4** **Years of School Completed by Occupational Groups of Employed White Men, 1976, in Percent**

|  | With less than 4 years of high school | With 4 years of high school or more |
|---|---|---|
| White collar | 15.9 | 53.8 |
| Blue collar | 63.3 | 36.8 |
| Service | 12.3 | 6.6 |
| Farm | 8.5 | 2.8 |
|  | 100% | 100% |

white-collar occupations, whereas only about 16 percent of those with less than four years of high school do white-collar work. Those with less education tend to work at blue-collar jobs, which, as we saw, are likely to pay less than white-collar work. The same relationship between education and occupation holds for white women and for black men and women.[24]

Thus the three usual socioeconomic indica-

**FIGURE 7.3** **Median income of year-round full-time workers by education and sex, 1976**

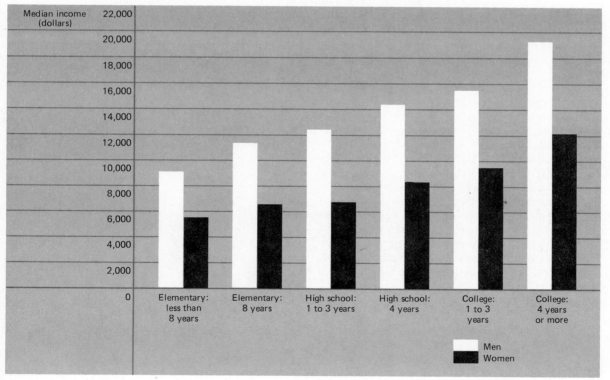

**FIGURE 7.4   One way of viewing the relationships among education, occupation, and income**

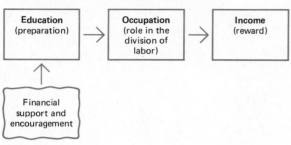

tors are related. Educational level varies with income level, and occupations vary with the general educational level of their workers and in the amount of their earnings; but even within occupations, education and earnings are positively associated. Education may be viewed as preparation for occupation, and income as a reward for fulfilling an occupational role (see Figure 7.4). High-status occupations generally are highly paid and require more education. Of course there are exceptions. The educational level of craftsmen is less than that of salesmen and men in clerical work, and yet their incomes are significantly higher, as we have seen.[25] We must also remember that the level of education attained is a product of many factors, including the financial support and encouragement of parents.

## Consequences of Stratification

**Life and Health**   Socioeconomic status is closely associated with many aspects of people's lives, even in such essential factors as life and health. Infant mortality rates and life expectancy are often used as indicators of the socioeconomic condition of a group. Persons with low family income are more likely to have poor health and decayed teeth than those with high incomes.[26] Lower-income persons have higher rates of pulmonary and heart disease, arthritis, whooping cough, diphtheria, and polio.[27]

This is not surprising if we consider how access to health care is associated with income. The poor are less likely to visit the dentist, for example, and when they do, they are more likely to need extractions. Similarly, when they go to the hospital, they are likely to stay longer than high-income persons.[28] Long life and good health do not entirely depend on access to medical aid, however. It is, after all, important to be healthy in the first place. Proper diet, sanitation, exercise, a clean environment, and freedom from undue stress are important to physical and mental health. Socioeconomic status is vitally related to where and how one lives and is thus related to one's chances for life and good health, and even happiness, at least insofar as happiness is related to life and health.

**Fertility**   Also **fertility** varies by socioeconomic status. Table 7.5 shows the number of children ever born to American women ages thirty-five to forty-four by level of education. You can see that the more highly educated a woman is, the fewer children she is likely to have. Income is also related to number of births. The lower socioeconomic groups have more children than the higher groups.

**Religion**   Even in the matter of religious choice, social class appears to have an influence. Some religious groups draw their membership primarily from the upper and middle classes, while others are composed predominantly of lower-class people. In the United States, Jews tend to rank highest in income, education, and occupational status, white Protestants occupy

One of the consequences of poverty is inadequate access to medical care. For many poorer Americans endless waiting in public health clinics like this one is a standard feature of "health care."

TABLE 7.5   Children Ever Born per 1000 Women, 1976

| Years of school completed | | Children ever born per 1000 women, 1976 |
|---|---|---|
| **Elementary:** | less than 8 years | 3,498 |
| | 8 years | 3,450 |
| **High School:** | 1–3 years | 3,432 |
| | 4 years | 2,846 |
| **College:** | 1–3 years | 2,620 |
| | 4 years or more | 2,217 |

**fertility:** the actual number of births in a given population in a given time period.

a middle position, and Catholics rank lowest. Among Protestants, however, there are other variations as well. For example, Episcopalians and Presbyterians tend to rank high in social class, while fundamentalists tend to rank lower. Even within the same religious denomination, there may be systematic differences in the type of religious involvement and style of participation according to the social class of members (see Chapter 13).

**Politics** Political preferences, too, are associated with social class, as we will see in greater detail in Chapter 14. Both major parties draw some members from all classes, but the working class has traditionally supported the Democratic party, and upper-income groups have generally joined the Republican party. Attitudes toward major political and economic issues vary by social class. In 1949 Richard Centers found striking differences in attitude between the professional, business, and white-collar group, on the one hand, and manual workers, on the other, in regard to such issues as the government's role in the economy and the value of greater influence of workers on government. A significantly higher proportion of the business, professional, and white-collar workers were ultraconservative on the political and economic issues he raised.[29] A study done three years later found essentially the same relationships.[30]

**Membership in Associations and Recreation** Differences in organizational membership by social class have long been noted. Persons in the professions and business and those with higher incomes are more likely than others to belong to formal associations.[31] Persons of

lower socioeconomic position are less likely to participate in voluntary associations.[32] There are also differences in the type of associational life engaged in by social class. Upper-income persons are more likely to join social clubs, charitable groups, professional associations, and organizations like Rotary and Kiwanis, whereas working-class persons tend to join labor unions and religious groups.

Recent data show that income makes a difference in the kinds of recreation people enjoy. Lower-income people are more likely to hunt and drive four-wheel off-the-road vehicles, whereas sailing and golfing are upper-income activities.[33] Watching television is also related to income (see Figure 7.5). More than half of those with incomes under $7,000 reported that television viewing was their favorite evening pastime. Of course, people with more money have more real choice with regard to how they spend their evenings, but educational level is also related to television viewing. Those with more education are likely to watch less TV.

**Marital and Family Patterns** A number of investigations of family life have focused on social-class differences. One important finding is that the female-dominated family structure is more characteristic of the lower class and affects the socialization of males in lower-class households.[34] Strict differentiation of male and female roles and structured barriers to communication between husband and wife are also characteristic of blue-collar marriages.[35]

The socialization of working-class children to different roles according to sex may account for the kind of family relationships found in working-class households. Working-class mothers appear to set different standards of acceptable and punishable behavior for girls and for boys. Middle-class mothers, on the other hand, tend to punish boys and girls similarly for similar misbehavior.[36] Reasons for punishment also differ by social class. Middle-class children tend to be punished only when it can be determined that their intentions are bad. Working-class children tend to be punished when behavior has disruptive consequences, regardless of the child's intention.

FIGURE 7.5    Income and education of persons reporting television viewing as favorite pastime, 1974

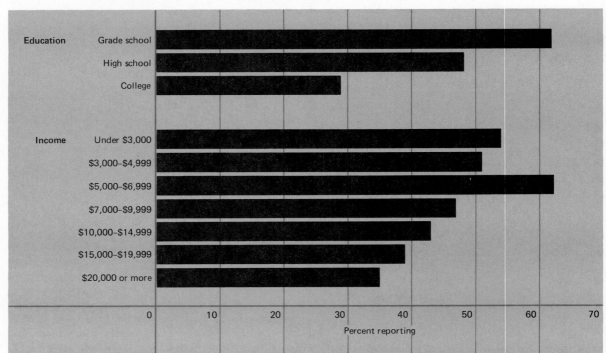

**Values**    Values can be defined as *the principles or standards people use in determining their behavior*. People express their values when they do what they feel they ought to do, when they act according to ethical standards. Values develop as a response to the situation in which a group finds itself. For example, in societies that must constantly defend themselves against unfriendly neighbors, military leadership and service are likely to be highly valued. Social and economic groups also develop values appropriate to their circumstances, and different social and economic circumstances elicit different beliefs about correct behavior. Joseph Kahl has distinguished five social classes and the values typically associated with each.[37]

The *upper class,* according to Kahl, that is, those, who rank highest in prestige, economic standing, and power in the community, value gracious living; making money is not as important to them as spending it well. Appreciation of the past is considered important to the refined way of life. Family lineage is significant, ancestors are revered for their accomplish-

ments, and bad behavior on the part of a family member is seen as a disgrace to all.

The *upper middle class* — college educated and well-to-do career people in the professions and in business — value initiative, planning, and good organization. Unlike the upper class, they look to the future and are little concerned with tradition. Their own accomplishments, rather than those of their forebears, are most significant to them.

Those in the *lower middle class* — moderately successful high school educated, middle-income business people, professionals, government employees, and manual workers — value respectability, because it distinguishes them from the lowest group, the chronically unemployed. Education, religious affiliation, and home ownership are the marks of their respectability.

The *working class* is composed of factory workers and semiskilled laborers. They value "getting by," and making a living. Chances of occupational advancement are slim, so the worker relies on seniority to bring income in-

It is doubtful that this man has anything in the vault behind him. Is his behavior related to his economic position?

white Anglo-Saxon Protestant, or WASP, among others. Membership in some of these groups is associated with class, status, and power ranking, and may be a key factor determining rank on these dimensions of stratification. We proposed in Figure 7.1 a model relating ethnic and racial differences to roles in the division of labor, and in turn to class, status, and power ranking. We have also discussed such differences as a basis for status distinctions and caste relationships.

Chapter 8 will discuss these matters in considerable detail, but we can indicate the point briefly by considering here the roles generally allocated to black Americans in the division of labor in the United States and the effects of that allocation on blacks' stratification rankings. Economially, the class standing of most blacks is markedly below that of whites. With regard to status and power, we have only to search honors lists such as *Who's Who*, to know that black Americans are socially less valued than whites by the white majority. No one with any knowledge of the United States would hold that black men and women occupy many positions of power in the country. In most communities, and certainly on the national scene, Black Power remains an ideal rather than a reality.

creases and job security. A key to understanding the behavior of working-class people is their search for security and stability.[38] This accounts for their reliance on the seniority system, their attachment to the extended family, their traditionalism, utilitarianism, and antiintellectualism. Unlike the upper-middle-class career person, workers usually do not find their jobs satisfying, and get through the workday merely to get home.

The *lower class* is composed of the unstably employed and those in the lowest paid manual positions. Most have little schooling. Because they view their situation as hopeless, they become apathetic and tend to rely on help from family and friends in times of economic hardship.

## ETHNIC-RACIAL DIFFERENTIATION AND STRATIFICATION

The United States is composed of many ethnic and racial groups, including blacks, Chicanos, Native Americans, Irish Catholics, Jews, "white ethnics," Asians, and of course the celebrated

## SEXUAL DIFFERENTIATION AND STRATIFICATION

Early in this chapter, we noted that task assignment in the division of labor is often determined by whether one is male or female. Here we shall look closely at some data on occupational, educational, and income differences between the sexes, and then consider the important issue of how sexual differentiation develops.

Like racial differentiation, sexual stratification is a reflection of institutionalized inequalities. Women are thought to have a "place" in "man's world" with proper attitudes, roles, and other characteristics. Society keeps them in that "place" through differential socialization and opportunity structures. The roles, tasks, and characteristics allocated to women result in their having less power than men generally, and being dependent on men (their fathers and husbands) for their class standing and social status in the community.

*"John, you are the best secretary I've ever had, and I would like to confide a personal problem in you. You see, my husband doesn't understand me . . ."*

Reprinted by permission of Newspaper Enterprise Association.

**Most of us have pretty stereotypical ideas about sex roles. This cartoon is funny because it switches them: the boss who makes passes at secretaries is usually male.**

## Occupation, Education, and Income

The proportion of the American female population participating in the labor force has increased steadily in this century. In 1900, 20 percent of women eighteen through sixty-four years of age were working outside the home; in 1940, the proportion was 30 percent; and by 1976, almost half were in the labor force. The stage of life when women enter the labor force has also changed. Before 1940, women tended to work only before marriage and childbirth. After 1940, the proportion of married women and mothers who were working showed significant increases.

By 1976, 37 percent of married women with preschool children were working outside of the home (compared to 12 percent in 1950) and 47.3 percent of all women were in the labor force.[39] Compare this with the 20 percent of all American women eighteen through sixty-four years of age, both married and unmarried, who were working in 1900.[40] The participation rate of women is still far below that of men (77.5 percent),[41] but the increase for women has been dramatic.

The presence and age of children affects the labor force participation of women, as does the income of their husbands. As you can see from Figure 7.6, women with children are more likely to work if their husbands' incomes are low. Highly educated women are also more likely to work than the less educated. In each income category, mothers with greater education are more likely to work. Increased education, of course, generally increases the financial benefits derived from a job. It appears, then, that a woman's decision to work is influenced by a number of factors: the ages of her children, the income of her husband, and her own educational level. In addition, many women simply enjoy working outside the home. In a national survey, three-fifths of employed women aged thirty to forty-four said that they would continue to work even if they were financially well off.[42]

The occupational distribution of women in the labor force differs markedly from that of men. A higher proportion of women are white-collar workers, but women tend to be concentrated in the lower-paid white-collar occupations, especially in clerical and sales work. Some occupations, usually low-status ones like household work, are overwhelmingly filled by women. In recent years, women have made some headway in becoming judges, lawyers, and college teachers, but even here their numbers remain comparatively low. Women made up 7 percent of all lawyers and judges in 1974 (compared to 3.7 percent in 1965) and they were 30.9 percent of all college and university teachers in 1974 (compared to 23.8 percent in 1965).[43] Figure 7.7 shows both the overrepresentation of women in some occupations and their underrepresentation in others.

Differences in male and female income are partially accounted for by differences in occupational distribution by sex. In 1975 over half of full-time female employees were engaged in clerical, service, and farm occupations (com-

**FIGURE 7.6** **Proportion of mothers in the 1976 labor force by their educational attainment, ages of their children, and the 1975 income of their husbands.**

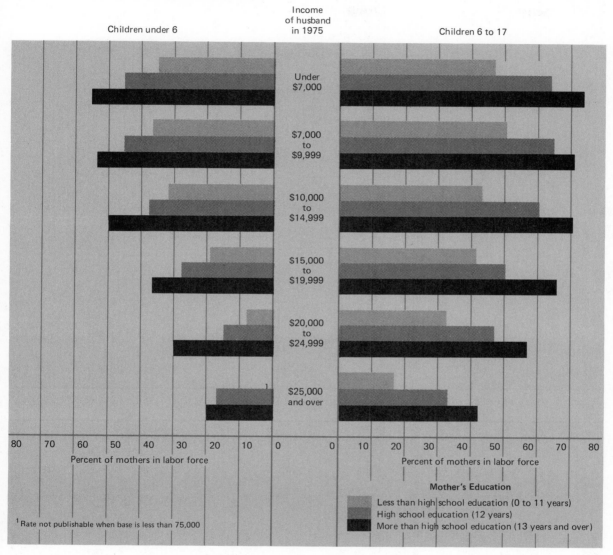



pared to 16 percent of employed males). These occupational categories had the lowest median earnings.[44] Figure 7.3 shows that the median earnings of women are below those of men in each occupational category. This discrepancy is largely due to the concentration of women in the lowest ranks of these broad occupational groupings. For example, in the health professions, women tend to be dieticians and nurses rather than dentists or physicians. The majority of women service workers are in personal service, food, or cleaning, whereas men fill the more highly paid protective service jobs, such as fire and police work.

Among blue-collar workers, men dominate the more highly rewarded craft occupations, while women tend to be machine operatives. Blue-collar women are particularly disadvan-

FIGURE 7.7 Representation of women in various occupational categories

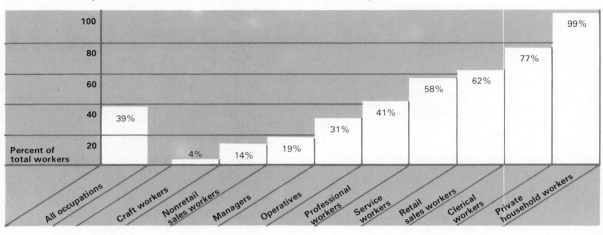

Women are more and more filling nontraditional occupation roles today, but do not achieve income equality with men no matter what their lifetime work experience.

taged by their lack of skills and seniority,[45] but not all of the differential in income is due to the *kinds* of jobs they have. For example, in 1970 the salaries of men who were full-time chemists exceeded those of their women counterparts by 31 percent.[46]

Even when men and women have the same educational levels, men are more likely to get greater rewards for their work. As you saw from Figure 7.3, the median income of full-time women workers with four years or more of college was less than the income of men with only one to three years of high school. Women high school graduates were making only 59 percent of the income of their male counterparts. Part of this differential is accounted for by the kinds of training women receive and the kinds of occupations into which they are directed.

A common explanation for sex-based income differentials is that women do not have as much work experience, even if they do have comparable educational levels. A recent study of 30–44 year-old women showed that the percentage of adult life spent in the labor force did make a difference in income.[47] The median income of those women who had worked 100 percent of their adult lives was higher than that of women who had worked only a proportion of their adult lives. The more the women had worked in the past, the higher their current incomes. Even when women worked 100 percent of their adult lives, however, they still did not achieve income parity with males. The ratio of women's median income to the median income of men of the same age when both had four or more years of college was 64.0. This means that the women's median income was only 64 percent of the median income of comparably educated men. For women who had worked all of their adult lives and who had four years of high school, the ratio was 74.9. Even when controls for occupation were introduced, women did not achieve income equality with men, no matter what their lifetime work experience.

What, then, explains the income gap between men and women? A number of factors. Women are concentrated in low-paying occupational categories and, within the higher occupational categories, they tend to be in the lowest ranks. The training and counseling that women receive direct them to lower-paying jobs. Women have less work experience than men, and men work more overtime than women.[48] Studies show,

## RESEARCHERS FIND PAY GAP WIDENS FOR MEN, WOMEN

The earnings gap between men and women has continued to widen during the last 20 years, despite some effort toward equal pay for both.

As a group, women working full-time now average only $6,800 a year, or 43 per cent below the $11,800 average earnings of men holding full-time jobs.

Twenty years ago, working women were earning only 36 per cent less than their male counterparts, according to a report by The Conference Board of New York, a private business research group.

Fabien Linden, a Conference Board economist, said the widening gap is largely explained by "a change in the occupational mix of working women" over the last 20 years and the fact that women generally are paid less because of less experience in the labor force.

Even among the college-trained there is a sizable earnings gap between men and women workers, he said.

College-trained women working full-time earned an average of $9,300 last year, compared with $15,200 for men. Among college graduates, women earned $10,400 compared with $17,200 for men.

Women college graduates, in fact, earned less on the average than men who did not finish high school.

Twenty years ago, most working women were either well-educated or worked because of a need to support themselves. Since then, however, because of changing attitudes toward work, a much broader base of women has entered the labor force, representing virtually all ages and all levels of education.

By contrast, males who have entered the labor force traditionally have come from the younger age brackets, since most men in the older age categories are already working. These young workers are increasingly better educated than those who preceded them into the work force.

The number of college-trained working women has risen significantly, but they account for only 42 per cent of the growth in the total female work force. Women with a high school education or less made up 58 per cent of the increase over the last 20 years, the majority taking relatively low-paying jobs. . . .

*Chicago Tribune,* November 30, 1975. Reprinted courtesy of the Chicago Tribune.

however, that even taking into consideration all these factors, the earnings gap can only be fully explained by outright discrimination; that is, qualified women are not paid as much as qualified men for doing the same work simply because they are women. This is comparable to discrimination based on race or color. As with all forms of discrimination, many rationalizations are given for practicing sex discrimination: women are inherently inferior; woman's place is in the home; in a tight job market, women should not take jobs that men need; men are more often heads of households. However unobjective and unfair many of these views are, they are widespread enough to set limits on what women can achieve.

### Nature or Nurture?

There is continuing controversy concerning the relative effects of biological differences and socialization on sex differentials in occupations and roles. As we saw in Chapter 4, some sex differences have been documented. But what is the source of these differences? The case for socialization, rather than genetics, is impressive. In general, there is considerable consistency in the sex-role messages transmitted to children by the major socialization agents—parents, teachers, friends, books, and other media.[49] Boys should be active, achieving, aggressive, independent, ambitious, rational. They are encouraged to succeed, to attain higher education, higher prestige, and higher-income jobs. They are, in short, socialized to compete for the occupational goals and to adopt the attitudes and personality traits that exemplify the values most prized and rewarded in American society.

By contrast, girls are socialized to be passive, nuturing, dependent, pretty, responsive, emotional, and "nice," all traits that are not so highly valued in society and that do not lead to positions and occupations of high prestige, power, and material benefits. If a woman does seek gainful employment, she is often limited in her choice to the jobs considered appropriate for women. These consist principally of occupations like nursing, teaching, secretarial and clerical work, and household work—all jobs that involve caring for other people or performing low-status occupations for which female competition is sanctioned by the society as a whole. Many high-status careers, such as

*"Dear Lord, was I put here on earth to cook, clean, sew, raise children, attend PTA meetings and be a loving wife, or was I put here on earth to pull down $30,000 a year as an executive for a top New York-based firm? Send me a sign."*

fashion model and movie star, are generally open only to women of outstanding physical attractiveness.

Needless to say, discrimination also operates against males who aspire to some social and occupational roles. Male nurses are still a rarity, while men who perform jobs traditionally associated with female activities, such as dress design or hair styling, are often considered "queer." Men who manifest personality traits associated with femininity, such as emotional sensitivity and tenderness, are unlikely to occupy positions of high social reward.

But sex discrimination is predominantly a female problem. Despite the fact that certain individual women have achieved jobs, pay, and status equal to those of men, women *as a class* are still largely confined to lower paid, lower status occupations. They are denied equal access to professional training, they are discouraged from competing with men for positions of pow-er and prestige, and, in almost every occupa-tional category, they receive less pay than a man would receive for the same job. Who is more likely to become the first "minority" Vice President of the United States—the Presidency remains unthinkable—a black male or a white female?

Even today, despite the gains made by the women's movement, the typical American woman continues to be socialized to internalize and display passivity, dependence, and emo-tionality in a culture that values and rewards aggressiveness, self-sufficiency, and rationali-ty. She takes home economics rather than shop, becomes a cheerleader rather than an athlete, and is advised to marry a doctor rather than become one. If, despite all this, she elects the traditional masculine achievement goals, she is likely to experience social disapproval and self-doubt for pursuing a deviant pattern. If she succeeds in entering the male-dominated occu-pational world, she may suffer educational, occupational, and income discrimination and may not expect the same levels of success and reward as her male counterparts. Although women constitute a majority of the American population, they remain a minority group in the sense in which that word is used in Chapter 8: a group socially dominated by another.

## STABILITY AND CHANGE WITHIN THE STRATIFICATION SYSTEM

What makes for stability within a stratification system—the maintenance of class, status, and power rankings for families from one genera-tion to the next? Many social scientists contend that the desire to pass on the benefits one has received or acquired to one's own children is the key to understanding continuity of social rank through the generations. Let us examine just how this is accomplished.

**Direct Inheritance** Direct inheritance of money, title, family business, or, in some cases, political power, is one way of maintaining con-tinuity of social position from one generation to the next. Little more need be said concerning this form of social inheritance. The benefits re-ceived are direct. It only remains for the indi-vidual receiving them to be able to hold onto and use them to advantage.

**Inheritance of Unequal Opportunities** An-other form of social inheritance—probably the most important one in American society—is the inheritance of unequal opportunities. While relatively few of us directly inherit great wealth, we do inherit differential access to the opportu-nity to attain high class, status, or power as a consequence of family position and home envi-ronment. Legally any native-born citizen of the United States may have the opportunity to be-come President, for example, but we all know that it also helps to be Protestant, white, male, well educated, and reasonably wealthy. Non-whites, females, Jews, and the poor have inherit-ed a reduced chance of attaining that particular goal. To use a similar example, a law degree from Harvard or Yale is very useful in attaining a position with a Wall Street law firm. While there are graduates of those schools who came from poor familes, the opportunity for admis-sion to Harvard and Yale is much reduced for the working-class teenager from a midwestern or southern industrial city. The inheritance of unequal opportunity is most marked with re-spect to occupational and educational attain-ment.

**Occupational Attainment** Occupational achievement may be passed on from generation to generation as a form of social inheritance, as shown in Figure 7.8. Families with high social position are able to give their offspring finan-cial, behavioral, and attitudinal advantages that enable them to enter occupations associated with high class, status, and power, and thus to become adults with high social position. They in turn establish families of their own, giving the same advantages in the occupational world to *their* children, and so the dynamics of social inheritance can continue through the genera-tions, with the result that great-grandchildren may find themselves in the same relative social rank as their great-grandparents were eighty years before. Of course, social inheritance does not operate perfectly in American society; fami-ly rankings may change somewhat over time—in either direction.

**Educational Attainment** Education is close-ly related to occupational position and earnings. But what determines the educational level one attains? Intelligence is one factor. The results of a study by William Sewell and Vimal

**FIGURE 7.8** Social inheritance through occupational achievement

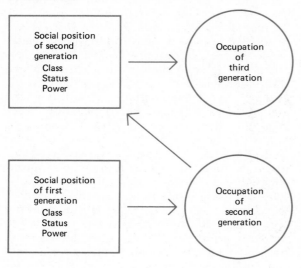

Shah indicate that intelligence, as measured by IQ tests, is a significant predictor of who will complete four years of college.[50] But they also found another important predictor: the socioeconomic position of the family of origin. Sewell and Shah used four categories for both IQ and socioeconomic classifications: low, lower middle, upper middle, and high. A higher proportion of high school seniors who scored low on IQ tests but high on the socioeconomic indicators completed college than did seniors who had low IQ scores *and* low socioeconomic status. Among those with the highest IQs as well, more than three times as many persons of highest socioeconomic status than those of lowest completed college (see Table 7.6). In each IQ category, socioeconomic status was an important predictor of plans to attend college and actual completion of college. Likewise, IQ made a difference in plans to attend college and college completion in each socioeconomic level.

**TABLE 7.6** Socioeconomic Status and IQ of High School Seniors who Graduated from College (in percentages)

| | IQ | |
| Socioeconomic status | Lowest | Highest |
| --- | --- | --- |
| Lowest | 0.3 | 17.0 |
| Highest | 9.2 | 57.6 |

Figure 7.9 also shows clearly the effect of the family's socioeconomic status on college plans. Those high school seniors whose families have higher incomes are much more likely to plan to go to college than are young people from lower income households. Other research strongly supports the link between family background and the amount of education received, although other factors, such as sex, may also affect educational attainment.

**Social Inheritance and the Functional Interpretation of Stratification** Social inheritance casts considerable doubt on a functional interpretation of stratification. The functional theory, as we have seen, proposes that unequal rewards are necessary to motivate the most qualified persons to assume the most important occupational and social positions. But social inheritance means that persons from families with high social positions, on the average, will *be* the most qualified. How do individuals acquire the specific abilities and qualifications? Some abilities are natural, such as musical genius, and some are acquired, such as administrative skills. The acquired abilities presume some native intelligence and ability to learn, but we know that such levels of intelligence and aptitude are widespread in the population in comparison to genius-level aptitude for music.

**FIGURE 7.9** College plans of high school seniors 14 to 34 years old, by family income, 1974

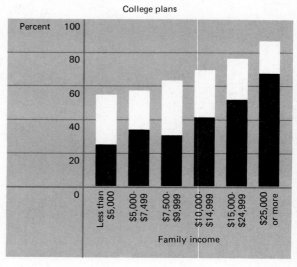

Now if appropriate aptitudes are widespread, but relatively few people achieve the highly rewarded positions that require those aptitudes, three conclusions are possible. First, relatively few people may want the most highly rewarded positions. We can dismiss this possibility as nonsensical on its face. Second, there is direct discrimination on the basis of ethnicity, religion, race, sex, and so forth. This, of course, is true, but it cannot account for those who are not discriminated against but who still fail to attain highly rewarded positions.

The third explanation is that some persons have acquired better qualifications and thus have achieved higher positions. Many children growing up in humble socioeconomic circumstances have the basic intelligence and aptitudes to perform almost any task or occupation, but their social inheritance denies them the opportunity to acquire the specific qualifications necessary for performing the highly rewarded tasks. They are, therefore, beaten in the competition by those who have had better opportunities to become qualified. This pattern is especially evident within the culture of poverty.

**The Culture of Poverty**   Social characteristics passed on to the next generation through socialization promote stability of social rank. The **culture of poverty,** as Oscar Lewis points out, is a response to a marginal position in a society that stresses free enterprise and achievement.[51] It is characterized by apathy, hopelessness, one-parent homes, and distrust of institutions, such as education and government. By means of socialization, the culture of poverty is passed on to succeeding generations. Thus the children of the poor share the characteristics of the culture of poverty. Even though they may have better economic opportunities than their parents, they are kept from taking advantage of opportunities for advancement.

The culture of poverty exerts an especially strong influence on attitudes and values. It is characterized by apathy and cynicism. Children who have been socialized to believe that they are controlled by a fate they are powerless to resist and that all important aspects of life are determined by others ("the bosses" or "the big guys"), are less likely to attempt to change their lot than are optimistic children. For example, even if a poor boy is told by a high school counselor that he has the ability to go to college, his

**culture of poverty:**   the hypothesis that the very poor establish behavior patterns to accommodate to the difficulties and insecurities of their lives which may differ considerably from those practiced or considered desirable by others.

**social mobility:**   movement of persons from one social group or position to another.

cynicism may prompt him to believe that "college is for rich guys and sissies," and his apathy may prevent him from applying for a scholarship. Of course, apathy and cynicism are not totally unrealistic responses to the situation in which the poor find themselves.

### Social Mobility

**Social mobility** refers to *the movement of persons from one social group or position to another.* Americans have always been concerned with social mobility. White Americans see themselves as an ambitious, pioneering people who tried and succeeded. It is difficult and painful for them to admit that institutionalized inequalities, such as unequal access to education, unequal pay for work done, job discrimination, and the social exclusivity of status groups frequently block dreams and goals for themselves and others.

We shall now explore the kinds and measures

Poverty: A city play area.

of mobility, as well as the experience of mobility in industrial societies.

**Horizontal and Vertical Mobility**   Movement between groups on the same social level is called **horizontal social mobility;** movement from one level to another is called **vertical social mobility.** When a company transfers a plant manager from one large city to another, the manager moves from one social grouping to another but remains in the same relative social position or rank because the occupational status has remained the same. This is a case of horizontal mobility. Vertical mobility, by contrast, does involve a change in social rank, as when a salesperson is promoted to personnel manager or when an executive becomes a farmer.

Vertical mobility is either upward or downward. Moving to a higher or lower level may be called ascending and descending mobility, or more colorfully, social climbing and social sinking.[52] Climbing presumably takes some effort whereas sinking seems passive. High economic standing, status, and power are valued in the United States. Social climbing, then, has the goal of attaining generally valued social ends, while social sinking probably represents either the repudiation of these ends or the inability to attain or retain them.

**Group Mobility**   Not only individuals but also whole groups may experience upward or downward mobility. The early Christian clergy, for instance, had relatively low social status because the church was not recognized by the state. Later the church gained importance and prestige, and the clergy as a group experienced upward social mobility. To take a modern example, scientists in the United States now have somewhat higher social status than they did in 1947; so we can say that scientists as a group have changed in status position in relation to other occupational groups.[53] Caste groupings may also experience vertical mobility.

**Status Inconsistency**   An individual or group may experience mobility along any one of the three dimensions of stratification—class, status, or power. A person may acquire a great deal of money, for example, and still be denied higher social status and access to power in the community. Mobility on a single dimension of stratification may result in **status inconsistency:** the situation of an individual or group that has inconsistent rankings on the stratification differentials. The inconsistency between ethnic status and class standing is a good example. A doctor may rank high in economic standing, but be accorded low social status because of his ethnicity.

Status inconsistency may cause people to seek political change, as when members of groups of declining social significance, such as WASPS, join reactionary movements like the John Birch Society. It may also affect interpersonal relations. Persons experiencing status inconsistency may wish to interact with others on the basis of the highest status they possess, but others may choose to interact with them in terms of their lowest status. A classic example is the case of the black doctor and the white laborer. If each operates out of a desire to be socially superior, the doctor will strive to make occupational standing most important in the relationship and the laborer will try to make race primary. There is evidence that status-inconsistent people commit suicide more often than others as a consequence of lack of social integration.[54]

**Intragenerational and Intergenerational Mobility**   Social mobility may be experienced by a single individual within one lifetime or by a family line over a number of generations. The former case is called **intragenerational** mobility and the latter, **intergenerational** mobility. Sociologists have used the amount of intergenerational mobility in a given society as an indicator of the strength of social inheritance in that society and of how open or closed it is.

**Frequency and Distance**   Both the *frequency* of social mobility and the *distance* moved are measures of social mobility in a society. The proportion of persons moving up or down the socioeconomic scale indicates the frequency of social mobility in a society. The degree of change in income and property, social status, and power indicates the distance moved. Together, these two measures give us some idea of how open or closed a society is.

**Social Mobility in Industrial Societies**   The amount of social mobility varies from one society to another and within the same society at different periods. Factors like economic stabili-

*"I just hope it drops in a decent neighbourhood."*

© 1975 Punch (Rothco).

**Aspirations for social mobility.**

**horizontal social mobility:** movement between groups on the same social level. Sometimes referred to as "lateral mobility."

**vertical social mobility:** social movement upward or downward on the class or status ladder; social climbing or sinking.

**status inconsistency:** the condition of having inconsistent rankings on the different stratification variables; for example, the black physician or the wealthy criminal.

**intragenerational mobility:** vertical social mobility experienced by an individual during his or her own lifetime.

**intergenerational social mobility:** vertical social mobility experienced by a family lineage over the course of two or more generations.

ty, prevailing ideologies, and the political situation may account for the variations. A classic study of social mobility in industrial nations done by Seymour Martin Lipset and Reinhard Bendix in 1959 revealed similarities in the frequency of actual upward mobility between generations.[55] Similar occupational structures in industrialized societies coupled with the desire of individuals to rise in status seemed to be responsible for the similarities. Another cross-national analysis of intergenerational mobility, done by S. M. Miller, concludes that the United States, France, and the Soviet Union have similar upward mobility rates.[56] In only five of the seventeen nations Miller studied did upward mobility exceed downward mobility,

however. These were the United States, France, Brazil, India, and the Soviet Union. Miller characterizes the United States and the Soviet Union as having a general pattern of upward mobility with limited downward mobility.

In the United States, a study of over 20,000 men found more upward than downward mobility both within and between generations. The distance moved, however, did not tend to be great. In general, offspring were not far removed from their parents, and persons at the end of their occupational careers were not greatly advanced from their first occupations.[57]

Change in the distribution of income over the years is a good indicator of how egalitarian or stratified a society is and whether it is chang-

**TABLE 7.7   Distribution of Family Income in the U.S., 1950–1976 (percent)[1]**

| Income rank | 1950 | 1955 | 1960 | 1965 | 1970 | 1976 |
|---|---|---|---|---|---|---|
| All families | 100.0 | 100.0 | 100.0 | 100.0 | 100.0 | 100.0 |
| Lowest fifth | 4.5 | 4.8 | 4.8 | 5.2 | 5.4 | 5.4 |
| Second fifth | 12.0 | 12.3 | 12.2 | 12.2 | 12.2 | 11.8 |
| Middle fifth | 17.4 | 17.8 | 17.8 | 17.8 | 17.6 | 17.6 |
| Fourth fifth | 23.4 | 23.7 | 24.0 | 23.9 | 23.8 | 24.1 |
| Highest fifth | 42.7 | 41.3 | 41.3 | 40.9 | 40.9 | 41.1 |
| Highest 5 percent | 17.3 | 16.4 | 15.9 | 15.5 | 15.6 | 15.6 |

[1]Beginning 1974, not strictly comparable with earlier years due to revised procedures.

ing. Table 7.7 shows the distribution of income for each fifth of U.S. families, beginning with the fifth that has the lowest income. There has been very little change in the distribution of income among segments of the population between 1950 and 1976. The highest 5 percent of families continued to receive over 15 percent of all the income. Figure 7.10 shows the percentage of various kinds of personal wealth possessed by individuals in the top one percent. Although their proportionate share of total corporate stocks has declined, their share of total net worth has remained fairly stable throughout the years shown. Using these indicators, we can say that the United States has become neither greatly more egalitarian nor more highly stratified in recent years.

**Factors Affecting Social Mobility** We have already discussed some of the institutionalized inequalities that block mobility aspirations. A number of other factors affect actual mobility. Some of these operate on the societal level and affect the objective opportunities of all or some groups for upward mobility. Others work on the individual level to determine who will benefit from opportunity and actually achieve higher social position. On the societal level, when the supply of highly ranked occupations expands or when the upper strata do not re-

produce in sufficient numbers to fill the highly ranked positions, the possibilities for upward social mobility are increased. Ethnic discrimination in a society may hinder some groups and enhance the competitive positions of others. The state of the economy and the stability of the government also can influence the opportunity structure.

On the individual level, such factors as family size and sibling position appear to affect occupational achievement and thus social mobility. Individuals from small families tend to achieve higher-status occupations than those from large families, even when the socioeconomic standing of the families is the same. Family size is important mainly because it affects the amount of education received. The higher educational attainments of children from smaller families may be a result of there being fewer persons to share in the financial, emotional, and time resources of the parents.

The amount of education attained is, as previously noted, a significant factor in socioeconomic status. Access to education can be a gateway to upward social mobility. Earlier, we saw that attainment of a high level of education is related to ability as expressed through IQ scores and to the socioeconomic position of the family of origin. Educational attainment is also related to sex and race. Women are less likely

**FIGURE 7.10** **Shares of the top one percent of persons in total personal wealth (net worth) and in selected asset holdings, selected years: 1953–1972**

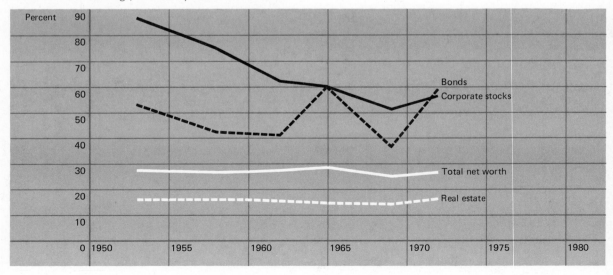

than men, and blacks are less likely than whites, to receive a higher education.

Aspirations contribute to social mobility. If aspiration is lacking, all the opportunity and ability in the world will not advance the individual. Members of the working class who do move upward in class ranking tend to be the most highly motivated.[58] Socialization in the home and by peers seems to be decisive. For example, one study found that among working-class boys with high IQs, those whose families gave them more direct encouragement to get a higher education in order to advance were the boys who did indeed intend to go to college.[59]

Other research suggests that parents have the greatest effect on aspirations to attain a high level of education and a high-status occupation; friends have slightly less effect than parents; and teachers have less effect than friends.[60]

There is by no means a perfect correlation between the socioeconomic standing of parents and that of their children in the United States and other industrialized nations. In other words, there is intergenerational social mobility, and much of it is upward. It is evident that there are opportunities to advance, although many factors affect the extent of these opportunities and who benefits from them.

## SUMMARY

This chapter explored social and economic inequality. Why are there inequalities? How are they perpetuated? If people advance, what factors aid them? We found that social inequality is built upon social differentiation and that sexual and racial/ethnic differentiation are particularly important bases of inequality in our society. Stratification, or unequal rank in class, status, and power position, has been perpetuated through the institutionalized inequalities that affect racial/ethnic groups and females. The stratification system is also perpetuated through the inheritance of social position from one generation to the next.

Although the American ideal is one of liberty and equality, stratification persists. In fact, we noted the near universality of some form of stratification. Reasons proposed for this vary greatly. Some maintain that unequal rewards are *necessary* to motivate people while others contend that the greed of human nature or the evil of human institutions has kept people in conflict over resources, thus perpetuating inequalities.

We explored the major types of stratification

systems—caste, estate, and class—and the types of inequalities associated with each. Even in a class system such as our own, where social mobility is valued, we noted the blocks to economic and social advancement. We also explored some of the consequences of stratification in the United States—differential access to medical aid, varying family patterns and fertility, and a host of other differences.

Finally, we addressed the question of social mobility, both upward and downward, in a class system. We saw that there is indeed group and individual mobility, although it is somewhat limited. Societal factors, such as the state of the economy, and individual factors, such as sibling position, have some influence on advancement.

Social factors strongly influence the lives of individuals. No more may we take the simple view—you can make it if you try. Not *all* can make it if they try unless there is substantial change in social structures. Having some sense of the profound influence of social structures on the lives of people is the beginning of attaining a sociological perspective.

## SUGGESTED READINGS

GREENE, BERT AND PHILLIP STEPHEN SCHULZ. *Pity the Poor Rich*. Chicago: Contemporary Books, 1978. Greene, at one time a caterer to the very wealthy, and Schulz take an irreverent look at how the privileged survive in America. Topics discussed include who the rich are, what they do, and other elements of their life style—what they eat, where they vacation, which

psychiatrists they see, how much their life style costs them.

KANTER, ROSABETH MOSS. *Men and Women of the Corporation*. New York: Basic, 1977. In her study of a large manufacturing firm, Kanter explores how the corporation "produces" people—their sense of themselves and their potentialities. The work experience of managers, professionals, secretaries, and unpaid corporate wives are explored in some detail. Kanter discusses the effect that opportunity, power, and the relative numbers of different social types (women, blacks, etc.) have on the behavior of individuals in the corporation.

LIEBOW, ELLIOT. *Tally's Corner*. Boston: Little, Brown, 1967. A study of poor Negro men who frequent a particular urban streetcorner. Liebow analyzes the routines and relationships of these men as a response to their low social and economic status.

RYAN, WILLIAM. *Blaming the Victim*. New York: Pantheon, 1971. Ryan explores the ideology of blaming the individual victim (the poor) for what is essentially a problem of our own social institutions. He discusses the institutionalization of unequal opportunity for the poor, particularly in the educational and economic systems; and he offers a biting critique of the culture of poverty concept.

SENNETT, RICHARD AND JONATHAN COBB. *The Hidden Injuries of Class*. New York: Vintage, 1972. Using personal interviews in Boston working-class communities, Sennett and Cobb allow us to see the lives and frustrations of working-class people through their own eyes. We learn how workers value themselves in relation to the social evaluations placed on the work they do.

WINSTON, SANDRA. *The Entrepreneurial Woman*. New York: Newsweek Books, 1979. A popular account of how the author and other women have overcome such obstacles as male chauvinism and the double duties of home and store to become successful business women.

# Chapter 8
# Minority
# Group
# Relations

Children carrying white flags were slaughtered, and pregnant women were cut open. The slaughter and mutilation continued into the late afternoon over many miles of the bleak prairie. Both male and female genitals were later exhibited by the victors as they marched into Denver, and some were made into tobacco pouches.

> Massacre of a village of eastern Sioux, Sand Creek, Colorado, 1864[1]

The Italian race stock is inferior and degraded. . . . It will not assimilate naturally or readily with the prevailing "Anglo-Saxon" race stock. . . . Servility and filthy habits of life . . . have been ingrained in Italians. . . . The greater part are illiterate and are likely to remain so.

> Popular stereotype, 1900[2]

Nigger! The white people do not want you to vote Saturday. Do not make the Ku Klux Klan take a hand. Do you remember what happened two years ago, May 9? George Hughes was burned to death, the country house destroyed. . . . For good reason.

> Handbill passed out to blacks, Dennison, Texas, 1932[3]

Treachery [and] loyalty to the emperor [are] inherent Japanese traits.

> Editorial, *Los Angeles Examiner*, May 10, 1943

Mexicans ought to be sent back to Mexico. Maybe Hitler was right. The animals of our society ought to be destroyed. Mexican people after seventeen years of age, think it's perfectly all right to go out, and act like an animal.

> Superior Court Judge, Santa Clara, California, September, 1969[4]

These quotations provide a harsh

introduction to the subject of this chapter. The American society is one of the most heterogeneous in the world. Most of us learn very young to differentiate among people according to race, ethnicity, religion, prestige, and worth. We learn this, not in the way we master arithmetic, but as a part of a complex socialization process, much of it involving a conditioning routine that shapes our attitudes, our unconscious predisposition to respond positively or negatively to racial, ethnic, and religious symbols. It is probably a rare American who is not familiar with terms such as nigger, coon, darkie, kike, hebe, chink, jap, nip, gook, dink, slope, greaser, honkie, and kraut.

Some readers of the last line above may have cringed inwardly as their eyes fell upon the words, knowing too well how it feels to be called by such names, and what it means to live in a society where whole groups of people are pigeonholed in such ways. How did this state of affairs come to pass in the United States? Does not the Declaration of Independence, the ringing rhetoric of which sparked the revolution in which our country was born, claim it is "self-evident" that "all men are created equal"?

And what is wrong with people that they are willing to treat one another in such ways? How can individuals who perceive themselves as kind, even loving, forthright and democratic, equal under the law and so forth, at the same time deny other people opportunities for decent housing or medical care, an adequate job or even fair treatment in the courts simply because the others are of a different skin color, ethnicity, or religion? The answers to these questions constitute the subject matter of this chapter. Many Americans might answer that it is "just human nature" to hate or be suspicious of someone who is "not like" themselves, but we know from Chapters 3 and 4 that this is not true. The

Key Concepts
Minority Group
Prejudice
Discrimination
Segregation
Ethnic Group
Race
Structured Social Inequality

Group Subordination in the United States
Absorption versus Inclusion
The Self-Fulfilling Prophesy and the American Dream
The Making of Subordinate Groups
Minority Responses to Dominant Group Policies

Minorities in American Society
Native Americans
Black Americans
Asian-Americans
Hispanic-Americans
White Ethnics

The Continuing Dominance of White Northern European Protestants
Racial and Ethnic Pluralism
Subcultures and Supercultures

Summary

Suggested Readings

attitudes and behaviors that constitute prejudice and discrimination are learned within a social and cultural context, and it is apparent that such a context exists in the United States at the present time.

In this chapter we will look at the social and cultural conditions that cause individuals to use such highly charged expressions; we will see the sources of institutional prejudice and discrimination, and finally, we will see how prejudice and discrimination have been imposed upon the American minorities and analyze the present status of each of these groups. It is our hope that the more we learn about prejudice and discrimination, the more difficult it will be for us to tolerate such patterns—in ourselves as well as in others.

## KEY CONCEPTS

### Minority Group

A **minority group** is *any group of people against whom categorical (absolute, unqualified) discrimination is practiced by those who control the economic or political institutions of the society.*[5] Although the term *minority* implies that the subordinate group is smaller than the dominant group, this characteristic need not be present in dominant-minority relations. In South Africa, for example, blacks constitute approximately 78 percent of the population, but they are clearly the ones against whom categorical discrimination is practiced by the dominant whites. *Majority* is the term frequently used for the group that controls the economic and political institutions. But it is the control of the institutions that serves as the basis of dominance, not mere numbers. England, France, Spain, and Ger-

many have controlled colonial peoples throughout the world by virtue of their military and economic power rather than by possessing larger populations, as have the dominant group in America, the white Anglo-Saxon Protestants.[6]

Any group that controls economic and political institutions will resist sharing that privilege with others. The white British Protestants who settled the United States and Canada established their language, their economic and political institutions, and their legal structure.[7] Varying degrees of institutional prejudice and discrimination have been directed in these countries against Native Americans, blacks, Orientals, Chicanos, Puerto Ricans, and the so-called white ethnics—usually Catholics and Jews. In Canada, people of French-Catholic origins are discriminated against, even in Quebec, where the 80 percent French-Catholic majority dominates the government.[8] In Northern Ireland, Irish Protestants control the economic and political institutions and discriminate against Irish Catholics. In Israel, the European Jews dominate the government, the economy, and the labor unions. They tend to be prejudiced and discriminatory not only against the Arabs but against Jews of Mid-Eastern and African origins.[9]

If the dominant group in a society is relatively homogeneous in its racial, ethnic, and religious attributes, you may predict that any subordinate groups that do not possess one or more of the attributes of the dominant group will experience differing degrees of economic and political prejudice and discrimination. In 1822, the freed American slaves who purchased land from West African chiefs and founded the independent nation of Liberia formed an aristocracy that controlled the economic and political institutions and monopolized wealth, power, and prestige. The two million native black Africans became the minority, discriminated against by a few thousand black families of American origin.[10]

### Prejudice

**Prejudice** is *"an antipathy based upon a faulty and inflexible generalization. It may be felt or expressed. It may be directed toward a group as a whole or toward an individual because he (or she) is a member of that group."*[11] There are two basic components to prejudice: the cognitive (or intellectual) and the emotional. When members of a minority group are primarily lower class, they tend to be labeled or stereotyped as inferior in native intelligence as well as having inherent tendencies toward laziness, filth, crime, alcoholism, rioting, and high fertility rates. Read the following quotation and guess which minority the author is talking about:

It is not astonishing that with a million—in the city, perhaps half the criminals should be of that race . . . they are burglars, firebugs, pickpockets. . . . Among the most expert of all the street thieves are . . . boys under sixteen who are brought up to lives of crime. . . . The juvenile—emulates the adult in the matter of crime percentage, 40 per cent of those arraigned at the House of Refuge and 37 per cent of those arraigned in the Children's Court being of that race.[12]

You probably guessed that the author was writing about blacks, Chicanos, Puerto Ricans, or Native Americans. Wrong! The date was 1908, the writer was a New York City Police commissioner, and the people he was complaining about were Jews, recent immigrants from Eastern Europe, primarily members of the working and lower classes. Today American Jews are predominantly in the middle class and have the highest median income of any religious category in the nation. Since they have become increasingly competitive in the educational and occupational systems, Jews are more likely to be

> **minority group:** any group against whom categorical discrimination is practised by those who control the economic or political institutions of the society.
>
> **prejudice:** an antipathy to an individual or group based on a faulty and inflexible generalization.

criticized today for being too achievement-oriented and too successful. For example, a former chairman of the Joint Chiefs of Staff, on October 10, 1974, advised the American people to

get tough-minded enough to set down the Jewish influence in this country and break that lobby. It's so strong. . . . They own the banks in this country, the newspapers, you just look at where the Jewish money is in this country.[13]

This allegation is as false in its time as the police commissioner's was in 1908. Reliable data show that

. . . Jews comprise less than 1 percent of the top officers and members of the boards of directors of the commerical banks in the United States. Jews are the principle stock holders or owners of only 3.1 percent of the 1,700 newspapers in the United States. . . . Of the American Society of Newspaper Editors' 800 members, less than 20 are Jews.[14]

**A minority group is one dominated socially, politically, or economically by those who control the society's institutions. Consequences of minority status: black and white residential neighborhoods in Fort Myers, Florida.**

Jews are as underrepresented in the elitist positions in the society as the other minorities, as we shall see below.

## Discrimination

**Discrimination** is the differential and unequal treatment of people because of their perceived physical or cultural characteristics.

Discrimination may be said to exist to the degree that individuals of a given group who are otherwise

---

### THE OTHER MINORITIES

This chapter focuses upon prejudice and discrimination based upon race and ethnicity. Clearly, other social categories are discriminated against by those who control the economic and political institutions — women, the aged, the physically and mentally handicapped, homosexuals, and others. Some sociologists have labelled these social categories "The New Minorities" or "The Other Minorities."[16] There are institutionalized patterns of prejudice and discrimination against each of these minorities. Let us look at women as an example of a minority.

Women constitute a numerical majority in the United States (about 51 percent of the population). Yet women are a sociological minority, categorically discriminated against by those who control the economic and political institutions. Women are underrepresented in the professional and managerial occupations (21.8 percent of the labor force to 28.3 percent for men) and are heavily represented in low-level white-collar jobs (35.1—6.2 percent for males).[17] The median income of women in the labor force is 59 percent of the median income of working men.[18] When women of the same age, with the same time in the same occupation are compared, women still earn only 73 percent as much as men.[19] Many prejudices exist to justify discrimination against women: females are inferior in native intelligence, irresponsible, inconsistent, emotionally unstable, and they are most satisfied in subordinate roles in the labor force or in the home.[20] Different but comparable patterns of prejudice and discrimination are imposed upon the aged, the physically handicapped, homosexuals, and others to put them at a disadvantage in competition for jobs, housing, and other desired goals of the society.

---

formally qualified are not treated in conformity with . . . nominally universal institutionalized codes.[15]

The history of most societies that have a relatively homogeneous dominant group within a heterogeneous population is filled with examples of discrimination.

## Segregation

*Segregation means holding apart or keeping separate.* Social **segregation** exists in two forms. *De jure* segregation is segregation sanctioned by law. *De facto* segregation is segregation that exists without legal sanction, as a matter of chance or circumstance. When the Supreme Court ruled in 1954 that *de jure* segregation in publicly supported educational facilities was unconstitutional, many Americans thought the problem had been solved. But *de facto* segregation of racial minorities in both the labor force and in residential housing continues much as before.

## Ethnic Group

It is useful to distinguish between ethnic groups and races. An **ethnic group** is *a population socially identified according to cultural criteria, such as language, religion, or national origin.* The social identification of ethnicity may be either imposed by others or self-generated from within the group in question. In the United States, any adherent of Judaism is likely to be classified by others as a Jew, that is, a member of a single ethnic group. In Israel, important distinctions are drawn among Sabras (native-born Israelis), Sephardim (Jews of Spain and Portugal and their descendants), and Ashkenazim (Jews of western, central, and eastern European origins).

Another definition would be that ethnics are *people who share a common cultural origin, real or imagined.* If people think of themselves as having a common origin, they are defining themselves as ethnics. If others perceive them that way, they are being defined as ethnics. To the extent that a fourth-generation Italian-American man identifies with Italian ancestry and cultural practices, for example, he is emphasizing his ethnic heritage, although he might hate Italian food, be unable to speak the language, and have anglicized his name. But even if he personally felt no tie with Italian culture, he might still be treated by others as if he did.

Jews wearing the Star of David in Nazi Germany. The Nazis were unable to distinguish Jews from other people on the basis of the "racial" characteristics they believed in. Thus they had to resort to artifical distinctions, principally the yellow Star of David sewn on clothing.

## Race

The phenomenon of race is widely misunderstood, mainly because, in the Western world at least, it has a peculiar double character. There are popular views of what race is and what it means, and there is a biological definition of race. The popular concepts are largely wrong. In studying minority groups, sociologists must consider both the biological aspects of race and the popular—social—interpretations of race.

**The Biological Meaning of Race** The term *race* first appeared in scientific literature in 1749. At first, skin color was used as an index for classifying human differences. But biologists soon realized that skin color was not a reliable criterion for classifying races because there is no sharp dividing line between one color and another. Scientists then developed categories that included the shape of the head, lips, and

**discrimination:** the differential and unequal treatment of people because of their perceived physical or cultural characteristics.

**segregation** (social): the physical separation of persons on the basis of group membership. *De jure* segregation is separation sanctioned by law; *de facto* segregation is separation as a consequence of fact or circumstance.

**ethnic group:** a population socially identified according to cultural criteria such as language, religion, or national origin.

nose, the texture and shape of hair, and the predominant blood type. But with most of these characteristics, too, there is no clear division between one group and another.

Biologists have now recognized that racial classification based on physical type is arbitrary—that is, it depends on the criteria chosen, and different scientists choose different criteria. Some biologists define three or four races, some twenty to thirty, depending on which characteristics they use to construct racial categories.

Underlying all these racial classifications, however, is the basic biological definition of race perhaps best stated by the noted population geneticist and biologist Theodosius Dobzhansky. Dobzhansky defines *races* as "*Mendelian (interbreeding) populations which differ in the incidences of some genetic variants in their gene pools.*"[21] Put more simply, this means that all human beings belong to one species, because they share the same *basic* genetic makeup; but different populations of human beings show different amounts of *specific* genetic variants, such as differences in skin color and other physical characteristics. For example, light eyes, light, wavy hair, light skin, and narrow noses and lips occur among all people, everywhere. But they are found occurring together, *in combination*, more frequently among the so-called white race than among other peoples.

The difficulty, of course, is deciding which characteristics can best be used to categorize races. It is easy to see that if scientists have trouble defining race, the public is likely to hold confused and wrong ideas about race. And indeed popular views of race are largely inaccurate.

**Popular Misconceptions** Among the many

erroneous interpretations of race, none is more pervasive than the tendency to call ethnic, cultural, and linguistic groups racial groups. This is clearly seen in Nazi mythologies about the Aryan and Jewish "races." Neither of these groups is a biological category, hence the Nazis required all Jews to wear the Star of David. Since they had no unique physical characteristics that would infallibly distinguish them from "Aryans," an observable basis for discrimination had to be constructed.

Perhaps as widespread as the error attributing racial characteristics to ethnic, cultural, or linguistic groups is the error ascribing particular attributes to all members of given racial groups. For example, whites are often thought to be mechanically gifted and warlike; Asians weak-eyed and crafty; and blacks emotionally childlike, lazy, stupid. There is no factual basis for any such beliefs.

A third popular error concerns the nature of race itself. In common American usage, the word *race* is often used as an equivalent of the biological term *species*, and the different races are assumed to be as biologically distinct as different species of animals, say, dogs and cats. This idea, too, is wrong. All human beings are members of a single species, *Homo sapiens*.

**Social Race.** Physical differences, defined either biologically or popularly, are often used as grounds for social differentiation, prejudice, and discrimination. What is important to the sociologist is the way races are defined by *society*. The significance of racial concepts is not their scientific accuracy, but their social reality: whether people believe in and act on their concepts of race.

For this reason, many sociologists have adopted and defined a category called **social race,** a *population whose members share certain inherited physical traits by which they are socially identified.* The essence of this definition is that it is *social.* Thus, skin, eye, and hair color are considered socially significant as indicating race membership, while other inherited physical traits, such as a tendency to freckles, are not. Like the biological definition of race, the definition of a particular social race depends on the criteria chosen by the definers — in this case, society. For the remainder of this chapter, when we refer to race, we will use the term in the sociological sense of social race.

### Structured Social Inequality

Although racial and ethnic groups may both constitute minorities, they are often treated quite differently, as we can see in the United States. In order to understand why and how this happens it is necessary to look at the way American society is organized. *Social inequality means that some persons or groups have greater access to the rewards and benefits of social life;* they are privileged in various ways: politically, economically, and socially. We are most familiar with inequalities and privileges among individuals. All of us know, for example, that the Kennedy and Rockefeller children are born into positions of almost unlimited opportunity. They may be no more competent and ambitious than anyone else, but they have access to resources and opportunities that most people can only dream of. This is how inequality among individuals is expressed, but the notion of inequality and privilege goes beyond individuals.

When social inequality is built into societies and affects entire social groups, it is structured. *Structured social inequality is the creation of inequalities in life chances by the social organization of a society* without regard to the capabilities of individuals. All societies are structured along *some* lines, and all establish basic divisions among their members. The criteria used to make these divisions differ according to what is valued in a particular society. In feudal Europe, and in modern England, a division that separates the aristocracy from commoners is built into British society, and members of the aristocracy have certain special privileges and rewards. A commoner can sometimes share in some of these rewards by earning them; but for the aristocracy, they are an inherited privilege.

Some societies are organized on the basis of racial or ethnic ancestry. These societies are organized so that one race or ethnic group occupies a superior position and others are subordinated. Physical and cultural characteristics are the basis of participation and exclusion. *When race, usually signified by skin color, is the factor determining subordination,* **racism** *is the organizing principle of the society.* Currently, the most obvious example of such a society is South Africa. The black African population there occupies a subservient position politically and economically. One set of rules exists for the white population and different sets for the black and mulatto populations. In an economically stratified society, privileged members may acquire or lose the resources that have placed them above the rest of the population. But in a racially stratified society, members cannot change their skin color, which is the basis of reward or deprivation, and so they cannot change their position in society. In South Africa, neither the whites nor the blacks can change their positions, because racial divisions are part of the basic organization of South African society, a closed system with inescapable effects.

In British aristocracy and South African

**social race:** a population whose members share certain physical traits by which they are socially identified.

**racism:** discrimination based on "racial characteristics," usually skin color.

apartheid, privilege and inequality are organizing principles. Participation and reward are distributed in much the same way as a playground see saw operates. For one group in the system to be elevated or rewarded, another is

---

### 'WAARS U PAS?'—BLACK MAN'S CONSTANT DREAD

The black man in South Africa dreads being stopped by the white policeman who demands in Afrikaans, "Waars u pas?"—Where's your passbook?

Every black who lives in an area "prescribed" by the government—in effect, nearly 90 per cent of the nation—must carry his or her multipaged passbook at all times.

Issued at the age of 16, it contains the bearer's name, address, sex, photograph, vaccination record, government identity number, and proof of tax payments.

Employers must sign it monthly. It also must include stamped approval to live outside one of the nation's ten small tribal homelands.

The passbook is the cornerstone of the detailed pass laws by which South Africa's 4 million whites exercise rigid control over its 18 million nonwhites.

Thus it is unquestionably the most immediate—and most deeply hated—symbol of white authority.

Running afoul of the complicated law is not difficult. If the passbook is missing or not in perfect order, a black person faces a trial as short as thirty seconds and a jail term as long as six months.

Police records show more than 500,000 pass law violations a year. It is estimated that since 1950, there have been more than 10 million arrests.

Chicago Tribune, June 27, 1976. Reprinted courtesy of the Chicago Tribune. Photo by Ernie Cox, Jr.

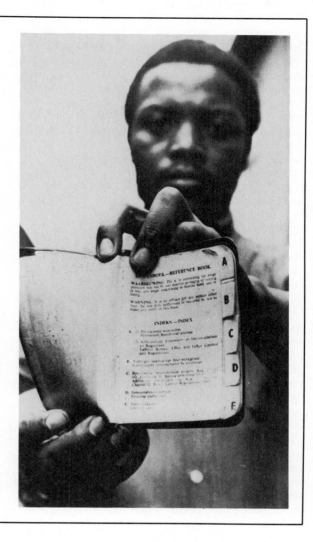

Whites in South Africa do not have to carry passes.

pushed down or depressed. It is difficult for a person with characteristics of either the privileged or the oppressed group to escape the mechanism. Privilege and inequality are not a function of individual determination, but a reflection of group position.

## GROUP SUBORDINATION IN THE UNITED STATES

Every measure of socioeconomic status indicates that certain racially defined groups are consistently at the bottom of the American ladder. The *structural* basis for this group subordination lies, at least in part, in the history of the United States as a host nation to various immigrant groups. All host nations establish a pattern of acceptance or rejection of newly arriving groups. One way to understand the past and present subordinate position of various racial and ethnic groups in the United States is to distinguish between the *absorption* and *inclusion* of those groups.

### Absorption versus Inclusion

In an ideal sense, *inclusion* implies that incoming groups can participate fully in developing new cultural, political, and economic realities. But rather than participating equally in the creation of a new society, racial and ethnic groups in the United States tended to be *absorbed* into a preexisting Anglo-Saxon structure. In all cases, the dominant groups in the host society controlled the absorption of the incoming groups so that preexisting social relationships and organizations would be altered as little as possible. Absorption ranged, with varying degrees of success, from dispersion throughout the various layers of society to total subordination in the position of slave.

**Racial Minorities and White Ethnic Groups**
In the United States, white ethnic and racial groups have experienced widely different degrees of absorption. Originally, there was no intention of fully including the African slaves within the fabric of American society. Graphic evidence of this is the section in the U.S. Constitution, now superseded, stating that a black slave was to be counted as three fifths of a man for the purpose of apportioning Representatives.

While racial groups were placed in a subordinate position based on physical type, white ethnic groups were placed in a subordinate status based on economic position. The implications of these differences between racial and white ethnic groups have been compared by Robert Blauner.[22] The most obvious difference in the experience of racial and white ethnic groups is *how they entered* American society. Most racial minorities—blacks, Native Americans and Chicanos (or Mexican-Americans)—were brought or absorbed into the United States involuntarily. (We treat Chicanos as a racial group because that is the way they have popularly been defined in the United States, even though the U.S. Census classifies them as white.)

Black Africans were taken by force from their homelands and brought to the United States as slaves. During the eighteenth and nineteenth centuries, Native Americans and Chicanos were forcibly incorporated into this country by westward territorial expansion. For both groups, entry into the dominant society was involuntary and was experienced by the group in question more or less *en masse*. By contrast, most European white immigrants entered the United States voluntarily and individually, or in small groups such as the family. Their differences in entry into American society contributed significantly to the different treatment later accorded these groups.

Racial and white ethnic groups were also treated differently *in the labor market*. Europeans in the developing capitalist economy could enter relatively freely into the wage-labor system. As the American economy developed, so did the immigrants' mobility and occupational prestige. The involuntary, unpaid labor done by slaves is in dramatic contrast. A somewhat mixed case would be that of the early Chinese immigrants, who were often brought over *en masse* by labor contractors to work for specific employers at fixed wages.

As a consequence of slavery, the black American was not absorbed into the economy until the beginning of the twentieth century. Slavery also led to the development of two kinds of employment. In the advanced sectors of the labor market—industrial work—entry was voluntary, wages were paid, and there was some mobility across occupational lines. At the opposite end of the spectrum, in the least developed sectors of the economy, labor was often not voluntary, wages were not paid or were very low, and there was little or no opportunity for mobility. Until recently, the best jobs in the voluntary labor market have been reserved for whites. Throughout the periods of increased immigration and absorption of white Europeans into the voluntary labor market, the society largely prevented other racial groups from participating in the advanced sectors of the economy.

Another major difference in the experience of these groups is the amount of *control* they were allowed to exercise over their lives and culture. The white European immigrants faced prejudice, discrimination, and ridicule, but they were allowed to maintain a sanctuary where they could express their cultural traditions. This was the ethnic community. Ethnic newspapers, schools, churches, and theaters grew in these communities; and life, culture, and people were respected within them, if not by the dominant society. The situation of racial minorities was different. Their culture was not tolerated; it was attacked. Slave families were often forcibly dislocated, and slaves were prohibited from speaking their native languages. Both slaves and Native Americans were prohibited from practicing their religions. Native Americans and Chicanos were forced off ancestral homelands that often had deep cultural and religious significance.

These are the structural bases of group subordination in the United States, the lines along which American society is divided. Since these divisions are basic to the social structure of American society, they are re-created in each generation. Thus the subordination of racial and ethnic groups is reproduced over time. The mechanisms through which this occurs are discussed below.

## The Self-Fulfilling Prophesy and the American Dream

When a dominant group assumes that a minority is inherently inferior in intelligence and systematically discriminates against that minority in education and in the economy, then many minority group members are likely to remain or become socially inferior to the dominant group. This *acquired social inferiority* is likely to affirm the assumption of *innate intellectual inferiority* and over the course of time, systematic prejudice and discrimination against the subordinate group will produce a group whose members are actually inferior in education,

---

### A BIOGRAPHY

Crow, James ("Jim"). (No photograph available.) Born about 1870 (exact date and place uncertain). Nationality: American; originally southern. Parents: unknown, but multiple, white, Protestant, probably of Anglo-Saxon stock. Education: public institutions. Widely traveled, Crow became a turn-of-the-century man of affairs. Always particularly active in law as well as national and local politics, he also engaged in medicine, the arts, science, education, religion, sports, entertainment, industry, and labor in addition to long service in the armed forces. By middle-age his influence had been felt on almost every aspect of the American scene and there were few places in the United States which he had not visited. His death has been prematurely announced on many occasions but latest reports indicate that, although enfeebled with age and partially incapacitated by *civil rights,* he is still alive and endeavoring to keep up with his lifelong pursuits. For detailed biographical information, see C. Vann Woodward, *The Strange Career of Jim Crow* (New York: Oxford University Press, 1955).

---

occupation, and income when compared with the dominant group. Unable to acquire education and jobs, they are likely to be unemployed, go on welfare, and resort to crime. They are more likely to live in inadequate housing, get lower scores on standardized tests, and have higher rates of alcoholism and mental illness than the dominant group.

These conditions confirm prejudiced members of the dominant group in their assumptions about the inferiority of the subordinate group. *Such a vicious circle constitutes a self-fulfilling prophesy: An incorrect assumption is accepted as true, and behaviors are adopted that produce the very conditions that make the initial assumption come true.*

Members of minorities tend to be socialized for subordinate roles. If they aspire to roles deemed inappropriate by the dominant group, then prejudice and discrimination are likely to be used to prevent them from gaining professional and managerial positions. *Supporting the self-fulfilling prophesy is the American Dream, the belief that if a person is intelligent and industrious, he or she can succeed—regardless of race, ethnicity, class origin, or other inherited social character-*

*istics.* If this ideology is true, then those who fail have only themselves to blame for their failure. The American Dream thus deflects criticism from the social institutions and the dominant group that controls them. It discourages criticism of our institutions and prevents institutional reform. It perpetuates the system in which opportunity to succeed is dramatically influenced by race, ethnicity, class origin, and other inherited social characteristics, even in America.

### The Making of Subordinate Groups

With the development of modern nationalism and imperialism, expansionist European governments came into contact with subordinate groups of different racial and cultural characteristics.[24] When a relatively homogeneous dominant group comes into contact with subordinate groups of different racial and cultural characteristics, the ruling group must develop policies for the treatment of the minorities. What are these policies?[25]

**Assimilation** *The process in which the minority gives up its own cultural patterns and acquires the cultural patterns of the dominant group,* is called **assimilation.** It may be forced upon the subordinate group if the dominant group punishes the minority for behaving according to its own cultural patterns. Anyone considered incapable or unworthy of being assimilated might be segregated from the rest of the population, expelled from the country, or exterminated. All three of these procedures were imposed upon minority groups in Nazi Germany. Millions of Jews, gypsies, Catholics, communists, and handicapped persons were segregated, subjugated, and exterminated during the Hitler period.

Assimilation may be encouraged without being forced upon the minority. In the United States, assimilation has taken the form of "Anglo-conformity." The dominant group has assumed" the desirability of maintaining English institutions, . . . the English language, and the English-oriented cultural patterns as dominant and standard in American life."[26] As white ethnics migrated to the United States, the educational, economic, and political institutions rewarded those who most readily could learn the English language and assimilate the other Anglo-American cultural patterns. It is no surprise that those immigrants who were most easily assimilated and who suffered the least prejudice and discrimination, were those who were most like the dominant group.[27] Thus immigrants of white British Protestant origins experienced the smallest amount of prejudice and discrimination. Despite the dream that all racial and cultural subgroups would intermingle in a single **melting pot** of American culture, in reality, assimilation has most often been primarily a matter of Anglo-conformity.

**Pluralism** Some minorities resist assimilation. *The policy of* **pluralism** *is the recognition of the persistence of cultural differences in subgroups in the population with no single subcultural group dominating the others.* A good example of cultural pluralism is found in Switzerland. The German, French, and Italian Swiss have retained their separate languages and cultural patterns, but all are bound together in a common political and economic framework. In the United States, some subgroups have maintained cultural differences within the overall framework of the American culture. Many of these groups have their own foreign-language and English publications to promote the interests and identity of the group. These manifestations of cultural pluralism are being given support by civil rights legislation, government programs for minorities, and affirmative action policies.

**Population Transfer** Sometimes the dominant group adopts a policy of physically separating a minority from other segments of the society. This may be an explicit policy in which the dominant group requires the minority to move from one part of the country to another. United States government policy often required Native American tribes to leave their own territories for other specified regions, usually because their land was desired by white interest groups for farming, cattle-raising, railroads, and other purposes. When Japan attacked Pearl Harbor, the United States Government transferred about 110,000 Japanese-Americans to special "relocation camps"; the Nazis transferred millions of persons to concentration camps in Germany and the countries it occupied.

The policy of population transfer is sometimes indirect. The dominant group may impose such severe restrictions upon a minority that they choose to leave the country. This strategy was used by the Nazis in the early 1930s before they adopted overt transfer policies. Similarly, many Russian Jews left their native land for the United States around the turn of the century because of harassment by the Czarist Russian government.

**Continued Subjugation** Sometimes the dominant group retains the minority in a position of continued subordination. In South Africa, for example, although only 19 percent of the population is white and 78 percent is black, the oppressive power of the dominant group is remarkably effective:

South Africa is held together in a condition of "static equilibrium" through a grim mixture of political coercions and economic interdependence. However exploited the Africans are, they depend for sheer physical survival on wage employment in the money economy. To withdraw one's labor is to face nearly immediate starvation. The price of survival at the minimum subsistence level is exploitation, oppression, and degradation.[28]

The policy of subjugation has been applied to all minorities at one time or another in United States history. It was most overtly applied to the racial minorities, Native Americans, blacks, Japanese, and Chinese. Social and economic advantages still accrue to members of the dominant group and to more privileged white mi-

**assimilation:** the process in which a minority gradually gives up its own cultural patterns and acquires those of the dominant group.

**the melting pot:** the belief and concept that the plurality of racial and ethnic minorities in the United States would eventually blend into a new and different "American" compound, their differences disappearing in the process.

**pluralism:** the belief and concept that racial and ethnic minorities can maintain distinctive subcultures and at the same time participate with relative equality in the larger society, with no particular group's culture dominating.

norities, because of the continued subordination of the racial minorities. These minorities are a source of cheap labor for employers and are less likely to compete with more privileged members of the society if they continue to experience systematic discrimination in education, jobs, and housing.

**Extermination** Complete destruction, is, of course, an ultimate solution to the problem of a minority, as perceived by a dominant group. It is estimated that approximately two-thirds of the Native American population was destroyed in the course of establishing the American na-

The Mess hall in a Japanese-American internment camp in World War II. Although the government jailed them for being Japanese, none of these American citizens were accused of any crime. The internment was a pure example of population transfer.

tion-state before policies were changed.[29] A more recent example of extermination as official government policy was that of Nazi Germany. Approximately six million people were systematically destroyed merely because they were Jewish.

Any of these policies may be adopted by a dominant group separately or in various combinations. The policies may change over time and may be implemented with differing degrees of commitment and success. Various leaders of governmental and economic organizations may differ in their commitments. There may be considerable discrepancy between official policy and the informal positions taken by those who control the institutions. There may be a discrepancy between the official policy articulated by those in control and the informal treatment of minorities by individual members of the dominant group. And, of course, all of these policies have been applied individually and in various combinations to the many groups of racial and ethnic minorities in the United States.

*Minority Responses to Dominant Group Policies*[30]

**Assimilation**   Members of a minority group may desire to give up their own cultural patterns in order to avoid the prejudice and discrimination imposed upon them by a dominant group. Their success in achieving assimilation is closely dependent on the dominant group's support and on the minority group's ability to make itself relatively indistinguishable from the dominant group. Those groups that are most different from the dominant group in race, ethnicity, and religion are likely to experience the greatest difficulty in assimilation.

**Pluralism**   The minority may seek to retain its own cultural patterns, but at the same time be given equal opportunity and be integrated into the educational, economic, and political institutions of the dominant group. Some minorities which in the past sought assimilation are now experiencing pluralistic movements on the part of some of their membership. Many blacks are asserting the dignity and merit of the racial and cultural characteristics of their subgroup.

Ethnicity is evidently an important source of community and personal identity for many Americans. On a remote reservation in northern Wisconsin, for example, the author saw large lapel pins with statements such as "Chippewa Power" and "I am proud to be a Sioux." For minorities who do not anticipate the likelihood of successful assimilation, or who do not value the way assimilation may take place, or who fear the social-psychological consequences of assimilation, pluralism may well be a more desirable goal.

**Secession**   If a minority is frustrated in its attempts to assimilate or to achieve a satisfactory pluralistic coexistence, it may seek to separate itself from the society that discriminates against it. In the 1920s Marcus Garvey, a black, sought to create a separate nation in Africa for American blacks. The initial separatist goal of the Black Muslims was that the American government grant them a few states in which to set up their own nation. The movement to create a separate Jewish state in Israel was primarily a consequence of Jews having no sovereign territory in the world where they might be the dominant group and control the economic and political institutions.

**Militancy**   Minority group members who attempt to transform or change societies in radical and revolutionary ways are responding to domination with militancy. Unlike secessionists, the militant wants to stay in the society and change it. But unlike the assimilationist and the pluralist, who also want to stay in the society, although on different terms, the militant insists that the situation be altered drastically. The Puerto Rican activist group, the Young Lords, is an example.

Listing these four ways in which minority groups respond to their situation may be misleading. For one thing, minority groups do not respond to domination in unified or cohesive ways. Each of the four responses may be expressed by different members of a particular minority group at the same time. Although certain kinds of responses may be more appropriate for some groups than others, no one minority group has a monopoly on a particular type of response. During different periods in a minority group's history, certain responses are more appropriate than others, but we can find examples of each type of response during a group's history. The Black Muslims, for example, began as a secessionist movement, went through a militant period, and now, since the death of Elijah Muhammad, appear to be moving toward pluralism.

How minority groups cope with their situation is largely influenced by what they are allowed to do. A modern example makes this point dramatically. Various federal, state, and municipal agencies effectively destroyed the militant response of the Black Panthers by killing some of their leaders, driving others into exile, and jailing the rest. At the same time, the national government encouraged pluralism among black people by offering financial aid to black organizations that were politically acceptable to it. The ways in which minority groups come to grips with domination, then, are heavily influenced by circumstances beyond their control.

**Minority Subcultures**  A subculture is a set of unique customs, rituals, and ways of associating that make a group different from the larger society and the other groups in it. Often these customs are rooted in a foreign cultural tradition. But in many cases, the customs are developed in response to conditions imposed on the group by the dominant elements of society. The Italians who reached American shores at the turn of the century were often as strange to each other as they were to the Americans who met them. They came from many remote areas of Italy, spoke different dialects, and expected different things. Their common experience in America transformed them into a group called Italian-Americans, and the shared expectations they developed became the Italian-American subculture. The same is true for the black subculture. The Africans who were brought to America as slaves came from many different tribes and spoke many different languages. What is known today as black culture was largely created in the United States.

Although minority subcultures have frequently developed as the result of conditions forced on groups, they have often become prized possessions. Many minority group members wish to maintain their subculture. They see themselves as different from the majority of

The Black Panthers are a militant response to minority status. Here the Des Moines group holds a press conference in which they blamed police for a disturbance (1969).

society, and they like their differences. They reject the idea of becoming like the majority. This sentiment is captured by slogans like "Black is Beautiful" and "Kiss Me, I'm Irish."

## MINORITIES IN AMERICAN SOCIETY

So far we have discussed the general concepts and ideas of ethnic and racial relations. Now we can anchor these abstract ideas in concrete realities by focusing on the different experiences of specific minority groups in America.

### Native Americans

**Historical Background.**  Before the white Europeans came, the Americas were peopled by small nations and tribes. They were organized as political units with territorial boundaries. Some nations were full-blown civilizations (the Aztecs and Maya of Mesoamerica and the Incas of South America); others were small societies of farmers and agriculturalists (the Hopi and the Zuni of the Southwest). Some were suc-

---

## HOOVER FEARED PANTHER MEALS
### Richard Philbrick

J. Edgar Hoover viewed the Black Panther Party's free breakfast program for children as a threat to attempts by the FBI to "neutralize the Black Panther Party and destroy what it stands for," a jury learned Friday in Federal District Court.

The late FBI director's opinion of the program was disclosed in an official memorandum by Hoover which was read to a six-member jury hearing evidence in the $47-million suit against the city and various agencies and individuals stemming from a Dec. 4, 1969 police raid on a Black Panther apartment on the West Side.

Fred Hampton, Illinois head of the party, and Mark Clark, a Panther organizer from Peoria, were killed in the raid and some other occupants of the apartment were injured or wounded by gunfire.

Hoover's 1969 memorandum to several dozen FBI field offices was one of a number of government documents surrendered to attorneys for the plaintiffs in the case, survivors of the raid, and relatives of Hampton and Clark.

Hoover instructed FBI agents to investigate funding of the free breakfast program in a way that it would "insure that no implication is created we are investigating the BCP [Breakfast for Children Program] itself or the church where it is being held."

Hoover advised FBI agents there was some indication that donations to the program were being used for other Black Panther activities. Of the breakfast program itself, he wrote in the memorandum:

"The resulting publicity tends to portray the Black Panther Party in a favorable light and clouds the violent nature of the group and its ultimate aim of insurrection."

In his memorandum, Hoover ordered FBI bureaus to consider "appropriate counterintelligence action" which included investigating the source of funds for the program.

Chicago Tribune, May 8, 1976. Reprinted courtesy of the Chicago Tribune.

How minority groups cope with their situation is in part a matter of what the majority allows them to do. Federal, state, and local authorities all responded violently to the Black Panthers' early aggressiveness. Later, when the Panthers turned to such innocuous activities as feeding inadequately nourished children, that too was viewed with suspicion.

cessful fisherfolk (the Tlingit of the Canadian Northwest); others were hunters and gatherers. The diversity of Native American tribes extended to their social organization and cultural beliefs. Each tribe had its own religious beliefs, art forms, and family structure.

The first major thrust of Western contact came with the relatively rapid movement of the Spanish conquistadors in the sixteenth century and later. The Spaniards used a superior technology (including horses, armor, and gun powder) and a political policy of divide and conquer. Moving into the Southwest, they subjugated the Pueblo tribes and placed them in servitude.

The pattern of contact in the colonial Northeast differed in several ways. First, the tribes were caught in the competition between France and England, each of which tried to make allies out of them. Second, there was no cohesive movement of conquerors against them, only a gradual encroachment of settlers into their territory.

The Nation of the Iroquois is a prime example of this pattern of encroachment and hostility. Initially admired by the settlers, the various tribes of the Iroquois nation were soon caught in the struggle between France and England. The tribes managed to maintain their unity up to the American Revolution, but shortly after 1800, torn by internal rivalry, the Iroquois nation disintegrated.

The period from 1849 to the turn of the century marked the opening of the American West and the great Indian wars. By 1890, the major campaigns were over. A half century of upheaval and bloody warfare had resulted in the defeat and subjugation of the Native Americans. Domination proved expensive: perhaps as much as $1 million dollars for every dead Native American.[31] A new policy emerged for physical and cultural control of the tribes. Demoralized and defeated, they were made wards of the state and were placed on reservations.

Three key legislative events made this possible. The first was the Indian Removal Act of 1830, which resulted in the removal of the Cherokee people from their ancestral lands in the mountain country of Georgia, Tennessee, and North Carolina. The congressional declaration of 1871 carried the process one step further. Not only could Native Americans be removed by the will of the American government, but they would no longer be "acknowledged and recognized as an independent nation, tribe, or power with whom the United States may contract by treaty."[32] The last step in the policy was the Dawes Act of 1887. In order to "civilize" the Native Americans, tribal lands were divided among the members of the tribe to fit the pattern of Western private ownership. Native Americans lost 90,000,000 acres of land within forty-five years, as white farmers and real estate speculators bought their holdings or swindled them away from individual Native Americans who often did not understand what their land sale implied.[33]

**Present Status** The past history of the Native American is one of exploitation and oppression, and the present situation is worse than that of any other American minority. They have been left only 2.9 percent of the land area of the United States. The Bureau of Indian Affairs estimates that 14 million acres are "critically eroded," 17 million "severely eroded," and 25 million "slightly eroded." In short, all 56 million acres of reservation land are marginal or submarginal.[34] As Will Rogers, the well-known humorist and a Cherokee, said, "In wars the slogan is Honor, but the object is land. They are always fighting for Independence, but at the finish they always seem to be able to use quite a snatch of the defeated opponent's land to be Independent on."[35]

It is estimated that in 1492 the number of Native Americans living in what is now the United States was from 700,000 to 1,000,000. Approximately two thirds of this population was destroyed by the white settlers' diseases and policies. Recent United States census figures for the contiguous states show a steady increase:

| 1890 | 248,000 |
| 1910 | 266,000 |
| 1930 | 332,000 |
| 1950 | 422,000 |
| 1970 | 793,000 |

Unfortunately the census figures are only available at the beginning of each decade, so our data come only as far as 1970. In 1968 approximately 452,000 Native Americans (57 percent) lived on or near existing or former reservations,[36] where life is grim for most of them.

In 1970, high school graduation rates were 23 percent for rural and 42 percent for urban Native Americans.[37] Of the rural Native Americans (male and female) who headed households, 64 percent had incomes of less than $4000 per year. Only 9 percent had incomes of $10,000 or more. The unemployment rate for rural males was 3.6 times the national rate. Table 8.1 shows how the incomes of Native American males compare with those of the total population.

TABLE 8.1 Median Incomes 1939–1970

| | Native American males (on reservation) | All American males |
|---|---|---|
| 1939 | $ 500 | $2,300 |
| 1949 | 825 | 3,475 |
| 1959 | 1,475 | 5,050 |
| 1970 | 2,749 | 6,614 |

In 1970 one-third of all Native American families were officially classified as poor, as compared to about 10 percent for all American families. The most basic amenities are unavailable to our poorest of minorities, a people who once possessed the continent: 48 percent of those in rural areas and 9 percent of those in urban areas have no toilet facilities. Two-thirds of those who live in rural areas have no plumbing at all.[38]

With these data in mind, we should not be surprised that in the 1960s, Native Americans had a death rate from tuberculosis 400 times that of the general United States population. The life expectancy had risen from 44 years in 1955 to 63–64 years in 1970, but this is still about six years less than the national average. In the 1960s, the adolescent suicide rate was 100 times that of the general population.[39]

Native Americans have increasingly moved to urban areas such as Chicago, Minneapolis, San Francisco, and Los Angeles. Two factors have contributed to this urban movement. The first is the termination of the tribal reservations. In some cases, cash settlements are offered to tribes in exchange for withdrawing all rights and claims to their ancestral lands. The second factor is the desire to find a better life than can be achieved on the reservations. Driven by poverty, Native Americans have often moved to the cities only to find conditions almost as harsh as those on the reservations. In

The shift to an urban environment has offered Native Americans little in the way of opportunity. Homeless people on the sidewalk in Gallup, New Mexico.

many cases, they merely shifted their dependency from the federal government, which administers the reservations, to local and state agencies, which administer urban welfare programs.

### Black Americans

**Historical Background**  If the essential feature of minority group status is social subordination, black people are the classic minority in the United States. Brought to this country against their will and forced to work without compensation, black people experienced the ultimate subordination: slavery.

Slavery warped all aspects of black life, not simply issues related to work. The culture Africans brought with them was systematically undercut. People from the same tribe were placed on different plantations so they could communicate with no one unless they learned English. Black families had no legal status, and family members could be sold away from each other when economic necessity dictated.

Slavery was abolished in 1865, but circumstances still prevented black people from competing with whites on an equal footing. Reconstruction of the South along democratic lines was defeated by compromises worked out between southern reactionaries and northern political interests. Sharecropping replaced slavery. Instead of the slave owners, the state now disciplined blacks and not much changed in the lives of southern black people.

Legally, the former slaves worked for themselves. But in fact they were still enslaved in many ways. Sharecropping was simply a new kind of bondage. By the time sharecroppers paid the farm owner for the use of the land, and for housing, food, and seed, they had very little left. In some cases, they owed the owner more at the end of the year than at the beginning.

Legally, blacks were free, but by 1900 a new structure of law had emerged to keep them powerless. "Jim Crow" laws restricted blacks to "separate but equal" public facilities. Vagrancy laws sprang up that effectively regulated the physical movement of blacks in the South. Blacks needed passes to travel, and if they did not have a certain amount of money they could be declared vagrants and thrown in jail. When laws proved ineffective, extralegal and illegal ways were developed to keep blacks in a subordinate position.

The situation of black people changed significantly in the twentieth century, when large numbers of them began moving north. Pushed by poverty in the South and drawn by industrialization in the North, between 400,000 and 1,000,000 black people migrated northward.[40] There they entered the labor force as service workers and unskilled laborers. While their incomes increased, their participation in the labor force was not complete. Black people were excluded from many unions on the basis of their skin color. The areas in which they could live were also limited as racial ghettos began to emerge in the North.[41]

Residential segregation had two somewhat contradictory but related effects on the black experience. Because of gerrymandering and outside political pressure, blacks could not control the political affairs of their own communities. But they turned the liability of residential segregation to advantage. Prevented from wider participation, black people turned their cultural efforts inward. The 1920s saw an explosion of black literary and musical talent, a period known as the Negro Renaissance.

Black advances were effectively checked by the Depression. Migration essentially ceased, and by the mid-1930s in some sections of the country, nearly 80 percent of black people were on public assistance.[42] Nevertheless, President Franklin Roosevelt's New Deal efforts to deal with the Depression and his appointment of a

"Black Cabinet" were somewhat beneficial to black people. But segregation and discrimination continued. There was discrimination in federal works projects, and housing financed by the Federal Housing Administration was segregated.[43]

The concern for the problems of black Americans that began with the New Deal carried over to the period between 1940 and 1955. Pressured by a march on Washington threatened by black leaders, Roosevelt issued an executive order on fair employment practices in the early 1940s. The combined effects of this order and the wartime economy led to further social and economic gains. By 1948, the armed forces were desegregated and President Truman had issued an executive order banning discrimination. In 1954 the Supreme Court declared unconstitutional the doctrine of separate but equal facilities in public education. The efforts begun in the 1940s culminated in the birth of the modern civil rights movement. On December 1, 1955, Rosa Parks, a black seamstress living in Montgomery, Alabama, refused to give up her seat to a white man on a public bus. Her refusal sparked a massive boycott that was eventually led by Dr. Martin Luther King, Jr.

The 1960s were marked by hope and optimism. The civil rights movement resulted in the passage of civil rights legislation in many states, and a national voting rights act was passed in 1965. Urban unrest was answered in part with federal aid. President Lyndon Johnson declared a War on Poverty. Although it

An old drawing of slaves at work. Despite Emancipation, the social conditions of black Americans did not change significantly until well into the twentieth century.

Martin Luther King, Jr., leads the March on Washington, August 28, 1963.

provoked serious internal dissension, the war in Vietnam provided jobs for many unemployed people. The National Alliance of Businessmen, in conjunction with the federal government, promised programs to employ the hard-core unemployed.

Recent years have seen steady economic progress for many black people. Between 1947 and 1976, black families earning $6,000 or more a year increased from 4 percent to 70 percent.[44] The median annual income of black families went from approximately $1,869 in 1950 to $9,264 in 1976. There was also progress in the black housing situation. Between 1960 and 1975, the number of blacks owning their own homes increased 83 percent[45] with 44 percent of all black families being home owners by 1975.

These figures indicate that, relative to the past, progress has occurred within the black community. But is *equality* — the elimination of the gap between the black and white life situation — occurring?

**Present Status: The Consequences of Racism** The essence of the black experience in the United States has been *racism:* exclusion from the society and its social resources on the basis of skin color. Inclusion, at best, has been reluc-

tant. American society has been organized around the principle that there is a special place for black people, a place separate from and not equal to that occupied by whites. The special limits put on the opportunities available to black people have insured that whites have advantages.

Racism operates on two levels: the individual and the institutional. *Individual racism* consists of individual attitudes and actions that are recognized as prejudice and discrimination. **Institutional racism** is the operation of impersonal, social institutional forces or policies in such a way as to produce outcomes consistent with racial discrimination. Examples of institutional racism include the long history of exclusion of blacks from the craft unions; the reluctance, until recently, to admit black people to colleges and universities or the professions; and the limits placed on participation in professional organizations.

In a highly industrialized economy, formal education is an important way for people to prepare for complex occupational roles. How would you like to be in the labor force today without a high school diploma? Your opportunities for stable, meaningful work with a chance for advancement would indeed be bleak. After more than 400 years of systematic prejudice and discrimination, 56.1 percent of the adult black population — compared with 33.8 of whites — are in exactly this predicament: they lack a high school diploma (see Table 8.2). While only 15.6 percent of blacks go to college, 28.9 percent of the white population do so. Of those who start college, far fewer blacks than whites complete four years. Even these statistics understate the educational problems of blacks. The academic quality of schools in black neighborhoods tends to be substantially lower than that of schools in white neighborhoods. The effect of many years of socioeconomic disadvantage contributes to blacks entering colleges of lower academic quality.

The percentage of nonwhites (87 percent of whom are black) employed in white-collar jobs rose 116 percent between 1960 and 1976, as compared to an increase of only 11.2 percent for whites.[46] As important as this improvement has been, its significance is diminished by the fact that 56.5 percent of the nonwhite population are in unskilled and semiskilled jobs, as compared to only 34.7 percent of the white population. If the white-controlled institutions do not provide the black subgroup with the necessary educational and occupational skills, then it should not surprise us that blacks have an unemployment rate twice as great as that of whites: 12.7 percent for nonwhites, as compared to 6.4 percent for whites, in 1976.[47] For nonwhites aged 16 to 19, the unemployment rate was 35.4 in 1976, as compared to 17.3 percent for whites of the same age. The median income of black families in 1976 was only 59 percent as much as that of white families.[48] While only 9.1 percent of whites were below the poverty level, 29.4 percent of blacks and other nonwhites were below the poverty level.[49]

As we have noted, the dominant group's treatment of a minority frequently involves a self-fulfilling prophesy. In the seventeenth century, whites brought blacks to America to exploit them economically. After centuries of blacks being assumed inferior and being systematically discriminated against in all spheres, black inferiority seems amply supported by objective measurements. The American Dream further supports the myth of inherent black inferiority by placing responsibility for success or failure upon the individual, rather than on the social system. If you are worthy and you work hard, you will succeed. Logically, it follows that if you fail, you have no one to blame but yourself. If blacks are substantially less successful than whites, it must be their fault. Such an analysis conveniently deflects attention, criticism, and action away from the institutions and those who control and benefit from them.

*Asian-Americans*

According to popular mythology, Asian-Americans have overcome racial adversity; they are proof the American Dream comes true. In many ways, however, the treatment received by Asian-Americans duplicates the experiences of

**institutional racism:** the operation of impersonal, social institutional forces or policies in such a way as to produce outcomes consistent with racial discrimination. For example, the neighborhood school concept is probably a sound one in elementary education and was certainly invented without regard to race. But its use in American cities today perpetuates racial segregation in the schools since urban American neighborhoods are segregated.

other racial minorities. To complicate matters, there are important differences *between* Asian-American groups. The experiences of Japanese- and Chinese-Americans highlight these issues.

**Chinese-American History** The first large-scale immigration of Chinese began in the 1850s. During the next thirty years, more than 300,000 Chinese made the difficult voyage across the Pacific to America. They left China because of floods, famines, and revolution, and came to the United States because of the discovery of gold in California, cheap passage, and the possibility of indentured labor. The Chinese were not universally welcomed. White miners in California, fearing unfair competition from the cheap Chinese labor, organized to keep the Chinese out of the mines. White businessmen tried to legalize serfdom by making the Chinese "contract laborers." The Chinese faced harassment of all sorts, including mob violence, miners' "taxes," and expulsion from some towns. By the time they began to migrate to the Midwest and East, they were the focus of a full-scale anti-Chinese movement.

This movement resulted in three types of anti-Chinese legislation.[50] The first restricted or excluded Chinese immigration to the United States. After years of trying to limit Chinese

TABLE 8.2   Levels of Education, by Race, for Persons 25 or Older, 1976

| Race | Elementary | | | High school | | College | | Median years completed |
|------|-----|-----|---|-----|-----|-----|---|-----|
| | 0–4 | 5–7 | 8 | 1–3 | 4 | 1–3 | 4 | |
| All | 3.9 | 7.1 | 9.7 | 15.3 | 36.3 | 13.0 | 14.7 | 12.4 |
| White | 3.0 | 6.4 | 9.7 | 14.7 | 37.3 | 13.5 | 15.4 | 12.4 |
| Black | 11.3 | 13.9 | 9.2 | 21.7 | 28.2 | 9.0 | 6.6 | 11.1 |

An anti-Chinese riot in Denver, Colorado, 1880.

immigration through state taxes, the Congress in 1882 passed a measure that suspended the immigration of Chinese laborers for ten years and made Chinese born in China ineligible for American citizenship. The Geary Act of 1892 extended the restriction another ten years, and in 1904 Congress extended the exclusion of the Chinese indefinitely and unconditionally. That was the situation until 1943, when the Chinese exclusion act was repealed. In 1968, a new immigration act was signed that repealed quotas based on national origins.

A second kind of legislation was used to eliminate Chinese competition with whites. California levied taxes on Chinese miners and fishermen. A "police tax" required that all "mongolians" who had not paid the miners' tax pay the state $2.50 a month. Such legislation usually proved to be unconstitutional, but it stimulated other ways of keeping the Chinese from competing with white workers. With few exceptions, the labor movement organized to push Chinese workers out of the mines. Racially inspired strikes, riots, and boycotts forced the Chinese out of numerous occupations and into crowded Chinatowns.

The third type of legislation attacked the Chinese community and its culture. The queue, or braid—a badge of citizenship worn by males in China—was effectively eliminated by an ordinance specifying that male prisoners have hair only one inch long. Since the Chinese were frequently arrested, few braids survived. Similarly, the Chinese tradition of burying the ashes of the dead in the home village in China was virtually eliminated by an ordinance that required permission from coroners to remove the dead from cemeteries; permission was seldom granted. By 1910, the Chinese population was limited in size, restricted to marginal occupations, and powerless. Their status remained basically unchanged until the 1940s.

**Present Status**   The 1970 census listed 432,002 Chinese in the United States. Most are concentrated in three states: 39.5 percent in California; 19.0 percent in New York; and 12.2 percent in Hawaii. Seventy percent of the Chinese live in central cities.[51] In spite of over a century of prejudice and discrimination, the Chinese have achieved a high level of success. They have attained a higher level of median education (12.4 years) than the total population (12.1 years).[52] In 1970, 55.8 percent of adult Chinese males were in white-collar jobs, as compared to 41.2 percent of white males.[53] The median family income of Chinese-Americans was a little over $10,000, as compared to the national median of $9,500.[54] Nonetheless, college-educated Chinese compete less successfully with college-educated whites, earning less money with the same amount of education.

The integration of the Chinese into the society has been through formal education and the occupational system. Traditional Chinese culture placed a high value upon industriousness and education as a means of occupational advancement.[55] These values were integrated into a cultural framework that encouraged the subordination of the self to the interests of the family. This has contributed to Chinese educational and occupational success within the American society. Yet their primary group patterns are more characteristic of pluralism.[56]

Approximately 85 percent of the Chinese marry within their racial and ethnic groups. Most Chinese marriages are no longer arranged by the parents, and much greater heterogeneity and freedom are evolving among the various subgroups that constitute the American Chinese. Yet it is doubtful that the dominant group in the American society desires and will accept the full assimilation of the Chinese-American. The experience of prejudice is still common, as the following quotation illustrates: "As a third generation American, a Korean War G.I., a Stanford doctorate, I am typical of other Asian-Americans who are outraged by statements such as: 'How long have you been in the U.S.?' and 'You speak English quite well.' "[57]

**Japanese-American History** Japanese immigrants began arriving on the mainland, usually in California, in the 1880s. The anti-Oriental sentiment directed at the Chinese quickly focused on them as well. In the opening years of the 1900s, business and labor leaders in San Francisco organized an anti-Japanese movement intended to exclude them from the United States. In 1906, the San Francisco school board directed all Asian schoolchildren to attend one school designated the Oriental School. When the Japanese government protested this treatment, President Theodore Roosevelt negotiated a bargain with them that came to be known as the Gentlemen's Agreement. Japan agreed to stop the emigration of its workers, and the president agreed to discourage a law limiting Japanese immigration.

In 1922, the Supreme Court ruled that Japanese born in Japan could not become citizens of the United States. The Court based its decision on the first naturalization act of 1790, which stated that citizenship was available, under certain conditions, "to any alien, being a free white person." This decision was later cited to sanction legislation specifying that people who were not eligible to become citizens could not own or lease land. Thus, the Japanese were prevented from voting, and their chances for competing with white farmers were severely limited.

This was not the last time the Japanese received harsh treatment because of their color and national origin. Three months after Pearl Harbor was attacked, President Franklin Roosevelt signed Executive Order 9066. This gave military authorities the power to designate certain parts of the country as military areas and to remove "any or all persons" from such locations. Although the United States was at war with Germany and Italy as well as Japan, and despite the fact that there were numerous instances of German subversion on the East Coast and none on the part of Japanese in the West, *all* mainland Japanese—aliens and citizens alike—were ordered to leave the west coast and move inland. One month later, they were placed in relocation centers for the duration of the war.

The Japanese internment or relocation camps of World War II are sometimes referred to as concentration camps, but the implications of that term are inaccurate. The Japanese-Americans were neither killed, starved, nor physically mistreated by the authorities. But they were unconstitutionally interned and deported from their homes, which they were forced to dispose of with losses estimated to average $10,000 per family,[58] and they were kept confined against their will without due process of law. A final irony is that the threat they supposedly represented never materialized. No Japanese-American in the continental United States or in Hawaii was ever convicted of sabotage or espionage during World War II. Financial restitution was made by the U.S. government only years later, and then it was only partial.

**Present Status** In 1970 there were 373,983 Americans of Japanese descent living on the mainland, 64 percent of whom resided on the West Coast. Although the Japanese have experienced high levels of prejudice and discrimination, they have made an extraordinary adjustment to life in the United States. The Japanese immigrants brought with them a unique complex of beliefs, values, and norms. The culture of nineteenth-century Japan was a mixture of tradition and modernity. On the one hand, the Japanese were socialized to subordinate themselves to the interests of family, community, and nation. Superimposed on the traditional values were those fostered by the industrial revolution in Japan: ambitious pursuit of educational and occupational success, rationality, risk-taking, and tolerance for insecurity.[59] This complex of attitudes has contributed to a remarkable level of success for the Japanese in America.

In 1970, Japanese-American adults had

achieved a higher level of median education (12.5 years) than the national total of 12.1 years. The percentage of Japanese-Americans who had completed high school and college was greater than that of the total population.[60] Japanese-Americans are more likely to have white-collar jobs than the total U.S. population. Similarly, the median income of Japanese families was $2,900 higher than the national average.[61] But in spite of the level of success attained by the Japanese in the United States, Japanese-Americans still achieve a lower level of success when compared with non-Japanese of the same education and age.[62]

The Japanese pattern of accommodation has been interesting. They have succeeded within the framework of the American educational and occupational systems, yet they have not apparently sought or attained assimilation at the primary group level. Most Japanese marry within their subgroup, and a large majority (about two-thirds) have other Japanese as their best friends.[63] The response seems to be a complex amalgam of partial assimilation and pluralism.

### Hispanic-Americans

We suggested earlier that minority groups are created and defined by their historical experience. Chicanos (Mexican-Americans) and Puerto Ricans are the most obvious example of this process. Though geographically and culturally distinct, these two groups share two important experiences. The early explorations of the Spanish conquistadors in both Mexico and Puerto Rico resulted in a merger of Hispanic with indigenous Indian culture. This merger created a distinct cultural unit. The other element these groups share is their proximity to their territorial homelands.

**Chicano History.** When English-speaking "Texicans" successfully revolted against Mexico in 1846 and then a few years later brought Texas into the Union, thousands of Spanish-speaking Texans became American too. Later, the Mexican-American War led to great portions of the Southwest and California becoming part of the United States.

The treaty that ended the conflict between Mexico and the United States in 1848 specifically guaranteed the property rights, political

Chavez leading a boycott of nonunion farm products.

rights, and cultural autonomy of the Chicano population. But these rights were quickly violated. First, the treaty promised early statehood, but while California and Nevada were quickly admitted to the Union, New Mexico and Arizona did not become states until sixty-four years after the treaty was ratified.

The second violation revolved around the question of land. According to the treaty, original land grants made to individuals by the Republic of Mexico were to be honored by the United States. But the growing westward migration of "Anglos" (English-speakers) made it increasingly difficult to uphold the treaty. By the close of the nineteenth century, the Chicano population, once a numerical majority holding parcels of land in the Southwest, was reduced to the status of a disenfranchised minority.

In the twentieth century, the changing conditions of farm labor have played a significant role in Chicano life. At the close of World War I and again during World War II, the United States actively recruited farm labor from Mexico. This *bracero* program was supposed to guarantee good working conditions and reasonable wages. But these guarantees were largely farcical.[64] At least one aspect of the agreement, however, was rigidly enforced: the braceros were not allowed to accept employment in the industrialized sector of the economy. This provision had the effect of forcing them to compete at fixed low wages against Chicano agricultural workers who were United States citizens. The result was that the braceros tended to drive the Chicanos out of the market.

**Present Status** Mexico and the United States share over 2,000 miles of border. An estimated 600,000 Mexicans have illegally crossed this border every year since 1973. In 1973 alone 480,000 illegal aliens were apprehended and returned by the Border Patrol. There are at least one million illegal Mexican nationals living in the United States.[65] Why? Mexico has a per capita income about one-sixth that of the United States, and it has one of the world's highest unemployment rates (almost 50 percent by some estimates).[66] The choice for many native Mexicans is to live in grim poverty at home, or to emigrate to the United States in search of work.

Some say this illegal migration relieves the Mexican government of some of its employment problems. Thus Mexico may be less than diligent in restraining the traffic. Because the United States is now interested in Mexico's vast resources of natural gas and oil, caution must be exercised in handling the issue. Further, there is evidence that some illegal Mexican immigrants take low-paying temporary jobs that Americans do not compete for, and that few settle permanently in the United States.[67]

In 1976 there were 6,590,000 Americans of Mexican origin in the United States, 76.8 percent of them living in metropolitan areas.[68] Sixty-seven percent of the adult Chicanos had not completed high school, as compared with only 33.9 percent of the white population.[69] In 1972 their median family income of $7,908 was about $3000 lower than that of the total population.[70] In 1976 the median income of households of Spanish origin (59 percent of whom are Chicano) was only 75.4 percent of the national average.[71] Twenty-two percent of all families of

Mexican-American origin were below the poverty level in 1976, as compared with 9.3 percent of all families.[72] These statistics show that the Chicanos are one of the poorest minorities; only Native Americans, blacks, and Puerto Ricans among the larger minorities have lower median incomes.

**Puerto Rican History** Puerto Rico became an occupied territory of the United States at the end of the Spanish-American War (1898). A civil government was established, but the President of the United States appointed all government officials, including the governor of the island. At the onset of World War I, Puerto Ricans were made citizens of the United States. On the island, Puerto Rican nationalism began to assert itself, and two important factions developed within the nationalist movement. One segment sought full independence for Puerto Rico and an end to U.S. rule. A second group was willing to accept a sort of commonwealth status under the protection of the United States. In 1948, the first free elections were held in Puerto Rico, and Luiz Munoz Marin, a supporter of the commonwealth, was elected governor. In 1952, the Puerto Rican people voted to accept the status of an "associated free state."

Because of poverty and limited economic opportunity, many Puerto Ricans migrated to

Many Puerto Ricans on the mainland live in or near New York City where they have created a Latin society.

the mainland hoping to better their life chances. First as inhabitants of a territory, and later as citizens of an associated free state, they were able to migrate without restriction. In the 1930s, there were less than 55,000 Puerto Ricans in the United States. Today, there are approximately 1.7 million, thanks largely to the development of air travel.

One sociologist estimates that "an average of 20,000 contract farm laborers have been coming to the mainland each year."[73] The Puerto Rican government has attempted to negotiate and control basic protection for these laborers, but even so, the conditions of employment are often exploitive and harsh. Many Puerto Ricans leave farm labor as soon as they can.

**Present Status** In 1976, 97 percent of the 1,753,000 Puerto Ricans living in United States lived in metropolitan areas, primarily in and around New York City.[74] Seventy-seven percent of the adults had not graduated from high school.[75] In 1972, their median family income was $7,163, or 64 percent of the median family income of the total population.[76] In 1976, 23.7 percent of all families of Spanish origin were below the poverty level, as compared with only 9.3 percent of all families in the population.[77] The Puerto Ricans are one of the poorest minorities, ranking behind only the Native Americans and blacks.

### White Ethnics

**Historical Background** **White ethnics** *are whites of European origin who are not from northern Europe or are not Protestant.* From the very beginning of the American republic, "foreigners" have often been regarded with suspicion and treated with prejudice and discrimination. The Alien and Sedition acts, passed in 1798, helped discourage easy naturalization for the new immigrants by requiring them to live in the United States for fourteen years before they could become citizens. In the first half of the nineteenth century, the largest number of immigrants were from Great Britain, Ireland, and Germany. As more and more came, resistance began to develop. The phrase "No Irish Need Apply" appeared on many job notices.

As the twentieth century approached, the tide of immigration changed. New immigrants began to arrive from southern and eastern Europe. The Italians, the Poles, and the Russians arrived in time to catch the last glimmers of the great urban-industrial expansion, but unskilled labor was still needed. This last major wave of immigration was confronted by renewed Anglo ethnocentrism. By the turn of the century, some Bostonians had formed the Immigration Restriction League, a group devoted to excluding southern and eastern Europeans because of their alleged racial inferiority. One influential advocate of this movement was Madison Grant, the author of *The Passing of the Great Race in America.* The great race was, of course, the "Nordic race."

The southern and eastern Europeans were portrayed as mentally defective, criminal, and vulgar. Intelligence tests were indiscriminately given to many of the immigrants from southern and eastern Europe, without considering that most of them knew no English, were totally unfamiliar with American culture and came from the lowest social classes in their countries of origin. The test results "proved" that the immigrants were inherently inferior: 83 percent of the Jewish immigrants and 79 percent of the Italian immigrants were labeled "feebleminded."[78] Such "evidence" led to harsh prejudicial stereotyping of these white ethnic groups.

It is urged that the Italian race stock is inferior and degraded; that it will not assimilate naturally or readily with the prevailing Anglo-Saxon race stock of this country; that intermixture, if practicable, will be detrimental; that servility, filthy habits of life, and hopelessly degraded standards of needs and ambitions have been ingrained in Italians by centuries of oppression and abject poverty; that they are incapable of any adequate appreciation of our free institutions and the privileges and duties of citizenship; that the greater part are illiterate and likely to remain so."[79]

The assumption of the biological inferiority of southern and eastern Europeans prompted the adoption in 1914 of a restrictive immigration policy based on a quota system. The system favored immigrants from Great Britain and the Scandinavian countries at the expense of the newer immigrants from southern and eastern Europe. The quotas were based on the population figures of the 1890s, which meant that "twelve out of fifteen newcomers had to be from Britain, Ireland, Germany, The Netherlands, and Scandinavia. Victory had gone to the Nordics."[80] It is no small irony that some of these allegedly inferior ethnic minorities have in the 1970s outstripped all or most of the white, northern European, Protestant groups in education, occupation, and income.

**Religion and Ethnicity**   There is no way to understand the experience of ethnic life outside the context of religious affiliation. America was not only dominated by an Anglo-Saxon elite; it was also predominantly Protestant. Many of the nineteenth century immigrants to the United States were members of two important religious minorities: Roman Catholicism and Judaism.

Much of the discrimination faced by the Irish immigrants stemmed from hostility to Roman Catholicism. In the 1840s and 1850s, the Know-Nothing party gained many adherents because of its antiforeign stance and the fears it expressed about Catholic loyalty to the papacy. The Ku Klux Klan also expressed strong anti-Catholic sentiment.[81] This recurrent fear of papal loyalty appeared as late as 1960, when some Americans questioned John Kennedy's loyalties. Was he Catholic or American?

Anti-Semitism has been even stronger. As late as the 1880s, the American Jewish community, made up largely of German Jews, was not singled out for harassment. But with the growing migration of eastern European Jews, anti-Semitism began to flourish in America, gaining strength in the first quarter of the twentieth century. In the 1920s, the Ku Klux Klan expanded its horizons to include Jews in its diatribe of hate. Jews were described as belonging to the ''Semitic race,'' obviously different from, and inferior to, the ''Aryan race.'' They were associated with radical and foreign ideologies, such as Bolshevism and anarchy. Many notable Americans have expressed anti-Semitic views, including Henry Ford, publisher of the *Dearborn Independent,* who warned his readers of the ''Jewish menace.'' He publicized a discredited document known as *The Protocols of the Elders of Zion,* that outlined a conspiratorial plan allegedly developed by Jewish leaders, to enslave the Christian world. Overt discrimination against Jews remained widespread until after World War II, with many organizations excluding Jews and some universities limiting the number of Jewish students.[82]

While religious differences often were the object of discrimination and persecution, reli-

> **white ethnics:**   there is no conventional agreement among sociologists on precisely what this term means, but it may be usefully defined to refer to whites of European origin who are not from northwest Europe or are not Protestant.

gion also acted as a basis of solidarity for ethnic communities of both Jews and Roman Catholics for a century after 1850. In the case of the Jews, religion was the common bond for three distinct groups of immigrants: the Sephardic Jews from Spain and Portugal, who first arrived with America's earliest settlers; the German Jews, most of whom arrived between the 1820s and the 1870s; and the eastern European Jews, who followed them. Each of these groups had a distinct national culture, but their religion bound them together. Within the framework of religion, they established numerous projects to aid newly arriving immigrants. And as anti-Semitism grew, American Jewry consolidated its ranks and resources in order to survive.

Religion played a similar role in the transition from immigrant group to ethnic group among Roman Catholics. In an attempt to maintain its hold on the newly arrived immigrants, the Roman Catholic church allowed the devel-

Immigrants.

opment of ethnically defined local parishes, and the church became a center for social and recreational activities within the ethnic community. Perhaps the most significant contribution was the development of a Catholic education system, which provided upward mobility for generations of white ethnic groups. By encouraging the ethnic parish, the church not only helped define the meaning of ethnic identification, but also provided a structure that tied various ethnic groups together.[83]

**Present Status** Tables 8.3 and 8.4, based on studies conducted by the National Opinion Research Center at the University of Chicago between 1963 and 1972, show the degree to which many white ethnics have moved into the middle class. The two ethnic groups with the highest average education and the highest average family income are the Jews and the Irish Catholics. The Jews have, as a group, 2.4 years more education than the national average and a mean family income $3,324 higher than the national average. Irish Catholics have achieved an average education 1.3 more years than the national average and an average family income $1,667 over the national average. Americans of British Protestant origins have the third highest level of average education and average family income, but these statistics do not mean that people of white British Protestant origins do not dominate the economic and political institutions.

**The Continuing Relevance of Ethnicity** An ethnic group is a population socially identified according to cultural criteria, and whose "social identification" might be self-generated or imposed by others. Thus, more informally, ethnics could be called people who share a common ancestral origin, real or imagined. Until very recently, sociologists generally assumed that in the United States, at least, ethnic origins would become less and less important socially as time passed and that ethnicity would diminish in significance as a sociological variable, perhaps eventually disappearing altogether. This, however, has not occurred. Several factors seem to have contributed to the persistence of ethnicity in American life, all having to do with the quality of social identification.

One is the matter of self-identification. If people *think of themselves* as ethnics, they will remain ethnics. Ethnicity arises from and is continually re-created by shared experience and cultural tradition and may be expressed in political and marital patterns, social practices, and so forth. Another factor is the reactions of others. If other people persist in treating a group as ethnic, and the others are in a position of social dominance, the definition will persist. The subordinated group may even adopt and cling to this definition in fierce defiance, thus reinforcing the continuing ethnic identification. Ethnicity also has political uses. Many of the immigrant groups used ethnicity as a basis for political power and advancement.

Perhaps the most important factor in the persistence of ethnicity in the United States is the elemental yet profound need of most humans for a group that validates their sense of belonging, uniqueness, and self-worth. American society is highly industrial, urban, secular, bureaucratic, and heterogeneous. Most of us live

**TABLE 8.3** Education among Selected Ethnic Groups (in percentages)

| Religious-ethnic group | Not completing high school | High school graduates | With some college | College graduates | Average years of education completed |
|---|---|---|---|---|---|
| British Protestant | 31.8 | 31.0 | 21.1 | 16.1 | 11.9 |
| Irish Protestant | 48.8 | 28.7 | 15.7 | 6.7 | 10.6 |
| Catholics | | | | | |
|   Irish | 26.3 | 34.1 | 22.6 | 17.0 | 12.2 |
|   Italian | 46.2 | 35.8 | 10.7 | 7.3 | 10.7 |
|   Polish | 51.5 | 33.1 | 10.3 | 5.1 | 10.0 |
|   Slavic | 46.0 | 38.4 | 10.5 | 5.1 | 10.4 |
| Jews (Eastern European) | 15.7 | 30.6 | 19.4 | 34.4 | 13.3 |
| National average | 44.2 | 30.0 | 15.0 | 10.8 | 10.9 |

TABLE 8.4   Occupation of Heads of Household and Income Deviation from
National Average, by Ethnic Group

| Religious ethnic group | Unskilled and service jobs | Crafts and skilled jobs | Clerical, sales | Professional, managerial, farm owners | Deviation of family income from national average family income |
|---|---|---|---|---|---|
| Protestant | | | | | |
| British | 22.3% | 19.2% | 16.0% | 42.7% | +$   721 |
| Irish | 30.7 | 23.4 | 13.6 | 32.3 | −$   566 |
| Catholic | | | | | |
| Irish | 23.1 | 25.3 | 12.5 | 39.2 | +$1,637 |
| Italian | 36.0 | 24.5 | 12.6 | 26.9 | +$   391 |
| Polish | 36.5 | 28.6 | 17.5 | 17.4 | +$   351 |
| Slavic | 36.3 | 29.6 | 11.2 | 22.9 | +$   165 |
| Jew (Eastern European) | 11.0 | 10.3 | 28.3 | 50.4 | $3,324 |
| National average | 34.0 | 20.2 | 13.1 | 32.7 | $7,588 |

in large urban areas where we can neither know nor care about most of the people around us. We work in impersonal bureaucracies and are primarily valued only insofar as we can contribute to the impersonal goals of groups and individuals with whom we come into contact. According to Erich Fromm,

The physiologically conditioned needs are not the only imperative parts of man's nature. There is another part just as compelling, one which is not rooted in bodily processes but in the very essence of the human mode and practice of life: the need to be related to the world outside oneself, the need to avoid aloneness. . . . Religion and nationalism, as well as any custom and any belief however absurd or degrading, if only it connects the individual with others, are refuges from what man most dreads: isolation.[84]

For many people ethnicity remains an important basis of group support and of social identity.

## THE CONTINUING DOMINANCE OF WHITE NORTHERN EUROPEAN PROTESTANTS

Although increasing numbers of Orientals and white ethnics have moved into the middle and upper middle class; the economic and political institutions are still heavily dominated by Americans of white British Protestant origins. In his research on the national upper class in the 1960s, one researcher found that most of the largest corporations were still controlled primarily by men of Anglo-Saxon Protestant backgrounds: "Top management is predominantly Protestant, with Catholics poorly represented, and Jews virtually excluded."[85]

A more recent study of the most important elites in the nation identified 4,000 people in private corporations, government, and education who make the major decisions that affect the well-being of the entire nation:

Great power in America is concentrated in a tiny handful of men. A few thousand individuals out of 200 million Americans decide about war and peace, wages and prices, consumption and investment, employment and production, law and justice, taxes and benefits, education and learning, health and welfare, advertising and communication, life and leisure.[86]

The social characteristics of these elites were "at least 90 percent Anglo-Saxon" and "there were very few recognizable Irish, Italian, or Jewish names." There "were only two blacks and apparently no Mexican-Americans, Native Americans, or Japanese-Americans among the top 4,000."[87]

### Racial and Ethnic Pluralism

Horace Kallen, the man who introduced the concept of cultural pluralism into the American vocabulary, used the image of the orchestra to describe the United States. Just as each instrument in the orchestra makes a distinct contribution to the musical composition, each minority group makes its particular contribution to American society. Kallen conceived each instrument—each group—as participating equally in this orchestration of social life.[88] But the image of an orchestra and the pluralist perspective derived from it are misleading. There is a tendency toward pluralism in America, but all groups have not shared equally in the society. Equality in America is a goal, not a fact. The relationship between minority and majority groups has not been based on equality; it has been based on power.

The concept of pluralism has to be modified to be faithful to American reality. There seem to be two kinds of pluralism: a pluralism of equality and a pluralism of subordination. In pluralism of equality, subcultural groups would interact in harmony, like the instrumentalists in the orchestra to which Kallen refers. Ethnic and racial subcultures would coexist on an equal basis, and no group would be able to force its way of life on others. Power and status would not be a function of ethnic or racial ancestry, and groups would be able to choose which, if any, aspects of another group's culture they wished to adopt. There would be agreement on who conducted the orchestra and how that conductor was chosen. The criterion for being conductor would not be ethnic or racial ancestry.

A different picture emerges from the pluralism of subordination. In this situation, ethnic and racial subcultures are not treated equally, and the relationship between them is not harmonious. Some subcultures are encouraged or permitted to flourish; others are attacked or co-opted. Perhaps more important, a group's ethnic or racial background is crucial in determining how it will share in a society's social resources. Some groups are included in, and others excluded from, full participation in society on the basis of their racial or ethnic ancestry. Subordination is not a random occurrence; it is systematically related to a group's race or ethnic background. Finally, to return to the orchestra analogy, consensus does not determine the conductor or the music to be played; power does. And that power is derived in large part from ethnic and racial status.

Pluralism in the United States is often a pluralism of subordination. The persistence of racial and ethnic distinctiveness does not occur in an egalitarian setting, despite an ideology to the contrary. As we have seen throughout this chapter, racial and ethnic differences have tra-ditionally structured the basis of social reward. Racial minorities have been either excluded from, or restricted to the margins of, society. Some ethnic minorities are isolated and often work at low-status occupations. Only ethnic groups whose cultures resemble Anglo-Saxon values—or at least do not conflict with them—have managed to excel.

## Subcultures and Supercultures

The pluralists are correct in pointing out that ethnic and racial subcultures persist. But their contention that people can be both ethnics and Americans minimizes the costs and consequences involved. They do not take seriously enough the push toward assimilation. The melting pot notion is instructive, for it does suggest that there is a culture with which all Americans have to contend. This culture might be called an American superculture: a culture that crosses racial and ethnic boundaries and that must be accepted if one is to operate in the larger society, even when acceptance means the end of ethnic identity.

The superculture that pervades American life is not the new nationality to which the melting pot referred. Nor is it the American Creed assumed by the pluralists. Essentially, it is a culture rooted in the western European tradition. Unless groups are willing and able to accept crucial aspects of this culture, they are denied complete access to American life. In this respect, the black essayist Harold Cruse has a more accurate perception of the American superculture than either the melting pot advocates or the pluralists. "America," he says, "has grown up planlessly and chaotically, leaving her racial and ethnic minorities to shift for themselves while she cultivates the idea that America is an all white Anglo-Saxon nation."[89]

Cruse is correct. But in fact the United States is neither all white nor all Anglo-Saxon nor all Protestant. Indeed, the WASPs who dominated American social, political, and economic life for so long are numerically a small minority in the American population. The great promises of the Declaration of Independence and Emma Lazarus's poem enshrined on the Statue of Liberty have not yet been kept, but it is too early to conclude they never will be. Structured social inequality is under attack on many fronts in the United States and may yet be overcome.

## THE NEW COLOSSUS
**Emma Lazarus**

Not like the brazen giant of Greek fame,
   With conquering limbs astride from land to
     land;
   Here at our sea-washed, sunset gates shall
     stand
A mighty woman with a torch, whose flame
Is the imprisoned lightning, and her name
   Mother of Exiles. From her beacon-hand
   Glows world-wide welcome; her mild eyes
     command
The air-bridged harbor that twin cities frame.
"Keep ancient lands, your storied pomp!" cries
   she
   With silent lips. "Give me your tired, your
     poor,
Your huddled masses yearning to breathe free;
   The wretched refuse of your teeming shore.
Send these, the homeless, tempest-tost to me.
   I lift my lamp beside the golden door!"

Inscribed on the pedestal of the Statue of Liberty,
1903.

## SUMMARY

A minority group is any social aggregate against whom categorical discrimination is practiced by those who control the economic or political institutions of the society. The source of institutional prejudice lies in the dominant group's control of the institutions. Prejudice, discrimination, and segregation are used as mechanisms to subordinate the minority. Prejudice is the prejudgment of a group on false assumptions. Negative emotional components are usually an integral part of prejudice. Discrimination is the differential and unequal treatment of a category of people because of their alleged physical or cultural characteristics. Segregation is the separation of dominant and subordinate groups to sustain advantages for the dominant group. Segregation may be sanctioned by law (*de jure*) or exist without legal sanction (*de facto*). Prejudice and discrimination toward minorities frequently results in a self-fulfilling prophesy. False prejudgments are made about the minority but, because of the discriminatory treatment of that minority, the dominant group may produce the social conditions which give plausibility to the initial prejudgment. The American Dream gives support to the self-fulfilling prophesy by placing the burden of success or failure upon the individual, rather than upon the social system.

The creation of dominance and subordination among heterogeneous groups within the same society became a problem with the creation of nation-states in the post-Medieval Period. Dominant groups may adopt different policies toward subordinate groups: assimilation, pluralism, population transfer, subjugation, and extermination. These policies may all operate together or in different combinations toward one or a number of different minorities at the same time or at different times. In the United States the official policy has tended to shift over time from subordination to assimilation or pluralism. Assimilation has been most applied to white ethnics. Subjugation was applied most harshly and for the longest periods to Native Americans and blacks, both racial minorities.

A minority may adopt different responses in its relations with the dominant group: assimilation, pluralism, secession, and militancy. Most minorities have taken all four postures at one time or another in their histories, and all four may exist within a given group at one time.

The major racial and ethnic minorities in the United States were surveyed. A brief history was given of each, with an analysis of its present position within the class structure. The Native American is the most disadvantaged of all minorities in the United States. The blacks are second although they are the largest of all minorities, with 11.5 percent of the total population. The Puerto Ricans and Chicanos are predominantly in the lower strata, but the Chinese, the Japanese, and many of the white ethnic groups have achieved educational, occupational, and income levels that place them above the national average. This upward mobility has been primarily into the middle class, rather than into the controlling positions in the economy and government.

Popular conceptions of the United States depict it as possessing a unified culture based on essentially Anglo-Saxon values and practices,

and these certainly are national norms. But the United States is, in fact, a plural society composed of a great variety of racial and ethnic minorities. To a considerable extent, although in varying degree, these groups remain separate but unequal in the social structure. The idea of the nation as a melting pot implies that racial and ethnic groups have been blended into a *new* cultural compound, but in fact this has not occurred. Some partial blending has occurred, particularly in white groups, but it results from the acculturation of minority group members to the dominant Anglo culture. Subcultures still coexist uneasily with the American superculture, and minority group members experience varying strains toward both assimilation and separatism. Social inequalities, some of them severe, persist on the basis of minority group membership. And although many of these have been notably reduced in the past half century, the promise of equality has not yet been fulfilled.

## SUGGESTED READINGS

BLAUNER, ROBERT. *Racial Oppression in America.* New York: Harper & Row, 1972. This book offers a provocative analysis of the treatment of blacks in America as a form of "internal colonialism," that racial oppression has been a guiding principle of American society.

FEAGIN, JOE R. *Racial and Ethnic Relations.* Englewood Cliffs, N.J.: Prentice-Hall, 1978. This is a very readable, comprehensive, and systematic survey of the minorities in the United States. Particular focus is given to the institutional sources of prejudice and discrimination.

GREELEY, ANDREW M. *Ethnicity in the United States: A Preliminary Reconnaissance.* J. Wiley, 1974. An outstanding analysis of the different patterns of accommodations of white ethnics to the American society. This book offers pertinent data on the different degree to which minorities have succeeded in the United States.

MOORE, JOAN W. *Mexican Americans,* 2d ed. Englewood Cliffs, N.J.: Prentice-Hall, 1976. An excellent brief analysis of Mexican Americans as a minority.

ROSE, PETER I. *They and We: Racial and Ethnic Relations in the United States.* 2d ed. New York: Random, 1974. This is a very brief and readable introduction to the problem of minorities in America.

SKLARE, MARSHALL. *American Jews.* New York: Random, 1971. This is an excellent brief sociological analysis of the position of Jews in the United States.

# Chapter 9
# Cities and
# Social Life

I saw the skyline grow, and I saw the city grow, and sometimes I wonder if it was worth the price we paid. In those days we did not need interracial movements or good-will groups. Then a neighborhood meant so much.

Here in the most cosmopolitan community since the beginning of time, a city composed of sons and daughters of every one of the forty-eight states, and with men and women from every country in the civilized world, we worked together. Here where there were and are more Irishmen than in Dublin, more Italians than in Rome, more Germans than in any other city than Berlin, and more Jews than in Palestine—here we lived together in peace, like one great family, and should so live today and tomorrow.

We all went to school and to the fields of sport—with little rancor, no real hatred. We lived like human beings, who asked only the opportunity to work out our earthly existence and worship our God according to the dictates of our conscience.

This I hold to be humanity. This is democracy. This was New York of the yon days.

James J. Walker, former mayor of New York, speech, 1946

How is the faithful city become an harlot! it was full of judgement; righteousness lodged in it; but now murderers! Thy silver is become dross, thy wine mixed with water: Thy princes are rebellious and companions of thieves: everyone loveth gifts and followest after rewards: they judge not the fatherless, neither doth the cause of the widow come unto them.

Isaiah 1:21—23

These very different commentaries introduce the subject of this chapter: the intriguing, complex, dangerous, and perhaps ungovernable phenomenon we call the city, where it came from, where it is now, and where it may be going. Cities are as old as civilization (the two words have the same linguistic roots and the same root meaning), and have always been its glory and despair. Many city people have looked back upon their early years with the kind of nostalgia displayed by Mayor Walker in the quote above, and it has only been in this century that the ancient division of the human population into city people and rural dwellers that is mirrored in Isaiah's lament has disappeared among the industrial nations.

Cities are rapidly becoming the dominant form of human settlement. Whereas in 1950 only 16 percent of the world's population lived in large cities, by 1970 nearly 24 percent did, and current population trends suggest that by the year 2000, 40 percent of the earth's inhabitants will be metropolitan dwellers. Not only are more people living in cities, but the number and size of cities are increasing. For example, in 1975 the world had approximately 1,950 large cities, a rise of 103 percent during the preceding 25 years; by the end of the century, 3,600 such cities are expected. While the average size of ''large'' cities (100,000 or more inhabitants) in 1950 was 422,000, by 1975 this average had risen to 523,000 with a projected average of 645,000 by the year 2000.[1] In short, residence in increasingly large cities is becoming the norm for the majority of the human population. Indeed, by the year 2000 much of the population of the world is expected to live in sprawling **urban** concatenations like Calcutta, which already has 177,000 persons to the square mile, roughly three times the number crowded into present-day Manhattan. What life will be like then—whether it will even be *possible*—is not at this time clear.

But that cities themselves will be with us, we may be sure. They have been on the scene for 6000 years or more, and in their essence are probably not much changed. They have tended to dominate the thought and life style of every society in which they have occurred, and they dominate the entire world today. Such peace as there is between the major nations is bought by holding one another's cities hostage to the threat of thermonuclear holocaust; and every advance in science, art, literature, medicine, music, philosophy, and even theology is the product of urban minds and urban ideas. No matter where we live, we are the people of the city and its captives.

The trends in the size and concentration of urban populations raise two fundamental questions. First, *as cities grow in size and number, how will patterns of behavior and social relationships be affected?* For example, it has long been known that crime rates are higher in cities than in less populous areas. Are crime and other forms of deviant behavior inevitably linked with urban living? Must the growth of cities be halted in order to preserve the social order? Other problems also arise as cities grow. The recent fiscal crises in New York City and Cleveland are examples. Can cities grow so large that the necessary services they provide, like garbage collection, police protection, and recreational facilities, become too costly? Or are there explanations and solutions to these problems that are independent of the urbanization process? These issues are some of the concerns sociologists have about cities.

A second set of issues is suggested by another question: *Is urban organization so complex that the common person cannot adapt satisfactorily?* Much has been written about the stress of urban living. Anyone who has waited thirty minutes for a traffic jam to clear, or pleaded with an unresponsive bureaucrat to get a cracked sidewalk repaired, has experienced the complexity of urban social organization. Do such conditions lead to alienation, feelings of powerlessness, estrangement, and isolation? Is the social climate of the city so oppressive and hopeless that people tend to withdraw from social interaction and community involvement? Many sociologists explore the problems of the social

Calcutta today.

psychology of urban life, that is, the relationship between urban organization and individual predispositions and behavior.

This chapter will focus on both the sociological and the psychological aspects of cities. It will begin with an introduction to the basic concepts of the nature of cities and a brief history of urban development. Attention will then be turned to a review of research on the modern city, with emphasis on the United States. The chapter will close with some observations on the future of the city.

## BASIC CONCEPTS AND DEFINITIONS

Of the several criteria that have been used to define the city, none provides a universally acceptable definition.[2] One definition is based primarily on population size, but there is wide

> **urban:** of or relating to *cities.*
>
> **urbanized area:** a U.S. Census term meaning a *city* or two contiguous cities of 50,000 or more inhabitants, plus any densely populated surrounding territory.

international variation as to the size a population must reach in order to be defined as a city or urban unit. The United Nations uses 20,000 inhabitants as the lower limit for defining an "urban agglomeration".[3] Davis arbitrarily chooses 100,000 inhabitants as the minimum number constituting a city.[4] The U.S. Bureau of the Census currently recognizes two types of urban units. An **urbanized area** consists of *a city (or two contiguous cities) of 50,000 or more inhabitants plus the surrounding densely settled territory.* **A Standard Metropolitan Statistical**

**FIGURE 9.1    Standard Metropolitan Statistical Areas**

SMSAs (shown in white) cross state boundaries as well as local governmental boundaries. The size of the SMSAs reflects the size of counties. Note the large Phoenix-Tucson area, which covers more land area than any of the Atlantic seaboard SMSAs, which have much larger populations.

**Area (SMSA)** consists of *one or more contiguous and functionally integrated nonagricultural counties containing at least one city (or a pair of cities) with at least 50,000 inhabitants.*

Another way to define the city is in terms of administration: A city is normally established in law or in governmental practice as a corporate entity of some kind with a set of administrative mechanisms and clearly defined jurisdiction limits.[5] Thus the city consists of the territory lying within these administrative boundaries, but again there is no international agreement on the political or administrative criteria to be used.

Sociologists generally define the city in terms of its social institutions and interpersonal relations. In a classic article, Louis Wirth defines the city as "a relatively large, dense, and permanent settlement of socially heterogeneous individuals."[6] Social institutions like the educational system and the division of labor become highly specialized and differentiated; primary groups, like the family, are weakened; social relations tend to be impersonal, and social norms lose their power of constraint so that diverse forms of behavior arise and come to be generally tolerated. Sociological definitions of the city are intuitively compelling, but difficult to formulate.

The city has also been distinguished in terms of the psychological attributes of its inhabitants.[7] The city dweller is exposed to a variety of social and physical stimuli, leading to "psychic overload." Adaptations to these diverse stimuli are sometimes said to result in a distinctive "urban personality," characterized by traits such as aloofness, distrust, anxiety, and individualism.

In short, the city can be defined in various ways. A comprehensive definition would include all of the criteria mentioned above—population size, administrative boundaries, social diversity, and individual orientations—and perhaps others as well, for example, the absence of agriculture, and a highly developed communication and transportation technology. The relevance of these criteria will become apparent in the discussion that follows.

### Urban Processes

Cities can also be considered in terms of the processes through which they are created and maintained. **Urbanization** is the *concentration of population in localities defined administratively as urban.* It can involve both an expansion of the *number* of points of concentration (that is, the number of cities) and an increase in the *size* of individual concentrations. In most societies today, both kinds of urbanization are evident, albeit in varying degrees. Urbanization is the result of two demographic processes: natural growth (the excess of births over deaths within the locality) and net migration (the excess of immigrants over emigrants).

Not to be confused with urbanization is **urbanism,** *the psychological and behavioral characteristics of urban dwellers that distinguish them from rural inhabitants.* Urbanism can be seen as a response to the demographic and social structural climate of the city. The development of a distinctively urban way of life may be reflected in "how people dress and speak, what they believe about the social world, what they consider worth achieving, what they do for a living, where they live, whom they associate with, and why they interact with other people"[8] The manifestation of urbanism varies considerably in different people and in different cultural settings.

A great deal of sociological attention has been devoted to the organizational changes that accompany urbanization. One of these is increasing *social differentiation.* In rural communities, economic and social functions necessary to maintain the population are carried out by a few groups, for example, the family and the church; but the city gives rise to a myriad of highly specialized groups and organizations. Socialization of the young, for instance, is no longer handled exclusively by the family, but primarily by the schools, youth associations, and the mass media. Community administration no longer resides with a council or elders or a single kin group, but is divided among a variety of officials, agencies, and public interest groups. In brief, the institutional and organizational bases of urban society, dramatically evident in the modern city, are characterized by a high degree of social differentiation.

Social differentiation of urban society, then, results from institutional and group specialization. Paradoxically, however, specialization and differentiation increase the interdependence among groups and institutions and lead to another characteristic of the city, *functional integration.* This means that a network of linkages—in communication, exchange, transportation, and systems of social regulation—underlies the urban social order. The urban family, for example, depends upon schools, retail and wholesale suppliers, recreational facilities, and a host of additional organizations to meet the needs and desires of its members.

Thus the city is not easily characterized. Most obviously, it is a concentration of population centered within more or less identifiable administrative boundaries. The social organization of cities tends to be more complex than that of towns and rural areas. Personal orientations and life styles in the city are correspondingly diverse and distinct from those of rural populations. In later sections of this chapter, these generalizations will be discussed and elaborated.

## THE GROWTH OF CITIES

Population concentrations require an adequate supply of food. The development of the first villages was thus dependent upon innovations in horticultural and agricultural technology, as well as natural resources and a benign climate that would permit the production of a food surplus. Only then was it possible to withdraw labor from food production and apply it to the production of other goods.[9] These innovations included the domestication of plants and animals (100,000–7000 B.C.), the development of irrigation techniques (around 5000 B.C.), the invention of the plow (around 4000 B.C.), and the development of metallurgy (around 3000 B.C.). Each of these additions to the cultural heritage of humankind made it possible to support increasingly large sedentary populations.[10]

### The Preindustrial City

The earliest "cities," which emerged in Mesopotamia around 3500 B.C., would hardly be called cities today. Nevertheless, they were ten times as large as the Neolithic villages that preceded them.[11] The city of Ur (The Biblical Ur of the Chaldees) may have housed almost 34,000 inhabitants by 2000 B.C.[12] It is possible that prior to the Roman Empire no city exceeded 200,000 residents.[13] Generally, these early cities were relatively small in both population and land area.

The preindustrial city was characterized by quite distinct and universal patterns of spatial and social organization, whether it was located

> **Standard Metropolitan Statistical Area (SMSA):** A U.S. Census term meaning one or more contiguous and functionally integrated nonagricultural *counties* containing at least one city or pair of cities with 50,000 or more inhabitants.
>
> **urbanization:** the concentration of population in localities defined administratively as urban. The word may refer either to growth in number of cities or increase in city size.
>
> **urbanism:** the psychological and behavioral characteristics of urban dwellers distinguishing them from rural inhabitants.

in the Near East, the Orient, or the New World.[14] The nexus of social life was the center of the city, where the major governmental and religious buildings were located and the elite resided. This concentration of the important people and public buildings was due to the rudimentary level of communication and transportation. Interaction among the elite required face-to-face contact. Further from the city center was an area where shops and the residences of craftsmen were located. The poorest urbanites and the farmers lived on the periphery of the urban settlement.

The social organization of preindustrial cities was highly stratified. Power resided with governmental and religious leaders, and social status was ascribed rather than achieved. Accordingly, there was little occupational mobility; a person learned a trade and practiced it for life. Social contacts were limited to others of the same caste or class. Social control was maintained through primary groups, especially those based on kinship. Status differences were extreme. People were either rich or poor, and life chances were promising only for the rich. Health, wealth, and education were the prerogative of the few.

### The Transition to Industrialism

European urban development was uneven from the fall of Rome in the fifth century A.D. through the middle of the eighteenth century.[15] During the feudal period (about 550–1100 A.D.), cities declined to a maximum of 2000–3000 inhabitants. In the Middle Ages, cities began to grow again, but even during the Renaissance they frequently had populations of only 20,000–

Above: The walls of Jericho. These may be the first city walls ever built.
Below: Ancient Jericho as it appears today.

30,000. A few cities during this period—Paris, Florence, Venice, and Milan—may have reached 100,000 inhabitants.[16]

A recent analysis of historical population data estimates that between 100 and 1850 A.D., there was little increase in the proportion of the world's population living in cities.[17] This figure hovered around 4–6 percent for nearly seventeen and one-half centuries. Then, primarily in Europe, urban populations began to grow rapidly. The major stimulus was the industrial revolution, a turning point in the world's urban history.

### The Industrial City

The major consequences of the industrial revolution, which is generally dated between 1750 and 1850, were the substitution of machines for hand tools and the replacement of animate sources of energy by inanimate sources. These developments "broadened the economic capacity of society. With the application of new and revolutionary forms of technology to manufacturing, transportation, and warfare, the basis was laid for the growth of cities larger than the world had ever seen before."[18]

Industrialization led to the rise of factories, and factories required workers. Thus began the migration of rural folk to the cities, a process that continues unabated today in most countries. Early industrial cities continued to expand primarily through migration until the early nineteenth century. At that time, death rates, which had been as high or higher than birth rates in most industrial cities, began to fall as a result of improvements in sanitation, nutrition, and medical care (see Chapter 10). As mortality declined, without a concomitant drop in birth rates, urban populations increased in size and number even more rapidly.

By about 1920, 14 percent of the world's population was living in cities of 20,000 or more inhabitants, ranging from 5 percent in Africa to 41 percent in Northern America.[19] By 1975, 30 percent of the human population was residing in localities with a population of 20,000 or more. Northern America again showed the high figure (65 percent), but the lowest proportion (17 percent) was in South Asia.[20] The growth of large cities, those of 100,000 or more, shows a similar pattern (see Chapter 10).

The spatial organization of early industrial cities was similar to that of preindustrial cities. As communication and transportation technology began to improve, however, this pattern changed. The advent of the telephone, trains, and automobiles made the urban population much more mobile. No longer was it necessary

A medieval European city.

for the elite to live near their place of work, so the more prestigious residential areas began to shift toward the periphery of the city. The major administrative, commercial, and financial offices were also freed to move away from the city center, although the trend was less evident for these nonresidential structures. Cities that developed after modern innovations in communication and transportation have a spatial structure quite different from that of the older urban centers, with a much wider dispersion of commercial, industrial, and administrative centers.

As we would expect, the typical industrial city manifests a distinctive social organization. Industrial cities are characterized by:

1. extensive division of labor
2. emphasis on innovation and achievement
3. lack of primary ties to a localized neighborhood
4. breakdown of primary groups, leading to social disorganization
5. reliance on secondary forms of social control, such as police
6. interaction with others as players of specific roles rather than as total personalities
7. destruction of close family life and transfer of its functions to specialized agencies outside the home
8. tolerance for diversity in values and religious beliefs
9. encouragement of social mobility and working one's way up
10. universal standards applicable to all, in such matters as the law, weights and measures, and prices.[21]

This profile of urban social organization in the modern world purposely exaggerates for purposes of contrast, but there can be little doubt that most industrial cities more or less conform to this model.

It should be evident that today's urbanite faces a different experience from that of his counterpart in Mesopotamia, Classical Greece, or even nineteenth-century England. This is not to say that urban life is uniform in all contemporary cities. Quite the contrary, the urban experience varies considerably among nations and cultures, as well as among cities within a particular country. Nevertheless, it is possible to describe general patterns of social organization and individual conduct that are applicable to a variety of urban settings in the modern world. The following sections will do so, drawing primarily on research conducted in the · United States.

## SOCIAL ORGANIZATION OF THE MODERN INDUSTRIAL CITY

One perspective on urban social organization reflects an interest in the spatial differentiation of the metropolitan community. It is often referred to as urban ecology.[22] The ecological approach to metropolitan structure has a long tradition in sociology, beginning in the early part of this century with the work of Robert E. Park and his colleagues at the University of Chicago.[23] As cities increase in size and density, social processes such as competition, dominance, succession, and segregation result in a sifting and sorting of the population into functional areas of land use, economic activity, socio-economic status, and cultural heritage.

Not only has the spatial organization of the city changed during the process of urban development, but so too have its social institutions.[24] Some of these transformations are reflected in institutional structure, for example, decreasing family and household size, and the growth of governmental bureaucracies. The functions of urban institutions have also changed, evidenced by the increased variety of activities encompassed under the umbrella of formal education and the diverse goals of voluntary groups to which urban residents may belong. Institutional change can be interpreted as a necessary adaption to new conditions created by the ongoing processes of urbanization and industrialization, but one must be extremely cautious in assigning causal significance.

### Metropolitan Structure

Several models have been developed for describing the ecological structure of cities (see Figure 9.2). It should be remembered that these models are ideal types that approximate the general configuration of a particular class of cities. They do not correspond perfectly to any particular city.

The *concentric zone model* was developed by Ernest W. Burgess, based upon his observations of Chicago's growth pattern.[25] According to Burgess, urban expansion follows a pattern of concentric zones, each defined by characteristic land use. At the core of the city is the central business district (CBD), an area of retail trade, light manufacturing, and commercialized recreation. Surrounding the CBD is a "zone of transition," primarily a residential area populated by marginal types—the very poor, recent immigrants, and social outcasts—although it may also contain some luxury housing. This zone is transitional because it is in the path of the expanding CBD, and land is frequently purchased on speculation so that it can be sold to commercial developers. The third and fourth zones are residential locales for working people and the middle class, respectively. Slightly further from the CBD is an area of upper-class housing, while on the periphery of the city's political boundaries is a ring of satellite towns and suburbs whose residents commute daily to places of work in the city.

An alternative model, proposed by Homer Hoyt, is called the *sector theory* of urban growth.[26] After examining data on sixty-four small and medium-size U.S. cities, as well as several larger cities, Hoyt concluded that growth patterns assumed the shape of pie-shaped sectors. The characteristics that best defined each sector were rental value and type of land use. Historically, high-rent residential areas have moved outward from the CBD along one or more sectors, generally following lines of transportation. Areas abandoned by the upper income groups are later taken over by lower income populations. A similar pattern would hold for the movement of industrial and commercial patterns of land use.

A third model of urban structure, the *multiple nuclei theory* differs from the zonal and sector approaches in postulating not one but several centers for the city.[27] Urban growth expands from the various centers, each of which specializes in an activity such as retailing, wholesaling, finance, or government. Multiple centers are postulated because of the need for specialized facilities, the benefits to be gained from co-location of similar activities, and the inequalities among the ways different activities

**FIGURE 9.2   The internal structure of cities**

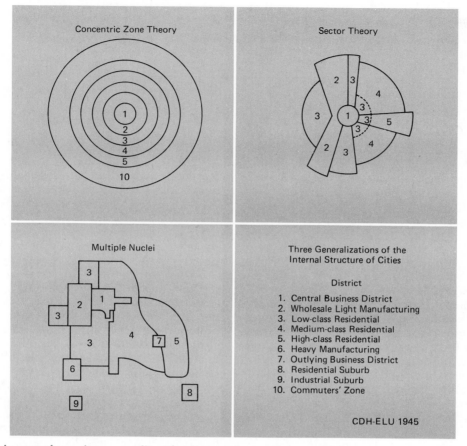

The concentric zone theory is a generality. The diagram for multiple nuclei
represents one possible pattern among innumerable variations.

compete for the most desirable locations. The multiple nuclei pattern is more characteristic of newer cities.

None of the three models provide a universally applicable description of the structure of all industrial cities, though each is more or less applicable to some cities. What these models do convey is the idea that cities do not grow randomly, but rather assume identifiable configurations that, once formed, influence future patterns of growth. Moreover, each of the three models shows how the internal structure of all cities is functionally differentiated into commercial, manufacturing, industrial, and residential areas.

The process by which residential areas of the city come to be differentiated is commonly referred to as *segregation*. Segregated communities may arise from personal choice, as when members of a particular ethnic group choose to reside in the same area, or from factors over which residents have no control, for example, land values or racial discrimination. The principal bases of segregation in industrial cities are the socioeconomic characteristics of residents— race, ethnic affiliation, occupation, income, and religion. Numerous studies have been conducted to determine the degree of residential segregation in American cities and to ascertain whether local communities are becoming more or less segregated.[28] Results from these studies are not totally consistent, varying in terms of the measure of segregation they employ, the characteristics they examine, and the cities they include. Generally, however, there is agreement that residential areas in American cities are relatively highly segregated in terms of residents' race, ethnic background, and occupation. For example, for 207 cities in 1960, the average index of dissimilarity (the percentage of whites or blacks who would have to change their residential block to produce an unsegregated distribution) was 86.1.[29] More recent studies suggest that residential segregation has probably declined slightly through the 1970s, but is unlikely to disappear in the near future.[30] Finally, residential segregation appears to be most evident in very large cities (over 500,000 inhabitants).

As cities grow, the distinction between the central, or *inner*, city and the suburbs becomes increasingly apparent. The extent and pattern of differentiation varies considerably according to the age and location of the city. The older cities of the Northeast, such as New York and Baltimore, are more likely to correspond to the Burgess concentric zone model, with residents' socioeconomic status (SES) increasing with distance from the city center. In newer cities, like Tucson and Albuquerque, this pattern is completely reversed, with the highest SES levels in the city rather than the suburban area. Of course, many cities do not show city-suburban differences that conform to these distinctive patterns.[31]

The changing composition of cities and suburbs is largely a function of population redistribution. Although by 1975, nearly three-quarters of the United States population resided in SMSAs (compared with less than one-third in 1900, had such units been recognized then), growth has been increasingly concentrated in suburban rings rather than in central cities for at least the past fifty years. By 1970, 54 percent of the SMSA population resided outside central cities, and the figure estimated for 1977 is 58 percent.[32]

Population decline is especially evident for the older and larger cities (see Table 9.1). A recent Census Bureau report shows that 13 of the 20 largest United States cities—mostly in the Northeast and Midwest—lost population between 1970 and 1976. Significant gains were evident, however, in southwestern and western cities.[33] Overall, between 1970 and 1977, central cities showed a population decline of 5 percent while suburban areas increased their number of inhabitants by 12 percent.[34]

Several factors may be responsible for the declining population of central cities—high rents and land values, shortages of desirable housing, crime, racial conflict, congestion, and pollution—but the chief influence has been a shift of jobs toward the suburbs. Between 1948 and 1967, 85 percent of the new jobs in manufacturing, retail and wholesale sales, and selected services were located in suburban areas.[35] Moreover, between 1947 and 1972, metropolitan central cities in this country lost a net total of 1,146,845 manufacturing jobs while their suburban rings gained 4,178,230.[36] Again these trends vary by age and size of the city. Contrary to the national trend, younger and smaller central cities are experiencing gains in manufacturing and retail trade jobs.[37]

By no means, however, is the central city losing its economic functions. It serves as a service center, coordinating the specialized activities distributed throughout the metropolitan region.[38] These include administrative offices, government agencies, the professions, finance, insurance, and real estate.

As urbanization proceeds, cities, suburbs, and nonmetropolitan areas are increasingly integrated into regional and national units. Communication and transportation networks link people and organizations widely dispersed in space. Goods and services are exchanged between city and countryside, resulting in a functionally integrated hierarchy of metropolitan areas and intermediate localities.

**Suburbanization: Nassau County, New York.**

TABLE 9.1    Estimated Population Change, 1970–1976, for the Twenty Largest U.S. Cities

| 1976 Rank | 1970 Rank | City | Estimated 1976 population | Absolute change, 1970–1976 | Percent change, 1970–1976 |
|---|---|---|---|---|---|
| 1 | 1 | New York | 7,422,831 | −472,732 | −6.0 |
| 2 | 2 | Chicago | 3,074,084 | −295,273 | −8.8 |
| 3 | 3 | Los Angeles | 2,743,994 | −65,819 | −2.0 |
| 4 | 4 | Philadelphia | 1,797,403 | −199,395 | −6.6 |
| 5 | 7 | Houston | 1,455,046 | +222,244 | +18.0 |
| 6 | 5 | Detroit | 1,314,206 | −199,395 | −6.6 |
| 7 | 8 | Dallas | 848,829 | +4,428 | +0.5 |
| 8 | 6 | Baltimore | 827,439 | −78,348 | −8.6 |
| 9 | 14 | San Diego | 789,059 | +92,032 | +13.0 |
| 10 | 15 | San Antonio | 783,765 | +129,612 | +20.0 |
| 11 | 11 | Indianapolis | 708,867 | −37,435 | −5.0 |
| 12 | 9 | Washington | 700,130 | −56,380 | −7.4 |
| 13 | 20 | Phoenix | 679,512 | +97,950 | +17.0 |
| 14 | 17 | Memphis | 667,880 | +44,350 | +7.0 |
| 15 | 13 | San Francisco | 663,478 | −52,196 | −7.0 |
| 16 | 12 | Milwaukee | 661,082 | −56,290 | −7.8 |
| 17 | 10 | Cleveland | 625,643 | −125,236 | −17.0 |
| 18 | 16 | Boston | 618,250 | −22,821 | −3.6 |
| 19 | 19 | New Orleans | 580,959 | −12,512 | −2.0 |
| 20 | 31 | San Jose | 573,806 | +112,594 | +24.0 |

Metropolitan areas, the units in the functional hierarchy, are differentiated and linked in sequences ranging from areas specialized in administration on a national scale, through regional to subregional and local areas. Here and there within the areas encompassed in the intermetropolitan system are small central-place hierarchies, subordinate usually to a nearby metropolitan area.[39]

## Metropolitan Institutions

The changing structure and functions of industrial cities are reflected in the organization of their social institutions. Trends in population size, distribution, and composition, along with economic differentiation and improvements in transportation and communication, have resulted in institutional adaptations to meet the changing needs of groups and individuals. For some institutions, the transformation has been so drastic that there is little resemblance to their counterparts in nonmetropolitan areas. For others, there has been only slight modification of earlier institutional forms.

**The Family**    Though it varies widely in form and functions in different cultures and societies, the family is a key institution in all communities. Some sociologists have argued that urbanization weakens family solidarity through the development of groups and institutions that compete with the family for the allegiance and time of its members.[40] Others contend that while living arrangements and family structure may be altered by urbanization, relationships within larger kinship networks are not necessarily diminished.[41] With a few exceptions, students of the family have assumed that it is directly influenced by urbanization.[42]

Recent data for the United States show differences in family structure between metropolitan and nonmetropolitan areas and, within the metropolitan component, between central city and suburban populations (see Table 9.2). Contrary to popular belief, there are no significant differences among residential types in average family size, average number of children, or in the proportion of families with children under 18 living at home. Trends toward smaller families and fewer children are evident in all three areas, when data for 1977 and 1970 are compared. However, there are significant differences by area of residence in the proportion of families headed by women and the proportion of households consisting of primary individuals (persons maintaining a household while living alone or with nonrelatives). Both of these

**TABLE 9.2** Selected Characteristics of Families and Households, by Race and Type of Residence, for the U.S. Population, 1977 and 1970

| | Metropolitan areas | | | | Nonmetropolitan areas | |
| | Central cities | | Suburban areas | | | |
| | 1977 | 1970 | 1977 | 1970 | 1977 | 1970 |
|---|---|---|---|---|---|---|
| **All Races** | | | | | | |
| Mean size of family | 3.30 | 3.50 | 3.42 | 3.68 | 3.39 | 3.58 |
| Mean number of children for families with children | 2.10 | 2.29 | 2.05 | 2.34 | 2.16 | 2.42 |
| Percent without children under 18 years old | 46.3 | 45.1 | 42.8 | 39.5 | 45.2 | 43.1 |
| Percent maintained by women | 20.7 | 15.7 | 10.9 | 8.4 | 11.0 | 9.6 |
| Percent primary individuals[a] | 32.0 | 26.1 | 19.2 | 15.1 | 21.1 | 17.9 |
| **White** | | | | | | |
| Mean size of family | 3.18 | 3.35 | 3.39 | 3.60 | 3.32 | 3.49 |
| Mean number of children for families with children | 1.99 | 2.21 | 2.03 | 2.30 | 2.09 | 2.34 |
| Percent without children under 18 years old | 50.7 | 48.3 | 43.9 | 40.0 | 46.7 | 44.2 |
| Percent maintained by women | 15.4 | 12.3 | 9.9 | 7.9 | 9.0 | 8.3 |
| Percent primary individuals[a] | 32.9 | 26.6 | 19.2 | 15.0 | 21.2 | 17.8 |
| **Black** | | | | | | |
| Mean size of family | 3.69 | 3.96 | 3.80 | 4.23 | 4.23 | 4.55 |
| Mean number of children for families with children | 2.39 | 2.66 | 2.31 | 2.80 | 2.74 | 3.20 |
| Percent without children under 18 years old | 31.5 | 31.5 | 27.0 | 29.2 | 30.2 | 30.2 |
| Percent maintained by women | 41.4 | 30.5 | 28.7 | 22.2 | 34.0 | 25.2 |
| Percent primary individuals[a] | 29.5 | 23.9 | 19.8 | 17.4 | 21.4 | 19.9 |

[a]Based on number of households. All other figures based on number of families.

types of household are considerably more prevalent in central cities.

Several differences in family structure are evident between blacks and whites. Blacks have larger families, more children, and a much higher proportion of families headed by females. The fact that more black families live in central cities than in suburban areas suggests that the increase in the rate of female-headed families in the suburbs could be an indicator of significant structural change in the white American family.[43]

Other trends in family structure are evident in (1) a recent rise in the age at marriage, (2) a slow but continued increase in the divorce rate, (3) an increase in voluntary childlessness, and (4) a greater variety of living arrangements, particularly as reflected in the number of unmarried couples living together.[44] Precise connections between residential type and family structure have yet to be identified. Certainly the differences we observe between central city, suburban, and nonmetropolitan populations in the United States do not provide evidence of sweeping effects of urbanization on the family institution. Nor does an examination of historical data lead to such a conclusion.[45]

The expectation that urbanization leads to a breakdown in family integration can also be questioned.[46] Studies suggest that even though kin are more likely to live in different households and to be more geographically dispersed, there is still relatively frequent contact among them. Even in large cities, relatives depend more on one another for advice and aid than on nonrelatives. In short, studies of urban families

While urban families do not differ much from other families, the proportion of households maintained by women is higher in the city than elsewhere.

The belief that urbanization leads to family breakdown is questionable, but it *is* accompanied by changes in traditional functions. More and more urban families, for example, are taking meals outside the home.

show that "relatives are seen more often, cared about more, and relied on more for assistance than friends, coworkers, or neighbors."[47]

The most convincing evidence for the impact of urbanization on the family bears upon the functions the family serves for individual members and the larger society.[48] In preliterate and peasant societies, and many contemporary rural communities, the family is the central social institution. Family functions include socialization, economic production and consumption, religious indoctrination, political decision-making, and social control. In industrial cities, however, the urbanite is served by an array of organizations that supplement or replace the family. In contemporary urban settings, the family serves, first, as the primary consumption unit toward which the market economy is oriented. Second, it serves, with varying degrees of effectiveness, to fill members' psychological needs for recognition, security, affection, and companionship.

**Voluntary Organizations** An increasing number of voluntary membership associations cater to the diversity of individual and group interests in the city. According to the "theory of mass society" these organizations counterbalance the isolation and anomie of urban life.[49] Voluntary associations provide a network of relations among people with similar interests and reduce the divisive tendencies in the social system.

A large variety of associations are available to urbanites. Church groups, ethnic and political organizations, civic action groups, fraternal societies, labor unions, and professional associations have long provided bases of affiliation and social participation. Numerous voluntary associations provide leisure activities such as hunting and fishing, jogging, stamp collecting, sports and cultural events. In short, the typical city in industrialized countries offers people the opportunity to identify with and participate in a vast array of groups and organizations.[50] Nevertheless, membership and participation rates are not so high as might be expected. For example, only 43 percent of a representative sample of U.S. adults belong to at least one association.[51] Moreover, the expected relationship between urbanization and voluntary association membership is weak at best. Studies conducted in the United States, Great Britain, West

**TABLE 9.3** Affiliation with Voluntary Associations (Excluding Unions) by Community Size for Four Industrialized Nations

| Community size | United States | Great Britain | West Germany | Italy |
|---|---|---|---|---|
| | **Percent with One or More Affiliations** | | | |
| Less than 5,000 | 50 | 38 | 37 | 22 |
| 5,000 – 20,000 | 56 | 31 | 36 | 32 |
| 20,000 – 50,000 | 60 | 40 | 28 | 28 |
| 50,000 – 100,000 | 41 | 23 | 26 | 22 |
| 100,000 – or more | 48 | 32 | 28 | 19 |
| | **Percent with Multiple Affiliations** | | | |
| Less than 5,000 | 28 | 12 | 11 | 4 |
| 5,000 – 20,000 | 30 | 9 | 11 | 5 |
| 20,000 – 50,000 | 39 | 18 | 5 | 4 |
| 50,000 – 100,000 | 26 | 3 | 4 | 4 |
| 100,000 – or more | 26 | 6 | 6 | 3 |

Germany, and Italy show inconsistent differences in association memberships according to community size (see Table 9.3). The stereotype of urban dwellers as joiners is not supported by available evidence.[52]

**Education** While the family is the key social institution in nonindustrial societies, in industrial societies the system of formal education comes closest to filling that role. Education provides a pool of workers capable of filling the diverse occupational roles necessary for the industrial economic system. It is also regarded as essential in preparing the individual to lead a satisfying and rewarding life. In the United

States and elsewhere, formal schooling has been extended to cover most of the period from youth to early adulthood. Moreover, educational programs are increasingly available for adults who want to improve their occupational skills or simply to learn more about some topic of special interest.

Data on educational attainment for the United States population show the **modal** level to be completion of high school (See Table 9.4). In 1977 approximately one-third of American adults 25 years of age or older had finished four years of high school, but had not completed at least one year of college. However, nearly two-thirds were high school graduates. College

**TABLE 9.4** Years of School Completed by the U.S. Population 25 Years Old and Over, by Type of Residence: 1977 and 1970 (1970 Metropolitan Area Definition)

| | | Metropolitan areas | | | | Nonmetropolitan areas | |
|---|---|---|---|---|---|---|---|
| | | Central cities | | Suburban areas | | | |
| Years of School Completed | | 1977 | 1970 | 1977 | 1970 | 1977 | 1970 |
| **Elementary:** | 0–4 years | 4.5 | 6.0 | 2.2 | 3.6 | 4.9 | 6.8 |
| | 5–7 years | 7.5 | 10.7 | 4.8 | 7.6 | 8.8 | 11.9 |
| | 8 years | 9.1 | 11.8 | 7.3 | 10.5 | 11.9 | 15.8 |
| **High school:** | 1–3 years | 16.3 | 20.5 | 13.5 | 18.5 | 16.1 | 19.0 |
| | 4 years | 33.2 | 29.3 | 38.2 | 34.4 | 36.1 | 29.5 |
| **College:** | 1–3 years | 13.8 | 10.8 | 15.3 | 12.2 | 10.9 | 9.1 |
| | 4 years | 9.1 | 5.9 | 10.9 | 7.5 | 6.8 | 4.7 |
| | 5 years or more | 6.7 | 5.0 | 7.7 | 5.6 | 4.4 | 3.2 |
| Total percent | | 100.0 | 100.0 | 100.0 | 100.0 | 100.0 | 100.0 |
| Percent high school graduates: | | 62.7 | 51.4 | 72.1 | 59.3 | 58.3 | 46.4 |

graduates are very much in the minority, constituting about 17 percent of the adult population.

The pattern of educational attainment varies by type of residence. Metropolitan areas have many more high school graduates and slightly more college graduates than nonmetropolitan areas. Within metropolitan areas, suburbs have significantly higher levels of education, for both high school and college graduation, than do central cities. Finally, between 1970 and 1977, educational attainment has increased for all three residential types.

Since the middle 1950s a number of significant changes have taken place in metropolitan education.[53] The most publicized, hotly debated, and volatile events have been associated with school desegregation. Initially aimed at eliminating the southern system in which black and white children were assigned by law to separate schools, desegregation programs have in recent years been designed to make the racial balance in a school correspond with the racial composition of its school district. Many white parents respond to desegregation programs by sending their children to private schools or moving to another school district; but the public response to school desegregation efforts has varied widely among cities. For example, Boston suffered a great deal of disruption when parents opposed plans to bus children away from neighborhood schools to achieve racial balance. Seattle, on the other hand, has instituted busing without serious protest.

**Occupations and Employment**  The most socially significant aspect of modern industrialism is its occupational structure.[54] Cities exhibit a much greater variety of occupations than do smaller communities, and some occupations are found only in cities. Labor force participation rates differ significantly for men and women, but only slightly by type of residence. In 1977, approximately three-quarters of American men and just under half of American women were employed in the civilian labor force.[55] The female participation rate had increased significantly since 1970, especially for suburban women. Employment rates were slightly higher for both sexes in suburban areas than in central cities or nonmetropolitan areas. The unemployment rate, reflecting the proportion of people seeking but unable to find work, was approxi-

**modal:**  of or pertaining to *the mode*, the value in a numerical distribution that is most frequent. One form of average.

mately 8 percent and slightly higher in central cities, especially for men. In central cities, suburban areas, and nonmetropolitan areas, blacks constituted a disproportionate share of the unemployed.

While there are some significant differences in the occupational composition of metropolitan and nonmetropolitan areas, there is little variation between central cities and suburbs within the metropolitan population ( see Table 9.5). As we would expect nonmetropolitan areas have fewer professional, technical, and clerical workers, and higher proportions of farmers, farm managers and supervisors, and farm laborers. However, the common image of suburbanites as white-collar workers (professional, managerial, sales, and clerical workers) is not reinforced by the data. The percentage of central city and suburban workers in this category does not differ significantly. In fact, the only major occupation group on which central city and suburban populations differ much at all is service workers (central city higher, as would be expected).

**Politics and Government**  Sociologists have been concerned for many years with the organization of politics and government in the city. The relevant issues and trends are highly complex, and can only be touched upon here. As indicated earlier in this chapter, one way of defining a city is in terms of administrative criteria—the land area and resident population under the jurisdiction of a governmental unit. A city's government is responsible for maintaining order (through its police department), providing services (fire protection, garbage pickup), and making a variety of decisions that determine the pattern of community organization and influence individual welfare (zoning restrictions, property tax assessments). A central issue in the political sociology of the city is the effect of urban expansion on the conduct of these administrative functions.

Metropolitan government has become increasingly fragmented. First, local control is threatened by the large share of the operating budget obtained from state and federal sources.

TABLE 9.5 Percent Distribution of Employed Persons 16 Years Old and Over, by Major Occupation Group and Type of Residence: 1977 and 1970 (1970 Metropolitan Areas Definition)

| | Metropolitan areas | | | | Nonmetropolitan areas | |
| | Central cities | | Suburban areas | | | |
| Occupation | 1977 | 1970 | 1977 | 1970 | 1977 | 1970 |
|---|---|---|---|---|---|---|
| Employed | 100.0 | 100.0 | 100.0 | 100.0 | 100.0 | 100.0 |
| Professional, technical and kindred workers | 15.8 | 15.4 | 17.5 | 17.0 | 12.5 | 12.0 |
| Managers and administrators, except farm | 10.5 | 7.7 | 11.8 | 9.4 | 9.9 | 7.9 |
| Sales workers | 6.4 | 7.5 | 7.2 | 8.1 | 4.9 | 5.8 |
| Clerical workers | 20.9 | 21.7 | 19.1 | 19.0 | 13.8 | 13.1 |
| Craft and kindred workers | 11.1 | 12.2 | 13.2 | 15.0 | 13.7 | 14.5 |
| Operatives, except transport | 10.8 | 13.0 | 9.7 | 12.4 | 14.6 | 16.7 |
| Transport equipment operatives | 3.7 | 3.9 | 3.5 | 3.6 | 4.4 | 4.3 |
| Laborers, except farm | 4.3 | 4.5 | 4.1 | 3.9 | 5.1 | 5.3 |
| Farmers and farm managers | 0.1 | 0.1 | 0.6 | 0.8 | 4.1 | 5.2 |
| Farm laborers and supervisors | 0.2 | 0.3 | 0.7 | 0.8 | 2.8 | 2.9 |
| Service workers, except private household | 14.9 | 11.9 | 11.5 | 9.1 | 12.7 | 10.5 |
| Private household workers | 1.4 | 1.8 | 1.0 | 1.0 | 1.4 | 1.9 |

During the period 1965–1973, this figure exceeded half of the total revenue for Newark, Baltimore, Buffalo, New York, Memphis, and Boston,[58] though there has been a trend toward a decrease in federal aid in recent years. Dependence upon external sources of revenue means that administrative decisions are often contingent upon the approval of those who will actually pay the bill—federal or state agencies, banks and so on.

Second, the changing composition and distribution of the metropolitan area contributes to political disunity. Racial cleavages result from the growing concentration of blacks in central cities as whites move to the suburbs. Suburbanization results in the growth of political structures in villages and townships, creating a "polycentric metropolis."[59] City, suburban, and county governmental units often compete with one another for funds and frequently lack coordination in the delivery of services.

Finally, there has been a tremendous growth of "limited purpose governmental units" and special interest groups that play a role in the administration of metropolitan areas. For example, "The Chicago area, from a purely formal standpoint, can hardly be said to have a gov-

ernment at all. There are hundreds, perhaps thousands, of bodies, each of which has a measure of legal authority and none of which has enough of it to carry out a course of action which other bodies oppose."[60] These subgovernments deal with sewage disposal, fire protection, library services, flood control, public health, and so on.

The fragmentation of urban governments creates serious administrative difficulties for central cities as well as suburban areas. Urban populations are faced with a multitude of complex and growing problems—crime, housing, waste disposal, urban blight, and transportation are a few examples. Formulation and implementation of policies aimed at remedying these conditions requires coordinated governmental leadership, which is hard to find in the fragmented political structure characteristic of today's cities.

## PROBLEMS OF THE MODERN INDUSTRIAL CITY

Our discussion of the structure and social organization of the modern city described a number of changes associated with urbanization. Increased population concentration and growth of the industrial sector results in territorial expansion and segregation of the population. The form and functions of social institutions gradually alter to meet the demands of an increasingly complex urban environment. Indeed, change is a ubiquitous feature of urbanization, reaching into all aspects of collective life.

Change, especially when it is rapid, creates strains on existing conditions. In the case of urbanization, many of these strains are directly attributable to the increased size, density, and heterogeneity of the population. Increased numbers of people create pressures on housing, school facilities, transportation systems, and public services agencies. The mix of racial, ethnic, and socioeconomic status characteristics in a population can influence the amount of intergroup conflict as well as the kinds of demands placed on governing bodies. In short, a variety of problems may accompany urbanization.

A 1975 survey of urbanites in the United States showed that crime was the most frequently recognized problem, followed by unemployment, transportation, education, housing, and high taxes.[61] The perceived seriousness of particular problems may vary among cities and regions of the country, and from one year to the next as well. This section will describe some of the major collective problems facing American cities, problems that are experienced by urban populations as a whole, as opposed to the private troubles of individuals. Two types of problems emerge—some manifested in the physical and others in the social environment.

## The Physical Environment

As cities age, they usually begin to deteriorate physically. Though difficult to measure precisely, serious physical deterioration is commonly referred to as *blight*. A blighted area is one that has lost its attractiveness for all its former uses; consequently, its buildings and installations have been allowed to fall into deterioration."[62]

**Housing** The older, central cities are most likely to contain deteriorated structures. A common practice is for owners to convert obsolete buildings into housing units while waiting for some commercial enterprise to bid for the land, thus generating slums. A **slum** may be

> **slum:** a residence area characterized by structural decay, overcrowding, lack of recreational space, and neglect of neighborhood facilities. When a slum is inhabited largely or exclusively by persons of a single ethnic or racial group, it may be called a "ghetto."

defined by physical as well as social characteristics, including structural decay, lack of plumbing, and a high ratio of occupants to rooms.[63] In addition to inadequate housing, slums are also characterized by congestion, lack of recreational space, and neglect of neighborhood facilities.

The considerable amount of attention social scientists and policymakers have given to blighted areas of inner cities can be misleading.[64] Recent data show that the majority of housing units in the United States, urban as well as rural, both inside and outside metropolitan areas, is evaluated as "excellent" or "good" (see Table 9.6). The major difference revealed by these data is between owner- and renter-occupied units, with the latter much more likely to be judged of fair or poor quality. As might be expected, renters are more likely to reside in urban areas and to be poor. But even for poor renters, housing conditions have been improving: "In 1950 one poor renter in five did not have running water and the exclusive use of a toilet or shower; by 1970 it was one in twelve.[65]

The improvement of housing conditions in the inner city is largely due to federally funded

Urban Landscape I.

**TABLE 9.6** Quality of Housing Structure, Owner and Renter Occupied, by Residential Type, United States, 1976 (Percentages)

| | | Residential type | | | |
| | | Urban | | Rural | |
| | Total | Inside SMSAs | Outside SMSAs | Inside SMSAs | Outside SMSAs |
|---|---|---|---|---|---|
| **Owner occupied** | | | | | |
| Excellent | 41.5 | 43.2 | 40.0 | 46.1 | 36.0 |
| Good | 47.6 | 47.5 | 48.7 | 43.7 | 49.1 |
| Fair | 9.6 | 8.2 | 9.8 | 9.0 | 13.3 |
| Poor | 0.9 | 0.7 | 0.8 | 0.9 | 1.2 |
| Not reported | 0.4 | 0.4 | 0.7 | 0.3 | 0.4 |
| **Renter occupied** | | | | | |
| Excellent | 19.4 | 19.5 | 19.5 | 23.3 | 17.2 |
| Good | 47.9 | 47.8 | 47.8 | 48.5 | 48.0 |
| Fair | 25.9 | 25.9 | 25.3 | 22.7 | 27.8 |
| Poor | 6.2 | 6.2 | 6.9 | 5.0 | 6.5 |
| Not reported | 0.6 | 0.6 | 0.5 | 0.4 | 0.6 |

slum clearance projects that began in the 1950s. Called "urban renewal," the projects were intended to raze slum areas and construct highrise apartments for the poor and the middle class. Although urban renewal programs have had some positive impact on central city areas,[66] they have received a disproportionate amount of criticism.[67] A basic deficiency is that while substandard housing was destroyed, it was frequently replaced by upper-middle-class residences or commercial buildings. In many cases the promised relocation of the poor to new and improved housing either never oc-

curred or greatly inconvenienced them by moving them far from their original neighborhoods. Moreover, the cost of housing for relocated families was increased by 7–15 percent.[68] Generally, it can be concluded that the "urban renewal program has failed to achieve its major purpose, to help those who lived in the slums."[69]

**Transportation.** One consequence of urbanization and industrialization has been the physical separation of home and work. With few exceptions, urbanites must engage in a daily journey to and from their place of employment.

**TABLE 9.7** Indexes of Economic and Population Growth and Transport Trends, United States, 1950–1970 (1950 = 100)

| Year | Gross national product[a] | Population | Motor vehicle registrations[b] | Transit riders[c] |
|---|---|---|---|---|
| 1950 | 100.0 | 100.0 | 100.0 | 100.0 |
| 1955 | 123.3 | 108.9 | 127.4 | 66.4 |
| 1960 | 137.3 | 118.7 | 150.2 | 54.3 |
| 1965 | 173.9 | 127.8 | 183.7 | 49.1 |
| 1970 | 202.6 | 134.5 | 221.5[d] | 42.8 |

[a]In 1958 dollars
[b]Publicly and privately owned vehicles
[c]Revenue passengers
[d]Estimated

The concentration of retail businesses in cities and suburbs also increases the need for efficient means of transportation.

City dwellers view transportation as a major problem. The 1975 Gallup Poll showed transportation-related concerns to be more important than problems of education, housing, and taxes.[70] The urban transportation problem has several dimensions, but most of them can be traced to a single source: the automobile.

Since World War II automobile ownership in the United States has increased sharply, while use of public transportation systems has decreased (see Table 9.7). As family incomes have risen, it has become possible for most households to have at least one car. The proportion of carless families in 1970 was reported to be 17 percent, as compared with 41 percent in 1950.[71] In 1970, 18.5 million families had two or more cars.[72]

A 1976 study of travel to work in twenty metropolitan areas shows that 80 percent of those surveyed went by auto or truck, and of these travelers, 72 percent drove alone. Between 1970 and 1976, the use of public transportation for travel to work declined by nearly 6 percent from its already reduced level.[73]

Increased automobile usage has created several serious problems for urban populations. First, there is a great deal of congestion on city streets, especially during peak hours when workers travel to and from the job. Not only are traffic jams frustrating, they are also costly.[74] It has been contended that congestion stimulates population deconcentration, that is, suburbanization "with a resulting loss of land values and rising costs of maintaining and administering municipal services within central cities."[75]

Second, most cities lack adequate parking facilities. Much congestion results from the number of automobiles clogging city streets while searching for a parking space. High-rise parking lots have not resolved this problem adequately. Third, automobiles compete with the more cost-efficient public transportation systems—bus, subway, and railway. While greater usage of public transit facilities would surely alleviate much of the traffic problem in our cities, Americans appear to be unwilling to sacrifice the convenience of the private automobile to achieve greater ease of movement. In contrast, Europeans rely much more heavily on public transportation,[76] though in recent years

Urban Landscape II.

the rate has declined somewhat. It should be recognized, however, that European systems of public transportation are much more extensive than ours, largely because they have been generously subsidized.

Finally, automobile transportation in the United States has been encouraged by government policies that promote and finance highway construction, while support for public transit has been minimal.[77] "Highway engineers . . . create new expressways to serve cities that are already overcrowded within, thus tempting people who had been using public transportation to reach the urban centers to use these new private facilities."[78] Unless federal and state governments recognize that current transportation policies are outmoded, urban transportation problems are bound to become increasingly intolerable. It is also possible, of course, that the current and increasingly petroleum shortage will force Americans once more to rely more heavily on public transportation. Unfortunately many once-efficient public systems have been dismantled or drastically curtailed since the nineteen-thirties.

## The Social Environment

Underlying many, if not most, social problems of urban society is social inequality—the uneven distribution of wealth and power among groups and categories of people. Social inequality is evident in all types of communities, rural as well as urban, but it differs considerably in both degree and kind in metropolitan areas.[79] The segments of the United States population that appear to be most disadvantaged are the young and the very old, racial minorities, and women—especially those who head families—although additional bases of social inequality can be identified.[80]

TABLE 9.8 Percentage below the Poverty Level by Family Status, Race, and Type of Residence, United States, 1976 and 1969[a]

| | Metropolitan areas | | | | | | | | Nonmetropolitan areas | | | |
| | Central cities | | | | Suburban areas | | | | | | | |
| | White | | Black | | White | | Black | | White | | Black | |
| Family status | 1976 | 1969 | 1976 | 1969 | 1976 | 1969 | 1976 | 1969 | 1976 | 1969 | 1976 | 1969 |
|---|---|---|---|---|---|---|---|---|---|---|---|---|
| All persons | 11.3 | 11.1 | 31.0 | 29.1 | 5.9 | 7.0 | 21.5 | 29.5 | 11.4 | 15.7 | 38.2 | 52.6 |
| In families | 9.4 | 8.3 | 30.2 | 27.7 | 5.0 | 5.6 | 20.3 | 28.1 | 9.5 | 13.3 | 36.8 | 51.4 |
| Head | 8.4 | 7.9 | 28.0 | 24.9 | 4.9 | 5.6 | 19.0 | 25.2 | 8.9 | 13.1 | 34.7 | 47.0 |
| Male | 5.0 | 5.6 | 11.7 | 14.3 | 3.0 | 4.2 | 8.8 | 18.0 | 7.1 | 11.3 | 21.4 | 40.5 |
| Female | 26.9 | 24.5 | 51.1 | 49.1 | 22.0 | 21.8 | 44.2 | 50.1 | 27.4 | 32.9 | 60.5 | 66.5 |
| Wives | 5.0 | 5.5 | 11.3 | 13.9 | 2.9 | 4.1 | 8.6 | 17.6 | 6.9 | 11.1 | 21.1 | 40.0 |
| Related children | | | | | | | | | | | | |
| Under 18 years | 16.1 | 11.7 | 42.1 | 36.5 | 7.6 | 6.8 | 27.8 | 35.0 | 13.1 | 15.2 | 46.2 | 59.4 |
| Other family members | 4.6 | 5.6 | 19.8 | 18.9 | 2.6 | 4.1 | 13.4 | 21.6 | 6.6 | 12.3 | 30.1 | 42.1 |
| Unrelated individuals | 21.6 | 31.2 | 36.4 | 41.7 | 16.8 | 30.3 | 35.3 | 46.9 | 30.7 | 47.5 | 55.9 | 69.7 |
| Male | 17.1 | 25.4 | 31.6 | 32.6 | 13.0 | 22.6 | 23.7 | 38.6 | 23.1 | 38.8 | 39.9 | 58.8 |
| Female | 24.9 | 34.8 | 41.4 | 50.0 | 19.6 | 35.1 | 49.9 | 54.5 | 35.5 | 52.6 | 69.6 | 79.4 |

[a]"Families and unrelated individuals are classified as being above or below the poverty level using the poverty index adopted by a Federal Interagency Committee in 1969. This index is based on the Department of Agriculture's 1961 Economy Food Plan and reflects the different consumption requirements of families based on their size and composition, sex and age of the family, head, and farm-nonfarm residence. It was determined from the Department of Agriculture's 1955 survey of food consumption that families of three or more persons spend approximately one-third of their income on food; the poverty level for these families was, therefore, set at three times the cost of the economy food plan. For smaller families and persons living alone, the cost of the economy food plan was multiplied by factors that were slightly higher in order to compensate for the relatively larger fixed expenses of these smaller households. The poverty thresholds are updated every year to reflect changes in the Consumer Price Index (CPI). The poverty threshold for a nonfarm family of four was $5,815 in 1976 compared with $3,748 in 1969." (U.S. Bureau of the Census, 1978c:134).

Poverty has been a concern in American society for well over a century[81] and attention has often been focused on the urban poor. Between 1969 and 1976, the proportion of the poverty population located in metropolitan areas increased from 56 to 61 percent. Four-fifths of this increase occurred in central cities, which in 1976 housed 38 percent of the nation's poor.[82]

Data reflecting recent trends in poverty status highlight the problem for different population segments (see Table 9.8). While the proportion of both whites and blacks in central cities who are below the poverty level has increased slightly (more for blacks), reductions are seen for suburban and nonmetropolitan populations (again, more for blacks). Family heads who are female are much more likely to be below the poverty level than male heads. This situation has been worsening in central cities for both whites and blacks, while there has been improvement for suburban blacks and for both races in nonmetropolitan areas. No change is evident for white female heads in suburban locations. A larger proportion of central city white and black minor children were below the poverty level in 1976 than in 1969; this percentage decreased significantly for blacks in both suburban and nonmetropolitan areas and for nonmetropolitan whites. Finally, there is a trend for all residential types toward a lower percentage of unrelated individuals who are below the poverty level. Compared to persons in families, however, unrelated individuals (especially blacks, women, and nonmetropolitan residents) are particularly likely to be poor, partly because this category is composed largely of elderly people.

Social inequality is also reflected in the differential ability of groups and individuals to exercise power, that is, to command or influence the behavior of others. Studies of urban communities show considerable variation in how decisions are made, by whom, and with what outcomes.[83] An early study of Atlanta found that community decisions were controlled largely by a small group of elites — corporation executives, government officials, labor leaders, professionals, leaders of civic organizations — whose influence was not commonly recognized by the general public.[84] A different conclusion was reached after a study of decision making in New Haven, Connecticut. Instead of a monolithic power structure such as At-

lanta had, there was a diffusion of power among a variety of groups and individuals — in short, a pluralistic system of community power.[85] While there are many unresolved issues — theoretical, conceptual, and methodological — in the study of community power, one conclusion stands out. Regardless of *"who* governs," the fact is that certain classes of residents have little voice whatsoever in community decisions. This mass of powerless individuals includes the poor, the young and the elderly, blacks and other racial minorities, women, and a variety of special interest groups.

**Racial Conflict**   Racial conflict is particularly evident in the city because of the concentration of blacks in metropolitan areas and the underlying problem of inequality. Blacks are disadvantaged in at least five different realms: legal rights, political power, housing quality, employment, and education.[86] Although improvements are evident over the past two decades, this has not been sufficient to prevent the occurrence of riots and civil disorder.

In contrast to urban race riots prior to the 1960s, which involved direct clashes between mobs of blacks and whites, recent black aggression has been directed against white-owned property, not white people.[87] Although the economic and political gain from rioting has been very limited, blacks have recently increased their political participation and gained political leverage.[88] For example, the proportion of blacks registered to vote is now almost equal to that of whites. The result has been that black officials have been elected in increasing numbers at local, state, and federal levels, though they still account for less than one percent of the country's elected officials.[89]

Whether these gains in the social, economic, and political position of blacks will be sufficient to ward off future riots is an open question. But in any case, "It is clear that blacks are fed up with the rhetoric of opportunity and promises; they want results."[90] If black inequalities cannot be reduced through peaceful and legal means, violence may be unavoidable. Prevention of urban race riots is largely in the hands of the white majority, particularly the politicians. They must take the steps necessary to ensure blacks rapid and equitable access to the opportunities and rewards now enjoyed by whites.

**Crime and Delinquency** In recent years, crime has been the most pressing problem for urbanites in the United States. Metropolitan newspapers report daily murders, robberies, muggings, car thefts, rapes, and other offenses. In many cities, residents are reluctant to go out after dark for fear of being attacked. Bus drivers and gas station attendants in a growing number of metropolitan areas do not carry cash in an effort to discourage robbers. In short, "part of the urban experience is to feel anxiety about crime."[91]

The ratio of serious crimes to inhabitants increases with community size, not only in the United States, but in Europe and Canada as well.[92] Data for the United States in 1970 show that the number of all violent crimes per person was 9.6 times greater in the largest cities than in rural places.[93] Of course one must remember that not all crimes are reported, and we do not know whether this underreporting varies by

Urban Landscape III.

community size. Nevertheless, the large rural-urban differences are unlikely to be eliminated by completely accurate reporting.

Some types of crimes are more closely associated with community size than others, and the rate for a few crimes is higher for smaller communities. For examples, "In American cities of over 250,000, murder and rape are about five times as high as in towns of 10,000; burglary, larceny, and aggravated assault are three times as high; automobile theft is over six times as high; and robbery about twenty-five times as high."[94] On the other hand, murder rates are higher in rural areas than in small cities.[95]

Although some observers suggest that the long-term trend in the United States has been toward a reduction in crime,[96] the increasing concentration of population in cities has meant that more people are exposed to conditions that provoke and facilitate criminal activity. Various characteristics of urban life have been proposed to explain the higher crime rate: (1) The greater wealth of city residents makes crimes such as robbery and burglary more profitable; (2) moral constraints are weaker in cities; (3) a larger proportion of urbanites see themselves as socially or economically disadvantaged, and see criminal acts as perhaps their only means of getting the things denied them; and (4) criminal subcultures are created in the city through the aggregation of "clients" for illegal services, "victims," and a "critical mass" of criminals.[97] In spite of increased efforts to control urban crime, involving the expenditure of millions of dollars of public and private funds, the situation doesn't seem to be improving. Urban-rural differentials persist for most types of crimes, and the urban rates continue to increase.

## THE INDIVIDUAL IN THE MODERN INDUSTRIAL CITY

Urban residence is an individual experience as well as a collective one. People *interpret* their physical and social surroundings and behave accordingly.[98] The same objective circumstances may result in quite different responses from different individuals. For example, while one person may view urban crowding as an opportunity for making new friends, another may see nothing but a confrontation with hostile strangers. Many sociologists have investigated the social psychology of city life in order to understand how individual behavior is related to the perception of social circumstances.

## Social Contexts of Personal Experience

One condition that differentiates cities from smaller communities is mobility. Urban residents are mobile geographically and socially. The two most important patterns of migration in the United States are rural-urban and urban-urban, respectively.[99] Migrants come to the city for various reasons. The possibility of earning more money through a better job is usually the dominant factor, but others include better schooling, an improved material life, cultural attractions, a wish to reunite with kin, and the desire to escape constricting families.[100] Movement within the city—from house to house, from one part of the city to another, or from the central city to the suburbs—is usually motivated by the same desires. In short, the majority of urban residents move in search of a better life, that is, "for the objective reason of opportunity or the subjective one of hope."[101]

**Social Mobility**  In addition to moving between geographic locations, people also change their locations in the social status hierarchy. Cities provide opportunities for social mobility. The larger the city, the more opportunity. For example, in the case of occupational mobility, because there is greater functional specialization and differentiation of the occupational structure, large cities have more white-collar occupations than smaller localities.[102] As expected, the average level of occupational status attainment varies directly with city size.[103] What is surprising, though, is that city size does not influence an *individual's* chances for occupational mobility.[104] The major determinants are family background, level of educational attainment, and size of community of birth. Thus although there is considerable occupational mobility in American society, and the amount does not appear to have changed much for the past half century,[105] it does not appear to be much different in cities of varying size.

Cities, then, are characterized by individual mobility, geographic as well as social. But to what extent and how are city dwellers aware of their potential mobility? Does it give them the impression of instability and a lack of social integration in the urban setting?[106] Can behavioral and psychological pathologies like alienation, mental illness, and unhappiness be traced to individual interpretations of urban mobility patterns? Evidence on these matters will be considered below.

**Ambition and Achievement**  Another aspect of the urban setting that may have significant effects on the individual is the emphasis on achievement. Personal success, especially in the occupational world, is a central theme in American culture.[107] Writing three decades ago, Kingsley Davis suggested how the modern city generates mobility aspirations:

> Just as the city requires and promotes geographical mobility . . . so it requires and promotes great social mobility as well. Its elaborate division of labor, its competitiveness, its impersonality—all tend to emphasize achievement rather than ascriptions of status. . . . The urban person can therefore raise or lower his status to a remarkable degree during his lifetime, and the competition for status (and with it the insecurity of status) becomes a perpetual preoccupation. . . . Today the city is a place where social climbing is most prevalent.[108]

High, often unrealistic, ambitions are characteristic of today's youth reflecting the cultural pressure to achieve.[109] Given the relative openness of the American class system, many will succeed in at least maintaining a better than average job or income. But others will remain at the bottom levels of the status hierarchy or will be downwardly mobile. Many of these nonachievers are found among the chronic poor concentrated in our central cities. This segment of the population may be perceived as "disreputable" by the larger society. Disrepute is a social pathology, a stigma, inflicted on the poor by those who have been more fortunate. Their worth constantly in question, the poor may respond with apathy, alienation, or antisocial behavior.[110]

The disreputable poor are an extreme case of the consequences of the cultural prescription to achieve in the face of limited opportunities. But less dramatic effects are felt throughout the society, probably more generally by urbanites. An example is "status insecurity." City dwellers exhibit a strong concern over status distinctions, comparing their achievements with those of their relatives, neighbors, and co-workers, and worrying about how others judge them. In brief, the orientation to achieve is a pervasive element of the culture of cities.

**Population Density**  Early sociological conceptions of the city emphasized high population density as a major characteristic. During the past few decades social scientists have studied intensively the effects of urban density on human behavior.[111] Underlying their investigations is the assumption that the number of persons in a given area influences patterns of social interaction and communication, and may have significant effects on individuals.

Population density can be measured in a variety of ways. We can measure "physical density," that is, the distribution of physical structures over a given land area. This includes the proportion of all buildings devoted to residential purposes, the average number of dwelling units per building or rooms per dwelling unit, and the ratio of single-family to multiple-occupancy units in an area. Of greater interest and utility to the sociologist is a measure that represents "social density," that is, the "number of interactions or messages exchanged per unit of time."[112] The extremes of social density — crowding and isolation — are of particular in-

Urban Landscape IV.

terest in urban studies. Measures such as the average number of persons per room and the proportion of one-person households are relevant here.

The Annual Housing Survey conducted by the U.S. Bureau of the Census provides information on population density levels and trends (see Table 9.9). The proportion of single-unit structures decreased slightly between 1970 and 1976, reflecting the national trend toward multiple-unit structures. About half of the housing units in central cities are single-unit structures, while for suburban metropolitan locations and nonmetropolitan areas this fraction is much higher, around three-quarters. The average number of rooms per dwelling unit did not change over this six-year period, but the figure is somewhat lower for central cities and considerably lower for rental units. Thus, central cities have higher population density.

Examination of indicators of social density leads to an equivocal conclusion. Regardless of the type of residence, the absolute percentage of dwelling units with more than one person per room is small and has decreased since 1970. (Dwelling units with a ratio of persons to rooms greater than 1.0 are[113] usually defined as crowded). The figure is higher for central cities than suburban areas, but approximately equal to that found in nonmetropolitan areas. It would appear, then, that central city households are not much more crowded than households in other areas. But central cities also have a higher proportion of one-person households than do suburban and nonmetropolitan areas, though this proportion has increased in all areas since 1970. Regardless of residential type, renters are more likely to live alone than owners, but especially in central cities.

These indicators of population density suggest that although the physical structure of the inner city seems to promote crowded households more than other areas, the actual differences are not large. Moreover, social isolation, as reflected in the proportion of one-person households, appears to be greater in central cities. Nevertheless, these measures of population density do not tell us about the actual frequency of interaction between people at different levels of urbanization; nor do they provide any indication of subjective feelings of crowding or loneliness, which are perhaps the most important consideration. In short, the implica-

TABLE 9.9    Selected Indicators of Population Density by Type of Residence, United States,
1976 and 1970 (1970 Metropolitan Area Definition)

| | Metropolitan areas | | | | Nonmetropolitan areas | |
|---|---|---|---|---|---|---|
| | Central cities | | Suburban areas | | | |
| | 1976 | 1970 | 1976 | 1970 | 1976 | 1970 |
| Percent single-unit structures[a] | 49.8 | 50.6 | 72.1 | 74.9 | 79.5 | 82.2 |
| Median number of rooms per dwelling unit (all units)[a] | 4.7 | 4.7 | 5.3 | 5.3 | 5.2 | 5.1 |
|    Owner occupied | 5.7 | 5.6 | 5.9 | 5.8 | 5.5 | 5.4 |
|    Renter occupied | 3.8 | 3.8 | 4.0 | 4.1 | 4.2 | 4.3 |
| Percent dwelling units with more than one person per room[a] | 5.0 | 8.2 | 3.7 | 8.9 | 4.8 | 7.9 |
| Percent one-person households (all units)[a] | 26.6 | 23.5 | 16.2 | 18.3 | 19.2 | 17.4 |
|    Owner occupied | 15.4 | 13.3 | 10.5 | 9.1 | 14.5 | 14.1 |
|    Renter occupied | 38.0 | 33.4 | 30.3 | 24.4 | 32.8 | 26.7 |

[a]Excludes trailers and mobile homes

tions of urban population density are still a matter of conjecture.

**Diversity of Life Styles**    Perhaps the single most distinctive feature of the city is the diversity of life styles it encompasses. Life styles are reflected in values, tastes, and consumption patterns[114] A given life style may be characteristic of a group with an obvious social and cultural identity, for example, an ethnic subculture or a religious sect; or it may be typical of a status group or population category lacking such an identity, like professionals or young people.

A generally accepted, if not entirely demonstrable, proposition suggests that the larger the city, the greater the variety of life styles represented. This is partly due to the population differentiation associated with urbanization and partly due to the apparently greater tolerance of urbanites for unconventional behavior.[115] Only in larger cities does one generally find such diverse groups as gay liberationists, Jesus freaks, greasers, singles, urban guerrillas, and prostitutes living in relative harmony with the more conventional components of the population.[116]

While the typical urban family still consists of the husband-wife-dependent children arrange-

ment, a variety of family forms have become increasingly prominent, including the unmarried living alone, childless couples, separated and divorced persons who do not remarry, and couples living together without marriage.[117] The urban commune constitutes another family form that has arisen in this century.[118]

Further evidence of diverse life styles is seen in urban patterns of work and leisure.[119] Cities provide a greater variety of occupations and greater opportunity of employment for women, as we have seen. But there are other variants as well. The amount of time devoted to work, as well as the work schedule, depend upon an individual's occupation and interests. Although the average work week is forty hours, perhaps a quarter of the work force exceeds this. For some the underlying cause is genuine commitment to the job, while for others, pressing responsibilities demand more of their time. Still other urbanites find it impossible to support themselves or their families without "moonlighting," that is, holding two or more jobs that may require fifty to sixty hours per week, sometimes more.

Daily work schedules of urbanites have become increasingly varied. The typical schedule still covers approximately eight hours between

Urban Landscape V.

6 A.M. and 6 P.M. However, some industrial plants have "swingshift" (4 P.M. to 12 A.M.) and even "graveyard" (12 A.M. to 8 A.M.) crews. Commercial establishments — department stores and supermarkets, for example — may be open 12 to 14 hours per day, including weekends, thus requiring employees to begin early or work late from time to time. The point is that work time in the city is decreasingly associated with the nine-to-five, five-days-a-week pattern characteristic of the recent past.

In spite of the fact that the city presents an image of work being done — that is, jobs being performed round the clock — urbanites actually have much more leisure time than agricultural populations. Leisure time activities assume many forms and take on a variety of meanings.[120] Spectator sports are a major diversion for some city residents, while others prefer to relax through participation in active sports, such as jogging, tennis, or swimming. Suburbanites have a reputation for preferring home-centered, family activities, while central city residents are seen as being more involved in community-based, commercial locations and events. Additional distinctions reflect differences between individual- and group-oriented activities, and those that are linked to particular age, sex, and status groups. Although participation in many forms of leisure is dependent upon relative affluence, the city nevertheless offers a wide variety of alternatives for the use of "free time."

The trend in urban life styles has been toward increasing diversity, in the family, religion, work and leisure, and the so-called "ultra-life styles" that may be characterized by the unconventional individual behavior of prostitutes, pool hustlers, panhandlers, radical political groups and religious sects.[121] This context of diversity is at the same time liberating and constraining. It offers individuals the opportunity to find support for their beliefs and values, no matter how much they diverge from social norms. On the other hand, it produces stereotypes of particular life styles — the ethnic neighborhood, the middle-class suburbanite, the drug culture — that often result in a perceived separation of urban social worlds. How does this mixture of freedom and constraint influence individual adaptations to the urban environment?

## Individual Responses to the City[122]

The conditions of urban life are often described as stressful. Many residents, especially migrants from rural areas, have difficulty adjusting to the pace and diversity of urban living.[123] The urban environment appears to the individual like a loosely integrated and rapidly changing social order. Urbanites assume multiple, sometimes conflicting, social roles; they are parents, employees, shoppers, PTA members, and their daily routine is composed largely of brief contacts with people they know only casually or not at all. Geographic and social mobility, as well as the diverse and continually shifting composition of the urban population, give an impression of instability. The urban resident is bombarded with a multitude of stimuli—automobile horns, bright lights, advertisements, construction noises, and so on. The city seems to promote social differentiation and psychological stress, both of which isolate people from one another. While providing freedom for individuals to pursue their own interests and life styles, such conditions also result in a weak moral order, which "permits social disruption and promotes personality disorder."[124]

There are two major alternatives to this *determinist* view of the effects of urbanization on the individual. *Compositional* theory holds that urbanization does not weaken primary social relationships and that size, density, and heterogeneity do not have necessarily adverse consequences for individuals.[125] "The dynamics of social life depend largely on the nonecological factors of social class, ethnicity, and stage in the life cycle"[126] These social structural factors account for the behavioral and social psychological differences found among city residents.

A third, *subcultural*, theory synthesizes ideas from the determinist and compositional positions.[127] The fundamental assumption is that urbanization generates and strengthens a variety of subcultures, "inhabited by persons who share relatively distinct traits (like ethnicity or occupation), who tend to interact especially with one another, and who share a relatively distinct set of beliefs and behaviors."[128] In some cases these subcultures coexist in relative harmony, but in others there is competition and conflict. Whether individuals will be adversely affected by urbanization thus depends upon the degree to which they are protected by belonging to one or another subculture, as well as the characteristics of the subculture in question.

The three perspectives discussed above offer alternative interpretations of the behavioral and psychological consequences of urban life. It should be emphasized, however, that the evidence does not provide any solid basis for choosing among them.[129] What *can* be assessed is the extent to which city dwellers manifest certain attributes that we associate with the urban experience.

**Alienation and Anomie**   Does mass society, exemplified by the urban industrial city, generate feelings of alienation and estrangement?[130] Impersonality, rationalism, heterogeneity, mobility, diversity, and increased size are thought to produce in individuals one or more of the following: a sense of *powerlessness*, a sense of *meaninglessness*, a sense of *normlessness*, *value isolation*, *self-estrangement*, and *social isolation*.[131] In brief, the alienated person feels a sense of separation from the social and cultural milieu.

Empirical studies of alienation have produced mixed results, partly because we lack standardized ways to measure it. We cannot conclude that urbanites are more alienated than residents of smaller communities.[132] Rather, alienation appears to be consistently associated with certain personal characteristics—lower education, poverty, marital dissolution, and unemployment—regardless of the size of the community. Only to the extent that urbanization influences these and other variables can it be said to indirectly produce alienation.

**Psychological Disorders**   Does urbanization increase the rate of psychological disturbance? Poor mental health has been associated with both overcrowding and social isolation,[133] social and geographic mobility,[134] lack of sociocultural integration,[135] and various measures of social inequality.[136] It has not, however, been demonstrated convincingly that these effects are at all unique to cities. One recent study based upon a national sample of 7,000 adults, "finds that residents of larger

Urban Landscape VI.

communities report fewer, not more, symptoms [of mental disorder] than residents of smaller communities.[137]

The problem is a familiar one: definitive studies, incorporating the controls necessary to eliminate competing explanations, are lacking.[138] There is no doubt that urban conditions can be stressful and frustrating; but most urbanites learn to cope with these difficulties and to ward off serious psychological damage. In short, the image of the city as a "behavioral sink" appears to be overdrawn.[139]

**Lack of Involvement.** Urban residents are frequently characterized as aloof and withdrawn, unfriendly to strangers, and unhelpful in times of trouble. Underlying this contention are assumptions that urbanites are concerned only with meeting their own personal needs, that they are afraid of being taken advantage of or attacked, and that they simply wish to avoid people from different subcultures.[140] While these assumptions may be true, the real issue is whether people are much different in smaller communities. Newspaper reports and popular novels to the contrary, "we can only assume that city people are—no less or no more than country people—their brothers' keepers."[141]

Does the separation of urban life into "social worlds which touch but do not penetrate"[142] result in self-conceptions related to subcultural

membership? Again, the available evidence does not lead to any firm conclusion. On the one hand, some urbanites—blacks, women, Chicanos, homosexuals—have recently declared the uniqueness of their situations and used this as a basis for coordinated action. On the other hand, some members of distinctive subcultures appear to stress that they are really no different from anyone else.[143]

To summarize, the city has many contextual features that distinguish it from smaller communities. While any one of these is likely to be stressful for some people, there is no evidence that city life is *systematically* related to pathological individual responses, such as alienation, mental disorder, social withdrawal, or deviant identities. On the whole, urbanites appear to be capable of coming to terms with their social environment, no matter how stressful it might appear to an observer.

## THE FUTURE OF THE CITY

Any discussion of the modern city concludes with speculation—hopes and fears for cities of the future. Regardless of whether one sees the modern industrial city as the source of all that is new and good in human civilization or as the source of problems that threaten all economic and social life, there can be little doubt that metropolitan concentration will be the dominant pattern of human settlement for the foreseeable future. Urban growth has its own momentum, like a snowball rolling down a mountain. Given the inevitability of continued large-scale urbanization, an important task for the social scientist is to identify factors that are likely to shape the city of the future.

### Demographic Considerations

By the year 2000, the world's population is likely to be somewhere between five and eight billion, depending upon the success of efforts to control fertility in the developing countries (see Chapter 10). One estimate suggests that approximately 25 percent of this number will live in cities of one million or more inhabitants (as opposed to about 12 percent in 1970).[144] In the United States the metropolitan population is expected to reach 85 percent of the total by the turn of the century.

As cities increase in population, they grow in

FIGURE 9.3 **The future of megalopolis**

By the year 2000, approximately 70 percent of the American population will live in just six megalopolitan areas: The northeastern seaboard, the Florida complex, the Houston-Dallas complex, the Great Lakes complex, the California complex, and the Northwest complex.

scale. This phenomenon, typically referred to as "urban sprawl," is seen in the territorial spread of the growing metropolitan area. An important consequence is that less land is available for agricultural purposes. Another result is that urban concentrations envelop previously separated corporate units, giving rise to *conurbations* e.g., the Atlantic Coast Region stretching from Bangor, Maine, to Norfolk, Virginia.

Although cities continue to grow, a countertrend has apparently been taking place since 1970. Several recent studies show a reversal of the long-term net flow of migrants from rural districts into metropolitan areas.[145] Nonmetropolitan areas are now growing more rapidly and gaining net migrants at a higher rate than are metropolitan areas. It is too soon to tell whether this trend will persist, but its effects are already significant.[146] Perhaps a growing minority of urbanites are rejecting the pace and complexity of metropolitan life. If this is borne out, it will have far-reaching implications for the economy and social organization of metropolitan areas as well as the newly growing nonmetropolitan localities.

## Technological Considerations

The survival of urban populations depends upon a food surplus in the countryside, capital-intensive modes of employment, and readily available energy supplies.[147] Rapid population growth during the past half century, accompanied by a disproportionate rate of urbanization, has resulted in serious worldwide shortages of food, capital, and energy. These problems now appear most vividly in the developing countries, but they will ultimately affect the quality of life in the industrialized nations as well, unless remedies are found.

New technology is frequently proposed as the solution to these (and numerous other) scarcities. However, there is a growing body of evidence that this argument is fallacious.[148] Despite extensive and costly efforts to develop new fertilizers and high-yield wheats and rices, world grain production has fallen in the past few years. With the inevitable exhaustion of fossil fuels, scientists have sought alternative sources of energy, emphasizing nuclear technology. The result has been far from successful. The availability of capital for industrial development has not kept up with the demand, resulting in increasing rates of global unemploy-

ment. The facts are much more complex than can be presented here, but the viability of the city is threatened because the resources necessary to support large urban concentrations are becoming increasingly scarce. Some observers feel that the most effective means to save the city lie in the improvement of living conditions and productivity in the countryside.[149]

## Political Considerations

Problems of governing the metropolis are serious constraints on urban growth throughout the world. Maintenance of social order requires that cities be guided, managed, and financed.[150] Otherwise, large-scale urbanization can only lead to chaos.

Few cities of the world are changing in accord with a formalized, rational plan. Urban policies regarding growth, housing, and transportation, for example, are practically nonexistent. Nowhere is this more evident than in the United States. The result has been a continuing series of urban crises that are commonly dealt with reactively, in the style of fire fighting.[151] Daniel Moynihan has suggested that we urgently need a national urban policy to define the goals of urban development and to provide a strategy for combating anticipated problems.[152] Some of the goals of the proposed policy are (1) to reduce the poverty and social isolation of minority groups in central cities, (2) to reorganize local government in response to the reality of metropolitan conditions, (3) to restore the fiscal vitality of urban government, and (4) to preserve the natural resources and the aesthetic qualities of the urban environment.[153]

That large cities are with us to stay is quite clear. Although the movement back to the countryside may continue, it is unlikely to alter significantly the economic and political centrality of the city in industrial societies. However, as we indicated, the oldest and largest cities can be expected to decline in population for at least the next few decades. Urban growth will be greater in the newer and middle-sized cities.

The real issues have to do with the quality of life for tomorrow's urbanites. Since city populations are dependent upon food, jobs, and energy for their survival, the availability of these resources must be closely evaluated. If agricultural production continues to fall, if rates of industrial growth cannot be maintained, and if inexpensive and efficient new sources of energy are not developed, the city may be in for some hard times.

In spite of efforts toward urban planning, urban renewal, and similar schemes, few nations have shown a desire to develop rational policies for long-term urban development. The principal reason cities are in trouble throughout the world is that decisions about urban problems have been divorced from those affecting the larger society. New concepts are called for to place the city within a national, if not global framework. Interdependencies between city and countryside must be recognized and used to inform growth policies.[154] Whether or not such steps are taken by local and national governments may well determine the quality of urban life in the next century.

## SUMMARY

By the end of this century over half the human population will be living in urban localities, and 40 percent will reside in cities with at least 100,000 inhabitants. Moreover, cities will exert a dominant influence on the quality of life in towns and rural communities. In short, to understand the human future one must give special attention to the demographic, economic, political, social, and cultural organization of cities.

The city is a complex organizational phenomenon, and its definition encompasses a number of attributes: a relatively large, densely settled population; a governmental entity with specified jurisdictional limits; a differentiated yet functionally integrated institutional structure; and a diverse set of norms, beliefs, values, and life styles that constitute a relatively distinct cultural system. Nonetheless, there is wide variation among cities, within as well as among nations.

The earliest cities emerged about 5500 years ago. Change in urban organization was gradual until the Industrial Revolution, which marked a major turning point in the world's urban history. Industrialization drastically altered the bases of human subsistence, broadening the economic base of society and creating conditions that both permitted and required increasingly large and concentrated resident populations.

This chapter has been focused on the modern industrial city in the United States and has addressed two broad issues. First, it has examined the distinctive organizational features of the modern city and related them to contemporary urban problems. The spatial organization of the metropolitan community has been described in terms of three alternative configurations. The *concentric zone model* assumes that the city radiates outward from the central business district, with each successive zone defined by different patterns of land use. The *sector model* assumes a pie-shaped configuration, with land use patterns following lines of transportation. The *multiple nuclei model* assumes the city to have several centers, each of which specializes in a different functional activity.

Residential segregation appears to be a fairly persistent feature of the modern city. The principal bases of segregation are socioeconomic status, race and income. Racial and ethnic minorities, and the poor are concentrated in the central city, with whites and higher SES groups more heavily represented in the suburbs.

Metropolitan population growth has been concentrated in suburban rings for the past half century. Population decline is especially characteristic of larger and older U.S. cities and is partly the result of high rents and land values, housing shortages, and problems of crime, congestion, and pollution in the inner city. More significant, however, is the fact that job opportunities have been much greater in the suburban rings. Metropolitan expansion has led to increasing interdependence among central city, suburban, and rural areas.

Urban social institutions are in some ways relatively distinct but not to the degree sometimes believed. Metropolitan families are more likely to be headed by women and to consist of primary individuals, but are not distinctive in terms of average family size or average number of children. Generally, there is little evidence to suggest that urbanization has had either major or detrimental effects on the American family.

In some ways, however, the family's social functions have been altered by organizational changes associated with urbanization. A significant factor has been the rise of voluntary associations—church groups, fraternal societies, civic action groups, etc.—that satisfy the needs of groups and individuals. Additionally, the formal system of education has taken over many of the socialization functions formerly left to the family.

Educational attainment is higher for metropolitan residents, especially suburbanites. Nevertheless, educational systems in some cities have experienced severe problems in recent years. Public response to racial desegregation is the primary example, but lack of adequate financing and challenges to the authority of teachers and administrators are also important.

The occupational structure of the city is much more diverse than that of rural areas. An increase in employment opportunities for women has been the most significant change in recent years, especially in suburban areas. Unemployment is highest for black men, particularly in the inner city.

Metropolitan government has become increasingly fragmented, as reflected by the variety of sources from which operating funds are obtained, the growing number of special interest groups attempting to influence political decisions, and the considerable overlap among jurisdictional boundaries. Governmental fragmentation has created serious problems for the coordination of leadership and administration in the city.

City growth and changes in the institutional organization of the metropolitan area are associated with the emergence of urban problems. Problems evident in the physical environment include blight and deterioration, housing shortages and inequities (particularly for blacks), and congestion due to the growing number of private automobiles in use.

There are also some serious problems with the city's social environment. These include poverty (highest among blacks, women heads of households, and the elderly), an inability to influence community decisions for large segments of the population, racial conflict, and growing crime rates.

The second broad issue examined in this chapter has to do with individual responses to urban living. The city has been viewed traditionally as detrimental to personal well-being. Urban conditions often identified as being stressful for individuals include social and geographic mobility, the importance placed on achievement, high population density, and the increased likelihood of contact with diverse—sometimes deviant—life styles.

Studies of the behavioral and personality characteristics of urbanites suggest that, other things being equal, city residents are no more likely to exhibit pathological responses than inhabitants of smaller communities. Stated otherwise, there does not appear to be any clear relationship between the correlates of urbanization and conditions such as alienation, mental disorder, aloofness, and social withdrawal. Urbanites appear to cope with their environment as well as anyone else.

A final consideration raised in this chapter involves the future of the city. That urban growth is bound to continue is a foregone conclusion. The real issue is what the quality of life will be like in the city of tomorrow. One important determinant will be the availability of the natural resources upon which the city is so dependent. Another factor is whether or not policies to guide the development and administration of cities can be devised and implemented. These and related issues will require the full attention and imagination of politicians, planners, scientists, and citizens if the city is to continue to be a livable habitat for humankind.

## SUGGESTED READINGS

Davis, Kingsley, ed. *Cities: Their Origin, Growth, and Human Impact.* San Francisco: Freeman, 1973. A collection of essays originally published in the *Scientific American.* Topics covered include early cities; population, health, and the city environment; urban transportation and city planning; cities in the developing world; and group relations in cities.

Fischer, Claude S. *The Urban Experience.* New York:

Harcourt, 1976. A comprehensive summary of the social and psychological consequences of urban life. The author concludes that while cities do produce distinctive subcultures as well as some unique social psychological consequences, they do not generate pathological behavior and personalities to the extent frequently argued by sociologists.

Jacobs, Jane. *The Death and Life of Great American Cit-*

*ies*. New York: Vintage, 1961. An influential attack on orthodox principles of city planning. The author emphasizes the benefits of social, economic, and physical diversity in cities and argues for policies that will save existing urban neighborhoods.

UROFSKY, MELVIN I., ed. *Perspectives on Urban America*. Garden City, N.Y.: Doubleday, 1973. An interdisciplinary challenge to the view that American cities are dying. The book covers topics such as the frontier heritage of the city, psychological problems of the poor, citizen participation, urban education, and the federal impact on cities.

WARD, BARBARA. *The Home of Man*. New York: Norton, 1976. A synthesis of issues raised at the 1976 United Nations Conference on Human Settlements (Habitat). Emphasis is placed on urban structure and design, resource availability, transportation, housing, and the economy of cities. The book places urban problems in a global context.

WHYTE, WILLIAM H. *The Last Landscape*. New York: Doubleday, 1968. This volume presents a strategy for preserving open space in and around cities, and argues that by saving open space for people, higher density settlements can be developed.

# Chapter 10
# Population and Demography

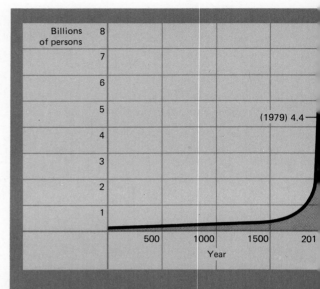

It took more than a million years for the world's human population to reach about a quarter billion at the year 1 A.D.

It took an additional 1650 years for that population to double to about one-half billion.

But it took only about 200 years for it to double again to a billion in 1850

Less than 100 years after that, it reached 2 billion in 1930.

It doubled again to 4 billion only 46 years later in 1976.

At the current rate of population growth, there will be 8.5 billion people living on this planet by the year 2015 — 35 years or less away.

How will *your* life be affected by the increasing number of people on earth?

The facts are stark. For the thoughtful reader, they may also be frightening. If you are a typical college freshman in 1980, you will be nearing age 40 at the turn of the next century. Today people in their forties are generally affluent enough to enjoy "the good things in life"—travel, recreation, fine food, nice homes, and so on. Will this be true for people who reach middle adulthood in the twenty-first century?

The answer to this question depends on many things that we cannot anticipate with any precision: developments in technology, political decisions, the choices people make among alternative life styles. Nevertheless, some important clues can be uncovered by examining current and projected population trends and their implications for the quality of life.

Currently, with just over four billion human beings on this planet, we are beginning to realize that the earth's "carrying capacity" is being strained, if not overtaxed.[1] The earth's biological systems form the foundation of the global economic system, providing food for people as well as raw materials for industry. Severe stresses on these biological systems— fisheries, forests, grasslands, and croplands—are now evident. The world food supply is lower than it has been in many years, and in the poorer countries, thousands of people die of starvation each year. Gasoline shortages and the threat of rationing are headlined in the mass media. The rising cost of housing, transportation, and food adds up to double-digit inflation in most of the world's economies. Industrial production has decreased because of shortages of raw materials. In short, the quality of life on earth is being undermined by the increasing demands we make on the earth's resources.

How serious these threats will be ultimately depends on population growth trends. Will, for example, the current rate of population growth continue, resulting in the projected eight billion people by early in the next century? Or, will that number be significantly altered, upward or downward, as a result of increases or decreases in the growth rate?

Two issues dominate discussions of population trends. First, *what are the dimensions of the population problem?* How large is the world's population and how is it distributed? What is the current rate of population growth and how is it likely to change in the future? How do the figures break down, for example, in terms of age and sex or geographic distribution? What causes differences in the size, growth, distribution, and composition of population?

The second major issue is *what are the consequences of the population problem?* How do population size and growth affect the food supply, economic development, the natural environment? How do governments and individuals respond to population trends?

## DEMOGRAPHIC DATA AND METHODS

**Demography** is *the scientific study of population.* The demographic phenomena include *structural aspects of populations*—their size, their rate of growth, their geographic distribution, and their composition, like sex, race, occupation, and education—and *population processes*—fertility, mortality, migration, and social mobility. How do demographers collect such data?

### The Population Census

The primary source of demographic data is the *population census,* an inventory of selected facts about the people who fall within the jurisdiction of a given administrative unit, such as a nation, county, or city. Most population censuses are conducted periodically by national governments to assess the needs of the population and to determine how national resources can best be used.

Censuses have been taken since ancient times, but only within this century have they counted the majority of the world's population. In the decade 1955–1964, eighty-five national censuses were taken, covering an estimated 68 percent of the earth's inhabitants. Four of the population giants—China, India, the Soviet Union, and the United States, which contain nearly half of the world's population—had censuses around 1960 and 1970. In the United States, a census of the population has been taken every ten years since 1790. A page from the form to be used in the United States population census for 1980 is shown in Figure 10.1.

The information collected for a population census varies from one nation to the next. Table 10.1 lists the information usually obtained in a national census. Additional facts may include income, place of work, number of times married, age at marriage, and religion. The questions are determined by what the government needs to know, and changes in a nation's

**TABLE 10.1  Information Typically Covered in a National Population Census**

A. Geographic items
   1. Location at time of census and/or place of usual residence
B. Household or family information
   2. Relationship to head of household or family
C. Personal characteristics
   3. Sex
   4. Age
   5. Marital status
   6. Place of birth
   7. Citizenship
D. Economic characteristics
   8. Type of activity
   9. Occupation
   10. Industry
   11. Status (as employer, employee, etc.)
E. Cultural characteristics
   12. Language
   13. Ethnic or nationality characteristics
F. Educational characteristics
   14. Literacy
   15. Level of education
   16. School attendance
G. Fertility data
   17. Children—total live born
H. Topics derived from the questionnaire
   18. Total population
   19. Population by size of locality
   20. Urban-rural classification
   21. Household or family composition

Population and Demography 259

**FIGURE 10.1  Sample page from 1980 United States Census form**

Page 2 — ————————→ Also answer the hous...

**Here are the QUESTIONS ↓**

**These are the columns for ANSWERS** ——→

*Please fill one column for each person listed in Question 1.*

| PERSON in column 1 | PERSON in column 2 |
|---|---|
| Last name | Last name |
| First name — Middle initial | First name — Middle initial |

**2. How is this person related to the person in column 1?**

*Fill one circle.*

*If "Other relative" of person in column 1, give exact relationship, such as mother-in-law, niece, grandson, etc.*

Column 1: START in this column with the household member (or one of the members) in whose name the home is owned or rented. If there is no such person, start in this column with any adult household member.

Column 2: If relative of person in column 1:
○ Husband/wife  ○ Father/mother
○ Son/daughter  ○ Other relative
○ Brother/sister

If not related to person in column 1:
○ Roomer, boarder  ○ Other nonrelative
○ Partner, roommate
○ Paid employee

**3. Sex** — *Fill one circle.*
○ Male  ○ Female  (×2)

**4. Race** — *Fill one circle.*

Each column:
○ White  ○ Asian Indian
○ Black or Negro  ○ Hawaiian
○ Japanese  ○ Guamanian
○ Chinese  ○ Samoan
○ Filipino  ○ Eskimo
○ Korean  ○ Aleut
○ Vietnamese  ○ Other — *Print race*
○ Indian (Amer.)
Print tribe →

**5. Age, and month and year of birth**

*a. Print age at last birthday.*
*b. Print month and fill one circle.*
*c. Print year in the spaces, and fill one circle below each number.*

Each column:
a. Age at last birthday
b. Month of birth
○ Jan.–Mar.  ○ Apr.–June  ○ July–Sept.  ○ Oct.–Dec.
c. Year of birth: 1 8 _ _
Digit columns: 0 ● / 1 ○ / 2 ○ / 3 ○ / 4 ○ / 5 ○ / 6 ○ / 7 ○ / 8 ○ / 9 ○

**6. Marital status** — *Fill one circle.*
○ Now married  ○ Separated
○ Widowed  ○ Never married
○ Divorced  (×2)

**7. Is this person's origin or descent —** *Fill one circle.*
○ Mexican-Amer.  ○ Cuban
○ Mexican or Chicano  ○ Other Spanish
○ Puerto Rican
○ Not Spanish  (×2)

**8. Since February 1, 1978, has this person attended regular school or college at any time?** *Fill one circle. Count nursery school, kindergarten, elementary school and schooling which leads to a high school diploma or college degree.*
○ No, has not attended
○ Yes, public school, public college
○ Yes, private, church-related
○ Yes, private, not church-related  (×2)

**9. What is the highest grade (or year) of regular school this person has ever attended?**

*Fill one circle.*
*If now attending school, mark grade person is in. If high school was finished by equivalency test (GED), mark "12".*

Highest grade attended:
○ Nursery school  ○ Kindergarten
Elementary through high school (grade or year)
1 2 3 4 5 6  7 8  9 10 11 12
○ ○ ○ ○ ○ ○  ○ ○  ○ ○ ○ ○
College (academic year)
1 2 3 4 5 6 7 8 or more
○ ○ ○ ○ ○ ○ ○ ○
○ Never attended school — Skip question 10  (×2)

**10. Did this person finish the highest grade (or year) attended?** *Fill one circle.*
○ Now attending this grade (or year)
○ Finished this grade (or year)
○ Did not finish this grade (or year)  (×2)

D-2 (X)  Fosdic 26.1:1

| CENSUS USE ONLY | A. ○ Inmate ○ Other | ○ ○ | CENSUS USE ONLY | A. ○ Inmate ○ Other | ○ ○ |

census reflect new problems confronting the society.

**Errors** Population censuses are not always free from error. Occasionally, census results are purposely falsified for political purposes. More often, errors are due to methodological inadequacies in collecting and processing the information. These can be classified as either errors of coverage or errors of classification.

*Errors of coverage* involve either incomplete enumeration, the most frequent mistake, or duplicate counting. Isolated households or communities are likely to be overlooked; and some categories of persons, such as very young children, sometimes go unreported. Further complicating enumeration is the fact that population counts may be based on two different criteria. The **de facto census method** counts the population according to where it is on the night preceding the census, while the **de jure census method** distributes people on the basis of their usual place of residence. Under the *de facto* system, a traveling salesman would be counted at his location for the night regardless of whether that was his permanent residence. Each method has advantages and disadvantages, and both are widely used. In the United States, the *de jure* method is standard, although *de facto* statistics are also collected.

*Errors of classification* result from the incorrect recording of population characteristics. Some of these inaccuracies are due to misreporting by the informant; others occur when the enumerator has to guess about a particular piece of information because the appropriate question was not asked, or was not answered, or was answered incorrectly. Age, income, marital status, and occupation are particularly likely to be erroneously reported.

### Vital Registration Systems

The population census provides a record of the characteristics of a population *at a given time* and is taken only periodically; *vital registration systems* record selected population events *as they occur.* Under ideal conditions, summaries are published monthly or annually. Events registered may include births, deaths, marriages, divorces, adoptions, and legitimations of minor children. For each event, supplementary information on race, age, occupation, and so forth may also be obtained, but not all of this information is recorded in all countries, and the accuracy of the statistics varies widely. Although errors in reporting and recording sometimes occur, the major problems with vital registration data are incomplete coverage and the vast amount of data to be recorded and analyzed. In 1965, for instance, complete birth registration statistics were available for only about 35 percent of the world's population.[2]

**Population Registers** Comprehensive procedures for continuously recording individual events and characteristics have been developed by many countries, but not the United States. Any change of characteristics, like occupation and place of residence, or any vital event, must be reported within a specified time. Although such population registers are usually established for purposes of policing or social control, they can provide demographic statistics as well.

**Sample Surveys** In recent years, sample surveys have been used increasingly to supplement census and registration data. In the developing countries, they supplement the data from incomplete census and registration coverage. The major advantage of sample surveys is that they provide a wider range of information than is available from census or vital registration sources. Surveys also permit more detailed analysis of the social and psychological factors associated with demographic events.

### Publication of Demographic Data

The main published sources of demographic information are the census and vital statistics prepared by individual nations. Census data, especially for the developing countries, are subject to several limitations. First, there are long periods (usually ten years) between censuses, during which population characteristics are changing, often rapidly and at unknown rates. Second, it often takes many years for the data collected in a census to be analyzed and published. In the developing nations, where government personnel and money are severely limited, only the most basic analyses may ever be published. Recently, however, technical and financial assistance from the United Nations and other organizations has increased the availability and quality of census information for many such countries. International vital statistics are even less accessible, and probably subject to greater error as well.

A major source of international data is the *United Nations Demographic Yearbook*, published annually since 1948. It includes basic population figures from censuses or estimates, vital statistics, and special topics presented in more detail, for instance, births and deaths, marriage and divorce rates, and population trends. For the relatively few countries that have population registers, reports are available and can be quite useful. Other sources of demographic data are the records of such programs as social security, military conscription, voter registration, and school enrollment.

### Demographic Analysis

Although the analysis of demographic data often involves the quantitative techniques common to most types of social research, certain unique procedures are particularly important in dealing with population variables. Of fundamental importance are the basic indicators of population growth, distribution, and composition, as well as fertility, mortality, and migration.

**The Balancing, or Demographic, Equation** Underlying the study of population is the **balancing equation,** sometimes called the **demographic equation:** Population size at the end of a given period equals population size at the beginning of the period, plus the number of entries into the population via births and immigration, minus the number of departures from the population via deaths and emigration. Any inaccuracies in the figures will, of course, affect the accuracy of the calculation. To illustrate, suppose that the population of Utopia was 100,000 on July 1, 1970, and we want to know the size of Utopia's population on July 1,

**demography:** the study of population including the structural characteristics of size, rate of growth, spatial distribution, and composition, and the population processes of fertility, mortality, migration, and social mobility.

**de facto census method:** counting people for census purposes as residing in the place where they spent the night preceding the day they are enumerated.

**de jure census method:** counting people for census purposes as residing in their usual or normal place of residence.

**balancing, or demographic, equation:** the basic equation used by demographers to analyze population size or distribution. The equation is

$$P_t = P_o + (B - D) + (I - E) + e$$

where $P_t$ = population size at the end of some specified time interval; $P_o$ = population size at the beginning of that interval; $B$ = number of births; $D$ = number of death; $I$ = number of immigrants; $E$ = number of emigrants; and $e$ = the residual error resulting from inaccuracies in census and vital registration statistics.

1980. We have records of 60,000 births and 30,000 deaths in Utopia over the ten-year period. Utopia's Immigration and Naturalization Bureau reports that between 1970 and 1980, 20,000 people entered the country through immigration, but only 5,000 emigrated to other nations. Assuming the figures are correct, then the population of Utopia on July 1, 1980, can be calculated as in Table 10.2

The importance of the demographic equation for population analysis cannot be overstated. It is principally used to understand the factors that contribute to population change. In addition, it can be used to project future population figures by making assumptions about future

**TABLE 10.2   The Balancing Equation For Utopia, 1970–1980**

| 100,000 | + | (60,000 | − | 30,000) | + | (20,000 | − | 5,000) | = | 145,000 |
|---------|---|---------|---|---------|---|---------|---|--------|---|---------|
| $P_o$ | | $B$ | | $D$ | | $I$ | | $E$ | | $P_t$ |
| Population on 7/1/70 | | Number of births | | Number of deaths | | Number of immigrants | | Number of emigrants | | Population on 7/1/80 |

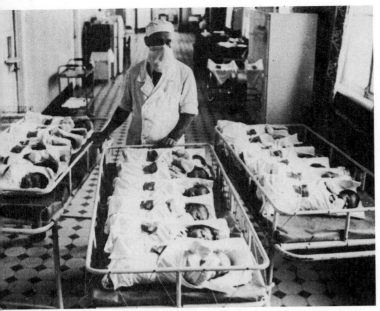

A cohort: newly borns in a hospital in Leningrad.

births, deaths, migration, and compositional changes.

The demographer sometimes focuses on particular subgroups within a population, such as blacks or workers. In these cases, the components of the balancing equation have to be specified accordingly. For some subgroups, such as those differentiated by sex or place of residence, it is only necessary to collect the appropriate statistics on births, deaths, migration, and so on. But with age groups, special considerations are necessary.

A **cohort** *is a group of persons within a given population experiencing the same event during a given year or interval of time.* For example, all people born during the period 1960–1964 constitute a five-year birth cohort, and all people who will marry in 1985 will belong to the marriage cohort for that year.

Many demographic analyses focus on age cohorts, particularly when changes over time are being studied. For instance, it might be useful to project to the year 2020 the effect on American society of the high survival rates among the cohort of those now aged twenty to thirty. This group is the largest single age category in the American population. If they survive in large numbers (as they are expected to do), and present birth rates do not change much, in

2020 they will still be the largest group. But at that time, of course, instead of being young, economically productive workers, they will be elderly, retired persons, with all that that implies for the labor force, medical care, social security, and so forth, all of which must be planned for ahead of time.

**Rates and Ratios**   Demographic statistics are frequently presented as *rates:* the number of events in a given period of time divided by the population in question during that period. The period of time used is usually a year, and rates are expressed per 100, 1,000, or even 10,000 members of the population. There are two types of rates: crude and refined. **Crude rates** measure the frequency of an event per unit of the whole population. **Refined rates** measure the frequency of an event per unit of population relevant to the event in question. Crude rates are not very useful because the denominator includes all members of the population, some of whom are not at risk of experiencing the event in question. The crude birthrate, for example, includes in the denominator women above and below childbearing age, as well as men of all ages. Refined rates are more valuable because in them the denominator is limited to population members who actually do risk experiencing the event being measured, like birthrates for women of childbearing age or marriage rates for previously unmarried persons.

Other types of demographic statistics are presented in terms of ratios, for instance, the **dependency ratio** is the number of persons of nonworking age divided by those of working age. Generally, rates are used in the analysis of population change, while ratios are employed for descriptive purposes.

## POPULATION THEORIES

Not until the eighteenth century did anyone consider population in a systematic or scientific way. The most important of these early writers were Thomas Malthus and Karl Marx and his followers.

### Thomas Malthus

The first person to write systematically about population was Thomas Malthus, an English clergyman and economist who published an analysis in 1798 in which he argued that a "natural law" governed the growth of populations.[3] Population, Mathus thought, would always increase faster than food production unless it was prevented by moral restraints, "vice," or natural disasters and disease. According to Malthus, the means of subsistence increase in arithmetic progression (1, 2, 3, 4, 5) because, at a given level of food-producing technology, the only way to increase the food supply is to increase the number of acres under cultivation, the number of fish caught, and so on. Population, however, increases in geometric progression (1, 2, 4, 8, 16), because two individuals can and normally do produce more children than the 2.1 required to replace themselves. (Any married couple must produce more than two children in order statistically to reproduce themselves because, in any population, some people will remain childless.) Thus, if unchecked, population would soon outstrip the resources necessary to sustain it, and there would be widespread famine.

Malthus recognized only two effective means of curbing the growth of population. The first he called *preventive checks*—including deferral of marriage, abstinence, and "vice"—extramarital sexual relations and prostitution, which would presumably avoid the birth of children. The second were *positive checks*, including epidemics, wars, plague, and famine, all of which would reduce the normal duration of life. Contraception within wedlock was generally regarded as immoral in Malthus's time and would thus have been labeled vice. For Malthus, individual human decisions and natural disasters were the only means of curbing population growth. No amount of social or governmental reorganization could affect it.

## The Marxian View

The Malthusian doctrine created a great deal of controversy and alerted followers and opponents alike to the need for a better understanding of population trends. An opposing view was presented by Karl Marx and other socialist writers. They argued that there is no natural law of population but that population size and growth are determined by social and economic conditions. Capitalism not only creates unemployment or underemployment because it cannot provide jobs for all, but it requires a readily available labor force that can be guaranteed

**cohort:** a group of persons within a given population experiencing the same event during a given time interval, for example, a specific age or degree of formal education.

**crude rate:** the frequency of an event, such as birth or death, per unit of population, usually per 1,000 or 10,000.

**refined rate:** the frequency of an event per unit of population at risk of experiencing that event, for example, births per woman of child-bearing age.

**dependency ratio:** the number of people of nonworking age in a population per 100 people of working age.

only if there is surplus population. Capitalism also requires consumers for its products, so there is even more demand for a large population. Population problems, therefore, are due to social and economic conditions, not to any lack of moral restraint in human heings. They can be resolved only through a reorganization of the social and economic bases of society.[4]

## The Demographic Transition

Modern theories of population growth are largely based on the decline in rates of growth in Europe following the Industrial Revolution. The most prominent of these is the **demographic transition theory** (see Figure 10.2). According to this theory, populations pass through a series of stages. First there is a period of high birth and death rates, producing a stationary condition with little or no net growth (Period A on Figure 10-2). This is followed by a series of transitional stages: In the first (Period B), mortality is reduced, causing the population to increase. Then (Period C) fertility declines, causing a decrease in the rate of growth. Finally (Period D), with birth and death rates both low, the rate of growth becomes relatively stable. Depending on the balance between mortality and fertility, the population may increase or even decrease slightly.

According to demographic transition theory, fertility had to be high in traditional societies because the mortality rate was so high it threatened societal survival. As mortality rates fell, families no longer needed to have so many children. Nevertheless, the institutional factors

FIGURE 10.2  The demographic transition

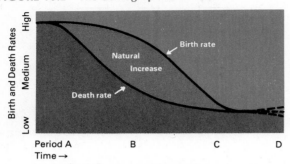

The theory of demographic transition, based largely on the European experience with industrialization, assumes that societies go through similar population stages as a consequence of modernization. In the original preindustrial stage, both birth and death rates are high and the population is usually relatively small, and stable (period A). With the beginnings of industrialization, improvements in medicine, sanitation, and so forth, death rates drop rapidly while, for a time, birth rates remain high. This results in a population explosion (Period B). After a time however, birth rates drop too, with the result that the rate of population growth decreases (period C), and population size becomes relatively stable once more, although it is larger. The relation of births to deaths may vary somewhat thereafter, resulting in a steady state, a slight increase over a long period of time, or even a slight decline in size (period D).

that supported high fertility—religion, morality, laws, customs, and habits—could not be altered rapidly. The result was a lag between the onset of mortality decline and the reduction of fertility, as shown in Figure 10.2.

These declines in mortality and fertility are the result of social and economic modernization. Mortality declines as improvements take place in public health, medical care, and the standard of living. Fertility declines, by contrast, as the result of a more complex interaction of social, psychological, cultural, economic, and demographic processes. Some of these are urbanization, individualism, and rising levels of aspiration, the decline of traditional norms governing familial organization and the status of women, industrialization, and increasing geographic and social mobility.

The institutional supports for high fertility were gradually undermined as a society modernized. Urbanization resulted in large, mobile city populations in which the small, nuclear family proved more responsive to the demands

of industry and people's rising personal aspirations. Children were no longer an economic asset, as they had been in agricultural society. Strong religious doctrines were replaced by a rational and secular point of view, and individual advancement was enhanced by formal education and the opportunity for women to work outside the household. In short, demographic transition theory states that fertility declines when social and economic changes increase the individual and familial advantages of having fewer children.

**Refinements in the Demographic Transition Theory:** The demographic transition theory provides a convenient description of the historical experience of European nations, but it has not proved very useful for predicting growth trends in the currently developing countries.

In the third phase of the demographic transition, children cease to be an economic asset: a family planning poster.

Although mortality rates have decreased as expected in many developing countries, fertility has not declined as predicted. Recent reformulations of transition theory have therefore focused on the biological, technological, political, social, cultural, and economic factors that affect human decisions regarding reproduction.

The demographic transition can be observed in the modern world in societies undergoing modernization. Under what conditions do some individuals become "demographic innovators" who limit their fertility in spite of a cultural tradition of large families? John C. Caldwell, who has studied the family and fertility in Sub-Saharan Africa, offers one answer:

'What distinguished the demographic innovators from others was not their lack of superstition or rationalism but their attitudes toward family and children. They have emotionally nucleated their families; they are less concerned with ancestors and extended family relatives than they are with their children, their children's future, and even the future of their children's children. They are more likely to have been "spoilt" themselves in that their parents gave them more emotion and wealth than they expected back, and this is the way they tend, although usually to a greater extent, to treat their own children.'[5]

Emotional nucleation, whereby parents live for and give to their children rather than the reverse results from several factors, one of which is the diffusion of Western culture, with its emphasis on the nuclear family and the responsibility of parents to oversee the welfare of their children. In economic terms, the distinction is that in posttransition societies, the flow of wealth has been reversed. Rather than children being economically useful to parents by working in the fields or taking care of them in their old age, posttransition parents use their wealth to enhance the well-being of their children. The smaller the number of children among whom the available resources of money, land, time, and emotional energy must be divided, the better.

## POPULATION SIZE

Population size is, obviously, the absolute number of inhabitants occupying a specified area at a given time, although we should remember that this number may vary according

> **Demographic Transition Theory:** the idea that societies go through a set of stages in population growth and decline associated with industrialization. The first stage is characterized by stability in size based on equally high rates of both birth and death. This is followed by a population explosion caused by rapidly declining death rates while birth rates remain high, through a later downswing in growth when birth rates decline, and a final period of stable size produced by low rates of both birth and death.

to whether the count is based on a *de jure* or a *de facto* definition. We must also note that except when census-year data are used, population size is based on estimates. Population change can be represented in a variety of ways.

The simplest indicator is the absolute difference between two dates. A more useful measure is the *intercensal percent change* (IPC): the relative amount of change in a population between census periods. It is computed by dividing the amount of change between two censuses by the population at the earlier census and converting the resulting number to a percent. For example, the United States population between 1960 and 1970 increased from 179,323,175 to 203,211,926, or about 13.3 percent; while the population of the world in the same period increased from about 2,982,000,000 to 3,632,000,000, or 21.8 percent. To compare different populations meaningfully, the interval between censuses must be equivalent, though it does not necessarily have to refer to the same years.

It is also useful to express population change in terms of the components of the basic balancing equation. **Natural increase (or decrease)** is *the net difference between births and deaths*. It is usually expressed as a rate per 1,000 population during a specified period. Net migration is the absolute difference between immigration and emigration and can also be expressed as a rate.

*Trends and Differences in Population Size*

Considering the length of time human beings have been on earth, the so-called population explosion is very recent. It is estimated that the human population did not reach 1 billion until approximately 1800–1860, but the second billion was reached around 1925, the third by

1960, and the fourth by 1975. As Table 10.3 shows, this trend is directly associated with an increasingly high rate of growth from about 1750 to the present and is uniform in one respect: absolute size has continually increased.

But the long-term trend in average annual rates of growth is not uniform among regions. In the period since 1750, the population growth rate declined in North America, remained stable in Europe, fluctuated in the Soviet Union and China, and increased in the remainder of Asia, Latin America, and Africa.[6] Paradoxically, then, the most rapidly growing nations are those that can least afford increasing numbers of people. For developing countries (in Africa, Latin America, and Asia excluding Japan), annual growth rates averaged 0.3 percent during the period 1850–1900, 0.9 percent for 1900–1950, and 2.1 percent in the years 1950–1965. Corresponding figures for the developed nations (Europe, the Soviet Union, North America, Oceania, and Japan) are 1.0 percent, 0.8 percent, and 1.2 percent, respectively.[7] If the most recent rates continue, the population of the developing nations will double in approximately thirty-three years, while the developed nations will double in about fifty-eight years.

The first national census taken in the United States (1790) showed a total population of just under 4 million. By 1850, this figure had grown to a little more than 23 million; in 1900, it was 76 million; and in 1950, it was just over 151 million. The most recent census, conducted in 1970, reported a population of 203,211,926. In early 1979, the Census Bureau estimated the United States population to be just under 220 million. The average annual rate of growth in the United States has declined considerably during the past two and one-half centuries, the peak being approximately 3.2 percent in 1820, while the lowest rate, near 0.6 percent, was recorded during the mid-1930s. The overall trend shows a sharp decline from the end of the Civil War to the beginning of World War II, followed by an equally sharp increase to the late 1950s. Since then, annual rates of growth have steadily fallen.

**Causes of Population Size** Population size and rates of growth are direct results of interaction among the components of the demographic equation—fertility, mortality, immigration, and emigration. These are in turn related to a wide variety of biological, social-structural, cultural, and other demographic factors. It should be evident that world population prior to the eighteenth century grew by gradual increase. Following the Industrial Revolution, the world rate began to climb more steeply, principally in the nations directly and immediately affected by industrialization, and chiefly because of changing relationships among fertility, mortality, and migration.

A decline in death rates initiated the increases in population. In the developed nations, the death rate began to fall in the early eighteenth century and continued to decline gradually for a period of 75 to 150 years, after which it stabilized at the current level. The birthrate also declined, but more slowly. The result has been

**TABLE 10.3   Estimates of Historical Population Growth**

| | Population (millions) | Average annual increase since preceding date (percent)[a] | Appropriate number of years required for population to double at given date |
|---|---|---|---|
| B.C. | | | |
| 7000–6000 | 5–10 | | |
| A.D. | | | |
| 1 | 200–400 | 0.0 | |
| 1650 | 470–545 | 0.0 | |
| 1750 | 629–961 | 0.4 | 173 |
| 1800 | 813–1,125 | 0.4 | 173 |
| 1850 | 1,128–1,402 | 0.5 | 139 |
| 1900 | 1,550–1,762 | 0.5 | 139 |
| 1950 | 2,486 | 0.8 | 86 |
| 1978 | 4,365 | 2.0 | 35 |

that natural increase remained relatively low and stable, averaging between 0.5 and 1.5 percent. Contrasting with this pattern, the death rate in Asia, Africa, and Latin America did not begin to fall sharply until about 1940, but then it declined dramatically, becoming equal to, or even lower than, the death rate in the industrialized nations in fifteen to thirty years. At the same time, the birth rate has remained at a level above that prevailing in western Europe in the early 1800s.

The reduced mortality brought about by the industrialized nations during the Industrial Revolution was associated with increased productivity, whereas the dramatic reduction of death rates in the developing nations since 1940 has been primarily due to medical technology imported from the more industrial nations, without the associated increase in internal economic productivity experienced earlier by the industrial nations. The result of this drastic shift in the balance between births and deaths has been a spectacular acceleration in the overall increase of population in the developing world during the past three decades—the population explosion.

Migration also may contribute to population increase. For example, the growth of European nations was curtailed somewhat by heavy emigration, primarily to the United States, between 1880 and 1930. But nowadays, net migration has relatively little influence on population growth, except in a few nations like Australia, Brazil, Canada, Israel, and New Zealand.

**Consequences of Population Size**    The consequences of variations in population size and growth can be viewed from two perspectives. In the short run, some distinct advantages can be seen in large size and rapid growth. If a nation has abundant natural resources, food, and habitable land, then an increasing population can be good for national development. People are needed to settle the land, to produce and consume goods, to provide and utilize services, and to coordinate the activities of groups and institutions. Such was the case with many, if not most, nations prior to the twentieth century, the United States being an obvious example.

But when land, food, and other resources are not abundant, continued population growth can be detrimental to national development, and sometimes even disastrous. Unfortunately, this situation prevails for most of the contem-

> **natural increase/decrease:**  the net difference between births and deaths in a given period, usually expressed as a rate per 1,000.

porary world. Natural resources have been depleted far beyond our capacity to replace them, millions of people suffer from malnutrition, and the numbers who die from starvation increase annually. In short, the era when rapid population growth was advantageous to national development has passed and is unlikely to be repeated in the foreseeable future.

Problems of population growth are not limited to developing nations. The United States has the highest per capita standard of living in the world and is the world's leading food exporter. But many of the problems facing it today result directly or indirectly from population size. The "baby boom" after World War II produced a tidal wave of children. School buildings had to be dramatically enlarged to accommodate them, as did the teaching profession. As the cohort aged, however, it left behind empty schoolrooms, some still unpaid for, and teachers without jobs, while it overwhelmed the colleges, creating a corresponding demand for college teachers. Similarly, the energy shortage, unemployment, pollution, and water shortages also in part stem from population growth. The United States now has too many people to maintain the standard of living that became conventional in the 1940s and 1950s. Today's college students probably cannot expect in maturity to enjoy the affluence to which most became accustomed in childhood.

To a large extent, the social chaos of the contemporary world is a product of population growth. Social institutions are increasingly unable to meet the needs of increasing numbers of people; but workable solutions themselves depend heavily on a reorganization of these same collapsing social institutions.[8] That is the dilemma presented by increasing population growth.

## POPULATION DISTRIBUTION

Along with increases in the size and rate of growth of the human population has come a change in the distribution of people over the earth's surface, largely as a result of increasing urbanization.

**Environmental pollution is often an indirect consequence of overpopulation.**

The distribution of a population has several important implications for social organization. A widely dispersed population is likely to lack social integration and to foster differences in culture and social structure. Urbanization permits collective efforts to deal with the necessities of societal survival, for example, a division of labor leading to occupational specialization. At the same time, densely concentrated populations may create stresses in their natural environments—resulting in depletion of resources or environmental pollution—or in their social environments because of the frequency of social interaction (see Chapter 9).

## Measures of Population Distribution

Population density, as we saw in Chapter 9, is the number of people per unit of land area (per square mile or kilometer, for instance). Density ratios are crude, however, because they do not reflect variations in the habitability or *support potential* of the land.

More useful and more frequently used are measures of population distribution within and between specified geographic or political areas. The most important criterion of population distribution is the urban-rural distinction. Although everybody recognizes significant differences between city and country populations, no criteria are universally agreed upon for the definition of an urban locality. Urban residence is generally associated with predominantly nonagricultural employment and a total population of at least 5,000. Obviously, there are drastic differences among those localities classified as urban, many more than exist between rural areas.

## Trends and Differences in Population Distribution

The pattern of distribution of the world's population according to major regions has changed only slightly over the past two centuries. As Table 10.4 shows, slightly more than half of the world's population has been in Asia, during that time. The remainder has been dispersed among the other major land areas. The proportion residing in the Americas has increased from 2.3 percent in 1750 to 14.1 percent in 1970, while moderate declines have occurred in Asia, Europe, and Africa.

**TABLE 10.4    Estimated Distribution of the World's Population 1950–1978 (Percent)**

| Area | 1750 | 1800 | 1850 | 1900 | 1950 | 1965 | 1970 | 1978 | Net change 1750–1978 |
|------|------|------|------|------|------|------|------|------|------|
| World[a] | 100.1 | 99.9 | 100.1 | 100.1 | 99.9 | 99.9 | 100.1 | 100.0 | |
| Africa | 13.4 | 10.9 | 8.8 | 8.1 | 8.7 | 9.2 | 9.5 | 10.4 | −3.0 |
| Asia | 63.0 | 64.4 | 63.5 | 56.1 | 54.4 | 55.7 | 56.6 | 58.3 | −4.7 |
| Latin America | 2.0 | 2.5 | 3.0 | 4.5 | 6.5 | 7.5 | 7.8 | 8.1 | +6.1 |
| North America | 0.3 | 0.7 | 2.1 | 5.0 | 6.7 | 6.5 | 6.3 | 5.7 | +5.4 |
| Europe | 15.8 | 15.5 | 16.5 | 17.9 | 15.8 | 13.5 | 12.7 | 11.0 | −4.8 |
| USSR | 5.3 | 5.7 | 6.0 | 8.1 | 7.2 | 7.0 | 6.7 | 6.0 | +0.7 |
| Oceania | 0.3 | 0.2 | 0.2 | 0.4 | 0.5 | 0.5 | 0.5 | 0.5 | +0.2 |

[a]Deviations from 100 percent are due to rounding.

Population densities are highly variable, as shown in Table 10.5. Although high densities are evident for some of the more industrialized nations, average densities are actually higher among the developing countries. As world population continues to grow, overall density must inevitably increase. Even by a conservative estimate, world population density will double between 1960 and 2000, resulting in over 7 billion people on the earth.[9] Furthermore, the density differential between develop-

ing and developed nations will increase about sevenfold. Once again, the pattern of population change will continue to present grave problems for those nations least able to cope with the pressures.

The most dramatic shift in the distribution of human population in modern times is in the growth of cities, as we saw in Chapter 9. In 1800 no more than 3 percent of the world's people could be considered urban and probably no single city contained a million inhabitants.[10]

**TABLE 10.5**  Population, Area, and Density for the World, Major Areas, and Regions, 1978

| Area | Estimated mid-year population (millions) | Area (km² in thousands) | Density (population per km²) |
|---|---|---|---|
| **World total** | 4,365 | 135,781 | 29 |
| Less developed regions | 3,203 | 74,468 | 38 |
| More developed regions | 1,162 | 61,312 | 19 |
| **Africa** | 455 | 30,319 | 13 |
| Western Africa | 141 | 6,142 | 19 |
| Eastern Africa | 126 | 6,338 | 18 |
| Middle Africa | 50 | 6,613 | 7 |
| Northern Africa | 106 | 8,525 | 12 |
| Southern Africa | 31 | 2,701 | 10 |
| **Asia (excluding USSR)** | 2,547 | 27,532 | |
| East Asia | 1,200 | 11,757 | 86 |
| People's Republic of China | 1,004 | 11,129 | 87 |
| Japan | 115 | 370 | 294 |
| Other East Asia | 81 | 258 | 32 |
| South Asia | 1,347 | 15,775 | 79 |
| Middle South Asia | 902 | 6,771 | 124 |
| Southeast Asia | 353 | 4,498 | 72 |
| Southwest Asia | 92 | 4,506 | 20 |
| **Europe (excluding USSR)** | 480 | 4,936 | 96 |
| Western Europe | 153 | 995 | 153 |
| Southern Europe | 137 | 1,315 | 101 |
| Eastern Europe | 108 | 990 | 107 |
| Northern Europe | 82 | 1,636 | 50 |
| **Latin America** | 352 | 20,566 | 16 |
| Tropical South America | 196 | 13,700 | 13 |
| Middle America (mainland) | 87 | 2,496 | 32 |
| Temperate South America | 40 | 4,134 | 10 |
| Caribbean | 28 | 236 | 114 |
| **Northern America** | 248 | 21,515 | 11 |
| **USSR** | 261 | 22,402 | 11 |
| **Oceania** | 22 | 8,511 | 3 |
| Australia & New Zealand | 17 | 7,955 | 2 |
| Melanesia | 3 | 525 | 6 |
| Polynesia & Micronesia | 2 | 30 | 44 |

**TABLE 10.6   Percentage of Population Living in Urban Areas for Major World Regions, 1950–2000**

|  | *1950* | *1960* | *1970* | *1975* | *1980*[a] | *1990*[a] | *2000*[a] |
|---|---|---|---|---|---|---|---|
| World Total | 29.0 | 33.9 | 37.5 | 39.3 | 41.3 | 45.0 | 51.3 |
| Less developed regions | 16.7 | 21.8 | 25.8 | 28.0 | 30.5 | 36.5 | 43.5 |
| More developed regions | 52.5 | 58.7 | 64.7 | 67.5 | 70.2 | 74.9 | 78.8 |
| Africa | 14.5 | 18.2 | 22.8 | 25.7 | 28.8 | 35.7 | 42.5 |
| East Asia | 16.7 | 24.7 | 28.6 | 30.7 | 33.0 | 38.6 | 45.4 |
| South Asia | 15.6 | 17.8 | 20.4 | 22.0 | 24.0 | 24.1 | 36.1 |
| Europe | 53.7 | 58.4 | 63.9 | 66.4 | 68.8 | 73.2 | 77.1 |
| Latin America | 41.2 | 49.4 | 57.4 | 61.2 | 64.7 | 70.7 | 75.2 |
| Northern America | 63.8 | 67.1 | 70.4 | 72.0 | 73.7 | 77.2 | 80.8 |
| Oceania | 61.2 | 66.2 | 70.8 | 73.4 | 75.9 | 80.4 | 83.0 |
| USSR | 39.3 | 48.8 | 56.7 | 60.9 | 64.8 | 71.3 | 76.1 |

[a]Projected

**TABLE 10.7   Percent of Total Population in Large Cities for Selected Years, 1920–2000**

| *Cities of 100,000 or more* | | | | | | | |
|---|---|---|---|---|---|---|---|
|  | *1920* | *1950* | *1960* | *1970* | *1980*[a] | *1990*[a] | *2000*[a] |
| World | 9.1 | 15.6 | 16.4 | 22.9 | 26.6 | 30.4 | 33.3 |
| Less developed regions | 2.6 | 7.9 | 11.5 | 14.9 | 19.0 | 23.6 | 27.4 |
| More developed regions | 22.8 | 30.5 | 36.4 | 41.8 | 47.2 | 52.0 | 55.7 |

| *Cities of 1,000,000 or more* | | | | | | | |
|---|---|---|---|---|---|---|---|
|  | *1920* | *1950* | *1960* | *1970* | *1980*[a] | *1990*[a] | *2000*[a] |
| World | 3.6 | 7.1 | 9.4 | 11.6 | 14.4 | 18.2 | 20.9 |
| Less developed regions | 0.1 | 2.9 | 5.0 | 7.2 | 10.3 | 14.4 | 17.7 |
| More developed regions | 10.0 | 15.1 | 18.5 | 21.8 | 25.8 | 30.0 | 32.9 |

| *Cities of 5,000,000 or more* | | | | | | | |
|---|---|---|---|---|---|---|---|
|  | *1920* | *1950* | *1960* | *1970* | *1980*[a] | *1990*[a] | *2000*[a] |
| World | N.A. | 1.9 | 3.2 | 4.6 | 5.8 | 7.8 | 9.9 |
| Less developed regions | N.A. | 0.3 | 0.6 | 2.5 | 4.1 | 6.4 | 9.0 |
| More developed regions | N.A. | 4.8 | 8.5 | 9.5 | 10.3 | 12.5 | 13.4 |

[a]Projected

During the past 175 years, the proportion of people living in cities has steadily increased, as has the number of localities classified as urban. Recent figures for the world and selected regions are shown in Table 10.6. These data show that by the year 2000 half the world's population will be living in urban areas.

The pace of urbanization differs considerably from one region to the next. Between 1950 and 1975 world urbanization increased by 36 percent; the developed regions increased by 29 percent, and the less developed by 68 percent. Not only is the world's population more urbanized; it is also increasingly concentrated in large cities (see Table 10.7), with the rate of increase higher for the developing nations.

Changes in population distribution within the United States reflect both the world pattern and the pattern for the industrialized countries. Population density at the time of the first census in 1790 was 4.5 persons per square mile; this increased to 7.9 in 1850, 21.5 in 1900, 50.5 in 1960, and 57.5 in 1970.[11] The increasing urbanization of the United States also reflects world trends, growing steadily since the beginning of this centruy. Seventy-five percent of the population is now urban.

## Causes of Population Distribution

Population distribution is influenced by a wide range of factors. In general, the more complex a society becomes, the less directly geographical and physical factors influence the distribution of its population. Since the Industrial Revolution, the significant determinants have been changes in demographic and social organization.

The most direct causes of population distribution are, of course, levels of natural increase and net migration. If births exceed deaths and immigration is greater than emigration, an area will grow and become more densely populated. Under normal conditions, population distribution changes relatively slowly, so the pattern of distribution existing at any time has important consequences for future change. At the international level, population distribution is largely a consequence of differences in rates of natural increase, although alterations in national boundaries may play a significant role.

Less direct causes of population distribution are social organizational factors and adminis-

trative decisions. The Soviet Union, for example, has deliberately populated Siberia through forced emigration as well as incentive plans. Economic activities, technological advance, and political decisions also influence patterns of population distribution. All national governments have laws that regulate migration to and from other countries, and some have policies that affect the internal distribution of population. For example, rural colonization schemes, government programs to encourage the decentralization of industry, and the development of "new towns," such as the unsuccessful Brasilia, aim at relieving demographic pressure on large cities.

## Consequences of Population Distribution

Variations in population distribution, especially around borders shared by two nations, may have important social, political, and economic consequences for international relations. Larger, more densely populated nations often desire to expand their territorial boundaries at the expense of smaller, less densely populated ones. Indeed, one of the major causes of international conflict is population pressure, for example, the recent Chinese movements into India and the Soviet Union, and the extended conflict in Indochina during the past quarter century. People are viewed not only as producers and consumers of material goods but also as the basis of national security. Territorial expansion, however, is usually a less feasible way to relieve population pressure than social reorganization.

At the national level, the principal trend in population distribution has been urbanization. Philip Hauser refers to this as population implosion and argues that as size and density increase, the potential for human interaction in any area is drastically increased.[12] For example, if we assumed an average density of 1 person per square mile for the United States in 1500, there would have been 314 persons within any circular area with a ten-mile radius. If there are 8,000 persons per square mile in the average central city in 1970, the number of persons within the same circular area would be 2,512,000. Finally, Manhattan Island, with a density of approximately 75,000 persons per square mile has 23,550,000 potential contacts within a circle

**FIGURE 10.3    Increasing population density**

1 person per square mile = 314
in a 10-mile radius
(U.S. in the year 1500)

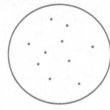

8,000 per square mile =
2,512,000 in 10-mile radius
(average density of American
central city in 1970)

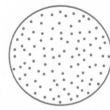

75,000 per square mile =
23,500,000 in 10-mile radius
(Manhattan Island in 1970)

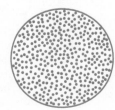

having a ten-mile radius! (See Figure 10.3.)

Although many of the problems associated with urbanization result from population diversification, others result directly or indirectly from the sheer numbers and density of urban inhabitants. In many cities unemployment is on the increase, land values and housing costs are skyrocketing, and pollution is reaching a level where life itself may be endangered.

The major problems of urban living are housing, employment, education, and poverty. When too many people are concentrated in relatively small areas they lack the resources to satisfy their collective expectations regarding human welfare. Whether cities continue to be the focus of the creative aspects of human culture, or degenerate into Hobbes's state of nature — where life would not only be poor, nasty, brutish, and short, as Hobbes said, but also *crowded* as well — would depend upon our ability to develop improved modes of urban social organization.

Rural areas have also been affected. While the proportion of people living outside cities has been declining, absolute numbers of rural dwellers have been increasing in the develop-

ing nations. The result is an excess of rural population in relation to the land cultivated, and thus considerable unemployment. This problem is made worse by the inequitable distribution of land ownership in many rural areas. Rural poverty is a significant problem in both developed and developing nations. Furthermore, rural-to-urban migration is selective: migrants are frequently younger, better-educated, and more ambitious, leaving on the land the aged, the illiterate, and the apathetic.

## POPULATION COMPOSITION

In addition to size and territorial distribution, populations differ in the distribution of personal characteristics among their members. This component of demographic analysis is called **population composition.** The characteristics considered are of two basic types. Ascribed characteristics include attributes such as age, kinship, sex, race, ethnic status, and place of birth, that are assigned to individuals by the circumstances of their birth. They are, except under unusual conditions, not subject to change. Achieved characteristics, by contrast, are determined by a person's efforts and social experience and are more clearly subject to change. Examples include marital status, nationality, language, religion, place of residence, occupation, education, and income.

Variations in population composition influence the basic population processes of fertility, mortality, migration, and social mobility. If many males have been killed in a war, for example, many women will have to remain single, and both fertility and the composition of the labor force will be affected. (The German population will show the effects of World War II for decades, as will the British.) Variations in population composition also influence social and economic organization.

### Measures of Population Composition

One technique for representing age and sex composition is the **population pyramid,** a diagram of the age distribution of a population, differentiated by sex. The pyramidal shape results from the fact that there are usually fewer older people in the population than younger people, although the degree of variation is dependent on fertility and mortality rates. Figure 10.4 shows the three basic types of population pyramids. The pyramid for Mexico is typical of populations with high and fairly constant fertility and larger numbers of people in the younger ages. The pyramid for the United States reflects a recent decline in fertility, resulting in smaller numbers of people in the younger ages. The pyramid for Sweden exhibits patterns associated with long-standing low fertility.

Two other measures of age and sex composition are available. The *dependency ratio* shows the ratio of people of nonworking ages (generally those below fifteen and over sixty-four) to those of working age (between fifteen and sixty-four). It is usually computed in terms of the number of persons of nonworking age per 100 persons of working age. For some purposes, it is useful to calculate youth and old-age dependency ratios separately.

The **sex ratio** represents the number of males in the population per 100 females. At birth, this ratio is approximately 105 for the human population in general, indicating a higher proportion of male births. But men have higher death rates than women, so the initial proportion is gradually reduced until the sex ratio is approximately even near middle age. From that point onward, females outnumber males. Social and cultural factors can influence the sex ratio for any population.

**population composition:** the distribution in a population of both ascribed characteristics (such as age, sex, and race) and achieved characteristics (such as marital status, education, and occupation).

**population pyramid:** a graphic representation of a population's age-sex distribution.

**sex ratio:** the number of males in a population per 100 females.

*Trends and Differences in Population Composition*

Until about 1850, most of the world's population had age structures similar to the classical pyramidal age-sex distribution seen in Mexico in Figure 10.4 Since that time, substantial changes have occurred in the age structures of the now-developed countries, with a fewer young people and more old people. In the developing countries, where fertility remains relatively high, the pyramidal shape has been maintained. Abbreviated age distributions for various regions of the world are shown in Table 10.8. One important consequence of the differences in these data is a variation in the dependency measures, shown in the last three columns. Generally, the total and youth dependency ratios are considerably higher for the developing countries, where a substantial pro-

**FIGURE 10.4    The three general profiles of age composition: Mexico, United States, and Sweden:** ca. 1976

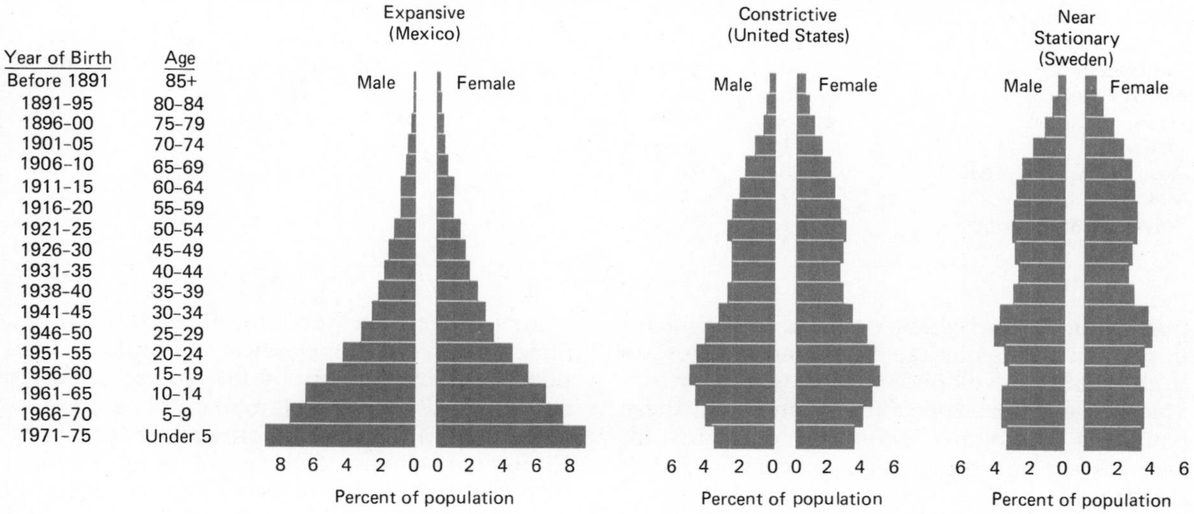

**TABLE 10.8** Estimated Age Distribution and Dependency Ratios of the Population of Major Areas of the World, 1975

| | Percentage distribution by age | | | Dependency ratio (number of persons in dependent age groups per 100 aged 15–64 years) | | |
|---|---|---|---|---|---|---|
| Area | Under 15 years | 15–64 years | 65 years and over | Under 15 years | 65 years and over | Total (under 15 plus 65 and over) |
| **World total** | 36.0 | 58.3 | 5.7 | 61.7 | 9.8 | 71.5 |
| Less developed regions | 40.4 | 55.8 | 3.8 | 72.4 | 6.8 | 79.2 |
| More developed regions | 25.0 | 64.5 | 10.5 | 38.8 | 16.3 | 55.1 |
| **Africa** | 44.2 | 52.9 | 2.9 | 83.6 | 5.5 | 89.1 |
| Western Africa | 44.8 | 52.7 | 2.5 | 85.0 | 4.7 | 89.7 |
| Eastern Africa | 45.0 | 52.4 | 2.7 | 85.9 | 5.2 | 91.1 |
| Middle Africa | 42.6 | 54.5 | 2.9 | 78.2 | 5.3 | 83.5 |
| Northern Africa | 44.2 | 52.5 | 3.3 | 84.2 | 6.3 | 90.5 |
| Southern Africa | 41.1 | 55.0 | 3.9 | 74.7 | 7.1 | 81.8 |
| **Asia (excluding USSR)** | | | | | | |
| East Asia | 32.7 | 61.5 | 5.8 | 53.2 | 9.4 | 62.6 |
| People's Republic of China | 33.4 | 61.0 | 5.6 | 54.3 | 9.2 | 63.5 |
| Japan | 24.5 | 67.7 | 7.8 | 36.2 | 11.5 | 47.7 |
| Other East Asia | 38.5 | 57.8 | 3.7 | 66.6 | 6.4 | 73.0 |
| South Asia | 43.2 | 53.8 | 3.0 | 80.3 | 5.6 | 85.9 |
| Middle South Asia | 43.0 | 54.1 | 2.9 | 79.5 | 5.4 | 84.9 |
| Southeast Asia | 43.6 | 53.4 | 3.0 | 81.6 | 5.6 | 87.2 |
| Southwest Asia | 43.1 | 53.0 | 3.9 | 81.3 | 7.4 | 88.7 |
| **Europe (excluding USSR)** | 23.9 | 63.8 | 12.3 | 37.5 | 19.3 | 56.8 |
| Western Europe | 23.1 | 63.3 | 13.6 | 36.5 | 21.5 | 58.0 |
| Southern Europe | 24.0 | 62.3 | 13.6 | 38.5 | 21.8 | 60.3 |
| Eastern Europe | 23.1 | 65.4 | 11.5 | 35.3 | 17.6 | 52.9 |
| Northern Europe | 23.8 | 62.8 | 13.5 | 37.9 | 21.5 | 59.4 |
| **Latin America** | 42.0 | 54.1 | 3.8 | 77.6 | 7.0 | 84.6 |
| Tropical South America | 43.1 | 53.8 | 3.1 | 80.1 | 5.8 | 85.9 |
| Middle America (mainland) | 45.7 | 50.9 | 3.4 | 89.8 | 6.7 | 96.5 |
| Temperate South America | 30.4 | 62.3 | 7.3 | 48.8 | 11.7 | 60.5 |
| Caribbean | 40.7 | 54.2 | 5.1 | 75.1 | 9.4 | 84.5 |
| **North America** | 25.5 | 64.3 | 10.2 | 39.7 | 15.9 | 55.6 |
| **USSR** | 25.8 | 65.1 | 9.1 | 39.6 | 14.0 | 53.6 |
| **Oceania** | 31.5 | 61.1 | 7.4 | 51.6 | 12.1 | 63.7 |
| Australia & New Zealand | 28.6 | 62.8 | 8.6 | 45.5 | 13.7 | 59.2 |
| Melanesia | 42.4 | 54.5 | 3.1 | 77.8 | 5.7 | 83.5 |
| Polynesia & Micronesia | 41.4 | 55.8 | 2.8 | 74.2 | 5.0 | 79.2 |

portion of resources are devoted to caring for dependents. The old-age dependency ratios are higher in the developed nations, where fertility is lower and life expectancy is longer. In these countries, there are increasing demands for services for the elderly, such as extended medical care.

Like other developed countries, the United States showed the classical pyramid-shaped population in 1900; but by 1970, it had begun to shift toward a more rectangular shape. In 1970, 28 percent of the population was under fifteen, 62 percent between fifteen and sixty-four, and 10 percent sixty-five or over. The resulting dependency ratios are 61.5 (total), 45.6 (youth), and 15.9 (oldage).[13] Compared with the figures in Table 10.8, the United States currently has an age structure like those of the other developed countries, but with a higher dependency ratio than the European countries or Japan.

Sex ratios do not usually vary much over time, but they do differ somewhat among the nations of the world, and considerably among the various age groups in a population. Generally, sex ratios are lower—that is, there is a higher proportion of females—in the developed nations and in successively older age categories (see Table 10.9.) In 1970, the United States had a sex ratio of 105.0 for the population under fifteen, 94.6 for those fifteen to sixty-four, and 72.1 for those sixty-five years of age or more. The total sex ratio for the population was 95.8.[14]

## Causes of Population Composition

Trends and differences in age and sex characteristics have a number of causes. As indicated earlier, the sex ratio at birth is approximately 105 males for every 100 females. Many explanations for this difference have been proposed, but the evidence is often contradictory and is by no means comprehensive. Differences in sex

TABLE 10.9   Estimated Sex Ratios (Males per 100 Females) for Major Areas of the World by Selected Age Categories, 1975

| Area | Under 15 years | 15–64 years | 65 years and over | Total |
|---|---|---|---|---|
| **World total** | 104 | 101 | 75 | 100 |
| Developing regions | | | | |
| More developed regions | | | | |
| **Africa** | 101 | 98 | 83 | 99 |
| Western Africa | 100 | 100 | 84 | 100 |
| Eastern Africa | 101 | 97 | 81 | 98 |
| Middle Africa | 100 | 94 | 74 | 96 |
| Northern Africa | 104 | 99 | 88 | 101 |
| Southern Africa | 100 | 97 | 77 | 97 |
| **Asia (excluding USSR)** | 105 | 105 | 90 | 104 |
| East Asia | 103 | 105 | 85 | 103 |
| People's Republic of China | 103 | 107 | 87 | 104 |
| Japan | 105 | 96 | 78 | 97 |
| Other East Asia | 104 | 100 | 69 | 100 |
| South Asia | 105 | 104 | 98 | 105 |
| Middle South Asia | 107 | 107 | 105 | 107 |
| Southeast Asia | 103 | 97 | 84 | 99 |
| Southwest Asia | 104 | 102 | 91 | 103 |
| **Europe (excluding USSR)** | 105 | 98 | 68 | 95 |
| Western Europe | 105 | 100 | 64 | 94 |
| Southern Europe | 104 | 96 | 72 | 95 |
| Eastern Europe | 105 | 96 | 69 | 94 |
| Northern Europe | 105 | 100 | 67 | 96 |
| **Latin America** | 103 | 100 | 85 | 100 |
| Tropical South America | 102 | 99 | 83 | 100 |
| Middle America (mainland) | 104 | 100 | 87 | 101 |
| Temperate South America | 103 | 100 | 82 | 99 |
| Caribbean | 103 | 98 | 96 | 100 |
| **North America** | 104 | 97 | 70 | 96 |
| **USSR** | 104 | 88 | 44 | 87 |
| **Oceania** | 105 | 105 | 79 | 103 |
| Australia & New Zealand | 104 | 104 | 77 | 102 |
| Melanesia | 106 | 111 | 104 | 109 |
| Polynesia & Micronesia | 106 | 107 | 100 | 106 |

composition at later ages as well as differences in the composite age structure of a population are much better understood.

Higher male mortality rates result in a gradual reduction in the sex ratio, so that it reaches 100 males for every 100 females approximately during the fifth decade of life and continues to fall with advancing age. Because migration may be more likely for one or the other of the two sexes, the sex compositions of migrant and native populations may differ accordingly. For example, the sex ratio is often lower in urban areas than in rural areas, reflecting the greater in-migration of young females as in many Latin American cities.[15] Some African cities, however, have an excess of males, because of the movement of younger men to the city from rural areas.[16] Young populations have higher sex ratios than older populations.

A population's age structure is most significantly affected by variations in mortality and fertility and war. The differential effects of birth and death rates are best illustrated by using **stable population models.** These are hypothetical populations of equal sizes for which an assumed level of mortality or fertility is held constant while the other is allowed to vary. If, for example, we hold fertility constant in both, we can observe the effects of different mortality rates. The population with lower mortality will have larger proportions of its members in the childhood and elderly groups because more will survive the traumas of childhood and the winnowing of aging. It will have smaller proportions of members in the middle-aged groups, because, of course, the total cannot exceed 100 percent. The influence of lowered mortality decreases as life expectancy increases, however, particularly beyond the age of sixty, when age begins to catch up with almost everyone.

During the past century, most of the industrialized countries have greatly reduced mortality in the younger age groups, thus reducing the average age of the population. But mortality in infancy and early childhood cannot be expected to go much lower, so future changes in the age structure of these populations can be expected to result in an increase in the proportion of older persons.

Much more extreme differences in age structure occur between stable populations having similar mortality rates but different levels of fertility. High fertility results in a higher proportion of younger people, and therefore lowered fertility will eventually increase the proportion of older persons.

The effects of migration are more difficult to pinpoint. Migration does not generally exert much influence on age composition, except in cases of sizable and long-lasting migratory movements that are highly age-specific. In Latin America during the past quarter-century, for example, most of those migrating from rural to urban areas have been young, thus affecting the age composition in both areas.

Finally, war affects age distributions. Heavy losses in particular age groups, such as men of military age, affect age composition directly. There is also an indirect effect in the form of lowered fertility in succeeding years. Recent population pyramids for France, Czechoslovakia, and West Germany show irregularities in age structure that reflect the effects of World War II.

### Consequences of Population Composition

Variations in age structure have dramatic effects on mortality, because death occurs more frequently at the youngest and oldest ages. They have a smaller impact on fertility and migration, because very young and very old people are, of course, infertile and they tend not to be migrants. Age composition also affects natural increase, because fertility increases with the proportion of people in the childbearing ages. For example, if the age distribution of the United Kingdom for 1961 were standardized to correspond with that of Mexico in 1960, the crude birthrate would increase about one-third, the crude death rate would increase about one-half, and the rate of natural increase would triple. If we reversed the procedure so that the Mexican age structure resembled that of the United Kingdom, Mexico's crude birthrate would fall, the crude death rate would increase, and the rate of natural increase would decline.[17] Mexico's age composition is typical of the developing world, and these calculations therefore illustrate how youthful age structures contribute to high rates of population growth.

Age composition affects social organization in a number of ways. First, changes in age composition can lead to the redistribution of political power and hence to changes in governmental policies, such as employment and welfare programs. Second, a concentration of younger persons means that personnel and resources have to be devoted to education and the creation of new employment opportunities. Third, populations with a relatively high proportion of older people must try to include the elderly in employment and in social and political activities, as well as provide adequate housing and leisure-time activities for them.

In recent years there has been considerable debate over the consequences of the changing age structure for our society. In 1975 the median age of the United States population was 28.8

**stable population models:** hypothetical populations of the same size in which assumed levels of mortality or fertility are held constant while the other is varied.

years; by the year 2000 this figure is projected to be 37.0 years, with a further increase to 42.6 years by 2050.[18] At the end of this century there are likely to be more than 29 million Americans over age 65 and 12 million over age 75.

The increasing numbers of older people will require some changes in economic and social policy. First, the social security system, which supports the majority of the older population, faces a real crisis. A growing number of people are drawing pensions, and doing so longer, as life expectancy at the older ages increases. At the same time, fewer people are paying into the system because of lowered fertility. Clearly, new means of supporting pensioners must be derived. Second, as older people live longer, they require facilities and services appropriate to their needs and ability to pay. Recreation, housing, medical care, and public transportation are examples. Third, not all older people are ready for retirement at age 65 or even 70. Some may desire or be forced by poor health to retire earlier, but many more will want to continue to be active in the labor force, if only on a part-time basis. Finally, as the proportion and number of older people continue to increase, their political strength will grow. Politicians are responsive to power blocs within the voting public, and the older population will doubtless become increasingly organized in order to influence public policy and government spending to satisfy their interests.

Sex composition in most populations is less variable, and therefore shows fewer consequences. One exception, however, is the so-called "marriage squeeze" experienced in the United States since about 1960. The steadily increasing birthrate from the mid-1930s through the late 1950s resulted in significant differences in the size of birth cohorts. Because brides are normally three to five years younger than their grooms, the number of females reaching marriageable age since 1960 has been considerably larger than the number of males. Consequently, many young women must now either marry outside the normatively defined

As significant number of people age, special services must be provided for them. This care used to be given by the extended family system. Now we confine the elderly to high-cost nursing homes.

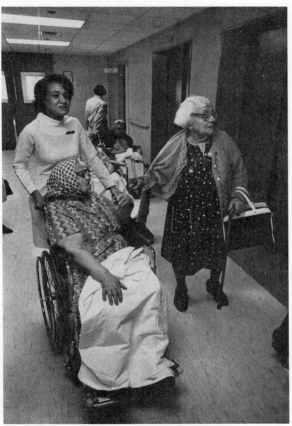

age range or remain single. Only after a lengthy period of relatively stable fertility rates will this discrepancy be eliminated. A similarly unbalanced sex ratio is seen at the older ages because of the longer life expectancy for women. This is why there are many more widows than widowers.

## POPULATION PROBLEMS

During the past 25 to 30 years, we have come to recognize that many of the problems faced by contemporary societies are directly or indirectly the result of demographic conditions. A universal concern in the modern world is improving the quality of life. How can we guarantee that all human beings will have sufficient food, clothing, and shelter, opportunities for employment and recreation, and the freedom to pursue their interests with a minimum of external constraint? Definitions of the "good life" differ, but those basic features are generally agreed upon.

Current population conditions, more serious in some areas of the world than others, inhibit attempts to improve the quality of life. Rapid rates of population growth (and the absolute number of people in some countries), increasing population densities, and imbalances in population composition endanger the conditions for human existence. The issues discussed below represent some of the basic features of the population problem.

### Food for the World

Malthus defined the population problem largely in terms of an increasing imbalance between food supplies and numbers of people. He foresaw a time when the world would be faced with the threat of widespread famine. Although this gloomy prediction has not yet come true, there is cause for concern, or even alarm, over the current world food situation. The major problems include an imbalance in food production between the developing and the developed nations, insufficient food reserves, malnutrition, and the lack of coordination in national food policies.

Although gross food production has increased during the past decade by about the same amount (30 percent) in both developed and developing countries, inequities in rates of population growth have resulted in a sizable difference in per capita food production. For the developed countries, the increase in per capita production has been about 15 percent, but in the less developed nations there has been virtually no improvement in per capita food production.[19]

Approximately 60 percent of our food energy is supplied by grains, including roots and tubers, with wheat and rice accounting for about 40 percent of total food consumption.[20] Available grain stocks therefore provide a useful index of world food reserves. If reserves fall below 100 million tons, it is likely that prices will increase sharply and severe shortages will develop. In 1961, world grain reserves totaled 222 million metric tons, equivalent to ninety days of consumption; 1974 estimates showed only 90 million tons of reserves, sufficient for only twenty-six days.[21] Most of these reserves are concentrated in the more developed nations.

Estimates of the extent of chronic hunger in the world vary greatly, with most experts putting the number of malnourished people somewhere between 1 and 2 billion.[22] In spite of the differences in the figures, it is clear that anywhere from one-quarter to one-third of the world's population, concentrated in Asia, Africa, and Latin America, suffers from an inadequate diet.

National food policies frequently conflict with one another, and this conflict seriously impedes resolution of world food problems. The issues at stake include government price supports for farm products, restrictions on grain imports and exports, international support for agricultural development in the poorer nations, fishing rights in national and international waters, and the establishment of a world food reserve. Clearly, increased international cooperation would help improve the quantity and quality of food resources.

Viewed quite simply, population growth can be directly translated into additional food demand. A population that increases by 2 percent during a given period must increase its food supplies by an equal amount, through internal production or imports, if per capita consumption is to remain unchanged. Some experts hope to increase food production through the application of modern technology.[23] They point to the great reservoir of unexploited food po-

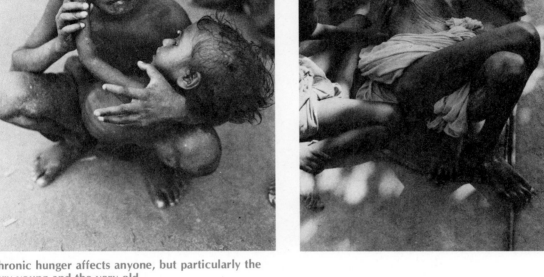

Chronic hunger affects anyone, but particularly the very young and the very old.

tential in the developing countries and to the recent increases in grain production achieved through the use of new high-yield seeds and improved fertilizers. This development, known popularly as the "Green Revolution," was heralded as the answer to world food problems in the early 1970s.

But a growing number of scientists recognize that technological solutions, including the Green Revolution, are themselves subject to a number of constraints.[24] A major concern is the serious shortage of four basic agricultural resources: land, water, energy, and fertilizer. In addition, some critics have pointed to the ecological stresses—soil erosion, pollution of lakes and streams from overfertilization, depletion of fish stocks—that have resulted from technological innovations aimed at increasing food production.[25] Finally, institutional factors govern-

ing the diffusion of knowledge necessary for using the new technology, the extension of credit, and the distribution of profits and products can influence the outcome of technological solutions to food problems.

In short, the world is faced with the potential worsening of an already serious imbalance between population and food supply. Solutions based on improvements in food-producing technology have been explored. "That there is a vast technological opportunity for expanding food supplies is not debatable, but this is not the real problem. The critical issue is at what price the additional resources will be brought into use."[26] Dwindling resources, environmental pollution, and ineffective governmental policies make the costs so high that the ultimate solution must be to reduce population rather than to increase food supplies.

Fertilizer is a basic agricultural resource. It is in increasingly short supply and has risen radically in cost as a consequence of OPEC oil price increases.

## Natural Resources and the Environment

The food problem is only one aspect of a larger issue. The survival of human populations depends on a continued supply of all our natural resources—air, water, land, minerals, and animals—and the maintenance of a habitable environment.

Resource problems can be understood in terms of (1) current and projected supplies and (2) rates and patterns of consumption. It is also useful to distinguish between two types of resources: those that are renewable, such as water and forest products, and those that are nonrenewable, like minerals and fossil fuels. Present concern is highest over the future availability of nonrenewable resources, but in the long run, both types may fall short of world demands.

Unfortunately, reliable estimates of ultimate reserves are not available for most natural resources, especially those that are ordinarily replenished by natural processes. The earth's supply of natural resources is probably limited. Moreover, most resources are unequally distributed among the regions and nations of the world.

A population's stock of natural resources is affected not only by natural endowment but by the level of technological development achieved and by patterns of international trade. Advanced technology may result in the discovery of new supplies, increased efficiency in extracting and processing, and the capacity to recycle resources for further use. Through international trade, populations deficient in a given resource can theoretically maintain a supply sufficient to meet their needs, if they can obtain foreign exchange with which to purchase it. But technological development thus far has depleted natural resources more than it has increased them, and equalization through international trade has been hindered by political and economic factors.

Although we can only estimate the absolute stock of world resources, trends and patterns of consumption are relatively well documented. A few examples suffice to indicate the overall trend toward increased resource utilization. For nonfuel minerals, world output rose by about 74 percent during the period 1953–1966, while population increased by only 28 percent.[27] In the United States, per capita water consumption increased from approximately 10 gallons per day at the beginning of this century to the current average of 160 gallons, and this figure is two or three times higher in some large cities.[28] Finally, between 1950 and 1968 the average annual rate of increase in energy consumption per capita for the world was 3.5 percent.[29] Clearly, with few exceptions, the human population is consuming more and more of the available natural resources, and projections for the foreseeable future show no indication of any significant change.

Furthermore, resources are consumed disproportionately by the various nations of the world. Generally, the higher the level of technological and economic development, the greater the share of resources utilized. For example, a 1970 estimate showed that the United States, with 5 percent of the world's population, consumes 42 percent of the world total of aluminum, 44 percent of the coal, 28 percent of the iron, 25 percent of the lead, 63 percent of the natural gas, 38 percent of the nickel, and 33 percent of the petroleum.[30]

The increased use of natural resources has been accompanied by a trend toward environmental deterioration, as evidenced by the great increase in waste products in the air, land, fresh waters, and oceans. Human activities of all kinds—residential, recreational, agricultural, industrial, military—contribute to the build-up of pollutants. The manifestations of pollution can be usefully divided into four categories:

1. Direct assaults on human health (e.g., lead poisoning or aggravation of lung disease by air pollution).
2. Damage to goods and services that society provides for itself (e.g., the corrosive effects of air pollution on buildings and crops).
3. Other direct effects on what people perceive as their "quality of life" (e.g., congestion and litter).
4. Indirect effects on society through interference with services that are provided for society by natural ecosystems, such as ocean fish production and control of erosion by vegetation. Examples of such indirect effects are destruction of vegetation by overgrazing and logging, and poisoning of coastal water with oil and heavy metals.[31]

Environmental deterioration is most evident in highly industrialized nations, and only these countries have developed organized measures, such as the United States Environmental Protection Agency, to deal with pollution and its consequences. In the developing nations, pollution is often viewed as an unavoidable consequence of efforts to raise the standard of living.[32]

Growing pressures on resources and the environment are directly related to two dominant population trends: increased size and concentration in cities. A growing population means a greater demand for resources of all kinds, and, with the exception of land, urban populations consume more resources per capita than those in rural areas. Furthermore, because environmental deterioration is largely a result of human activities, continued growth and concentration of population can destroy natural habitats unless measures are taken to counteract or control destructive practices.

Most observers agree that unless measures are taken to reduce the rate at which resources are consumed and natural processes disrupted, the quality of human life will sooner or later be threatened. Several solutions have been proposed. First, population growth and distribution could be controlled. Second, advanced technology might provide substitutes for natural resources and more efficient means of waste disposal. But each of these solutions takes a considerable amount of time to implement, and neither deals with resource and environment problems directly.

A third solution involves an organized, two-stage effort to conserve natural resources and to maintain the quality of the environment[33] *Resource management* involves governmental attempts to encourage an increase in the yield from a particular resource process, but under rational guidance aimed at minimizing harmful effects. *Environmental management* goes further. The goal of this stage is to exploit resources while simultaneously maintaining environmental quality and ecological stability. Recent American attempts to restrict porpoise kills by tuna fishermen is an example.

The relationship among population, resources, and the environment is complex. Population growth and urbanization increase the pressures on resources and the environment. Thus any reduction in these trends would be beneficial. But even if the human population could somehow be frozen at current levels, existing rates of resource use and environmental deterioration would still threaten the quality of human life within a few centuries. Although optimists continue to anticipate technological solutions to these problems, the more likely prospect is that we will have to adopt rather stringent environmental conservation measures.

**Another effect overpopulation is the depletion of nonrenewable natural resources. Strip mining in Arizona.**

This Objiway Indian suffers from mercury poisoning he contracted from consuming fish caught in a polluted lake.

## Economic Development

There are many ways to achieve the common national goal of raising the living standard and improving the quality of human life. Success is usually measured in terms of economic development. Standard indicators include per capita income, gross national product, the industrial distribution of the labor force, and levels of savings and investment.

Since about 1850, economic growth has increased very rapidly, compared with advances in earlier times, but not all nations have shared equally in the trend toward affluence. In fact, the economic gap between the rich and poor nations is increasing. In 1958, for instance, the developed nations produced about 82 percent of the world's goods and services; by 1968 this figure had increased to 87 percent.[34] Incomes have also increased much more in rich nations than in poor ones. The ratio between incomes

in the industrializing countries and all other nations in 1850 was about 2 to 1. If recent trends continue, that ratio could be 30 to 1 by the end of this century.[35]

Economic development is affected by many factors, but few have as much significance as population growth. Until the 1930s, population and economic growth were positively related: the more developed countries grew more rapidly than the rest of the world. The past four decades, however, have produced a reversal in this relationship. Rapid population growth now appears to be an obstacle, rather than a stimulus, to economic development.

How does rapid population growth impede economic development? First, prolonged high fertility results in a youthful age structure. This then creates a "dependency burden" with a lower proportion of the population available for the work force. Second, a country with a rapidly growing population must use resources and capital to meet subsistence requirements rather than for investment or for upgrading production technology and education. Third, many people in a rapidly growing population will be unable to find work or will work at tasks that are relatively unproductive.

As high fertility impedes economic growth, so a low level of economic development hinders significant reduction of fertility. Two factors are especially important. First, a stagnant economy offers few opportunities for women to enter the labor force. Their principal alternative is early marriage and motherhood. Second, slow economic growth inhibits attempts to raise levels of educational attainment, and education shows a significant inverse relationship to fertility. Almost everywhere, the educated have lower fertility rates than the uneducated.

It should now be evident that problems of population and economic development constitute a vicious circle. Rapid population growth impedes economic improvement, and economic problems tend to increase the strains generated by growing populations. The problem now facing the developing countries is where efforts to break this potentially catastrophic relationship should be concentrated: on population, the economy, or both? Although opinions are divided, there is some evidence that the most crucial immediate task is somehow to control the rate of population growth.[36]

High fertility impedes economic development: slum housing in India.

## Political Conflict

Changes in a variety of population variables, such as size, density, and composition, can have political consequences, but rates of growth are currently the most important factor. This is evident at both national and international levels.

Problems are more severe in the developing countries, where most governments lack the resources necessary to satisfy citizens' rising expectations for improvements in the quality of life. Jobs are scarce, hunger is a way of life, housing is inadequate, and public services are often disorganized. Under these conditions, there is little public confidence in government officials, and the resulting social and political unrest often leads to political instability, social disintegration, and even civil war.

Of even greater significance, in the long run, are the international problems generated by rapid population growth. As we saw earlier, large and growing populations were thought until recently to be necessary for power in international relations; consequently, many governments adopted policies favoring high birthrates. Imbalances in population and resources often generate border wars, such as the recent conflicts in the Middle East and Central America. Competition for resources influences international trade relations. Nations with a relative advantage in the supply of key resources can blackmail other members of the international community. The current activities of the oil-producing countries of the Middle East are a prominent case in point.

Robert Heilbroner has said that we currently face three principal dangers: runaway population growth, massively destructive war, and potential environmental collapse.[37] To a large extent, the latter two result from the first. Rapid population growth makes international conflict and environmental deterioration increasingly likely, if not inevitable. The control of population growth may be the most important political issue in the world today. The relationship between population pressures and political tension deserves far more attention than it has received to date.[38]

> **family planning:** the general name for publicly or privately sponsored programs to reduce population growth rates through encouraging individual citizens to limit family size.

## PROSPECTS FOR POPULATION CONTROL

Despite widespread agreement that rapid population growth is a major world problem, there is little consensus as to the optimum size or rate of growth of population, or the means by which population goals, however defined, might be achieved most effectively. Most discussions focus on the developing nations, but the issues are relevant to all countries of the world. While population growth is an immediate problem for the developing countries, it is only a matter of time before the developed countries find themselves under similar pressures.

### Family Planning

Earlier, we saw that high fertility is the major cause of rapid population growth. Recognition of this has led some countries to introduce **family planning** programs. These involve the distribution of contraceptives on a national basis, usually through the public health services. There are also many private family planning programs, such as Planned Parenthood in the United States.

Those who rely upon family planning make a number of assumptions: First, they assume that contraceptives are technically efficient—that by using them correctly, people can prevent births. Second, they assume that contraceptives can be distributed widely and economically; third,

283

The family planning program at work in Indonesia: explaining the I.U.D.

that there is a demand for contraceptives among that segment of the population having the greatest risk of producing children, primarily women aged 15–29; and finally, participation in family planning programs must be voluntary.

As you can see, some of these are big assumptions indeed. Although it is certainly true that modern contraceptives are technically quite efficient, the assumption that people will use them, and use them properly, is clearly weak. (Even many American college girls believe that The Pill may be used as "morning-after" protection.)

Despite the problems, the number of countries with family planning programs has increased steadily since the 1950s. Of 130 developing countries surveyed in 1976, 64 provided financial support for family planning activities, and many others at least tolerated such programs under the auspices of private organizations.[39]

Assessment of the success of family planning programs is hindered by the lack of adequate data. A 1967 evaluation by Donald Bogue heralded "the end of the population explosion." Bogue predicted that "from 1965 onward the rate of world population growth . . . will slacken to such a pace that it will be zero or near zero at about the year 2000, so that population will

not be regarded as a major social problem except in isolated and small 'retarded' areas."[40] The major justification for this optimism was a belief that family planning programs were becoming increasingly widespread and effective in the developing countries of the world.

In the same year, 1967, Kingsley Davis criticized several features of the family planning approach. These included allowing couples to have the number of children they want, failure to take reproductive motivation into account, and lack of attention to institutional factors that reinforce the large-family pattern. In particular, he maintained that socioeconomic changes are more effective in changing fertility patterns than family planning efforts.[41]

In 1975, Walter Watson and Robert Lapham classified changes in the birthrate during 1970–1974 for eighty-one developing countries according to a crude socioeconomic index. They concluded that fertility was not likely to decline among those living at very low socioeconomic levels, unless determined, sustained efforts to reduce fertility were carried out.[42] Of the thirty-one countries included in the "low" category, many of which had very active family planning programs, only India and Indonesia showed a possible or probable decline in the birthrate over the four-year period. This supports Davis's assertion that social and economic changes have a greater influence on birthrates than do contraceptive programs.

It should not be concluded, however, that family planning programs have no effects on fertility. Societal modernization may increase the demand for fertility limitation. Colombia has significantly reduced its birthrate during the past 15 years,[43] and a recent analysis of family planning programs in 20 other developing countries indicates that "The direct effects of socioeconomic indicators and the program outputs were substantial and about equal."[44] The real question is whether family planning programs *and* socioeconomic change will be sufficient to reduce population growth in the absence of explicit national, even international, population policies.

*Population Policy*

The relative lack of success of family planning programs suggests that we need a more comprehensive approach to problems of population growth. The United Nations defines population policy as "programs designed to contribute to the achievement of economic, social, demographic, political and other collective goals through affecting critical demographic variables, namely the size and growth of the population, its geographic distribution (national and international) and its demographic characteristics."[45] Although all nations have implicit policies along at least some of these lines, few have taken explicit stands to provide enforcement.

Of 130 countries whose official views on population were evaluated in 1976, only 33 had policies aimed at reducing the population growth rate.[46] But some of these are among the world's most populous nations—Egypt, Bangladesh, China, India, Indonesia, Mexico, Pakistan, the Philippines, Thailand, and Turkey. Japan is one of the most densely populated countries in the world. From 70 million in 1935, its population climbed to 84 million in 1950 and in 1977 was estimated to be 114 million. Recognizing an acute population problem, the Japanese government took steps to control population growth shortly after World War II. Abortion was legalized and made affordable to all. The government publicly promotes contraception and distributes contraceptives free of charge. Japan was the first country to officially advocate

sterilization to control population growth. In short, the Japanese government has successfully implemented an antinatalist policy.

---

**NO EASY WAY OUT?**

MYTH: WARS, DISEASE, AND NATURAL DISASTERS WILL CONTROL POPULATION SURPLUS.

Fact: In Five Years of Terrible War, Population of North and South Vietnam Grew More than 3 Million

Fact: Giant Tidal Wave Killed More than 500,000 in East Pakistan in 1970, but This Number Was Replaced in Just 35 Days

Fact: Improved Health Care and Modern Medicines Have Lengthened Western Man's Life-Span by Two Decades since 1900

MYTH: TECHNOLOGY AND OCEANS WILL FEED WORLD

Fact: Green Revolution Is Shot in Arm, but Population Growth is Neutralizing Food Production Gains.

Fact: Oceans Are 90% Biological Deserts, with Other 10% in Danger of Being Over-exploited

MYTH: PLENTY OF ROOM—MAN IS ONLY USING A FRACTION OF THE LAND

Fact: Much of Land Is Too Hot, Too Cold, Too Wet or Too Dry for Agriculture or Human Habitation.

---

The population problem will neither go away nor resolve itself. It can only become worse if we do not attack it systematically in the near future. Wishful thinking is not enough.

China, the largest country in the world, has also attempted to reduce population growth through official government action. It has been claimed that no other country has

. . . committed itself so firmly and unequivocally to the control of population growth . . . mounted such an ambitious campaign to alter traditional values relating to marriage and family formation . . . gone as far toward making family limitation an object of sustained community interest and pressure . . . developed such a comprehensive system for the delivery of birth control services, including contraceptives, sterilization, and abortion.[47]

Attempts to evaluate China's success in population control are hampered, however, by the lack of recent objective data. The last population census in China was taken in 1953. Much of our information on the population control efforts is propaganda and not subject to critical evaluation. Nevertheless, it appears that the Chinese birthrate has declined significantly, from 38–42 per thousand in the 1920s to 16–25 per thousand in the 1970s.[48]

The key to the Chinese birth control campaign is reindoctrination of the population to eliminate traditional values that favored early marriage, large families, male children, and family privacy. New values are promoted through publicity campaigns, local study sessions, and traveling propaganda groups. Modern methods of contraception, abortion, and sterilization are used to achieve desired family size. In addition, societal modernization, as indicated by increasing literacy and educational attainment, may have had some effect on fertility. But the overwhelming influence on reproductive behavior has been in the form of political pressure to conform to governmentally defined standards.

Almost without exception, population policies are concentrated on fertility. Recently, however, a few countries, such as Colombia and Venezuela, have adopted policies aimed at obtaining a better territorial distribution of the population. China's population policy seeks to maximize female labor force participation.

The idea that population policies should go beyond family planning is certainly not new. A wide variety of alternative measures have been suggested, including postponement of marriage, encouraging women to seek rewards from nonfamilial roles (primarily in the labor force), substantial fees for marriage licenses, taxes on children, legalization of abortion and mandatory abortion for out-of-wedlock pregnancies, and compulsory sterilization for men with two or three children, to mention just a few. Some of these suggestions are now being incorporated into official population policies. For example, there has been a slow trend toward legalizing abortion in developing countries, especially those that have attained a higher level of socioeconomic development. In a few countries, such as Colombia, there is some evidence of efforts to improve the status of women. Various incentives have been offered

**The earth can't handle many more birthday parties.**

ZPG poster. The Zero Population Growth movement offers a radical solution to the problem of overpopulation. It may be the only solution.

in India to encourage voluntary sterilization. In short, efforts to develop national population policies are increasing, with some positive results. But it is not clear whether the problems can be resolved in time to avoid disaster.

A growing movement, called Zero Population Growth (ZPG), has as its goal stopping world population growth as soon as demographically feasible. The principal mechanism for achieving zero growth is social regulation of the rights and obligations of childbearing. This involves reordering people's views of personal freedom. Emphasis is placed on our obligations rather than our rights as members of society. Private interests are given a lower priority than those of the society. In effect, people would be socially restrained from having children, or would be limited to having one or two, in order to allow available services and resources to be used for raising the standard of living of the earth's existing population.

Ultimately, the choice is up to each of us. Population policies are no different from any other guidelines for human conduct. If they are to succeed, they must call forth a sense of obligation and a recognition that compliance offers many benefits. If population control is seen in this light, however, the social definition of parenthood will undergo some drastic changes. How that might be accomplished remains to be seen.

## SUMMARY

Demography is the study of human population. It is of importance to sociologists because of its close, reciprocal relation with social organization. The principal demographic variables—birth, death, migration, social mobility, population distribution, and composition—deeply influence a society's social organization and are in turn influenced by it.

The fundamental demographic data are facts about a given population at a particular time or in a particular time period, their number, ages, sex distribution, marital statuses, number of children, occupations, educational characteristics, places of residence and employment, numbers of births and deaths. This information is obtained in a variety of ways, the most common of which are the population census, vital registration systems, population registers, and sample surveys. These data are published in many ways, usually by national governments or the United Nations.

The three major areas of demographic interest are population size and growth, population distribution, and population composition. Population size and growth did not become a matter of public and scientific concern until the late eighteenth century, when Malthus argued that population growth would always increase faster than the means of subsistence. If unchecked by certain moral restraints, "vice," or natural disasters and disease, population growth would inevitably lead to widespread famine. This general view remains popular today, although Marxians deny it, arguing that there are no natural laws of population growth, but rather that it is determined by social and economic conditions.

Modern scientific views do not particularly reflect either of these positions. They are derived from the observation that rates of population growth—in European history, at least—were profoundly affected by the Industrial Revolution. The concept of demographic transition involves moving from a stage of high birth and death rates and relatively stable population through a transitional stage of continued high birthrates together with lowered death rates (a population explosion), to a final stage of much reduced birth and death rates, resulting in a relatively stable population size once again.

Population size is calculated by counting, of course, and although there are many ways of measuring changes in it, all basically compare births to deaths with allowance for changes due to migration. For the world population as a whole, size has continually increased in a geometric fashion, although there are important regional differences. In recent times, the least industrially developed countries have been increasing at the greatest rate. The rapidity with which world population has been increasing in the past century is generally attributed to a decline in mortality rates. In many parts of the world, birthrates have remained high while death rates have dropped steeply. Where this is coupled with lack of technological development, the resulting problems have seriously interfered with efforts at further development.

The basic measure of population distribution is density, usually calculated as the number of persons per square mile or kilometer. The rural-urban distinction calls attention to the fact that the principal and most important change in population distribution in recent years has been the increasing urbanism of the world's population, with consequent increases in the number and sizes of cities everywhere. Particularly in the developing countries, rapidly increasing urbanization is producing social dislocations and a decline in the quality of life.

Population composition has to do with both ascribed characteristics, such as age, sex, race, ethnicity, and place of birth, and achieved characteristics, such as labor force status, marital status, nationality, education, and income. Age and sex are particularly important compositional variables. The population pyramid is a diagram of the age and sex distribution in a population at a given time. Population pyramids are significant because the shape of the pyramid in a given society reflects its fertility and mortality and such things as the dependency ratio: the ratio of those of nonworking age to those of working age. A society with a high dependency ratio will have to devote significant proportions of its resources simply to caring for its dependents, with important proportions of its work force laboring to that end. In general in the world today, dependency ratios are higher in the underdeveloped countries than in the more developed. The sex ratio, the proportion of men to women, is also an important measure of population, as is age structure.

The significance of these matters is apparent when we examine a number of worldwide social problems. It is mathematically inevitable that if world population continues to grow at its present rate, the world will run out of food. Even if new technologies made an adequate food supply available, numerous problems of distribution and preference would remain. The depletion of natural resources and environmental problems are also related to population size and increase. In the developing nations, economic and technical progress is hindered, and sometimes crippled, by very high birthrates and dependency ratios, so that expectations for improvements in the quality of life cannot be met. Political turmoil and conflict appear the inevitable result.

Population control of some kind may be the only answer to problems of this kind. Two proposals for control are family planning and national population policy. The former refers to efforts by governments and private organizations to encourage individuals to reduce family size, thus diminishing the birthrate and, eventually, maintaining population at levels capable of permitting a desirable quality of life. The latter refers to rational programs for manipulating variables that national governments can control, such as distribution, employment, education, and so forth, all of which affect fundamental demographic variables like birth and death. A private organization in the United States that has taken a forthright population policy stand is Zero Population Growth, which advocates social regulation of childbearing.

## SUGGESTED READINGS

*Demographic Dynamics* (1979– ), published monthly by American Demographics, Inc., Ithaca, N.Y. The journal includes articles written for the educated layman and covers a variety of issues related to current U.S. population trends.

HAUPT, ARTHUR, AND THOMAS T. KANE. *Population Handbook.* Washington, D.C.: The Population Reference Bureau, 1978. A clear and concise guide to basic demographic measures. Topics covered include age and sex composition, fertility, mortality, morbidity, nuptiality, migration, urbanization and distribution, and population change. Also provides a glossary of key demographic terms.

LITTLEWOOD, THOMAS B. *The Politics of Population Control.* Notre Dame, Ind.: University of Notre Dame Press, 1977. An insightful examination of the influence of government agencies, the Catholic Church, private foundations, and special interest groups on efforts to control population dynamics in the United States. Written by a veteran journalist, the book covers broad issues of population policy regarding fertility, contraceptive services, immigration, and internal migration. In-depth case studies provide a real sense of the political context of population issues.

MAMDANI, MOHMOOD. *The Myth of Population Control: Family, Caste, and Class in an Indian Village.* New York: Monthly Review Press, 1972. An Indian anthropologist's analysis of why a village family-planning program was unsuccessful. The author links decisions regarding contraceptive use and family-size limitation to village social organization, particularly the family and socioeconomic status. Provides an informative counterbalance to technological and educational strategies to achieve control of population growth in less developed nations.

McGRAW, ERIC. *Population Today.* London: Kaye and Ward, 1979. This volume includes a summary of the origins of the population explosion and discusses effects of continuing population growth on the struggle to meet people's basic needs, for example, food, energy, water, education, employment, and housing.

ZEISSET, PAUL T. *Reference Manual on Population and Housing Statistics from the Census Bureau.* Washington, D.C.: U.S. Bureau of the Census, Data User Services Division, 1977. An appropriate and up-to-date starting point is provided for the new or prospective user of demographic data from the Census Bureau.

# FOUR
## Social
## Institutions

Part 3 talked about some major elements of the societal organization of most societies, what is sometimes called social structure. In the five chapters that follow, we examine major *social institutions*, what are probably the most significant specific structural or organizational elements of any society anywhere. These are the family, education, religion, politics, and economics. Although societies have social structural elements beside these that can properly be called institutions, these five are certainly universal; no society can exist without them.

A social institution occurs when some set of social organizational relationships becomes so "frozen" by custom as to become normative, "the way things are" in a particular society. The "freezing process" is called "institutionalization." Thus a social institution has normative values attached; not only is it how things are done by a particular people, it is the right, just, moral, and proper way to do them.

Most sociologists who analyze social institutions adopt a functional approach to understanding them, perceiving them as existing to fulfill imperative social needs, things that must be accomplished if the society in which they exist is to survive. (The rearing of children and the production and distribution of food are classic examples.) The argument is simply that some activities are so essential to a society that specific arrangements for getting them accomplished *must* be established and adhered to. Institutions are the product of this necessity. All five chapters in this part adopt this view to some extent. In these chapters, too, we tend to concentrate upon American society, but will occasionally contrast American institutions with others elsewhere.

291

# Chapter 11
# The Family

You would expect the opening illustration of a chapter about the family to depict a family, but if you consider for a moment, you'll probably agree that nothing in this picture makes it certain that the group shown *is* a family. There's no way to tell for instance, that the people in the picture are not a babysitter and a friend taking their charges for a walk.

The point is, of course, that a family is not just a group of people. A special relationship distinguishes the family from other types of social groupings. To define those unique social relationships, however, is very difficult. Common sense suggests that a family is composed of a mother, a father, and their children. This is a good start, but it clearly does not include many familiar family patterns. What about adopted children? What about single-parent families? What about old Aunt Minnie who lived with your mother and father for years? What about your older sister now that she and her husband have "a family of their own?" The family is obviously not so simple to define as it may at first have seemed.

Sociologists normally define the family

either by reference to a specific form of social *organization* or by reference to a particular set of social *activities*. Bell and Vogel, for example, choose the first option, proposing that the family exists in any society where the related positions of husband and wife, or mother, father, and children, are recognized and shared notions.[1] Zelditch also stresses *structural* factors, noting the primacy of the parental role as the crucial characteristic of the family system.[2] Other scholars focus on the universal *functions* that distinguish the family institution from other institutions. For example, Reiss claims that the legitimate procreation and nurturing of offspring is the central feature of the family group that serves to separate it from all other institutions.[3]

Neither approach to defining the family is more correct than the others; each simply emphasizes contrasting aspects of family life. Our definition combines structural and functional elements. We regard the *family* **as** *a kinship-structured institution normally composed of an adult male and female along with their offspring who live together in a more or less permanent relationship approved by society as marriage.* This special social group, found in variant forms, provides children with a legitimate social position and has the responsibility of nurturing infants until they are able to function as fully developed members of their society. This formula leaves a number of issues unresolved, but it should become clearer, as we survey the major ways sociologists classify families into types. Each of our models is based on a distinct analytical principle, thus any particular family may fit into more than one type at a time.

## PRINCIPAL TYPES OF FAMILY ORGANIZATION

The family is without question the oldest human institution. It arose sometime during the prehistoric experience of humankind, and every society of which we have any knowledge has evidenced some form of family life. The family is truly a universal institution. No society has managed to survive without it, and the few that have tried, have had to give up the experiment or face extinction.

The universality of the family has not, however, resulted in a uniform pattern of social organization for this institution. Differing societal systems have produced widely varying types of family structures. For those of us nurtured in the culture of the West, it is difficult to comprehend how family life would be tolerable in the polygamous organization of the Australian aborigines or in the arranged marriage system of classical China or in the patriarchial pattern of the Old Testament Hebrews. Yet each of these arrangements has met the needs of its society, perhaps more efficiently than our nuclear family pattern meets our needs. We need to keep in mind, therefore, that this institution participates in a wider social order where it assumes certain specialized tasks. Domestic labor patterns, kinship structures, and marital arrangements fitting for one society might well be disruptive if transplanted into another cultural system. Variety among family types is more than the spice of life; it is often a social necessity mandated by the differing constitutions of societies themselves.

Family types may be described from a number of different angles, each of which discloses an important aspect of family organization. Some family patterns are based on structural differences while others are based on differences in function, in leadership, and in marriage arrangements. In the course of studying them, it should become clear that family practices in the United States are by no means typical of families everywhere, particularly of those outside the orbit of Western social experience. Some styles of family life may strike us as exotic—who, for example, has not marveled at the goings-on in the bushes of Samoa? No doubt others will impress us with their stifling restrictions compared with our own relative freedom in family affairs. Becoming familiar with these different styles is not only fascinating in its own right, but it also has a practical relevance as well. We frequently heighten our awareness of our own family organizational patterns— which otherwise we simply take for granted as somehow inevitable—by seeing them in stark opposition to styles practiced in other parts of the globe. Like all cultural units, the family is a product of social forces that fashion its form and purpose.

### Kinship Structures: Nuclear and Extended Families

A **kinship system** *is a complex of social relationships established by marriage and descent from a common ancestor as well as by such related issues as inheritance, succession, sexual relations, and residence. A kinsman, therefore, is a person to whom one is socially defined as related.* There are two conventional distinctions among one's relatives. *Persons with whom one shares a blood lineage* are normally regarded as *consanguineal kin,* while *those to whom one is related by marriage* are called *affinal kin.* (The popular name for affinal kin in American society is *in-laws.*) Kinship is clearly a larger category than the family, for it includes not only husband, wife, and their children, but also grandparents, aunts, uncles, cousins, and so forth. This has prompted the designation of two types of families that set different limits for the number of relatives recognized as participants in the immediate family group.

The first type is called the **extended family,** that is, *three or more generations included in a functional family unit, namely, grandparents, parents, and granchildren, including all the brothers and sisters of the second generation, along with their spouses and offspring and some-*

This, too, is a family.

*times the in-laws from several of these marriages.* Members of the extended family typically live together in a single household or in adjacent households and function together as an integrated economic unit.

The polar opposite to the extended family is the **nuclear family.** Organizationally, it is far less complex. The nuclear family consists of *a married couple and their children.* This is the basic building block of most kinship systems, and in contemporary Western civilization, it is the most important unit in terms of the social functions of the family.[4]

Generally speaking, the nuclear family (sometimes called the conjugal family) fits the needs of industrial societies more adequately than extended family structures. Indeed, the pattern in which nuclear families live in relative isolation from the rest of their kinship network predominates in most economically advanced societies. This does not mean that industrialization causes the rise of the nuclear family pattern, or, conversely, that a nuclear family system causes the emergence of industrial societies. All that we can assert with some degree of certainty is that the ideal of the nuclear family is an almost universal, empirical correlate to technologically advanced societal systems.[5]

In contrast, extended families exist in, and fit with, agrarian, traditional societies. Consequently, the extended family form is probably the most common one in the world, and until 1900, it typified the American family as well, particularly in rural areas. The degree to which the extended family has disappeared from American life is a measure of social change in the society and structural change within the family. Today, the typical American identifies far less with the extended family as an important focus of activity or personal identity than with the nuclear family. Nowadays, the extended kinship network is usually significant only on ceremonial occasions: births, weddings, funerals, and major holidays, such as Thanksgiving. "Over the river and through the woods, to Grandmother's house we go. . . ." But note that grandmother's house in the nostalgic jingle is only "over the river and through the woods" and accessible by sleigh; one needn't take a jet to Miami or Los Angeles. The extended family does not usually play an important role in day-to-day family life. Most Americans perceive a difference between their

**family:** a kinship-structured grouping normally composed of an adult male and female and their offspring living together in a more or less permanent relationship approved by their society as marriage.

**kinship system:** a complex of social relationships established by marriage and descent from a common ancestor. Social scientists distinguish two types, *consanguineal* kin (persons with whom one shares "blood" lineage) and *affinal* kin (persons to whom one is related through marriage).

**extended family:** three or more generations included in a single, functional family unit consisting of grandparents, parents, and grandchildren, brothers, sisters, and their spouses and children, and so on.

**nuclear or conjugal family:** a married couple and their children residing together.

**family of orientation:** the family into which one is born.

**family of procreation:** the family established by one's marriage and production of children.

*families* and their *relatives,* and resist being drawn into the activities and responsibilities of the latter. ("Why should I bail my brother-in-law out of his financial difficulties?")

## Life Cycle Functions: Families of Orientation and Procreation

Another set of distinctions is based on the functional relationship of the family to the individual. The **family of orientation** is *the particular grouping into which the person is born and from which he or she receives primary socialization.* The family of orientation is the one that nurtures the individual for future participation in society.

A **family of procreation** is *established when one is launched from the family of orientation, marries, and produces children of one's own.* The family of procreation for parents is simultaneously the family of orientation for their offspring. Every family containing both parents and children is a family of both orientation and procreation. The proper designation depends upon whether the individual we are concerned with is the parent or the child. Most of us participate in both family types during our life cycle, with the family of orientation dominating our childhood and the family of procreation our adult years. Our rights, obligations, and social responsibilities within the family vary according to our placement in one type or the other, and the transition from one type to the next does not always proceed smoothly. All of us are familiar with the parents who find it difficult to admit that their children are, in fact, grown, that the old parental authority cannot be wielded anymore.

*Marriage and Household Arrangements:*
*Monogamous and Polygamous Families.*

It would be difficult to describe every form the marriage relationship has taken in human societies. Yet throughout the world, the phenomenon we call **marriage** involves *a stable set of socially recognized relationships between husband and wife, including, but not limited to, sexual relations.* A more technical definition would be that marriage is *a contract between spouses of the opposite sex that makes children born to them legitimate.* (The legitimation, of course, is accorded by society, not the parent couple.) Two elements are noteworthy in this definition. First, marriage is a *contract.* It is a legally sanctioned and public agreement between people for an exchange of goods and services. Americans may well take offense at such an unromantic understanding of marriage, but that is, when you get right down to it, what marriage is all about. Quarrels between husband and wife about how money is to be spent—on a dress for the wife, a set of golf clubs for the husband, or a carpet for the living room—and quarrels about the assignment of tasks—who is to take out the garbage or who is to bathe the baby—are all stereotypical because they recur almost universally between spouses. Yet it is out of such minutiae of living together that a marriage is made. Second, our definition says the contract is *between spouses,* but it does not say how many. This raises the distinction between two

How work is divided is part of the essence of marriage.

forms of marriage, monogamy and polygamy.

**Monogamy** means *the marriage of one man to one woman.* It is the marital form practiced by most people throughout the world and is virtually universal in industrialized societies. **Polygamy** is a general term that covers *any form of marriage of three or more persons.* It is not uncommon in preindustrial societies, and in fact, more cultures around the world permit polygamy than restrict marriage to the monogamous form.[6] The apparent contradiction between this statement and the previous one is easily resolved: Even in societies that permit polygamy, most people do not practice it because they cannot afford to.

Each of the two basic marital forms has a number of possible subtypes (see Figure 11.1). A monogamous society may allow *serial monogamy,* in which individuals are permitted to remarry after an original marriage is terminated by death or divorce; this, of course, is the custom in the United States. A society may also practice *straight-life monogamy*, in which remarriage is not permitted.

The variations of polygamy are *polygyny*, marriage of one man to two or more women (the most common form of polygamous marriage); *polyandry*, the marriage of one woman to two or more men (less frequent than polygyny and usually occurring where there is a shortage of women); and *group marriage*, the marriage of several men to several women simultaneously, all of one sex regarding all of the other sex equally as spouses. Polygyny and polyandry have been practiced in various societies throughout history and in some societies are still allowed today. Islamic law, for example, permits men to marry as many as four wives—if the husband can adequately support them. The Mormans in nineteenth-century America were also polygynous. It is doubtful that group marriage ever occurred among preliterate peoples, although early anthropologists believed they had found some instances of it. The difficulties in making group marriage work suggest that it would never be very popular. The American press occasionally reports the practice, often in

**marriage:** a stable set of socially recognized relationships between husband and wife including, but not limited to, sexual relations.

**monogamy:** marriage of one man to one woman. Monogamy appears in two forms, *serial* monogramy, in which the individual may remarry after divorce or the death of a spouse, and *straight-life monogramy* in which remarriage is not permitted.

**polygamy:** marriage of three or more persons. Polygamy may appear in three forms, (1) *polygyny,* marriage of one man to two or more women; (2) *polyandry,* marriage of one woman to two or more men; and (3) *group marriage,* simultaneous marriage of several men and women, with all of one sex regarding all of the other equally as spouses.

combination with group living experiments. At least one sociologist, Ira Reiss, has documented it in a few instances.[7] Of course, no such "marriages" are recognized as legal by any American jurisdiction.

**FIGURE 11.1    Monogamy and polygamy**

Monogamy:
Marriage of
one man to
one woman

Straight-life
monogamy:
Remarriage is
not permitted

Serial
monogamy:
Individuals may
remarry after
death or divorce
of a spouse

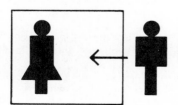

Polygamy: Marriage of three or more persons

Polygyny: Marriage of one man to two or more women

Polyandry: Marriage of one woman to two or more men

## *Leadership Roles: Patriarchal, Egalitarian, and Matriarchal Families*

Family organization involves more than simply what form of marriage is practiced. A whole set of structural questions must be resolved: How is the newly created household to be set up? Where will the children fit in the kinship system? To whom will they be related? How will problems or quarrels be settled? Who will "wear the pants" in the family? Each of these issues is a major element in any marriage, and every society develops conventional solutions for them.

**Descent** The issue of descent—who will be related to whom and how—is not so simple as it might seem. There are three different systems for reckoning descent: **matriliny** *(tracing kinship through the female line),* **patriliny** *(tracing kinship through the male line),* and **bilaterality** *(tracing kinship through both lines).* In the United States, we use a bilateral system; we see ourselves as descended from (related to) the families of both our parents. The only favoritism shown the male line is the passing on of the husband-father's family name to other members of the family. Yet even the practice of the wife taking the husband's last name is currently undergoing some change. Many couples are now hyphenating the last names of marriage partners, so that, for example, if Cybil Craven marries Donald MacDonalds, their family name would be Craven-MacDonalds. Moreover, if their daughter, Ima, marries the son of another hyphenated couple, say, Virginia Hamm and Thomas Bergers, then when Ima and her husband hyphenate their last names, her married name could sound like an advertising slogan: Ima Craven-MacDonalds-Hamm-Bergers. Obviously, in a couple of generations the business of hyphenating last names could get out of hand.

Problems of this sort are reduced if one follows a strictly patrilineal or matrilineal system. Such systems also greatly reduce the number of one's relations. In America, we have grandparents on both our mother's and father's sides of the family because we follow a bilateral system. But if we were a matrilineal society, you would not have paternal grandparents; that is, you would not acknowledge your father's family as related to you. Your father, of course, would be related to you, but at birth, you would have joined your mother's family tree, and taken her family name, not his. Descent, then, is a social, not a biological, relationship—although in this country we tend to think of it as biological.

**Authority** Another major structural element of the marriage system is authority, the pattern of dominance and subordination in marital decision making. The American folk phrase "wearing the pants in the family" pinpoints the issue, although changes in clothing styles have robbed this expression of its former clarity. Authority is still an important issue in families for the simple sociological reason that in order for a group to work or live together, decisions must be made, and people must be convinced or coerced to carry them out. Some kind of authority or leadership has to be exercised. Someone must plan, initiate, and oversee the completion of family tasks.

The major leadership types may be located on a continuum ranging from patriarchy at one pole, through two types of egalitarianism, to matriarchy at the other extreme (see Figure 11.2). **Patriarchy** is an extreme form of male dominance in which *the male head of the family not only exercises the highest authority and power but also possesses a number of important legal rights, such as total claim to family property and assets.* Pure patriarchy is found only in small tribal groupings still largely untouched by modernization. Much more common is the **husband dominant** pattern, in which *the male spouse makes the major decisions,* but his power is based on cultural norms rather than legal traditions. This pattern was the predominant leadership style of American families from Colonial times through the nineteenth century, when it was reinforced by the massive infusion of immigrants into American society. It persists today among some working class groups.[8]

In middle-class American families, the leading form of governance is **egalitarian.** *Power is jointly shared so that decisions are reached by both marriage partners.* Sociologists normally distin-

**FIGURE 11.2  Range of control in family dominance**

| PATRIARCHAL | EQUALITARIAN | MATRIARCHAL |
|---|---|---|
| Husband-dominant | (Syncratic--Autonomic) | Wife-dominant |

guish between two subtypes of egalitarianism. In the first subtype, called *syncratic, both spouses decide all major issues together.* Since neither one dominates the other, this form represents a consensual balance of power. It is also somewhat difficult to achieve, because partners invariably bring to the decision-making process differing interests, expertise, and creative ideas. The other subtype of egalitarianism, the *autonomic,* takes into account those inevitable differences and attempts to turn them to the family's advantage. Accordingly, *decision areas are allocated to spouses on the basis of their experience and competence, and each holds the controlling power in appropriate areas of expertise.* Thus the husband may decide whether to buy a Ford or a Plymouth, while the wife may decide whether to buy a Maytag or a Whirlpool. Autonomic decision making recognizes the superior competence of each spouse to resolve issues within a clearly specified domain.

The **wife-dominant** type of leadership structure is similar to the husband-dominant pattern, except that *the female spouse makes the major family decisions.* This pattern is embraced by a relatively small number of societies. In American social experience, it normally appears when the husband is weak or absent. In these cases, the households are wife-dominant by default.

**matriliny:** the practice of tracing descent through the female line.

**patriliny:** the practice of tracing descent through the male line.

**bilaterality:** the practice of tracing descent through both male and female lines.

**patriarchy:** the form of family authority structure in which the father or eldest male exercises greatest power and holds title to all family assets.

**husband or male dominance:** the form of family authority structure in which the male spouse makes major decisions as a matter of cultural tradition.

**egalitarian:** the form of family authority structure in which power and decision making are shared equally between spouses. Egalitarian structures may be *syncratic,* in which all decision making is shared, or *autonomic,* in which each spouse has separate spheres of decision making.

**wife or female dominance:** the form of family authority structure in which the female spouse makes major decisions as a matter of cultural tradition.

**FIGURE 11.3  Types of families, by race of family head: 1960, 1970, and 1975**

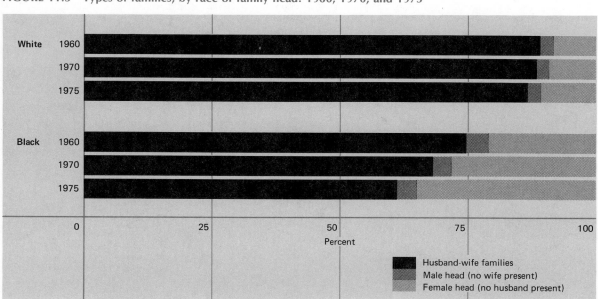

This pattern is clearly on the increase, especially within the black community (as evidenced by Figures 11.3 and 11.4.[9]

**Matriarchy** is the final type. As the polar opposite of patriarchy, it is a *leadership system in which women reign supreme and hold full possession of all legal rights and family power.* This type is included more for the sake of analytical symmetry than for empirical descriptiveness, since no pure form of matriarchy is currently known to exist.[10]

Certain variations in leadership patterns correlate closely with particular descent systems in a society or culture. A patriarchal pattern is usually found in societies that trace lineage through patriliny; egalitarian forms normally follow bilateral lineage systems; and matrilineal societies are usually arranged toward the matriarchy pole of the family leadership continuum. Most societies have favored patriarchy or husband-dominance coupled with a patrilineal or bilateral descent system. In modern societies everywhere, social and cultural change is tending to establish more egalitarian patterns of decision making in which the expression of authority is not rigidly linked to gender. Such changes are visible in almost all the institutions of the modern world and they are particularly evident, in the United States at least, in the primary relationships of contemporary marriage. Decision making is no longer the sole province of the male, and the subordination of wives in the American family is rapidly declining.

The many types of social structure out of which a society creates the family institutions best fitted to its social order go a long way toward explaining the enormous diversity found in family systems around the world. For American society, family organization combines a nuclear pattern with a monogamous marriage system, an egalitarian leadership structure, and a bilateral means of reckoning descent, all of which may characterize a family of orientation or procreation. This pattern is typical of most modernized societies, but the majority of people still live where family life is organized to include extended or patriarchal or polygamous practices. No analysis of a society's family system is ever complete moreover until its leading characteristics have been studied and clearly documented.

FIGURE 11.4   Families with female head, by race and marital status of head: 1960, 1970, and 1975

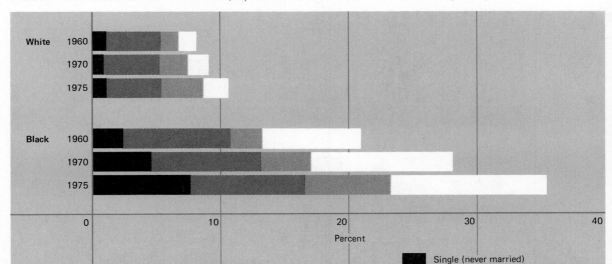

# PROCESSES OF FAMILY CHANGE: THE EMERGENCE OF THE WESTERN FAMILY

The sort of family organization we have just described as typical of America and the modernized West—nuclear, monogamous, and egalitarian—is the end result of a long social history. Edward Shorter, a social historian has proposed a theory to account for this development[11]

## The Traditional Family

Shorter describes the traditional family as the product of village life, a subsistence economy, and a provincial outlook. Marriage was subjected to rigid community controls. Families selected marriage partners for their offspring on the basis of economic concerns and in the interest of strict social control over individual behavior. Romance was unimportant, children were little valued, and privacy for intimate relations was virtually impossible to obtain.

## The Advent of Industrialization

The traditional family was totally undermined by the industrial revolution. Jobs attracted many young people to the cities, where they enjoyed much greater freedom from community controls. Almost immediately there was a dramatic rise in the rate of illegitimate births. This, according to Shorter, was the first sexual revolution of modern times. Karl Marx also observed the pattern, but his interpretation was that young women were being sexually exploited by their urban employers. Shorter's data show that peasant girls more often had working class men for partners. The rise of illegitimacy was not therefore a function of exploitation, but of the newly acquired opportunity for sexual experimentation.

Of larger significance, however, was the dramatic shift—first among lower-class people—toward selecting marriage partners on the basis of romantic attachment rather than economic or communal interests. The establishment of romance as the basis for marriage slowly spread through the whole population, moving from the lower classes all the way up.

Closely allied to this was a change in the value attached to children. Peasant women in traditional society had little time for their children

**matriarchy:** the form of family authority structure in which the mother or eldest female exercises greatest power and holds title to all family assets.

because of their work loads in the house and fields. Upper class city women often sent their babies into the countryside to be tended by a wet nurse until they were about two years old. Poor diet, swaddling (binding children in strips of cloth to limit their activity), and outright neglect produced the staggering infant death rate—25 percent perished before they reached their first birthday. Among foundlings the rate sometimes exceeded 50 percent. The development of romance between spouses helped trigger, Shorter asserts, a revolution in maternal love. During the latter part of the nineteenth century, maternal nursing along with an improvement in the general quality of maternal care radically reduced infant mortality. An increase in emotional attachment to offspring eventually produced the child-centered ethos of the world as we now know it.

The combined influence of romance and maternal love generated yet another transformation in family life: Domesticity increased as the home became a shelter from public surveillance for the nuclear family unit. Work was transferred from the home to the factory, office, or shop; newly wedded couples moved out of their parents' homes and into apartments or houses of their own; access into another person's domicile became contingent on invitation. All of this increased the freedom of the nuclear family, but it also laid exclusively upon the parents' shoulders the full responsibility for nurturing their own offspring. The family unit thus emerged as a tightly knit group bound by strong emotional attachments.

## The Making of the Modern Family

By the beginning of the twentieth century, the modern family had come to prevail as the norm in all Western societies. Everywhere it tended to exhibit the same features: love as the basis for marriage, privacy and intimacy among family members, intense concern for the welfare of children, isolation from the larger kinship network, greater freedom and independence for

Family portraits, then and now. The degree to which the extended family has disappeared in America is a measure of the radical degree of recent family change.

of strong emotional ties. Most people today regard these arrangements as beneficial, and the nuclear family has become one of the most respected, cherished, and valued institutions of the modern world. Once the power of traditionalism had been broken on the wheel of industrial progress, a family life based on sentiment, mutual concern, and personal independence could emerge as a liberating ideal and an empirical reality.

*Toward the Postmodern Family.*

No institution is ever immune to social change. In the mid-1960s, Shorter contends, we went through a second sexual revolution. Sexual activity increased in premarital, marital, and extramarital relations. As in the first revolution, there was a marked increase in the rate of illegimate births—even though effective contraceptive measures were now widely available. Shorter sees the second sexual revolution as a prelude to the emergence of the postmodern family. Although it is still too early to define it exactly, some characterisitics are already discernible. First, the expanding influence of the adolescent subculture increasingly curtails the ability of parents to guide their children. Second, the norms of the peer culture tend toward a new hedonism or pleasure-seeking. This is reflected in the increased use of alcohol and drugs, greater sexual activity, an emphasis on sports for boys and popularity for girls as means of acquiring status among one's peers, and a loss of academic discipline so that high grades and diplomas are valued more highly than the knowledge and skills which those symbols are meant to denote.

A third feature of the postmodern family is the spiraling divorce rate. Although a vast majority of those who divorce eventually remarry— indicating that marriage is still valued highly— the chances are growing that couples will not spend their entire married lives together. This trend extends beyond the United States throughout most industrialized societies (see Figure 11.5) In part, this may be because more women are now working and hence have the economic freedom to extricate themselves from unhappy marriages; or it may mean that the mothering role is changing as the peer group soon snatches the young from the family nest;

the nuclear family unit, and a high degreee of specialization with respect to family functions. No longer was the family a miniature society whose rhythm of activity was established by tradition and whose members went about their affairs with little feeling for one another. Now the family performed a singular set of activities unique unto itself and couched within a matrix

FIGURE 11.5   Divorce rates, selected countries: 1955–1975

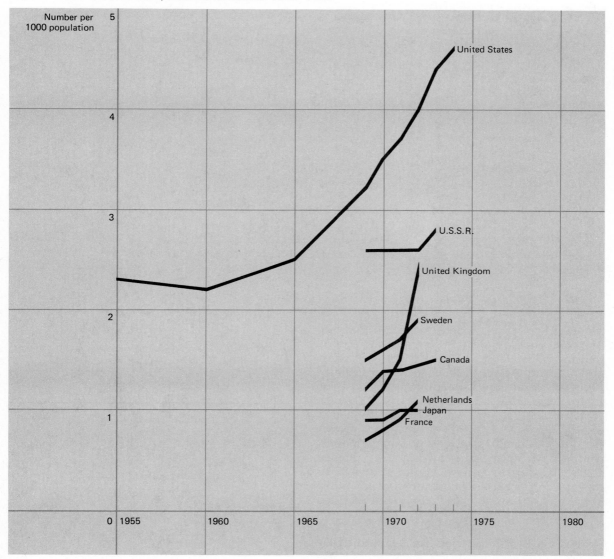

or it may be because people are living longer and thus have more opportunity to divorce and remarry (see Table 11.1).

Whatever the cause, Shorter sees the basic structure of the family as shifting in the post-modern world. Just where it is going is uncertain, and why it is changing is unclear. Shorter believes that one of our most vital and cherished institutions is slowly deteriorating. Perhaps he is right. Or perhaps he is too pessimistic. Only our children will know for sure.

## SOCIAL FUNCTIONS OF THE FAMILY

Thus far our discussion has covered some of the major structural forms of the family along with several sources of change affecting this institution. Now we turn to consider the social activities or functions which the family is responsible for performing. The reasons for the endurance and universality of the family are based on the functions it carries out on behalf of society, the family as a unit, and people as individuals.

**TABLE 11.1  Expectation of Life at Birth: 1920 to 1976[a]**

| Year | Total | | | White | | | Black and other | | |
|---|---|---|---|---|---|---|---|---|---|
| | Total | Male | Female | Total | Male | Female | Total | Male | Female |
| 1920 | 54.1 | 53.6 | 54.6 | 54.9 | 54.4 | 55.6 | 45.3 | 45.5 | 45.2 |
| 1930 | 59.7 | 58.1 | 61.6 | 61.4 | 59.7 | 63.5 | 48.1 | 47.3 | 49.2 |
| 1940 | 62.9 | 60.8 | 65.2 | 64.2 | 62.1 | 66.6 | 53.1 | 51.5 | 54.9 |
| 1950 | 68.2 | 65.6 | 71.1 | 69.1 | 66.5 | 72.2 | 60.8 | 59.1 | 62.9 |
| 1955 | 69.6 | 66.7 | 72.8 | 70.5 | 67.4 | 73.7 | 63.7 | 61.4 | 66.1 |
| 1960 | 69.7 | 66.6 | 73.1 | 70.6 | 67.4 | 74.1 | 63.6 | 61.1 | 66.3 |
| 1965 | 70.2 | 66.8 | 73.7 | 71.0 | 67.6 | 74.7 | 64.1 | 61.1 | 67.4 |
| 1970 | 70.9 | 67.1 | 74.8 | 71.7 | 68.0 | 75.6 | 65.3 | 61.3 | 69.4 |
| 1971 | 71.1 | 67.4 | 75.0 | 72.0 | 68.3 | 75.8 | 65.6 | 61.6 | 69.7 |
| 1972 | 71.1 | 67.4 | 75.1 | 72.0 | 68.3 | 75.9 | 65.6 | 61.5 | 69.9 |
| 1973 | 71.3 | 67.6 | 75.3 | 72.2 | 68.4 | 76.1 | 65.9 | 61.9 | 70.1 |
| 1974 | 71.9 | 68.1 | 75.8 | 72.7 | 68.9 | 76.6 | 67.0 | 62.9 | 71.3 |
| 1975 | 72.5 | 68.7 | 76.5 | 73.2 | 69.4 | 77.2 | 67.9 | 63.6 | 72.3 |
| 1976 | 72.8 | 69.0 | 76.7 | 73.5 | 69.7 | 77.3 | 68.3 | 64.1 | 72.6 |

[a]**In years.** Prior to 1960, excludes Alaska and Hawaii. Data prior to 1940 for death-registration states only. See *Historical Statistics, Colonial Times to 1970,* series B 107–115.

## The Family and the Wider Society

The family is a specialized institution that differs from such other institutions as the economy, the polity, and so forth in both structure and function. As a subunit of society, the family possesses boundary lines from, and points of interchange with, other subunits of the wider social order. Bell and Vogel have provided a useful overview of the major linkages between the nuclear family and the economy, polity, community, and value system (see Figure 11.6).[12] This model will be a point of departure for exploring what the family does for the other social institutions and what rewards it receives in exchange.

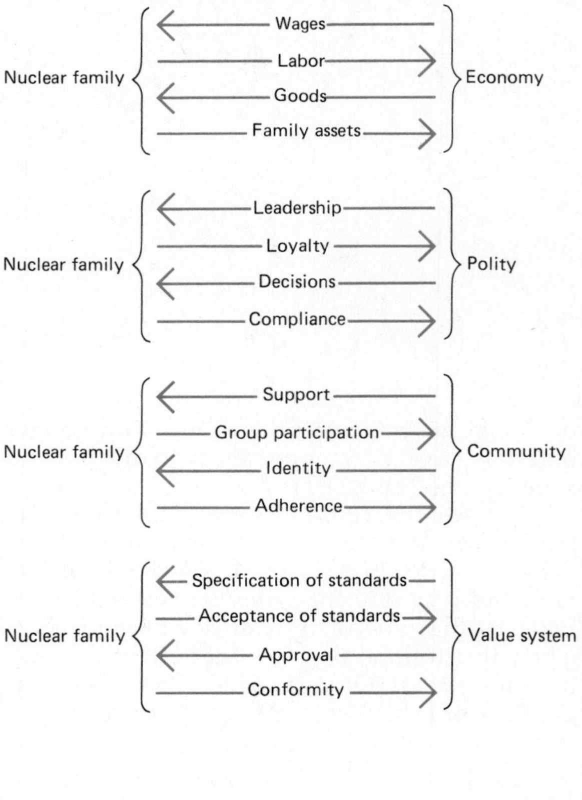

**The Family and the Economy**  Providing laborers for the economy is the family's first function, according to Bell and Vogel. It provides *member replacement* not only for the economy, but for society as a whole, which would soon die without the infusion of new members. The family is the only institution legitimately charged with the responsibility of procreation. The family controls the quality as well as the quantity of the new members through the socialization process. The family gives an individual a basic orientation toward the value of productive labor in general as well as the fundamental skills for entering the labor market.

FIGURE 11.6  The interchanges between the nuclear family and the functional subsystems of society

A poorly socialized individual may be an unreliable, irresponsible, or incompetent worker. Thus the family—not the economy—determines the quality of the labor force, and if the family fails to produce workers with the necessary social skills, the economy will be unable to alter that situation decisively.

In return for labor, the economy supplies the family with wages and income, in general rewarding with higher wages those who function better.

Family resources return to the economy through the purchase of goods and services. One family, of course, cannot affect the balance of supply and demand within the economy, but an aggregate of families can exert considerable influence. When concern over the ecology led many people to boycott phosphate detergents, for example, soap makers soon complied by producing biodegradable products. The exchange of family assets for consumer goods, thus has a significant impact on economic affairs.

**The Family and the Polity**  The **polity** is roughly equivalent to what we call *government* in contemporary societies. The central function of a government is to establish societal goals, such as national defense, eliminating poverty, conserving energy, ending racial inequalities, and so forth. Articulating these goals and marshaling the necessary human and fiscal resources to attain them falls under the general category of providing leadership (see Figure 11.6). The family responds by providing loyalty.

We are not born with a commitment to democracy; we acquire it largely through our training in the family. As we shall see in Chapter 14, the family shapes our political attitudes and our attachment to particular political parties. Even in the chaotic 1960s, sociologists observed a continuity in political attitudes that spanned the generations. Many young radicals proved to be the offspring of politically liberal or radical parents.[13] Individual families are not able to select policy options in quite the same way they can select among consumer goods, but they can shift loyalty from one party to another during elections and thus aggregates of families can influence the course of political affairs.

The family supplies the polity with compliance in return for decisions. Again, single fami-

> **polity:**  a body of persons having an organized government, or the system or principles of government; the state of the body politic.

lies have little control over specific decisions, but leaders must nonetheless concern themselves with the possibility that people will not abide by leadership decisions. Laws relating to marijuana use and the 55-mile-an-hour speed limit are two instances where widespread noncompliance has made political leadership virtually meaningless. Because a government's rules are not automatically accepted, leaders must try to discern the will of the people. In the process of evaluating political decisions, the family is the smallest social unit, but it is one of the most crucial in determining whether compliance will be forthcoming.

**The Family and the Community**  The bond between the family and the community is essentially integrative. The first set of functions (see Figure 11.6) concerns the overall orientation of the family toward the community and the neighborhood. Formal group participation includes voting, serving on the school board

Like charity, political socialization begins at home.

or civic committees, aiding in charity fund drives, or joining the volunteer fire department. Informal participation is likely to be more frequent: lending a neighbor a cup of sugar, carpooling to the commuter train or the nursery school, providing hints on home repairs, or even engaging in small talk over the back fence. The repayment for this participation is communal support in the form of reinforcement of the family's norms and a helping hand from community members when the family is in need.

The second set of functional relationships is somewhat more crucial. The community bestows an identity on the family in exchange for the family's adherence to community norms. The family's identity may be expressed in phrases like, "They're a hard-working family," or "They're rich, but they aren't snobbish," or "They're very good Catholics," or "They're kind of artistic—always into weird things." Behind these descriptions stands a fairly elaborate stratification system into which a family is placed on the basis of such variables as income and behavior patterns. Each class group subscribes to different behavioral norms, and status identity is awarded by the community according to a family's adherence to these norms. A college professor with a middle-class income, for example, is likely to be given a lower-class status position if he puts a battered 1965 Chevy up on cement blocks on the front lawn. Such behavior would be clearly deviant in a middle-class neighborhood, while in a lower-class neighborhood, it might not raise any eyebrows.

It is difficult to overestimate the importance of status placement. All families need to know where their members stand in relation to the community's stratification system. Not only does identity prevent anomie and generate a sense of belonging, it also helps a family discern what behavior would help the family unit achieve upward social mobility or prevent downward mobility. Persons in a family that lacks a social identity would be lost in community affairs, devoid of any sense of direction and unable to distinguish between normative and deviant behavior.

**The Family and the Value System**    The family is a value-carrying, rather than a value-generating, institution. It is the smallest social unit responsible for the internalization of value standards. Values are general orienting principles, and hence they serve as a higher reference point than the concrete patterns of behavior that are the object of community interest. Accordingly, the societal value system supplies the ultimate standards and the family responds by accepting those standards. The value system furnishes the criteria for judging specific patterns of behavior as appropriate or undesirable. For example, in American society, in-laws are treated with almost the same respect as blood relations and offspring within a nuclear family are treated impartially because of our societal commitment to the value of equality.

In the second set of interchanges, the value system gives approval and the family responds with conformity. Not only does the value system set standards, but it rewards those who conform to them. Values are usually sufficiently internalized so that family members feel guilt or esteem whenever they measure their behavior against the value criteria established by the larger society; no intervening agency is necessary to interpret the acceptability of concrete actions. Alongside these internal judgments, however, the community also gives external reinforcement. Together internal and external judgments give family members a sense that they are in good standing in relation to the value system.

## The Family as a Unit

The internal functions of the family meet its fundamental needs for survival. Four basic functions are absolutely essential to the well-being of the family as a unit—task performance, family leadership, integration, and value solidarity.[14]

**Task Performance**    In every family, certain activities must be performed for the family to endure and maintain the standard of living appropriate to its status position. Someone must shop for groceries, shovel snow, wash clothes, paint the house, pay the bills, and do a hundred other chores family living generates. To meet these responsibilities efficiently, families develop a division of labor—certain tasks are allocated to specific family members. Several criteria govern the allocation of tasks. Some are said to be assigned on the basis of *physical abilities*, but actually, the only task absolutely so determined is the bearing of children. Nonetheless jobs that require physical strength are

Task performance and social integration are essential to the family's well-being.

usually allotted to men. Another criterion is *expertise;* a wife who majored in accounting in college will probably manage the family budget. A third factor is *natural affinity.* A son may enjoy working with tools and therefore assume the endless repair jobs around the house. Fourth, *societal conventions* often prescribes the allocation of certain tasks to certain persons within the family. In most households, it is assumed the wife will take primary responsibility for preparing the meals. Generally, societal conventions are adhered to more strictly in blue-collar families than in white-collar households.[15] Finally, family *consensus* is responsible for a certain number of task assignments. This is more likely to take place when there is a drastic change in the family routine, such as a wife returning to the work force, going back to school, or having a baby. Adjustments are normally made by consensus to lighten her work load. As children grow older, they commonly assume more tasks around the house—although in this case the consensus is more often between the two parents than between parents and child. However the division of labor is accomplished, these functions are an important aspect of family life. No single member can possibly perform all the daily activities that are required to keep the family functioning smoothly.

**Family Leadership**  The natural leaders within the family are the parents. Not only do they have more social experience, more practical information, and the physical and financial

power to coerce their offspring, but they possess the legal responsibility of making decisions for their minor children. When the American family is described—quite accurately—as child-centered, this does not mean that children make the decisions that direct the family. A five-year-old is simply not capable of deciding to move out of the city and into the suburbs where there is more play space, better schools, and a safer social environment. Child-centeredness means that parents make decisions that take into account the children's needs, even though children lack the power or wisdom to lobby for their own interests in the decision-making process.

Family leadership, then, refers to the exercise of power within the organization to keep the group operating in an orderly manner. This entails making decisions and allocating tasks, as well as seeing that these decisions and tasks are carried out in actual practice. Family leadership is further complicated by the fact that this group is an emotionally bound social unit. Consequently sheer power is not usually regarded as an appropriate means for establishing order within the family. Parental leaders who assign tasks must also build into the family sufficient motivational support to encourage members to carry out their responsibilities. Because of the intimate relations among family members, leaders are susceptible to manipulation. When a distraught teenager explains that doing the dishes will prevent seeing a movie that just *everyone* in the crowd is going to see, even the sternest set of parents may find themselves up to the elbows in soap suds and dirty pots and pans. Child-centeredness has struck again.

**Social Integration** All social groups, including the family, need to maintain at least minimal solidarity. We might assume that, because the family is a close-knit group, integration is rarely a pressing problem. This is not really the case. Achieving integration is an ongoing activity on which families spend a good deal of energy.

One of the most important means for promoting family integration is rarely recognized as an integrative mechanism. It is the simple establishment of a routine for ordinary family affairs. Many families, for example, try to assure that at least one meal during the day—usually the evening meal—is taken together. The dinner hour thus becomes an occasion in which all members of the family can interact, share the day's experiences, and deal with problems. Similarly, special events in family life take on a ritual character. Family outings, vacations, birthdays, and holidays with unique family customs, all serve to bind the group together around a common stock of memories and experiences. At such times, family life can be celebrated and the group commitment reinforced.

"Keeping up with the Joneses" may be regarded as reprehensible on some grounds, but it can help promote internal family solidarity. Nothing promotes internal group cohesion as effectively as an external competitor. Families who feel their prestige or position threatened quickly close ranks and pull together as a team. Moreover, parents frequently use competitive appeals to enforce control over their children's behavior. "What will the neighbors think?" This question brings home the need to protect the family's good name, and thus usually suffices to curb our actions so as not to jeopardize family interests. Family pride is often important in maintaining family solidarity.

**Value Solidarity** Family value patterns are the normative expectations shared within a family and related to family goals and activities, for example, that all members will go to college or that all will attend church together on Christmas Eve. The family value system operates at a more specific level than the societal value patterns we discussed in the last section. They are concerned with how family members relate to one another and to outsiders. They often reflect the interests of particular ethnic, religious, class, or peer groups, many of whom may deviate significantly from the dominant societal value system. In legitimizing the family's division of labor, leadership functions, and social integration, the value system supplies meanings and a sense of direction for family life, along with the means of ranking family goals and setting the ground rules for their attainment.

Family values do not usually differ drastically between parents and children, since parents oversee the initial value socialization of their offspring. Yet differences may emerge as children mature and come under the influence of the peer group, the school, or other socializing agents. At this point, some agreement must be reached as to which values are to serve as the basis for family activities.

Family values sometimes conflict with values and mores outside the family. Families with strict religious beliefs often regard the larger society as permissive and attempt to preserve a value system that outsiders may view as peculiar or impractical. Religious sects such as the Amish or Hutterites are extreme examples. Conflicts sometimes arise out of circumstances beyond family control. For example, many families customarily allocate money for higher education for their sons, assuming that only their male children will one day support families of their own. This violates a value almost universal in American families that all children be treated equally by their parents. Maintaining value solidarity, then, is far from simple. Values can cause conflict or they can promote harmony. To accomplish the latter, families need good judgment, care, and concern for one another.

### The Family and Individual Needs

The many ways in which the family meets individual needs include such activities as reproduction and physical maintenance, socialization, social control, status placement, and the achievement of psychological balance.

**Reproduction and Physical Maintenance** As we have said, the family is the only agency for legitimately reproducing the species. Most

Family members must share values for the family to endure as a unit, and it is hardly surprising that they usually do.

of us owe our existence to the family, but our debt extends far beyond birth itself. The human infant is a remarkably unfinished animal at birth. Unable to fend for ourselves and survive, we require years of care and guidance. Normally, the family provides nurture and protection of the newborn, feeding, clothing, and sheltering us until we are ready to leave the family nest. Not all families provide equal physical care and maintenance, of course, but virtually all provide some. For most families, the cost is considerable. Recent estimates place the cost of raising a child from birth through four years of college between $45,000 and $65,000 (see Tables 11.2 and 11.3). A similar investment in IBM stock would generate a small fortune by the end

**TABLE 11.2** Direct Cost of Raising a Child to Age 18 in the U.S. at 1977 Prices[a] (by region, cost level, and type of residence)

| Region | Farm costs | | Rural nonfarm costs | | Urban costs | |
|---|---|---|---|---|---|---|
| | Low | Moderate | Low | Moderate | Low | Moderate |
| Total U.S. | $33,124[b] | $48,988[b] | $35,006 | $53,830 | $35,261 | $53,605 |
| North Central | 31,764 | 47,046 | 31,675 | 47,237 | 36,849 | 50,671 |
| South | 35,365 | 52,617 | 34,415 | 55,173 | 34,654 | 54,863 |
| Northeast | 32,382 | 45,840 | 37,618 | 57,355 | 31,861 | 53,586 |
| West | na | na | 40,476 | 58,255 | 38,243 | 56,065 |

[a]Undiscounted figures

[b]West excluded

**TABLE 11.3** Total Direct Costs of a Child in the U.S., about 1977 (by cost level)

| Cost level | Childbirth | Costs to age 18[a] | 4 years of college | Total |
|---|---|---|---|---|
| Low-cost | $1,443[b] | $35,261 | $7,452 | $44,156 |
| Moderate-cost | 2,194 | 53,605 | 8,416 | 64,215 |

[a]Based on U.S. average for urban areas.

[b]Assumed to be in the same proportion to the moderate-cost childbirth figure as the respective costs to age 18.

of twenty-two years, but couples continue having children anyway. As one expectant mother put it, "IBM stock is just no fun to cuddle."

**Socialization of Children**   Not only does the family create and physically maintain children, it also carries out the serious responsibility of socializing each child. In Chapter 4 we defined socialization as the process, beginning at birth, through which one eventually adopts as one's own the norms, values, and beliefs of one's culture, and the roles appropriate to one's social position. Although in American society we tend to think that children largely determine their own social development, socialization does not really proceed so freely and openly. Children are mostly taught by their families to conform to socially approved patterns of behavior. Exactly what behavior constitutes proper performance, of course, differs according to social class, religious, racial, ethnic, and other factors, and, of course, some parents fail to socialize children effectively at all. Societal demands for conformity are nonetheless powerful and pervasive.

Socialization is not merely learning to conform. It teaches us how and when *not* to conform or how to bend the rules in particular situations. Most parents have been in the awkward position of having to explain to a child why *this time* Mommy and Daddy are doing something they have previously told the child it is wrong to do.

**Social Control**   Although social control is closely related to socialization, it is different enough to warrant attention. Early sociologists tended to regard social control as little more than sexual control, but the regulation of sexual behavior is now considered only one important aspect of the whole process. Social control comes from external pressure and social sanctions administered primarily by parents, but also by school authorities, law enforcement officials, community leaders, and so forth. Socialization, by contrast, denotes the internalization of norms so that we become self-regulating. The source of the sanctions constitutes the difference between the two forms of behavioral control.

The importance of social control is that we learn the socially appropriate ways for realizing our personal interests. The family thus equips us for responsible participation in the society at large. Durkheim claimed that social controls tamed our essentially egoistic, selfish drives and transformed us into moral, civilized beings.[16]

**Status Placement**   In American society, social identity is fixed by family membership—by being born to parents of a given status position whose characteristics the children initially internalize. Class outlook is also acquired, so that children receive from their parents basic values, attitudes, and definitions of reality. Because children internalize family beliefs and attitudes, they are treated and defined by others as extensions of the social identity of their parents. The children of the "best family in town" are treated as such.

The ascribed social status acquired from one's family of orientation, however, does not automatically persist throughout one's life. Once launched from the nuclear family, an individual is responsible for achieving and maintaining a status that will prevail during the adult years. As a general rule, the social training acquired in the family of orientation fosters a continuity of status when a family of procreation is established. The likelihood of drastic upward or downward social mobility is thus significantly curtailed, but not prevented. Dur-

**Social control begins in the family.**

ing the late 1960s and early 1970s, many alienated young people from white-collar families dropped out of college and refused to take advantage of the opportunities afforded by their social position. But these opportunities did not go unfulfilled, for blue-collar youth quickly occupied those openings in college and in the job market. Peter Berger predicted that a good number of white-collar dropouts would experience downward mobility, while those who filled their positions from blue-collar families would enjoy upward mobility.[17] Thus high class position in the United States is never absolutely guaranteed, each individual must to some degree earn his or her own position in the stratification system.

**Maintaining Psychological Balance** Physical maintenance, socialization, social control, and status placement are all largely directed toward the needs of the young individuals in the family. Promoting psychological balance is a function that primarily meets the needs of adults. Of course, even children have psychological needs that require gratification. The nuclear family is an important source of affection, love, and social interaction.

The pressures experienced by adults in modern life intensify their need for a place where psychological balance can be restored. In the world of secondary relationships outside the home, adults have to be constantly concerned about the image they project. Role management takes a great deal of psychological energy and generates anxiety as well as frustration. The modern nuclear family, then, has become important as a place of refuge for adult members who need a release from the pressures of contemporary social life.

## ROLE RELATIONS IN THE FAMILY

Four major role patterns characterize the relationships among family members, namely, leadership, sexual, mating and parenting, and companionship roles.

### Leadership Roles

The analysis of small groups has helped sociologists interpret family role patterns. All small groups, including the family, appear to require two different types of leaders. These have been

designated the *instrumental* and *expressive* leadership roles. Although fundamentally different, they complement one another in the context of the small group. In most families, the husband performs one, and the wife performs the other, leadership role.[18]

**Instrumental Leaders** Because the nuclear family is subject to many demands—biological, economic, individual, and so forth—one leader typically assumes the administrative task of seeing that each of these demands is met in a socially approved manner. This person is called the instrumental leader. The central concern of this leader is behavior, that is, the achievement of goals necessary for the subsistence of the group. Normally the instrumental leader is not only responsible for allocating specific family tasks, but also for organizing the entire household to insure their successful completion. The instrumental leader need not accomplish these tasks alone, but should provide information and motivation for others to do so. The instrumental leader also has major responsibility for integrating the family with the ongoing society. Since the instrumental leader is usually the family's breadwinner, he or she is likely to have contacts beyond the residence and the context of the nuclear family, and thus provides the crucial linkage between the family and the community.

**Expressive Leaders** The activities of the instrumental leader are insufficient to ensure the persistence of the family as a small group. Rational, work-oriented, and demanding, the instrumental leader would produce a totally unlivable system, if there were not a supporting and complementary leader to resolve the tensions such behavioral demands arouse. This is the *expressive leader*. Home-based and intimate with the children, the expressive leader responds to the integrative and emotional needs of family members, some of which are created by the demands of the instrumental leader. Through warmth and affection, this leader aids in the psychological stabilization of the nuclear family unit. Because of the expressive leader's attachment to the home, the household itself is symbolically associated with the family's security, love, and personal support.

In most societies, the two leadership roles are divided between the sexes. The pattern in American society is for the husband-father to take the instrumental role while the wife-mother assumes the expressive role. It should be pointed out, however, no actual mother or father is expected to approximate fully the traits defined for each type. What distinguishes American society is a degree of flexibility that allows for a sharing of instrumental and expressive activities between the two parents. The father, for example, may diaper the baby or be a "soft touch" for spending money or prepare the meals from time to time, while the mother may hold a job outside the home, repair the torn screen door, or discipline the child whose baseball broke the storm window. Nevertheless, trading particular functions does not decisively alter the basic responsibilities allocated to the two leaders. The American father is still generally considered the breadwinner. A father without a steady job to support the family is still regarded as performing inadequately. The notion of a giving, loving "mom" who manages the household with sensitivity contrasts with the go-getting, activist, worldly wise "dad." An expressive man is likely to be pegged as an effeminate, henpecked husband, while an aggressive, instrumental woman may be regarded as a bossy, domineering wife. Thus, even in the more open patterns of American life, the ideal of a sexual division of labor between the instrumental and expressive leaders endures.

## Sex Roles

Male and female are biological concepts. Masculine and feminine, however, are culturally defined attributes. All societies make fundamental distinctions between the rights and obligations of the two sexes. Yet the variations in content of the two roles are also quite impressive. Not all societies assign heavy, physical tasks to men. Tasmanian women are traditionally the seal hunters, swimming out to kill those large animals. Arapesh women are expected to carry the heaviest loads on their heads because, as all Arapesh know, women have harder heads. In our society, women are expected and socially trained to be more emotional, aesthetically appreciative, and sympathetic. In classical China, these were purely masculine traits. Thus two overriding conclusions are warranted: (1) Everywhere a basic distinction between the sexes is socially recognized, justified, and taken very seriously, so that sexual differences are passed from generation to generation with a

care rarely equaled in other areas of social learning; and (2) the behavior considered appropriate for each sex differs markedly among cultures.

Although sex roles derive initially from biological differences, they include an ever-widening sphere of behaviors, including dress, carriage, attitudes, values, and self-image. Each new person in society must learn masculinity or feminity from his or her socializing agents. Often this is not an easy task and some role strain results. In American society, the masculine role has traditionally stood for strength, vigor, and the ability to meet the outside world head-on and deal with it effectively. The individualistic, macho role idealized in American culture is beyond the reach of many boys and men, and can cause genuine problems. The traits that spell success in one facet of the masculine role—strength, power, and aggressiveness— may spell disaster in another. During the adolescent years especially, young men are forced to come to grips with these competing role demands and work out a socially acceptable self-image.

Learning the feminine role appropriate to our culture is no easier. Not long ago every young girl knew exactly what part she was to play in life—wife, homemaker, mother. Her major decisions were made first by her parents and later by her husband. Society greatly limited her options. Early in this century, with more economic independence—always more important than the right to vote—and with greater equality between the sexes in marital decisions, the female role has experienced drastic transformation. Moving into the business world, politics, and the professions, women must reinterpret their role. The marked increase in the number of women who are unhappy or dissatisfied with what they take to be the feminine role may arise from the role ambiguity currently prevailing in American society. Consider, for example, the Virginia Slims cigarette slogan, "You've come a long way, baby." The obvious inference is that women have attained sufficient equality to smoke what men smoke. Instead, they are offered a slender, "feminine" cigarette. If you've come a long way, baby, why must you settle for anything less than what the cowboys smoke in Marlboro country? Ambiguity over the meaning of equality in sex roles still persists. Is it possible to be equal *and* different? Ann Oakley, a British sociologist, vehemently

Male and female are biological concepts, but masculine and feminine are culturally-defined attributes.

answers, "No." Her admittedly radical recommendation is to correct such inequality by abolishing gender roles, the housewife role, and the family as well.[19]

Even when they have gained access to the business world, women are still treated as second class citizens: Wages are lower and opportunities fewer. Many individual women are still not sure whether they should—or even want to—compete with men and win. In a study on male attitudes and role conflicts, Komarovsky discovered that the college men in her sample wanted to marry women less intelligent than themselves, although they ideologically favored equal rights for women. This finding led to the further discovery that many women "play dumb" in order not to jeopardize their relationship with a boyfriend.[20]

It is impossible to tell at the present time what direction the redefinition of the feminine role will take. Some sociologists predict a further blurring of sex roles, but it is doubtful whether complete unification can ever be accomplished. More important, socialization into sex roles is associated with preparation for instrumental and expressive leadership functions. Adjusting sex roles, then, can have profound effects upon the performance of other family role patterns.

### Mating and Parenting

These two social roles are closely related, since mating is the social process that leads up to marriage, and parenting is one of the major purposes for which marriages are established. Normally, mating precedes parenting, but the increased rate of marital disruption these days often results in some people operating in both roles simultaneously.

**Mate Selection**    The process of choosing marriage partners is called mate selection. It operates according to two sociological principles **preferential mating** and **marriage arrangement,** usually attributed to Murdock and Winch.[21] In preferential mating, cultural and behavioral patterns define the field of eligible mates for a given individual, but the responsibility for selecting a mate rests with the two persons who form the nuptial couple. In marriage arrangment, persons other than the nuptial couple influence or control outright the selection of a mate for an individual. Preferential mating is the norm in modern societies, while arranged marriages still persist in many non-Western cultures. In a sample of Algerian immigrants now living in and around Paris, for example, Michel discovered one of three women and one of five men had never seen their mates before marriage.[22] That may seem to some of us shocking, yet women from cultures where arranged marriage is a norm often pity American women for having no assistance in seeking a husband. Actually, a number of rules indirectly influence mate selection by narrowing the field of eligibles, even in the open system flourishing in the United States. These include heterosexuality, the incest taboo, and the rules of endogamy and exogamy.

The principle of *heterosexuality* is operative in every society. It requires that persons considering marriage be of the opposite sex. Although homosexuality has been permitted in various cultures, it has never been defined as a marital relation. By apparently universal definition, marriage must include at least the possibility of parenthood, which, of course, requires a heterosexual union. The effect of the heterosexual requirement obviously is to reduce the field of eligibles by approximately 50 percent.

The **incest taboo** forbids sexual relations with someone who is considered a close relative, although exactly what behaviors constitute incest and who is defined as a close relative may vary considerably. In some American states, one is permitted to marry anyone but a parent or sibling; other states prohibit marriage between second cousins.[23] The universality of the incest taboo is usually attributed to the fact that it prevents conflicts that would destroy the family and kinship group, and it forces offspring to satisfy their sexual drives outside the nuclear family, thereby laying the foundations for new families. As Talcott Parsons has pointed out,

the family is a self-liquidating group, and the incest taboo is the social mechanism for ejecting the young into the world to create new families.[24]

The rules of *endogamy* and *exogamy* limit the field of marriage eligibles further. **Endogamy** *requires an individual to marry within a culturally defined group of which the individual is a member.* **Exogamy** does the reverse, *requiring the individual to marry outside of his or her own kind.* Both the heterosexual marital requirement and the incest taboo are examples of a kind of exogamy, but the terms endogamy and exogamy usually apply to kinship units, such as clans, and to racial, ethnic, or religious groupings. All these requirements are learned through socialization and are so widely accepted that few ever consider violating them.

**The Parenting Roles**    All societies take a firm stand on who may or may not procreate because of the significance of legitimacy and social placement. Children play an important role in the family image—and often in prosperity—in almost all societies. In some cultures, young women are or were not considered married until they became pregnant with their first child. This requirement underscored the importance of procreation as a family function.

Children have been desired for both economic and noneconomic reasons. Espenshade has identified the direct and indirect monetary costs as well as the investment of time and emotional energy[25] despite which couples still strongly prefer to have children, although the desired number of offspring has been decreasing for several decades. Nine out of ten married couples in the United States have children and half of those who are childless desire them. As Blood and Wolfe have pointed out, however, there has been a shift from desiring a quantity of children toward desiring quality children.[26] Hence, the ideal number of children—as well as the actual number of children per household (see Figure 11.7)—has drastically decreased so that parents may invest more time, emotional support, and money in each of their children.

Preparation for parenthood begins with pregnancy. In the isolated nuclear family, young parents cannot learn from members of the extended family as previous generations did. Doctors, friends, child care classes, and 26 million copies of Dr. Spock's *Baby and Child Care* have filled the information gap. Having

**FIGURE 11.7**  Average size of families, by age and members: 1950–1990

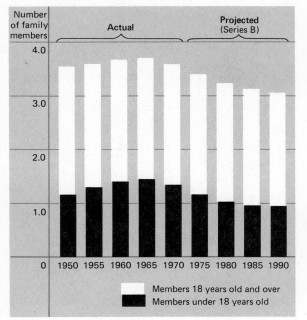

children greatly alters the husband and wife roles. Indeed, children can induce a case of cultural shock. No longer are parents free to pursue their interests at will—they can't dash out for a midnight pizza and leave the baby in the crib. The strain of parenting is frequently more intense for the mother, since she is ordinarily the person most responsible for the day-to-day care of the children. Yet mothering does have rewards. The mother-child bond is usually a strong emotional linkage which both mother and child find psychologically rewarding. By the same token, this emotional tie makes all the more difficult the launching of children. Just as the arrival of children represents a cultural shock, so too does their departure from the family nest. Mothers, in particular, may regard this event as signaling the completion of one of their major roles. But despite all the problems, most American parents prize their children as life's richest blessings.

## Companionship

The romantic basis of marriage and the emphasis on companionship are relatively recent innovations. Indeed, few changes within the family have been accepted as rapidly as the com-

**preferential mating:**  the cultural and behavioral patterns that define an individual's field of eligible mates; the social rules defining persons with particular characteristics as appropriate or inappropriate marriage partners.

**marriage arrangement:**  the process through which persons other than the nuptual couple influence or control mate selection.

**incest taboo:**  the norm forbidding marriage or sexual contact between persons defined as closely related.

**endogamy:**  the requirement that one marry within some group of which one is already a member. Racial, religious, and ethnic endogamy are common.

**exogamy:**  the requirement that one marry outside of some group of which one is a member, typically a kinship unit, family, clan, and so on.

panionate marriage ideal. Its pervasiveness is documented in an investigation by Blood and Wolfe in which roughly 50 percent of the wives in the sample chose "companionship in doing things together with the husband" as the most valuable aspect of marriage, outpacing such other features as understanding, standard of living, and the chance to have children.[27]

By companionship, we do not mean simply that couples spend most of their leisure time together, although this is certainly part of it. The emphasis is on sharing all of one's experiences with a mate. This implies greater intimacy between marriage partners, equality of power, privacy from the scrutiny of kin and neighbors, and the stabilization of adult personalities. Moreover, our increased life expectancy gives couples more time to develop close bonds of affection. The major responsibilities of parenting are completed in relatively few years, but companionship may continue from mating until death.

Part of the sharing that occurs in the companionship role is sexual. Society regulates our sexual behavior by sanctioning marriage as the appropriate context for its fullest expression. Although the rules for sexual conduct are sometimes violated—as, indeed, are many social rules—still no society has ever tolerated sexual anarchy. Rather, societies have channeled sexual drives through the institution of marriage in order to strengthen the husband-wife relationship, especially since the emergence of the isolated nuclear family in modern societies. Casual sexual activity outside marriage not only challenges social control; it also jeopardizes marriage as a socially sanctioned institution for intimate relationships, whether sexual or otherwise. Thus, while we understand the strength of sexual drives and are not surprised at the violations of the rules governing sexual conduct, this should not be interpreted as leading to a general reduction in the value of marriage as the proper institutional context for sexual relations. Indeed, Shorter regards the current trend toward sexual pleasure-seeking outside marriage as dangerous, precisely because it threatens the quality of family life.[28] So long as sexual relations and companionship are closely associated — by society and individuals — greater sexual activity outside marriage can be expected to undermine the companionship role which many American marriage partners now hold as the most valuable aspect of their life together.

## CHANGING SOCIAL ROLES AND THE LIFE CYCLE

So far, we have approached social roles from a thematic perspective, but they may also be viewed dynamically as movement through the life cycle. Lopata has taken this approach in a study limited to the social role of housewife.[29] She suggests that the housewife's life cycle consists of six stages of development:

1. The first period is from home-based infancy, where personality is formed among primary social groups, to school and work roles in a wider community context. In this period, women acquire socialization into their sex role, and they also participate in secondary social networks where their action is evaluated according to rational, competency-based, and achievement standards. The direction of change is from home-limited to pluralistic social roles.
2. The second period is somewhat shorter. It goes from the multidimensional, nonfamilial roles of the young adult to the roles of wife and housewife. During this period, some limitation of freedom occurs. Business or schoolwork may be replaced by full-time housework. The usual pattern, however, is for women to continue working outside the home until the birth of the first child.

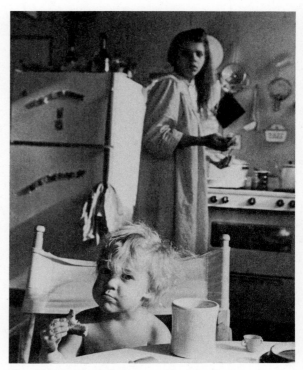

The third stage of the housewife role can be most distressing, tieing her to young children and confining her to the home

3. Drastic change occurs in the third period. It moves from the external-participating role of the young adult to the role of mother. The housewife is confined quite drastically to the geographical environment of the home. Her attention is directed toward young children who demand most of her energy and time. She is often severely isolated from other adult contacts. This can be one of the most psychologically distressing periods of her life cycle, since it involves a radical readjustment of her life style and a sharp reduction in social contacts.
4. The next period allows greater freedom to the housewife-mother. It begins with total immersion in the physical care of children and progresses to increasing competence as housewife, mother, and community participant. As the children mature, they no longer require the large investment of time, energy, and support that small children demand. Moreover, as with other social roles, experience produces a higher quality of performance with more ease and efficiency. Many housewives also reenter the work force during this period.
5. The fifth stage marks the near completion of the

mothering role as children become independent. It covers the period from full participation in family life to a "shrinking circle" when the nuclear family is reduced to husband and wife. The housewife is suddenly free to explore new interests, engage in community affairs, and spend more time with her husband. This is often curtailed by the death of the husband.

6. The final period extends from being the sole surviving member of the household until death. Today, about 11 million Americans are widows or widowers (about 5 percent of the population), and 80 percent of these are women, because (a) males have higher mortality rates in almost all ages; (b) widowed women are less likely to remarry than widowers; and (c) American women usually mar-

ry men somewhat older than themselves, thus increasing their chance of becoming widows. If this practice continues (and there is no reason to believe it will not), and if longevity continues to increase within the population, we can expect the proportion of widowed women to increase in the future.

Widowhood is thus essentially a female problem. Because of the status of women in the United States, simply making a living is likely to be much harder for the widowed female than the widowed male. She may be unemployable through lack of experience or skills, or simply because of age. If the younger widow has children to support and educate, her problems are simply compounded.

A number of social roles are available to the widowed woman, depending on her health, her financial resources, and her psychological strength. She may, of course, continue her career or develop a new one. She may be forced into involuntary isolation caused by illness, or dependency on her children or on the state's social services, if her own fiscal resources are not adequate. For some women, this stage provides freedom to travel, to participate in social activities, and to develop new interests. This period thus requires adjustment or resocialization into widowhood, and it may be a creative, liberating, multidimensional stage or a depressing, anxiety-ridden, lonely final chapter to one's life. Much depends upon the resources that are available and upon what the individual makes of them.

### Three Variations of the Housewife Role

This model for the housewife's life cycle is not, of course, a precise blueprint everyone follows to the last detail. Some sociologists would consider it hopelessly stereotyped. Lopata herself admits that a good deal of variation is possible. She distinguishes three types of performance within the housewife role, types that vary in regard to skill, creativity, outlook, and education. Class standing, however, represents the major differentiating principle, since this helps determine one's educational achievement, attitudes, and personal interactions.

First is the *restricted* housewife. She has little education, often lower-class standing, and a passive stance toward her role. She is task-oriented, homebound, and relatively uncreative

**Widowhood is essentially a female problem. How a woman adapts to it is largely a matter of what resources are available and what use she makes of them. She gets little reinforcement from society.**

in her performance as both housewife and mother. Often she holds some resentment toward the dominance of her husband and she feels incompetent or ineffective in many social relationships outside the home and neighborhood.

The *uncrystallized,* housewife reaps the benefits of more education and greater ease in establishing fruitful social relationships. She is less passive in accepting conventional housewife functions, shares power more equally with her husband, and is happier with the housewife role, partly because of her competence and social skills. This type of housewife is capable of organizing life rather than simply adjusting to it. Socially, she enjoys a lower-middle- to middle-class status position.

The *multidimensional* housewife—the third type—Lopata regards as the most satisfying and competent role variation. Women in this category usually have some higher education which they use as a resource for gaining creativity in their role. The home is not shut off from the world outside; it becomes a place for entertaining; through art and decorating, the world is brought into the family living space. The multidimensional housewife takes an interest in her husband's vocational endeavors and provides support, often as an adjunct to his job. In return, the husband tends to regard his wife as one with whom he shares equal authority, and decision making is a joint enterprise. Housewives in this group tend to be drawn from middle- to upper-middle-class status positions.

Lopata concludes that as competence in housewife and child-rearing skills increase, so too does creativity, role variation, and—perhaps most important—personal satisfaction with the housewife role. Hence lower-class women more often feel locked into a rigid role definition and experience the housewife role as unfulfilling drudgery, while women who possess greater social skills tend to approach the role as a creative opportunity and manage to find happiness and fulfillment in the occupation of housewife.

Unfortunately, few studies have been undertaken on role changes in the male life cycle. We may assume that the major stages for men parallel those of women. Where some women are oriented toward children, however, most men would undoubtedly be oriented toward their careers. The cultural shock of launching children for the woman may find its counterpart in the man's retirement. Beyond this, we have little concrete data. Clearly, more research is needed in this crucial area of family life.

## THE DECLINE OF THE AMERICAN FAMILY: A REVIEW OF THE EVIDENCE

The family is subject to the pressure of social change like all other institutions. The conviction that the family in our society is undergoing a crisis enjoys wide popularity. Such varied voices of public opinion as *Redbook* magazine, Billy Graham, and the FBI have all warned of the imminent collapse of the American family. Let us look critically at the evidence in order to ascertain whether the alleged decline is myth or fact.

The indications of deep-seated crisis most often cited include (1) the rising divorce rate, (2) greater sexual freedom (the new morality, an increased rate of illegitimate births, and a higher incidence of unmarried couples living together), (3) the rapid geographic movement of families creating a sense of rootlessness, (4) a decline in the number of offspring per nuclear family, (5) a loss of family functions, and (6) the generation gap. Some are clearly more important than others.

### Divorce

The issue of divorce is more complex than is commonly recognized. One cannot infer the health and stability of the family directly from the divorce rate. In pre-Communist China, the divorce rate was very low, but the suicide rate for wives was very high. Chinese women were often trapped in a tension-filled family situation where it was not uncommon for mothers-in-law to beat to death their daughters-in-law. They were advised by the old adage; "Good women should hang themselves; only bad women seek divorce."[30] Most Americans would surely agree that divorce is more humane than suicide as a means of reducing family tensions. But if a low divorce rate in a given society need not indicate a harmonious family life, what does the high divorce rate mean in America?

Several characteristics of divorce are worth considering. First, most divorces tend to occur in the early years of marriage before children appear. It should not be inferred from this that children hold marriages together, but rather that couples who have children seem to believe that their marriages will work. The data are on their side; once couples settle down to having children, there is a strong probability they will remain together.

Another important feature is the rate of remarriage. Currently 75 to 80 percent of divorced persons remarry. This may signify that couples have not given up on marriage as an institution. Some persons choose to divorce and remarry, until they achieve the ideal marriage they highly value. Perhaps the divorce rate should be viewed as an adjustment going on within the marriage system. As such it testifies to the value Americans attach to marriage, not to a denial of its significance as is so often inferred.

Divorce occurs most often where a wide divergence in background separates marriage partners. Couples drawn from dissimilar age cohorts, class standings, racial groups, ethnic communities, religious traditions, and educational levels possess a higher probability of divorcing. Conversely, couples of similar backgrounds are less likely to divorce. The reason is simple. With greater emphasis on companionship, similar backgrounds facilitate compatibility in marriage, since attitudes, values, and outlooks tend to be similar.

Finally, the divorce rate is lower for couples who have higher education, income, and class standing. In the 1950s, Goode demonstrated that divorce was related inversely to class stratification.[31] By 1975, this pattern had begun to change, particularly for college men. Men who have completed four years of college now divorce at about the same rate as all men whether they have been to college or not. For women with four years of college, however, the divorce rate is still 10 percent lower than that of the total population.[32]

To summarize the divorce phenomenon (see Figure 11.8), divorce occurs in 38 out of 100 marriages. This rate has been increasing gradually since 1955. The remarriage rate is still high, and the family institution is still highly valued in American society, even by those who divorce. Divorce occurs most often in couples of divergent social backgrounds, and it still correlates inversely with class standing, but not as

The custody of the children causes much pain in divorce proceedings.

much for college men as twenty years ago.

The divorce rate does not directly reveal the "health" of the family system. As the divorce rate has gone up, so too has marital happiness and satisfaction with family life in recent years (see Figures 11.9 and 11.10). As long as preferential mating is the norm and intimate personal relationships between spouses is the ideal, we should expect some persons to make mistakes in selecting marriage partners. Divorce is a mechanism for correcting uncongenial marriages. This is by no means a recommendation for divorce; at best, it merely suggests that divorce may not be the worst thing that can happen to a marriage. A conflict-ridden marriage may produce more unhappiness than divorce and remarriage.

Closely associated with the divorce phenomenon may be another issue gaining increased public attention: physical violence between spouses. More overt conflict between mates is being reported than previously. This probably does not signify that physical fighting is on the increase. What now is reported as "wife beating" (and less frequently "husband battering") was previously regarded as a routine part of married life. This form of behavior is no longer tolerable. Ironically, there is evidence that couples who physically fight are likely to express affection in physical forms as well. In severe cases of wife abuse—and also in child-abuse—

**FIGURE 11.8   Rates of first marriage, divorce, and remarriage for U.S. women: 1921–1977**

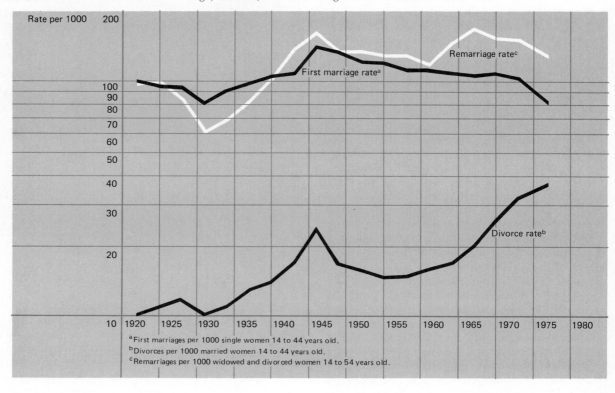

ᵃFirst marriages per 1000 single women 14 to 44 years old.
ᵇDivorces per 1000 married women 14 to 44 years old.
ᶜRemarriages per 1000 widowed and divorced women 14 to 54 years old.

**FIGURE 11.9   Marital happiness: 1973–1975**

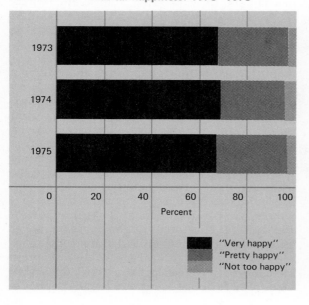

**FIGURE 11.10   Satisfaction with family life: 1973–1975**

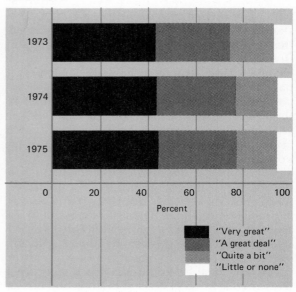

FIGURE 11.11 Attitude toward ease of divorce: 1974 and 1975

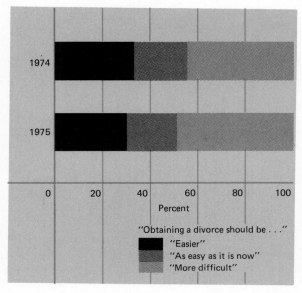

"Obtaining a divorce should be . . ."

- ■ "Easier"
- ▨ "As easy as it is now"
- ▨ "More difficult"

violence no doubt indicates an inadequate adjustment to social or familial pressures. At any rate, physical conflict between spouses is undoubtedly both a cause of divorce and a manifestation of the frustration people experience in trying to cope with an increasingly complex set of social forces surrounding contemporary family and social life.

Family conflict and incompatibility were among the major justifications for easing divorce laws over the last two decades. The emergence of marriage dissolution through "no-fault" divorce raises the question of whether social controls can any longer promote the norm of monogamy. Social pressure to work out problems instead of divorcing has been relaxed. There appears to be a trend toward making divorces more difficult to obtain (see Figure 11.11). Of course, a good deal of trauma, per-

sonal anxiety, and disruption still accompanies even the most amicable divorce. Ultimately couples must decide for themselves whether the cost is really worth the likely benefits. Groups like the Family Section of the American Sociological Association are taking steps to improve counseling and social programs to help people work out their family problems without resorting to divorce.

### Sexual Freedom

Many Americans associate the rising divorce rate with the increased sexual freedom that has emerged since the mid-sixties. As Shorter suggested, however, the sexual revolution pervades the whole of American life—influencing premarital, marital, and extramarital sexual relations.[33] No direct connection has been established between the sexual revolution and divorce, although many are convinced the connection exists. What troubles many students of family life is that the sexual revolution may signal a move toward greater hedonism and pleasure-seeking, and this could undercut the discipline needed for family living.

One discernible result of the sexual revolution is the higher incidence of couples living together "without benefit of clergy." Of course, this practice was not invented in the last fifteen years. What has changed is that once this was a lower-class phenomenon, but now it is spreading into the middle and upper classes, and especially into the college population. One needs to keep this practice in perspective, however. Projections by Glick and Norton suggest that considerably less than 10 percent of the total adult population will ever live together like man and wife without being married[34] (see Tables 11.4 and 11.5). Those who go even further to experiment with group marriage constitute a much smaller minority. Students have evidenced a good deal of interest in alternate

TABLE 11.4 Unmarried Couples Living Together: United States, 1960, 1970, and 1977

| Year | All unmarried couples | In 2-person households | In households of 3+ persons |
|---|---|---|---|
| 1960 | 439,000 | 242,000 | 197,000 |
| 1970 | 523,000 | 327,000 | 196,000 |
| 1977 | 957,000 | 753,000 | 204,000 |

TABLE 11.5    Proportions of Adults Living as Unmarried Couples: United States, 1977

| Unit of comparison | Total, millions | In unmarried couples | |
| --- | --- | --- | --- |
| | | Millions | % of total |
| Total population | 216.0 | 1.914 | 0.9 |
| Unmarried adults | 52.63 | 1.914 | 3.6 |
| Divorced men | 3.17 | .171[a] | 5.4 |
| Divorced men under 35 | 1.3 | .085[a] | 8.3 |
| Total households | 74.14 | .957 | 1.3 |
| Couple households | 48.43 | .957 | 2.0 |
| 2-person households | 17.81 | .753 | 4.2 |
| Husband or man under 25 | 3.3 | .248 | 7.4 |
| Husband or man 35 to 44 | 9.37 | .090 | 1.0 |
| Husband or man 65 and over | 6.79 | .085 | 1.3 |

[a]Estimated for all such men on the basis of data for those in 2-person households.

family arrangements, but actual practice has remained so limited that the nuclear family ideal has not been challenged.

Although much of the opposition to unmarried couples living together, of course, is based on moral grounds, one important group has sternly opposed the practice on the basis of a practical rationale. Some feminists argue that women are inviting exploitation when they enter housekeeping arrangements out of wedlock. Should a pregnancy result from such a union, the woman is likely to be left with the sole responsibility, with few legal sanctions to constrain the father to shoulder his share of the obligation. Whether she decides to have the child or get an abortion, the risks and expenses — both monentary and emotional — are likely to be borne by the woman. The increase in the rate of illegitimate births and abortions cannot be considered primarily a function of unmar-

TABLE 11.6    Pregnancy Outcomes: U.S., 1970–1975 (pregnancies resulting in legitimate and illegitimate live births, legal and illegal induced abortions, and spontaneous abortions)

| Year | Total pregnancies | Live births | | Fetal deaths | | Spontaneous abortions and still-births |
| --- | --- | --- | --- | --- | --- | --- |
| | | Legitimate | Illegitimate | Induced abortions | | |
| | | | | Legal | Illegal | |
| Number (in thousands) | | | | | | |
| 1970 | 5,682 | 3,332 | 399 | 193 | 530 | 1,228 |
| 1971 | 5,462 | 3,155 | 401 | 480 | 250 | 1,176 |
| 1972 | 5,060 | 2,855 | 403 | 587 | 130 | 1,085 |
| 1973 | 4,998 | 2,730 | 407 | 745 | 54 | 1,062 |
| 1974 | 5,156 | 2,742 | 418 | 899 | 12 | 1,085 |
| 1975 | 5,288 | 2,692 | 448 | 1,034 | 10 | 1,100 |
| Percent | | | | | | |
| 1970 | 100.0 | 58.6 | 7.0 | 3.4 | 9.3 | 21.6 |
| 1971 | 100.0 | 57.8 | 7.3 | 8.8 | 4.6 | 21.5 |
| 1972 | 100.0 | 56.4 | 8.0 | 11.6 | 2.6 | 21.4 |
| 1973 | 100.0 | 54.6 | 8.1 | 14.9 | 1.1 | 21.2 |
| 1974 | 100.0 | 53.2 | 8.1 | 17.4 | 0.2 | 21.0 |
| 1975 | 100.0 | 51.0 | 8.5 | 19.6 | 0.2 | 20.8 |

ried couples living together (see Table 11.6), but the increased opportunity for sexual experience can be expected to affect such rates to some extent.

## Geographic Mobility

Increased geographic mobility among American families helps break up the family as a residential unit and generates a sense of rootlessness. When one of every three or four families moves each year there no longer is a "Home, Sweet Home" to look back on nostalgically. The truth is, however, that geographic movement tends to be either a family's response to opportunities in the job market or its effort to mark monetary gains by moving into a better neighborhood. Families still hold to the ideal of owning a home of their own. Indeed, the evidence suggests that families are much concerned with where and how the family is housed. The mobility rate, therefore, is more a reflection of economic forces than evidence for a decline in family life.

## Family Size

A decrease in the number of children each nuclear family has is often cited as a measure of disenchantment with family life. As we noted earlier, however, such a reading really misses the point. A decline in the birthrate is a response to the reduced need for large numbers of children to work the farm, perpetuate the species, and care for aged parents. Thus, a shift has occurred, with families desiring fewer children and being more concerned about the quality of their children. More time, money, and emotional support can be invested in children if the number is two or three instead of ten. Children are, however, still highly valued in American society.

## Loss of Family Functions

Many activities once undertaken by the family have now been transferred to other institutions. Many skills once taught in the home are now taught in school in home economics, industrial arts, sex education, and other classes. Religious education, too, has largely been taken over by professionally trained experts. Information about health care is acquired more often from physicians, books, and special classes than from family members. Financial support of the aged is now shouldered by government, releasing family members from much of their responsibility in this area. This list could easily be expanded to cover other functional losses of the nuclear family.

Must the family now be less valued if so many of its activities have been allocated to other groups or institutions? Or is the family now becoming more specialized? By relinquishing many functions, it can perhaps perform better the tasks it still retains, such as socializing the young and stabilizing adult personalities. On the other hand, as the family becomes more proficient, its sister institutions may well be getting overburdened. We may have achieved greater proficiency in the family at the expense of our educational institution for example. At any rate, the loss of family functions, rather than impairing family life, has made possible its substantial improvement and specialization.

## The Generation Gap

A final issue in the decline of the American family is the celebrated notion of the generation gap. Initially developed in the 1960s, the idea of a widening division between parents and children in regard to values, political attitudes, sexual norms, and the like became widely accepted in the popular culture before it could be tested by social scientists. When research was undertaken, it revealed that there was considerable continuity between generations and, more importantly, that the real gap in American life was not generational but between the college and noncollege segments of the population. On several issues, this gap now appears to be closing.[35] It appears, then, that the division in American society was never exclusively a family problem: it was an issue that more directly affected the political, economic, and educational spheres of American social life.

## The State of the American Family

We are now in a better position to evaluate the quality of American family life. There is no denying that families, like all social groups, encounter difficulties, face periods of social strain, and sometimes function poorly. The per-

## ONE-PARENT FAMILIES OUTPACING TWO-PARENT ONES

Washington (AP)—In the past two decades, the number of families headed by one parent has increased more rapidly than two-parent ones, according to a new Census Bureau report.

The report, released Sunday, found that the overwhelming majority of single-parent families was headed by women.

The increase is blamed on the rapid rise in the divorce rate, which, the study found, climbed from 2 per 1,000 persons in 1940 to 5.1 per 1,000 last year.

And the study said:

"If the current level of divorce continues on a lifetime basis, the proportion of marriages ending in divorce may be close to 40 percent."

Last year, 19 percent of the families with children under age 18 were headed by one parent, all but 2 percent of those maintained by the mother, the report said. There was a total of about 30.4 million families with children under 18 in 1978.

In 1960, 7.4 percent of the families were maintained by mothers, and 1.1 percent by fathers.

The number of families headed only by a woman increased by 55 percent during the 1960s and by 78 percent from 1970 to 1978, said the bureau.

In comparison, the number of two-parent families increased 8.1 percent from 1960 to 1970, and declined 3.1 percent from 1970 to 1978.

With the rising number of divorces has come a tripling in the number of children affected by breakups.

In 1956, there were 361,000 children involved in divorces, but by 1976 the number had risen to 1.1 million.

The number seems to have stabilized in recent years, which may foretell a decline in the years ahead, said the Census Bureau.

"For most children in one-parent families, this living arrangement is a temporary one, spanning a period of a few years, usually until their custodial parent remarries, reconciles, or marries for the first time," the report said.

"Nevertheless, to the child living with only one parent for a few years, this period represents a psychologically and socially significant part of his or her life span."

Lafayette, (Ind.) Journal-Courier, July 2, 1979. Reprinted by permission of AP Newsfeatures.

sonal failures or maladjustments of family members account for some of these difficulties. Other problems, however, are a direct result of social forces that are simply too overwhelming to be coped with adequately. The pressure on families to fulfill the value of achievement, for example, often encourages family leaders to spend beyond their financial resources in order to attain a high status position, and this can put a severe strain on family relations. The ideal of companionship in marriage heightens expectations of sensitivity and psychological support which some spouses simply cannot produce. The growing influence of the peer culture often threatens to liberate the young from parental guidance before parents think their offspring are ready to make serious decisions on their own. Masculine and feminine roles are being redefined and realigned in relation to one another, and tension is an inevitable by-product of such basic transformations. And there are always the ongoing stresses of organizing the family and allocating tasks so that the group performs effectively and within the bounds of social norms. These are only a few of the more prominent pressures affecting family living at the present time.

In spite of the pressures impinging upon it, however, the American family appears to be remarkably stable as a social institution. The divorce rate, while high, has not undercut the American commitment to marriage, as is indicated in part by the substantial remarriage rate. Increased sexual freedom, geographic mobility, the decline in the birth rate, the loss of family functions, and the so-called generation gap, have failed to erode family life significantly. The evidence indicates that American family life is relatively stable and functioning efficiently. As long as Americans worry about the decline of the family, it will probably remain a healthy institution; when we stop being concerned with the quality of family life, that decline will probably have already begun in earnest.

## SUMMARY

The family is a basic social institution in all societies. It may be defined as an adult male and female living together with any of their offspring, in a more or less permanent relationship approved by their society as marriage. The family is universal; there are no societies where it is not a recognized and honored institution, and perhaps there can be none. So far as we know, none has ever existed.

Families may be organized in a wide variety of ways and according to many different principles. Family types based on kinship structures produce nuclear and extended systems. The nuclear family is comprised of only the married couple and their offspring, while the extended family includes the nuclear family plus all other kin who live with them. In families of orientation the individual is socialized, while in families of procreation the individual is one of the parental leaders. Families defined by marriage and household arrangements may be monogamous or have several kinds of polygamous organization. Family types based on leadership roles range from patriarchal through equalitarian to matriarchal types.

Family organization may be seen as developing from a traditional extended to a modern nuclear structure based on romantic love, maternal care, and domestic privacy that isolates it from the larger kinship group. These changes may have resulted from industrialization. Now we are moving toward the postmodern family in which the peer culture and pleasure-seeking are increasingly important. This may generate some unfortunate consequences for the stability of the post-modern family.

The social functions of the family vary widely. Some are performed by the family for society at large and involve interchanges with the economy, the polity, the community, and the value system. Other functions are related specifically to the family unit itself. These include task performance, leadership, social integration, and the attainment of value solidarity. The most commonly recognized functions are those performed by the family for individual members, including physical maintenance, socialization, social control, status placement, and, for adults especially, psychological support.

In order to survive and prosper as a small group, the family requires the performance of a number of social roles. Leadership is divided between the instrumental and expressive leader roles. The instrumental leader is the administrative, work-oriented, executive head of the household. This role is normally allocated to the husband-father. The expressive leader is the emotional-integrative complement to the instrumental leader, and this role is normally assigned to the wife-mother. Preparation for these roles begins early as persons are socialized into their appropriate sex roles. Masculine and feminine roles are culturally defined patterns of behavior deemed appropriate for each sex. All societies make basic distinctions between the sexes, but the behavioral patterns assigned to males and females vary considerably from one society to the next. Mate selection, operates through two processes: preferential mating and marriage arrangement. Parenting begins with pregnancy and involves the nurturing, socializing, and guidance of offspring. Once children are launched from the nuclear family, this role is curtailed—although parents may still influence their children in subtle ways. Companionship is now regarded as one of the most important reasons for marriage. This includes affection, love, and mutual sharing as the fundamental linkage between husband and wife. Romantic love converges with the companionate role to help stabilize adult personalities. Social roles also change as an individual moves through the life cycle.

Family living is not totally free of problems and social strains, but their impact does not appear to be drastically undermining family living for most Americans. The divorce rate, increased sexual freedom, geographic mobility, the decline in the birth rate, loss of functions, and the so-called generation gap, all indicate that important adjustments are going on within this institution, yet, the family is, by and large, emerging as a more specialized institution whose basic functions are as important now as they ever were. The deep-seated commitment to the quality of family life of a vast majority of Americans suggests that the family remains one of the most stable institutions within American society.

## SUGGESTED READINGS

COLES, ROBERT. *Children of Crisis.* New York: Dell, 1968. A sensitive and sometimes painful account of the effect on children, their parents, and teachers, of the racial integration of southern schools in the 1960s. Although the author is a psychiatrist, the study is free from technical jargon; it tells the story of conflict-ridden and frequently violent events in a straight-forward manner, using much of the language of the participants themselves.

GOLDBERG, STEVEN. *The Inevitability of Patriarchy.* New York: Morrow, 1973. A book calculated to provoke anger among members of the women's liberation movement, the author develops the bold thesis that men have dominated, still dominate, and will in the future dominate women in family and societal relationships. Goldberg argues that male superiority is inevitable because of the biological-hormonal differences between men and women, differences that necessarily must manifest themselves in social life.

HOWELL, JOSEPH T. *Hard Living on Clay Street: Portraits of Blue Collar Families.* Garden City, N.Y.: Doubleday, 1973. A contemporary study of two blue-collar, white families in Washington, D.C. The material presented in the book concerns the "everyday life of families struggling for some kind of equilibrium in the situation of rising expectations and declining opportunities." Told largely through the words of the participants, the narrative provides a fresh perspective which cuts across many stereotypes of blue-collar life.

LEWIS, OSCAR. *The Children of Sanchez: Autobiography of a Mexican Family.* New York: Random, 1961. This is one of several studies undertaken by Lewis on the culture of poverty. In this volume set in a slum tenement of Mexico City, the members of the Jesus Sanchez family each relate his or her own story of life experiences. Filled with pathos, violence, tragedy, and humor, the book reads more like a novel than social science research.

MILLER, ARTHUR. "All My Sons," (a play) collected in *Six Great Modern Plays.* New York: Dell, 1956. An intensely gripping drama about the conflict between a father who is prepared to act illegally in business in order to save his family from financial ruin and his son who insists that there are higher values beyond the family. At the climax of the play, the father realizes he has a responsibility to the larger brotherhood of mankind, acknowledges that the innocent people harmed by his schemes are "all my sons" too, and in his guilt commits suicide.

WILKES, PAUL. *Six American Families.* New York: Seabury, 1977. This book is based on the nationally televised series, "Six American Families." The families captured here are quite diversified: northern and southern, black and white, ethnic and WASP, poor and wealthy, stable and fragmented, urban and rural. None is portrayed as typical, but each reveals something significant about the peculiar strengths and weaknesses of contemporary American families.

# Chapter 12
# Education

Americans are not very philosophical people. They tend to be impatient with ambiguities, demanding instead decisive answers. Win or lose? Hero or villain? Credit or blame? They want precision, especially when it comes to evaluating their institutions.

Nowadays, education is in the center of the arena. Schools are blamed for everything from declining moral standards in youth to the careless squandering of taxpayers' money. The only redeeming feature is that the schools keep the kids off the street for about thirty hours a week and provide the community with entertainment in the form of sporting events, concerts, and theatrical productions on weekends.

Lurking behind such moments of relief and pride are enormously complex issues, such as busing, tracking, equality of opportunity, affirmative action, and, most importantly, financing. Since the first step toward enlightened social problem-solving is thorough analysis, the sociology of education poses the following questions:

1. What is the nature of education in a free society?
2. What functions does it perform?
3. How is education organized in the United States?
4. Does a college education make any difference to students in terms of earnings, career mobility, or life satisfaction?[1]
5. Why do some students have excellent chances of success in school at all levels, while others do not?
6. Under what conditions are schools likely to live up to contemporary educational challenges? For example, how can they help bring about social equality?

## WHAT IS EDUCATION?

To define education, we must first distinguish it from the more general process of learning we call socialization. Humans are born "unfinished,"[2] devoid of abilities that might distinguish them from other animals. In the process of social interaction, they acquire interactional competence,[3] and internalize their culture's patterns of behavior. Much of this learning—especially in the early stages—is informal; it is seldom organized by either parents or siblings. It is inclusive, multidimensional, and unplanned. Education, or formal learning, is a much more limited process. Education is the *organized, systematic and conscious behavior by which a society transmits its culture through teachers to learners.*

All social institutions are organized responses to deeply cherished social values and exist as part of a network of social relationships. Schools and colleges—the specific organizations that are assigned the teaching tasks of the culture collectively—constitute the institution of education. Teachers, administrators, school boards, trustees—all the people associated with making schools function smoothly—may be seen as "institutional actors."[4] They staff the organizations whose deliberate aim is to educate.

In this chapter we will examine the institution of education concentrating upon, although not limiting ourselves to, the way in which that institution performs in the United States. Four major topics will be considered: the ways in which various sociologists have examined education, the principal functions that American education performs for the society, the way in which the educational process is organized in the United States, and the important and controversial relationship between education and social stratification in our society. As you go through the chapter, you may wish to attempt to place your own educational history within the context of the discussion. Education is an institution in which every reader of this book is intimately involved and there may be no better way of acquiring the sociological perspective than to apply it to one's own life and experiences.

## SOCIOLOGICAL PERSPECTIVES ON EDUCATION

Sociologists agree on the importance of theoretical thinking, the search for relationships between divergent phenomena or events that might, to the untrained observer, appear to be unrelated. The sociological perspective can help us place problems in a larger context so that each problem does not appear discrete, isolated, and therefore subject to the error of simple solutions. For instance, if students are cheating or apathetic about school, who is to blame? Students? Teachers? Parents? The community? An isolated case involving one teacher and a few students may not be a sociological problem, but if cheating and apathy are widespread, the sociologist begins to examine the social matrix that includes all the persons involved. Viewed from this perspective, "blame" is scarcely an appropriate term. The situation is a good deal more complicated.

Figure 12.1 illustrates a basic premise of sociology—that social life operates as a *system of relationships* with various units in constant interaction and flux.[5] The school, as part of a system, is actually surrounded and controlled by the larger societal dynamic. Any analysis of educational organizations must take into account the values and resources of the environment in which they operate.

Theories of education, like all theories, are like a spotlight scanning a darkened landscape. A theoretical beam illuminates certain aspects of reality while neglecting or distorting others. For some time now, two competing theoretical perspectives have been seeking to promote their respective versions of the educational landscape. These are structural functionalism and conflict theory (see Chapter 2). The functional spotlight tends to focus on aspects of the educational system that lead to integration, consensus, and stability in the social order. Conflict theorists focus on aspects of schooling

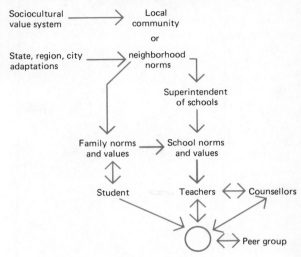

**FIGURE 12.1   The teaching/learning culture**

characterized by struggle, dominance, and dynamic change.[6] A brief discussion of the leading advocates of each position will make their theories clear.

### Functional Theorists

Until recently, structural functionalism, sometimes called consensus theory, has dominated the sociology of education. This is largely due to the tremendous influence of Durkheim on American sociology.

**Durkheim and Classic Theory**   Durkheim, you remember, was deeply concerned with the basic question of social integration (see Chapter 2). He believed that humans are born selfish, egoistic, and asocial. Each society must socialize its newcomers to be loyal citizens of the state and dutiful to things beyond themselves.[7] Taking for granted that each society has central, agreed-upon values and beliefs, Durkheim argued that the chief function of schools is moral education.[8] A child who has internalized societal values has a powerful system of self-control—an internal police force—since even thinking about violating the internalized moral codes will result in guilt and shame.[9] In traditional societies, Durkheim argued, the family, and later the church, performed the function of instilling this moral conscience. With the rise of urbanized industrial societies, however, the

Durkheim argued that the basic function of schools is moral education. This dimension is apparent in the parochial school, but it is no less present in public education, although the moralities taught may be somewhat different.

**education:** the organized, systematic, conscious behavior by which a society transmits its culture through teachers to learners.

school was charged with this task, since the church no longer reflected the moral values of the modern state. Although he was concerned with homogeneous morality, Durkheim believed that different classes of people were "destined for special milieus" and should be trained in the attitudes appropriate to these positions in life.

For Durkheim, then, the main function of education is to build moral fiber in each new generation. The schools should serve the purpose of maintaining the social system in an integrated, harmonious fashion. What about the teacher's role? On this point, Durkheim does not equivocate: "Just as the priest is the interpreter of his god, the teacher is the interpreter of the great moral ideas of his time and his country."[10]

As any observer of the average American classroom can verify, such priestly images of the teacher are clearly not shared by the current generation of students. Durkheim would interpret the prevailing irreverence as a clear sign of social disintegration and moral laxity.

**Contemporary Functionalism** From the late 1930s to the early 1960s, Talcott Parsons was the most influential American theorist writing in the functionalist perspective. In one of his well known essays,[11] Parsons analyzed the classroom and argued that the two major functions of the school are socialization and occupational selection. Since schools reward children on the basis of achievement, he argued, they are uniquely suited to the task of sifting and sorting individuals according to the physical and intellectual demands of different occupations. In traditional societies, occupations were assigned on the basis of ascribed characteristics such as family background, race, sex, and ethnicity. In complex industrial societies, a person should be rewarded according to individual achievement. In this way expertise and talent will be naturally selected for the most crucial positions and the whole society will benefit. Since the teacher is a neutral judge, and the selection process is scrupulously fair, students grow to accept the system and move into their designated slots. The obvious problem with this theory is that it ignores a vast amount of research that demonstrates that social class background, race, and sex have a major impact on the selection process.[12]

*Classic Conflict Theory*

In 1932, in a book called *The Sociology of Teaching*,[13] Willard Waller presented a very different picture of the classroom from that of Parsons. Conflict, change, and coercion typify the social relations between teacher and student. Far from being a stable institution, the school, in Waller's view, is "a despotism capable of being overturned in a moment, exposed to an instant loss of its stability and its prestige."[14] Waller took a dim view of the entire institution of education. He saw teachers and students in position of unavoidable conflict, since students did *not* share any of the concerns teachers were charged with transmitting to them. Waller was one of the first sociologists to suggest that children have a culture all their own and that the main business of that culture is peer interaction, which adults dismiss as "play." School and other adult ideas are merely rude intrusions into an otherwise spontaneous and enjoyable cultural existence.[15]

While Waller would agree with Durkheim and Parsons that the school functions to socialize children, he saw coercion rather than value consensus as the basic instrument of order in the schoolroom. Neglected in this view is a considerable slice of social reality in which the relations between teachers and students are often warm, supportive, and even loving. Social reality is complex. It becomes increasingly clear that neither the functionalist nor the conflict view alone tells the whole story.

### Contemporary Conflict Theory

*Schooling in Capitalist America,* by Samuel Bowles and Herbert Gintis, was published in 1976.[16] This work promises to be the center of lively debate for the next decade.[17] Its central target is the capitalist economic system of the United States and the role education plays in maintaining it. According to Bowles and Gintis, the history of capitalism begins when the economic demand for a flexible labor force brings about widespread geographic mobility. This weakens the extended family—the traditional basis of social order. At the same time the factory system throws together large numbers of workers under oppressive working conditions. This system is unresponsive to the traditional controls of community, church, and family. The situation is complicated by the waves of immigrants arriving in cities, with neither the education nor the discipline necessary for industrial labor.

The school, according to Bowles and Gintis, does not impartially reward achievement. Family class background plays a major role, regardless of talent. Children of the elite go on to prestigious occupations; children of the disadvantaged take up the same lower-class jobs as their parents. The educational institution serves to legitimate and perpetuate all the inequalities and injustices that prevail in the economic institutions under capitalism.

Bowles and Gintis call for nothing less than a complete overhaul of the educational system through a "frontal attack on institutionalized education."[18] Though they present a well-documented thesis, their theory does not satisfactorily explain a considerable body of research that demonstrates that schools do promote social mobility and have historically been a force for social reform.

## FUNCTIONS OF EDUCATION

While the general form of educational functions may be easy to agree upon, specific content is clearly a source of much debate. Theorists from both perspectives agree that schools should furnish moral instruction, cognitive development, and technical skills. But which values and beliefs should be presented? Are teachers agents of the state, or should they act in the best interests of the students? What of the families, or the teachers' own professional judgments? Should students be taught to think critically or trained to follow orders without question or reflection?

**FIGURE 12.2   A typology of educational functions**

|  | Order | Change |
|---|---|---|
| **Manifest (overt)** | Cultural transmission<br>Social integration<br>Social control<br>Training & development of workers<br>Screening and allocation | Cultural innovation<br>Cultural diffusion<br>Critical thinking<br>Altered socioeconomic hierarchies |
| **Latent (covert)** | Babysitting<br>Control of marriage prospects<br>Reduced unemployment<br>Social contacts | Revolutionary ferment<br>Minority awareness<br>An oversupply of "restless" intellectuals |

Intentionality

Social Function

**Shop. Is this the capitalist economic system at work?**

One way out of this dilemma comes with the recognition that in modern society, educational institutions must serve a dual function. On the one hand, they serve the state in the maintenance of *social order*. In this they function as a conservative force. On the other hand, they must be responsive to the enormous forces for *change* typical of modern societies: urbanization, industrialization, technology, and human liberation movements. Robert Merton suggests that any social institution serves both manifest and latent functions[19] (see Figure 12.2). Educational functions for either order or change are subject to this dichotomy, a duality that presents an overwhelming challenge to beleaguered educators.

*Manifest Conservative Functions*

As you may recognize by now, functional analysis tends to focus on the stabilizing aspects of social institutions. Several such functions can be identified for the educational institution:

**Cultural Transmission** Every society must pass on its accumulated fund of cultural knowledge from generation to generation. Through language, humans maintain a cultural memory bank that predates early civilization. Cultural survivals in the forms of values, beliefs, and skills are central aspects of contemporary social life. We can, for example, readily trace our preoccupation with sports to the ancient Greeks and our sexual mores to our Puritan heritage.

Before the Industrial Revolution, formal enculturation (education) was restricted to the elite. The common expression that a person or group is "cultured" reflects those times. With the advance of the industrial state in the nineteenth and twentieth centuries, knowledge grew more complex, specialized, and difficult to communicate. At the same time, a need arose for a broader base of educated people to run the society. Transmission of technical knowledge and skills could no longer be left to the family and the church, as in earlier times. Although the family still serves important socialization functions, schools are expected to take over early in the child's development. After primary socialization in the family, the school is charged with transmitting not only basic literacy, but also the ideals on which societal institutions depend. In the United States, such ideals would

Cultural transmission function of the schools. Fifth graders reenact the World War II flag-raising on Iwo Jima.

include democracy, freedom, *laissez-faire* capitalism and monogamous heterosexual marriage.[20] Though we tend to think of indoctrination as something practiced only by totalitarian states, all societies engage in it to some degree. Imagine, for example, the case of an American schoolteacher who advocated socialism, anarchy, or homosexuality; few communities would tolerate such "subversive" advocacy. Schools, then, clearly operate to conserve and transmit knowledge, beliefs, and sentiments from the past, but sometimes they do so at the expense of tolerance and independence of inquiry.

**Social Integration** One of the major problems confronting the modern industrial state is the cultural diversity of its population. The United States is an outstanding example of highly diverse racial and ethnic groups trying to live together.

Bringing the "hyphenated Americans"—German-, Chinese-, Irish-, Afro-, to mention but a few—into the mainstream has been a central concern of recent times. The only vehicle available for this assimilation is public school education, where common language, history, and values are taught. This is crucial, particularly in a democratic society that depends on some degree of political and economic concensus. Heterogeneity, of course, does not result only from recent immigration. In many African states, whose borders were often the result of arbitrary colonial politics rather than tribal compatibility, the schools must also serve the manifest function of social integration.

**Social Control**   We often associate the idea of social control with the police, riot squads, or the National Guard. As Durkheim pointed out, however, the most effective kind of social control is an internalized set of norms that make an individual self-policing. Any society that neglects to produce this process does so at its cultural peril. The schools are admirably suited to this kind of socialization. President Kennedy's admonition, "Ask not what your country can do for you, but what you can do for your country!" is an example of a call to social control. The charismatic young president was suggesting that we forget our individual concerns and make a commitment to something bigger than ourselves: our nation.

As Philip Jackson points out in *Life in Classrooms,* the average American child has spent 7,000 hours in school *before* entering junior high school.[21] A main goal of school socialization during this period is to train the child to cope with waiting in line, frequent frustration, and constant interruptions. In short, the child must learn *patience.* Those who cannot conform to those social controls may be "referred" for more intensive training. Alternatively, the nonconforming student may drop out of school and thus be denied access to jobs and social contacts as an adult. School, then, serves as both an indirect and a direct mechanism of social control for the community and the society as a whole.

**Training and Development of Workers**
Every modern industrial society must have an educated and technically expert work force. The government may create scholarships, funding, and other inducements to fill specific needs, for example, for engineers or computer programmers. The school is the social supplier for such economic demands. On a less specific level, school credentials are required for most occupational placement, even when there is no necessary relationship between the job skills and those acquired in school. Garbage collectors being required to have high school diplomas is one example.

Training acquired in school goes beyond mere skill. Motivation to work for a living, as well as attributes like punctuality, responsibility, obedience to authority, and self-discipline make for a desirable industrial labor force—at least from the employer's perspective. Schools spend much of their resources assuring that graduates have these attributes.

**Screening and Allocation**   Who finishes high school? Who goes to college? Who goes on to graduate or professional schools? The school is the key sifting and sorting mechanism by which these channels of social mobility are managed in industrial society. We have seen that formal education was formerly reserved for the elite. The rise of compulsory education in modern societies, while eliminating that inequality, clearly creates others. Screening tests of academic performance serve to track students into particular channels that have direct occupational consequences. Since occupations are major determinants of earnings, prestige, and power, as we saw in Chapter 7, the school effectively loads the dice on the individual's entire life chances.

In Britain until recently, children were definitively screened by a rigorous examination at age eleven. Such systems do not leave much leeway for "late bloomers." Even in the United States, where schools are more flexible, there is considerable evidence that the sifting and sorting process is less than impartial, and may serve to perpetuate the cultural *status quo.* Social mobility has been shown to result much more from changes in labor force composition than in personal characteristics of those competing in the race to the top.

*Latent Conservative Functions*

Some latent maintenance functions are also served by schools. While never openly articulated, these functions are built into the school system, especially at the college level, where social class backgrounds tend toward homogeneity.

**Baby-sitting**   Schools have always had the effect of relieving parents of several hours of child care each day. This may be viewed as a type of systematic baby-sitting service. This function has important implications for family life as more women seek economic independence through full-time employment.

**Control of Marriage Prospects** One important consequence of school attendance is the shaping of attitudes toward the opposite sex. Not only are students socialized into their respective gender roles, they are also given a prolonged opportunity for dating and courtship in an atmosphere that is socially competitive. The intensity of competition controls the pool of eligibles during the period of mate selection, thus maintaining the distinctions between the social classes into the next generation. For example, at one small liberal arts college in the midwest, where 94 percent of the students are from upper middle-class families, 68 percent of the students intermarry, though not always before graduation, of course.

**Reduction in Unemployment** With more than 9 million students in American colleges and universities and a decreasing demand for

Many college students meet their future mates on campus.

their services upon graduation, it is clear that higher education serves to keep students from either displacing employed persons or swelling the unemployment statistics themselves. Though it is clear to many educators that a large proportion of students are not serious about learning, and escape the process whenever the opportunity presents itself, it is neither economically nor politically feasible to educate only those who are genuinely motivated. College, in other words, works to keep large numbers of people out of the labor force.

**Social Networks for Career Mobility** In spite of major attempts in recent years to make career opportunities more accessible to women and minorities, it is widely known that school-tie networks still influence actual placements. Many friendships formed in groups such as fraternities, clubs, teams, and residence halls continue beyond graduation, especially if such contacts can help promote career interests. Elite schools, such as those in the Ivy League, have clubs in many major cities where their graduates can continue to interact socially. Many national fraternities maintain employment offices in major cities, to serve their alumni exclusively. The range and quality of such networks is directly related to the prestige of the college or university attended. This is another way that societal positions are maintained within particular groups and passed on intergenerationally to those who are members of the networks.

*Manifest Change Functions*

The second type of function demanded of modern educational systems accounts for many of the tensions experienced by today's educators. These functions serve to *change* the social system.

**Cultural Innovation** One of the widely endorsed values in contemporary civilization is that of progress. With half of all the scientists in human history currently alive and productive, the rate of technological change and its social ramifications are enormous. Colleges and universities have always been a source of new ideas and knowledge. Elementary and high schools are also expected to create opportunities for new discoveries and creative achievements. Rather than teaching specific content, many educators feel that the best service they can render to students is to teach what Alvin Toffler calls a "modular mentality," that is, a habit of coping with rapid change without becoming disoriented.[22] To the extent that schools can accomplish this, they are a force for social change. Whether or not change constitutes "progress" is debatable, of course, but Americans tend to equate the two.

**Cultural Diffusion**  When ideas are created or taught in the school, a process of diffusion is underway. The "new math," novel hypotheses about the origins of the life, "simulations," all such activities provide not merely knowledge, but attitudes and skills that may lead to further inquiry and change. For example, the introduction of Darwin's evolutionary hypothesis into the school curriculum had a revolutionary impact on the advancement of scientific thinking. In the developing countries, the tension between ideology and religious dogma on the one hand, and science on the other, is often resolved in favor of science. This tends to undermine traditional belief structures.

**Critical thinking**  Schools have not always sought to produce active, questioning minds. The church was the main source of education in Medieval Europe and its emphasis tended to be on religious dogma rather than independent inquiry. Though schools later became secularized, the old method of rote memorization was retained. Critical thinking contrasts sharply with rote learning. Its orientation is toward change and independence, not toward tradition and authority. It is found mostly in industrial democracies and is still not widespread even today. A Soviet educator remarked about the American school system, for example:

It's obvious to me from reading your books that you Americans don't agree on a set of values to be transmitted to your children. Your books try to deal with every side of the question. Ours, admittedly, present only one side. It seems to me that you must create unimaginable confusion.[23]

Though scarcely presenting "every side of the question," it is true that Western schools often allow or even encourage critical analysis of their institutions. This necessarily increases the possibility of change.

**Alteration of Socioeconomic Hierarchies**  Although power, privilege, and prestige traditionally tend to be concentrated in the upper strata of society and to be passed on intergenerationally, the process of industrialization changes this pattern. As industrialization gains momentum, its demands go beyond the niceties of social rank and family background. Industrial systems require competent technical and professional personnel—usually more than can be supplied by the relatively low reproduction rates of the existing elite. This opens the social system to the sons and daughters of lower-class families, *if* they can acquire the requisite educational qualifications. In their 1967 study of social mobility in the United States, Blau and Duncan demonstrated that education is the key to upward mobility.[24]

While certainly no guarantee of success in the labor market, a college degree is a basic requirement for entry into the higher occupational levels in industrial nations. Education is a major factor in support of Pareto's proposition that "history is a graveyard of aristocracies."[25] We will have more to say about the amount of change educational institutions are likely to affect when we discuss educational stratification.

*Latent Change Functions*

Several unintended change functions seem to be served by the educational institution. Universities and colleges have often been the breeding ground of revolutionary ferment in the modern world. France, Germany, Italy, Japan, India, Cuba, and the United States are recent examples. Minority groups are inclined to develop an enhanced awareness of their outgroup status and become more militant in the school setting than in work environments. The production of an "over-supply" of college trained individuals (who have no vocational skill to sell in a technological economy) sets up a constant threat to the *status quo*.[26] Many drop out completely in frustration. At times, these dropouts form a radical counterculture which refuses to endorse the traditional work ethic of the mainstream.

We have seen that educational institutions not only help to maintain social stability but are also a direct force for change. They produce new knowledge, values, and attitudes; they diffuse these to groups outside the school system;

they often foster critical analysis of institutional traditions and serve as a channel by which new blood may transfuse the elite. Finally, they sometimes stimulate the awakening of militant and revolutionary consciousness among minorities and unattached youth.

## THE ORGANIZATION OF AMERICAN EDUCATION

There are many ways in which a society can organize its school system. One is implied in the (probably apocryphal) story that, at one time in France, the Minister of Education could tell by looking at his watch exactly what every French child in every grade in every school was reading at that instant. The United States has chosen a much more decentralized system, in which the states are responsible for setting standards of education and local communities are responsible for establishing and supporting public schools that meet those standards. Private schools are also permitted, so long as they meet state requirements.

### Primary and Secondary Schools

In the highly decentralized United States school system, federal legislation sets very general guidelines for the states, which, in turn, allow wide local autonomy. States are broken up into districts, or communities, which elect a School Board to act in behalf of the community. The Board then has full authority to set policy which must be implemented by administrators and teachers. The Board appoints as chief administrator of the district a superintendent, who is responsible to the Board for the management of all schools in a local district. Within the school building, the principal is the boss and has authority over the teachers and other administrative assistants. The teachers, in turn—needless to say—exercise authority over students. The formal system is depicted in Figure 12.3.

**Community Control and Financing** While local control keeps school systems responsive to community values, this arrangement has some serious drawbacks. Financing for most school expenses is tied to local property taxes. Thus the school budget often becomes the focal point of political and economic disputes that may

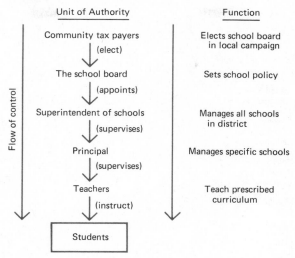

FIGURE 12.3   Authority relations in public education

have little to do with education. Furthermore, since property values are tied to the racial and occupational characteristics of a community, the quality of an American child's education is directly related to parental life chances. A comparison of taxable property per student by region reveals a startling pattern of inequalities, with some school districts having ten thousand times the tax base of others.[27] This is a major factor in the kinds of educational variations revealed in Table 12.1.

In 1978, a "taxpayers' revolt" which originated in California began to gain momentum. Some Ohio communities voted down a bond issue without which their public schools would be unable to remain open, and many states and districts across the country were in similar predicaments. Meanwhile, private secondary school enrollments soared as upper-middle-class parents purchased education beyond the reach of the general public. Such discrepancies in educational opportunities are expected to create an institutional crisis which may result in greater federal funding and a corresponding loss of community control.

**Endorsement of Mass Education** In spite of many imperfections, the United States has the most accessible and comprehensive educational system in the world. Since it endorsed the idea of publicly supported education early in this

**TABLE 12.1  Percent of Draftees Who Failed to Meet the Mental Requirements for Induction into the Armed Services, by State: 1972**

| State or other area<br>1 | Total<br>2 | Failed mental requirements only | | | Failed<br>mental<br>and<br>medical<br>requirements<br>6 |
|---|---|---|---|---|---|
| | | Total<br>3 | Failed<br>mental<br>tests<br>4 | Train-<br>ability<br>limited<br>5 | |
| **United States** | **9.9** | **6.7** | **3.5** | **3.2** | **3.2** |
| Alabama | 28.6 | 18.3 | 8.6 | 9.7 | 10.3 |
| Alaska | 9.8 | 3.8 | 1.9 | 1.9 | 6.0 |
| Arizona | 7.8 | 4.4 | 1.2 | 3.2 | 3.4 |
| Arkansas | 16.4 | 10.8 | 7.7 | 3.1 | 5.6 |
| California | 6.3 | 4.4 | 1.7 | 2.7 | 1.9 |
| Colorado | 4.5 | 3.0 | 1.6 | 1.4 | 1.5 |
| Connecticut | 4.4 | 2.1 | 1.2 | 0.9 | 2.3 |
| Delaware | 9.6 | 6.5 | 5.5 | 1.0 | 3.1 |
| District of Columbia | 20.4 | 12.5 | 11.1 | 1.4 | 7.9 |
| Florida | 11.3 | 8.0 | 5.5 | 2.5 | 3.3 |
| Georgia | 24.8 | 19.8 | 11.6 | 8.2 | 5.0 |
| Hawaii | 14.7 | 10.6 | 4.8 | 5.8 | 4.1 |
| Idaho | 3.6 | 2.3 | 1.4 | 0.9 | 1.3 |
| Illinois | 6.5 | 4.8 | 2.4 | 2.4 | 1.7 |
| Indiana | 6.5 | 4.6 | 1.9 | 2.7 | 1.9 |
| Iowa | 3.3 | 2.1 | 0.6 | 1.5 | 1.2 |
| Kansas | 2.5 | 1.7 | 0.6 | 1.1 | 0.8 |
| Kentucky | 17.5 | 10.0 | 5.7 | 4.3 | 7.5 |
| Louisiana | 23.7 | 17.2 | 12.3 | 4.9 | 6.5 |
| Maine | 4.9 | 2.9 | 1.0 | 1.9 | 2.0 |
| Maryland | 7.3 | 4.8 | 4.3 | 0.5 | 2.5 |
| Massachusetts | 4.0 | 2.4 | 1.0 | 1.4 | 1.6 |
| Michigan | 5.4 | 3.2 | 1.7 | 1.5 | 2.2 |
| Minnesota | 1.9 | 1.1 | 0.5 | 0.6 | 0.8 |
| Mississippi | 35.2 | 26.6 | 17.1 | 9.5 | 8.6 |
| Missouri | 3.9 | 2.2 | 1.2 | 1.0 | 1.7 |
| Montana | 2.0 | 1.2 | 0.3 | 0.9 | 0.8 |
| Nebraska | 2.5 | 1.8 | 0.7 | 1.1 | 0.7 |
| Nevada | 7.0 | 4.1 | 2.0 | 2.1 | 2.9 |
| New Hampshire | 4.3 | 2.0 | 0.6 | 1.4 | 2.3 |
| New Jersey | 7.8 | 5.8 | 2.8 | 3.0 | 2.0 |
| New Mexico | 12.1 | 8.6 | 3.4 | 5.2 | 3.5 |
| New York | 8.6 | 5.3 | 2.2 | 3.1 | 3.3 |
| North Carolina | 20.4 | 15.2 | 8.3 | 6.9 | 5.2 |
| North Dakota | 3.5 | 2.1 | 0.5 | 1.6 | 1.4 |
| Ohio | 6.8 | 4.2 | 1.5 | 2.7 | 2.6 |
| Oklahoma | 9.8 | 6.3 | 0.5 | 5.8 | 3.5 |
| Oregon | 2.7 | 2.0 | 0.0 | 2.0 | 0.7 |
| Pennsylvania | 5.7 | 3.7 | 2.0 | 1.7 | 2.0 |
| Rhode Island | 6.0 | 5.1 | 2.4 | 2.7 | 0.9 |
| South Carolina | 33.8 | 25.5 | 14.3 | 11.2 | 8.3 |
| South Dakota | 2.7 | 1.6 | 0.3 | 1.3 | 1.1 |
| Tennessee | 20.3 | 13.5 | 7.1 | 6.4 | 6.8 |
| Texas | 12.9 | 8.3 | 3.8 | 4.5 | 4.6 |
| Utah | 4.1 | 2.9 | 1.7 | 1.2 | 1.2 |
| Vermont | 4.3 | 2.1 | 0.6 | 1.5 | 2.2 |
| Virginia | 16.0 | 11.5 | 7.8 | 3.7 | 4.5 |
| Washington | 4.0 | 1.8 | 0.2 | 1.6 | 2.2 |
| West Virginia | 17.3 | 9.4 | 5.1 | 4.3 | 7.9 |
| Wisconsin | 4.9 | 3.2 | 1.3 | 1.9 | 1.7 |
| Wyoming | 2.4 | 1.8 | 0.7 | 1.1 | 0.6 |
| **Outlying areas:** | | | | | |
| Guam and Mariana Islands | 37.1 | 25.0 | 10.2 | 14.8 | 12.1 |
| Puerto Rico and Virgin Islands | 76.3 | 59.6 | 48.9 | 10.7 | 16.7 |

century, the educational growth rate has been phenomenal. In 1910, 15 percent of the 14–17 age group were in high school; by 1957 this figure had risen to 90 percent. In 1900, about 7 percent of Americans in the 18–20 age group were graduating from high school; today the figure is over 80 percent. About two-thirds of the American population, or 75,000,000 persons, had high school diplomas as of 1978; about 40 percent of those have also pursued some kind of postsecondary program.

American education is usually compulsory until age 16. In Europe, only 20 percent of the 16-year-olds are still in school, compared to 90 percent in the United States. The median of formal schooling completed is now 12.1 years for all Americans 25 and older.[28]

An objective measure of the American commitment to education is that the country spends 142 billion dollars annually on its public education system. As Figure 12.4 shows, this amount has increased steadily since World War II, but has leveled off at about 8 percent of the Gross National Product in the 1970s.

## Higher Education

Only one-tenth of European secondary school students go on to college, whereas United States colleges accommodate half of that age group. Three major forces account for the explosion of higher education in the United States since World War II. First, the population pressures brought on by the postwar baby boom created a huge demand, beginning in the early 1960s. Second, increasing technological sophistication in industry and business set up a demand for a more highly educated labor force. Third, the civil rights movement not only enhanced the awareness of blacks and other minorities regarding the central role education plays in occupational mobility, it also supported their more militant demands for increased access.

The complexity of higher education has grown with this increasing demand. A public-private dichotomy prevails, with hierarchical ranking within and between the structures. The major difference is the source of financing and, of course, the degree of autonomy from state or federal control which is afforded the private college or university.

**Status Ranking** Though sometimes based more on tradition than on the actual quality of education available, there is a distinct status order in American higher education. The privately endowed northeastern Ivy League (Brown, Columbia, Cornell, Dartmouth, Harvard, Penn, Princeton, and Yale) and the Seven Sisters (Barnard, Bryn Mawr, Mount Holyoke, Radcliffe, Smith, Vassar, and Wellseley) rank highest. They maintain high admissions standards and charge relatively high tuition.

Next in the hierarchy are a number of large state universities. Among the leaders in this group are the University of California at Berkeley, the Big Ten schools in the Midwest, and

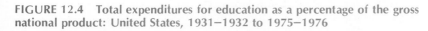

FIGURE 12.4 Total expenditures for education as a percentage of the gross national product: United States, 1931–1932 to 1975–1976

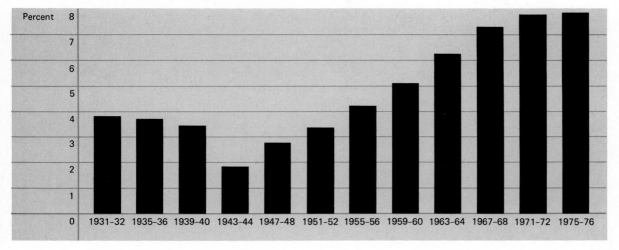

many other institutions across the country from Rutgers to the University of Washington. In about the same position are a number of small, select, private liberal arts colleges, such as Williams, Oberlin, and Swarthmore. State colleges, such as teachers colleges, are next in line. These schools have a decidedly more local orientation than the large universities and are not, therefore, well known outside their regions. Finally, junior colleges, with their open admissions policies and generally heavy vocational orientation, have the lowest status among institutions of higher learning.

Smaller classes and opportunities for personal contact with professors make the private liberal arts college—like all private education—very attractive to those who can afford it. Publicly supported colleges and universities appear in a variety of forms and sizes. The giants are the multiversities—universities so large and so complicated as to have multitudes of functions, interests, and effects on the society, as well as multiple ties to a variety of social institutions. The basic difference between a college and a university is that a college is a four-year institution granting a bachelor's degree, while a university offers graduate and professional education and degrees as well as undergraduate. A community college, however, is almost always a two-year institution.

**Enrollments and Diversity**  Three features of higher education in America distinguish it from any other in the world: rate of growth, accessibility, and diversity.

In 1870, 1.7 percent of 18–21-year-olds were enrolled in 563 degree granting institutions in the United States, totaling 52,000 students; in 1976, we find more than 50 percent of 18–21-year-olds enrolled in 3046 colleges and universities; total enrollment: 9,731,431. About half of these institutions are controlled by private organizations, although about 80 percent of all college students attend public institutions. The number of two-year colleges has doubled in the past twenty years; there are now 897 public and 231 private junior colleges, enrolling fully 26 percent of all students.[29] Table 12.2 shows the diversity and concentration of schools across the country.

**Profile of the College Freshman**  In the vocabulary of statistics, the mode is the most frequent score in a frequency distribution. For example, in a study of incomes, if the largest group in the sample had incomes in the $10,000–$12,000 bracket, we would say that the modal income was $11,000. Taking the freshman class of fall 1976, the following profile emerges of a modal student:

The student is likely to be a white, 18-year-old male. He is single and has earned a B average in high school. He is the first member of his family to attend college, though both his father and mother have high school diplomas. The family earns $15,000–$20,000 or less, and the student will probably major in business. His political orientation is "middle-of-the-road".[30] Table 12.3 presents further data on the 1976 entering class.

**Trends in Higher Education**  Trends now observable in American colleges and universities will have major social consequences during the next decade. The most dramatic shift taking place in traditional patterns is in the *age distribution* of college students. Starting in 1972, the proportion of students under twenty-five years old began to decrease, going from 72 percent to 67 percent between 1972 and 1976. This 5 percent decrease in the younger age group contrasts with the increase in the proportion of enrollment for those over twenty-five. Most of this increase is accounted for by females over thirty-five. Between 1972 and 1976, the actual number of enrolled women in this age group went from 418,000 to 700,000 for an increase of 67.5 percent. This trend is likely to continue as

**TABLE 12.2  Number of Institutions of Higher Education and Branches, by Type, Control, and State: 1976–1977**

| State or Other Area<br>1 | Total<br>2 | All Institutions | | Universities | | All other 4-year Institutions | | 2-year Institutions | |
|---|---|---|---|---|---|---|---|---|---|
| | | Public<br>3 | Private<br>4 | Public<br>5 | Private<br>6 | Public<br>7 | Private<br>8 | Public<br>9 | Private<br>10 |
| **United States** | **3,046** | **1,455** | **1,591** | **95** | **65** | **455** | **1,298** | **905** | **228** |
| Alabama | 56 | 36 | 20 | 2 | 0 | 14 | 15 | 20 | 5 |
| Alaska | 9 | 7 | 2 | 1 | 0 | 2 | 1 | 4 | 1 |
| Arizona | 22 | 17 | 5 | 2 | 0 | 1 | 4 | 14 | 1 |
| Arkansas | 29 | 16 | 13 | 1 | 0 | 9 | 10 | 6 | 3 |
| California | 252 | 134 | 118 | 2 | 4 | 29 | 104 | 103 | 10 |
| Colorado | 39 | 27 | 12 | 2 | 1 | 11 | 11 | 14 | 0 |
| Connecticut | 46 | 22 | 24 | 1 | 1 | 5 | 19 | 16 | 4 |
| Delaware | 10 | 6 | 4 | 1 | 0 | 1 | 1 | 4 | 3 |
| District of Columbia | 19 | 3 | 16 | 0 | 5 | 3 | 10 | 0 | 1 |
| Florida | 73 | 37 | 36 | 3 | 1 | 6 | 32 | 28 | 3 |
| Georgia | 67 | 35 | 32 | 1 | 1 | 16 | 24 | 18 | 7 |
| Hawaii | 11 | 8 | 3 | 1 | 0 | 1 | 3 | 6 | 0 |
| Idaho | 9 | 6 | 3 | 1 | 0 | 3 | 2 | 2 | 1 |
| Illinois | 149 | 61 | 88 | 3 | 5 | 10 | 75 | 48 | 8 |
| Indiana | 64 | 23 | 41 | 4 | 2 | 9 | 35 | 10 | 4 |
| Iowa | 61 | 22 | 39 | 2 | 1 | 1 | 33 | 19 | 5 |
| Kansas | 52 | 29 | 23 | 3 | 0 | 5 | 19 | 21 | 4 |
| Kentucky | 38 | 9 | 29 | 2 | 0 | 6 | 21 | 1 | 8 |
| Louisiana | 31 | 20 | 11 | 1 | 2 | 13 | 9 | 6 | 0 |
| Maine | 25 | 10 | 15 | 1 | 0 | 6 | 14 | 3 | 1 |
| Maryland | 52 | 30 | 22 | 1 | 1 | 12 | 19 | 17 | 2 |
| Massachusetts | 119 | 33 | 86 | 1 | 7 | 14 | 55 | 18 | 24 |
| Michigan | 94 | 45 | 49 | 3 | 1 | 12 | 40 | 30 | 8 |
| Minnesota | 65 | 30 | 35 | 1 | 0 | 9 | 31 | 20 | 4 |
| Mississippi | 45 | 27 | 18 | 2 | 0 | 7 | 12 | 18 | 6 |
| Missouri | 83 | 28 | 55 | 1 | 2 | 12 | 48 | 15 | 5 |
| Montana | 12 | 9 | 3 | 2 | 0 | 4 | 3 | 3 | 0 |
| Nebraska | 29 | 16 | 13 | 1 | 1 | 6 | 11 | 9 | 1 |
| Nevada | 6 | 5 | 1 | 1 | 0 | 1 | 1 | 3 | 0 |
| New Hampshire | 24 | 10 | 14 | 1 | 0 | 2 | 12 | 7 | 2 |
| New Jersey | 65 | 31 | 34 | 1 | 2 | 13 | 26 | 17 | 6 |
| New Mexico | 17 | 14 | 3 | 2 | 0 | 4 | 3 | 8 | 0 |
| New York | 287 | 84 | 203 | 2 | 12 | 39 | 156 | 43 | 35 |
| North Carolina | 116 | 73 | 43 | 2 | 2 | 14 | 29 | 57 | 12 |
| North Dakota | 15 | 11 | 4 | 2 | 0 | 4 | 3 | 5 | 1 |
| Ohio | 131 | 61 | 70 | 8 | 1 | 5 | 63 | 48 | 6 |
| Oklahoma | 44 | 29 | 15 | 2 | 1 | 12 | 10 | 15 | 4 |
| Oregon | 43 | 21 | 22 | 2 | 1 | 6 | 19 | 13 | 2 |
| Pennsylvania | 179 | 62 | 117 | 3 | 4 | 20 | 102 | 39 | 11 |
| Rhode Island | 12 | 3 | 9 | 1 | 0 | 1 | 9 | 1 | 0 |
| South Carolina | 56 | 32 | 24 | 2 | 0 | 10 | 19 | 20 | 5 |
| South Dakota | 17 | 7 | 10 | 2 | 0 | 5 | 8 | 0 | 2 |
| Tennessee | 67 | 23 | 44 | 1 | 1 | 10 | 37 | 12 | 6 |
| Texas | 146 | 92 | 54 | 6 | 4 | 30 | 45 | 56 | 5 |
| Utah | 14 | 9 | 5 | 2 | 1 | 2 | 2 | 5 | 2 |
| Vermont | 23 | 6 | 17 | 1 | 0 | 3 | 16 | 2 | 1 |
| Virginia | 72 | 39 | 33 | 3 | 0 | 12 | 29 | 24 | 4 |
| Washington | 48 | 33 | 15 | 2 | 0 | 4 | 15 | 27 | 0 |
| West Virginia | 28 | 17 | 11 | 1 | 0 | 11 | 8 | 5 | 3 |
| Wisconsin | 58 | 30 | 28 | 1 | 1 | 12 | 25 | 17 | 2 |
| Wyoming | 8 | 8 | 0 | 1 | 0 | 0 | 0 | 7 | 0 |
| U.S. Service Schools | 9 | 9 | 0 | 0 | 0 | 8 | 0 | 1 | 0 |
| **Outlying areas** | **28** | **12** | **16** | **1** | **0** | **7** | **7** | **4** | **9** |
| American Samoa | 1 | 1 | 0 | 0 | 0 | 0 | 0 | 1 | 0 |
| Canal Zone | 1 | 1 | 0 | 0 | 0 | 1 | 0 | 0 | 0 |
| Guam | 1 | 1 | 0 | 0 | 0 | 1 | 0 | 0 | 0 |
| Puerto Rico | 23 | 7 | 16 | 1 | 0 | 4 | 7 | 2 | 9 |
| Trust Territory of the Pacific Islands | 1 | 1 | 0 | 0 | 0 | 1 | 0 | 0 | 0 |
| Virgin Islands | 1 | 1 | 0 | 0 | 0 | 0 | 0 | 1 | 0 |

**TABLE 12.3   Selected Characteristics of First-time Students in Institutions of Higher Education: United States, Fall 1976 (Percentage Distribution)**

| Item<br>1 | First-time students | | | Item<br>1 | First-time students | | |
|---|---|---|---|---|---|---|---|
| | Total<br>2 | Men<br>3 | Women<br>4 | | Total<br>2 | Men<br>3 | Women<br>4 |
| **Total** | **100.0** | **100.0** | **100.0** | **Political orientation:** | | | |
| | | | | Far left | 2.2 | 2.6 | 1.8 |
| **Age by December 31, 1976:** | | | | Liberal | 25.6 | 26.7 | 24.5 |
| 16 or younger | .1 | .1 | .1 | Middle-of-the-road | 56.0 | 51.9 | 60.5 |
| 17 | 3.8 | 2.9 | 4.9 | Conservative | 15.2 | 17.6 | 12.6 |
| 18 | 74.1 | 71.5 | 77.0 | Far right | 1.0 | 1.3 | .6 |
| 19 | 16.6 | 19.2 | 13.7 | **Year graduated from high school:** | | | |
| 20 | 2.1 | 2.6 | 1.5 | 1976 | 92.6 | 91.6 | 93.7 |
| 21 | .7 | .9 | .5 | Did not graduate in 1976 | 7.4 | 8.4 | 6.3 |
| 22-25 | 1.5 | 1.9 | .9 | **Average grade in high school:** | | | |
| 26 or older | 1.2 | 1.1 | 1.3 | A or A+ | 8.4 | 6.7 | 10.3 |
| **Racial background:** | | | | A⁻ | 11.3 | 9.0 | 13.8 |
| White, Caucasian | 86.2 | 87.1 | 85.2 | B+ | 20.6 | 17.7 | 23.8 |
| Black, negro, Afro-American | 8.4 | 7.3 | 9.6 | B | 26.6 | 25.7 | 27.6 |
| American Indian | .9 | 1.0 | .9 | B⁻ | 13.2 | 15.6 | 10.6 |
| Oriental | 2.0 | 2.2 | 1.9 | C+ | 11.6 | 14.6 | 8.5 |
| Mexican-American, Chicano | 1.7 | 1.6 | 1.7 | C | 7.8 | 10.1 | 5.3 |
| Puerto Rican-American | .5 | .6 | .5 | D | .4 | .6 | .2 |
| Other | 1.8 | 1.9 | 1.7 | **High school program:** | 85.8 | 86.4 | 85.2 |
| **Marital status:** | | | | College preparatory | 14.2 | 13.6 | 14.8 |
| Married | 1.8 | 1.6 | 1.9 | Other | | | |
| Not presently married | 98.2 | 98.4 | 98.0 | **Standardized tests taken:** | | | |
| **Veteran status:** | | | | S.A.T. | 71.8 | 72.6 | 70.9 |
| No | 97.9 | 96.7 | 99.1 | A.C.T. | 50.7 | 50.5 | 50.8 |
| Yes | 2.1 | 3.3 | .9 | P.S.A.T. (11th grade) | 73.2 | 72.0 | 74.4 |
| **Father's education:** | | | | **Distance from home to college:** | | | |
| Grammar school or less | 7.5 | 7.0 | 8.0 | 5 miles or less | 14.5 | 14.9 | 14.1 |
| Some high school | 13.0 | 12.7 | 13.2 | 6 to 10 miles | 15.1 | 15.3 | 14.8 |
| High school graduate | 28.5 | 29.0 | 28.0 | 11 to 50 miles | 26.0 | 25.1 | 26.9 |
| Postsecondary other than college | 4.3 | 4.1 | 4.4 | 51 to 100 miles | 13.0 | 12.6 | 13.4 |
| Some college | 13.3 | 13.3 | 13.4 | 101 to 500 miles | 23.9 | 24.0 | 23.8 |
| College degree | 18.5 | 18.6 | 18.4 | More than 500 miles | 7.5 | 8.1 | 6.9 |
| Some graduate school | 2.3 | 2.3 | 2.3 | **Highest degree planned anywhere:** | | | |
| Graduate degree | 12.6 | 12.9 | 12.3 | None | 3.2 | 3.1 | 3.3 |
| **Mother's education:** | | | | Associate (A.A. or equivalent) | 8.1 | 6.7 | 9.7 |
| Grammar school or less | 4.9 | 4.5 | 5.3 | Bachelor's (B.A., B.S.) | 35.6 | 34.2 | 37.2 |
| Some high school | 11.2 | 10.7 | 11.7 | Master's (M.A., M.S.) | 28.6 | 27.9 | 29.4 |
| High school graduate | 42.2 | 43.7 | 40.6 | Ph.D. or Ed.D. | 8.7 | 9.8 | 7.6 |
| Postsecondary other than college | 6.8 | 6.2 | 7.3 | M.D., D.O., D.D.S., or D.V.M. | 7.1 | 8.3 | 5.7 |
| Some college | 13.8 | 13.3 | 14.2 | LL.B. or J.D. (law) | 4.8 | 6.0 | 3.5 |
| College degree | 14.5 | 14.7 | 14.4 | B.D. or M. Div. (divinity) | .6 | .7 | .4 |
| Some graduate school | 1.9 | 1.9 | 1.9 | Other | 3.3 | 3.3 | 3.3 |
| Graduate degree | 4.8 | 4.9 | 4.7 | **Probable major field of study:** | | | |
| **Estimated parental income:** | | | | Agriculture (incl. forestry) | 3.6 | 5.3 | 2.0 |
| Less than $4,000 | 6.3 | 5.5 | 7.3 | Biological sciences | 6.2 | 6.7 | 5.7 |
| $4,000 to $5,999 | 4.4 | 3.8 | 5.1 | Business | 20.9 | 22.5 | 19.2 |
| $6,000 to $7,999 | 4.8 | 4.5 | 5.3 | Education | 9.3 | 4.5 | 14.3 |
| $8,000 to $9,999 | 6.1 | 5.9 | 6.2 | Engineering | 8.5 | 15.2 | 1.6 |
| $10,000 to $12,499 | 11.1 | 10.7 | 11.5 | English | 1.0 | .6 | 1.4 |
| $12,500 to $14,999 | 12.2 | 12.5 | 11.9 | Fine arts | 6.1 | 6.0 | 6.2 |
| $15,000 to $19,999 | 17.2 | 18.1 | 16.1 | Health professions | 6.9 | 1.5 | 12.4 |
| $20,000 to $24,999 | 13.6 | 14.1 | 12.9 | History, political science | 3.1 | 3.7 | 2.4 |
| $25,000 to $29,999 | 7.5 | 7.9 | 7.1 | Humanities (other) | 2.2 | 1.8 | 2.5 |
| $30,000 to $34,999 | 5.5 | 5.6 | 5.4 | Mathematics and statistics | 1.0 | 1.1 | .8 |
| $35,000 to $39,999 | 3.3 | 3.3 | 3.3 | Physical sciences | 2.7 | 3.9 | 1.4 |
| $40,000 or more | 8.0 | 8.0 | 8.0 | Social sciences | 5.6 | 3.2 | 8.2 |
| **Current religious preference:** | | | | Other technical fields | 7.5 | 8.6 | 6.5 |
| Protestant | 44.7 | 42.7 | 46.6 | Other nontechnical fields | 10.7 | 11.2 | 10.3 |
| Roman Catholic | 35.5 | 35.6 | 35.3 | Undecided | 4.7 | 4.3 | 5.1 |
| Jewish | 3.6 | 3.9 | 3.4 | **Reasons noted as very important in selecting this college:**[1] | | | |
| Other | 6.2 | 6.3 | 6.3 | Relative wanted me to come here | 6.8 | 5.9 | 7.8 |
| None | 10.0 | 11.7 | 8.3 | | | | |

**TABLE 12.3** (continued)

| Item | First-time students | | | Item | First-time students | | |
|---|---|---|---|---|---|---|---|
| | Total | Men | Women | | Total | Men | Women |
| *1* | *2* | *3* | *4* | *1* | *2* | *3* | *4* |
| Teacher advised me | 4.2 | 4.4 | 4.0 | Basic Educational Opportunity Grant | 14.3 | 13.7 | 15.1 |
| Has a good academic reputation | 43.1 | 40.0 | 46.5 | Supplemental Educational Opportunity | | | |
| Offered financial assistance | 13.6 | 13.4 | 13.9 | Grant | 2.6 | 2.5 | 2.6 |
| Not accepted anywhere else | 2.9 | 3.5 | 2.3 | College work-study grant | 4.8 | 4.5 | 5.2 |
| Advise of someone who attended | 14.4 | 13.6 | 15.4 | State scholarship or grant | 6.5 | 6.3 | 6.5 |
| Offers special education programs | 25.3 | 21.2 | 29.8 | College grant | 5.6 | 5.5 | 5.5 |
| Has low tuition | 18.0 | 17.7 | 18.3 | Private grant | 2.6 | 2.6 | 2.7 |
| Advice of guidance counselor | 7.5 | 7.7 | 7.4 | Federal Guaranteed Student Loan | 5.4 | 5.7 | 5.2 |
| Wanted to live at home | 11.6 | 11.1 | 12.1 | National Direct Student Loan | 4.5 | 4.4 | 4.7 |
| Friend suggested attending | 7.2 | 6.7 | 7.7 | College loan | 1.8 | 1.8 | 2.0 |
| College's representative recruited me | 3.9 | 4.5 | 3.3 | Other loan | 2.8 | 2.7 | 2.8 |
| **Major reasons for receiving financial aid:**[1] | | | | Full-time employment | 3.2 | 4.5 | 1.9 |
| Financial need | 77.9 | 75.1 | 80.7 | Part-time employment | 18.0 | 21.8 | 13.7 |
| Academic talent | 29.7 | 28.6 | 30.9 | Savings | 13.1 | 14.8 | 11.1 |
| Athletic talent | 7.5 | 12.5 | 2.1 | Spouse | .5 | .5 | .6 |
| Other special talent | 6.5 | 7.4 | 5.5 | Personal G.I. Benefits | .8 | 1.5 | .2 |
| **Sources of financial support for** | | | | Parent's G.I. Benefits | .7 | .7 | .5 |
| **college of $500 or more:**[a] | | | | Social Security Dependent's Benefits | 2.9 | 2.8 | 3.0 |
| Parental or family aid | 46.0 | 44.5 | 47.8 | Other sources | 1.8 | 2.0 | 1.5 |

[a]Because some students gave multiple responses to this term, percents add to more than 100.0.

NOTE: Data are based upon a sample survey of full-time freshman enrolled in college for the first time. Because of rounding, percents may not add to 100.0.

**Portrait of the college freshman.**

colleges seek to fill the spaces left by the declining pool of eighteen-year-olds available in the population.[31]

*Coeducation* is another significant trend. In the mid-1960s, single-sex colleges reached a peak with 236 all male and 281 all female. By 1976, the number of men's colleges had decreased 49 percent, and the number of women's colleges had decreased 54 percent. Together, these single-sex colleges accounted for only 9 percent of the total. Most were religiously controlled, private colleges. Only nine were public institutions and four of these were United States military academies. We predict that with the desegregation of such traditional male bastions as West Point, the others will not be far behind. The trend is shown in Figure 12.5.

*Undergraduate choices of major fields of study* have also undergone changes in recent years. In 1976, there were 925,700 bachelor's degrees awarded in the United States. Five years earlier, 839,000 had been granted. Twelve fields accounted for 90 percent of the degrees in 1970–71; the leading areas were education, the social sciences, business management, English, and engineering. In 1976, the leaders were education, business management, the social sciences, the biological sciences, and the health professions.[32] As the national interest in environmental issues and health care gains momentum, we would expect this trend to sharpen.

Since one of the main criteria for getting into the mainstream of American life is education, we can expect to find women acquiring a greater proportion of bachelor's and master's degrees than ever (45 percent in 1975). They are now earning nearly twice as many Ph.D.'s as they earned ten years ago. Over the same period, the percentage of females earning professional degrees tripled. For example, in 1965 women received only 3 percent of all law degrees, whereas they earned 15 percent in 1975. Other fields where women are making significant inroads at the doctoral level are communications (28 percent), architecture and environmental design (16 percent), mathematics (11 percent), physical sciences (8 percent), and computer science (7 percent). Fields such as business management and engineering are slower in opening their doors to women, with only 4 percent and 2 percent, respectively, in 1975. (see Figure 12.6).

With Affirmative Action, the push for E.R.A., and changing attitudes toward women in the work force, we can predict a quickening of this trend. All of these trends in the demography of American education will have major consequences on the dynamics of family life and patterns of socialization in the next generation. We can expect, however, that while the content of socialization may change, one major agency of socialization—the student

**FIGURE 12.5**  **Institutions of higher education for men, for women and coeducational: United States, 1945–1976**

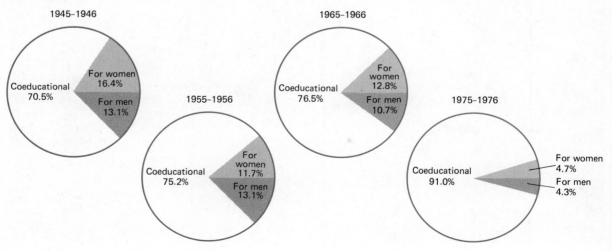

FIGURE 12.6    Percent of bachelor's and higher degrees earned by women: United States, 1964–1975

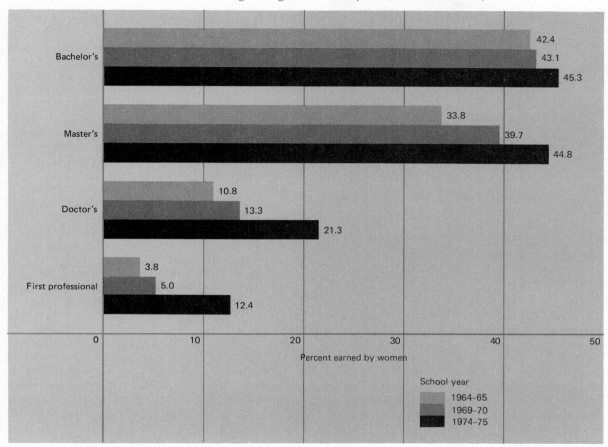

peer group—will remain powerful in the student experience. We turn now to an examination of the dynamics of peer subcultures.

*Student Peer Groups*

**High School**    How would you most like to be remembered by your high school classmates? Would you prefer to evoke memories as "brilliant," "gorgeous," "a star athlete," "the most popular" or "a leader in activities"? Answers to this kind of question can be very revealing of student values. James Coleman conducted such a study among ten Illinois high schools and reported his findings in a classic study, *The Adolescent Society*, in 1961.[34] Coleman's findings on the question were clear: males wanted to be remembered as athletes;

females fluctuated between wanting popularity and leadership in activities.

What this and a number of other studies[35] reveal is the presence of a student subculture, at both the high school and college level, with its own set of norms, values, and statuses that often conflict with adult expectations and values. The conclusion of most youth research is that extracurricular participation and peer popularity in school far outweigh academic concerns. In fact, scholastic achievements alone, without any extracurricular involvement, usually detract from a student's popularity. High grades are viewed as icing on the cake, while nonacademic success is the staff of life.

What does it take, specifically, to be a member of the in-crowd in high school? As anyone who has survived the experience can attest, the

The peer culture probably has as much to do with what happens to the student in high school as anything else.

criteria are well defined. A profile of the in-crowd male in a typical school might look like this: He has a good personality and reputation, plays a major varsity sport, is well dressed, handsome, and has a car. His female counterpart has a similar description. She, too, has a good personality and reputation; she is a cheerleader at those varsity games, wears nice clothes and, of course, is good-looking. Coleman's findings also confirmed that the brightest girls play down their intelligence in order to get dates, presumably in deference to the fabled male ego. Another interesting finding was a pattern of dominance by students from well-educated, middle-class homes, although this did not hold in schools with predominantly working-class students. The problems of being left out socially were greatest for working-class students in upper-middle-class school environments.

Why do teenagers develop a peer culture separate from the dominant adult society? Coleman reasoned that in a highly complex industrial society, the family loses many of its traditional functions—such as moral indoctrination—to the school. However, the school bureaucracy leaves little room for individual and affective relationships in its formal structure; so the student is "forced inward toward his own age group, made to carry out his whole social life with others his own age. With his fellows, he comes to constitute a small society, one that has the most important interactions within itself, and maintains only a few threads of connection with the outside adult society."[36]

Presumably this is true for males and females alike. You recall that Waller described a childhood culture as early as 1932—one that was in conflict with the school authority. What is happening, apparently, is that childhood is being prolonged as industrialization advances. One possible explanation is that "the adolescent society" is a human adaptation to stress. The stress in this case is that of being age-segregated, dependent, and unproductive in a society that values independence and productivity. Though extracurricular activities in school may be just a game, adolescents can at least determine their own rules.

The main sociological insight provided by Coleman's work on adolescence has a practical application; rather than focusing on motivation, I.Q., and other personality factors when trying to explain academic achievement, it seems more useful to look at the value climate—the norms—of the school, and at the organization of peer influences. A sociological model of Coleman's theoretical explanation is shown in Figure 12.7. This sociological model suggests that patterns of behavior should be viewed in

**FIGURE 12.7  Schematic model of high school interactions**

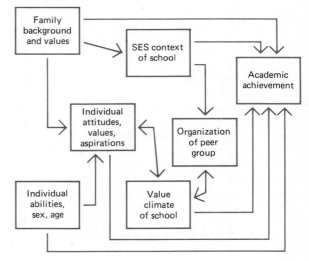

the context of family, school, and peer group interactions. Research findings do change over time as new factors and strains enter the social equation, but the principle represented in this model should remain valid.

As we shift our focus to a discussion of college student subcultures, it would be a mistake to draw any sharp distinction between high school and college peer cultures, since at least one study indicates that the major reason for extracurricular involvement in high school is to have it on the record for college admission.[37]

**College and University** Residential college environments are much more complex than those of high schools. New factors enter the social matrix: roommates, fraternities, personal freedom—all of which call for considerable adaptation. However, the major difference between high school and college is found in the emphasis on academic performance. Since higher education is not compulsory, faculty members feel free to exert pressure for scholastic commitment; yet distinctive student subcultures exist, complete with differing emphases, attitudes, and life styles. To succeed, students must balance the demands made by these competing forces; they must learn, without much practice, to play the student role.

A number of researchers have studied the

The results of a fraternity-sorority soap battle. College peer culture is an important influence on student behavior.

process by which college students manage this juggling act.[38] Since many day-to-day demands are in conflict, one could readily predict some creative performances. Vassar College was the subject of an intensive study of peer group influence on academic commitment. When Nevitt Sanford and his associates did the study in the late 1950s, Vassar was still a women's college. Although it had the reputation of being a first-rate liberal arts school, Vassar students evidenced a wide range of academic orientations. Sanford found peer influences to be dominant, often operating to confirm such stereotypes as "superintellectual," "science-major type," "debutante," or "Yale weekend girl." Vassar women resisted socialization to faculty norms, not by rebelling against scholastic work—in fact good grades were respected—but by holding back on full commitment to academics where they might interfere with social relations. The ideal student was one who could play the role gracefully; she got good grades consistently while having a full social life, without appearing to work too hard at keeping a high grade point average, and, in fact, exerting considerable effort to appear nonchalant. In this way, student norms served as a mechanism by which students maintained a *status quo* they found comfortable.

In a similar study of Kansas medical students in 1962, Hughes, Becker, and Geer[39] found the same struggle: to balance academic demands with social existence. The peer group functioned as a buffer against what were often impossible academic demands. Rather than becoming competitive in a "survival-of-the-fittest" struggle, the students soon reached an informal consensus on what *all* of them would learn for exams; informal norms also emerged to set the number of case studies they would submit—a small proportion of the total assigned. Other adaptations by the Kansas peer group involved a number of shortcuts in laboratory and clinical exercises. Through such mutually reinforcing actions, students were able to gain collectively some power in a situation where students are formally powerless.

The same group of researchers published a study of the general student culture at the University of Kansas in 1968.[40] Their goal was again to analyze patterns of adaptation students make in the face of conflicting demands on their energies, intellect, and emotions. Though they came from a wide range of backgrounds and were enrolled in dozens of different programs, the students at Kansas shared one adaptation: a "G.P.A. (grade point average) perspective."

Once again, grades were a dominant part of student consciousness. Everything depended on keeping a G.P.A. above the various requirements for scholarships, sports eligibility, and membership in fraternities and sororities. Familiar strategies were employed in pursuit of grades: taking "gut" courses, apple polishing, playing to professors' prejudices, cramming, quibbling about minor test details, and, with great regularity, cheating.

This last practice brings up a point that interests sociologists of education. Why is it that some student groups have high rates of cheating while others do not?

*The problem of cheating* among undergraduates is well researched.[41] High rates of cheating were found in a variety of college and university settings, which is not in itself surprising. However, the data suggest considerable variation in the degree and seriousness of the offense. Can the variation be explained by "personal-background factors" — such as the individual's age, sex, G.P.A., or motivation? Or can the variation be explained by "situational characteristics" — the student's perception of rules, peer group attitudes, etc.? In testing the predictive power of these two hypotheses, the research findings have overwhelmingly supported the situational hypothesis; that is, that the social context in which cheating occurs is a better predictor of this behavior than the personal characteristics of the students themselves. Under an honor system, where the norms are clear, there is less cheating than in proctored systems. In one study, cheating dropped from 81 percent to 30 percent of the student body after an honor system became institutionalized.[42] Even honor systems are vulnerable, however, as recurrent scandals at West Point and the Air Force Academy indicate.

The fact that more than half of most student populations admit to cheating suggests a deeper cultural explanation. Anti-intellectualism is common in American tradition and in contemporary life. A combination of pity and scorn is reserved for "the egghead," "the bookworm," "the absent-minded professor," and "the school marm" — all stereotypes of intellectuals. If knowledge can be normatively discredited in this fashion, it is predictable that the aim of college attendance is not always the pursuit of knowledge; it is more often the pursuit of a negotiable credential or a contact network for the job market. This culturally amoral orientation to the means by which the credential is earned may also be the reason that the major concern of students is not that they cheat, but that they may get caught. The ghost of Durkheim lurks in the background calling for a return to moral education.

We have seen that the college peer culture plays a significant role in the behavior patterns of students. The pervasive reality of grades, and not necessarily what they represent, shape the adaptations that get passed on from one student generation to the next. Some modes of adaptation — e.g., the fraternity "file" — are institutionalized; others are rediscovered by each new group. Every individual student must confront the fact that campus existence is governed by group structures that often circumscribe personal choice. The best antidote to such structures is to become conscious of the norms that maintain them.

## EDUCATION AND STRATIFICATION

Sociologists interested in stratification ask, "Who gets what and why?" The "what" refers to valued resources in the society: wealth, power, and privilege; the "why" refers to the social process by which such resources are allocated.

As we saw in Chapter 7, stratification exists when the allocation of resources becomes patterned so that some classes are more privileged than others, and the privileged classes have sufficient control over the social environment to transmit their privilege to their offspring. One of the obvious consequences of this process in practically every modern society is the formation of an elite. In Europe, we still find the remnants of feudal aristocracy; in India, we find Brahmans of high caste; and in the United States we find "old families" — descendants of business barons of the nineteenth century.

What is the relationship between the elite and education? Most importantly, they have historically controlled the routes of educational access for the less privileged classes. It is possible to measure societal rigidity by the way educational opportunities are made available to the nonelite.

In the United States, although the reality of class privilege is often visible, the ideal of social equality always prevails. This belief system suggests that merit, based on ability and motivation, is the only acceptable criterion for educational and occupational advancement. It is true that the single most important predictor of both occupational prestige and income is the number of years of formal education an individual has completed. The process by which one acquires those years of formal education is complicated, however, and education is hardly the only relevant variable, as we saw in Chapter 7.

The greater the level of industrialization, the closer the relationship between education and occupation. In the United States, one of the most highly industrialized nations in the world, it has become crucial to acquire educational credentials if one is to become part of the mainstream. Since we endorse mass education and competition for the privileged positions, the school becomes the processing center in which students are tested, evaluated, graded, and tracked for most occupational destinations. In the end, after high school, some will go on to higher education and elite positions; others will go on to vocational or technical schools; and

others will go directly into the work force. What are the main determinants of such different life chances? To answer this question, we turn to a schematic depiction of the stratification process and research evidence of the hypothesized relationships.

### Who Goes to College?

The relationships diagramed in Figure 12.8 have been thoroughly documented. Sociologists of educational stratification are particularly interested in variables that have strong influence on educational attainment. Four such variables—socioeconomic status of family (SES), race, ethnicity, and gender—combine to affect the different educational experiences and evaluations that young people experience in school. These in turn affect their relative success in the schooling process, which, in the long run, determines how far they go up the educational ladder.

**Socioeconomic Status** One of the most thoroughly researched relationships in sociology is that between socioeconomic status and academic achievement. An individual's SES is usually measured by the parents' occupations, income, and education. It is closely related to all forms of scholastic achievement—standardized I.Q. test scores, classroom grades, assignment to academic rather than vocational programs, graduation from private school, matriculation in professional colleges and university programs.

In a national study of high school seniors conducted by the government in 1972,[43] this relationship was consistently demonstrated on six standardized tests. On each test, students in the higher SES groupings had higher average scores while the least affluent students scored lowest. Similarly, only 18 percent of the lowest SES students had plans to attend a four-year college, whereas 60 percent of the most advantaged students did. In a follow-up study conducted one and one-half years later, less than half of the low SES students who had planned to go to college were actually enrolled, whereas 87 percent of the highest SES group were carrying out their college plans. Even when lower SES students succeed in going beyond high school, as they are doing in increasing num-

FIGURE 12.8    The process of stratification in schools

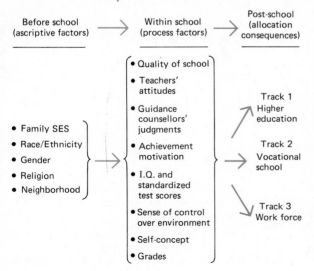

bers, it would be a mistake to assume equality of educational attainment. If the admissions criteria do not present an obstacle, tuition usually does, as is evidenced by the differences in class composition at different types of institutions (see Table 12.4).

What role does ability play in educational success and the probability of going to college? As Table 12.5 indicates, although achievement is important, it is not as important as SES. For example, if we hold aptitude constant and compare the highest 25 percent and the lowest 25 percent on the socioeconomic scale of high school students, we find only 75 percent of the high ability, low SES males plan to go to college, whereas 92 percent of the high ability, high SES students make plans to attend. At the other extreme, we find 33 percent of the low ability, low SES group aspiring to higher education, whereas 57 percent of the low ability, high SES group have college plans.[44] It should be remembered in interpreting these data that SES is never neutral: in terms of academic achievement, it works *for* those at the high end and *against* those at the low: High achievers from deprived backgrounds are truly notable, while low achievement in the high SES category is probably more descriptive of actual academic potential than it would be in the case of a low SES student.

Though family income is the strongest determinant of college attendance, other correlates of SES are also influential. The college aspirations

TABLE 12.5 Percentage of 1967 High School Graduates Planning College Attendance by Academic Ability, Sex, and Socioeconomic Status (SES)

| Socioeconomic status | | Academic ability | Gender | |
|---|---|---|---|---|
| | | | M | F |
| Highest 25% | + | Highest 25% | 92 | 93 |
| Highest 25% | + | Lowest 25% | 57 | 37 |
| Lowest 25% | + | Highest 25% | 75 | 60 |
| Lowest 25% | + | Lowest 25% | 33 | 25 |

of one's high school friends,[45] role models in the home, sibling college attendance, one's high school counselor's values and attitudes[46] all interact in intricate, though predictable ways to affect outcomes. But socioeconomic status outweighs all other social influences in the educational process.

**Race and ethnicity** The Coleman Report, which we will discuss in more detail later, was a response to a congressional mandate that inequalities in educational opportunity be investigated in terms of race, religion, color, and national origin. Some of the results, summarized in Table 12.6, demonstrated a clear rela-

TABLE 12.4 Social Class Composition of Students in Various Types of Postsecondary Institutions (in Estimated Percentages)

| Class status | Cosmopolitan university[a] | Ivy college[b] | Opportunity college[c] | Warnell[d] | State college[e] |
|---|---|---|---|---|---|
| Upper and upper-middle | 30 | 75 | 5 | 40 | 20 |
| Lower-middle | 45 | 20 | 40 | 50 | 50 |
| Working | 25 | 5 | 55 | 10 | 30 |
| TOTAL | 100% | 100% | 100% | 100% | 100% |

[a]Large state or municipal institutions with low tuition and high standards maintained by large freshman failure rate.
[b]Private liberal arts colleges for men and/or women, with high standards and high prestige.
[c]Colleges and junior colleges with lower admission standards and low tuition, oriented toward middle class vocational skills.
[d]A general name for small-city liberal arts colleges, often church-related or -originated, which provide good quality education for middle-class youth.
[e]State or local institutions with low tuitions, often founded as teacher training centers and oriented toward upwardly mobile farm and lower-middle-class youth.

TABLE 12.6   Nationwide Median Test Scores for 1st and 12th Grade Pupils, Fall 1965

| Test | Racial or ethnic group | | | | | |
|---|---|---|---|---|---|---|
| | Puerto Ricans | Native-Americans | Mexican-Americans | Oriental-Americans | Blacks | Majority (White) |
| **1st grade** | | | | | | |
| Nonverbal | 45.8 | 53.0 | 50.1 | 56.6 | 43.4 | 54.1 |
| Verbal | 44.9 | 47.8 | 46.5 | 51.6 | 45.4 | 53.2 |
| **12th grade** | | | | | | |
| Nonverbal | 43.3 | 47.1 | 45.0 | 51.6 | 40.9 | 52.0 |
| Verbal | 43.1 | 43.7 | 43.8 | 49.6 | 40.9 | 52.1 |
| Reading | 42.6 | 44.3 | 44.2 | 48.8 | 42.2 | 51.9 |
| Mathematics | 43.7 | 45.9 | 45.5 | 51.3 | 41.8 | 51.8 |
| General information | 41.7 | 44.7 | 43.3 | 49.0 | 40.6 | 52.2 |
| Average of the 5 tests | 43.1 | 45.1 | 44.4 | 50.1 | 41.1 | 52.0 |

tionship between minority status and depressed academic achievement.[47] The outstanding exception is the performance of Oriental Americans. In 1977, 67 percent of whites over 25 were high school graduates, whereas only 46 percent of blacks and other minorities had this level of attainment.[48] Race and ethnicity, then, continue to be a major factor in answering our crucial stratification question, "Who gets what and why?"

**Gender**   How does gender affect academic achievement?[49] Unlike race or ethnicity, a student's gender is unrelated to class background for the obvious reason that the sexes are about equally distributed across socioeconomic strata. Since there is also no theoretical or empirical reason to associate gender with general scholastic ability, any relationship we find between academic achievement and sex must be attributed to aspects of the stratification process outlined in Figure 12.8. The power of this process to cause differential performances between the sexes is demonstrated by a large body of research evidence. Girls generally get higher grades in both elementary school and high school than boys. They seldom have truancy or misbehavior problems and require much less remedial work than boys. In a 1972 study of high school seniors, 40 percent of the boys reported a B or better average, whereas 60 percent of the girls had this level of achievement.[50] On standardized tests, the outcome depends heavily on the content being tested. At the high

school level, boys score higher then girls in mathematics, science, social studies, and citizenship. Girls excel in reading, writing, music, and literature.[51]

Throughout most of this century, women have had greater success in graduating from high school than men. For example, in 1950, 60 percent of the females, but only 54 percent of the males, earned high school diplomas.

However, a dramatic reversal takes place in the relative performance of males and females as the end of high school approaches. After superior performance through all of the lower grades, girls begin to fall behind as advanced education approaches. Women have, until recently, demonstrated lower aspirations toward college and, if they do enroll, have had a higher tendency to drop out before college graduation.

How can this pattern be explained? The explanation is not genetically based feminine predispositions; rather, an answer is to be found in traditional sex-role socialization patterns. As school progresses, males are encouraged to link education to career goals, whereas females are encouraged to value popularity over academic performance. Females are more likely to be taught to inhibit competitiveness, ambition, and tenacity—traits that are associated with masculinity. Instead, females are encouraged to demonstrate obedience, nurturance, and a desire to please.[52] Such traits do not facilitate academic achievement, especially in a competitive environment.

As Figure 12.6 showed, these patterns are

The proportion of women taking graduate and professional degrees is increasing but remains low relative to men.

changing rapidly. The proportion of bachelor's degrees awarded to women is increasing more rapidly than for men and this is also true for professional and advanced degrees. Nonetheless, it is important to recall that, in 1975–76, only 21 percent of doctorates and 12 percent of first professional degrees were awarded to women.

Recent increases in the percentage of older women returning to school and changes in socialization patterns can be expected to weaken this strong association between gender and educational attainment. In the meantime, the fact remains that gender is a powerful factor in educational stratification.

## Education and Social Mobility

Social mobility, as we saw in Chapter 7, is the movement of an individual or group, upward, downward, or laterally among social strata. Changes in occupational prestige are often used as a general indicator of mobility, though we

have seen that property ownership, wealth, income, power, and education can also be important measures. As a basic prerequisite to occupational entry, education is often cited as the most crucial requirement for upward mobility in an industrial society. How valid is this claim? We have already seen that the longer one stays in school, the more one can expect in yearly and lifetime earnings (see Chapter 7). Is it true that a college graduate has a better chance of landing a good job in the first place than someone without a degree?

**Education and Jobs** Before 1970, the answer would have been a resounding "Yes!" However, by the late 1970s advanced education was no longer a guarantee of suitable job placement.[53] The data in Figure 12.9 support this contention.

In recent years the number of college graduates has begun to exceed the demand for college-trained individuals. The National Center for Education Statistics predicts that 16.1 million college degrees will be awarded between 1974 and 1985, but only 12.2 million college-level jobs will be available. Though only 13.1 million graduates will compete in the labor force directly, this still leaves a surplus of approximately 1 million college graduates who will have to settle for relatively less prestigious jobs or remain unemployed.

This pattern is already having critical effects in the labor force. Employers, operating in a buyers' market, are simply increasing the formal educational requirements for low-skill jobs, in the belief that this is an "investment in human capital." This belief is not well founded. Researchers have shown that there is no relation between formal education and work performance.[54] It has also been calculated that only 15 percent of the increase in educational requirements for jobs during this century can be attributed to any need for greater expertise. Berg calls this educational inflation "the great training robbery." He argues that the main function of formal education is no longer training; it is, rather, to act as a barrier to occupational access for those who cannot afford a college education.

The implications of these trends are serious. Although college graduates still have a competitive edge over those without a degree, they must often settle for unchallenging work or

**FIGURE 12.9   Number of college graduates in relation to number of "college-level" jobs**

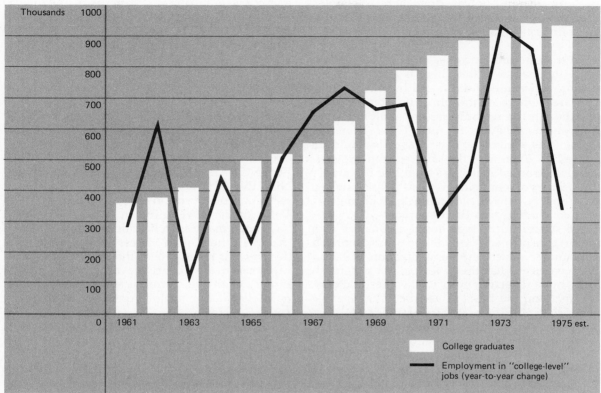

unemployment. Family background, school prestige, and social contacts can increasingly be expected to be larger factors in job placement than academic performance. Finally, channels of social mobility will probably become less accessible, as white-collar positions are filled from the upper social strata.

It would be a mistake to conclude from all of these trends that education is a waste of time. On the contrary, as the job market tightens,

*Degrees no longer guarantee high status employment.*

education becomes a basic necessity. The practical conclusion one can draw here is simple: though education is no guarantee of a job, the lack of it is a guarantee of unemployment.

**Education and Income** We have already seen (in Chapter 7) that there is a strong association between education and income. This is one area where education quite literally pays off, though the rewards are not at all the same for women as they are for men. The demonstration of this systematic discrepancy is found in Table 12.7. Even with the same educational credentials, women make less than half the median incomes of men, though there is still a strong relationship between education and income.

In concluding this brief summary of educational stratification, we should emphasize the importance of specifying the sociological conditions under which any generalization is valid. We have seen that the school is not a neutral force, but a reflection of societal values that discriminate on the basis of ascribed characteristics such as SES, race, ethnicity, and gender. As one might expect, there is widespread disagreement between consensus and conflict theorists about how much inequality exists and how to explain such patterns. Consensus theorists emphasize the extent of upward mobility offered by the public education system and the opportunities now available for women, the poor, and minorities. Conflict theorists emphasize the persistent relationships between minority status and educational disadvantage, and vice versa. They argue that the systematic pattern of disadvantage is exacerbated by several other factors in the school system: teachers' expecta-

tions, testing, grading, counseling, teaching, and curriculum content. Patterns of inequality do exist and persist in the scholastic achievements of American students, regardless of the perspective from which we view them.

### Educational Opportunity: A Continuing Controversy

"COURT-ORDERED INTEGRATION RAPPED BY SOCIOLOGIST WHO STARTED IT ALL," announced a June 1, 1975, headline in the Lansing, Michigan *State Journal*. "HAS FORCED BUSING FAILED? JAMES COLEMAN OFFERS NEW INSIGHTS FROM RECENT RESEARCH," reads the cover caption of the October, 1975 *Phi Delta Kappan*. Beginning in April, 1975, there have been many such headlines in major newspapers in the United States. Behind the media declarations raged one of the most heated controversies in the history of American education. In the eye of the storm were the findings and opinions of one major American sociologist, James S. Coleman.[55]

The origin of the controversy was the 1954 Supreme Court decision in *Brown vs. Board of Education*. This ruling struck down the doctrine of "separate but equal," thus making racial segregation in schools illegal, even where school facilities were equal. In *Brown 2 (1955)*, the justices ordered desegregation with "all deliberate speed" and so began the controversy.

**The Coleman Report** By 1964, the rising impatience of blacks and other minorities moved President Johnson and the Congress to appoint a commission headed by James Cole-

---

TABLE 12.7 Median Annual Income by Years of School Completed and Sex, 1975

| Years of school completed | Men | Women | Ratio Women/Men |
|---|---|---|---|
| Less than 8 | $ 4,665 | $ 2,252 | .48 |
| Elementary school (8 years) | 6,642 | 2,641 | .40 |
| 1–3 years of high school | 8,825 | 3,308 | .37 |
| High school diploma (4 years) | 11,834 | 4,549 | .38 |
| 1–3 years of college | 13,060 | 5,403 | .41 |
| College (4 years) | 15,659 | 7,489 | .48 |
| Postgraduate study (5 or more years) | 17,914 | 10,421 | .58 |

man to study educational opportunities in American public schools. Coleman and his colleagues surveyed 570,000 students and 60,000 teachers in nearly 4,000 public schools. Their report, *Equality of Educational Opportunity*, was published in 1966 and is commonly known as "The Coleman Report." As is often the case in the social sciences, Coleman's data supported some, but challenged most, of the ideas we take for granted about American education. Though immensely detailed, the report may be summarized as follows:

1. Schools remained "largely segregated,"[56] not only in terms of students, but also in the distribution of teachers. Blacks taught blacks; whites taught whites. Desegregation was not proceeding with "all deliberate speed." Not only were schools still segregated racially, but they were segregated socioeconomically. The average black child came from a large and poorly educated family, was seldom enrolled in a college-bound program, and was exposed to only a limited number of standard academic courses. These findings surprised no one.
2. On a series of achievement tests, whites outperformed all other groups, with the exception of Oriental-Americans. This again, was no surprise.
3. On several measures of school quality, Coleman did not find the wide discrepancies many had expected. Black schools did have some deficiencies in certain facilities, such as science and language laboratories, but these differences were small. Regional variations in quality were inconsistent enough to defy any form of generalization. For example, in the nonmetropolitan North and West, 47 percent of blacks but only 26 percent of whites attended schools with accelerated curricula, while in the metropolitan Southwest, the situation was reversed: 76 percent of whites and only 34 percent of blacks attended such schools. In short, no significant pattern of disadvantage in school characteristics was discernible at the national level.
4. Coleman found no significant relationship between the quality of the schools and variations in levels of student achievement. This has been the most controversial finding of all. It is difficult for many people to believe that school quality does not matter very much in the learning outcomes of children. School quality was measured in terms of curriculum, facilities, teachers' academic aptitude and training, student-teacher ratio, and even the educational level of teachers' mothers. If these factors do not have a significant effect on students' achievement, one might reasonably inquire, what does? The answer Coleman offered was the social

composition of the student body, for example, the proportion taking a college preparatory program, the proportion from college-educated families, the proportion who are white—all strong correlates of socioeconomic status. One important qualification of this general conclusion—and one often forgotten in the furor—is that schools *do* make a difference in the degree to which they affect the achievements of different groups. Minority students benefit much more from an improvement in school quality—for example, in teachers' qualifications—than do the already advantaged white majority.[57]

Coleman reasoned that since the explanation of low achievement does not lie in the school, we must look elsewhere—in the home, the neighborhood, and the peer environment. It took only a brief theoretical step to reach the conclusion that if disadvantaged students could be immersed in advantaged social—though not necessarily academic—environments, overall aspirations and achievements would improve. This became known as the "integration hypothesis." However, since public schools are dependent on neighborhood composition, integration could only be accomplished if the racial and socioeconomic boundaries were redrawn to bring about the necessary balance.

**Busing**  Based largely on the Coleman findings, busing was selected as the best mode of achieving racial balance by the administrators who were charged with implementing change. Under this plan, school districts could make adjustments in their racial composition to correct segregated environments. Students would be bused randomly, regardless of ethnic background, family SES, or literacy level. The theoretical predictions were that, after initial resistance and tension, blacks and other minorities would soon achieve at the same level as whites. Racial prejudice was also expected to be reduced.

Since 1966, public reaction to desegregation in general and busing in particular has been inconsistent and often confusing. For example, while 75 percent of the population favors integrated education, only 15 percent of whites and 49 percent of blacks favor busing to achieve it.[58] In a series of studies on the effects of busing, the evidence suggests that blacks are not necessarily helped by attending desegregated schools.[59] It seems important to distinguish

Busing in Boston. Can the schools correct societal inequities?

between types of integration—for instance, there are schools that are integrated because they are in a naturally heterogeneous neighborhood, and there are schools that are artificially mixed by busing. In the latter type, which is likely to be racially tense, the effect on student learning may be negative. Some of the data suggest that integration often damages minority students' self-concepts, aspirations, and self-confidence by placing them in competition with white students who have the advantage of better academic preparation and development.[60] There is also evidence that all-black high schools can produce excellent students, not because they are segregated, but because they get enthusiastic support from the community, faculty, and students for the school's academic goals.[61]

The most ferocious response to busing has come from white ethnic neighborhoods. In south Boston, for example, where the population is largely Irish Catholic, busing was greeted with sustained violence. It is clear that in such neighborhoods, busing may have been a poor choice as a mode of desegregation.

**White Flight** An even more significant problem, however, is white migration from cities to the suburbs, which not only abandons urban schools to the poor and minorities, but also erodes the tax base for other social services as well as education. Coleman has called for an end to busing since he believes it causes "white flight."[62] However, his methodology has been challenged on this point; his critics have demonstrated that there is no causal relationship between desegregation and the shifting residence pattern of whites.

A recent analysis of Coleman's data revealed that middle-class parents (both black and white), often send their children to private schools or move to the suburbs. This kind of "class flight" was taking place long before desegregation or busing. Many sociologists and educators now advocate the popular political preferences: voluntary desegregation, community self-determination, and parental control of educational decisions.

**Inequality in Education** The desegregation and busing controversy began over one injustice: inequality of educational opportunity. Americans have assumed that if only educational access could be equalized, all other social inequalities would be rectified. Is this a valid assumption?

In a major study, Christopher Jencks and his associates at Harvard challenge the assumption that equalizing educational opportunities can reduce the income gap between socioeconomic groups.[63] They provide sound evidence that even if schools were to provide the same educational experiences for all, economic inequality would still prevail. Jencks argues that we cannot expect schools to cure social ills that are part of the structure of other institutions. Although he supports expenditures on schools to make them "pleasant places," Jencks believes that educational outcomes cannot be equalized until a guaranteed income is provided for all Americans.

These data and interpretations suggest that

356

we are asking too much of our educational organizations. Schools, colleges, and universities serve individuals with varied backgrounds, abilities, and motivations who represent the entire social system. Education is intrinsically valuable at both personal and societal levels, but it cannot be held responsible for the inadequacies of other institutions in American life. Education can be civilizing, democratizing, and humanizing, but only when these attributes are valued and practiced in wider social relations.

The degree to which education can fulfill its promise depends entirely on the wisdom, integrity, and compassion that govern the allocation of all our scarce social resources. Any discussion of educational inequality that does not acknowledge its relation to economic, political, and family inequalities is bound to be unproductive. The sociological perspective, thus, can make a practical contribution to personal and public decisions on the future of education.

## SUMMARY

Education is not an independent institution, but rather an organized response to the twin problems of sociocultural continuity and sociocultural change. Schools have a number of functions, both manifest and latent. In the process of maintaining the continuity of the culture, schools are charged with the task of cultural transmission, social integration, social control, training of a work force, and screening individuals for allocation to desegregated positions in the occupational structure. The latent conservative functions served by the schools are those of baby-sitting, pooling of marriage prospects, reducing unemployment, and promoting career mobility in social networks.

The change functions of the school also have manifest and latent components. Manifestly, the schools are expected to promote innovation, diffusion, critical thinking, and social equality. Latently, schools often breed revolutionary ferment, raise the consciousness of minorities and give rise to leadership which articulates the concerns of the underprivileged, though otherwise passive, "masses." Educators and educational outcomes must be studied in relation to other societal dynamics.

American primary and secondary education has several distinguishing features, notably its emphasis on local control and financing and, of course, its overwhelming commitment to mass education.

The demography of American education is highly stratified in terms of prestige and relative access. This has significant life-chance consequences for those being exposed to the different school environments. Three major characteristics are the trend toward increasing vocational programs, the shifting age structure toward an older undergraduate population, and a marked increase in the proportion of women earning degrees at both undergraduate and graduate levels.

Four major variables have high predictive power in answering the question, "Who goes to college?" Family socioeconomic status, race, gender, and ethnicity all continue to be critical sociological variables. While educational credentials no longer guarantee a job, the lack of them is usually a guarantee of unemployment or marginality in the labor force.

Regarding equality of educational opportunity, we saw that formal learning, like all human learning, takes place in a social context and cannot be divorced from the powerful influences of family life, neighborhood, and peer interactions.

It seems clear that social life is immensely complex; if we are to use our scientific expertise to solve the educational problems confronting our society, we must begin with what Durkheim called "that larger social matrix."

## SUGGESTED READINGS

BERG, IVAR. *Education and Jobs: The Great Training Robbery.* New York: Praeger, 1970. This volume explores the relationship between educational credentials required for job access and the actual demands of the positions. The findings demonstrate a trend of credential inflation which leads to underemployment and boredom of the most highly trained.

BOWLES, SAMUEL, AND HERBERT GINTIS. *Schooling in*

*Capitalist America: Educational Reform and the Contradictions of Economic Life.* New York: Basic Books, 1976. Based on elaborate research of both the authors and others, a soundly Marxian thesis is documented which argues that American schools function to serve the capitalist class by reproducing social inequality rather than altering it.

BRONFENBRENNER, URIE. *Two Worlds of Childhood: U.S. and U.S.S.R.* New York: Russel Sage Foundation, 1970. A useful comparison of the schooling experience in the United States and the Soviet Union. The book shows the impact on personality formation and approaches to group life which is likely to result from the respective school systems.

KOZOL, JONATHAN. *The Night Is Dark and I Am Far From Home.* New York: Houghton Mifflin Co. 1975. This book is a dramatic indictment of the American public school system. Schooling is depicted as a process of systematic deceit in which students are taught a progression of myths and half-truths. The final outcome is argued to be one of trained incapacity to either reason or differentiate between knowledge and ideological programming.

MARIN, PETER, VINCENT STANLEY, AND KATHRYN MARIN eds. *The Limits of Schooling.* Englewood Cliffs, N.J.: Prentice-Hall, 1975. A fine collection of articles on the issue of freedom in educational institutions in America. Contributors, including Jonathan Kozol, Paul Goodman, John Holt, and Ivan Illich, are agreed that contemporary society needs "deschooling" such that children can experience the world in richer form than is offered in today's classroom. A thoroughly critical volume.

PARELIUS, ANN P., AND ROBERT J. PARELIUS. *The Sociology of Education.* Englewood Cliffs, N.J.: Prentice-Hall, 1978. A first-rate text which covers the history of American education and offers a data-based analysis of contemporary educational issues. Cross-cultural descriptions of China, Africa, and the U.S.S.R. are also presented in excellent detail. This is singularly the best introduction to the sociology of education in print.

# Chapter 13
# Religion

The institution of religion, like that of the family, is universal among human societies. No contemporary society exists, and no historical society is known, without some institutionalization of religious phenomena. Religion is probably not so old in human experience as the family (which may have come with the race in its evolutionary journey from the prehuman state), but there is persuasive evidence that something very like it was in existence even before humans took their present physical form more than 100,000 years ago.

Unlike the other social institutions, religion focuses on something beyond the natural and cultural world—the interaction between people and their gods, sacred principles, or ultimate powers. The supernatural aspect of religion complicates the sociological study of this institution. Gods are simply not available for interviews, nor susceptible to other forms of sociological measurement. Accordingly, sociology cannot tell us anything about the validity of religious beliefs. But by scrutinizing religious behavior, it can tell us something about human society and ourselves.

Mark Twain once observed, "Man is the Religious Animal. He is the only Religious Animal. He is the only animal that has the true religion—several of them"[1] The great American humorist was implying that religion is a universal activity, practiced in all human societies, that its forms are extremely varied, and that it is regarded with great seriousness by those who adhere to it.

What, however, is meant by *religion?* Does *universal* imply that all people are religious? What are the social dimensions of religion? How does religion function? And finally, does religion today retain the importance it had in earlier periods of American life?

Virtually all sociological discussions of religion begin with or soon come to the classic treatment of the subject by Durkheim. Durkheim saw the essence of religious belief and experience as the differentiation in all societies between *the sacred* and *the profane* or secular. All people, he said, find things of which they stand in awe, and to which they give reverence, and that feeling of awe before what they find inexplicable or incomprehensible is the essence of religion. Not everything inexplicable or incomprehensible is necessarily awesome, of course, but the awesome is always, at bottom, inexplicable. That before which we do *not* stand in awe is the usual or practical or explicable, and the contrast between the two attitudes or sets of feelings, Durkheim wrote, "is the distinctive trait of religious thought."[2] We will return to this matter later.

## WHAT IS RELIGION?

At first glance, this question appears elementary. Surely we all have some commonsense knowledge of religion. But we need some familiarity with the basic premises of the major world religions to insure that our sociological definition will encompass the full spectrum of human religious experience.

### The Major World Religions

Religion emerged sometime before the beginning of recorded history. Archeological evidence indicates that it arose so early in social experience, that it is clearly among the oldest of our social institutions.[3]

The religious communities of human beings are often distinguished by reference to their central object of worship. Around this sacred object, person, or concept, belief patterns, ritual practices, ethical systems, and social organization take form. Hence we commonly speak of religions as being **monotheistic** (*believing in one god*), **polytheistic** (*believing in several gods*), **ethical** (*religions of the way*), and **ancestral** (or *nationalistic*) religions.

**Monotheism** Most Americans are familiar with two major monotheistic faiths: *Judaism*, with about 14.5 million adherents, which centers on the worship of Yahweh, the God of the Old Testament as revealed to Moses and the prophets; and *Christianity*, which sprang from Judaism and is now divided into Protestant, Catholic, and Eastern Orthodox branches to form the largest religious body in the world, with over 951 million believers (see Table 13.1). Most Christians believe in the Trinity (God is One in Three Persons, namely, Father, Son, and Holy Spirit), accept the Bible as a sacred scripture, and adhere to the teachings of Jesus.

A third monotheistic faith is *Islam*. This originated in the sixth century A.D. from the teachings of the prophet Mohammed. The object of worship is Allah whose revelations are recorded in the Koran, the sacred scriptures of Islam. Islam is today the second largest world religion, with 538 million members, called Moslems, located primarily in the Near East, Africa, and Asia. Islam has shaped Arab culture in much the same way as the Judeo-Christian tradition has informed the culture of the West.

**Polytheism** The most prominent polytheistic faith is *Hinduism*. Its followers believe in a hierarchy of gods ranging from local deities through regional gods to gods associated with large caste groups. Hinduism is probably the oldest religion, dating back to the late Stone Age. Most of its 519 million members live in India, Pakistan, and Bangladesh.

**Ethical Religions** Buddhism, Confucianism, and Taoism reflect an outlook quite different from that of Western faiths, stressing ethics instead of ideas, adjustment more than change, and the past more than the future. They are often called the religions of the way. All lack the notion of a personal god, and their doctrines have developed from a set of principles that define the ultimate order of the universe. These sacred principles encourage followers to practice an ethical life so as to fulfill the ultimate order and produce harmony in personal and social life.

*Buddhism*, which is closely related to Hinduism, arose in India during the sixth century B.C. when the "enlightened one," or Buddha, discovered the means for achieving spiritual excellence (Nirvana) through meditation. Each of Buddhism's various sects emphasizes different aspects of the sacred texts and has its own rituals and moral codes. Today, these groups include 245 million practitioners.

*Confucianism* is the religion founded on the ethical teachings of Confucius, who lived in China from 551 to 479 B.C. Urging the moral and physical harmony of all things, Confucianism attracts many different kinds of people. Since it lacks priesthood, a theological system, and other features common to religions. Max Weber, C. K. Yang, and others have questioned whether Confucianism should be viewed as a religion or as a philosophy possessing an ethical system.[4] Although this is a valid question, we follow the usual procedure of including Confucianism, with its 175 million adherents, as one of the world religions.

Closely allied with Confucianism is *Taoism*. Beginning as a philosophical school in China 2,000 years ago, Taoism is now a religious community of 29 million. More mystical than Confucianism, Taoism has its own sacred scriptures, ethics, and especially political theory. Like other religions of the way, however, Taoism is concerned with the quality of one's

**TABLE 13.1  Religious Population of the World**

| Religion | N. America[1] | S. America | Europe[2] | Asia | Africa | Oceania[3] | Totals |
|---|---|---|---|---|---|---|---|
| Total Christian | 228,479,000 | 161,872,500 | 358,732,600 | 86,358,000 | 98,326,000 | 17,290,000 | 951,058,100 |
| Roman Catholic | 130,789,000 | 151,017,000 | 182,087,000 | 44,239,500 | 31,168,500 | 3,230,000 | 542,531,000 |
| Eastern Orthodox | 4,121,000 | 55,000 | 62,145,600 | 1,786,000 | 16,335,000 | 360,000 | 84,803,200 |
| Protestant[4] | 93,569,000 | 10,800,500 | 114,500,000 | 40,332,500 | 50,822,500 | 13,700,000 | 323,724,500 |
| Jewish | 6,356,675 | 675,000 | 3,960,000 | 3,186,460 | 274,760 | 80,000 | 14,532,895 |
| Moslem | 248,100 | 197,800 | 8,277,000 | 427,035,000 | 101,889,500 | 66,000 | 537,713,400 |
| Zoroastrian | 250 | – | 3,000 | 224,700 | 530 | – | 228,480 |
| Shinto | 60,000 | 92,000 | – | 61,004,000 | – | – | 61,156,000 |
| Taoist | 16,000 | 12,000 | – | 29,256,100 | – | – | 29,284,100 |
| Confucian[5] | 96,100 | 85,000 | 25,000 | 175,440,250 | 500 | 42,000 | 175,688,850 |
| Buddhist[5] | 155,000 | 195,300 | 220,000 | 244,212,000 | 2,000 | 16,000 | 244,800,300 |
| Hindu | 80,000 | 547,000 | 330,000 | 516,713,500 | 473,650 | 650,000 | 518,794,150 |
| Sikh | – | – | – | 10,000,000 | – | – | 12,000,000 |
| **Totals** | **235,491,125** | **163,676,600** | **371,547,600** | **1,553,430,010** | **200,966,940** | **13,144,000** | **2,545,256,275** |
| **Population[6]** | **347,934,000** | **224,154,000** | **733,454,000** | **2,304,929,000** | **412,183,000** | **21,729,000** | **4,044,433,000** |

[1]Includes Central America and the West Indies. [2]Includes the USSR where it is difficult to determine religious affiliation. [3]Includes Australia, New Zealand, and islands of the South Pacific. [4]Protestant figures outside Europe usually include "full members" rather than all baptized persons and are not comparable to those of ethnic religions or churches counting all adherents. [5]Statistics for Confucianism and Taoism are undeterminable in China since the Maoist-Marxist revolution. [6]Continental total populations are United Nations data.

life in relation to the ultimate order of the universe and one's individual destiny.

Unlike Western religions, religions of the way are nonexclusive. It is not considered bad faith to worship in a Confucian temple one day, a Taoist the next, and a Buddhist the following day. This complicates the task of estimating the strength of Eastern religions. An individual may be Taoist, Buddhist, and Confucian at the same time. Moreover, the Maoist revolution in China has confused the tabulating of religious adherents even more. More reliable information from China may force a readjustment of the numerical estimates for all three religions of the way.

**Ancestral Religion**   By far the largest ancestral religion is *Shintoism*, the traditional faith of Japan. Just before and during World War II, Shinto ancestor-worship became a means for showing loyalty to the state as represented by the emperor. After the war, the nationalistic aspects of Shinto were deemphasized in favor of the more ancient belief in honoring the ancestral spirits who guard individual and collective life. Shinto followers number about 61 million persons in Japan and throughout the world.

**Primitive Religion**   *Animism* is the belief in spirits and ghosts who move about the world working good and ill in person's lives. According to Sir Edward Tylor, one of animism's chief interpreters, such universal experiences as death, dreams, and visions lead primitive peoples to assume the existence of a soul that can roam about detached from the body.[5] From this notion arises concept of spiritual beings who, can be appeased or invoked in times of distress. Elaborate religious ceremonies develop as people seek to come to grips with crises in their lives. Few today accept Tylor's theory that all religions originate in animism.

*Totemism* is the belief that sacred power, or *mana*, dwells in specific objects—usually common plants or animals. These objects serve as the focus of religious veneration in ritual activities. Durkheim suggested that primitive people did not worship the actual snake, bird, or tree that was their totem, but regarded these objects as symbols of the sacred force standing behind them.[6] By identifying with a totem, a person can participate in the realm of the sacred.

Durkheim also observed a close association between totemic religion and the kinship network. Members of the same clan in the kinship system share a totemic emblem. When an individual receives a totemic symbol it is an assignment of a place in the religious sphere, as well as a social location within the family system. Durkheim believed this connection was the key to understanding the function of religion in modern as well as primitive societies. Symbols such as the cross of Christianity give the members of a particular religious group something to identify with, just as primitive people identify with a totem in order to find a place in the social order.

Thus "primitive" religion is not so different from "modern" religion as one may assume. Indeed, Durkheim theorized that religion everywhere shares fundamentals that promote social cohesion and solidarity by uniting people with the values and norms of their society. Religion is thus one important way a society makes moral demands on its members. Just as primitive people find themselves drawn to society through religious participation, so modern people are attracted to the collective norms of their societies in religious practices.

### The Sacred as The Hallmark of Religion

We are now in a better position to address the question, "What is religion?" Clearly, some of our commonsense responses now seem inadequate. We can no longer define religion as belief in God, since several religions of the way really have no gods as such; nor will *theology*, a formal system of ideas about the divine, always serve as a distinguishing mark of religion, since some religions have no such doctrinal system. Neither will priestly activity suffice, because some religions exist without developing a professional priesthood.

Common to all religious structures and practices, however, is one outstanding feature. This element is the *sacred*, the focal center for religious veneration. For theistic religions, the sacred is defined as a supernatural deity, a personal God who exists above and beyond the world. In ethical and primitive religions, the sacred often seems more abstract. It may be understood as the ultimate structure of the universe, either as symbolized in sacred principles or as reflected in totemic objects. However differently religious communities may have perceived and depicted the sacred, all have some explicit notion of sacredness at the center of their tradition.

Durkheim defined religion as "a unified system of beliefs and practices relative to sacred things, that is to say, things set apart and forbidden—beliefs and practices which unite into a single moral community called a church, all those who adhere to them."[7] The sacred should be seen in opposition to all things secular (worldly or temporal). Thus the sacred is a powerful, extraordinary, awe-inspiring, and transcendent reality above and beyond the material universe.

In *The Idea of the Holy*, the German scholar Rudolf Otto isolated the major features of the sacred: otherness, mystery, tremendousness, and awe-inspiring capabilities.[8] Durkheim and Otto agreed that the sacred was the source of religious sentiment—although in Durkheim's theory society and not God stood behind sacred manifestations. For both of them, the sacred remained a general category, with specific meanings filled in by each religious community according to its own history and needs. Around the sacred center, beliefs, practices, and social organization mark the distinctive characteristics of each religious tradition and its unique interpretation of the sacred.[9]

## The Basic Dimensions of Religiosity

Durkheim and Otto explained how religious institutions respond to the sacred by generating beliefs, rituals, ethical codes, and social organizations. While the sacred is not available for scientific investigation, the concrete features of the religious institution are, and they become, the focus for sociological inquiry.

**Belief Patterns** The sacred reality people experience through revelation, reflection, or divine illumination is defined by a set of ideas called *belief patterns*. Of course, religious beliefs vary considerably in content, clarity, and precision. Some belief patterns are logically organized, like the theology of the medieval church. Others, like the religious legends of the Australian aborigines, are loosely related collections of myths with only a vague doctrinal system, if any. Some belief patterns—however vague—must be developed to provide direction

for the religious movement, but beliefs are not necessarily the basic element of the religious institution. Sometimes they arise to explain certain rituals and sometimes the ritual or social organization takes its form from the beliefs.

Once framed, beliefs generally develop from myth to doctrine as the religion develops from primitive to modern. To be sure, myths are never totally eliminated from belief systems, even among the "advanced" religions. The story of Adam and Eve, or Buddha under the Bo tree, for example, still convey profound religious meanings even for believers who doubt the historical literality of these accounts.[10]

**Ritual Practices** Closely related to belief patterns are rituals prescribed for believers as appropriate human responses in the relationship to the ultimate source of being or value. Like belief patterns, rituals display consider-

Moslems at prayer. Religious ritual fosters collective participation.

able variation, from making deep scars on the face to praying five times a day. Some rituals bestow thanks and praise on a deity, others petition for special blessings, and still others seek to appease the wrath of the gods or attain forgiveness for impious deeds. Some rituals, such as meditation and yoga, are practiced in isolation, while others, like dancing, feasting, or preaching, require a social setting. Rituals tend to foster collective participation and encourage collective enthusiasm as a means for reaffirming commitment to a faith.

Ritual practices differ in structure and requirements. Some rituals, like Quaker meetings, are relatively free and spontaneous, while others, such as the Latin Rite of the Roman Catholic Church, remain uniform over long periods of time and across many cultural frontiers. Regardless of their structural specificity, however, rituals provide occasions for remembering and celebrating the meanings of a religious tradition, and they reinforce the attachment of believers to the content and organizational framework of their religious group.

**Ethical Codes**  While rituals are behavior patterns directed toward the worship of deity, ethical action is behavior addressed toward other persons. The ethical life is informed by the religious ideas contained in the belief system. The Roman Catholic belief in the sanctity of life, for example, produces an ethical norm prohibiting abortion. Ethical norms often mold the members of a religious group into somewhat similar character types. Thus, participants in a religion often develop patterns of behavior that help distinguish them from members of other religious communities. Quakers, for example, are noted for their ethical commitment to pacifism, while Islam values the ethical virtues associated with the "holy war." For the sociologist interested in how religions control or direct the behavior of their followers, the structure of a group's ethical system is a crucial object of analysis.

**Cultic Organization**  The word *cult* is often used popularly as a synonym for "sect," but technically the cultic organization of a religious group is its institutionalized patterns of social organization and structure. The cultic structure perpetuates and safeguards the group's central religious experience. It prescribes such matters as the conduct of ritual activities, the establish-

ment and maintenance of places of worship, the selection of specialists in religious affairs — priests, monks, nuns, seers, ministers, cantors, and so forth — and the ranking of religious offices, as in the hierarchy of a priesthood. The cult also defines the proper roles for laity and clergy for groups that make such distinctions.

Cultic organization is necessary for the social and institutional expression of religious faith. No religion can long endure without cultic organization. It insures the continued life and vitality of a religious tradition. Of course, individuals can and do initiate new religious ideas and transform old ritual practices. But individuals are unlikely to persist very long or make much impact without cultic order to transmit the innovations to others. Any religion that survives its founder must become a social movement complete with a cultic organization.

**Sociological Analysis and Religious Truth**  Science cannot assess the validity of theological claims, nor can theological explanations be regarded as binding on sociologists. That is, in studying Islam, we are not forced to accept the doctrine that Allah was the creator of this religious institution; it is sufficient for sociology to acknowledge that Mohammed believed this was so. Sociology can neither affirm nor deny the theological claims of believers, so sociologists must suspend judgment about whether religious beliefs are true or false. For example, we may develop a political interpretation of the doctrine of Papal Infallibility and demonstrate how well this dogma serves the needs of high officials in the Roman hierarchy by consolidating their control over the church. This demonstration, however, does not "prove" that the doctrine is untrue or that its establishment is not a legitimate unfolding of divinely inspired tradition. Scientific analysis may or may not influence belief but sociology has no grounds for evaluating the validity of religious claims. Sociologists studying the social dimensions of religion should recognize that they are treating only one set of factors that may be active in this institution.

*A Working Definition of Religion*

We can now formulate a working definition of religion. **Religion** is *a set of activities organized around the sacred — that nonempirical source of power, transcendence, mystery, and awe.* In the process of becoming institutionalized, religion establishes, around this sacred center, belief systems, ritual practices, ethical codes, and cultic organizations. All religions that endure over time eventually become social movements capable of exerting tremendous influence as realities that bestow meaning and significance on the lives of individuals and groups.

### What Religion Is Not

We should now be able to identity some endeavors that resemble, yet do not actually qualify as, religious belief or conduct. Magic, science, political ideology, and secular philosophy all belong to this category.

**Magic**  Magic parallels religion in its desire to manipulate the unknown for the achievement of human goals. Unlike religion, however,

Magic, like that practiced by this voodoo priestess, is usually a practical affair directed toward specific objectives for individual clients.

> **religion:** the human activity consisting of belief systems, ritual practices, ethical codes, and cultic organization organized around ideas of the sacred.

magic engages in special and often secretive activities in order to attain private goals for individual clients. The rituals of magic typically try to defeat enemies, cure diseases, increase rainfall, and so forth.

Religion, by contrast, is oriented toward the common or collective good, providing people with a sense of ultimate meaning or deepening their commitment to a faith and its ethical standards. Religion is concerned with the question of humanity's relation to the sacred, while magic seeks to manipulate nature and the supernatural for the specific advantage of individuals who are the clientele for occult practitioners.

It is easier to distinguish magic from religion intellectually than to separate them neatly in practice. Some scholars believe that magic in some form almost invariably accompanies religious practices. Having a priest bless your car or placing a plastic Jesus on the dashboard does not differ substantially from securing a talisman from a witchdoctor to ward off evil spirits, yet you may regard the first acts of piety and the last as primitive superstition.

Generally, religion addresses issues of ultimate importance rather than questions of narrow personal interest. Religion also generates a system of myths and rituals more complex, creative, and universal than the simple techniques of magic with their secret formulas, spiteful motives, and hostility.

**Science**  Like magic and religion, science is a human approach toward the unknown. Where magic attempts to manipulate aspects of the world by mysterious rituals, science seeks to understand the natural realm by constructing universal laws that operate independent of human will and supernatural intervention. According to Malinowski, the rudimentary science of primitive people complemented their belief in magic.[11] Science dealt with the secular and practical unknown, with the technology of subduing nature, while magic and religion dealt with the supernatural aspects of the unknown.

Curiously enough, while we know more

about the natural world than our ancestors did, the scope of the unknown has not decreased proportionately. It has expanded. The author of Genesis could precisely delineate the nature of the heavens and how the sun, moon, and stars were suspended in the firmament. Now that we understand the physical constitution of some parts of the universe better, we have endless questions about black holes in space, quasars, galaxy formation, and a host of other puzzles that only twenty years ago could not have been entertained as scientific problems. As we learn more, we discover how inadequate our previous understanding was and how much more there is to learn. Thus science is not diminishing but expanding the sheer scope of the unknown.

The growth of science has served to disenchant the world so that the need for magic has been decisively reduced. As a part of this disenchantment science has also challenged some religious views of long standing. Many biblical reports, from the creation of the world in seven days to miracle stories, have either been refuted by natural science or their historical character enshrouded in a cloud of doubt.

The history of the warfare between science and religion has not been entirely negative, however.[12] Nor has science destroyed religion, as some scholars and churchmen predicted it would. While science has assumed a larger and larger role in describing the physical order, religion has continued to concentrate its attention on the moral and spiritual aspects of reality.

### Political Ideologies and Secular Philosophies

Political ideologies (such as communism and fascism) and secular philosophies (like the thought of Bertrand Russell, Albert Camus, or Jean-Paul Sartre) are often compared with religion. But political and philosophical idea systems lack a concept of the sacred. Without this element, such movements do not satisfy the most important criterion in our working definition of religion. Indeed, magic, science, and political-philosophical ideologies all stand apart from religion largely because their attempt to provide systems of meaning are not organized around a sacred center. For some individuals, secular philosophy or political ideology may serve as a substitute for religion, but that does not make these idea systems religious.

## THE SOCIAL FUNCTIONS OF RELIGION

Because religion is a complex phenomenon, the social functions it performs are quite diverse. Some religious functions are manifest—intended and immediately observable—and some are latent—unintended and not immediately discernible. If an activity helps the integrative performance of an organization, then we call this activity functional—as, for example, when religion preaches tolerance, peaceful cooperation, and love and then promotes these aims through its ministerial and lay practices. Some religious activities must be called dysfunctional because their consequences frustrate the stated goals of the group. Racist discrimination in a church that preaches brotherly love and equality among believers is a case in point. In general, religion is functional or dysfunctional, depending on the extent to which it contributes to the achievement of societal goals. In part, of course, this depends on whether religious goals and societal goals are compatible. In Northern Ireland, the political conflict between Protestants and Catholics has proved dysfunctional for society as a whole. In the United States, most religious communities are regarded as contributing moral depth and wholesomeness to society at large.

Our discussion of religion's social functions includes the empirical research inspired by each of several theoretical viewpoints. Throughout the discussion, we should bear in mind that no one theory can account for all religious behavior.

### Alienation: The Marxist Tradition

Karl Marx had a profound influence on the sociology of religion. He asked many questions that subsequent interpreters had to try to answer—whether or not they agreed with him.

**Marx's Thought** Marx based his analysis of the social functions of religion on the work of the theologian Ludwig Feuerbach. Feuerbach had proposed that the idea of God was of human origin and creation.[13] Human beings projected into the heavens an ideal image composed of the noblest human traits. The purpose of this ideal was to provide individuals with a model of moral excellence. Before long, however, people lost sight of the fact that this god was their own creation. They began to worship and fear the created ideal as though it were a supernatural being.

Marx carried Feuerbach's thesis further. If it causes people to live in fear of an object they themselves have constructed, religion must be perceived as an alienating force in human life — perhaps the primal alienating force.[14] By terrorizing people with the fear of a nonexistent god, religion prevents complete self-realization and deprives people of the opportunity of becoming fully human. The world created by religion is a false world; it condemns those who accept it to live within a "false consciousness" in fundamental opposition to their basic human nature. This is the alienating dynamic of religion, Marx argued. Once alienation became established, it soon spilled over and debased other social relationships. It manifested itself in economics, politics, family life, and education. To overcome the alienating influence of religion required nothing less than the total rejection of all religion.

**Social Class and Religious Alienation** Marx next turned to an analysis of the concrete functions religion performs. Here economic factors — the core of any Marxist analysis — play a larger role: Religion serves to sustain the interests of the dominant class in society. Thus it contributes to the exploitation of the lower classes.

Marx divided reality into two major forces — the ideal and the material. Ideal forces, or the "superstructure of society," consist of all mental forms, such as legal ideas, moral values, philosophies, political ideologies, and religious beliefs. Material forces, or the "substructure of society," include those economic relations derived from production — in short, one's class position. Marx asserted that the material situation — the class location — one acquires through accident of birth determines one's ideals and values, including one's religious beliefs. Religion, therefore, is first and foremost a reflection of the socioeconomic situation.

Religion maintains the prevailing class structure, with its unequal distribution of wealth and privilege. The working classes suffer under an exploitive system imposed from above by the ruling class, but religion snuffs out the fires of angry resentment and helps the working classes tolerate their misery. Religion teaches the lower classes that this world is a vale of tears to be endured with humility and piety; those who suffer without complaint will receive their reward in heaven, and "There'll be pie in the sky by and by when we die." Religion, Marx declared, "is an opiate to the people," a tranquilizer that dulls the senses and lulls them into passive acceptance of the injustices of a capitalist economy.

**The Legacy of Marx** Modern sociologists are skeptical about any analysis whose findings or conclusions can be reached before the research is undertaken. Yet Marx has taught us a great deal about religion. Material forces — and especially social-class influences — have a powerful impact on what a religious community believes and how its members practice their faith. Thanks to Marx we can understand why some people worship with Bach and others sing nothing but gospel songs. In each instance, class perspective determines what music is appropriate. But Marx could have understood even more clearly how some people find beliefs comforting — because they justify their privileged social position — and how other people use religion as an escape from the harsh reali-

Marx's observation that religion and social class (or ethnicity) were related has been thoroughly documented by the sociology of religion. "Saved" worshipper of the Pentacostal Faith being baptized in Harlem.

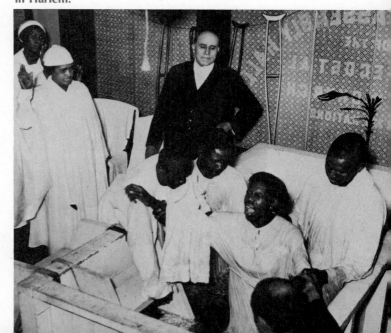

ties of social inequality. Indeed, there is ample evidence to lend support to the thesis that religion often bestows an aura of sacred legitimacy on the cultural perspectives of its adherents. During the American Civil War, it may be recalled, the southern churches actively condoned slavery, while the northern churches raised their voice to champion the cause of abolition. These facts neatly conform to Marx's idea of the class- and interest-bound character of religion.

Sometimes, however, the churches act in accord with their moral teachings rather than with the vested interests of their members. Consequently, sociologists have modified the Marxist thesis. Religion is *sometimes* a reflection of the class outlook of its members. This revision retains Marx's major insight without perpetuating its errors.

**Denomination and Social Class** One of the most scathing critiques of religion's surrender to material factors is a 1929 study by H. Richard Niebuhr, *The Social Sources of Denominationalism*.[15] Niebuhr maintained that material factors and social class played a more significant role than religious doctrines in dividing the church into **denominations.** Members of the lower class—the "disinherited" Niebuhr called them—are in effect excluded from participation in middle-class denominations because they feel socially out of place and uncomfortable there. This forces them to create smaller, more conservative **sects** to minister to their needs. The sects often develop an unusual theological position and a strict set of ethical standards that place them in opposition to middle-class culture.

Gradually, as the lower-class sect encourages its members to practice such virtues as honesty, hard work, abstention from alcohol, and responsibility to family obligations, individual members—and sometimes the whole group—experience upward social mobility toward a middle-class life style. As the sect approaches middle-class status, extreme features of its theology are modified in favor of more moderate beliefs and practices. This helps attract converts who are already middle class. But once middle-class status is achieved, the new denomination no longer ministers to the disinherited, making necessary the formation of yet another sect to address the religious needs of the lower class, and the cycle begins anew. Niebuhr concluded

that it is almost impossible for the churches to overcome the class divisions of secular culture.

Other material or social factors exercise a divisive influence like that of social class. Among them are race, ethnicity, sectionalism, and the frontier, which fostered rural revivalism in contrast to the urban religion of the commercial East. The common feature of many schisms in church structure is their dependence on sociological foundations rather than doctrinal differences. Thus, while Niebuhr was not a Marxist, he nonetheless recognized the force of material factors in church structure and religious behavior.

Recent studies reveal that we are only beginning to understand the links between social class and religious behavior (see Table 13.2 for social class profiles of American religious groups). In a study completed in 1965, N. J. Demerath, III, observed that social class affects denominations in several ways.[16] For example, religion tends to reinforce the secular values and pursuits of the middle and upper classes, while it fosters withdrawal from the secular world for lower-class believers.

In 1970 Rodney Stark and Charles Y. Glock made a curious discovery relating to upward social mobility and the tendency for people to switch denominational affiliation.[17] Previous research had established that Protestant denominations can be arranged hierarchically in terms of the class standing of their members.

**TABLE 13.2 The Social-Class Distribution of Major American Religious Denominations (percent)**

| Denomination | Upper class | Middle class | Lower class |
|---|---|---|---|
| Christian Scientist | 24.8 | 36.5 | 38.7 |
| Episcopal | 24.1 | 33.7 | 42.2 |
| Congregational | 23.9 | 42.6 | 33.5 |
| Presbyterian | 21.9 | 40.0 | 38.1 |
| Jewish | 21.8 | 32.0 | 46.2 |
| Reformed | 19.1 | 31.3 | 49.6 |
| Methodist | 12.7 | 35.6 | 51.7 |
| Lutheran | 10.9 | 36.1 | 53.0 |
| Christian | 10.0 | 35.4 | 54.6 |
| Roman Catholic | 8.7 | 24.7 | 66.6 |
| Baptist | 8.0 | 24.0 | 68.0 |
| Mormon | 5.1 | 28.6 | 66.3 |
| No preference | 13.3 | 26.0 | 60.7 |
| Atheist, agnostic | 33.3 | 46.7 | 20.0 |

Fundamentalist or conservative groups tend to minister to the lower class; the majority of denominations are solidly middle class; and Episcopalianism is generally regarded as having the highest status membership. Glock and Stark showed that upward social mobility by individual church members was positively correlated with shifts in denominational affiliation. Conservative sects (as well as Roman Catholics and Southern Baptists) draw most of their new converts from unchurched lower-class people. Middle-class congregations, such as Methodists, Presbyterians, and Congregationalists, attract their new members largely from lower-class churches, while the more liberal Episcopalians recruit their converts from the moderate, middle-class churches.

A striking pattern of membership fluidity emerges from this research. Social class mobility correlates positively with denominational affiliation, switching, and disaffiliation, so that the middle class manifests a stronger commitment to religion than members of other class groups. Moreover, social class mobility, and not religious ideas, appears to be the critical factor in explaining why church-goers switch denominational affiliation.

## Cohesion: The Durkheimian Tradition

Emile Durkheim identified the major social function of religion as the symbolic and institutional integration of human groups in a unified social order.

**Durkheim's Thought** While most Americans view society as the result of individuals banding together for their mutual benefit or protection, Durkheim asserts that individuality is itself a product of society. People need moral norms, language, conceptual abilities, and so forth, in order to be more than humanoid animals. All of these attributes are derived from culture as conveyed by society. Society, then, "is a reality *sui generis*,"[18] that is to say, it is unique, one of a kind. What makes any society extraordinary is its *collective representations* or conscience, the set of beliefs, values, and norms shared by the members. The collective conscience molds both institutional structures and individual action. It integrates as well as directs how one should act within the societal context. Durkheim believed that the collective conscience

> **denomination:** a conventional, widely accepted religious organization without "establishment" in the form of state support; a "respectable," although not "official" church. Methodism or Roman Catholicism in the United States are examples.
>
> **sect:** a small grouping of great religious orthodoxy characterized by stress on withdrawal from secular society, lay leadership, often of a charismatic nature, informal services, adult conversion, and strict personal ethics. The original Black Muslims were an American example.

was a reality beyond human control, a social element that arose spontaneously out of interactions among the members of society to define their cultural norms. The collective conscience is the highest moral standard specifying the rules that the members must accept in order to interact in a stable social life. Durkheim spoke as though this cultural control center at the heart of society could act and impose its demands in a somewhat suprahuman fashion.

How can people be made to control their natural egoism and submit to the demands of collective rules? Durkheim believed that no person voluntarily gives up personal interests in favor of more binding collective requirements. Religion is the overwhelming force necessary to convince us to obey the rules. Indeed, the idea of force is born of religion, Durkheim claims, for through power religion separates the sacred from the profane or secular. When one enters a great cathedral, it is not the same as entering a large office building, auditorium, or football stadium. One feels in the cathedral the power of the sacred, for the cathedral symbolizes the awesomeness of religious reality.

Sacredness can be infused in or superimposed on anything. The sacredness we feel in the cathedral comes not from the building itself, but from the power it symbolically represents. In the primitive religions examined by Durkheim, ordinary objects — birds, plants, or animals — serve as the totem, the sacred emblem, of the clan. The object, however, is not important; the sacred character infused into it sets it apart. Durkheim claimed that the same patterns are observable in the Roman Catholic mass, for

**According to Durkheim, sacredness can be infused in anything: two sacred objects.**

example, when ordinary elements like the wine and water are infused with sacredness so that they become the body of Jesus. Thereafter they must be treated differently. In a similar fashion, the aborigines take a bone or a piece of wood, and emblazon on it their sacred symbol to make a Churinga, a ritual object. Before going into battle, they rub themselves with their Churinga in order to become stronger. And they *are* stronger, Durkheim declares, because the sacred power of religion is conferred on them. This power is not merely psychological; it is sociological because the collective power of the social group is instilled in them.

The heart of Durkheim's interpretation of religion is that the sacred is actually the concentrated force of society. The collective conscience inspires commitment to its moral norms by clothing its ideals in sanctity. By committing ourselves to religion, we are actually committing ourselves to the rules of society itself. This is the context of Durkheim's famous assertion that religion is society worshipping itself.

Like Marx, Durkheim believed that the theological claims of religion were a social fiction. But unlike Marx, he was not opposed to the religious community and its operations. The attachment of people to the religious community was simply a way for them to manifest their attachment to the norms of the larger social order. Since societal unity was very important in Durkheim's view, religion could be tolerated as a social fiction, so long as it promoted social solidarity.

Religion performs this integrative function efficiently because it places human action in a sacred framework of meaning. During the late Renaissance, for example, citizens believed that kings ruled by divine right. To challenge the king's authority was to question the wisdom of God. Religion bathes secular institutions, ideas, and norms in the legitimating glow of the sacred. It gives them a sense of "rightness" so that people are less inclined to question them than rules which are obviously secular. (Many Americans today support democracy not only because they think it is a good political theory, but also because they regard it as the form of government ordained by God as "right for Americans." Consider the phrase "One nation under God," and the frequent assertion that the United States is a "Christian country," in spite of the fact that it was the first to adopt separation of church and state as a fundamental principle.)

Durkheim saw other reasons for the effectiveness of religious institutions in promoting social solidarity. In secular life the collective conscience must rely largely on its coercive power to impose order on society. Religion functions through the magnetic charm of the sacred, persuading rather than forcing people to fulfill the demands of the collective conscience. Religion transforms external pressures into internal compulsions, so that people obey not because they *must* but because they feel they *should*. This is why societies express their social norms as principles that come from the divine order.

Religious ritual reinforces social integration by promoting commitment to the sacred and to the collective conscience behind it. But since the fires of religious enthusiasm require periodic rekindling, Durkheim said, public ceremonies assume a preeminent role in religious life. They afford opportunities for collective memory, celebration, and reassertion of the meaning of the sacred events that provide a society's identity. Rituals also supply occasions for voicing the vital concerns of the society and appealing for divine help. Rituals put people back in touch with the collective forces on which religious affirmations are based. In the afterglow of a ritual experience, people feel invigorated, with a newfound sense of power for coping with the realities of life. This is no illusion, Durkheim maintained, for they really *are* better equipped to deal with life's problems. The power that believers encounter under the guise of the sacred is a real power: it is the collective power of society itself.

**The Legacy of Durkheim** Durkheim's theory of religion has been as influential as that of any other figure in the sociology of religion. Although the thesis that religion is society worshipping itself has been largely rejected as something that cannot be tested by scientific means, Durkheim's emphasis on the role of the sacred, his theory of the close connection between religious beliefs and moral norms, and his stress on ritual in reinforcing commitment to religious and secular values, have all weathered the test of critical scrutiny. Above all, Durkheim made us aware of how the religious institution generates loyalty to the authority of secular society. He would immediately have understood why Americans print "in God we trust" on our currency, Englishmen sing "God save the Queen," and the Nazis rallied around the slogan "Gott mit uns" (God with us) and tried to replace the cross with the swastika.

**Religion and the Integration of American Society** A number of Americans have applied Durkheim's insights to analyses of American

Is this a sacred object?

society and its religious communities. W. Lloyd Warner in 1961 contended that beyond the churches there exists a basic symbolic order where sacred beliefs and secular rituals overcome the tensions and conflicts of communal life.[19] Memorial Day observances, for example, bring into focus this higher realm of collective experience, for this holiday—at least in the earlier decades of this century—took on the character of a religious ceremony. It was an occasion for celebrating the sacrifices of those who died for the "the American way of life." Parades, patriotic speeches, prayers, and other rites were designed to stimulate a renewed commitment to the ideals of American society. (Do not reject this thesis if the Memorial Day celebrations with which you are familiar do not seem this elaborate. The holocaust of World War II, followed by further bloodletting in Korea and Vietnam, have made it harder for Americans to celebrate death in war as gloriously sacrificial, but the analysis of the *functions* of such ceremonies remains as valid as ever.)

Warner's interpretation of Memorial Day became an opening wedge for understanding a whole series of semireligious phenomena. Not only do we Americans commemorate the major events of our social history with holidays like Thanksgiving, the Fourth of July, and Washington's and Lincoln's birthdays, but we also revere quasi-sacred artifacts such as the flag, and the Tomb of the Unknown Soldier.

Our quasi-sacred scriptures include the Constitution, the Declaration of Independence, and the Gettysburg Address. We have elevated men like Washington, Lincoln, and Jefferson to the status of demigods. Warner believed American civil ceremony sustained the basic norms of society in precisely the way Durkheim had predicted.

### The American Way of Life as Religion

Another analysis of American religion, still in the Durkheimian tradition, was suggested by Will Herberg in *Protestant-Catholic-Jew* (1960).[20] Noting that church membership was increasing rapidly in the early 1950s, along with almost all the major forms of social disorganization, from crime and delinquency to family disruption and suicide, Herberg sought to explain this startling state of affairs.

Americans were participating in religion more but heeding its teachings less, Herberg said, because *belonging to* a religious community had become more important than sharing its beliefs or living by its ethics. Individuals needed an organization in which to establish an identity for their personal life and derive a "place" in American society. Not belonging to a religious community was tantamount to being un-American.

Thus membership in the three major religious bodies increased substantially, but the average participant was more interested in "having a religion" than in being religious. The beliefs and morals informing everyday life were the secular principles of the American Way of Life, not the teachings of a religious community. In short, the primary function of religion had become more social than religious. This led Herberg to denounce American religion as idolatrous and to ask whether religion can serve two masters, whether it can faithfully perform its religious function and at the same time fulfill a social function.

**Civil Religion** What function does religion serve in unifying society today? In 1967, Robert Bellah addressed this question in a landmark essay called "Civil Religion in America."[21] Bellah describes civil religion as a religious sanctification of American political ideals, historical leaders, and the ultimate destiny of the society.

President Kennedy's grave has become a quasi-religious shrine. Visited by thousands every year, it is one of the most popular tourist attractions in Washington.

Civil religion is not an organized church like Roman Catholicism, but rather a religious dimension to political society that sets American experience within a transcendent frame of reference. No real conflict emerges between this religious aspect of the society and the religion of the churches because civil religion advances no doctrine apart from the democratic creed. The god it serves is somewhat unitarian. Civil religion supplies sacred legitimation for the ideals of democracy. Without civil religion Bellah believes, American society might suffer disintegration and lose its sense of direction.

### The Creation of Meaning: The Weberian Tradition

Max Weber coined the term "sociology of religion" and, along with Durkheim, helped set the discipline on its current course. Weber was primarily concerned with how religious institutions generate systems of meaning that possess the authority and legitimacy to direct social action and control behavior. Through both of these modes of influence, religion has been a creative and a stabilizing institution in society.

**The Creation of Meaning**  Weber proposed that religions respond to a basic need—the need to understand the purpose of life. The Old Testament figure, Job, for example, suffered terrible calamities—the loss of his family, the destruction of his worldly possessions, and the affliction of painful sores. Throughout his ordeal, Job's most pressing question was not "How can I regain what I have lost?" but "Why has this trouble descended on me?" We can tolerate terrible suffering, Weber observed, if it is meaningful. Religion furnishes the meaning that makes life worth living.

Yet in pursuit of this purely religious goal, the religious institution makes a valuable contribution to secular social life. To impart meaning to personal existence, religion must first define the world where human action is set, create a *world view*. Consider, for example, the world view of the New Testament. Here reality is depicted in terms of a three-story universe with hell below, earth in the middle, and heaven above. This reality structure helps people learn how to act on earth so as to escape hell and enter heaven.

Religious world views define a social reality whose influence is not confined to religious matters alone. Once religion defined the world as flat, people acted on the assumption that it was flat. Similarly, most Americans firmly believe that people by nature strive to get ahead. This commonplace assumption about human nature has religious origins. The Puritans preached that all human achievement was for the glory of God. The secularized Puritan value of achievement has been institutionalized as a permanent feature of the American character. In this way, religious institutions often lay the foundations of meaning on which social orders are constructed.

**The Protestant Ethic**  In *The Protestant Ethic and the Spirit of Capitalism*, Weber described the connection between the theological doctrines of the sixteenth-century Protestant reformer John Calvin and the secular behavior characteristic of modern capitalism.[22] The Calvinists believed in predestination, the idea that God selects certain persons for heaven and others for hell before they are born. Nothing we do in life can affect God's decision for our salvation

or damnation. Nevertheless, Calvinists were under tremendous psychological and social pressure to live righteously, not in order to change God's decision but in order to prove to themselves and others that they were among the elect marked for salvation.

Calvin claimed that the chief purpose of human life was to glorify God and give Him honor. This obligation applied to more than

**JOHN CALVIN**

John Calvin (1509–1564) was one of the great Protestant theologians. His doctrines, Weber argued, provided an essential and fertile underpinning for the development of capitalism. Calvin preached thrift, hard work, temperance, plain living, and perhaps most important, the doctrines of calling and predestination. These doctrines implied that all people were ordained to be whatever they were; thus, it became an act of worship and obedience to divine command to do one's job well. From this doctrine also sprang the notion of work as worship. These ideas formed a complex unit which lent itself very easily, according to Weber, to the creation of a capitalist mentality and economic rationality in business. Working hard and thriftily to make a business prosper became a religious activity.

Sunday worship. Those other six days when they labored in their secular vocations could also be dedicated to God's glory. Working for the glory of God, however, required nothing less than the believer's best effort. Hence, economic achievement through honest, disciplined, rational labor constituted a major portion of the Calvinist ethic, not for economic motives alone, of course, but for the ultimate purpose of the glory of God.

This ethic of diligent labor produced the psychological mind-set essential for productive capitalist activity. Not only did Calvinists work hard, they worked like rational, calculating entrepreneurs rather than skilled craft workers. The Calvinists' adventurous spirit was fired by their ambition to give God glory. This fitted them with the proper mental attitude for lively participation in modern, rational capitalism.

Weber was fully aware that capitalism in some form had been present in economic relations for centuries. He contended, however, that modern, rational capitalism is a product of the Reformation and is qualitatively different from previous forms of capitalist endeavor.

Later in his career, Weber produced a set of studies of the other major world religions. These studies revealed that the patterns of ethical life, along with the close relations among religion, state, and the family, actively prevented the development of a business mentality like that found in modern Western economies. In India, for example, it might be unthinkable not to take one's brother-in-law into one's business even if he is a lazy good-for-nothing who will eat up the profits while contributing nothing. The traditional norms supporting kin relations above all others might make the profit calculation irrelevant. In Western societies, by contrast, economic considerations are central, and a businessman who hired a relative under such circumstances would be regarded as foolish. These comparative studies reinforced Weber's faith in his theory of the unique relationship between Calvinism and modern capitalism.

**The Legacy of Weber**   Weber's chief contribution was his insight into the ability of religions to establish world views. Calvinism, quite unintentionally, offered a view of reality that stimulated rational economic activity. Hinduism, Confucianism, Buddhism, and Judaism, by contrast, developed world views that discouraged aggressive business behavior of the Western type. Religious institutions frequently generate ideas that later transform the way people think and act in secular affairs. Indeed, some of a people's most important sentiments — especially those relating to the purpose of life — originally spring from religious sources. The significance of religion goes far beyond the institutional limits of the churches; its ideas often penetrate social life to influence many activities we regard as entirely secular.

**Puritanism and Science**   In an imaginative essay, Robert K. Merton sketched the role of Puritan attitudes in fostering scientific development.[23] Puritanism, a later branch of Calvinism, stressed inner-worldly activity, which, Merton noted, led to a deepened interest in nature and science. In Britain, where Puritanism was strong in the seventeenth century, the Royal Society for scientific research had many Puritan members who emphasized the twin virtues of rationalism and empiricism in the analysis of nature.

As science progressed, however, its theories and data ultimately conflicted with some of the events narrated in the Bible — the creation, the flood, miracles, and other supernatural events. Ironically, Puritan endeavors in natural science undercut the credibility of Puritan religious beliefs. Merton concluded that this pattern may not be unusual. Secular activities stimulated by a religious orientation may often give rise to strife within the religious community. Once new religious ideas have changed the world, that newly defined world is likely to alter substantially the way the religious institution pursues its purely religious tasks.

**The Protestant Ethic in Contemporary Life**   Since the publication of Weber's thesis, scholars have wondered whether Protestantism still encourages greater economic success among its followers than, say, Catholicism or Judaism. Gerhard Lenski explored this question in a study of metropolitan Detroit.[24] Lenski was interested not in the historical connection between Calvinism and capitalism but in the influence religious perspectives exert on secular success in contemporary American life.

Lenski's findings confirm the view that religious beliefs still play an important role in developing orientations that lead toward success

"My Protestant work ethic made me a bundle, but my Puritanical guilt complex won't let me enjoy it."

New Yorker, May 5, 1973. Drawing by H. Martin; © 1973 The New Yorker Magazine, Inc.

in the wider social sphere. For example, Protestantism nurtures individualism, independence from familial ties, and a powerful drive toward upward social mobility, while Catholicism reinforces the reverse sentiments of obedience to authority and reliance on the extended family. Although Protestants and Catholics are not very different in the United States, they are different enough to reduce Catholics' upward social mobility as compared with that of their Protestant neighbors. Lenski concluded that religion is still a significant factor in motivating secular behavior.

**Religion and Culture** Weber identified some of the ways religious ideas influence secular processes. Ernst Troeltsch, his colleague and friend, pointed out that the reverse was also true; culture affects religion. Religion can adopt one of three possible attitudes toward culture; it may embrace it, reject it, or dismiss it as irrelevant. Each choice results in a different institutional structure: church, sect, or mysticism.[25]

A **church,** to use Troeltsch's categories, is an established ecclesiastical system financially supported by the state and enrolling most of a society's members. At one time, Anglicanism

> **church:** in Ernst Troeltsch's terms, an established ecclesiastical system supported by the state and enrolling most of a society's members. The Church of England in Britain and Lutheranism in Sweden are examples. More commonly, simply a conventional religious organization.
>
> **mysticism:** a highly individualistic form of religious behavior focusing on subjective experience and tending to regard both the secular world and religious structures as irrelevant. The search for personal, supernatural experience.

in England, Lutheranism in Sweden, and Roman Catholicism in France all conformed to this pattern. All religious communities are faced with the hard choice of maintaining rigorous standards of belief and practice, so that only those few who possess the deepest faith qualify for membership, or lowering standards in order to impart a modest degree of religiosity to a large number of people. A church decides for the masses. It chooses to embrace culture, the state, and the support of the ruling classes so that some faith, however limited, may be dispensed to all.

The *sect* confronts the same problem, but chooses the other alternative. The sect limits itself to a small group of believers who adhere to very rigorous standards of doctrinal belief and ethical practice. The sect rejects the contemporary secular culture. Examples of this approach are to be found among the Amish and Jehovah's Witnesses. Sects tend to withdraw from the world of secular society, rely upon lay leadership, an informal liturgy, a membership based on adult conversion, and strict ethical discipline in daily life. Church and sect, then, represent two diametrically opposed forms of religious expression.

The third form, **mysticism,** regards culture as religiously irrelevant. It opposes in principle all formal worship and social organization that might limit the free movement of the Spirit. Believers focus on an inner experience, a highly individual vision of God. Compared with this, culture is unimportant, so mystics remain indifferent toward secular affairs. Although they sometimes unite in loosely formed groups, they quickly dissolve these communities when group life threatens the free access of the individual Spirit to personal illumination.

Church, sect, and mysticism are thus three mutually exclusive forms of social organization within Christianity. Each represents a valid expression of the Christian ideal. Troeltsch points out the many ways the religious institution can organize the interplay between faith and culture, with religion modifying culture even as culture sets the conditions for the course of religious development.

**Church and Sect**   Troeltsch based his three-fold model on the social patterns Christianity had developed through the nineteenth century. Recent studies have updated and expanded his ideas. As we have seen, Niebuhr described a continuum starting with sects of the disinherited and moving toward churches of the established middle class. Liston Pope carried this further by describing twenty-one stages of the transition from sectarianism to church status.[26]

More recently J. Milton Yinger replaced the church-sect distinction with a model based on four institutional types: ecclesia, denomination, established sect, and sect.[27] This corresponds more closely to contemporary patterns in the churches. The **ecclesia,** like Troeltsch's church, reaches out to the boundaries of society and embraces members from all socioeconomic levels. It is usually an established, or state church, like the Church of England.

The *denomination* is neither an established church, nor does it withdraw from society like a sect. Rather, denominations ally themselves with political and cultural forces, while remaining somewhat circumscribed by class lines, regional differences, and racial boundaries. Such American religious bodies as the United Methodist Church, the Southern Baptist Convention, Roman Catholicism, and other mainstream churches fall within this category.

The **established sect** is more inclusive and less alienated from· secular culture than Troeltsch's sect type. It does not, however, possess the sophistication and social influence of the denominations. Examples of this type in North America include the Church of God, the Church of Christ, Missionary Alliance Churches, and a number of smaller religious bodies.

The fourth type, the *sect,* includes very small and normally unstable groups seeking converts, quite often, under a charismatic leader. These

One of the common hallmarks of the sect is the storefront church.

sects come and go, but if they can solve the difficult organizational problems that plague them at the beginning, they can develop into established sects. The Black Muslims began as a sect and have now moved into the status of an established sect.

### The Social Construction of Religious Reality

Fashioning the varied functions of religion into a general framework of analysis is far from simple. Peter Berger and Thomas Luckmann have recently combined the insights of Marx, Durkheim, and Weber with some of their own, and have achieved a new synthesis of the many functions performed by religion.[28]

Berger and Luckmann describe their framework as a *social construction of reality perspective.* By this they mean that the social meanings and structures of reality are humanly created and maintained. This is important because we often regard the church as deriving from supernatural forces and forget that it is social actors who actively engage in its formation and perpetuation. We must recognize both subjective and objective aspects of religious reality.

**The Subjective Level: Individual Religiosity**
When we enter society, we begin a long and complex learning process. In swift order, we must learn a language, master the symbols of our culture, assume social roles, internalize

group norms, and establish an identity. Through the same socialization process, we also acquire a religion, with its sacred beliefs, rituals, and ethical requirements. To show how this occurs, Berger suggests a threefold process of reality construction.[29]

In the first stage, *externalization*, individuals project meanings into the world by creating nonmaterial ideas or fashioning material objects. Producing a philosophical system, a work of art, or an automobile are all examples of externalization, because each entails a purposive effort of creation or production.

In *objectification*, our projections or externalizing activities generate an object which takes on an existence apart from us. Once an object has become a real thing—whether an idea or a material object—it may no longer be controllable by its creator. For example, a group of physicists projected the plans for a nuclear fission bomb during World War II. Under government sponsorship, the atomic bomb was then actually created; it became objectified and assumed a concrete existence in our arsenal of weapons. Fearing its destructive force, however, many of the scientists who built the bomb strongly urged that it should never be used. Dropping the bomb was a frightful reminder that objectified ideas cannot always be controlled by those who produce them in the first place.

The final stage is *internalization*. Meanings in the external world—objectified ideas—are absorbed into the self to form the subjective, conscious concepts, personality structures, and identity that constitute selfhood. Through socialization, persons internalize meanings that were previously norms and ideas that came from the culture.

This threefold process, however, actually begins in personal experience with internalization. We can explain this by means of a concrete example: Most of us acknowledge the Golden Rule as an excellent guide for living. None of us, however, thought up that norm and articulated it entirely on our own. We first internalize it by virtue of our training in the home, church, or synagogue. Once internalized, it can be projected as an idea to which we are firmly committed. If we and others did not project this norm, it would cease to exist. This is what Berger and Luckmann mean when they say reality is socially maintained. Without human actors to perpetuate and maintain them, religious ideas,

**ecclesia:** one form of religious organization in Yinger's model; very similar to Troeltsch's "church"; an established, state-supported, national religious organization.

**established sect:** a sect in the process of becoming a denomination, more inclusive and less alientated than a pure sect.

norms, and social structures would not achieve objectification and be internalized by future generations. Thus we make religion through externalization. Through objectification religion takes on an existence apart from us, and through internalization religion makes us. We can now consider how individuals carry on the process in the life cycle.

In childhood, we accept almost uncritically the religious tradition given to us. We externalize meanings in almost the identical form in which we internalized them from the family and the church. But as we approach maturity, we may begin to raise questions about the adequacy of the religious beliefs acquired from our tradition. Once this occurs, the "fit" between the subjective religion we have externalized and the objective beliefs and practices espoused by the church can no longer be taken for granted. We may turn to other religious traditions, or we may decide that the beliefs we have already internalized from our tradition are still adequate after all. Meanwhile, the religious institution provides a number of mechanisms to increase the likelihood that believers will conform to the officially sanctioned patterns of their religious community. The most extreme pressure, of course, is the threat of excommunication, but other, more subtle, forms of persuasion and social control are available as well.

Of course, these controls are not always effective. The breakdown in social control can result either in the loss of an individual to another religious community or in the death of subjective faith altogether. A good deal of any church's energy is spent on nurturing the subjective religiosity of its members. Indeed, the success and survival of a religious institution depend to a large extent on its ability to keep individuals loyal to its beliefs and practices.

**The Objective Level: Institutions** Religious institutions are the objective structures which

Something all religions do is respond to the major events of the human life cycle.

groups of people project and maintain as the proper order for the religious life. The symbolic aspect of the religious institution includes the social meanings through which the nature of sacred reality is defined. Berger and Luckmann refer to this set of meanings as a "sacred cosmos," or world view, that not only establishes an "official version of religious reality," but also explains and justifies "the truth" as a religious group perceives it. Theology is a "plausibility structure," an organized rationale for accepting a religion's fundamental meanings. Consider, for example, how the Calvinists convinced people that the doctrine of predestination was fair. They reasoned that all people are by nature sinful and therefore deserve damnation. God in his grace, however, has selected some to escape their just punishment. That God should spare some is not unfair to those who are damned, however, for they are simply receiving what their sin merits. Thus theology made the doctrine of predestination plausible for Calvinists.

The religious institution is also composed of organizational structures. These arise because a series of offices and roles are required to fulfill the mission of the church. The sacred world view informs the organizational structure in quite explicit ways. The Lordship of Christ over the church in Catholicism, for instance, finds institutional expression in the office of the Pope, Christ's vicar on earth. Together, then, the symbolic and organizational features of the religious institution constitute the objective level of religious reality.

Keeping the subjective and objective, the personal and institutional, levels of religious reality integrated remains a perpetual problem. Yet this integration is attained despite the difficulties. One reason for this is that vast numbers of people rely heavily on religion to bestow meaning, purpose, and direction on life. The important events of life are frequently celebrated by religious ceremonies, from baptism or circumcision at birth to a funeral at death. Churches and synagogues also provide psychological, material, or spiritual help during times of individual crisis. On balance, Berger and Luckmann do not regard the aid given in times of crisis as the most important and valuable contribution to religious participants. The less obvious, but necessary, definitions of reality we get from religion affect our lives more directly and pervasively.

The variety of social functions performed by the religious institution prevent the reduction of religious activity to one set of simple functions. Religion at once creates meaning and destroys other meaning systems. It promotes social change on some occasions, while on others it retards change. Religion often exerts rigorous social control to maintain the *status quo,* while at other times it may legitimate change. Frequently, religion merely reflects socioeconomic patterns of stratification, yet at other times it challenges material inequalities as morally unacceptable. And through all this diversity, religion is constantly affecting secular culture and being affected by it.

## THE SOCIOLOGY OF AMERICAN RELIGION

The religious institution has always held a prominent place in the American experience. Indeed, few societies have fashioned a better environment for the growth of religious sentiments. The vitality and enthusiasm associated with our religious life has encouraged the formation of new denominations and experimentation with new forms of religious expression. One scholar has captured the essence of American religion in the simple phrase, "the lively experiment."[30]

### General Traits

Pervasiveness, secularity, and voluntarism characterize the American religious institution and differentiate it from religious life elsewhere.[31]

**Pervasiveness** Most Americans have never questioned the basic value of religion. The United States has been spared the anticlerical periods experienced in many other nations — most notably France in the eighteenth and nineteenth centuries. In part, the support Americans give to their religious communities can be explained by our history. Early English-speaking settlers fled England in 1620 to escape religious persecution, and their settlement here was motivated by religious sentiments. The second wave of immigrants, the Puritans of 1630, came voluntarily to establish a holy commonwealth in Massachusetts, free from the interference of either bishop or king. Other colonies were likewise founded on religious principles.

During the first century of American history, however, the vitality of the churches waned. The first settlers had been devoutly religious, but later immigrants showed more interest in acquiring land and in making money than in developing piety. In the 1690s, church membership slipped to no more than one-fifth of the population.[32]

The great revivals of the 1740s and the early 1800s started a long process of recovery. Church membership rolls swelled impressively, and identification with some religious community gradually became the norm in American society. Reviewing the data since the 1830s, Seymour Martin Lipset concluded that American religion has experienced an almost continuous "boom" since that time.[33] Now, according to the best available data, 95 – 98 percent of Americans believe in God, about 60 percent belong to a religious organization (see Table 13.3), and about 45 percent regularly participate in worship, more than in other industrialized countries (see Figure 13.1).

The figures are particularly striking when compared to the rates of belief and participation in other Western or industrialized societies. A Gallup poll taken in several Western countries revealed a thirty-eight percent point spread between the United States, with the highest rate of belief in God, and Sweden with the lowest (see Table 13.4).[34] In the United States (1955 – 1966), 44 to 49 percent of the population attended church services in an "average" week.[35] Americans consider religious beliefs more important than do members of most other modern societies (see Figure 13.2). The growth of modern life styles and thought forms, often suspected of being hostile to religion, does not

**TABLE 13.3** **Religious Affiliation of the American Population, 1974**

| Religious group | Members |
|---|---|
| Protestant | 72,485,146 |
| Roman Catholic | 48,701,835 |
| Jewish | 6,115,000 |
| Eastern churches | 3,695,860 |
| Old Catholic, Polish National Catholic, Armenian | 849,052 |
| Buddhist | 60,000 |
| Other | 380,557 |
| **Total** | 132,287,450 |

**FIGURE 13.1** Percentage of adult population that attends church each week in various countries

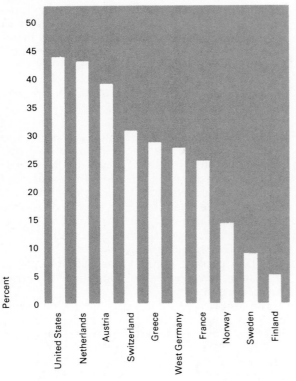

Percent

United States, Netherlands, Austria, Switzerland, Greece, West Germany, France, Norway, Sweden, Finland

**TABLE 13.4** Gallup Poll on Religious Beliefs, December 26, 1968

| *Asked in 12 nations: Do you believe in God?* | | |
| --- | --- | --- |
| | Yes | No | No Opin. |
| United States | 98% | 2% | —% |
| Greece | 96 | 2 | 2 |
| Uruguay (cities) | 89 | 8 | 3 |
| Austria | 85 | 10 | 5 |
| Switzerland | 84 | 11 | 5 |
| Finland | 83 | 7 | 10 |
| West Germany | 81 | 10 | 9 |
| Netherlands | 79 | 13 | 8 |
| Great Britain | 77 | 11 | 12 |
| France | 73 | 21 | 6 |
| Norway | 73 | 12 | 15 |
| Sweden | 60 | 26 | 14 |

yet appear to have eroded the American commitment to religious belief and practice.

**Secularity**  Surprisingly enough, pervasive religiosity and secularity have been mutually supportive in American religion. By secularity, we mean that the several denominations are all legally separated from the state, regard one another as equals, cooperate on matters of mutual spiritual concern, and readily enter into productive relationships with nonreligious institutions and organizations.

Such institutional behavior received impetus from the pluralism and moralism that have distinguished American religious life from the very beginning. Despite a number of denominational mergers in recent years, there are still some 223 religious organizations in America, and this does not include the innumerable storefront churches that have not yet reached established sect status. Such variety makes it difficult for one denomination to press the claim of being "the true faith" against all

others. The legal barrier against state support of any religion has also encouraged American denominations to relate to one another as equals. Thus American society has long encouraged church membership without ever showing much concern over which denomination one joined.

Since the early revivalist days, Americans have stressed ethics over doctrine, right living over right belief. In Europe, rigid doctrinal boundaries segregated religious communities into almost self-contained enclaves. The moralism of American religion has produced the opposite effect. The frequent exchange of pulpits by ministers of different denominations, the initiation of union prayer meetings and ecumenical organizations, and the relatively common practice of denominational switching of membership have given American religion a secular quality not present in the religious climate of other societies.

The depth of our secular orientation and moralistic cast is reflected in the low levels of religious knowledge prevalent in our society. A Gallup poll of 1954 showed that although virtually every American identifies with a religious community, very few know even the most commonplace facts about their faith. Consider these startling findings: In response to the question, "Who is the mother of Jesus?" 6 percent of all Catholics and 5 percent of all Protestants could not identify Mary; 67 percent of Protestants and 40 percent of Catholics in the

**FIGURE 13.2**   Religious beliefs in selected countries: 1975 – 1976

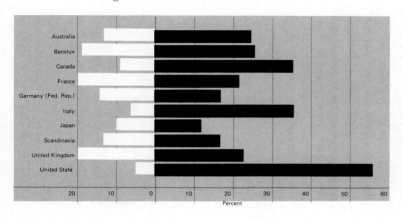

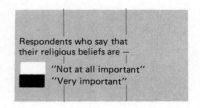

Respondents who say that
their religious beliefs are —

☐ "Not at all important"
■ "Very important"

same sample could not specify the three persons of the Trinity; 79 percent of Protestants and 86 percent of Catholics could not identify a single Old Testament prophet; 78 percent of Protestants and 94 percent of Catholics could not name Paul as the author of most of the books in the New Testament (Jews, who do not accept the New Testament as Scripture, did almost three times better than Catholics, with 17 percent answering correctly); 41 percent of Protestants along with 81 percent of Catholics could not identify Genesis as the first book of the Bible.[36]

These data do not speak well for the effectiveness of religious education in the United States. But American church members put a very small value on serious knowledge about their faith. Some scholars interpret this limited religious knowledge as indicating an increase in socially motivated (or "other-directed") — rather than religious inspired — church-going in the past few decades. But others note that Americans have always been far more interested in moral issues than religious knowledge or doctrinal distinctions. Secularity is an abiding characteristic of the way Americans practice and respond to their religious traditions.

**Voluntarism**   Membership in a religious organization in the United States is always a matter of personal choice. One is not legally a member of a given church by accident of birth, as is the case in societies possessing a state church. Voluntarism deeply affects the social environment in which the churches function. It thrusts all denominations into competition

with all other denominations for members. Talcott Parsons argues quite convincingly that denominational competition serves a positive function.[37] It forces a church to be responsive to the spiritual needs of its members. In state churches, where financial support is guaranteed, members may be taken for granted or even ignored. Denominational competition may thus be a part of the special genius of American religion that accounts for much of its dynamism.

**The Churches and Politics**   Perhaps because they could not assume their concerns would automatically gain a hearing in the councils of

Despite the constitutional separation of church and state, the voluntaristic nature of American religion has always insured the political involvement of the religious. Here, clergy march in support of civil rights in Selma, Alabama.

## THE CHRISTIAN WORLD LIBERATION FRONT

The Christian World Liberation Front (CWLF) emerged from the Jesus movement during the late 1960s in the San Francisco Bay Area. The evangelical organization—founded by Jack Sparks, his wife, and three other couples as a spin-off from Campus Crusade—sought to infiltrate radical political groups and the less organized Bay Area street people to communicate a conservative religious message in the graphic language of the hippie subculture. Consider, for example, this gospel according to the CWLF in counterculture lingo:

Dig it! God has really laid a heavy love on us! He calls us His children and we are! The world system doesn't recognize that we're His children because it doesn't know Him. Right on, brothers and sisters, we *are* God's children even though we're a long way from being what He's going to make us. Don't get hooked on the ego-tripping world system. Anybody who lives that system, doesn't really love God. For this whole gig—the craze for sex, the desire to love everything that looks good, and the false security of believing you can take care of yourself—doesn't come from our Father but from the evil world system itself. That world system is going to be gone some day and along with it, all desire for what it has to offer; but anyone who follows God's plan for his life will live forever. (Dig it! This whole plastic bag is exactly what Jesus liberated us from.)

The CWLF concentrated much of its early efforts on counteracting leftist politics with old-time religion. At political rallies, for instance, when the chant was taken up: "Ho, Ho, Ho Chi Minh, the NLF is gonna win," members of the CWLF would reply with their own chant: "Ho, Ho, Ho Chi Minh, Jesus Christ is gonna win." Actions such as this and endless conversations with radical students and counterculture participants quickly won the CWLF a growing number of converts. Considerable publicity brought financial support and an opportunity to expand their operations. Several houses were established in the Bay Area for transient youth and new members. A Christian family environment was to characterize these "homes" and provide the occasion for developing a sense of Christian community.

A newspaper called *Right On* was founded, providing the CWLF with a way to get its message quickly and directly to the street people and students. For the most part, *Right On* published articles of more substance than other "Jesus" newspapers. Although it dealt with current issues such as war, women's liberation, sex, and homosexuality, it tried to avoid any identification with liberal or conservative politics. The answer to the world's problems given by the paper was thoroughly religious; insofar as CWLF editors were concerned, secularism, materialism, and worldliness were the problems for which Jesus was the universal answer.

By 1975, CWLF had moved from its mission on the streets and campuses toward becoming a rapidly institutionalizing church. Bible study had expanded to providing à "Christian perspective" to balance out the largely secular orientation of the university. A coherent theology has not yet emerged. The CWLF speaks in personal and often literal terms about the Jesus who has brought them into the "Father's Forever Family." Jesus the Alternative, however, is often a symbol which means different things to different members of the group. To the ex-drug pusher, political radical, rootless street person, the alternative is usually defined in terms of rejecting a life style. In its place comes a disciplined ethical life, religious rapture, and a zealous "witnessing" to others still trapped in a meaningless existence.

Like other segments of the Jesus Movement, the CWLF has "divined the signs of the times" and prophesied that Jesus is coming soon. Rejecting the ways of this world, these Christians have concluded that this world will soon pass away to be replaced by the Kingdom of God. More and more, the CWLF has been preparing for the judgment day, not only in seeking a personal relationship with Jesus but also in warning others of His imminent return.

On balance, the CWLF is a relatively sophisticated "Jesus Freak" group. Its houses, newspaper, and personal evangelism have all made an impact on the religious environment of the Bay Area and beyond. Slowly it is moving toward developing a theology and a Christian life style for conveying the conservative gospel to alienated and counterculture youth. The question remains, however, whether the original charisma of the group will be lost once the social atmosphere of the streets of San Francisco in the early 1970s is finally gone. Will the group survive the ordeal of institutionalization, and, if so, will its mission and identity be changed? For the present, we wonder, we're asking, we don't know.

government, the American churches have for many years spoken out strongly on critical political questions. Political activity has differed, however, for the liberal and conservative churches. The liberals have moved freely into the political realm to lobby directly for decisions they considered morally significant. Usually, these were reform movements, such as the abolition of slavery in the 1840s and opposition to the Vietnam War in the 1960s. The lower-status churches and more conservative sects have often supported conservative political views. These groups have supported Prohibition, sought to suppress scientific teachings that conflict with Scripture, and strongly opposed communism and "un-Americanism," to cite a few examples. As might be expected, the political activity of churches frequently reflects the social class of their members.

Voluntarism has also affected the internal politics of the churches. In societies with a state church, the religious institution tends to be hierarchically organized and governs itself through ecclesiastical officials alone. The ordained priesthood normally shares little decision-making power with the laity. From the time of the Puritans, however, American religious institutions have had the laity deeply involved in the formal decision-making process. Because the members at large control the purse strings, they can influence church policies and activities.

No doubt American religion provides ample evidence of saints and sinners, moral earnestness and hypocrisy, good faith and bad. On balance, however, it would be difficult to find another society where religion as a social institution is so widely regarded as a good thing

**FIGURE 13.3  Selected characteristics of respondents reporting degrees of confidence in organized religion: 1975–1976**

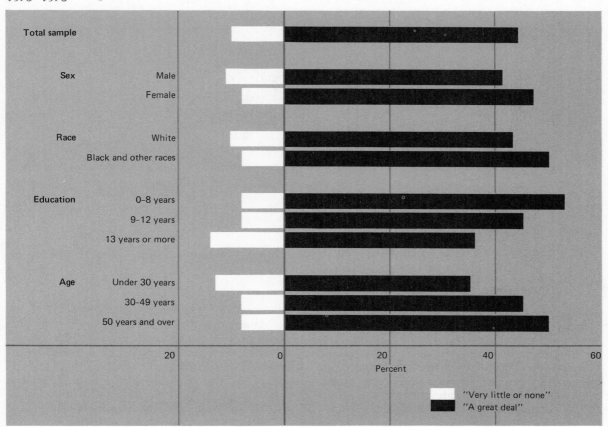

FIGURE 13.4    Importance of religious beliefs, by selected characteristics of respondents: 1975–1976

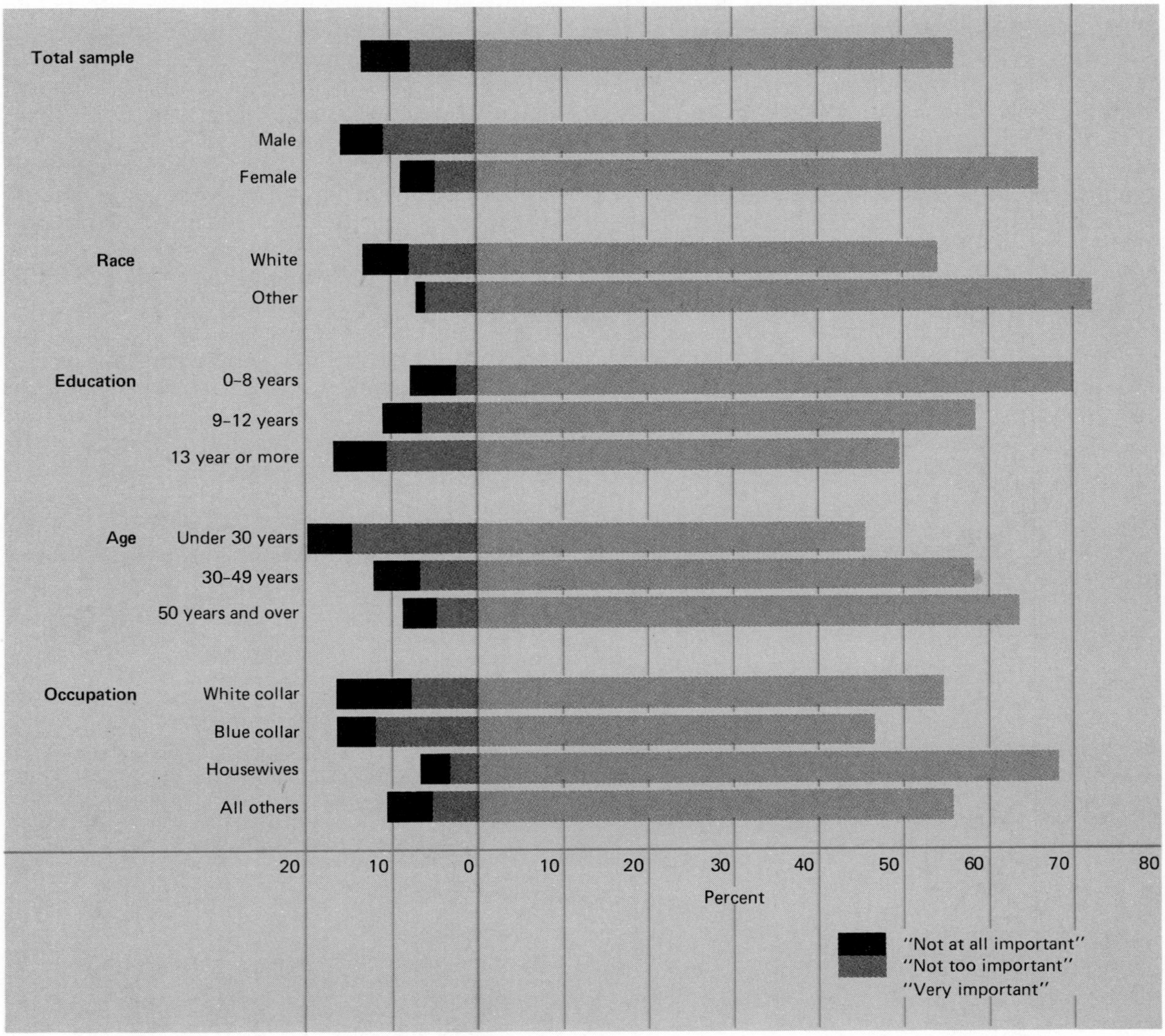

and where personal religiosity is so much a part of the life style of the people (see Figures 13.3 and 13.4). Certainly no other industrialized country approximates the level of commitment to or emphasizes the importance of religion as much as the United States (see Figure 13.2). If commitment and support are any measure of the strength and vitality of a social institution, then religion must be judged one of the more stable institutions in American society.

## Recent Trends

All social institutions confront pressures of social change and adapt to modifications that occur in the other institutions around them. American religion is no exception. Some recent trends can be identified: (1) increasing secularization and the emergence of a "post-Christian age," (2) further disputes over the meaning of church and state separation, and (3) the resurgence of evangelicalism and charismatic movements.

## Secularization and the Post-Christian Age

In the 1960s a group of theologians and social scientists reported that belief in the supernatural was declining at a rapid pace in the modern world. The great Judeo-Christian cultural era was drawing to a close because people no longer required the overarching religious symbols that once helped produce harmonious social life. The issue is far from simple and far from being sociologically confirmed.

Part of the problem is the fact that seculariza-

tion has no universal definition. If religion is the search for ultimate meaning, we would have to agree there is a great deal of religious activity in our society today.

We know that during the 1960s, church attendance declined somewhat, there was a decline in doctrinal orthodoxy, interfaith marriages increased in number, financial support of churches declined, and there was a general relaxation of moral codes—especially with regard to sexual behavior. Some of these changes proved to be slight setbacks from which the churches promptly rebounded. Seminaries are now enjoying higher enrollments, attendance and contributions in churches are up, and people generally believe religion is gaining in influence (see Figure 13.5); but other indicators such as moral codes and belief changes are still evident. In short, the evidence is mixed with respect to secularization.

The 1970s have witnessed a resurgence of supernaturalism. Occultism, spiritualism, and the "Jesus movement" sprang into existence among young, educated, middle-class groups—the very people alleged to be the avant-garde of encroaching secularization. A Gallup poll in 1976 counted 32 million believers in astrology alone.[38] If secularization is an empirical fact, it should undercut belief in the occult as well as religion. Whether supernaturalism in its various manifestations will persist very long, we cannot tell. But the evidence does raise questions about American loss of belief in the supernatural.

**Separation of Church and State** Although American society permanently institutionalized the separation of church and state in the Constitution, it is becoming clear that the two institutions are interrelated in a number of subtle ways. For example, the churches in America, like certain other institutions, enjoy tax-free status. Critics both within and without the churches charge that tax exemption constitutes informal state support and therefore violates the principle of separation. The tax revolt signaled by California's Proposition 13 has added new fuel to the fire as taxpayers look for new ways to generate revenue without raising personal taxes.

A related issue concerns the question of federal, state, and local financial aid to parochial

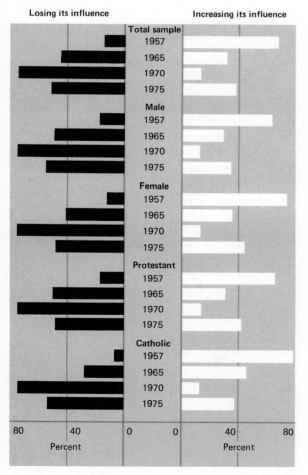

**FIGURE 13.5** Influence of religion, by selected characteristics of respondents, selected years: 1957–1975

schools. Ironically, when this issue first surfaced in the 1800s, Catholics tended to oppose the practice, while Protestants—who then had more religious schools than Catholics—largely approved the arrangement. Now the sides are very nearly reversed. Catholics, who have a sizable parochial school population, argue vigorously for state aid to religious schools, while Protestants are more likely to oppose it. The courts have so far ruled against parochial aid, but the issue does not appear likely to disappear.

Another volatile issue is the use of government funds for abortion. Liberals and representatives of the poor urge that welfare money be made available to all women who seek abortions, even if the mother's life is not in danger. Conservative Protestants and Roman Catholics vehemently oppose such payment. Politics, class interests, and religious values combine to make the issue tremendously complex and emotionally charged. This issue illustrates how difficult is the task of separating church and state.

**The Resurgence of Evangelicalism** Evangelicalism asserts a conservative or fundamentalist theology along with the immediacy of religious experience. Historically, evangelicalism has always been closely allied with revivalism. In the late 1960s and early 1970s, conservative groups suddenly experienced renewed vigor. In part, this may have been a reaction against the increasing secularity, and in part, it resulted from the recruitment of religious adherents from the ranks of the New Left and radical political groups. The most notable consequence, however, has been an increase in membership of conservative or charismatic sect groups.

Several features of the new evangelicalism are worth noting. First, many followers come from middle- and upper-middle-class backgrounds. This is a decided break from the lower-class composition of sects American society had come to regard as normal. The new evangelical movements are also different politically. Traditionally conservative religion went hand in hand with conservative politics. Now, however, many evangelicals are politically liberal and politically active.[39] And finally, pentecostal beliefs and practices—such as speaking in tongues, faith healing, frequent prayer meet-

ings, and so forth—have historically been associated with Protestantism, while the new evangelicalism has been widely successful in Roman Catholic circles.

The conservative sects—such as the Unification Church, the Children of God, and the like—along with new religious cults from the Orient including Hare Krishna and various Buddhist groups, are now the fastest-growing segment of American religion. If this pattern persists, American religion may well be entering an era of greater conservatism. Some authorities, however, think that the sects may soon lose their new converts to middle-class denominations. This would mean that the resurgence of evangelicalism will be less significant in the long run than current data indicate. Based on experience, this period of enthusiasm

Despite theological discussions of a post-Christian age, evangelicalism has experienced a sudden upswing in America, particularly among the young.

may leave the basic structure of American religion reinforced, but basically unchanged. The unusual qualities of the current pentecostal and holiness groups, however, make it difficult to predict what their long-range effects will be on American religious behavior.

## SUMMARY

Religion is a set of human activities organized around the sacred (the nonempirical source of religious power, transcendence, mystery, and awe) which creates a social institution comprised of beliefs, rituals, ethical codes, and social organization. By positing the sacred as the hallmark of religion, it is possible to distinguish religion sociologically from other social phenomena such as magic, science, and political or philosophical ideologies. Moreover, religion is a universal institution. This does not mean all people are religious, but rather that we know of no society where some form of religiosity, no matter how primitive, is lacking.

Marx conceived religion as an alienating force that merely reflected and rationalized the material inequalities produced by a capitalist economy. Research undertaken within this tradition does, in fact, reveal that religious beliefs and organizational membership follow class lines. Durkheim emphasized the integrative influence of religion. He regarded religious belief and practice as a mechanism society employs to nurture commitment to the basic moral norms contained within collective conscience. To the extent that people attach themselves to the religious community, they are really affirming their loyalty to society. In contemporary sociology, examples of this are found in the research on civil religion and the interpretation of the American way of life as a sacred belief system. Weber explored how religion establishes legitimate systems of meaning. For purely religious reasons, the major faiths define the world for their constituents, and these definitions have profound effects upon the way people behave in secular, social contexts. His classic work *The Protestant Ethic* *and the Spirit of Capitalism* showed how important is the religious creation-of-meaning function. Subsequent research in this tradition has confirmed an integral relationship between religion and culture, with the influence flowing both ways. Troeltsch's categories of church, sect, and mysticism, along with their contemporary refinements, help demonstrate that religion affects culture in a number of important ways, just as culture affects religion. Berger and Luckmann attempted to synthesize the discussion of religion's functions by describing the social construction of reality perspective. They show how religion is humanly created and maintained in both its subjective and objective aspects, meeting both individual and collective needs for meaning, order, and social explanation.

There is a widespread belief that religion is on the decline in the West. Is this true for America, and what is the sociological evidence? The pervasiveness, secularity, and voluntarism, characteristic of American religion reveal the source of that deep-rooted support Americans typically extend to religious life. Recently in the upsurge of evangelicalism, we have seen the prophets of secularism temporarily refuted in their suggestion that Americans no longer find the supernatural believable. Indeed, there are several areas where American religion is revealing new life and vitality as it moves beyond the radical events of the 1960s. How such issues as the separation of church and state and the new religious movements and secularization will be resolved, we cannot now predict. But it does appear to be a safe assumption that religion in America will remain a "lively experiment" for some time to come.

## SUGGESTED READINGS

BERGER, PETER L. *The Noise of Solemn Assemblies: Christian Commitment and the Religious Establishment in America.* Garden City, N.Y.: Doubleday, 1961. This early essay by a leading sociologist of religion is a critique of organized religion's failure to attain social relevance. In the second portion of the book, the author sketches out new responses for the church in addressing the issues of personal commitment, theological reconstruction, and the development of a vital ethical approach to the contemporary problems of modern social life.

Cox, Harvey. *The Secular City,* rev. ed. New York: Macmillan, 1967. A controversial yet landmark bestseller in the 1960s, this volume stimulated a flurry of debate over the theological meaning of secularization and the growth of urban culture. The central theme claims that the coming of secularization is a logical outcome of Biblical religion. Modern life, Cox concludes, should be celebrated by the church and critically probed for new modes of being religious.

Greeley, Andrew M. *Unsecular Man: The Persistence of Religion.* New York: Dell, 1972, 1974. Fr. Greeley, a noted sociologist and Roman Catholic priest, refutes the popular notion that religion is on the decline in modern societies—a victim of scientific, technological development. The lively thesis argued herein charges that the religious needs of humankind have not drastically changed, nor is the religious institution losing its ability to speak in a critical fashion to the questions of faith prevailing in the contemporary world.

Herberg, Will. *Protestant-Catholic-Jew,* rev. ed. Garden City, N.Y.: Doubleday, 1955, 1960. One of the most widely read interpretations of religion in America, Prof. Herberg develops the engaging thesis that the three major religious traditions in the United States—Protestantism, Catholicism, and Judaism—merely represent different ways of being American. The faith of Americans is no longer deeply committed to the distinct theologies of these three religious communities, but it is firmly fixed on the "American way of life" as the normative and underlying substance of our religiosity.

Lewis, Sinclair. *Elmer Gantry.* New York: Dell, 1927, 1954. A powerful novel about the exploits of a revivalist preacher with strong ambition and few ethical scruples. The historical figure on whom the story is based is Billy Sunday, a baseball player turned master revivalist who shocked, entertained, and converted Americans in massive numbers during the early decades of the twentieth century. Lewis depicts in graphic terms what sociologists often try to portray in more abstract language.

Needleman, Jacob, and George Baker. *Understanding the New Religions.* New York: Seabury, 1978. A wide-ranging survey of the new religious groups which have recently captured public attention by many leading authorities on American religious life. The articles are divided between descriptions of the new religious groups and interpretations of their social meaning and long-term importance for American society.

# Chapter 14
# Politics

This book was published during a national election year. The American people, through a process invented more than two hundred years ago and never postponed or defaulted even in the midst of civil war, were electing a president and numerous members of Congress and other offices. Indeed, although most Americans are not aware of the fact, the government of the United States is among the oldest continuously surviving governments in the world. (Only those of Great Britain and Iceland are older.)

We are all more or less aware of the immense influence that government has over our lives, and we are frequently impatient with its operations as they impinge upon our daily affairs, but even government, with its great significance for us, is just one aspect of the larger social phenomenon called *politics.* Every reader of this book, no matter how young, will have realized by this time that human life is immersed in politics, that social relations are almost by definition political, if we understand that word to mean the regulation or control of human interactions. You have no doubt heard people express the judgment that "it's all political" with reference to everything from how football seats are distributed at your college or university to the gasoline shortage or major issues of national and international policy, such as the SALT treaties or peace in the Middle East. Even family relations can sometimes be characterized as political when members bargain with one another about who is to have the car tonight, or quarrel about, and then work out rules for, the disposition of household chores.

Politics, then, is a term we encounter in a wide variety of contexts, sometimes referring to events of international importance and sometimes to local or even personal events, or activities within some organization to which we belong. These various usages raise the questions: What is politics? What does sociology have to tell us about it? How does it work? Are there commonalities in political behavior that can give us some clues to the nature of the general phenomenon?

For the sociologist, the answers to such questions involve such concepts as power and authority, political institutions, state, government, and regime. Once these terms have been defined (below), the general question of what sociology can tell us about politics can be broken down into somewhat more specific ones: What are political institutions supposed to do? What kinds of political regimes are there? How do governments and regimes change? How does the state affect other institutions of the society and how is it, in turn, affected by them? This chapter will provide some basic answers to questions of this kind.

## WHAT IS POLITICS?

In the broadest sense, **politics** involves *getting and using (or attempting to get and use) power and authority*. Power is the ability to get others to do what they would not do if left to their own devices. Max Weber defined power as: "the chance of a man or a number of men to realize their own will in a communal action even against the resistance of others who are participating in the action."[1] We have authority when others perceive our possession and use of power as right and proper. Authority is legitimated power. Governments have power to enforce the law, and muggers have the power to steal from their victims. A government also has the authority to enforce the law because it is perceived as proper that it should do so, but the mugger has only power, because his actions are perceived as illegitimate: He has no authority to steal.

### Power Resources

As we saw in Chapter 6, power comes from the possession of several kinds of resources.[2] The first, *utilitarian resources,* include goods, services, property, and income. With these we can get others to do something in exchange for a material reward. Employers have this kind of power over their workers.

*Normative resources* are social-psychological rather than material. They involve such attributes as honor, prestige, esteem, love, or acceptance. Individuals or groups with such qualities can often persuade others to do something they otherwise might not do. Persuasion involves getting others to change their intentions, not just "go along" in order to get a reward. The prestige of the office of president gives this sort of resource.

Finally, there are *coercive resources.* This involves the ability to do violence to others. An individual who possesses physical strength or weapons has such resources. A society's coercive resources include weapon stockpiles, military installations, manpower, and the police. The mugger's power depends entirely on this type of resource. Less obviously, the power of government ultimately rests on this base as well. Citizens comply with their government's orders not only because it provides them with goods and services but also because the government can force them to do so. Many citizens go to war or pay taxes only to avoid landing in prison. Under certain conditions, governments

**Politics involves getting and using, or attempting to get and use, power and authority. Victorious Sandinista troops with their leader Tomas Borjes, Nicaragua, 1979.**

exercise their power to take human life itself. Henry VIII of England had Anne Boleyn beheaded in 1536, and the state of Florida had a convicted murderer electrocuted in 1979.

## Bases of Authority

While all power is based on the possession of resources, authority is a special type of power that rests upon the belief of the members of a group that it is legitimate: Whoever is in charge *should* give directives and everyone else *should* obey. Recall (Chapter 2) Weber's three types of authority: *traditional, charismatic,* and *legal.*[3] These concepts are useful in the systematic study of political systems, past and present, although none by itself describes any actual political system. All real systems of rule involve combinations of traditional, charismatic, and legal elements.

**Traditional authority** is domination based on the belief that whatever has always existed is valid. It rests on ''an established belief in the sanctity of immemorial tradition and on the legitimacy of the statuses of those exercising authority under them.''[4] Those who live under traditional rule are subject to conventions but not to laws. Traditional rule is highly personal since obedience is owed to the person, such as a tribal chief or a king, who occupies the position of authority by virtue of inherited status and not by virtue of election or special technical qualifications.

**Charismatic authority** is rule opposed to the restrictions of routine, custom, and law. People submit because they believe in the extraordinary quality of the leader, whether this quality is real or imagined. The relationship between charismatic leaders and those who recognize their legitimacy resembles more closely the relationship between prophet and disciple than that between ruler and subject or between elected official and citizen. The relationship between Hitler and his Nazi followers is an example. Charismatic leaders are likely to arise during periods of social crisis when conventional politics fail to deal with extraordinary problems or during periods of massive collective effort. The leader establishes a claim to leadership by dealing with problems in unconventional ways that appear successful. If, however, the successes do not continue, the leader's legitimacy and rule are threatened.

> **politics:**  the attempt to secure and exercise power and authority.
>
> **traditional authority:**  rule based on tradition or the careful observation of tradition.
>
> **charismatic authority:**  rule based on the force of an individual's personality, ''personal magnetism.''
>
> **legal authority:**  rule based on the validity of a consistent set of abstract, impersonal principles.

**Legal authority** is rule based on the validity of a consistent set of abstract, impersonal principles. Such rules become established by the voluntary agreement of all concerned. The system of rules specifies the rights and obligations of those who rule and those who are ruled. The persons subject to commands obey the law itself, not the persons who implement the law. In bureaucratic organizations, for example, those in positions of authority are obeyed only so long as they themselves follow the formal rules. Richard Nixon had to resign the presidency when his contempt for the rules was discovered.

The governments of most modern nations base their claims of authority to rule on legal grounds. However, as Weber pointed out, laws can be imposed by some people or groups on others.[5] In some nations, the Soviet Union, the Philippines, Chile, South Korea, Rhodesia, and South Africa, for example, many citizens feel that their government rules in ways, and according to laws, that are neither right nor proper. Governments tend to rely on their coercive resources to achieve compliance from such citizens. When they do so, they commonly deprive them of the civil rights to which they, as citizens, are legally entitled. This has often led to their being subjected to cruelties far beyond the understanding of most of us.

## Politics in Social Relationships

All social relationships ultimately involve power and authority: A mother tells her children to go to bed, a teacher gives out homework assignments, a labor leader calls workers out on strike, a school board fires a teacher, a police officer writes out a traffic summons, a church

Traditional, charismatic, and legal authorities: Louis XIV, Ayatollah Khomeini, and President Jimmy Carter.

board increases church membership dues. All of these are using power and authority. Political sociologists, however, do not generally study personal relationships in private social settings. Their main concern is with the acquisition and use of power and authority in circumstances that affect the lives of comparatively large numbers of people in important ways. They study power and authority in complex organizations, in communities, and in nations.

## The Sociological Approach to Politics

Rather than conceiving of politics as a separate, independent part of social life, sociologists see it as influencing and being influenced by other features of the social setting in which it occurs. For example, a factory owner may be unable to get employees to work on a Sunday because of their religious beliefs. A mayor and city council may be able to complete a civic project only because it had the backing of local business leaders. Congress may be newly able to pass civil rights legislation because recent increases in the average level of education of the American public are associated with more tolerant attitudes toward minorities. In the first example, religion affected the use of power and authority; in the second, economics was important; and in the third, education played a role.

The use of power and authority on the societal or national level generally affects the lives of the largest number of people in the most significant ways. That is why many sociologists interest themselves in national politics. The structure of power and authority at the national level of social organization is called the *state*. As Weber defined it, the **state** is *the social institution that possesses the "monopoly of the legitimate use of physical force within a given territory."* The sociology of politics usually consists of the study of the reciprocal relationships between state and society, that is, the ways in which the state, as one social institution, affects and is affected by the other institutions of society: family, education, religion, and economics.

The **government** of a society is *the set of persons that, at a given time, exercises the power and authority of the state.* In our country, the most common purpose of elections is to change or retain some of the people who together make up the government. By way of contrast, a *regime*

**the state:** the social institution or organization possessing a monopoly on the legitimate use of physical force within a given territory; the highest (most inclusive) independent political unit.

**the government:** the set of persons who, at a given time, exercise the power and authority of the state.

**regime:** the principles or "rules of the game" according to which a given society's political life is conducted.

does not consist of people at all. Rather a **regime** is *the set of abstract "rules of the game" according to which the society's political life is to be conducted.* Some rules specify how the society's members should participate in influencing their government. Other rules indicate the responsibilities of the government to the society and its members. In the United States, we emphasize the rights of citizens to influence governmental policies through such activities as voting, participating in organizations concerned with public affairs, campaigning, and contacting government officials about issues and problems. The "rules of the game" tend to limit the strength of the government's control and the significance of the social and economic changes it can introduce. In certain totalitarian political systems, such as that of the Soviet Union particularly during the Stalinist era, regime rules allowed the government to transform the society but kept citizen participation at a minimum.

In focusing on the relationship between state and society, the sociology of politics is concerned with the impact of society on government somewhat more than with the impact of government on the other social institutions. This distinguishes sociologists from political scientists. Both might study the effect of a government program, such as Aid to Dependent Children, on the family, but the political sociologist would be more likely to explore the social conditions in the urban ghetto or the increasing political power of organized minorities that prompted enactment of the government program.

The sociology of politics also studies how regime norms affect and are affected by other social institutions. Here again a difference in

## THE BILL OF RIGHTS

**Amendment I**  Congress shall make no law respecting an establishment of religion or prohibiting the free exercise thereof; or abridging the freedom of speech, or of the press; of the right of the people peaceably to assemble, and to petition the Government for a redress of grievances.

**Amendment II**  A well regulated Militia, being necessary to the security of a free State, the right of the people to keep and bear Arms, shall not be infringed.

**Amendment III**  No Soldier shall, in time of peace be quartered in any house, without the consent of the Owner, nor in time of war, but in a manner to be prescribed by law.

**Amendment IV**  The right of the people to be secure in their persons, houses, papers, and effects, against unreasonable searches and seizures, shall not be violated, and no Warrants shall issue, but upon probable cause, supported by Oath or affirmation, and particularly describing the place to be searched, and the persons or things to be seized.

**Amendment V**  No person shall be held to answer for a capital, or otherwise infamous crime, unless on a presentment or indictment of a Grand Jury, except in cases arising in the land or naval forces, or in the Militia, when in actual service in time of War or public danger; nor shall any person be subject for the same offence to be twice put in jeopardy of life or limb; nor shall be compelled in any criminal case to be a witness against himself, nor be deprived of life, liberty, or property, without due process of law; nor shall private property be taken for public use, without just compensation.

**Amendment VI**  In all criminal prosecutions, the accused shall enjoy the right to a speedy and public trial, by an impartial jury of the State and district wherein the crime shall have been committed, which district shall have been previously ascertained by law, and to be informed of the nature and cause of the accusation; to be confronted with the witnesses against him; to have compulsory process for obtaining Witnesses in his favor, and to have the Assistance of Counsel for his defence.

**Amendment VII**  In Suits at common law, where the value in controversy shall exceed twenty dollars, the right of trial by jury shall be preserved, and no fact tried by a jury, shall be otherwise re-examined in any Court of the United States, than according to the rules of the common law.

**Amendment VIII**  Excessive bail shall not be required, nor excessive fines imposed, nor cruel and unusual punishments inflicted.

**Amendment IX**  The enumeration in the Constitution, of certain rights, shall not be construed to deny or disparage others retained by the people.

**Amendment X**  The powers not delegated to the United States by the Constitution, nor prohibited by it to the States, are reserved to the States respectively, or to the people.

Part of the American regime: The Bill of Rights guarantees public liberties.

emphasis distinguishes the sociology of politics from political science. Sociologists tend to interest themselves in the impact of society on regime, while the opposite is true for political scientists. American political sociologists have been centrally concerned with political democracy and the social conditions under which it is stable: "If the stability of society is a central issue for sociology as a whole, the stability of a specific institutional structure or political regime—the social conditions of democracy—is the prime concern of political sociology."[6]

Unlike both sociology and political science, political philosophy pursues explicitly norma-tive concerns: Who should govern? What are the most desirable regime norms? To what goals or ends should the state be directed? The empirical findings of sociologists concerning actual regimes and governments certainly help the political philosopher answer those questions.

## FUNCTIONS OF THE STATE

As previous chapters have pointed out, one way sociologists understand the social institutions that make up society is to see them as contributing to the solution of particular problems or sets of problems that all societies face. The political institution of society, the state, helps solve four related problems. Its four most important functions are: protection against external threat, maintenance of internal order, establishment of societal goals, and allocation of social goods and services.

### Protecting against External Threat

A society cannot survive and carry on its activities if another society invades and conquers it. Most conquerors permit the vanquished to survive (although some, like Genghis Kahn, do not); but they usually impose their own social and political order on the conquered nation, or simply divest it of its movable resources and depart. In either case, the survival of the invaded society is threatened. The only societies that can afford to ignore external threat are those that can depend on protection from another society. Mexico is a possible example.

For protection from external enemies, real, possible or imagined, most modern states have extensive coercive resources. In 1977, for example, 23.8 percent of our federal budgets went for defense; in 1968, at the height of American involvement in Vietnam, the figure was 43.3 percent. It is the responsibility of the government to maintain such resources and mobilize and direct their use when national security is threatened. The need to maintain coercive resources raises three questions for government: (1) How extensive should such resources be? (2) Under what conditions should they be used? and (3) How does meeting the need for coercive resources affect meeting other needs? In the modern world, the answers to such questions seldom are clear. In democratic nations they are often at the center of political debate.

### Maintaining Internal Order

The state maintains internal order by enforcing existing laws or enacting new ones, or through arbitrating conflict that could threaten social stability. Government has the coercive resources to ensure the routine flow of social life by forcing compliance with laws regulating force and fraud. When it does not have such a base of power, or when it fails to use it, anarchy may result. But whether or not a given situation involves illegitimate force and requires the intervention of government power is not always clear. An urban riot with extensive looting, the burning of buildings, and sniping at firemen involves threats against human life and social stability. It demands the use of police and possibly the military. Using force to break up a political rally is another matter. Differentiating between a peaceful political demonstration and a political meeting that precipitates a violent attempt to overthrow some constituted authority is a difficult matter of judgment. It depends primarily on one's own political perspectives and assessment of how one will be personally affected by the situation. Too rapid a decision to resort to force can have tragic consequences, as the killings at Kent State and Jackson State Universities in the early 1970s illustrate. Such use of force by the government can threaten rather than preserve internal order to the extent that it is seen as illegitimate by large segments of society. Such situations can seriously erode the normative resources of a government.

Fraud is a means of using deceit rather than force to get others to do what they would not ordinarily do. Though it is more subtle than force, its unregulated use would certainly be socially disruptive. The need for government to regulate fraud most commonly arises (1) with the development and widespread use of new technology, (2) when essential material resources become scarce, and (3) when demands for new social values appear.

Large corporations and the state itself are the major developers and users of new technologies. For example, government-sponsored projects led to the harnessing of atomic power, and private companies developed many of its commercial applications. Both government and private industry seek to promote the use of atomic power because of the increasing cost and unreliability of our sources of foreign and domestic petrochemicals. Both government and private industry have an interest in the public's belief in the safety of atomic power technology. While deliberate deceit may or may not be involved, many well-documented studies indicate that government and industry representations of the hazards of atomic power plants have been, at best, grossly understated. Consumer groups and environmentalists articulate the demand for protection from threats to health in the age of atomic technology. It is difficult to control

An important part of the state's function in maintaining internal order is the arbitration of conflict. In this case, members of the President's Commission on Three Mile Island investigating the cause of the accident at the crippled nuclear power plant, 1979.

giant industries with their massive public relations programs involving, or appearing to involve, fraud. It is ironic that government regulatory agencies may require close scrutiny to insure that they are not tools of private corporate interests on the one hand, or of a particular government on the other. To the extent that either of these occurs and is widely recognized, the normative resources of a government are diminished and internal order is that much less secure.

In addition to regulating force and fraud, the state must arbitrate conflicts among members of society, not merely repress them. The word conflict often suggests physical violence; but values can also be in conflict, and individuals, groups, or organizations with different values may also conflict. For example, the enrollment of James Meredith as the first black student at the University of Mississippi in 1962 involved both physical and value conflict. In the debate about the proper use of national forests and other government-owned land in the western states, three groups—conservationists, lumber interests, and stock raisers—all have aims that they regard as legitimate. All the aims are legal but contradictory. In such a case, the government must arbitrate because it is the only authority capable of doing so. Sometimes it simply provides time for a new value to become widely legitimated, as in the Meredith instance.

(Federal troops are no longer needed to enroll black students in universities.) Sometimes the government may seek to accelerate social change by making sure it does not bring about destructive consequences. This is often attempted through regulatory legislation.

In its important role as controller of social change through arbitration of conflict, the state may choose any one or more of four responses. First, it may *repress* change to avoid conflict, although this tactic, if prolonged, can bring about either social stagnation or revolution. In Czarist Russia, for example, both occurred. Second, the state can *arbitrate* and *guide* change in such a way that conflict is avoided. Once the Communist regime had been thoroughly established in the People's Republic of China, traditional Chinese social life was radically transformed without great bloodshed or traumatic upheaval. Third, government may *repress* conflict in order to avoid the social change that often accompanies it. The Nixon administration attempted this tactic to stop the antiwar movement of the late 1960s and early 1970s. This response is often unsuccessful, however, as it was in that instance. The American public's changing attitudes toward American involvement in the internal affairs of other countries clearly were affected by the unpopular distant war against an "enemy" who posed no obvious threat to American security. The repression of

**400**

dissent may only have hastened and hardened the change. Fourth, government can *arbitrate social conflict* to bring about guided change. The responses of the Kennedy and Johnson administrations to the civil rights movement are examples in point.

### Establishing Societal Goals

All groups, at various times, set and pursue collective goals. For example, a family seeks a new home, a union strikes for better working conditions, a school board floats a bond issue to buy expensive capital equipment, and a university alumni association devotes itself to recruiting a winning football team for their school. In each case, a decision is made for the group as a whole. In each of these decisions, the interests of various group members probably are taken into account, and each decision is likely to have some effect on all group members.

It is the responsibility of the state, and therefore of those who govern, to set and pursue collective goals for society. Only the state has the authority and the power to do so. Regime norms specify the areas of social life that the decisions of government may affect, how the interests of diverse social groups must be taken into account, and the degree to which government decisions can influence individual lives. For example, the governments of both the United States and the Soviet Union must establish and pursue collective goals for their societies, but in general, Soviet government may affect more areas of social life in more significant ways, while taking into account the interests of fewer social groups, than may the government of the United States.

To what extent do the decisions of American government concerning collective goals actually take into account the interests of the diverse groups that make up American society? According to C. Wright Mills, such interests generally get ignored.[7] Insofar as national events are decided, only those who have access to the command of major organizations, in particular the military, large corporations, and the government, have interests that are systematically taken into account. Whether or not this is as true today as it was in the 1950s when Mills wrote his book, the question continues to demand serious attention. In the United States,

however, regime norms do limit the extent to which any particular government can ignore public wants. In this respect politics in the United States and in the Soviet Union differ significantly.

### Allocating Goods and Services

In Western democratic nations, the state directly distributes from one-fifth to one-third of the gross national product and indirectly affects the remainder. This figure is even higher in totalitarian nations.[8] Recognizing how important this state function is, Harold Lasswell defines politics as dealing with "who gets what, when and how," and David Easton defines it as involving "authoritative allocation of values."

All societies need goods and services, such as schools, roads, transportation, health and sanitation facilities, economic security in old age, and so on. Nations vary in the degree to which meeting such needs is considered the legitimate task of government. Nations also differ with respect to how much support the state may require in taxes and other levies and services, such as labor on public works projects or in public agencies. The more extensive the goods and services provided by government and the greater the amount of support it demands, the larger the proportion of the nation's gross national product the government will administer. For the past several decades in the United States, the public sector of the economy has increased in size and importance. Whether this increase will continue or whether there will be a genuine widespread, significant taxpayers' revolt is a political question yet to be answered.

Many nations have comparable proportions of their gross national product administered by government, but they differ as to the particular goods and services for which the state takes responsibility. For example, Canada places a higher priority on health care than does the United States. Within any nation, groups often differ over the proportion of the public budget that should be assigned to different areas, such as transportation, health services, housing, protection, education, environment conservation, and so on. For example, Social Security programs are most preferred among lower-income groups while public works projects receive widest support among middle- and upper-income groups.

While all governments allocate goods and services, some invest primarily in present consumption and others invest primarily for future consumption. The former pattern prevails in most Western industrial democracies, while the latter is more common in nations with so-called planned economies, such as the Soviet Union and the developing nations of Asia, Africa, and Latin America.

## TYPES OF POLITICAL REGIMES

Our classifications of political regimes originated in ancient Greek social philosophy. Reflecting on the features of the Greek city-state, Aristotle made a basic distinction between **oligarchy** (rule by a few) and *democracy* (rule by a majority of citizens). He was critical of both political forms on the ground that neither was just. In Aristotle's view, oligarchy was a distortion of aristocracy (rule by the most capable members of society, for the common good). Oligarchy gave control to the property-owning minority who ruled in order to promote their own interests. Democracy was a distorted form of rule of the *polis* (rule by the most capable, in ways that rewarded citizens according to their contributions to the well-being of the community). Democracy, he believed, gave power and authority to the majority, who were not necessarily capable, and frequently violated the rights of the property-holding minority.

Although there are no "pure democracies" in the world today, several shared features characterize the regimes of nations such as Canada, the United Kingdom, New Zealand, Australia, France, Japan, the Scandanavian nations, Israel, and the United States—nations that are commonly regarded as democratic. Pure oligarchies—least in the form that Aristotle visualized—are also rare. In the twentieth century there have been tyrannical regimes such as those Aristotle condemned. Two obvious examples were Germany under Hitler and the Soviet Union under Stalin. These regimes, however, are not referred to as oligarchic but as *totalitarian*—a form of rule new to social history, since several of its traits rest on the use of modern technologies. The terms democracy and totalitarianism are not applicable to all regimes found in the world today, but they are useful for understanding the regimes of the most powerful nations of the modern world.

### Democracy

Edward Shils identified three qualities of political **democracy**[9]—civilian rule, representative institutions, and public liberties.

Democracy involves *civilian rule* in at least two senses. First, all citizens have the right to seek and hold political office. They have the right to participate in political life through activities such as voting, belonging to political organizations and interest groups, and contacting political officials. Such rights are the privilege of everyone, not just of an aristocratic elite or a professional class of civil servants. Second, political decisions have to be justified publicly. That is, democratic rule is based on the consent of the governed, not on the use of force or the threat of force, such as rule by the police or military.

Democracy involves *representative institutions*, that is, authority to govern is derived from election by citizens. In complex societies, democracy is expressed in the competitive struggle between officeholders or would-be officeholders. Each must seek, find, and maintain support by at least appearing to represent their constituents' interests. Thus the decisions they make and the policies they espouse must take into account citizen preferences.

Democracy involves the maintenance of *public liberties* in the sense that each citizen has certain rights, such as the rights of free communication and free assembly, which the state must respect. The state has limited authority based on uncoerced agreements. Violence, intimidation, and fraud are barred in principle, and the rights of minorities are guaranteed in principle. Only on occasions when there are genuine threats to external or internal security, as in the case of war or impending revolution, can such rights be suspended, and then only temporarily. Even under these extreme conditions, such action by the state is likely to meet significant opposition.

Related to political democracy is *social democracy*. A democratic society is one whose dominant culture and social structure directly or indirectly support democratic political processes.[10] The most widely known analysis of the relationship between state and society in America was written almost a century and a half ago (1835) by the French scholar Alexis de Tocqueville.[11] In his *Democracy in America*, de Tocqueville argued that the democratic regime was maintained not only by its constitutional structure, but also by the absence of a large military establishment, a prosperous economy, and the mores, customs, and religious beliefs of Americans.

## Totalitarianism

The most basic feature of **totalitarian** rule is suggested by the word *total*. Under totalitarianism, all social institutions are controlled by the state. This includes the economy, education, religion, and even the family. The state itself is run by a single political party. Since the state or party dominates all dimensions of social life, it totally dominates the life of the individual as well: work is assigned by, or must be acceptable to, the party; education involves the acquisition of knowledge, skills, and attitudes useful to the state; religion is ultimately loyalty to the state; and family life centers on state-supporting activities.

Carl J. Friedrich and Zbigniew K. Brzezinski distinguished six interrelated features of political totalitarianism: (1) Elaborate ideology. This is the official doctrine that specifies how members of the society are expected to live their lives. It is based upon a radical rejection of the existing society and promotes the development of a new idealized social order. (2) A single political party. Usually this includes less than 10 percent of the total population. The party, which typically is very well organized, vigorously promotes acceptance of the ideology. It is generally led by one individual, the dictator, and is either superior to, or completely intertwined with, the government bureaucracy. (3) A widespread system of terror carried out by the party and a secret police such as the gestapo or the K.G.B. The terror is directed not only against internal and external enemies of the regime, but also against more or less arbitrarily selected classes of the population. The forms of physical and psychological terror make use of modern science, particularly psychology. (4) Government and party control of all the means of mass communication, such as press, radio, and motion pictures. This control is historically

> **oligarchy:** the monopolization of power by a small group.
>
> **democracy:** the form of political regime characterized by civilian rule, representative institutions, and public liberties.
>
> **totalitarian:** the form of political regime in which all institutions of the society are controlled by the state.

unique because of its technological sophistication and complexity. (5) Technologically conditioned and virtually complete control over the military. (6) State control of the entire economy.[12]

**Communism and Fascism** Totalitarianism has taken two forms in the modern world—communism and fascism. *Communism* obviously has meant different things to different people in different places and at different times. In the developing nations it has often been associated with revolt against colonial rule. To the workers of some western European nations, such as France and Italy, it has meant defense of lower-class interests. To many of America's political conservatives it has meant an international conspiracy set on world domination. To the citizens of socialist countries, the term connotes a meaningful goal their society is striving to attain.[13]

Nazi Germany represented a completely totalitarian state.

Today the Communist parties in the Soviet Union, western Europe, eastern Europe, and China have very different ideas about the details of Communist rule. Many of these differences stem from variations in the historical, political, social, and cultural contexts to which the principles of communist rule had to be adapted. Karl Marx, whose writings provided many of the basic ideas, was concerned with the suffering of the working class in early industrial Britain and western Europe. But since both Russia and China had overwhelmingly peasant populations and low levels of industrial development, and still were able to develop communist regimes, we may assume that Marxist principles are capable of a great range of interpretation and application.

Despite this diversity, the term **communism** can be defined as a *political system in which the chief instruments of economic production, distribution, and exchange are common rather than private property.* In principle, the ultimate responsibility of those who legislate the economic affairs of the community is to the citizens of the nation.

According to doctrine, communist regimes are pitted against capitalism and against the bourgeois-democratic regimes that support it. Capitalism is conceived as a system of production whose object is the profit of a small property-owning class rather than meeting the needs of the majority. Also according to communist doctrine, the so-called political freedoms of capitalist workers are, in reality, nothing more than the right to be exploited, the inevitable consequence of a political-economic system based on principles of unregulated, private enterprise, free competition, and freedom of contract.

Fascism arose in Europe during the 1920s and 1930s. The term *fascism* is used primarily to identify the political systems by which Italy was ruled from 1922 to 1945 under the dictatorship of Benito Mussolini, and by which Nazi Germany was led by Adolf Hitler from 1933 to 1945. Defining **fascism** is as difficult as defining communism, but most fascist regimes share the following characteristics: First, they are strongly *nationalistic.* The primary functions of the state are to maintain domestic law and order (often relying on force and terror) and aggressively to support national interests in foreign affairs (often through military means). Second, fascist regimes are strongly *anti-communist.* They stand for the maintenance of private property and for

the supremacy of experts over politicians. Third, fascist regimes usually are ruled by a *single party led by a dictator.* All political parties except the fascist party are abolished. The party and its subsidiary organizations affect all aspects of society from teaching schoolchildren the slogans and ideology of the regime, to cultural and sports activities, the legal system, and even individual matters such as job advancement. Fourth, fascist regimes control all major financial, commercial, and industrial organizations in the country.

### The American Political System

The United States political structure was established to embody the basic features of political democracy and to guard against tyranny. First, it is a *constitutional system.* Democratic government requires an effective set of rules that specifically define the rights and obligations of citizens and of those who govern them. It subjects rulers to the control of the ruled and imposes what Weber termed a system of rational-legal domination. In a constitutional system there is a sharp distinction between office and incumbent. This was clear during the Watergate period when many Americans continued to respect the presidency although they had little respect for President Nixon.

The Constitution itself specifies procedures for replacing incumbents, usually in the form of periodic elections by universal adult suffrage. It specifies procedures for changing the principles of the regime, usually by modifying the Constitution itself. There are, however, limits as to how a constitution can be changed. To guarantee that civil liberties cannot be taken away, an independent judiciary protects the rights of citizens against the government. Responsible opposition is a necessary part of the political system as are a continuing commitment to the principles of free expression and association, equal access to government, and responsiveness of government to citizen demands. Thus democracy is not, strictly speaking, majority rule, since even a majority may not eliminate its civil liberties.

Second, it is a *federal system.* In theory the federal government can exercise only those powers given to it by the Constitution, whereas all other powers are reserved for the states. Of course, great bodies of law and precedent have grown up delineating the rights and powers of both the central government and the states. Legal contests between the two sets of authorities still continue. The ultimate meaning of the federal system is that power is shared between the central and state authorities.

Third, it is a *pluralistic system*. American society is socially heterogeneous and pluralistic. This great diversity makes Americans receptive to membership in groups organized on many different bases: age, sex, race, social class, geographic region, religious preference, income, occupation, and the like. Some of these groups become politicized—they focus attention and activity on political objects and political goals. This is the phenomenon of political pluralism so characteristic of American politics, the heterogeneity and competition among political groups.

To appreciate the full meaning of this political pluralism, recall the immense diversity of organized groups active in recent presidential, senatorial, and congressional election campaigns. These include, ethnic and racial groups, feminist groups, pro-choice and anti-abortion groups, conservationists and industrialists; gun-control and pro-gun groups, urban interests and farm groups, and many others.

Fourth, it is a *competitive, two-party system*. A political party is "any political group that presents at elections, and is capable of placing through elections, candidates for public office."[14] Political competition ceases to exist whenever contestants and opponents are deprived of equal rights. Competitive systems vary as to the amount of actual competition going on within them at any time. For example, an election may involve a number of candidates for public office going unopposed. At the other extreme, an election may involve a bitterly fought contest in which one political party wins by a very thin margin. Whatever the actual state of competitiveness at any time, however, there is always the *potential* for competitiveness in the system.[15]

Parties serve as instruments for democratic government when they effectively convey to authorities the demands of the public as a whole. This can occur within a competitive party system in which parties balance, to some extent, loyalty to themselves and to the state, party interest and general interest and, when in power, partisanship and impartial governing.

> **communism:** the political system in which the chief instruments of economic production, distribution, and exchange are common rather than private property.
>
> **fascism:** the European political systems of the 1920s and 30s, characterized by intense nationalism, opposition to communism and democratic practice, elitism, autocracy, and authoritarianism. Italy under Mussolini and Germany under Hitler are outstanding examples.

For all practical purposes, the American political system operates within the structure of two great political parties, the Republican party and the Democratic party, that have dominated American politics for close to a century. No law forbids the formation of new parties, and third (or fourth or fifth) parties can, sometimes with great difficulty, get on the ballot. Most of these parties are short-lived, having been formed by people who are interested in a single special issue that they feel is being ignored by both major parties.

There are only five or six other two-party systems in the world today, including those of New Zealand, Australia, Canada, and possibly Austria since 1966. In these systems, both parties must accommodate as many groups, interests, and demands as possible in order to remain competitive. This tends to minimize ideological conflict within the society. In the United States, there is rarely any intense and prolonged political conflict between "liberals" and "conservatives" in any of the common or historically specific meanings of these terms.

Fifth, the American political system is an *expanding system*. Over many decades it and its components have grown larger and more structurally complex. For example, in 1940 the federal government had 1.1 million civilian employees. By 1950 that number had increased to 2.1 million, by 1960 to 2.4 million, and by 1976 to 2.9 million.[16] Independent agencies, such as the Consumer Products Safety Commission, the Environmental Protection Agency, the Equal Employment Opportunities Commission, and the Nuclear Regulatory Commission have arisen. The vast expansion of federal welfare services is reflected in the enormous increase (even after allowing for inflation) in public expendi-

The Populist party convention in 1896 and the Democratic and Republican party conventions in 1976. Third parties do not fare well in American politics because of the requirement that the President be elected by a majority vote.

tures for social welfare, from 23.5 billion dollars in 1955, to 52.3 billion in 1960, 145.9 billion in 1970, and 331.4 billion in 1976.[17]

Part of this expansion is a response to population growth and economic growth. There are more people and more groups to serve and more social and economic transactions to regulate. Part of the growth is the result of technological change. Thirty years ago there was no need for an agency to oversee the production, use, and disposal of radioactive materials or to administer a national space program. Part of the growth is due to changes in the social and physical environment. For example, the emergence of multinational corporations like IBM, ITT, and EXXON has prompted the development of congressional subcommittees to oversee the role such organizations play in domestic politics and international affairs. Finally, and possibly most important, part of this expansion is a result of changing definitions of the legitimate tasks of government in providing for the

general welfare. Examples of relatively new demands for services to be provided by the state include protecting the physical environment, insuring racial and sexual equality in the job market, and providing economic aid to families with dependent children.

Insofar as expansion of any political system meets new or continuing social needs, the expansion can be a reflection of the working of political democracy. But political expansion always carries with it certain antidemocratic threats. Robert Michels, a European sociologist of the early part of this century[18] studied the European trade-union movement and the political parties it developed in the late nineteenth century, in particular the German Social Democratic Party. His special interest in this party stemmed from his observation of the paradox that a party committed to democratic ideals became organized in such a way that it was unresponsive to its members and gave its leaders considerable freedom to make decisions on their own. Michels believed that such processes were inevitable in all political organizations, particularly as they developed mass support and a clear-cut leadership structure. After representatives of any organization have been in office, they develop expertise and a control over the means of communication well beyond that of rank and file members. As time passes, they become increasingly free to act on their own. Their ability to devote all of their time to political tasks puts them in a strategic position. They have the "inside track" and the knowledge of whom to know and what to do in order to get things done. They can use their skills to perpetuate themselves in office. They often attempt to keep the positions which give them power and privileges by co-opting future leaders and thereby prevent free choice in the selection of leadership. They may create additional positions within the leadership ranks, increase the benefits of holding office, and simultaneously reduce their contact with the general membership of their organization. When they are successful in perpetuating themselves, the organization becomes a rigid bureaucracy, entrenched in its own operations, and no longer responsive to its membership.

Michels believed that this evolution was inevitable, and spoke of it as an "iron law." The notion does have its critics. Michels may have generalized too broadly from too limited a sample. Furthermore, there are conditions which can, and do, reduce the likelihood that an organization will develop an oligarchic structure.[19] These include a concerned and active general membership (i.e., lack of apathy), relatively little disparity between the positions of members and leaders, a climate receptive to dissent and innovation, and a network of independent associations within the organization in which members can gain information and acquire social and political skills. It is apparent, however, that the organizational developments identified by Michels do often occur. Almost any leadership group has some tendencies toward self-perpetuation.

The government of the United States now leads more than 220 million citizens. It is vast, structurally complex, and employs almost 3 million people. Michels alerts us to the antidemocratic potential inherent in this situation. Steady expansion of the state, even to meet social needs as defined by citizens, ultimately can lead to domination by an unresponsive government.

Max Weber was also deeply concerned about the antidemocratic features that social organizations developed over time. Weber warned that the efficiency and effectiveness of their operating principles led major modern organizations to become bureaucratically structured. He observed that such organizations tend to grow larger and to become increasingly interrelated. Increasingly complex problems of coordination and regulation cause expansion of the state, government becomes the biggest bureaucracy in the society, and power becomes concentrated in the hands of legally constituted political leadership. As the number and technical complexity of government decisions increase, political leaders have to rely more heavily on "experts" within the bureaucracy to deal with such matters. Concentrated social power tends to slip from recognized political leaders to anonymous bureaucratic agents. Whereas Michels feared rule by a relatively small, self-serving, and self-perpetuating government, Weber feared rule by nonelected "experts" who made political decisions on the basis of "facts" rather than on the basis of the expressed will of the people. Weber alerts us to the antidemocratic potential inherent in bureaucratic rule — even bureaucratic rule in a supposed political democracy.

## POLITICAL CHANGE

Political change involves changes of government, or change of regime, or, in some instances, change in both. In the first case, a new set of people simply take over the government. This is not to say that such a change cannot have far-reaching consequences. A new government may be dedicated to initiating major new social and economic policies. A change of regime does constitute a major social transformation. It involves altering the rules of the political game. It replaces one set of citizen rights and obligations with another and redefines the responsibilities of the government to the society and its members. For example, a nation may move from a totalitarian to a democratic regime or vice versa. A change of both government and regime is the most drastic form of political change. This is exemplified by the political consequences of successful struggles for independence by nations in which colonial regimes are replaced by rule of the local population.

Political change can be quite routine or it can involve the disruption of the total society. Democratic regimes have built-in provisions for changing both governments and regime norms. Changes of governments in the United Kingdom, for example, are remarkably orderly and nondisruptive. Whenever a British government fails to maintain the parliamentary majority's belief in its capacity to govern effectively (as shown by a vote of no confidence in the House of Commons), it is obliged either to resign or to call for new elections. In either case, a new government is formed. In the United States, change of regime norms is accomplished through constitutional amendment. A regime with provisions for its own public review and for orderly change is likely to be relatively long-lasting. The American political system seems to

Political change is more likely to take violent forms, like the Bolshevik revolution, when the government is repressive and there is little routine political participation among the public.

have institutionalized satisfactorily the possibilities for change.

In other countries political change often takes violent forms. Studies indicate that violence is most likely to occur when there is government repression and relatively little nonviolent political participation such as voting.[20] Other studies show that the way political change is likely to occur in a society is related to the particular segments of the society that seek the change.[21] When a society's skilled, highly educated members attempt to bring about political change, political action is likely to be organized and intense. Such people possess the intellectual and organizational skills to initiate and direct collective action. When political change is sought by the less skilled and less educated, efforts are likely to be spontaneous and disorganized, to involve relatively large numbers of people, but to be of low intensity. Whether organized and intense efforts at political change are on a large or small scale is dependent on the extent of mass political discontent and the strategic access of members of skilled and educated strata to the existing government.

Political change—whether routine or disruptive—always involves the actions of social groups. Sometimes the group is small, as in the case of "palace revolts," where one government forcibly replaces another with little or no involvement of the mass public. Sometimes the entire citizenry can be involved, at least in principle, as in a national election. Whatever the situation, the acts of social groups oriented toward changing the political life of their society constitute one form of *political participation*. Such acts cause political conflict and change.

### Participation in Routine Political Change

*Routine* acts of political participation are those that are encouraged (as opposed to merely permitted), although not required, within a society. One "does one's duty," one is a "good citizen." Such participation expresses belief in the legitimacy of the structure of power and authority of the society. In the United States, voting for and writing to government officials are examples. (See Table 14.1.)

Routine political participation is related to political change in two ways. First, the purpose of participating can be to bring about change—

**TABLE 14.1** Percentage Engaging in Twelve Different Acts of Political Participation[a]

| Type of political participation | Percentage |
|---|---|
| 1. Report regularly voting in presidential elections[b] | 72 |
| 2. Report always voting in local elections | 47 |
| 3. Active in at least one organization involved in community problems[c] | 32 |
| 4. Have worked with others in trying to solve some community problems | 30 |
| 5. Have attempted to persuade others to vote as they were | 28 |
| 6. Have ever actively worked for a party or candidates during an election | 26 |
| 7. Have ever contacted a local government official about some issue or problem | 20 |
| 8. Have attended at least one political meeting or rally in last three years | 19 |
| 9. Have ever contacted a state or national government official about some issue or problem | 18 |
| 10. Have ever formed a group or organization to attempt to solve some local community problem | 14 |
| 11. Have ever given money to a party or candidate during an election campaign | 13 |
| 12. Presently a member of a political club or organization | 8 |

**Number of cases:**  weighted   3,095
unweighted  2,549

[a]Note that figures in Table 14.1 do not always correspond to those in the text since they do not always refer to the same patterns of behavior. For example, in Table 14.1 it is noted that 72 percent of the American population report regularly voting in presidential elections, while in the text it is stated that about 21 percent of the American public votes rather regularly, but do not try to influence the actions of government in any other way. What this means simply is that among those who vote regularly are many who are also politically active in other ways and some for whom voting is their only political involvement.

[b]Composite variable created from reports of voting in 1960 and 1964 presidential elections. Percentage is equal to those who report they have voted in both elections.

[c]This variable is a composite index in which the proportion presented above is equal to the proportion of those in the sample who are active in at least one voluntary association that, they report, takes an active role in attempting to solve community problems. The procedure utilized was as follows: Each respondent was asked whether he was a member of fifteen types of voluntary associations. For each affirmative answer he was then asked whether he regularly attended meetings or otherwise took a leadership role in the organization. If yes, he was considered an active member. If he was an active member and if he reported that the organization regularly attempted to solve community problems, he was considered to have performed this type of political act. Membership in expressly *political* clubs or organizations was excluded from this index.

as in the case of voting for a minority party. Second, by using existing mechanisms for change, such processes are reinforced. This occurs, for example, even in the case of voting for a "write-in" candidate or a "third party" candidate.

A study by Sidney Verba and Norman Nie found that the American public is not divided simply into more or less politically active citizens.[22] Many types of participants engage in different acts with different motives and different consequences. Political acts differ in how much influence they exert on members of government and in how much information they convey; they differ as to whether the activity is likely to bring the individual into open conflict with others, whether the outcome of the activity has individual or collective consequences, and with respect to the amount of initiative they require, that is, how much they demand of one's time, resources, and skills. There are several distinctive modes of participation:

Routine political participation reinforces the social mechanisms permitting it.

1. *Voting:* About 21 percent of the American public votes rather regularly, but do not try to influence the actions of government in any other way. Voting involves high pressure on political figures but it conveys little information; it may involve the individual in conflict with others who support different parties or candidates; it has collective results; and it requires little initiative.
2. *Citizen-initiated contacts:* About 4 percent of the population makes contact with political officials on matters which the citizens themselves define as important. These people vote in elections but do not engage in communal or campaign activity. Contacting members of government involves low to high pressure (depending on the resources of the person doing the contacting), conveys considerable information, does not usually involve the individual in conflict, has individual results, and requires some to considerable initiative.
3. *Campaign activity:* About 15 percent of the population are active partisans in political campaigns but engage in almost no community activity. Campaigning involves high to low pressure and information; it involves the individual in conflict, has collective results, and requires some initiative.
4. *Cooperative participation:* About 20 percent of the population is willing to be quite active in community affairs while staying out of the relatively conflicting realm of campaigning. This type of participation involves low pressure but conveys considerable information; it does not involve the individual in conflict; it has both collective and personal outcomes; and it requires considerable initiative.

In addition, 22 percent of the population initiates no political activity of any kind and, at the other extreme, 11 percent are "complete activists" who participate in all types of activity with great frequency. There are a number of ways to interpret these statistics. Twenty-two percent clearly is a significant proportion of the American population. Their lack of involvement may indicate their general satisfaction with the political and economic system, or conversely, it might be a symptom of alienation or withdrawal.

In any event, we know that politically inactive people come disproportionately from lower-social status groups while the upper-status groups are vastly overrepresented among the complete activists. As Verba and Nie point out:

Equal rights to participate are just that—*rights* not obligations. Some may take advantage of the rights, others may not. The result is that participation is

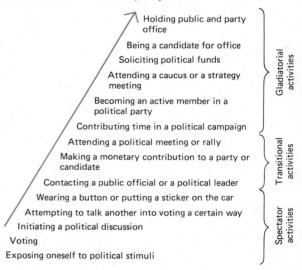

FIGURE 14.1   Hierarchy of political involvement

Holding public and party office
Being a candidate for office
Soliciting political funds
Attending a caucus or a strategy meeting
Becoming an active member in a political party
Contributing time in a political campaign

*Gladiatorial activities*

Attending a political meeting or rally
Making a monetary contribution to a party or candidate
Contacting a public official or a political leader

*Transitional activities*

Wearing a button or putting a sticker on the car
Attempting to talk another into voting a certain way
Initiating a political discussion
Voting
Exposing oneself to political stimuli

*Spectator activities*

unequally distributed throughout the society because the qualities that lead some to choose to participate—motives, skills, resources—are not equally distributed.[23]

While political participation is the source of political change, the consequences of participation depend on who takes advantage of it (see Figure 14.1).

## Participation in Disruptive Change

The likelihood, extent, and duration of nonroutine political activity in a society, as well as the outcome of such activity, is influenced by the resources possessed by those who would challenge the government and by the government itself.

According to Seymour M. Lipset, two of the most important resources a government can possess in conflict situations are *legitimacy* and *effectiveness*.[24] Effective and legitimate political systems, such as those of the United States, Sweden, and Great Britain, tend to be stable. Ineffective and illegitimate regimes, like those of Hungary and East Germany in the late 1950s, are by definition unstable and break down unless they are dictatorships maintaining themselves by force. In the short range, effective but illegitimate regimes, such as those of well-governed colonies, are more unstable than regimes that are relatively low in effectiveness and high in legitimacy, such as the governments of various Western democracies in the 1930s. However, prolonged effectiveness over a number of generations may give legitimacy to any government or regime.

There is some question about how, and to what extent, legitimacy and effectiveness are associated with disruptive political change. For example, Lipset shows that political stability depends more on legitimacy than on the satisfactory allocation of goods and services. A study of riots, strikes and demonstrations in Latin America, however, revealed that these break out just as frequently in highly legitimate political systems as in those with little legitimacy.[25] A review of data from 114 nations revealed that, although the legitimacy of a regime or a government does not reduce the likelihood of attempts at disruptive political change in response to some deprivation for which the political system is held responsible, lack of legitimacy can motivate citizens to collective violence.[26] Whatever the precise character of the relationship, legitimacy and the ability to satisfy social wants appear to reduce the likelihood of disruptive politics in a society.

When nonviolent means for expressing hostility are available, there is less likelihood of disruptive political change. If citizens have the opportunity to do such things as vote for extremist parties or participate in millenarian (evangelical or pentecostal) religious movements, they are less likely to participate in nonroutine politics.

Closely related is the manipulative ability of government. This includes the ability to persuade the dissatisfied to use routine political means in pursuit of their goals, or to accept limited concessions rather than pursue broader and more extensive goals, or to displace their aggression against minority groups or against other nations. It has been argued that America's so-called welfare state is really an attempt to "cool out" the poor and minimize the potential political danger they pose.[27]

Finally, one of the most important resources available to government in times of stress is its *coercive potential*—the size of the police and military forces it can use, taking into account the loyalty of these forces to government and regime. If such forces are used, they must be used fully enough to deter aggression and not used in so limited a way that their employment simply becomes another source of frustration for the politically dissatisfied. For example, using police and military force at civil rights and antiwar demonstrations in the late 1960s seemed to intensify activists' efforts at political change.

Groups which seek political change through nonroutine means are more likely to take action if they have these resources: a high level of motivation, widespread support, protection from the retribution of government, and the ability to inflict great costs and violence on authorities.

People are likely to be highly motivated if they feel that their government or regime has deprived them of important rights. While widespread, high levels of motivation may be essential for radical or disruptive political action, it is not essential for *reform*. For example, Michael Lewis pointed out in the case of the American Civil Rights Movement:

> Neither the N.A.A.C.P., nor the Urban League has ever fired the loyalties of the rank and file. Court tests, behind the scenes negotiations, and educational efforts are not the kind of activities which evoke passionate commitments from those who live their lives largely outside the middle class context.[28]

Widespread support for nonroutine or disruptive political action not only increases the probability of success, but by doing so, it also increases the motivation to participate. Widespread support means that individuals are more likely to receive social reinforcement for their political attitudes and participation. Widespread support may also make the government reluctant to attempt retribution for fear of increasing the political conflict. The conditions under which disruptive political action is likely to have broad support include the existence of long-standing discontent with the social-political order and the presence of a well-organized political movement with a clear, widely appealing program for social reform. Precisely these conditions, plus the added ingredient of a charismatic leader, contributed to the Nazi success in Germany.[29]

A variety of factors affect a government's ability to strike out against those attempting disruptive political change. First, there are general cultural factors, such as the toleration of society for coercion. Most Americans probably react with some horror to the sight of political

Mass arrest of antiwar demonstrators, May, 1971. Widespread support for disruptive political action increases the probability of its success and the motivation to participate. The American antiwar movement helped bring about the end of the Vietnam War.

demonstrators being physically attacked by baton-swinging police. Such a sight would be unlikely to evoke such a reaction in Japan, Turkey, or Argentina. A second factor is the attitudes of the authorities themselves. Some may be sympathetic to the demands of the discontented. Finally, as noted above, there are the related factors of the loyalty of the government's forces on the one hand and the number and motivation of the challenger's forces on the other.

Clearly in situations where a society has little historical experience with coercion, where the authorities are divided in their loyalties, and where the people who want vast changes are numerous and highly motivated, the likelihood of government retribution is small. Similarly, such factors increase the ability of those who seek political change through disruptive action to inflict costs on government.

## STATE AND SOCIETY IN AMERICA

The sociology of politics investigates the mutual influence of politics and the other institutions of society. Politics affects family, religion, education, and the economy in almost countless ways. Laws, regulations, and programs initiated by government are felt in every sphere of social life. For example, the family can be affected by laws governing marriage, adoption, abortion, and divorce, by programs of aid to dependent children, and by the social security system. Religion is legally limited in certain ways (especially in public schools), yet in others it is promoted by the state ("In God we trust" is stamped on our coins, the pledge of allegiance emphasizes that we are "one nation under God," and religious organizations enjoy special tax benefits). Formal education to a certain age is required by law, and the American public supports one of the world's most extensive educational systems. Government directly influences the economy through wage and price controls, monetary policy, regulation of interest rates, and as a major employer, producer, and consumer. These are but a very few examples of the bearing of the state on American society. While much of this is relatively well known, the other side of the coin—how society affects politics in America—probably is less obvious.

### The Family and Politics

In the family, people acquire the beliefs, values, norms, feelings, motives, and identities that are likely to influence the pattern of their participation in politics. Several factors contribute to the importance of the family as an agent of this type of learning, termed *political socialization*.[30] The family is a social group in which there is a considerable amount of interaction and to which generally there is deep emotional attachment. It is everyone's first agent of socialization. During the initial period of an individual's physical, intellectual, and moral development the family has virtually exclusive control. For a long period it is the sole source to which one can turn for the satisfaction of basic needs. People identify with, act, and think like those who regularly satisfy their needs. The family is hierarchically structured and serves as the first setting in which individuals observe and participate in the process of group decision making. Finally, through the family, individuals acquire many of their politically relevant social identities, such as religion and ethnicity.

A number of factors determine how much influence the family will have on the ways an individual plays adult political roles. These include (1) the relative attractiveness of the family to the child (particularly in relation to school and peer group), (2) the extent to which the parents agree with each other on politics, (3) the cohesiveness of the family, and (4) the interest the parents have in politics.

The more attractive a group is to us, the more likely we are to adopt its norms. For example, a young person can have parents who are staunch Republicans and good friends who are equally staunch Democrats. In a situation where a choice must be made, all things being equal, the individual will chose the norms of the more attractive group. Most political situations do not involve forced choices, however. In voting, for example, we can avoid making a choice by withdrawing from the situation. We can consciously choose not to vote, "forget" to vote, or fail to vote because of lost interest. This so-called withdrawal effect is a common reaction to such a decision-making situation. The person with Republican parents and Democratic friends is not likely to have strong partisan feelings or to maintain a high level of interest in politics. Such a person is not likely to be politically active.

Children also face conflicting norms if their parents disagree politically. In general, family influence tends to be stronger when members' viewpoints are homogeneous. Individuals whose parents support opposing political parties are less likely to have a strong party preference than are those whose parents both support the same party. In turn, weak party identification tends to be negatively associated with political participation.

The more cohesive a family is, the more likely it is that its young members will adopt the political views and identities of the parents. The higher the rate of interaction and the stronger the emotional ties between parent and child, the more likely is the child to adopt the party preference of the parents—assuming they have such a shared preference. While one is not born a Republican or a Democrat in the same sense in which one is born a Catholic or a Protestant, in cohesive families the situations are not very dissimilar.

Politically involved persons tend to be the products of politically interested families. Children reared in families where parents are interested in politics, discuss politics, and participate in political activities are more likely to develop a sense of being politically effective than children from less politically interested families. For adults, a feeling that one can have an impact on political affairs through one's own action encourages participation.

### Religion and Politics

In the United States, despite the importance of the separation of church and state, politics has a religious dimension.[31] There are, according to Robert Bellah, certain decidedly religious views that are neither sectarian nor in any sense Christian that the majority of Americans share. These have played an important role in the development of American politics. This public religion is expressed in a set of beliefs (Americans are the chosen people), symbols (the Statue of Liberty), and solemn rituals (the inauguration of the president), and has its own prophets (Washington and Jefferson), martyrs (Lincoln and Kennedy), sacred events (Memorial Day), sacred places (Arlington National Cemetery), and sacred scriptures (the Declaration of Independence and the Constitution). Bellah calls this the American civil religion (see Chapter 13). It has served, among other things (1) to reaffirm the legitimacy of the highest political authority, (2) to provide a basis for a national self-understanding, (3) to provide symbols of national solidarity, and (4) to mobilize deep levels of personal motivation for the attainment of national goals. It is often confused with Christianity by many Americans.

The family is an agent of political socialization.

Bellah argues that events such as the antislavery movement of the nineteenth century and American rejection of socialism ever since the 1850s cannot be fully understood without reference to religious motives. He also contends that the present threat of political control by unresponsive bureaucracies is, in part, to be accounted for in terms of the displacement of a religious national self-understanding by calculating reason. Such reason treats political issues as exclusively technical problems to be dealt with by experts rather than as indicators that national priorities and ultimate goals need public consideration.

### Education and Politics

While there is some subcultural variation, particularly among the very poor, among blacks, and Chicanos, family and school have tended to give even very young children a strong sense of national loyalty. Schools reinforce this with the recitation of the pledge of allegiance, the singing of patriotic songs, the celebration of national holidays, and so on.

Most American children begin early to idealize established political authority. By the time they are seven or eight years old, they become aware that there is an authority outside the family that demands some support, obedience, and respect. At first, children conceptualize this authority in terms of concrete persons such as the president and the police officer. Such figures are usually viewed as trustworthy, benevolent, and helpful. Later, as children develop the capacity to deal with less easily understood structures such as Congress and the Supreme Court, and with abstract concepts, such as government, they transfer to them some of the positive qualities they previously attributed to individual persons. They tend to agree with the blanket statement, "All our laws are fair," and tend to agree strongly that "What goes on in the government is all for the best."[32] As children grow older they become considerably less idealistic. Political figures seem less heroic and benevolent and some inequities in the law are understood. Nevertheless, children tend to remain less politically cynical than their parents—however cynical that happens to be. In fact, the widespread adult political cynicism and distrust does not seem to develop before eighth grade.[33]

Functionalists argue that these early attitudes are important because they enable the government and regime to persist despite a variety of stresses and strains. Deep-rooted attachment to the political regime established in childhood can provide support for a political system during times of crisis such as war and economic depression. More generally, trust, confidence, and affection are always needed by government and regime to assure that citizens will comply with the decisions of authorities, tolerate significant personal costs, such as taxes and military service, and exercise some self-restraint in making demands on their political institutions.

Family and school not only teach children "proper" attitudes concerning their country, they also teach about political roles. This can be seen by looking at children's understanding of "good citizenship." Second and third grade children make little distinction between a good person and a good citizen. Throughout elementary school, however, the concept of citizenship becomes more clearly defined and is located chiefly in the realm of the political. By eighth grade, children tend to characterize good citizenship in terms of three attributes: general interest in public affairs, participation in the electoral process, and obedience to laws—in that order of importance.[34]

A number of studies have measured the factual political information that children acquire in school. In knowledge of formal political structures, contemporary government officials, and basic political processes, the level of student information is remarkably low. For example, a recent national survey found that more than one-third of the thirteen-year-olds questioned could not identify the Senate as one of the two parts of the Congress. The survey also found that less than half of the seventeen-year-olds could name any of their congressional representatives and only 70 percent could name the governor of their own state.[35]

Political socialization in America is producing children who tend to be loyal and relatively idealistic, who define citizenship responsibilities in primarily passive terms, and who are politically uninformed. While their loyalty has not been shown to be of the "My country right or wrong" variety, it certainly does not indicate much interest in someday working to improve existing social conditions, however "improvement'' may be defined. While an idealized view of political authority does not necessarily mean accepting benevolent despotism, it does not facilitate understanding that in a political democracy the right to govern is derived from the expressed will of the people. A passive definition of "good citizenship" does nothing to encourage close scrutiny of political affairs with a view to having one's voice heard when important policies are being formulated and political decisions are being made.

### Economy and Politics

America's industrial economy helps sustain its democratic regime. While industrialization in no sense causes the development of democratic political forms, it does create conditions favorable for their growth.[36] This is suggested by the fact that the vast majority of the advanced industrialized nations have universal or virtually universal adult suffrage, organized political opposition protected by law, and the right of disadvantaged persons to organize and engage in collective action in their own behalf.

Unlike an agricultural economy, an industrial economy requires a large labor force able to read and write. Widespread literacy means that most citizens may have a better ability to understand and follow the workings of their government and to communicate their political views to each other and to authorities. It also means that they may be better able to organize to take collective political action. A high literacy rate requires the development of a system of schools, in which—in addition to the ability to read and write—other politically useful skills are learned. These include the ability to deal with abstractions, to think critically, and to communicate ideas verbally.

Industrialization also promotes *urbanization.* Concentration of workers in comparatively small areas facilitates communication and organization. In an urban setting, workers are more likely to become aware of the political interests they share and to recognize that together they possess political resources that can be used to their own advantage to influence how the state allocates goods and services.

Industrialization increases workers' productivity while it reduces the amount of time and physical effort they spend on production. It also tends to increase their wealth. In an industrial-ized economy, workers have more time, energy, and money to invest in political activity.

As a result of an advanced industrial economy, then, the United States has a low illiteracy rate, an extensive system of public education, a largely urban population, and a large and relatively prosperous middle class. In theory, at least, it has a citizenry with the skills and resources needed to keep the American political system democratic.

## DEMOCRACY AND POLITICAL POWER

Earlier in this chapter, political democracy was defined as a regime of civilian rule with representative institutions and public liberties. As useful as this definition is, it tells us nothing about how power, the central fact of politics, is actually distributed in a society with a democratic political system.

In a system of civilian rule, as in any other, some citizens have more resources and therefore more power than do others. That is, civilian rule does not produce political equality. The presence of representative institutions does not, and cannot, guarantee that the interests of all groups will be given equal consideration by those who govern. The existence of public liberties does not mean that all sections of the population will make equal use of them. Although universal public liberties may help reduce inequalities in power, they will not eliminate them.

Political democracy, then, is not equivalent to, nor can it produce, political equality. Thus the question of how much political equality any political democracy has remains an important question for research. Sociological thought is divided about how much political equality actually exists in the United States. One school, the *pluralist,* believes that power is distributed as equally as possible in the context of a modern, highly differentiated society. While not all individuals and groups have equal power, these sociologists maintain that most have some power to achieve their ends in areas of particular interest to them. The *elitists,* on the other hand, see the distribution of power, whether local or national, as anything but equal. In their view, the ability to decide important political issues is concentrated in the hands of a very few persons—the elite—who are not formally responsible to the mass public or to any sector of it whose interests are affected by their decisions.

### The Elitist Position

Elitists generally view power as participation in making social policy: Mills wrote that "Power has to do with whatever decisions men make about the arrangements under which they live . . . [and] insofar as decisions are made, the problem of who is involved in making them is the basic problem of power."[37]

Those who are reputed to participate in such decision making are those who control major social organizations in the United States. In the case of individual communities, this generally involves business leaders. In the case of the nation, it involves those who command major institutions, such as high-ranking leaders of the government and the military and the owners and executives of the largest corporations.

Floyd Hunter's study of Atlanta is the classic illustration of the elitist view with regard to the distribution of power in American communities.[38] Hunter found power concentrated in the hands of a group of leaders of the business community who interacted socially and who determined social policy informally and without publicity (see Chapter 7). The group consisted of forty industrial, commercial, financial owners, and top executives of large enterprises. There were no formal ties between this group and the city government. However, the presence of its members on policy-determining committees and their links with other powerful institutions and organizations of the community made government subservient to their interests—interests which were generally promoted by maintenance of the political-economic status quo.

Mills's *Power Elite* is undoubtedly the most widely cited study of the distribution of power in the United States. His thesis is that continuous and important social power resides with those who hold the highest decision-making positions in the nation's political, economic, and military institutions.

The unity of the power elite lies in the similarity of their social origins, education, and style of life, the criteria of admission, honor, and promotion that prevails among them, the common interests that connect their institutional areas (for example, industry and the mili-

tary) and, at times, some explicit coordination. Such sources of unity make it possible for members of the power elite to take one another's point of view and to interchange top roles. The corporation executive who was a leading war material producer and who later became Secretary of Defense, is one of Mills's prime examples. Members of the power elite "define one another as among those who count and who, accordingly, must be taken into account."[39]

According to the elitist image, at least as expressed by Mills, the American public is politically passive, disorganized, and unable to play a significant part in making public policy. It would seem that citizens would have some power through their involvement in organizations, such as labor unions, but according to Mills and others, such organizations have ceased being politically effective for their members. This is because of the enormous gap between the members and the leaders of mass associations. As soon as a person becomes a leader of an organization with significant resources, he or she is taken in by the elite and develops a self-perception as one of its members. The interests then taken into account are not the interests the leader supposedly represents, but rather the interests of the elite. The leader discusses, debates, and resolves issues with them and "sells" the products to the membership of the organization. The leader is no longer a delegate of the organization but a spokesman of the elite.

This analysis is intended to apply to political parties as well as to other mass associations. Elections are therefore viewed as contests between leaders who are not truly representative of their groups. Party leaders sell a political program to their supporters rather than work for their interests. Consequently, according to Mills, in the United States, "There is little live political struggle. Instead, there is administration from above, and a political vacuum from below."[40]

Another variety of the elitist image was developed by William Domhoff.[41] Domhoff claims that the United States has a distinctive upper class which controls or dominates its political life on the national level. His studies of the backgrounds of people in key decision-making positions in the federal government (such as cabinet members, presidential advisors, and members of the Supreme Court) and in large

**Members of the American power elite?** *(left)* **"Engine Charlie" Wilson left the presidency of General Motors Corporation in 1953 to become Secretary of Defense under President Truman while** *(right)* **Robert McNamara left the Ford Motor Company in 1960 to become Secretary of Defense under President Kennedy.**

corporations revealed that they disproportionately tended to come from a privileged class. The class is united by its members having attended exclusive schools and elite universities where they belonged to the "right" fraternities. Now they belong to exclusive clubs, visit the "right" resorts, support similar charitable and cultural organizations, and so on. According to Domhoff, the upper class exerts its influence to preserve the prevailing order of power and privilege in America not only by occupying key positions but also by making political campaign contributions, lobbying, and joining national policy-planning organizations such as the National Planning Association, the Committee for Economic Development, the Advisory Council, the Twentieth Century Fund, the Brookings Institution, and the Council on Foreign Relations.

### The Pluralist Position

Pluralists generally view power as the ability or potential of an individual or group to realize their own will in political conflict. Individuals or groups who possess the resources to impose their will on others are regarded as possessing power.

Pluralists observe that there are many power-relevant resources. These include, among other things, money and credit; control over jobs; control over the information of others; social standing; knowledge and experience; popularity, esteem, and charisma; legality and constitutionality; ethnic solidarity; and the right to vote. Such resources are not equally distributed. To the extent that they are dispersed or concentrated in the hands of a few, power is also dispersed or concentrated.

Pluralists emphasize that particular resources can have different political value in different contexts. For example, ethnic solidarity and the right to vote may be crucial in determining the outcome of a particular election but may have little bearing on the formation of economic policy. The opposite might be true for control over jobs.

Whether studying the distribution of power in an individual community or in the nation, pluralists tend to find that power-relevant resources are dispersed and that these resources have different values in different areas of political conflict. Dahl found this pattern in his study of the distribution of power in New Haven, Connecticut (see Chapter 7).[42] He also found that (1) individuals or groups best off in their access to one kind of resource are often badly off with respect to many other resources, (2) no one resource dominates all the others in all or in even most key decisions, and (3) virtually no one and certainly no group of more than a few individuals is entirely lacking in some politically relevant resources.

This does not mean that pluralists believe that political democracy and equality of power are inseparably linked. There are always inequalities in the distribution of political resources. There are always power differentials. However, pluralists do interpret the pattern of dispersed inequalities as representing a kind of political system in which, if there is not exactly equality, there is at least some approximation of it.

In addition, pluralists point out that other factors of the American political system reduce the possibility of concentrated power being used effectively by a small elite to further their own interests: (1) Competitive elections require elected officials to make some effort to support

Members of the Congressional Black Caucus talking to newsmen. That disadvantaged groups can combine resources to produce aggregate strength supports a pluralist interpretation of power.

policies desired by the electorate (in order to remain in office). (2) Disadvantaged groups can combine resources to produce aggregate strength. (3) Major social forces often shape issues in ways beyond the control of any one group, no matter how powerful it is. (4) Social norms limit the political objectives that can be pursued. (5) There are constitutional and other forms of legal constraint on power. (6) There are often counterelites pursuing individual or group interests. The powerful have to contend with each other when their interests do not coincide. At times the elite also have to contend with organized opposition, such as civil rights groups, women's groups, environmental groups, youth groups, trade associations, and other voluntary associations.

Arnold Rose's study of the distribution of power in America presents a view similar to Dahl's view of power in New Haven.[43] Rose concluded that American society is composed of many small elite groups, each exercising power in a different area of political life. Some have economic power, others use political control, and still others have military, associational, religious, and other power. Rose acknowledges that in American society many individuals have no social ties to give them any political influence. Nevertheless he maintains that the majority of the population consists of groupings of individuals who have some political information, interest, and concern, who have varying degrees of power, and who communicate their opinions to government. As a result, Rose maintains that the majority is not readily susceptible to manipulation or control by a political elite. For Rose, Dahl, and other political pluralists, political inequality is dispersed in the United States.

### Some Recent Findings

Both pluralists and elitists present considerable empirical data to support their diverse positions. Since each school uses a somewhat different set of concepts, methods, and measures, their conflicting findings may be reflections of these differences.

John Walton reviewed thirty-three studies of the distribution of power in fifty-five American communities. He found that the **reputational method** (in which informants are asked to identify the most influential people in their community, the method most often used by elitists) tended to list power structures that were monolithic, monopolistic, or in which there was a single leadership group. The **decision-making method** (in which the focus is on specific community issues and on the persons active or instrumental in their resolutions, the method most often used by pluralists) tended to identify power structures with at least two durable factions, or in which there were changing coalitions of interest usually varying with issues.[44]

Several more recent studies draw on the previous research, use some new research methods, and have produced some new findings on the distribution of power in American communities: (1) Socially integrated, heterogeneous populations have less concentrated power structures. (2) In the United States there are regional differences in the distribution of power. (3) The more industrial the community, the less concentrated its power structure. (4) Communities with a high proportion of absentee ownership tend to have less concentrated power structures. (5) It is not the power of any individual or set of individuals that best depicts the structure of power in any community, but the network of ties that exist between major community organizations. For example, the banker who also sits on the executive boards of three other community organizations will be more powerful than the banker who does not hold other executive positions. The presence of such situations and their interrelationships define the structure of community power.[45] (6) The greater the economic and social differentiation of a community, the greater the importance of organizations versus persons as significant political actors. (7) The larger and more differentiated a community, the more formal and regular the pattern of contact between power holders.[46]

> **reputational method:** the means of studying power or status that asks people to identify others as influential members of the group, community, organization, and so on.
>
> **decision-making method:** the means of studying power or status that identifies influentials by actual activity in specific decision-making cases.

Such findings suggest a picture of the distribution of power in American communities which is neither pluralist nor elitist in detail. They also suggest, by extrapolation, that the distribution of power in the nation as a whole cannot be described adequately in terms of either the pluralist or the elitist models. We need further research on the distribution of power. Such studies should involve data from communities of varying sizes, location, economic bases, and population characteristics. They should use measures of power that do not automatically produce findings of a particular type.

As we saw at the beginning of this chapter, power rests on the possession of resources. Since power resources are never equally distributed in any American community, some individuals or groups or organizations will have more power than others. Elitists and pluralists alike point out that in any political situation, some group will be in a better position to get what it wants than others. They disagree only about whether it is always the same group that dominates, or whether different groups dominate different issue areas. Whatever the case, there is general agreement that only a small number of people actually shape public policies.

## SUMMARY

When we speak about politics, sometimes we are talking about national or international events, sometimes about state or local events, and sometimes about activities occurring in the small groups to which we belong. Politics is concerned with *power* and *authority* in social relationships at all those levels.

Power is the ability to get others to do what they ordinarily would not do. It comes from the possession or control over a wide variety of resources such as wealth, honor, esteem, and instruments of force. Authority is legitimated power. Power is legitimated when those who are subject to its use share the belief that those who use it have the right to do so.

All social relationships at some time or

another involve politics. However, sociologists particularly interested in politics tend to focus on the uses of power and authority that affect relatively large numbers of people in important ways—such as in complex organizations, in communities, and in the nation.

The state is the social institution that has a monopoly of the legitimate use of physical force within a given territory. The government of a society is the set of people who at any given time exercises the power and authority of the state. A regime is a set of abstract rules that specify the rights and responsibilities of a society's political leaders and citizens.

The sociology of politics focuses on the relationship between state and society, particularly on how regime and government are affected by the other institutions of society— family, religion, education, and economy. Many political sociologists study how these institutions sustain a particular type of political regime— political democracy.

The state performs four major activities: (1) protecting the society against external threat; (2) maintaining internal order; (3) establishing societal goals; and (4) allocating goods and services.

While there are many different types of political regimes, those of the nations which are presently among the world's most powerful can be classified into two broad types: democracy and totalitarianism. Political democracy is a regime of civilian rule with representative institutions and public liberties. A totalitarian regime has an elaborate ideology, a single political party made up of a small proportion of the total population, a widespread system of terror, and government and party control of the media of mass communications, the military, and the economy. The two major forms of totalitarianism in the modern world are communism and fascism.

Political change in a nation involves a change of government or a change of regime, or, in some instances, a change of both. Political change can be routine or it can involve the disruption of the total society. Democratic regimes have built-in provisions both for changing government and for changing regime norms. In contrast, attempts to bring about political change in many societies are often violent affairs. Violence is most likely to occur when there is government repression and where there is little opportunity for routine political participation, such as voting. The likelihood of violence is also influenced by the particular segments of the society that seek political change.

A wide variety of laws, regulations, and government programs directly relate to the family, religion, education, and the economy. In turn, each social institution has its influence on politics. In the United States, the family and school are major agents of political socialization, religion supports the highest political authority and provides symbols of national unity, and the economy produces conditions favorable to the maintenance of political democracy.

Political democracy is not equivalent to, nor does it produce, equality of political power. There are two different schools of sociological thought about the extent to which anything resembling political equality is actually found in American communities and in the nation as a whole. The *elitists* see power as concentrated in the hands of a very few persons who are not formally responsible to the mass public. The *pluralists* see political inequalities as dispersed. Individuals or groups powerful in one area of social life generally are not the same individuals or groups powerful in other areas. The combination of the inequality of the resources possessed by various social groups and the underinvolvement of the less affluent in politics produces major inequalities in the political power of the various segments of American society.

## SUGGESTED READINGS

BALL, GEORGE W., ed. *Global Companies*. Englewood-Cliffs, N.J.: Prentice-Hall, 1975. A short paperback containing excellent essays on the promises and threats international corporations present to the political economies of all nations.

GREENSTEIN, FRED I. *Children and Politics*. New Haven, Conn.: Yale University Press, 1965. A classic study of political socialization, richly illustrated with interviews with children ages nine through thirteen. It deals with such questions as: What political ideas are held by children? From whom do their ideas come, and do they vary between boys and girls, between upper and lower socioeconomic classes?

MILLS, C. WRIGHT. *The Power Elite.* New York: Oxford, 1956. Possibly the most widely read study of power in America ever written. Mills's thesis is that there are three major areas of power in American society: economic, political, and military. Within each of these areas a small elite exercises effective power. These three elites, taken together constitute the national power elite who makes the decisions having national and international importance.

*Newsweek* editors. "Big Government." *Newsweek,* December 15, 1975, pp. 34–46. The article raises the question of why there have been continuing and growing complaints about "Big Government" ever since the 1960s.

SKOLNICK, JEROME H., and ELLIOT CURRIE, eds. *Crisis in American Institutions.* Boston: Little, Brown, 1979. A collection of readings including: "Pinto Madness," "Keeping the Poor Poor," "The Bakke Case: Affirmative Action or Distraction," and "Delusions of Power: The Benefits, Costs and Risks of Nuclear Energy." All of these illustrate how social problems are produced by the "normal" working of our political and economic system.

# Chapter 15
# Economics

Human beings of our kind have roamed this planet for approximately 100,000 years. But only in the last hundred years have a majority of the people in the most highly industrialized societies been freed from worrying about obtaining an adequate food supply and protecting themselves from the physical environment with adequate clothes and housing. If you had a book 1,000 pages long, with each page representing 100 years of human social and cultural development, you would have to read 910 pages about the nomadic, subsistence-level existence of hunters and food gatherers before reading about the development of a simple horticultural economy based on the hoe or the digging stick.

You would have to read through to page 950 before encountering an agricultural economy based on the invention of the plow. It was also in this period that the first written language appeared.

You would have to turn approximately 998 pages before you would read about the Industrial Revolution, around 1800.

The last page of the book, of course, would represent the last 100 years of human history. It would include half of the entire recorded history of the United States. It would only be on this final page, and then only in the most highly industrialized nations of the world, that a majority of the population would not be preoccupied with the task of securing basic economic subsistence.

As you are probably aware, the structure and functioning of the economy affects almost every facet of your life. For example, you may be in school—and reading this book—for distinctly economic reasons: to acquire skills that will qualify you for a job, or because you cannot obtain the kind of job you want without further education.

You have already read chapters about culture, groups, socialization and personality, social stratification, and the institutions of the family, religion, education, and government. All of these sociological phenomena are so directly related to the structure and functioning of the economy that many seem almost determined by it. It is no wonder that some of the most important theories of human behavior have been based on an economic analysis.

In this chapter, we will briefly survey modern economic evolution and then consider the dramatic effect that industrialization has had on the institutions of education, government, the family, and religion; we will survey the central characteristics of the American economy; and finally, we will consider the economy and society of the future.

The economy is so important to all other facets of social life that we will be forced to review some material we have previously mentioned. The sociological significance of the economy lies in the inextricable degree to which it is interrelated with almost all other features of the society and culture.

## WHAT IS THE ECONOMIC INSTITUTION?

The **economy** is *the institution that organizes land, labor, and technology for the production, distribution, and consumption of goods and services.*

### Factors of Production

When we speak of *land*, we refer to all of the natural resources that are usable in productive processes — territory for hunting, horticulture, and farming, water resources, forests, and raw materials like oil and copper. *Labor* refers to all of the intellectual and physical activities related to producing goods and services. In some societies the economic roles are very simple — all men are hunters, all women are food gatherers; in others they are very complex — today in the United States, there are over 30,000 categories of occupations. *Technology* refers to all of the man-made tools that are used in the production of goods and services, from the digging stick of the food gatherer to the cyclotron of the nuclear physicist. In the simplest economies, the technology of the entire community may be composed of portable and readily replaceable things like baskets, spears, and stone axes. In modern industrial societies, the technology of an urban community is often composed of thousands of factories, machines, storage facilities, vehicles, and communication devices.

### Functions of the Economy

**Production** Labor, capital, and technology may be applied to the raw materials of land to produce food and nonedible material goods (anything from a pot to an intercontinental jet plane). Another function of production is to provide services for humans and their possessions. In subsistence societies, almost everyone in the community is engaged in the production of food. In advanced industrial societies, about two-thirds of the people sell their services and most have little to do with the direct manufacture of food or material goods. Most college students acquire little knowledge and few skills related to the production of goods. Most are in training for jobs related to the selling of some service on the labor market.

**Distribution** In most subsistence societies, those who produce goods and services are the very ones who consume them. Production is for use, not for sale in a marketplace. The modern industrial society is quite different. Did you grow, gather, and process the food that you consumed today? What about your clothes? Not only did you not grow the cotton, shear the wool, or make the synthetic fiber for your clothes, you probably did not even construct the garments you are wearing. The distribution of goods and services from all over the nation and world to consumers in a modern economy is incredibly complex. Our very survival is based upon the efficiency of impersonal distribution systems that bring us food, water, clothing, housing, medicine, transportation, energy, and other goods and services without which we could not survive. Few of us have the skills to live off the land.

**Consumption** refers to the patterns by which people in a society use the goods and services which are produced. In a simple hunting and gathering society, the best hunter may get the best cuts of meat from the hunt, while the less prestigious members get the less desirable pieces. In our own society, the difference in consumption between the wealthiest and the poorest citizens is dramatic. Compare the goods and services consumed by a billionnaire with those of a malnourished welfare family.

## CENTRAL PROBLEMS OF ALL ECONOMIES

The economic institution of a society specifies how it should organize its land, labor, capital, and technology. What is to be produced and in what quantities? Who is to own the land and the technology? The land may be owned jointly by all the members of the community, as in many preindustrial societies, or land and technology may be owned by some private citizens to the exclusion of all others as in most capitalist societies. Or they may be owned and controlled by the government in the name of the total population, as in socialist societies. Other issues concern how goods and services will be produced, who is to receive the items produced, and in what quantities.

These issues are abstract, but we are all affected profoundly by our economy's ways of resolving these problems. The economic institution is of such critical importance that societies are frequently classified by the types of economies they possess: (1) hunting and gathering, (2) horticultural, (3) agricultural, (4) industrial, and (5) postindustrial.

Although we will focus primarily on the contemporary American economy, it is important to realize how historically recent are the industrialization, urbanization, bureaucratization, and secularization that characterize the society of which we are a part.

## Hunting and Gathering Societies

The *hunting and gathering society* is usually relatively small, with most of its social **bands** having fewer than fifty members. The bands are normally nomadic, moving where food and game are plentiful. Each band usually moves within a limited territory whose boundaries are recognized by adjacent bands. Members of these societies have few permanent possessions because of their nomadic way of life. Their economy is subsistence-based. All ablebodied children and adults must engage in hunting and/or food-gathering activities. Adults cannot usually obtain more food than they, or they and their families, can consume. Because there is little economic surplus, the stratification system is simple. The most honored member of the band may be granted a second wife and receive deference from others, but few other social distinctions are likely to appear.

In hunting and gathering societies, the division of labor is usually based on age and sex. Men tend to do most of the hunting, while women and children do most of the food gathering. Although most of the food is obtained through gathering, hunting tends to be a more prized economic activity.

Because hunting is a male-dominated activity, most hunting and gathering societies tend to be *patrilineal* and *patrilocal*: children inherit their kinship group through the father's lineage, and women go to live with their husband upon marrying. Among the Arunta, an Australian hunting and gathering people, for example, a band would usually be composed of a man, his wife and children, his parents, his brothers and their wives and children, and his unmarried sisters.[1]

Sharing tends to be one of the central economic characteristics of a hunting and gathering society: the family shares food with other families in the band today so that others will

**the economy:** the institution that organizes land, labor, and technology for the production, distribution, and consumption of goods and services.

**band** or **social band:** the basic social unit of many hunting and gathering societies. Bands are small, nomadic groups, usually based on kinship, living and traveling together as a subsistence economic and social entity. A number of such kin-related bands may constitute a *clan*, and two or more clans may constitute what is called a *tribe* among American Indians.

**horticulture:** the form of agronomy in which land is broken with a digging stick or hoe with consequent limitation upon the amount of food that can be produced.

**agriculture:** the form of agronomy in which land is broken with a plow making possible large-scale food production.

share with them when necessary in the future. The fact that a woman moves to her husband's kinship group and band upon marriage further contributes to the potential for economic reciprocity in times of scarcity.

For over 90,000 of the 100,000 years of their existence, modern human beings lived in hunting and gathering societies; and *all* premodern human beings were hunters and gatherers.

## Horticultural Societies

Approximately 9000 years ago in the Middle East, in Asia Minor and Palestine, people stopped merely harvesting the grains that grew naturally and started replanting some of the seeds. In this seemingly modest development lies the beginning of a dramatic change in people's relationship to their environment. Instead of depending entirely on the caprice of nature for game and plant food, people began to produce their own food by cultivation with the digging stick and later the hoe. At first, **horticulture** merely supplemented the food obtained by hunting, fishing, and gathering, but eventually it replaced hunting and gathering as the major form of food acquisition.

The primary difference between *horticultural* and **agricultural** economic systems lies in the degree to which land tends to be permanently and continuously productive. Agriculturists usually farm the same land for many years. But horticulturists open new fields, use them for two to four years, and then abandon them as the yield declines.

In the horticultural society . . . people gain their chief livelihood by planting seeds, roots, or tubers and harvesting the product, but do so without the knowledge of fertilizer, terracing, irrigation, regular rotation of crops, or the use of draft animals. . . . The provision of fertilizer is thus not a conscious act but rather a secondary response to the techniques of clearing. This procedure makes possible the development of more or less permanent villages, but it limits both their size and productivity.[2]

Horticultural communities become more sedentary than hunting societies, because people do not have to move so often as planted crops increasingly become the major source of food. With greater productivity, these communities increase in size, and dwellings become larger and more permanent. Horticultural societies are usually organized around villages, frequently numbering in the hundreds. Each village usually consists of various clans, but the clan itself is normally the primary unit of economic organization, social control, and religious activity. The increase in economic productivity frees some individuals from food-producing activities and allows them to perform other functions. Social and institutional differentiation begins, as some people are able to specialize in economic, political, or religious activities.

Horticultural communities tend to be self-sufficient. Production is for use, not for sale in a market. In general, the women engage in the horticultural activities, while the men clear the bush, hunt, fight, and where there are domestic animals, take care of the livestock.[3] The complexity of the stratification system increases with increases in economic surplus and with increases in specialization in the political, economic, military, and religious institutions.

### Agricultural Societies

After approximately 4,000 years during which various societies reached different levels of horticultural development, some groups modified the hoe into a kind of plow. This seemingly modest adaptation of a traditional tool for exploiting the economic environment was in fact

Grain harvest in imperial Egypt. The plow, which made large civilizations possible, was invented in the Middle East. The workers shown in this ancient frieze probably used it.

a silent revolution, a development sometimes called "the dawn of civilization." Use of the plow is what distinguishes the agricultural economy from the horticultural economy. The plow was a great advance over the hoe used by the horticulturist. The hoe could not eradicate weeds or restore nutrients to the soil, and consequently, horticulturists who used it to replant the same land for several seasons found that the land became infertile or choked with weeds. The plow, by contrast, could overturn and kill weeds and could dig deep enough into the soil to restore nutrients to the surface. Unlike horticulturists who had to abandon their land after a few years of use, agriculturists could farm the same land for long periods of time.

The first plows of the Middle East were modified hoes. At first, they were probably drawn by people, but eventually draft animals were used. The use of the plow and draft animals, combined with increasing knowledge of crop rotation, fertilizer, irrigation, and terracing, brought about dramatic changes in society. The greatly increased food productivity freed many more individuals to specialize in commercial, political, military, and religious roles. This led to the development of cities, places where specialists could gather to sell their goods and services. The need for a common medium of exchange with which specialists could sell their own goods and services and purchase the goods and service of others led to the development of some form of money. The need for a complex accounting system to record the increasing number of economic, political, and military activities was probably the chief factor in the development of written language. (The earliest known specimens of writing are Sumerian account books and tax records from between 5000 and 6000 B.C.) As cities increased in size and complexity, bringing increased anonymity and impersonality, it could no longer be assumed that people shared the same values. The political institutions had to establish laws, law-enforcing agencies, and formal penalties to induce a conformity that might not otherwise be forthcoming, because of increasing differences in beliefs, values, and norms.[4]

Advanced agricultural societies had several characteristics in common. Most states were controlled by a small landed aristocracy. Through their control of the government and the military, these aristocrats controlled the farming land and those who worked on it. The ruling elite used the urban areas as their primary center of control over the surrounding hinterland. Often, they used the religious institution as a means of justifying to the illiterate masses their wealth, power, and prestige. These landed aristocrats occupied the top level of the stratification system, with only a small class of merchants and craft workers occupying an intermediate position. At the bottom was the vast bulk of the people, usually around 90 percent of the total population. They were illiterate and lived subsistence-level lives that—as Hobbes said—were "poor, nasty, brutish, and short."

## Industrial Societies

Not until 4,800 years or so after the invention of the plow did a series of dramatic changes occur in the means of production. The *Industrial Revolution* began in England in the latter part of the

One of the basic elements of the Industrial Revolution was widespread substitution of machines for human or animal labor. The mechanical reaper shown here replaced hundreds of hours of human work with scythe or sickle.

eighteenth century. Many social, cultural, and economic factors contributed to it. The English revolution of 1688 affirmed the ascendancy of Parliament, particularly the House of Commons, over the King. For almost two centuries after that, the property-holding class was dominant in Parliament. Their control of the government enabled these wealthy landowners to improve the techniques of farming and cattle raising. They initiated the use of fertilizers, developed new farming tools and new crops, and improved the system of crop rotation. They also passed a series of "enclosure acts," which forced small tenant farmers to relinquish their ownership or use of the land. The mass of agrarian land thus became concentrated in the hands of a very small class of wealthy landlords. The tenant farmers, no longer tied to the land by law and tradition, often migrated to urban areas and became workers in the factories established during the Industrial Revolution.

Other factors contributed to the development of the Industrial Revolution in England. England acquired a new set of colonies, developed markets throughout Europe and America, built up the largest navy and merchant marine in the world, and won control of the seas. Thus, England was wealthy from agriculture and commerce and had the capital to invest in the development of machinery.

The first important inventions in the Industrial Revolution were made in the textile industry: the fly shuttle, the spinning jenny, and the water frame. The newly developed steam engine provided the energy to drive these machines. In about seventy-five years, the production of textiles increased by more than 500 percent. In the same period, even higher increases occurred in the production of iron and coal. Steam engines were used to power ships, vehicles, and trains. Thus, the stage was set for changes that would have more profound effects on human beings and their institutions than all of the developments that had occurred in the preceding 100,000 years of human existence.

## THE EFFECTS OF INDUSTRIALIZATION ON CONTEMPORARY SOCIAL INSTITUTIONS

### Education

In preindustrial societies, the education of the young for adult economic, political, and military roles took place primarily within the family. Even in advanced agricultural societies, such as those existing in Europe immediately before the Industrial Revolution, the vast bulk of the population received their education for adult roles within the family. Formal education in advanced agricultural societies was only for the children of the nobility and the wealthier mer-

**FIGURE 15.1** The working population of the United States: 1820–1970

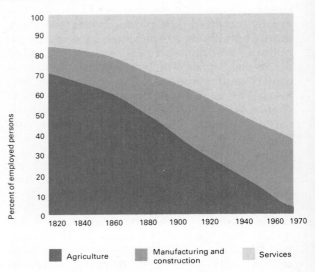

chants. Most people in such societies were illiterate. Only after industrialization occurred did those who controlled the political and economic institutions perceive a need for extending education to the masses. Thus, the development of public education was based less on democratic, humanistic ideals than on the perceived need to train the labor force for the increasingly complex tasks of an industrial society.

Figure 15.1 shows the changing nature of the American labor force. In 1820, 70 percent of the United States labor force was in agricultural

**TABLE 15.1**   Enrollments at Three Educational Levels, United States, 1870–1978 (in thousands)

| Year | Elementary and kindergarten | Secondary | College and university | Total |
|------|------------------------------|-----------|------------------------|-------|
| 1870 | 7,500  | 80     | 52    | 7,632  |
| 1880 | 9,757  | 110    | 116   | 9,983  |
| 1890 | 14,181 | 358    | 157   | 14,696 |
| 1900 | 16,225 | 696    | 238   | 17,159 |
| 1910 | 18,457 | 1,111  | 355   | 19,923 |
| 1920 | 20,864 | 2,496  | 598   | 23,958 |
| 1930 | 23,739 | 4,812  | 1,101 | 29,652 |
| 1940 | 21,127 | 7,130  | 1,494 | 29,751 |
| 1950 | 22,207 | 6,453  | 2,659 | 31,319 |
| 1960 | 32,441 | 10,249 | 3,570 | 46,259 |
| 1970 | 37,133 | 14,715 | 7,413 | 59,261 |
| 1978 | 35,021 | 15,633 | 9,023 | 59,677 |

occupations, and only about 17 percent was in service-oriented occupations. The next 150 years saw a continuous decline in the portion of the labor force in farming, with an associated increase in the portion of the population in service-oriented jobs. By 1970, almost as many people were in service jobs (about 66 percent) as had been in farming in 1820 (70 percent). One of the central educational tasks of the nineteenth and twentieth centuries has been to prepare the children of the less well educated for the increasingly complex occupational roles generated by an industrial economy. You yourself may be an example of this phenomenon, as are several of the authors of this book.

As Table 15.1 shows, the population has been given access on a continuing basis to greater and greater amounts of (primarily public) education. First, public elementary education was extended to the masses, then public high school education. Since World War II, colleges and universities have increasingly become institutions for educating those of the lower middle and working classes (see Chapter 12). As recently as 1940, only 15 percent of college-age people went to college. In the early 1970s, over 50 percent of those of college age were starting college. The number of students attending college more than doubled from 1960 to 1970 and increased by 152 percent between 1960 and 1975.

## Government

One of the antecedents for the development of a stable democracy is apparently the industrialization of the society. S. M. Lipset found a strong correlation between the level of economic development (industrialization, average wealth, urbanization, and education) and the evolution of democracy.[5] Lipset does not mean by this that these four characteristics cause democracy, but that they may be necessary for the development of a stable democracy. In a society where there is little economic surplus, where the vast majority of the population live under conditions of extreme poverty, and where there is no tradition that legitimizes the government, illegal and violent means are likely to be used to change the leadership or structure of the government. The small group composing the elite may be unwilling to compromise with the leaders of the masses because of the small

size of the economic surplus, the qualitative differences that appear to exist between the well-educated elite and the illiterate masses, and the often radical nature of the demands made by those leaders.

Figure 15.2 shows the stratification systems in three types of societies. In an agricultural, preindustrial society, there tends to be a very small ruling and middle class, while the rest of the population lives at the subsistence level.

As a society experiences industrialization, the shape of its stratification system changes to that of a pyramid. Elite roles become somewhat more open, and the middle classes expand, so that a smaller proportion of the population remains at the lowest stratification levels.

With industrialization the rural poor are forced or lured to cities, where new forms of employment are being created in the factories and workshops of the new industrial economy.[6] Most of the rural poor are gradually converted into the urban poor—the industrial proletariat. The middle class increases in size as more professionals, managers, and lower white-collar

**FIGURE 15.2  Stratification systems in three types of societies**

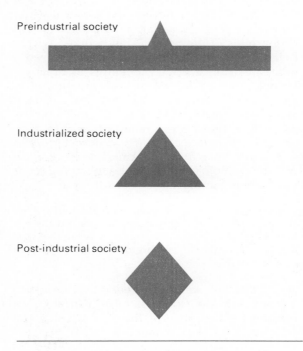

Preindustrial society

Industrialized society

Post-industrial society

Late nineteenth or early twentieth century industrial workers.

workers are needed to control and service the bureaucracies that run the new industrial activities.

During this "take-off period" of industrialization in the latter half of the nineteenth century and the early part of the twentieth, there was great economic exploitation of the urban work force. The "iron law of wages" prevailed, the philosophy that justified paying employees a bare subsistence wage so that they would have to keep working just to stay alive.

In 1903, 25,000 children, some as young as five or six years of age, were employed in the cotton mills of the South. They worked twelve hours per day at the machines and received a bare subsistence wage.[7] Attempts to organize unions and bargain collectively were viewed as illegal during this period. The courts usually sided with management, as did most of the other agencies of government.[8] It was in such an atmosphere that a group of men met in Pittsburgh in 1880 to form the American Federation of Labor (AFL). They wrote the following revolutionary preamble to their constitution:

A struggle is going on in all of the nations of the civilized world between the oppressors and the oppressed of all countries, a struggle between the capitalist and the laborer which grows in intensity from year to year.[9]

In 1955, the American Federation of Labor merged with the Congress of Industrial Organizations (CIO) to form the AFL-CIO. In the new preamble to their constitution, they proclaimed their allegiance to "our way of life and the fundamental freedoms of our democratic society."[10] The Marxian rhetoric of the 1880 preamble was omitted; there were no terms such as *struggle, oppressed, capitalist, and laborer.*

What are the reasons for this deradicalization of labor? The continued industrialization of the American economy has caused great increases in productivity and greater economic surpluses. Unions and collective bargaining have been legalized, legitimized, and integrated into the structure of the capitalistic economy and into the democratic party system. These changes have brought about dramatic changes in the degree to which workers—union and nonunion—benefit from the economy and thus support democratic capitalist society. In 1890, the average work week was 62 hours;[11] in April 1977 the average work week was 35.8 hours.[12] When the purchasing power of the dollar is kept constant (in 1968 dollars), the following data emerge: (1) in 1913, 61 percent of American families and individuals earned under $3,000, whereas only 17 percent of families and individuals earned under $3,000 in 1967; (2) in 1913, only 4 percent of families and individuals earned $10,000 and over, whereas in 1967, 27 percent of families and individuals earned $10,000 and over.[13] The median income of the American family (in dollars with constant purchasing power) almost doubled between 1950 and 1976 (an increase of 90.5 percent).[14]

Increased education and affluence also contribute to the economic security and rationality that enables a population to understand and use the complex instruments of democratic government. The stratification system in highly industrialized—postindustrial—societies tends to become diamond-shaped, as greater and greater proportions of the population share in the affluence and move into middle-class or skilled occupations and as the degree of economic differentiation diminishes.[15] (The typical American worker today lives on a scale far superior to that of a European feudal lord, while the difference between a worker's lifestyle and that of an employer is much less than that distinguishing lord from serf.)

There is now a large middle class: 50.2 percent of the present labor force is in white-collar jobs.[16] Members of the working class, which is declining in size, tend to have stable jobs with incomes and fringe benefits that give them a vested interest in economic stability. Legal organizations represent their interests: unions and (usually) the political party of the Left. Thus it is less likely that the proletariat will adopt illegal or violent means to achieve their ends.

If democratic governments tend to induce loyalty to the existing political economy by providing legitimate means through which the great mass of the population benefits, how do they induce loyalty—or at least nonviolent responses—on the part of the 11.8 percent of the population below the poverty level?[17] One effective way is to provide various forms of welfare to assist and control the poor. Meeting poor people's minimal needs for subsistence is one way of reducing their potential for political and economic radicalism. Welfare programs give the poor at least a minimal vested interest in the social system.

## The Family

For approximately 95,000 years, people depended on the extended family for the solution of all problems—economic, political, military, educational, and religious. Even in the most advanced agricultural societies, the family was the primary unit for the production of food, education, religion, protection, and recreation. With industrialization, many of the functions once served only by the family were taken over totally or partially by differentiated and specialized institutions.

**The Economic Function**  The production of goods and services, once accomplished within the family, is now almost entirely accomplished by specialized economic institutions. The family no longer works together as an interdependent economic unit of production; only one in twelve persons in the labor force is even self-employed. The bulk of the labor force must

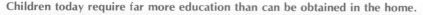

Children today require far more education than can be obtained in the home.

leave the home in order to work elsewhere. If the family is composed of both parents and offspring, this usually results in the mother taking over most of the socialization of children.

**The Educational Function**   Much of the education of the young is now carried out in formal institutions by trained specialists. Most young people do not inherit the jobs of their parents in an industrial society. Further, the young require more formal training than the parents would be capable of giving them.

**The Protective Function**   Most of the protective functions that were once primarily served by the family have been taken over partially or wholly by other institutions. Government agencies such as the police and fire departments and health and welfare organizations help protect private citizens and their property. Private insurance companies insure against ill health, death, and damage to personal and real property.

**The Religious Function**   The religious ideology and rituals that permeated all activities within the family in preindustrial societies have been eroded by the processes of secularization within the society. Most of the religious activities that family members participate in now take place within specialized institutions for about one hour per week, on holy days, or at births, weddings, and funerals.

**Recreational Functions**   In preindustrial societies, most recreational activities were performed within the family. In modern industrial societies, most recreation occurs outside the home, and children tend to depend on peers, rather than on members of the family, for it. Marital partners may have such specialized recreational preferences that they engage in recreation separately from each other, with the husband playing golf with his friends, while the wife plays tennis with hers. Even the advent of television has not necessarily shifted the focus of recreation to the family. Many families own more than one television set, so that different family members can watch different programs, according to their specialized interests. The family's loss of all these functions, has doubt-

less contributed to the rising rate of divorce in recent years. People increasingly marry primarily for personal satisfaction, or divorce because they have not attained that satisfaction. People are not so strongly bound in marriage by practical necessity as they once were.

## Religion

In preindustrial societies, religion was an important part of everyday life. When the extended family had to cope with all the basic societal problems, it integrated religious ideology and rituals into the everyday activities of the economy, social control, education, and recreation. But with industrialization and the institutional differentiation that accompanied it, religion became less and less important in everyday life. The industrialized economy emphasizes understanding the observable world in order to control it better and thus achieve secular ends in the different institutional spheres. Religious status loses most of its importance. In the economy, status is based increasingly on the possession of knowledge and skills that enable one to manipulate land, labor, or capital in order to increase the productivity of organizations. In government, status is increasingly based on the knowledge and skills that enable one to pass or enforce legislation for the benefit of a given interest group or for the society at large.

One predictable consequence of educating and socializing the bulk of the population to understand and manipulate the environment for their own and group goals is secularization, the habit of viewing things in a secular instead of a religious way.[18] *Secularism* is the *description and explanation of life in naturalistic terms, terms that refer to observable objects, events, and relationships.* Since religious beliefs generally focus on the supernatural, it is predictable that secularization will undermine the influence of religious ideology, institutions, and clerical personnel.[19]

## CAPITALISM, SOCIALISM, AND THE POLITICAL INSTITUTION

**Capitalism** is *an economic system characterized by private or corporate ownership of the means of production, where most investments are deter-*

mined by private decisions rather than by those in government, and where prices, production, profits, and the distribution of goods and services are determined mainly in a free market. Producers of goods and services are supposed to compete freely to provide consumers with the best product at the lowest price, to the benefit of all. This ideal description obscures the complex realities of modern economies. Some industries tend to be most efficiently served by monopolies—communications and utilities, for example. Most large industries are dominated by one to four companies that limit competition, set prices to guarantee profits, and attempt to shape consumer tastes. Problems from the evolving industrial economy have necessitated government intervention. Thus industrialized capitalist nations usually have mixed economies, with government ownership of some of the means of production and a considerable degree of government regulation and subsidization of those privately owned.

**Socialism** is an *economic system in which the government owns and controls the means of production—raw materials, factories, communication and transportation systems, etc.* Goods are supposed to be produced not for profit but for the "public good," which is defined by those who control the economy. Income is redistributed through the use of heavy taxes on high incomes and on inherited wealth. The less privileged get government welfare benefits from the cradle to the grave (guaranteed minimum wages, employment, medical care, etc.)

This is another ideal definition. The only nations that have total government ownership and control of the means of production are those with totalitarian and socialistic regimes. The democratic nations usually labeled socialistic—Britain and the Scandinavian countries—have most of their land and capital owned by private citizens, although there is much greater government ownership and control of the economy than in the United States. There is also much more redistribution of income through taxes and welfare benefits in those countries than in the United States. Most democratic industrial nations today have mixed economies with differing degrees of government and private ownership and control of the economy. These economies are neither purely capitalistic nor purely socialistic.

**capitalism:** the economic system characterized by private or corporate ownership of the means of production, investment by private rather than government decision, and the determination of production, distribution, price, and profit by a free market.

**socialism:** the economic system in which government owns and controls the means of production and distribution, makes decisions on investment, and controls price and profit for the public good.

**primary sector of the economy:** the sector that deals with raw materials, including agriculture, fishing, mining, and forestry.

**secondary sector of the economy:** the sector dealing with the transformation of raw materials into finished products, including manufacturing and construction activities.

## CENTRAL CHARACTERISTICS OF THE AMERICAN ECONOMY

### Changing Composition of the Labor Force

Economists usually divide the various parts of the economy into the *primary, secondary,* and *tertiary* sectors. The **primary sector of the economy** *processes raw materials and includes the activities of agriculture, fishing, mining, and forestry.* The **secondary sector** *deals with manufacturing and construction, transforming raw materials into finished products.* The **tertiary sector** *deals with the economic activities that contribute services to the society,* rather than raw materials or manufactured goods.

About 4 percent of the American population now produce food for the rest of us. In 1800 about 95 percent of all Americans were farmers.

TABLE 15.2  Percent of American Workers in Major Occupational Groups, 1900–1977

| | 1900 | 1910 | 1920 | 1930 | 1940 | 1950 | 1960 | 1970 | 1977 |
|---|---|---|---|---|---|---|---|---|---|
| Total labor force (in 1,000s) | 29,030 | 37,291 | 42,206 | 48,686 | 51,742 | 59,648 | 66,681 | 78,627 | 89,258 |
| White-collar workers | 17.6% | 21.3% | 24.9% | 29.4% | 31.1% | 37.5% | 43.1% | 48.3% | 50.2% |
| Professional and technical workers | 4.2 | 4.7 | 5.4 | 6.8 | 7.4 | 7.5 | 11.2 | 14.2 | 15.3 |
| Managers, officials, and proprietors | 5.8 | 6.6 | 6.6 | 7.4 | 7.3 | 10.8 | 10.5 | 10.5 | 10.4 |
| Clerical workers | 3.0 | 5.3 | 8.0 | 9.1 | 9.6 | 12.8 | 14.7 | 17.4 | 18.0 |
| Sales workers | 4.5 | 4.7 | 4.9 | 6.3 | 6.7 | 6.4 | 6.6 | 6.2 | 6.5 |
| Blue-collar workers | 35.8 | 38.2 | 40.2 | 39.6 | 39.8 | 39.1 | 36.3 | 35.3 | 33.1 |
| Craftsmen and foremen | 10.5 | 11.6 | 13.0 | 12.8 | 12.0 | 12.8 | 12.8 | 12.9 | 13.1 |
| Operatives | 12.8 | 14.6 | 15.6 | 15.8 | 18.4 | 20.4 | 18.0 | 17.7 | 15.3 |
| Nonfarm laborers | 12.5 | 12.0 | 11.6 | 11.0 | 9.4 | 5.9 | 5.5 | 4.7 | 4.7 |
| Service workers | 9.0 | 9.5 | 7.8 | 9.8 | 11.7 | 10.9 | 12.5 | 12.1 | 13.7 |
| Private household workers | 5.4 | 5.0 | 3.3 | 4.1 | 4.7 | 3.1 | 3.3 | | |
| Other service workers | 3.6 | 4.6 | 4.5 | 5.7 | 7.1 | 7.8 | 9.2 | | |
| Farm workers | 37.5 | 30.9 | 27.0 | 21.2 | 17.4 | 12.4 | 8.1 | 4.0 | 3.0 |

**Reduction of Agricultural Effort** One of the most dramatic effects of industrialization has been to reduce the number of individuals required to feed the population. In 1900, 37.5 percent of the labor force was in farming; in 1977 only 3 percent of the labor force was in farming. (See Table 15.2.) In 1940, the average farmer produced enough food to feed 10.7 people; in 1972, the average farmer produced enough food to feed 52.4 people.[20] Only in the last 200 years have most workers in the primary sector of industrial societies been able consistently to provide more food than their immediate families needed. The great economic surplus of food produced by American farms frees the bulk of the population to engage in other specialized occupations.

**The White-collar Explosion** The United States Department of Labor now lists over 30,000 different occupational specialties. Table 15.2 shows the dramatic increase in the number of workers in the white-collar occupations. In 1900, only 17.6 percent of the labor force was in white-collar occupations; in 1977, 50.2 percent of the labor force was in white-collar occupations. In 1974, service workers constituted 67 percent of the labor force.[21] The modern worker, then, is likely to be in a service occupation, as well as better educated and more affluent than the parent of his or her own sex.

**Women in the Labor Force** Another effect of industrialization has been the increased entrance of women into the labor force. As we saw in Chapter 7, the percentage of women in the work force has gone from 18 percent in 1900 to 41 percent in 1977.[22] Forty-seven percent of all women are now working with three-fifths of these women married.[23] Women tend to be concentrated in clerical occupations and in service jobs. Their median income is only 59 percent of that of the male worker.[24] Even when women and men of the same age, education, and time in the labor force are compared, women tend to earn only 73 percent as much as men.[25] Clearly, there is not equal treatment of women in the job market.

**Youth in the Labor Force** People like most readers of this book, who were born at the end of the so-called baby-boom of the late 1950s and

> **tertiary sector of the economy:** the sector contributing services to the society and the other sectors of the economy.

early 1960s, are now entering college, graduate schools, or the labor force. There is a distinct population bulge of those 25 to 44 years of age in the 1970s which will continue into the 1980s. Not only is the labor force younger than in the 1960s; it is better educated. In 1976 only 33 percent of workers aged 45 and older had finished high school, as compared with 86 percent of those under 34.[26] The economy is not producing as many new professional and managerial jobs as the colleges and universities are producing candidates for such positions. The Bureau of Labor Statistics predicts that by 1985 about 25 percent of recent college graduates will be unable to find jobs that require a college education. This pattern continues a trend that started in 1969.[27]

Thus intense competition is likely to increase for positions in professional schools and for jobs at professional and managerial levels. Many college graduates will have to take jobs for which they are overqualified. This is likely to place similar strains on those in lower strata, forcing them to take less desirable jobs than they had anticipated, because of competition from the better educated. Such dislocations are likely to produce lower levels of job satisfaction for those who feel dispossessed of their just rewards.

*Private Corporations*

**Separation of Ownership and Control** In the nineteenth century, few of the companies that later became national organizations were public corporations. Most began as family-owned businesses with names such as Du Pont, Swift, Armour, Ford, and so on. The shift from family-based capitalism to modern corporate capitalism managed by trained specialists occurred around the turn of the century because of a succession of financial crises. The bankers, who controlled the money and credit, intervened and reorganized many of the largest businesses in the country. They installed professional managers to administer the organizations, and thus brought about a separation of ownership from control that was to become institutionalized in the bulk of modern corporations.

The increasing size and complexity of the modern corporation made obsolete the traditional nineteenth century forms of family ownership and control. By 1932, the proliferation of shares of stock for the major companies and the wide diversification of stock holdings had resulted in a separation of ownership from control in the vast majority of cases.[28] This separation of ownership from control became even greater in the 1960s: "whereas six of the largest 200 corporations were privately owned (80 percent or more of stock) in 1929, in 1963 there were none, and 84.5 percent of the firms had no group of stockholders owning as much as 10 percent.[29] Paul Samuelson, the Nobel Prize-winning economist, says that "all management together—officers and directors—holds only about 3 percent of the outstanding common

stock. The largest single minority ownership groups typically hold about a fifth of all voting stock . . . more than enough to maintain a 'working control.'"[30] Thus, people who own only a small fraction of each corporation exert control over it.

**Oligopoly** One visible and controversial development of the American economy has been the development of **oligopoly**—*the domination of industries and markets by fewer and fewer corporations.* Table 15.3 shows the degree to which the four largest companies in selected industries dominate the markets for which they produce their goods. In twenty of the industries, four companies account for 65 to 94 percent of all production. To quote Paul Samuelson:

The largest 200 corporations hold more than one-fourth of income-producing national wealth. They

**TABLE 15.3  Percent of Production Accounted for by the Four Largest Companies in Selected Industries in the United States, 1972**

| Industry | Percent | Industry | Percent |
|---|---|---|---|
| Telephone and telegraph apparatus (1970) | 94 | Pulpmills | 59 |
| | | Wines, brandy and brandy spirits | 53 |
| Motor vehicles | 93 | Canned and cured sea foods | 50 |
| Primary lead | 93 | Industrial trucks and tractors | 50 |
| Flat glass | 92 | | |
| Cereal breakfast foods | 90 | Distilled liquor, except brandy | 47 |
| Chewing gum | 87 | | |
| Cigarettes | 84 | Shipbuilding | 47 |
| Tires cord and fabric | 84 | Surgical and medical instruments | 32 |
| Carpets and rugs | 80 | | |
| Primary aluminum | 79 | Petroleum refining | 31 |
| Calculating and accounting machines | 73 | Weaving mills, cotton | 31 |
| | | Bread, cake, and related products | 29 |
| Tires and inner tubes | 73 | | |
| Primary copper | 72 | Food preparation | 26 |
| Blended and prepared flour | 68 | Periodicals | 26 |
| Canned specialities | 67 | Pharmaceutical preparations | 26 |
| Explosives | 67 | Textile goods | 25 |
| Aircraft | 66 | House furnishings | 23 |
| Metal cans | 66 | Paints and allied products | 22 |
| Industrial gases | 65 | Book publishing | 19 |
| Roasted coffee | 65 | Household furniture | 19 |
| Guided missiles and space vehicles | 62 | Fluid milk | 18 |
| | | Newspapers | 17 |
| Soap and other detergents | 62 | Wood household furniture | 14(?) |
| Synthetic rubber | 62 | Concrete products | 10 |
| Cane sugar, refining | 59 | Women's dresses | 9 |

employ one out of every eight workers. The 500 largest industrial corporations have more than half the sales in manufacturing and mining and get more than 70 percent of the profits. Half-a-dozen industrial corporations each control more money than any one of our 50 states does.[31]

A new class of professional managers has evolved, a few hundred people who control the largest corporations, billions of dollars of resources, and the economic well-being of millions of investors and employees, and even entire communities.[32] These executives are not elected by the American people, nor are they directly accountable to them. The ideology of nineteenth-century capitalism proclaimed that the free competition of many manufacturers striving to offer the best product at the lowest price would make the consumer king. This prediction is challenged by the structure of the oligopolistic market, which shapes consumer attitudes and creates a demand for its products by spending billions of dollars for advertising and sales promotions.[33]

**Conglomerates**  Not only have corporations grown into massive organizations that dominate whole industries; the largest corporations frequently absorb other corporate entities in unrelated industries. For example, International Telephone and Telegraph (ITT) is a huge **conglomerate** operating over 150 affiliated companies, including the second largest car rental corporation in the world, the largest hotel chain in the world, the country's largest bakery products manufacturer, one of the leading suppliers of educational exhibit materials, the nation's leading maker of automatic fire protection equipment, one of the largest vending machine companies, a major insurance company, a home construction company, a book publisher, a glass company, and a major processor of chemical cellulose.[34] With this in mind, the following figures should not surprise us:

Of the almost two million corporations in America, one tenth of 1 percent controls 55 percent of the total assets; 1.1 percent controls 82 percent. At the other end of the spectrum, 94 percent of the corporations own only 9 percent of the total assets.[35]

**Multinational Corporations**  Many conglomerates conduct their business activities in more than one nation. One-fourth of total world

> **oligopoly:**  the domination of an industry and its market by a small number of sellers.
>
> **conglomerate:**  a business corporation that has diversified its interests through merger with or purchase of many different kinds of firms.
>
> **multinational corporation:**  a business firm incorporated in two or more nations, thus having its total operation subject to the laws of none.

production is now accounted for by **multinational corporations.** Their share of total world productivity is likely to increase to 50 percent by the year 2000.[36] About two-thirds of the multinationals have their headquarters in the United States. The annual productivity of these multinationals is the third largest in the world after the United States and Russia.[37] Many of these multinationals have annual gross sales greater than the gross national products of entire nations (see Table 15.4).

A number of factors contribute to large corporations becoming multinational:

1. Labor is frequently cheaper in other nations than in the United States, for example, South Koreans get fourteen cents an hour to assemble television components, and prisoners may be employed for less than $1.33 per day in Colombia—although it is against the law to use prison labor for private profit in the United States.[38]
2. Raw materials may be obtained and processed in some parts of the world far more profitably than in the United States.
3. Large corporations frequently produce more than their domestic markets can consume. They therefore seek to sell their goods and services in the markets of other nations.
4. There is frequently less regulation of corporate activity in other nations than in the home market. Some conglomerates sell pharmaceutical preparations in other nations that are banned by the Food and Drug Administration at home. Some of these drug companies charged foreign subsidiaries as much as eighty-two times the normal price.[39]
5. Tax credits are often extended to corporate income earned in other nations. "Bribery of public officials, illegal in this country, is a way of life in many parts of the globe. Conglomerates which conform to such local mores can deduct their expenditures as 'ordinary and necessary business expense,' in the unemotional language of the Internal Revenue Code."[40]

TABLE 15.4   Nations and Corporations: A Comparison of the Gross National Products of Selected Industrializing Nations and the Annual Sales Volumes of Selected Corporations, 1974, in Billions of Dollars

| Nation or corporation | GNP or sales | Nation or corporation | GNP or sales |
|---|---|---|---|
| Mexico | $48.7 | Philips Gloeilampenfab | $9.4 |
| Exxon | 45.0 | U.S. Steel | 9.2 |
| General Motors | 31.5 | Egypt | 9.1 |
| Austria | 27.9 | Israel | 9.0 |
| AT&T | 26.2 | Nippon Steel | 8.8 |
| Iran | 25.6 | Pakistan | 8.3 |
| Ford | 23.6 | Hoechst | 7.8 |
| Turkey | 22.0 | Chile | 7.6 |
| Norway | 18.8 | Nestle Chocolate | 5.6 |
| British Petroleum | 18.3 | Morocco | 5.0 |
| Standard Oil of California | 17.9 | Lockheed Aircraft | 3.3 |
| Greece | 16.3 | Ghana | 2.9 |
| Sears Roebuck | 13.1 | Colgate-Palmolive | 2.6 |
| South Korea | 12.4 | Burma | 2.4 |
| Portugal | 11.2 | Chicago Pneumatic Tool | 0.3 |
| ITT | 11.2 | Dahomey | 0.3 |

**Bureaucratization and the "Employee Society"**   Not only do the executives who run the large corporations control huge material reserves, they also control people. One major characteristic of American society is that every institution in it except the family is bureaucratized. Only 8.7 percent of the workers in the labor force are self-employed.[44] Upon completing your education, you are likely to enter a white-collar occupation in a formal organization that is either a private or a government bureaucracy. The very college or university that you are now attending is probably bureaucratic in structure, and, as remarked earlier, you may be here largely because you want to prepare yourself for bureaucratic participation.

Bureaucracy is frequently associated in the public mind with inefficiency. Yet, whether we like being manipulated by such structures or not, bureaucracy is in fact the most efficient way to organize and coordinate a large number of specialists working to achieve formally defined goals. What other principle of organization could coordinate the activities of the approximately 750,000 people who work for the American Telephone and Telegraph Company, owned by nearly 3 million stockholders? It is not a coincidence that bureaucratization is a central feature of all industrial societies, be they capitalistic or socialistic.

Bureaucratic landscape

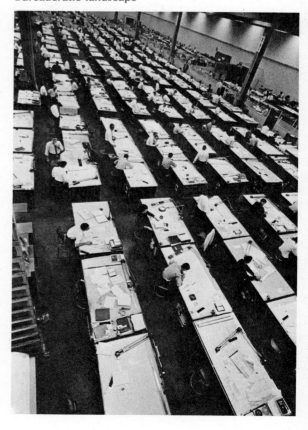

## CASE STUDY: THE WORLD OF I.T.T.

The multinationals have such great wealth and power that individually or collectively they have the potential for subverting or circumventing the authority of government and the public interest of a particular nation. For example, the chief of the United States Justice Department's antitrust division opposed International Telephone and Telegraph's merger with Hartford Insurance. Sheraton Motels, which are owned by I.T.T., pledged $400,000 to the Republican National Convention in San Diego. Shortly afterward, President Nixon explicitly ordered the Attorney General to have the Justice Department drop its antitrust suit against I.T.T.[41] In the international sphere, I.T.T. contributed to the overthrow by a military coup of the democratically elected socialist government in Chile, which resulted in the murder of the Chilean president, Salvadore Allende. Keeping a promise made to the Nixon administration, I.T.T. leaders worked closely with the C.I.A. to accomplish the downfall of the Chilean government. Eight-million dollars was spent to support Chilean groups opposed to the Allende administration.[42]

The implications that such mammoth multinationals have for nation-states are great. Those who head such organizations are not elected by the citizens of the nation where the corporations have their headquarters, nor are the organizations entirely subject to the laws of those governments. If the laws of the home country do not serve the profit-making goals of management, the corporate leaders may shift their activities to another nation. Such a decision may have implications for thousands of workers, several smaller companies, and governmental tax revenues. Collectively, many such decisions by multinationals could well affect the entire well-being of a small nation. Thus, within a relatively brief period of time in human history, an organizational form has evolved that transcends the boundaries and authority of most nations. The primary allegiance of these organizations is to their own economic self-interest. The vision of Carl A. Gerstacker, Dow Chemical's chairman, is as follows:

"I have long dreamed of buying an island owned by no nation, and of establishing the World Headquarters (caps in original) of the Dow Company on the truly neutral ground of such an island, beholden to no nation or society. If we were located on such truly neutral ground we could then really operate in the United States as U.S. citizens, in Japan as Japanese citizens, and in Brazil as Brazilians rather than being governed in prime by the laws of the United States. . . . We could even pay any natives handsomely to move elsewhere."[43]

### Labor Unions and Professional Organizations

**Unions** One response of workers to a society increasingly dominated by large corporate employers is to form their own organizations to bargain collectively for higher wages, better working conditions, job security, and fringe benefits. In 1974, there were approximately 20 million union members in a work force of about 93 million, or 21.7 percent.[45] A list of the eight largest American labor unions appears in Table 15.5. Although there are ninety-four unions with over 25,000 members each in the United States, the fourteen largest unions account for over half of all union members.[46]

Unionization, or something similar to it, is a necessity for many workers. Whereas a single employee would be unable to negotiate with a giant corporate employer, a union representing all the employees within the organization—if not within the industry—can negotiate effectively. A union's threat to withhold all truck

TABLE 15.5 Seven Largest Labor Unions in the United States, 1974

| Union | Number of members |
|---|---|
| Teamsters | 1,973,000 |
| Automobile Workers | 1,545,000 |
| Steelworkers | 1,300,000 |
| Electrical Workers | 991,000 |
| Machinists | 943,000 |
| Carpenters | 820,000 |
| Retail Clerks | 651,000 |
| Laborers | 650,000 |
| **Total** (8 unions) | 8,873,000 |

drivers, machinists, or steelworkers constitutes such a potential danger to a corporation's activities that employers are usually willing to negotiate seriously to reconcile differences.

In addition to negotiating with corporate management to improve job conditions and rewards, union leaders also attempt to influence the passage and enforcement of legislation that furthers the interests of union members and to block that which is disadvantageous to them.

**Professional Organizations** Most professional men and women form occupational groups to protect and further their interests. The American Bar Association represents two-thirds of the 300,000 lawyers in the country; the American Medical Association is composed of 210,000 doctors; and the National Educational Association represents 1,700,000 teachers.[47] These and similar professional associations pursue their members' interests by political endorsements and contributions and by lobbying those who hold executive, legislative, and judiciary positions in federal, state, and local governments.

### The Increasing Role of the Government in the Economy

**Regulation and Control** In the nineteenth century in the United States, there was little government intervention in the economy. Those who owned or controlled land, labor, and capital had great freedom to use these resources however they pleased, regardless of the consequences for others. This system, however, produced several undesired consequences: recurrent business recessions, the emergence and growth of oligopolies, indiscriminate waste of national resources, extreme racial and sexual discrimination, economic exploitation of the many by the few, and the corruption of government by those who controlled great resources.

In response to these and other problems, the federal government passed laws, set policies, and created regulatory agencies to control the operations of corporate enterprise. The chief regulatory agencies, such as the Interstate Commerce Commission, the Federal Trade Commission, and the Securities and Exchange Commission, have so much power that they have been called the fourth branch of government. Many observers, however, question the

effectiveness of regulatory bodies and laws in preventing abuses of the public good by corporations and private persons. The economist Daniel R. Fusfeld, for example, has pointed out the problems brought about by the antitrust laws:

> The dilemma of antitrust is that it has permitted the development of an economy dominated in large part by big business and has allowed that economy to structure itself in oligopolistic form. At the same time it has outlawed a variety of specific business practices that are the natural mode of behavior of giant firms and oligopolies. Yet the drive toward market control, price stability, and live-and-let-live attitude is the natural outcome of the oligopolistic structure that antitrust has failed to attack.[48]

**Expenditure of Tax Revenues** The federal government now spends over $400 billion per year. Because almost all of this money is spent directly or indirectly through the private sector of the economy, the distribution of such expenditures has substantial consequences for companies, industries, workers, communities, state and local governments, and even entire geographic regions. If, for example, a very large government contract went to Lockheed rather than to Boeing, the entire region that depends heavily on the Boeing Corporation might experience unemployment, business failures, regional recession, and even a cutback in local government services as public revenues from taxes decline.

**Control of Monetary and Fiscal Policy** In response to many bank failures and financial losses to the public, the federal government passed the Federal Reserve Act in 1913. This act created the Federal Reserve System, which, among other things, controls the money supply by buying or selling Treasury obligations (in the form of notes or bills) to banks. This increases the money supply because the Federal Reserve pays the banks in cash, which then becomes available for lending, investment, and so on. Similarly, when the Federal Reserve sells, it takes money out of the system, thus decreasing the money supply. Through its control of the monetary supply and other powers it has to regulate the banking system, the Federal Reserve can strongly influence the economic actions of corporations, labor, state and local levels of government, and you as a private consumer. In 1933 the Federal Deposit Insurance

Corporation (FDIC) was created to insure bank deposits and protect the private citizen from bank failures.

The **fiscal policy** of the government is *the way it determines income and expenditures and the relationship between them.* The income, of course, comes from taxes. The expenditures are all those expenses listed in the national budget. A *positive* fiscal policy is one that prevents extreme fluctuations in the business cycle and that maintains a high level of employment in the economy, without extreme inflation or recession. In time of recession, the government may attempt to stimulate the economy by encouraging corporate and personal spending and by spending more money than it takes in in tax revenues. The government may also temporarily lower income taxes to encourage spending. To ease the burden of the poor, it may increase welfare payments, and to ease unemployment and stimulate the economy further, it may spend money on public works — razing slums and rebuilding central cities, building hospitals, roads, and so on.

**Welfare Expenditures** Since the New Deal era of the 1930s, there has been almost a continuous increase in the percent of the federal budget allocated to aid the less privileged and disprivileged. In 1976, 43.5 percent of the federal budget ($161.4 billion) was allocated to health, labor, welfare, and education; 4.2 percent of the budget (or $15.6 billion) was allocated for veterans' benefits and services.[49] Although many people, especially the most privileged, object to such welfare expenditures, these expenditures indicate the degree of responsiveness of a democratic government to its electorate.

If you look at Table 15.6, you can see that in the industrial democracies, the largest taxes are

> **fiscal policy:** the principles a government uses to determine its income and expenditures and the relationship between them.
>
> **gross national product:** the total output of goods and services in a national economy.

taken as a percentage of the **gross national product** (GNP), the *total output of goods and services in the economy.* As Samuelson wryly pointed out,

> These [industrial democracies] happen to be the kinds of nations which have shown the greatest growth and progress in recent decades. Contrary to the law enunciated by Australia's Colin Clark — taking more than 25 percent of GNP is a guarantee of quick disaster — the modern welfare state has been both humane and solvent.[50]

### Government as a Tool of Group Interests

When we look at the major economic functions of the government, it is easy to understand why private corporations, labor unions, professional organizations, civil rights organizations and other interest groups are greatly concerned with how much they can influence the various economic activities the government affects. As we saw in Chapter 14, one of the central functions of a democracy is to translate the potential for conflict among many interest groups into legal and legitimate channels of competition and rivalry. These diverse interest groups are likely to be loyal to democratic capitalistic institutions if their leaders perceive that they have legitimate means of working to achieve their goals through the existing economic and political institutions. The data in Tables 15.7 and 15.8 show one way individuals and interest groups attempt to influence federal legislators.

Private corporations, labor unions, profes-

**TABLE 15.6  Taxes as a Percent of GNP in Various Countries, 1976**

| Developed countries | Recent average tax | Less developed countries | Recent average tax |
|---|---|---|---|
| Sweden | 43 | Spain | 21 |
| France | 38 | Jamaica | 17 |
| West Germany | 35 | Columbia | 16 |
| United Kingdom | 35 | India | 15 |
| Canada | 32 | Philippines | 11 |
| United States | 32 | Nigeria | 9½ |
| Switzerland | 23 | Mexico | 7 |
| Japan | 21 | Afghanistan | 6 |

THE BOSSES OF THE SENATE.

This nineteenth century political cartoon illustrates a common perception of the relative importance of lobbyists and legislators in the law-making process.

sional organizations, and other interest groups attempt to create an indebtedness to their interests on the part of those who hold executive and legislative positions in government. For example, in 1971–72 the Committee to Re-Elect the President (Nixon) collected $57.5 million, much of it from large corporations, and spent $55.2 million. Clearly, corporations that made large contributions hoped these donations would reduce the likelihood of the president appoint-

**TABLE 15.7  Special Interest Group Political Committees, 1974**

*Total contributions to 1974 congressional candidates*

| | | |
|---|---:|---:|
| Labor | | $ 6,315,488 |
| Business, professional, agriculture and dairy | | 4,804,473 |
| Business | $2,506,946 | |
| Health | 1,936,487 | |
| Agriculture and dairy | 361,040 | |
| Miscellaneous | | 682,215 |
| Ideological | | 723,410 |
| **Total interest group committees** | | $12,525,586 |

**Individual Interest Groups**
*Largest contributors to 1974 congressional candidates*

| | | |
|---|---|---:|
| 1. | American Medical Assns. | $1,462,972 |
| 2. | AFL-CIO COPEs | 1,178,638 |
| 3. | UAW | 843,938 |
| 4. | Maritime Unions | 738,314 |
| 5. | Machinists | 470,353 |
| 6. | Financial Institutions | 438,428 |
| 7. | National Education Assns. | 398,991 |
| 8. | Steelworkers | 361,225 |
| 9. | Retail Clerks | 291,065 |
| 10. | BIPAC (National Assn. of Mfrs.) | 272,000 |
| 11. | National Assn. of Realtors | 260,870 |

**TABLE 15.8  Individual Contributions of $500 or More to 1974 Congressional Candidates Broken Down by Occupation of Contributor**

| Occupation | House | Senate | Total |
|---|---:|---:|---:|
| Agriculture | $ 424,857 | $ 291,988 | $ 716,845 |
| Oil, gas, and other natural resources | 688,697 | 993,923 | 1,682,620 |
| Construction/real estate | 1,270,461 | 1,197,190 | 2,467,651 |
| Transportation | 131,126 | 226,909 | 358,035 |
| Manufacturing | 808,345 | 831,550 | 1,639,895 |
| Banking | 331,177 | 379,941 | 711,118 |
| Investments | 429,953 | 583,530 | 1,013,483 |
| Insurance | 225,077 | 339,756 | 564,833 |
| Financial industry | 986,207 | 1,303,227 | 2,289,434 |
| General business | 2,145,636 | 2,312,493 | 4,458,129 |
| Business total | $ 6,455,329 | $ 7,157,280 | $13,612,609 |
| Doctors | 350,110 | 228,685 | 578,795 |
| Attorneys | 1,123,019 | 1,528,809 | 2,651,828 |
| Other professionals | 793,369 | 774,606 | 1,567,975 |
| Professional | $ 2,266,498 | $ 2,532,100 | $ 4,798,598 |
| Business/professional total | $ 8,721,827 | $ 9,689,380 | $18,411,207 |
| Housewife | 485,982 | 779,352 | 1,265,334 |
| Retired | 411,183 | 584,813 | 995,996 |
| Others | 1,262,508 | 542,566 | 1,805,074 |
| Miscellaneous total | $ 2,159,673 | $ 1,906,731 | $ 4,066,404 |
| **Grand Total** | $10,881,500 | $11,596,111 | $22,477,611 |

ing as officials of regulatory agencies people who would control corporations in ways contrary to their interests. Corporations making large contributions also hoped to be looked on favorably when the government was deciding which companies to grant government contracts.

Whether fiscal and monetary policies are constructed to benefit the entire complex of interest groups or certain groups more than others is likely to depend on who the president is, whether he is a Republican or a Democrat, and whether Congress is controlled by a coalition of Republicans and southern Democrats or by a majority of Democrats from nonsouthern states. Obviously, how much welfare legislation is passed depends heavily on which party controls the presidency and what coalitions control Congress.

To repeat, political parties tend to represent the interests of the group that contribute funds or large blocs of votes to them. We should not be surprised, therefore, at the correlation between the source of a politician's campaign funds and the way that politician votes. In this century, most of the legislation that has benefited the lower and working classes, minorities, and unions has come from the Democratic party. The Republican party has been more likely to oppose legislation to benefit these groups.[51]

### Specialization and Economic Interdependence

One consequence of the great specialization of our industrial society is the economic interdependence that results. Most of us specialize in selling a service or goods to others in return for money. With this money, we have to pay other specialists for food, clothing, housing, transportation, and so on. A strike, drought, war, recession, or some other seemingly remote catastrophic event may hamper or prevent us from earning a wage or buying some good or service. For example, a series of poor harvests resulting from bad weather in Latin America can easily double the price of coffee in the United States in three or four years. When in 1973 the oil-producing nations of the Mideast increased the price of oil by over 300 percent per barrel and imposed an oil embargo on the industrialized world, all the nations of the world were affected—industrial and nonindustrial alike. The oil embargo was a major con-

tributory factor in the worst worldwide economic recession since the 1930s. The events in Iran in 1979 with the overthrow of the Shah, the further increase in oil prices by the OPEC nations, and the heightened energy crisis have further escalated the world's economic problems.

People in most preindustrial societies lived in self-sufficient little communities where they provided for all of their needs—economic, political, military, educational, and medical. In industrial societies, we live in complex networks of interdependence with people we don't know, but on whose support we depend for survival. This interdependence is as true for corporations, industries, unions, and all levels of government—local and national—as it is for you and me.

### Interlocking Institutions: The Military Industrial Complex

We have seen in previous sections how interrelated and interdependent are private corporations, labor, and government. The federal government has spent over $1,000 billion on the military since World War II.[52] Almost all of this money has been spent through private corporations. Approximately 3.8 million jobs, or one job in nine, depend on defense expenditures, and money from defense contracts is spent in more than three-quarters of the nation's congressional districts.[53] The one hundred largest corporations in the United States receive 75 percent of the defense contracts, and more than 80 percent of these contracts are awarded without competitive bidding. As John K. Galbraith puts it, the defense department

. . . provides contracts of long duration, calling for large investment of capital in areas of advanced technology. There is no risk of price fluctuations. There is full protection against any change in requirements. . . . Should a contract be cancelled the firm is protected on the investment it has made.[54]

In 1976 the Defense Department spent ninety billion dollars.[55] It is no small irony that so many millions of individuals and thousands of groups have vested interests in producing an awesome array of weapons of war capable of killing hundreds of millions of people. The same is true in the Soviet Union. Rather than an assessment of the diplomatic and military need for a given weapons system, other considerations frequently become important. What would be the effect of canceling such a contract upon the corporation's ability to survive financially? What would happen to the thousands of workers who would lose their jobs, the businesses that subcontract much of the work from the main defense contractor, and the businesses and governmental units that derive revenues from defense contractors and their employees? And, of course, the politician's own constituency may throw him or her out of office if an important military contract is canceled.

The issue of a military-industrial complex is not the nightmare of a paranoid but a well-documented reality.[56] President Dwight D. Eisenhower, a Republican and a former five-star general, warned in his last presidential address to the nation:

> The conjunction of an immense Military Establishment is new to the American experience. The total influence—economic, political, even spiritual—is felt in every statehouse, every office of the Federal Government. . . . Our toil, resources, and livelihood are all involved; so is the very structure of our society. In the councils of government we must guard against the unwarranted influence, whether sought or unsought, by the military-industrial complex. The potential for a disastrous rise of misplaced power exists and will persist.[57]

## THE DEVELOPMENT OF ECONOMIC THOUGHT[58]

Economic theory has changed along with the economic institutions and social conditions it describes.

### Mercantilism: The Economy as a Tool of Government

In mercantile theory, the dominant idea during the seventeenth and eighteenth centuries, wealth was equated with the amount of money that a nation possessed. Money was measured in terms of a nation's supply of gold and silver. By selling more goods and services to other nations than it purchased in international trade, a nation would build up its total fund of precious metals. Colonization was a source of gold and silver and raw materials that would be fashioned into products to be sold in international

trade, again with the goal of increasing wealth. Government granted legal monopolies to firms that produced for export. Under this government-administered economy, small businesses were at an extreme disadvantage in competition with the powerful, wealthy, and influential merchants. Mercantilism was not merely a theory, it actively served the interests of the wealthy and powerful.

### Adam Smith (1723–1790): Economic Competition without Government Controls

In *The Wealth of Nations* (1776), Adam Smith attacked mercantile theory. He believed that wealth is based upon the nation's capacity to produce goods and services. Money is merely a medium of exchange. In a *laissez faire* economy, the government does not regulate business people, but gives them maximum freedom to pursue their own profit. Smith's central thesis is that in a free market producers who give consumers the best product for the lowest price will be rewarded with the highest profits. Thus the absence of government restriction will encourage free competition among many producers that will reward consumers, competent producers, and the nation at large.

Smith's theory clearly served the interests of the middle-class businessmen who had suffered under the mercantile system:

> In a real sense, the rising bourgeois class needed a spokesman for their interests. Smith provided them with the ideology that served their purpose. Equally important, his ideology fed their self-esteem and moral needs.[59]

### Karl Marx (1818–1883): The Government as an Instrument of Economic Interests

As we saw in Chapter 2, Marx lived when dramatic transformations were being thrust upon many Western societies by industrialization. He analyzed the relationship between the structure of the economy and the overall institutional framework and concluded that the ownership of the means of production determines the distribution of wealth, power, and ideas. Marx projected that the capitalists would become wealthier and the masses would become poorer. The end of capitalism would occur when the masses revolted, gained control of the means of production, and created a workers' socialistic state.

The social conditions of Europe in the mid- and late-nineteenth century seemed to support Marx's view of capitalism. The masses lived in poverty, while those who controlled the economy seemed to dominate all the other institutions as well. Had these conditions continued into the twentieth century, there might well have been a worldwide revolution of the workers against the capitalists. However, governments intervened to eliminate or reduce many of the excesses of the capitalism of this period, unions have become part of the economic and political institutions of the society, and the masses have acquired a share of the increased productivity of the industrial economy.

*John Maynard Keynes (1883–1946): Government as a Regulator and Subsidizer of the Economy*

Adam Smith assumed that many producers would freely compete within a market for the money of the consumer. He also assumed that an economy unregulated by the government would be self-regulating in its use of land, labor, and capital.

John Maynard Keynes challenged these assumptions. In the early twentieth century, it had become obvious that in many markets there was no open competition among many suppliers for the purchases of consumers. Many large corporations were able to drive out competitors and set prices, usually with a few other suppliers, to the disadvantage of consumers. Furthermore, modern economies were not self-regulating. Serious imbalances could develop resulting in recessions and depressions. Keynes argued that government should intervene to correct the imbalances. It should manipulate fiscal and monetary policies to influence the growth of the economy, the rate of inflation, employment, and national income. In times of recession, the government may spend more money (on defense, roads, hospitals, etc.) in order to influence employment, consumption, investment, etc. With its monetary policy the government may reduce interest rates in order to encourage borrowing by consumers and producers to increase expenditures, investments, and employment. The governments of most industrialized nations recognize the inter-

dependence of economic and political institutions:

> The fruits of post-Keynesian economics have been the better working of the mixed economy. The era since World War II has witnessed a world growth in output and living standards unmatched in recorded history.[60]

## THE DARK SIDE OF THE AMERICAN ECONOMY

The United States is the wealthiest nation in the world. It has a total productivity more than twice that of the second wealthiest nation, the Soviet Union. Although Americans no longer have the highest per capita income of all other industrial nations, United States citizens are among the wealthiest in the world. Our economic situation is far from perfect, however. What are some of the major criticisms of the American economy?

*Poverty*

In 1976, 25 million persons were living below the poverty level, as defined by the federal government—9.1 percent of whites and 29.4 percent of nonwhites.[61] Most sociologists who study the poor believe that the government figures greatly underestimate those who are living marginal lives within our economy.

*Prejudice and Discrimination*

The cumulative and contemporary consequences of prejudice and discrimination result in minorities earning only a fraction of the income of white males as we saw in Chapters 7 and 8:

1. In 1976 the median income of black families was only 59.5 percent of the median income of white families.[62]
2. The median family income of those of Spanish origin was only 72 percent of the median family income of whites.[63]
3. Native Americans are the poorest of all minorities: Native American males who live on the reservation earn a median income that is 42 percent of that of all American males.[64]
4. In 1976 the median income of the year-round full-time adult female worker was 59 percent that of the adult male worker.[65]

### Unemployment and Underemployment

In 1976 over 7.5 million people were unemployed and seeking work (7.9 percent of the labor force of 97.5 million).[66] The unemployment rate was twice as high for nonwhites (12.7 percent) as it was for whites (6.4 percent).[67] These figures do not include those who are unemployed but have given up any hope of finding work, or those who are underemployed—working at a part-time job because of the unavailability of full-time work.

### Dissatisfaction with Work

Significant numbers of American workers are dissatisfied with their jobs and a majority would not choose to enter the same work if they had the choice. Younger workers, in particular, appear to be rebelling against the authoritarianism of their bureaucratic settings.[68] This dissatisfaction is likely to increase in the future for college-educated people. As stated earlier, it is projected that by 1985, 25 percent of those with college degrees will have to take jobs for which a degree is not required.[69]

### Bureaucratic Omnipotence and Individual Impotence

It is difficult for the individual in the United States not to feel powerless in attempting to cope with a social world dominated by large bureaucratic structures. These bureaucracies are controlled by small elite groups, most of whom seem unaccountable to the private citizen. According to traditional democratic and capitalistic ideologies, the private citizenry controls the political and economic institutions through their personal decisions in the election booth and the marketplace. These ideologies seem more fictional than real for many citizens in contemporary society.

### The Warfare State[70]

In a world where hunger, poverty, unemployment, and countless other human problems abound, it seems perverse that such a large portion of the wealth of the industrialized nations should be diverted to the development and production of instruments of war. It is disturbing that millions of American workers and thousands of companies, governmental units, and communities should have such a vested economic interest in preparation for war. Such preparations may produce the self-fulfilling prophecy of a nuclear holocaust in which no nation wins and everybody loses. These large military expenditures are, of course, not peculiar to the United States. The Soviet Union spends at least as much on its military forces. Such expenditure is spurred by reciprocal distrust among the major industrial nations.

### What Is Good for America May Be Bad for Much of the World

The population of the United States is only 6 percent of the total population of the planet, yet we consume over 30 percent of all the resources utilized in the entire world in a given year.[71] Economic, political, and military realities may enable the United States and the other indus-

Unemployment and underemployment remain a reality for millions of American workers.

trialized nations to exploit the raw materials and labor of the developing nations, but the pursuit of such national self-interest is likely to result in the people of the so-called developing nations continuing to exist in a state of hunger and disease, leading lives that remain at a subsistence level. These unfortunates of the developing nations constitute a majority of the people on the earth.[72]

## THE INDIVIDUAL WITHIN THE AMERICAN ECONOMY

The American people today are generally better educated and more affluent than their parents were. But how satisfied are they? The question is important, but it is also very difficult to answer. What is meant by satisfaction? How do you measure its presence in the labor force?

All industrial societies have created ideologies that place a high value on labor within the work force. Russia and Communist China praise the worth of labor for the national good. Manual labor is given high value in both of these nations. In China, urban white-collar workers must go back to rural communes to engage in manual labor in order to understand the importance of working with one's hands. In American society, males are socialized to judge their worth in terms of occupational criteria—they are expected to be employed, and their status is largely dependent on their occupational success.[73] One of the first questions usually asked of an adult male by someone he has just met is, "What do you do?"

The importance of one's work is not judged simply by the quantitative factors of obtaining an income to buy goods and services for oneself and possibly others. In our society, employment is a means by which a person's utility to society is judged and his or her worth as a human being is validated. Consider the effects of unemployment on the psychology and physical health of the unemployed. One study found that people who were out of work for over a year felt stigmatized by the community, friends, and relatives and tended to withdraw from participation in social events, including those with family and friends.[74]

In another study, Nancy Morse and Robert Weiss asked a representative sampling of American men the following question: "If by some chance you inherited enough money to live comfortably without working, do you think you would work anyway, or not?"[75] Approximately 80 percent of the sample said that they would continue to work even if they did inherit

TABLE 15.9 Percent of Those in Various Occupational Groups in Detroit Who Would Try to Get into a Similar Type of Work if They Could Start Over Again

| Professional and lower white-collar occupations | Percent | Working-class occupations | Percent |
|---|---|---|---|
| Urban university professors | 93 | Skilled printers | 52 |
| Mathematicians | 91 | Paper workers | 52 |
| Physicists | 89 | Skilled auto workers | 41 |
| Biologists | 89 | Skilled steelworkers | 41 |
| Chemists | 86 | Textile workers | 31 |
| Firm lawyers | 85 | Blue-collar workers, age 30–55 | 24 |
| School superintendents | 85 | Blue-collar workers, age 21–29 | 23 |
| Lawyers | 83 | Unskilled steelworkers | 21 |
| Journalists (Washington correspondents) | 82 | Unskilled auto workers | 16 |
| Church university professors | 77 | | |
| Solo lawyers | 75 | | |
| Diversico engineers | 70 | | |
| Unico engineers | 70 | | |
| White-collar workers, age 21–29 | 46 | | |
| White-collar workers, age 30–55 | 43 | | |

sufficient funds to live comfortably without working. A majority of the white-collar workers would continue in the same type of work. A majority of those in working-class occupations, although preferring to work, would not continue in the same types of jobs.

As Table 15.9 shows, occupations that require the greatest education and skills and offer the highest status, authority, and income tend to be most satisfying. People who are least satisfied with their jobs are those in occupations that require the least formal education and offer the least status, authority, and income. H. L. Wilensky found that at all occupational levels, those most likely to be dissatisfied were those who experienced the following:

1. work situation and organizational setting that provided little discretion in pace and schedule, and a tall hierarchy above (low freedom, high pressure)
2. career which has been blocked and chaotic
3. stage in the life cycle that puts the squeeze on [such as having large numbers of children living at home and low amounts of savings and investments.][76]

Conversely, "control over the workplace, opportunity for sociable talk on the job, and an orderly career foster work attachment."[77] The occupations most likely to possess these attributes, of course, are those of the professional and managerial categories. After conducting long interviews with a sampling of 1,354 men in diverse occupational categories and strata, Wilensky concluded that it appeared that "the vast majority of Americans are 'playing it cool,' neither strongly wedded to the job nor feeling it to be an intense threat to their identity."[78]

## THE COMING OF POSTINDUSTRIAL SOCIETY

What does the future hold for the American economy and society through the year 2000? A number of prestigious academics have written books on this subject.[79] Let us look at some of their projections.

### Affluence and Leisure

Herman Kahn and Anthony J. Wiener and others project that by the year 2000, affluence and leisure will have increased dramatically in the United States. Real per capita gross national product should increase by about 100 percent between 1965 and the year 2000. The projected average work week for the year 2000 is composed of four working days of 7.5 hours each. There will be thirty-nine working weeks per year, ten legal holidays, three-day weekends and thirteen weeks of vacation per year.[80]

These projections may not prove to be accurate because of a multiplicity of contingencies that cannot be foreseen. However, let us review some figures from the past in order to gain some perspective on projections into the future. In 1890, the average work week was 62 hours.[81] In April 1977, the average work week was 35.8 hours.[82] In 1913, in 1968 dollars, 61 percent of families and individuals earned under $3,000 per year; in 1967, only 17 percent of families and individuals earned under $3,000 for the year.[83] Just between 1950 and 1976 the per capita income in the United States increased 90.5 percent, the value of the dollar being held constant for purposes of analysis.[84]

### Projected Trends

**The Service Occupations**   It is projected that there will be a continued increase in the portion of the labor force that is in the service-related occupations. The increased automation of the industrial sector of the economy and the mechanization of the farm sector will further reduce the number of people needed to produce food and manufactured products.

**The Professional-Technical Strata**   There will be a continued increase in proportion of the labor force in scientific-technical work. As America increasingly moves into the postindustrial stage, the way for an individual to gain access to more power and prestige will increasingly be to acquire scientific and technical knowledge and skills.[85] See Table 15.10 for an analysis of the primary means of achieving power in preindustrial, industrial, and postindustrial societies. According to Daniel Bell, rather than the landowners or the businessmen being dominant in postindustrial society, scientists and professional technocrats will dominate society.

A person may achieve control of an organization through the inheritance of property. But without the technical skills to manage it, the

**TABLE 15.10   Stratification and Power in Three Types of Societies**

|  | Preindustrial | Industrial | Postindustrial |
|---|---|---|---|
| Resource | Land | Machinery | Knowledge |
| Social locus | Farm<br>Plantation | Business firm | University<br>Research institute |
| Dominant figures | Landowner<br>Military | Businessmen | Scientists<br>Researchers |
| Means of power | Direct control<br>of force | Indirect influence<br>on politics | Balance of technical-<br>political forces<br>Franchises and rights |
| Class base | Property<br>Military force | Property<br>Political organization<br>Technical skill | Technical skill<br>Political organization |
| Access | Inheritance<br>Seizure by armies | Inheritance<br>Patronage<br>Education | Education<br>Mobilization<br>Co-optation |

company will fail to compete successfully with more professionally run organizations. In large private corporations, as we have noted, there has already been a separation of control from ownership, with professional managers administering the complex bureaucracies. Those who use politics as the means to power must either be competent professional technocrats or hire technicians and experts who have the knowledge and skills to make technical judgments on complex issues. What all this adds up to is the increasing dominance of those with technical skills—the emergence of a technocratic elite. In Bell's words:

The members of this new technocratic elite, with their new techniques of decision-making (systems analysis, linear programming, and program budgeting), have now become essential to the formulation and analysis of decisions on which political judgments have to be made, if not to the wielding of power. It is in this broad sense that the spread of education, research, and administration has created a new constituency—the technical and professional intelligentsia.[86]

**The Increasing Role of Government** An ever-increasing number of people will be employed by all levels of government—federal, state, county, and city. The political institution will dominate the postindustrial society as the private corporations dominated the industrial period. In the United States, there is such an inextricable interdependence of economic units that there is an ever-increasing need for government coordination of the relations among

Workers at Social Security headquarters in Baltimore. A projected trend: More and more people will be employed by government.

corporations, unions, professional organizations, agricultural cooperatives, consumer organizations, and other interest groups. These groups increasingly seek to make their claims known and implement them through politics, to have the economic functions of government serve their interests. In Charles Reich's words:

The valuables dispensed by government take many forms, but they all share one characteristic. They are steadily taking the place of the traditional forms of wealth—forms which are held as private property. Social insurance substitutes for savings, a government contract replaces a businessman's customers and goodwill. . . . Increasingly, Americans live on governmental largess—allocated by government on its own terms, and held by recipients subject to conditions which express "the public interest."[87]

**The Future of Affluence and Leisure**  Only in this century, and only in the most highly industrialized nations, have a majority of the population been freed from the preoccupation of obtaining an adequate food supply and of protecting themselves from the environment with adequate clothing and housing. One might once have thought—naively—that affluence and leisure would have brought us satisfaction and optimism. Yet the national polls document a dissatisfaction with and pessimism toward our institutions and society that are disquieting to many observers. As long ago as 1930, Keynes, anticipated some of the problems of increasing affluence and leisure in a famous essay:

If instead of looking into the future, we look into the past—we find that the economic problem, the struggle for subsistence, always has been hitherto the primary, most pressing problem of the human race—not only of the human race, but of the whole of the biological kingdom from the beginnings of life in its most primitive forms. . . . If the economic problem is solved, mankind will be deprived of its traditional purpose. . . . I think with dread of the readjustment of the habits and instincts of the ordinary man, bred into him for countless generations, which he may be asked to discard within a few decades. . . .

Thus for the first time since his creation man will be faced with his real, his permanent problem—how to use his freedom from pressing economic cares, how to occupy the leisure, which science and compound interest will have won for him, to live wisely and agreeably and well. . . . There are changes in other spheres too which we must expect to come. When the accumulation of wealth is no longer of high social importance, there will be great changes in the code of morals. We shall be able to rid ourselves of many of the pseudo-moral principles which have hag-ridden us for two hundred years, by which we have exalted some of the more distasteful of human qualities into the position of the highest virtues. . . . The love of money as a possession—as distinguished from the love of money as a means to the enjoyments and realities of live—will be recognized for what it is, a somewhat disgusting morbidity, one of those semi-criminal, semi-pathological propensities which one hands over with a shudder to the specialists in mental disease.[88]

## SUMMARY

The economy is the institution that provides for the production, distribution, and consumption of goods and services for a given population. Of the approximately last 100,000 years of human existence, about 90,000 were spent in hunting and gathering societies, 4,000 years were lived in horticultural societies, and 4,800 more years passed with people living in agricultural societies. Agriculture, with its capacity to produce considerable surplus, gave rise to fully developed stratification systems, cities, permanent residences, and great gulfs in social distance between the small, wealthy elite and the mass of peasants.

Until the Industrial Revolution, 200 years ago, the vast bulk of the population lived at the subsistence level. Not until this century was a majority of the population freed from subsistence worries, and then only those in the most highly industrialized societies.

The effects of industrialization on the other social institutions has been dramatic. The increasingly machine-based economy has reduced the need for unskilled workers and increased the need for those in the skilled manual and white-collar occupations. Education has become the instrument for providing people with the knowledge and skills to fit into the increasingly complex labor force. Industrialization has produced a society that is urban, affluent, and well educated, conditions that appear to be necessary for the development of a stable democracy. The contemporary economy has stripped the family of many of its former functions, such as the economic, protective, and recreational functions. The increased emphasis on understanding and manipulating the observable world has brought about a general secularization of the society, which has undermined the influence of religion.

The American economy has six central characteristics: (1) the changing composition of the labor force, (2) private corporations, (3) labor unions and professional organizations, (4) the government, (5) specialization and economic interdependence, and (6) the military-industrial complex. The major change in the composition of the labor force in this century has been the increasing dominance of service-oriented occupations. Two-thirds of the labor force are in jobs that contribute services rather than raw materials or manufactured goods to the economy. The proportion of people engaging in agriculture has diminished dramatically. Almost half of the women are now employed in the labor force. Those born in the last years of the "baby boom" are now entering the labor market. More of these young people have college degrees than there are jobs for which a degree is a prerequisite.

Private corporations in the American economy are characterized by the separation of ownership and control. The control of private corporations has shifted from owners to professional technocrats who possess the managerial skills needed to coordinate the personnel and resources of the large, complex corporations. Along with corporate growth has come an increasing trend toward oligopoly, the domination of an industry by three or four of the largest firms. Many of these corporations have absorbed corporations from other unrelated industries, becoming conglomerates. Some of these huge corporations now conduct business in many countries, and two-thirds of these multinationals originated in the United States. The multinationals have wealth and power that transcend national boundaries and constitute a control problem for individual nations. The worker in the American society lives in an occupational world dominated by bureaucratic employers—private and governmental.

Workers and professional people have formed labor unions and professional organizations to protect and further their interests. These groups greatly increase their members' abilities to negotiate with employers and political bodies. The unions have become a major economic and political force in the United States, and over one-fifth of the labor force is unionized.

The government has played increasingly important roles in the economy by creating regulatory agencies, allocating expenditures to certain economic sectors, controlling monetary and fiscal policy, and funding welfare programs to aid ever-larger sections of the population. Because of these great economic powers, the government is increasingly viewed as a tool that may be influenced by diverse groups within the society—corporations, unions, professional groups, minorities, and so on.

The specialization of the labor force, industries, and regions of the nation and world has created an economic interdependence with profound consequences. Events remote from us, and possibly unknown to us, may affect our ability to obtain the most essential or trivial of goods and services.

One of the profound effects of institutional specialization and interdependence has been the development of a military-industrial complex where millions of people in government, private corporations, labor unions, and in the community at large have been given a vested interest in the expenditure of billions of dollars per year for the military. Such vested interests may prevent more humane uses of these vast financial resources. Further, such military expenditures tend to stimulate reciprocal responses in rival nations that contribute to a perpetual weapons competition which could lead to a nuclear holocaust.

The development of economic thought has paralleled the changing structure of the economy. Whereas mercantilists believed that the economy should be an instrument of the government, Adam Smith opposed all government regulation of the economy. In the nineteenth century, Marx viewed the government as an instrument of those who controlled the economy. Today in the industrial non-Communist nations, the government is primarily viewed as a regulator and subsidizer of mixed economies, which are neither purely capitalistic nor socialistic.

Although many benefits have been derived from the industrialization of American society, there are criticisms of the American economy: (1) Many Americans still live out their entire lives in poverty, (2) minorities are not deriving a fair share of the productivity of the economy, (3) millions of people are unemployed and underemployed, (4) many Americans have difficulty in finding meaning in their work, (5) seemingly omnipotent bureaucracies controlled by a relatively unaccountable elite appear to dominate the economy, (6) much of the wealth is expended for what can be labeled a permanent war economy, and, (7) some or much of the affluence in the United States seems to be derived from the exploitation of a disproportionately large share of the world's economic resources.

The economy has a profound effect on the individual in another way. Work in industrial societies has become one of the central activities by which a person's worth is judged — by the individual as well as by others. In spite of the importance of work as a basis for self-esteem, most Americans appear to be neither greatly committed to, nor alienated from, their jobs.

Most of the projections concerning the economy and society of the future state that Americans (and those in other highly industrial societies) will have great affluence and leisure. If these projections prove accurate, one problem of the future may well be that of finding a meaning for our lives in ways not related to the economic system. Other events expected to occur are a continuing enlargement of the service sector of the labor force, with corresponding reductions in the primary (extraction) and secondary (manufacture) sectors; an increase in the numbers and influence of the professional-technical stratum; and an increase in government domination of all economic activities.

## SUGGESTED READINGS

BARNET, RICHARD V., AND RONALD E. MULLER. *Global Reach: The Power of the Multinational Corporations.* New York: Simon & Schuster, 1974. This is an excellent documentation of the degree to which multinationals may develop vested interests which are in conflict with the interests of nations within which they do business and have their headquarters.

LEKACHMAN, ROBERT. *Economists at Bay: Why the Experts Will Never Solve Your Problems.* New York: McGraw-Hill, 1976. This book offers a penetrating analysis of the problems posed by multinationals for nations and for analysis by economists.

MINTZ, MORTON, AND JERRY S. COHEN. *America, Incorporated: Who Owns and Operates the United States.* New York: Dell, 1971. This is a detailed account of how private corporations attempt to translate their economic wealth into political power.

SAMPSON, ANTHONY. *The Seven Sisters: The Great Oil Companies and the World They Made.* New York: Viking, 1975. This book offers a disturbing analysis of how these oil companies have cooperated to form a cartel which furthers corporate interests across national boundaries.

SAMUELSON, PAUL A. *Economics,* 10th ed. New York: McGraw-Hill, 1976. This book offers the student a readable and interesting overview of economics by a Nobel Prize winner who possesses a social conscience.

SMELSER, NEIL J. *The Sociology of Economic Life,* 2d ed. Englewood Cliffs, N.J.: Prentice-Hall, 1976. This is an excellent brief overview of the development of economic thought.

# FIVE

## Collective Behavior and Social Change

We saw in Chapters 1 and 2 that the problems and models of sociological analysis have always been concerned with social order and change. These issues are simple in formulation but complex in implication. What makes social order and regularity possible? How do we account for the persistence of pattern in social life? With the weight of social order and regularity so consistent, how is it that things do change? What makes social alteration possible, and how does it come about?

Earlier sections of this book have largely been devoted to the problem of order. Scientific endeavor must have pattern and regularity with which to work. The three chapters that make up the last part of this book, however, are concerned with the kinds of social phenomena that produce change.

Chapter 16 discusses deviant behavior, crime, and social control. *Deviant behavior* is behavior that breaks social rules, abandons conventional patterns; it is often both the product of, and a force for, change in a society. To talk about deviance, or to define a behavior as criminal, is to say something about the *status quo* and those who maintain it; the forces of order and change. *Social control* means all the forces that are directed toward the regularization of behavior. Even though social control is intended to maintain order, by reacting to what is perceived as disorder, it must often introduce change as well.

Chapter 17 is about *collective or mass behavior* and the special variety called *social movements*. These phenomena are often deeply involved with social change and may, indeed, be major mechanisms through which it is accomplished. In Chapter 18, we take up the topic of change itself, the conditions under which it is likely to occur, the various social agents that manifest and promote or retard it, and the trends of change current in the modern world.

# Chapter 16
# Deviance, Crime, and Social Control

456

efforts were to no avail; doctors and nurses interpreted everything the pseudopatients did in terms of the original diagnosis. When some of the volunteers went about taking notes, the hospital staff made such entries in their records as "patient engages in writing behavior." The only people who realized that the experimenters were normal were some of the patients. "You're not crazy," said one patient. "You're a journalist or a professor. You're checking up on the hospital."

*Crazy:* During a psychiatric interview, a pseudopatient noted that he was closer to his mother as a small child, but as he grew up, became more attached to his father. Although this was a perfectly normal alteration of identity figures, it was taken by the psychiatrist as evidence of "unstable relationships in childhood." The hospital, Rosenhan concluded, distorts the perception of behavior. "In a psychiatric hospital," he says, "the place is more important than the person. If you're a patient you must be crazy."

Rosenhan and his colleagues were not exposed to the squalor and degradation of any modern snake pits, but they did witness incidents of abuse and brutality. One patient was beaten for approaching an attendant and saying "I like you."

All this, the Stanford psychologist point out, is part of a pervasive depersonalization and helplessness that afflicts patients in a mental hospital. The experimenters found much additional evidence that the staff didn't regard the patients as people, or even in some cases, acknowledge that they existed. On one occasion, a nurse casually opened her blouse to adjust her brassiere in the midst of a ward full of men. "One did not have the sense she was being seductive," said Rosenhan. "She just didn't notice us."

From their fellow patients, the volunteers quickly learned that they were caught up in a kind of Catch-22 paradox. "Never tell a doctor that you're well," said one patient. "He won't believe you. That's called a 'flight into health.' Tell him you're still sick, but you're feeling a lot better. That's called 'insight.'" "You've got to be sick and acknowledge that you're sick," says Rosenhan, "to be considered well enough to be released."

As it was, it took up to 52 days for the volunteers to get out of the hospital, even though most had been admitted voluntarily and the law in many states makes discharge mandatory on request in such instances on 72 hours' notice. Three of the volunteers finally walked out of the hospital. The other nine were ultimately discharged, but with the stigma of the diagnosis "schizophrenia in remission."

*Newsweek,* January 29, 1973. Study originally reported in D. L. Rosenhan. "On Being Sane in Insane Places." *Science,* 179 (January 19, 1973), pp. 250–258.

The *Newsweek* story is both fascinating and frightening. The situation *is* a common theme for horror films and nightmares. Sociologically, however, it raises some far-reaching questions: If specialists cannot distinguish between deviance and normality, who can? What do we mean by deviant behavior and how is it to be recognized?

Of course, as a matter of popular understanding "everybody knows" that some kinds of behavior are wrong or immoral or perverted or insane and that the kind of people who habitually engage in them are sick or depraved. Good folks sometimes go wrong for awhile under severe stress, but that is understandable and can be forgiven; it does not mean that they are not essentially "good." But we must distinguish between an occasional lapse on the part of someone "like us" and the willfully wrong behavior of "common criminals," who are clearly not "like us," or the "crazy" behavior of those who are obviously insane because they act in "bizarre" ways.

In the popular understanding, there are two kinds of people and two kinds of behavior, deviant and nondeviant. We recognize deviant people by the fact that they engage in deviant behavior, nondeviants by the fact that they do not. We recognize deviant behavior because it is wrong, illegal, immoral, or depraved. Any individual who is not a deviant would recognize these things. This minitheory in the sociology of deviant behavior implies that deviance is a quality that inheres in people, in behavior, or in both; deviant people and deviant acts are different from other people and acts; deviance is intrinsic; individuals or acts are either deviant or nondeviant in their very nature; deviance is a quality of people or actions—and a readily recognizable one, at that.

The Rosenhan experiment shows, however, that—as is often the case with "what everybody knows"—things may not be so simple as they first appear. Before exploring further, let us try to agree on the meaning of the word *deviance* itself.

## THE MEANING OF DEVIANCE

The dictionary definition of the verb *to deviate* is *to turn aside from a way or course, to depart or swerve from a procedure or line of thought or reasoning.* **Deviance,** then, involves variation. Deviant behavior is variant or unusual; a deviant person is one who is unusual or atypical, "different" from others. *To call something deviant thus implies a departure from norms for acceptable behavior.*

This dictionary definition does not seem to be inconsistent with the popular understanding until we confront the assumptions on which that understanding rests. Is it true that there are two kinds of people, the deviant and the nondeviant, who in their natures are different from one another and are distinguishable? This is an old idea and one that even scientists have accepted and attempted to investigate. The relations between deviant behavior and physical characteristics, body types, body chemistry, chromosomal structure, and so forth have often been studied. But no theory of this kind has

YOU KNOW NOTHING ABOUT WATERGATE. WHICH GROUP WOULD YOU MOST LIKELY SUSPECT OF BURGLARY, THEFT, BREAKING AND ENTERING, WIRETAPPING, ELECTION LAW VIOLATIONS AND CONSPIRACY?

Editorial cartoon by Paul Conrad. Copyright © 1976 Los Angeles Times. Reprinted with permission

**What do we mean by deviant behavior? How do we recognize it? Why would many people pick the second group in response to the question?**

been able reliably to distinguish so-called deviants from others, and none has been able successfully to predict deviant behavior.

"But," a defender of the popular understanding might argue, "people have free will; they can choose whether to engage in deviant behavior or not. No one makes someone steal. The difference is in motivation." This argument is, of course, a variation on the "different people" assumption. It seems plausible on the surface, but, again, it falls down when confronted with facts. It implies that the essence of deviation is intentional nonconformity, that deviants are people who want to violate norms. But, as Howard Becker asks, are those who have been defined as deviant the only people who have ever experienced the desire to commit a deviant act?[1] Clearly, the answer is no.

All of us occasionally have impulses to violate social norms. Honest appraisal of our mental lives would lead most of us to admit that larceny, assault, sexual experimentation, and per-

**deviance:** sociologically, departure or variation from a normative standard.

haps even murder are things we commonly imagine, not to mention smoking in forbidden places, walking on the grass, cursing in public, and so forth. Indeed an honest self-inventory would probably show that the vast majority of people not only experience impulses to deviate but that they often act upon them. Few of us have never stolen anything, violated a speed law, or engaged in some other illegal or socially forbidden behavior. One classic study of "law-abiding" people showed that more than 90 percent had violated the felony code at least once in their adult lives![2] The idea that there are two different kinds of people, the deviant and the nondeviant, simply will not stand up to objective inspection.

The other assumption on which the popular understanding rests, that some behaviors are intrinsically deviant, turns out to be equally false when we examine the facts. It is virtually impossible to specify any particular human behavior, any act, that is everywhere and at all times condemned. Murder, for example, is very widely prohibited. But murder is not an act, it is a set of circumstances. The act of killing another person is sometimes accepted (as in self-defense) and sometimes even praised and rewarded (as in war). Rape is sexual intercourse under a specific set of circumstances—with

**Shoplifting, a common crime among young people. Almost all of us have at some time committed an act which, if we'd been apprehended, would have been called deviant.**

threats or violence and without the consent of the victim. Cannibalism is the proper outcome of battle in some cultures. Incestuous marriage was required among royalty in ancient Egypt and in the Inca empire. Crimes are simply acts that have been prohibited by legislative bodies under specified conditions and the legal codes are not by any means entirely supported by social norms. Many people regard some laws as foolish or even morally wrong.

The popular understanding of deviance, then, is false in both of its underlying assumptions. Deviance is not a quality or characteristic of either people or behavior. It is, rather, as we said earlier, a judgment that an individual is engaging in behavior that departs from social norms.

### Norms and Deviance

The sociological definition of deviance as a judgment about norm violation seems clear enough, but as we saw in Chapter 3, there are two different dimensions to human acts, the behavioral dimension, that is, how people actually behave, and the normative dimension, or how we ought to behave. The traffic laws pose a familiar example of the two. A speed limit is normative: we ought to conform to it and we may be legally penalized if we do not. But behaviorally, most of us violate most speed limits (a little bit) most of the time, and, moreover, the police usually do not enforce them rigorously. A patrolman with a radar set will not normally pull you over for going thirty-two miles an hour in a thirty-mile zone. A citizen who always observed every speed limit precisely would clearly deviate from the behavioral norms by observing the normative ideal. Deviance is therefore relative.

### The Social Relativity of Deviance

*Deviance is a judgment by an individual or group that another individual or group is behaving in nonconforming ways.* Judgments are made on the basis of normative standards, which is to say they are cultural. The social conditions under which they are made vary immensely.

**Deviance Is Societally Relative**  What is seen as deserving of punishment in one society may be ignored or even rewarded in another. A

cultural abomination in one society may be a religious observation somewhere else. Even within a given society, different subcultures may have norms quite inconsistent with those of the general culture or other subcultures.

**Deviance Is Temporally Relative**  What is defined as deviant at one point in history may be ignored or even encouraged at another. At the turn of the century, for example, opium and morphine additives were widely used in patent medicines without social disapproval. In 1978 the legislature of the State of Wisconsin raised the legal age for drinking from 18 to 21. The day before the legislation came into effect, a nineteen-year-old could legally buy a drink; the day afterward, attempting to do so was a misdemeanor. Temporal relativity can also be seen in such matters as abortion, long hair on men, pants suits for women, and many other behaviors that were once viewed as deviant and were penalized with greater or lesser punishments.

**Deviance Is Spatially Relative**  Sexual intercourse between spouses in the bedroom is encouraged by church and state. Sexual intercourse on the front lawn will land you in jail. An eighteen-year-old may not purchase liquor in one state, but across the state line the purchase is legal; some states have dry counties where the sale of liquor is totally forbidden. The airlines may not serve alcoholic beverages to passengers in flight over Kansas.

**Deviance Is Relative to Social Status**  In many college towns, a professor apprehended by the police for driving while intoxicated may be released with a lecture or even be driven home. A student apprehended in the same condition is likely to spend the night in the pokey, and may be expelled from school as well. Richard Nixon was pardoned for involvement in actions for which his subordinates went to jail. Corporations may be fined relatively small sums for acts that, if committed by individuals, would result in long prison terms.

The status of victims is also relevant. In former times in the American South, a black who assaulted or killed a white was apt to be treated very harshly, while a white who assaulted or killed a black might never come to trial. White men raped black women with impunity, whereas if a black man was even suspected of

Deviance is societally and temporally relative.
*(Above)* **Marijuana smokers.** Specific subcultures
sometimes encourage, or at least define as
appropriate, behaviors that others—the general
culture—define as deviant. *(Below)* **This ad
emphasizes the temporal relativity of the deviant
label for marijuana users.**

raping a white woman, the act would be regarded as a hideous crime and the man might
not live to be arrested. At the same time, blacks

who raped or killed other blacks were apt to be
treated more leniently than whites who raped
or killed other whites.

**Deviance Is Relative to Its Consequences**
Some actions are punished as deviant only
when they result in certain consequences; at
other times, they are ignored. The classic example is that the social norms forbidding premarital sex are generally enforced for young people
only when the female partner becomes pregnant and then, as a rule, only against her. (The
male's social status among his peers may even
improve.) Drunkenness is normally reprimand-
ed only when the resulting behavior becomes
flagrantly offensive.

We can conclude that deviance is a characteristic of neither persons nor actions. It is, rather,
like most other human behavior, an interaction
process. Most of our behavior is conducted for
and before an audience of others, and the example of what is called deviant behavior makes it
clear that the meaning of a given act is in large
part defined by that audience of others. The
conditions under which that definition is made
determine what the definition will be. To understand deviant behavior, then, we must focus
neither on the behavior itself nor on the individual who committed it, but on the conditions
under which it occurred and the reaction of
others to it.

## DEVIANCE AND SOCIAL CONTROL

The concept of deviance is necessarily interwoven with the concept of social control. As we
noted in Chapter 4, social control consists of all
of the ways in which social norms are enforced,
the processes and mechanisms that contribute
to the maintenance of normative conformity.
Social control may be formal, as in police work,
or informal, as in peer pressure within social
groups. Its most effective form, however, is the
self-control produced by socialization.

### Social Control and Socialization:
### Self-Control

As we saw in Chapters 4 and 5, all of us play
different roles in which our behavior is fairly
predictable: student, teacher, father, daughter,
lover, spouse. Certain behavior is expected in

each role. There may be a variety of ways to play a given role, but each role has some boundaries. Socialization prepares us to behave in accordance with the expectations of the society we are entering. We usually think of this in terms of children and how they internalize the values of their society. But socialization also operates each time we enter a social situation where we have no precise understanding of what is expected of us. In selecting a career, we are usually socialized into a new language, one peculiar to that occupation. Along with the language come many other norms we are expected to observe in order to function efficiently within that occupation.

Leisure pursuits are another example. If you went to an opera for the first time, you would find that it is perfectly acceptable to leap to your feet and shout BRAVO! when an aria is especially well sung. This behavior would be inappropriate at a chamber music recital. How to behave as a plumber or an architect, what behavior is expected at an opera or a concert, is generally not learned in childhood. Socialization is an ongoing process, continuing throughout life.

The form of social control that results from the internalization of norms through socialization is most effective, and it provides the glue that holds society together. The norm we do not wish to violate is far more efficiently enforced than the one that requires police surveillance. Few American jurisdictions have laws prohibiting the eating of dogs. The norm prohibiting it is so widely and thoroughly internalized that legal restraints would be superfluous.

**Informal social control is based on social organizational reciprocity. We need the cooperation of others in order to enact our own roles.**

The popular understanding of deviance described above—and the American and British systems of criminal law as well—rest on the idea that deviance results from a failure of this internalization of social controls. Deviants are perceived as people for whom the socialization process has not worked properly, since they "choose" to violate social norms. Punishing them for their behavior should thus help them learn it is improper and harmful to themselves, as well as preventing others from following their example. The deviant is "different," but can be made to conform.

We have seen that this assumption is often erroneous. Almost every person raised in a given society internalizes its general norms to some degree. In many instances, the reason for "deviant" behavior is not that individuals have failed to acquire the norms, but that because of normative conflict, or role requirements, they must violate a norm in some way. When two or more norms conflict, the actor often has to violate one in order to abide by the other. For example, few students report one another for cheating. They prefer to abide by the norm that says you don't tell on friends and thus violate the norm against condoning cheating.

### Social Control and Social Organization: Informal Control

The type of social control involved with social organization could be called group control, but is more commonly labeled **informal social control.** You will recall that Chapters 5 and 6 described social organization as the web of relations and interactions between individuals in groups, social situations, organizations, social institutions, and society itself. Social organization, thus, is both a structural framework and an ongoing process, and its basis is *reciprocity*. In order to function at all, we must share reciprocal expectations with others. Many roles are themselves reciprocal, requiring the presence and cooperation of another. Many groups, in turn, exist only as parts of organizations, and both informal groups and organizations operate within institutional and societal frameworks. It is apparent, then, that for an individual, both self-interest and need satisfaction depend heavily upon the normal acting out of social organization.

Because we are all so deeply involved in what

Georg Simmel called "The Web of Group Affiliation," we must respond to the expectations that others have for us.[3] To the degree that we do not, we are likely to have satisfactions withheld and punishments applied. Most work situations, for example, require the cooperation of a number of people. A physician in private practice, for instance, depends just as much on receptionists, technicians, secretaries, and pharmacists for the successful outcome of his or her work as a factory worker depends on the dozens of co-workers who contribute to the finished product of the assembly line.

To the degree that this cooperation with others in the situation breaks down, all members are likely to experience reduced reward, and those responsible are likely to be called to task by the others. Thus, because we live in social groups and situations, other people exercise an informal social control over us by their

> **informal social control:** the enforcement of normative conformity through socialization and social organizational reciprocity.
>
> **formal social control:** the enforcement of normative conformity through formal means such as police, organizational rules, and so on.

ability to sanction and their influence on our own behavior. (The "rate-buster" on the assembly line can be quite satisfactorily controlled by a "slowdown" of other workers, tardy inspection by supervisors, delay at the tool crib, and so forth.) The expectations of others, which are a fundamental part of our own roles, are a major element in social control.

### Social Control and Social Structure: Formal Control

**Formal social control** has to do with *social structure* rather than with *social organization*. It is applied by agencies specifically designated to perform that function. The most obvious illustration of formal social control is the apparatus of police, courts, and prisons within the institution of law. Formal control is specifically and consciously designed to secure normative conformity. It is probably the least efficient of the three varieties of social control, but even brief consideration will show that it is hardly dispensable. Although formal controls are obviously not 100 percent effective, most people probably *are* sometimes prevented from doing things they might otherwise do by the threat of formal punishment.

### The Relation between Deviance and Social Control

Deviance is a function of social control. Social control creates deviance. Social groups create deviance by creating rules and then labeling those who violate the rules as deviant. Durkheim was the first to recognize and describe this connection.

You may recall from Chapter 2 that Durkheim devoted his professional career to the study of the social organization and the normative order of society. Crime, the kind of deviance he addressed in *The Division of Labor in Society*, was

Formal social control is applied by agencies of society. While it is probably the least effective of the three agencies, we cannot dispense with it.

for Durkheim a natural consequence of the existence of a collectively supported moral order.[4] Crime is thus a natural part of any society, because all society requires a moral order.

Durkheim's perception about crime applies to all kinds of deviance. Society cannot exist without a moral order, and this order is based on rules. Since the existence of rules of any kind makes their violation possible, the possibility of deviance is built into the very structure of society itself. The existence of a code of "right" conduct creates the possibility of "wrong" conduct by definition. Wrong gives meaning to right.

Kai T. Erikson's *Wayward Puritans*, a monograph in historical sociology, explains this principle as follows:

Now people who live together in communities cannot relate to one another in any coherent way . . . unless they learn something about the boundaries of the territory they occupy in social space, if only because they need to sense what lies beyond the margins of the group before they can appreciate the special quality of the experience which takes place within it. . . . To begin with, the only material found in a society for marking boundaries is the . . . networks of interaction which link [members] together in regular social relations. And the interactions which do the most effective job of locating and publicizing the group's outer edges would seem to be those which take place between deviant persons on the one side and official agents of the community on the other. The deviant is a person whose activities have moved outside the margins of the group, and when the community calls him to account for that vagrancy it is making a statement about the nature and placement of its boundaries. It is declaring how much variability and diversity can be tolerated within the group before it begins to lose its distinctive shape, its unique identity.[5]

According to Lewis Coser, because social norms are not always entirely precise and clear, the commission of what are later defined as wrongs is sometimes necessary to the clarification of what is right.[6] Limits are sometimes established only after the fact, when they have been violated. This is, of course, exactly the situation in a legal "test case": Someone deliberately violates a law in order to test the law's constitutionality.

Contrary to the popular (and legal) idea that deviance results from a failure to control individual behavior, deviance actually represents a measure of successful control. The definition of an act as deviant presupposes the existence of norms forbidding it. The amount of deviance in a society is not a measure of the breakdown of its moral order. It may be a measure of normative conflict and inconsistencies in social organization, but it also manifests the ongoing operation of social structure.

## VARIETIES OF DEVIANT BEHAVIOR

It is apparent that a wide variety of behavior may be considered deviant by at least some members of a society at any time and that the variety is wider still if we include interpretations of deviance across time and culture. Where there are norms regulating human behavior—which is to say, everywhere—there must be deviance of one kind or another. The varieties of deviance may be grouped according to three general categories: violations of law, of custom, or of manners. All three are subject to social change, of course, which means that in any category, the definition of deviance may alter over time.

### Violations of Law

In Western societies, there are two types of law, criminal and civil. A violation of criminal law is called a crime and may be classified as a *felony* or a *misdemeanor* depending upon its severity. In *misdemeanors* or *torts*, violators are not usually conceived by others as deviant or criminal. But to complicate matters the law distinguishes between acts that are *mala in se* and those that are *mala prohibita*, that is, acts wrong or evil in themselves, such as rape, and acts that are wrong merely because they are forbidden, such as traffic offenses. While most members of a society may agree that the commission of an act *mala in se* is a deviant behavior, many may not agree in defining as deviant many acts that are *mala prohibita*. It may be a crime to falsify one's income tax return, for instance, but many of us do not regard all people who do so as criminals. Thus crime and delinquency (which simply means the commission of a legally prohibited act by a person beneath the age of majority) must be treated as somewhat special instances of deviance, and we do so below.

## Violations of Custom

Most people agree that there is "something wrong" with people who commit violations of custom, especially those involving well institutionalized norms for common behavior. Even this agreement is complicated, however, by the same kind of distinction the law makes between acts *mala prohibita* and acts *mala in se*. We distinguish here between violations of *custom*, which might generally be regarded as wrong in themselves, and violations of *manners*, which may be regarded as improper merely because they are very unusual and, perhaps, uncivil. Homosexuality, bigamy, transvestism, and drug abuse are widely condemned. That these behaviors are also frequently illegal is beside the point because the laws forbidding them have been passed in response to custom and merely formalize it. Many other behaviors that are not against the law meet with equal or greater disapproval. To return to an example cited earlier, anyone habitually consuming dogmeat would probably be regarded as deviant in the United States although no law prohibits it, and anyone found raising dogs for the purpose of eating them would probably be stopped by the application of other laws such as those governing humane slaughter or the housing of animals. There seems little doubt that a person persisting in the behavior would sooner or later

**Young men kissing would be considered deviant by most Americans, but it is not against the law.**

be incarcerated, more likely in an asylum than a prison. Similarly, thirty years ago a man who wore pink satin clothing in public would unquestionably have been ostracized or even beaten. Some acts are considered "deviant," even evil, or wrong in themselves, simply because other ways of doing things have become completely traditional. Deviance of this kind is usually understood as involving morality. (Aside from its illegality, what is "wrong with" polygamy?)

## Violations of Civility or Manners

Sometimes behavior that merely violates accepted manners or civility may be seen as so unusual or bizarre as to constitute deviance. A woman who habitually stood in crowded elevators with her back to the door, facing the crowd, would be likely to be viewed as "crazy," and a man who persisted in crawling on all fours in public places would sooner or later confront the police. Taking a drink from a stranger's water glass in a restaurant might result in your removal, and if you blew your nose on your sleeve you would be shunned as a boor today, although such usage was recommended etiquette only a few centuries ago. Probably every small town in the United States has certain institutionalized deviant roles such as "town drunk" and "town crazy person." The latter is apt to be guilty of no more than breaches in civility, manners, and customary dress and public demeanor. (Wearing old-fashioned clothing in an unkempt state, talking to him or herself in public, and perhaps keeping "too many" pets.) Violations of manners or civility are usually not considered wrong in themselves, but because of their rarity or nonconformity, they are too far "out of step."

Since so much behavior may be perceived as deviant, any proper understanding of the phenomenon will necessarily be a sophisticated one. It should not surprise us that a fair number of rather different scientific explanations for deviance have been attempted. Before we turn to those, however, we must consider crime and delinquency at some length as special instances of deviation. This is necessary for two reasons, first because the two are so deeply confounded with other varieties of deviance, as noted above, and second, because a number of theories of the origins of crime, particularly early ones, are sometimes generalized to "explain" deviant behavior of any kind, regardless of its legality or illegality.

## CRIME AND DELINQUENCY AS SPECIAL INSTANCES OF DEVIANCE

Sociologists generally agree that crime and delinquency are simply special instances of deviant behavior, not a unique kind of nonconformity. Illegal acts differ from most other deviance, however, in being legislatively defined and thus may *not* be contrary to the social norms that most members of the society support. In a very special sense, the law creates crime (or can "uncreate" it again when laws are rescinded). This makes crime and delinquency special cases of deviance, because some illegal behavior may be considered deviant only because it is illegal. We noted earlier that at one time the use of opium and morphine was common in the United States. Although drug addiction was then considered unfortunate, perhaps on a level with alcoholism, drug users were in no sense deemed criminal. The passage of the Harrison Act in 1915 turned what had been acceptable (if not praiseworthy) behavior into criminal behavior. A reverse situation is occurring in contemporary American society with the move toward decriminalization of the use of marijuana.

### The Definition of Crime

How, then, does the sociologist of deviance, define crime? Since there is a general social norm that members of a society should obey the law, any criminal behavior is deviant in this sense. But most so-called law-abiding people in fact violate the legal code frequently and are not considered criminal or deviant. Self-report studies show that most Americans have, at one time or another, committed acts that could have qualified as crimes had they been brought to the attention of the authorities. Thus it is difficult even to decide when a criminal is a criminal. Are people criminals when they engage in behavior that violates the penal code or when they are arrested or when the courts find them guilty?

Most sociologists include three elements in a working definition of **crime:** (1) the actor must violate the penal code through either omission or commission of an act; (2) the actor must have acted voluntarily; and (3) the kind and degree of social injury to the state must be specified. This last point helps to distinguish between criminal and civil matters. In criminal matters, the charges are brought on behalf of the "People of the State of _____," emphasizing the idea that the action inflicted a social injury on all the citizens of the political jurisdiction.

In the case of juvenile delinquency, definition is even more difficult. Children violate the same laws that adults do, committing murder, rape, robbery and theft. (Often, in fact, they do it more.) But minors also come to the attention of the police and the courts for many acts that would be ignored if committed by an adult. These include such "children's crimes" as truancy, running away, incorrigibility, and curfew violations. Legally, then, *delinquency* is anything a legislative body has chosen to call delinquent. Sociologically, the term is almost meaningless.

While some crime or delinquency clearly fits the sociological definition of deviance—behavior judged by others to violate norms—some does not. While crime is popularly conceived to

Opium use in the last century was not illegal. It became illegal—and deviant—in 1915. If the laws are ever revised, it may become nondeviant again.

be the best and most obvious example of deviant behavior, and all early theorists addressed deviance *as* crime, many sociologists of deviance today study other kinds of acts instead. As we will see, theories of deviance that were originally addressed specifically to criminal behavior all fall short because they assume that criminals are somehow different from other people.

**Victimless Crimes**  One of the most controversial aspects of the definition of crime concerns **victimless crimes** or, as they are also called, crimes without complainants. These are activities that are positively valued by their perpetrators and in themselves cause no readily ascertainable social harm. The law defines them as crimes, but they have no victims. Classic examples are prostitution, gambling, and drug use. While few sociologists would deny that socially harmful activity is often associated with the provision of such activities as prostitution, illegal gambling, or drugs, many agree that to label as criminal participation in the activity itself is a matter of public morals rather than crime *per se.*

In a most comprehensive study, Winick and Kinsie estimated that prostitution grosses more than one billion dollars a year. It is believed to involve between 100,000 and 500,000 women.[7] Clearly no enterprise so widespread and so flourishing could exist without both a high degree of public—and police—acceptance. In what sense, then, can prostitution, or more particularly the patronization of prostitutes, be said to be deviant? Gambling is a similar example. Gambling is legal in some states, but throughout most of the United States, the activity is illegal. The most prevalent form of illegal gambling is "Playing the Numbers," in which bets from ten cents up may be placed on a three-digit number determined by the parimutuel results from a particular racetrack. About 32,000,000 Americans are believed to participate. Are they all deviants? The debate about the "criminality" of drug use—particularly marijuana—is similar.

**White-Collar Crime**  The problems of defining deviance are particularly acute in any consideration of **white-collar crime.** These are often crimes committed by persons in positions of social responsibility. They include violations of trust associated with high-status positions,

> **crime:**  a voluntary act of omission or comission that violates the penal code and results in a specified kind and degree of injury to the state.
>
> **victimless crimes:**  sometimes called crimes without complaints, this class of crime involves illegal behaviors positively valued by their perpetrators and resulting in no easily demonstrable social injury. Examples are prostitution, illegal gambling, drug use, and so on.
>
> **white-collar crime:**  a violation of criminal law occurring in the course of a legitimate occupation. Examples are tax evasion, embezzlement, price-fixing, and so on.

as well as all forms of crime committed in the normal course of otherwise legal occupations.

The concept of white-collar crime was conceived by Edwin H. Sutherland.[8] Through his work, it began to be taken as seriously by criminologists as robbery, arson, and assault. One consequence was the realization that all criminals were not lower class. Crimes are committed by the middle and upper classes as well as the lower, but they are likely to be crimes of different kinds.

*Tax evasion* is a common white-collar crime. One recent case involved former President Nixon: By backdating the donation of certain documents to the National Archives, Nixon attempted to take a tax deduction which was no longer allowable at the actual date of donation.

*Embezzlement,* another common white-collar crime, involves manipulation of bookkeeping and accounting records to conceal the theft of funds. Employee theft comes in all sizes, from the clerk who steals from the cash register to the inventory control administrator who diverts merchandise meant for an employer to a third party for profit.

*Misrepresentation in advertising* has been dramatically brought to the attention of the public through the efforts of Ralph Nader and others. It often involves a claim that a product does something that it does not do. For example, a Standard Oil television commercial showed an ex-astronaut conducting a demonstration that was later revealed to be a fake.

In *fee splitting,* one professional, such as a doctor or a lawyer, recommends to a client a

Reprinted by permission of Jules Feiffer.

**There is some question as to whether much white-collar crime should be considered deviant.**

second professional, whose fees are a good deal higher, to provide some specialized service. As a "courtesy" to the referring professional, the specialist "kicks back" an agreed-upon share of the fee.

*Price fixing* involves an illegal arrangement between two or more corporations to stifle competition by fixing the lowest bid price in advance of the submission of bids to the prospective customer. In this way, all the participating companies can take turns being the lowest bidder at various times, and at no time are the bids truly competitive. Thus the companies' risk is eliminated, and the unwary customer is victimized. A famous example of price fixing (and bid rigging) was the General Electric-Westinghouse swindle of the 1950s, which resulted in prison terms for some of the executives of these companies. Prison sentences are uncommon for the white-collar criminal, but in this case, the victimized customer happened to be the United States government.

Other types of occupational crimes include unfair labor practices, padding expense accounts, misappropriation of funds, influence peddling, and corruption in the management of trusts and receiverships.

White-collar crime is made possible for individuals by virtue of their possession of specific occupational positions. Opportunity thus influences both its frequency and type. People who never handle cash or keep books in the course of their work are unlikely to commit embezzlement. The decision to hold up a liquor store or gas station may say more about the narrow range of opportunities available than about the criminal's need for money. If he could take a bribe instead, the criminal would probably choose to do that because it might well bring in more money at much lower physical risk. And if he got caught, the possibility of a suspended or much reduced sentence would be greater. (Former Vice-President Spiro Agnew, who did not contest his conviction for taking a $2,500 bribe, was sentenced to unsupervised probation.) Thus the kinds of crimes an individual commits are in some part a function of the kinds of opportunities available.

What makes white-collar crimes particularly difficult to deal with as a form of deviance is that many of them are defined by the occupational cultures of their perpetrators as legitimate business practices. "Puffing" the client's product is what advertising is about, and so a certain amount of misrepresentation is normal and expected. The practice of not inquiring too deeply into the source of campaign funds appears to be normal among politicians. Thus, although some occupational crimes are clearly committed with criminal intent, others seem to result from conflicts between the occupational subculture's norms of profit at any price and ruthless competitiveness on the one hand, and the larger culture's norms forbidding law breaking on the other.

### The Incidence of Crime in the United States

The Federal Bureau of Investigation is the nation's official recordkeeper of crime. Every year the FBI publishes *Crime in the United States: Uniform Crime Reports,* a collection of statistics. These figures include data from approximately 8,000 police jurisdictions. What is watched closely are what the FBI calls the **index crimes,** those it judges most serious. Table 16.1 shows index crimes for 1976. Arrest rates differ from crimes "known to the police." Table 16.2 reveals where police have apparently been concentrating their efforts.

**Problems with Official Reports**  The validity of the statistics presented in Tables 16.1 and 16.2 as an accurate reflection of the extent of crime in the United States is problematic. First, these statistics necessarily leave out a large number of crimes that go unreported to the police. A murder is much less likely to escape the attention of the police than is a larceny, especially if little money is involved. Some crimes, such as forcible rape, often go unreported due to the reluctance of victims to complain.

Another problem is dependence on local po-

**index crimes:**  the serious offenses used by the FBI in its *Uniform Crime Reports* as indicators of the overall crime rate.

TABLE 16.2   Number of Persons Arrested for Ten Most Frequent Offenses, 1976

| Offense | Number |
|---|---|
| Drunkenness | 8,449,000 |
| Larceny | 7,485,000 |
| Driving under influence | 6,360,000 |
| Disorderly conduct | 4,277,000 |
| Drug violations | 3,973,000 |
| Burglary | 3,167,000 |
| Simple assault | 2,821,000 |
| Liquor violations | 2,456,000 |
| Aggravated assault | 1,441,000 |
| Weapons violations | 883,000 |
| **Total** | 41,312,000 |

lice jurisdictions for complete reporting. The 1967 President's Commission on Law Enforcement and Administration of Justice documented many cases of probable error in police reporting procedures.[9] In some cases, a local police administrator may be self-serving. For example, if the sheriff is running for reelection, it may be advantageous to show a decrease in crime during the previous term. On the other hand, for a newly elected sheriff who wants a computer center or some other expensive hardware from the county council, a rising crime rate would be a persuasive bargaining chip.

The President's Commission also noted an increasing tendency for ghetto crimes to be included in the statistical compilations. Previously, police had been reluctant to involve themselves in the investigation of crimes where both the perpetrator and the victim were black, and often ignored reports of all but the most serious crimes in ghetto areas. Recently, politically active American blacks have exerted pressure on the police for greater concern for the rights and property of the black ghetto residents with a resulting increase in reported crime.

**Unofficial Reports**  Social scientists and others have tried to assess the true incidence of criminal behavior in the population, as distinguished from the incidence shown by official reports. Almost all of these studies have shown

TABLE 16.1   Index Crimes for 1976

| Offense | Number known to police |
|---|---|
| Murder | 19,000 |
| Forcible rape | 56,000 |
| Robbery | 421,000 |
| Aggravated assault | 490,000 |
| Burglary | 3,089,000 |
| Larceny ($50 and over) | 6,271,000 |
| Auto theft | 958,000 |
| **Total** | 11,304,000 |

**TABLE 16.3  FBI Index Crimes, 1966–1977**

| Crime | 1966 | 1968 | 1970 | 1971 | 1972 | 1973 | 1974 | 1975 | 1976 | 1977 |
|---|---|---|---|---|---|---|---|---|---|---|
| | | | | | *Rate per 100,000 inhabitants* | | | | | |
| Murder and nonnegligent manslaughter | 5.6 | 6.8 | 7.8 | 8.5 | 8.9 | 9.3 | 9.8 | 9.6 | 8.8 | 8.8 |
| Forcible rape | 12.9 | 15.5 | 18.3 | 20.3 | 22.3 | 24.3 | 26.2 | 26.3 | 26.4 | 29.1 |
| Robbery | 80.3 | 131.0 | 171.5 | 187.1 | 179.9 | 182.4 | 209.3 | 218.2 | 195.8 | 187.1 |
| Aggravated assault | 118.4 | 141.3 | 162.4 | 176.8 | 186.6 | 198.4 | 215.8 | 227.4 | 228.7 | 241.5 |
| Burglary | 708.3 | 915.1 | 1,067.7 | 1,148.3 | 1,126.1 | 1,210.8 | 1,437.7 | 1,525.9 | 1,439.4 | 1,410.9 |
| Larceny ($50 and over) | 456.8 | 636.0 | 859.4 | 909.2 | 882.6 | 2,051.2 | 2,489.5 | 2,804.8 | 2,921.3 | 2,729.9 |
| Auto theft | 284.4 | 389.1 | 453.5 | 456.5 | 423.1 | 440.1 | 462.2 | 469.4 | 446.1 | 447.6 |
| **Total crime index** | 1,666.6 | 2,234.8 | 2,740.5 | 2,906.7 | 2,829.5 | 4,116.4 | 4,850.5 | 5,281.6 | 5,266.4 | 5,054.9 |

that much, much more crime exists than is indicated by official reports, such as the one shown in Table 16-3.[10] For instance, Jay R. Williams and Martin Gold studied the 847 adolescents surveyed in the 1967 National Survey of Youth to examine the differences between self-reported and "official" delinquency. They found that 83 percent had committed a chargeable offense within three years; less than 3 percent of the offenses were discovered by the police.[11] The National Opinion Research Center (NORC) surveyed 10,000 households in 1965 and concluded that the actual crime rate in the United States was about twice as great as the official crime rate. About half of those interviewed said that they had been victims of crimes they had not reported to the police.[12]

In 1974, the Law Enforcement Assistance Administration (LEAA) released the results of a sampling of about 200,000 citizens in eight cities. Because people do not always report crimes to the police and the police do not always report them to the FBI, individuals were asked for their own experiences with crime. In general, the citizens reported about twice as much crime as official statistics show.[13] A second LEAA report comparing cities showed that the crime rate as reported by citizens was five times as high in Philadelphia as that shown by the FBI reports; about three times as high in Chicago, Detroit, and Los Angeles; and twice as high in New York.[14] The degree to which crime victims underreport their experiences is indicated by Table 16.4.

These reports, however, are not conclusive. Although the NORC and LEAA studies were carefully conducted scientific investigations and may be presumed to be generally accurate, we do not *know* the real state of affairs and perhaps never can in any detail. Statistics on crime rates are notoriously inaccurate, and conclusions based on them must be carefully assessed. Victimization studies, for example, may overreport criminal activity as a result of misunderstanding of the event, ignorance of the law, memory failure, interviewer error, and outright lying.[15] But there does seem to be more crime in the United States in recent years than in previous times, and it is clear that there is more crime than the official statistics show. We do not know, however, how much more there is nor all of the reasons behind the recent increase. Simple explanations should be sus-

pected. There is a great deal more to the explanation of crime—or any other deviant behavior—than such popular explanations as moral breakdown, "mollycoddling," permissiveness, and so forth.

## The Matter of Punishment

In the United States, the aspect of the legal system that deals with persons convicted of crimes is called *corrections*. This includes everything

**TABLE 16.4   Percent of Victimization Actually Reported to the Police, for Selected Crimes, 1975**

| Type of crime | Percent |
|---|---|
| All Personal Crimes | 31.6 |
| Crimes of violence | 47.2 |
| Rape | 56.3 |
| Robbery | 53.3 |
| Robbery with injury | 65.0 |
| From serious assault | 66.7 |
| From minor assault | 62.5 |
| Robbery without injury | 47.9 |
| Assault | 45.2 |
| Aggravated assault | 55.2 |
| Without injury | 65.1 |
| Attempted assault with weapon | 50.1 |
| Simple assault | 39.1 |
| With injury | 47.9 |
| Attempted assault without weapon | 35.9 |
| Crimes of theft | 26.2 |
| Personal larceny with contact | 34.6 |
| Purse snatching | 48.7 |
| Pocket picking | 26.9 |
| Personal larceny without contact | 26.0 |
| All Household Crimes | 39.0 |
| Burglary | 48.6 |
| Forcible entry | 72.9 |
| Unlawful entry without force | 38.0 |
| Attempted forcible entry | 32.9 |
| Household larceny | 27.1 |
| Completed larceny[a] | 27.3 |
| Less than $50 | 15.4 |
| $50 or more | 53.2 |
| Attempted larceny | 23.1 |
| Motor vehicle theft | 71.1 |
| Completed theft | 91.1 |
| Attempted theft | 35.3 |
| All Commerical Crimes | 81.1 |
| Burglary | 79.6 |
| Robbery | 90.2 |

[a]Includes data, not shown separately, on larcenies for which the value of loss was not ascertained.

that happens to the defendant after conviction: sentencing, fine, probation, imprisonment, parole, execution. As the name suggests, the object or philosophy of the American judicial system is to "correct" a wrongdoer through some kind of punishment. Today, punishment usually means fines or imprisonment. Although capital punishment (execution) was not unusual in the United States in earlier times, the United States now may be in the process of abandoning it.[16]

The theory that punishment will "correct" a criminal was developed by the classical school of criminology in the eighteenth and nineteenth centuries. Classical criminologists believed in the *pleasure-pain principle*, the idea that the fundamental nature of human beings is to seek pleasure and avoid pain. Thus a person who is made to experience pain as a consequence of some action will thereafter avoid repeating the act in order to avoid the pain it caused the first time. To this hypothesis, the classical criminologists added the notion of **deterrence:** Others, seeing the pain inflicted on the wrongdoer, will be deterred from doing the

Whether punishment accomplishes "deterrence" of deviant behavior is open to debate.

same thing themselves in order to avoid the punishment.

Sociologists today reject the theory. Several studies have shown that punishment does not necessarily prevent convicted criminals from once again engaging in criminal behavior when they have the opportunity. The President's Commission on Law Enforcement and the Administration of Justice, for instance, reported that two-thirds of the persons entering prisons each year had been in prison before.[17] It seems clear that the "pain" of imprisonment is not sufficient to end criminal behavior.

The case against the theory of deterrence — that others will be prevented from committing crimes by observing the fate of criminals — is more difficult to make. The problem is that there is no way to find out whether or not another person has been deterred. If individuals abstain from criminal activity, it is extremely difficult to prove that they do so for fear of punishment. Would the crime rate be even higher than it is if punishments were more mild? Such questions cannot be easily answered.

The evidence we have indicates that the theory of deterrence is false. Unfortunately, most of the studies have concentrated on the deterrent effect of capital punishment, which is usually imposed only for murder. But statistically, murder is an unusual crime. It is normally a crime of passion committed among family members or close friends. Most killings are spur of the moment, committed in a fit of rage. Forethought about the consequences, which the idea of deterrence implies, would not occur. In any event, murder rates in American jurisdictions with and without capital punishment show no relation between the possibility of execution and the incidence of murder.

Most sociologists would argue that socialization and social organization are far more effective deterrents to all nonconforming behavior than punishment. As noted earlier, few of us refrain from eating dogs merely because we might be punished for it. For deterrence to be effective, punishment must be *certain*. Few people commit crimes with the expectation of being caught. At the present time in the United States, only about 5 percent of crimes known to the police are resolved by the conviction of their perpetrators. Punishment for criminal wrongdoing, then, seems far from certain.

To sum up, if the object of punishment is to

reduce the incidence of crime, it is evident that punishment does not work. Beyond the complexities of police investigation, arrest, trial, conviction, and the sociologies of who gets arrested, tried, and convicted or released—beyond all this—on a theoretical level, sociologists would not expect punishment to be an effective deterrent to crime or other deviant behavior. Recall that all deviance, and particularly crime, is in some respects a matter of definition by others, usually after the act in question has been committed. Deviants have no control over how their behavior will be defined. But if someone else (typically the district attorney) decides whether a particular action was a crime, for example, we cannot expect that punishing the criminal will affect the matter. The purpose of trial, remember, is to establish whether or not a specific individual was "the criminal" once it has been decided that a criminal act has occurred.

The crime rate in a society is the creation of the social organization and social structure of that society. Thus only that organization and structure can raise or lower it. For example, the decriminalization of marijuana use will reduce the crime rate for drug-related offenses. By comparison, punishment is irrelevant to the incidence of crime.

## THEORIES OF DEVIANT BEHAVIOR

Since the behavior defined as deviant is so various, there is an equal variety of ways to explain it. Many of these were originally addressed specifically to crime or delinquency, but have been broadened to include other forms of deviance as well. We can classify all of them generally as being either nonsociological or sociological.

### Nonsociological Theories of Deviance

**Free Will**   The classical school of criminology, on which American law is based, takes the position that people have free will to choose courses of behavior and thus can be held responsible for their acts. Deviance, or norm violation, derives not from personal characteristics or deficiencies but from the individual's deliberate choice of "wrong" over "right." Criminals are viewed as lacking will power or a sense of

> **deterrence:** the hypothesis that punishment of one person for a wrongful act inhibits others from doing the same thing for fear of similar punishment. This belief is still widely accepted in American law and public opinion but is largely rejected by social scientists.

morality and are therefore regarded as a menace to society. To deter others from criminal behavior, punishments should fit the seriousness of the crime and these punishments should be applied equally to similar offenders. From this view comes a system of universal and abstract justice in which the individual offender matters less than the offensive behavior.

As we have seen, this philosophy of choice is based on the belief that criminal acts and the people who commit them are different from other acts and other people. The act is seen as different because it is a "crime," the people, because they commit it. But, as we noted earlier, the behaviors involved in crime are usually normal behaviors; only the circumstances in which they are enacted makes them criminal. If

*"The Court takes cognizance of your plea that the very nature of the municipal accounting system invites fraud, and reminds itself that the very nature of the judicial system requires me to slap you in the jug."*

New Yorker, October 11, 1976. Drawing by Fisher; © 1976 The New Yorkers Magazine, Inc.

**The notion of free will holds people responsible for their acts.**

doing things forbidden by law is what differentiates criminals from noncriminals, then there are no noncriminals in the population. Virtually everyone violates a law at one time or another. Thus the free will theory is not an adequate explanation of deviance.

**Constitutional Theories**    Constitutional theories hold that crime is the result of defects in an individual's physical constitution. The first constitutional theorist was Cesare Lombroso (1836–1909), an Italian criminologist. Lombroso's brand of philosophical positivism rejected free will as an explanation of behavior and replaced it with biological determinism. People, Lombroso believed, were moved to act as they did because of their biology. Criminals were "atavistic anomalies," throwbacks to a type of primeval bestiality. Some people were born criminals and could be identified by their body structure and facial features. Indeed, Lombroso measured the length and width of convicts' noses and fingers, the thickness of their lips, the height of their brows, and so forth to prove his point.

Early in the twentieth century, an English criminologist named Charles Goring put Lombroso's hypotheses to the test and found them unsupported by the evidence. Nonetheless, Lombroso's influence remains stronger today than Goring's, although in later life Lombroso abandoned the constitutional approach. In 1949, William Sheldon, a psychologist and physician, developed a classification of three body types that he maintained were related to behavior. These three types of physique, called somatotypes, are: (1) endomorphs—soft and round and usually fat; (2) mesomorphs—muscular and athletic; and (3) ectomorphs—skinny and fragile. Mesomorphs, according to Sheldon, were more often delinquents than the other types.[18]

In 1952, sociologists Sheldon and Eleanor Glueck, tested the somatotype theory on samples of delinquent and nondelinquent boys. They claimed that the majority of the delinquents were mesomorphic—muscular, well-knit, and athletic.[19] But like Lombroso's work, the Gluecks' research has been criticized for logical and statistical inadequacy. Other researchers could not reproduce the Gluecks' results and found simple errors in computation as well. Furthermore, many pointed out, adoles-

cent male delinquency is in some respects a physical sport, and those who engage in it frequently, and thus come to the attention of authorities, might be expected to be muscular and athletic.

The latest entry in the deviance-through-physiology school is the chromosomal deficiency hypothesis. The Y chromosome carries male traits and the X chromosome female traits. The normal ovum contains one X chromosome. If the ovum is fertilized by a Y-bearing sperm at the time of conception, the baby will have one Y and one X chromosome in each cell and will therefore be male. If the ovum is fertilized by an X-bearing sperm, the baby will have two X chromosomes and will be female.

In the early 1960s, a certain human male was found to have an extra Y chromosome. Instead of having an XY combination, he possessed an XYY combination. Soon other examples of this anomaly were observed and described. XYY individuals were said to be tall, aggressive, antisocial males, with low IQs and severe acne. They were believed to be found in greater proportions in mental institutions or prisons than in the general population, and the public's temptation to embrace the "born criminal" hypothesis was once again encouraged. This was strengthened by the types of crimes some of these men had committed, crimes involving murder and rape in rather bizarre forms.

The XYY hypothesis in criminology is not merely an updating of Lombroso. It is an attempt to explore the field of criminal biology and is a logical extension of the work of Sheldon and the Gluecks on the possible relationship between physiology and deviant behavior. Research in this area is still sparse. Most researchers merely suggest the possibility of an increased risk of psychopathic personality in the XYY male. Recent research has even cast some doubt on this.

The constitutional theory of the "born criminal" has many problems. Modern social science from Durkheim and Freud to the present establishes the ambiguity of the distinction between criminals and noncriminals. The differences between the identified deviant and the nondeviant seem to lie in internalized controls and external constraints that modify the possibility of the deviant act more than any inherited differences. The primary weakness of the constitutional approach is that an act becomes criminal only when it is defined as criminal by law. Since law is not a part of nature or biology, but a part of the culture, an individual cannot be *constitutionally* disposed toward crime commission.

**Psychoanalytic Theories** According to psychoanalytic theory, deviance is a response to personality problems. Generally, deviants and criminals are considered "sick" or "maladjusted." Crime results from mental illness or psychological abnormality. George B. Vold, a sociologist of crime, summarizes the position as follows:

> Criminal behavior . . . is to be understood, simply and directly, as a substitute response, some form of symbolic release of repressed complexes. The conflict in the unconscious mind gives rise to feelings of guilt and anxiety with a consequent desire for punishment to remove the guilt feelings and restore a proper balance of good against evil. The criminal then commits the criminal act in order to be caught and punished. Unconsciously motivated errors (i.e., careless or imprudent ways of committing the crime) leave "clues" so the authorities may more readily apprehend and convict the guilty, and thus administer suitable cleansing punishment.[20]

Many early psychiatric studies found offenders to be generally "psychopathic" or "emotionally ill." The National Committee for Mental Hygiene published a summary of these in 1931 and found considerable variation in the extent of psychiatric deviation diagnosed in correctional institutions in various parts of the country. The committee concluded that this difference indicated a discrepancy among diagnosticians rather than some definitive description of those being diagnosed.[21]

The psychoanalytic theory of deviance poses the problem of whether psychological deviation is a cause of deviant behavior or the consequence of it. One is tempted to say that anyone who acts in a deviant manner is psychologically disturbed, and this is not uncommon among proponents of this approach. But this really explains nothing. It is understandable that someone suffering from a psychopathological disorder could commit a crime. But persons not afflicted with these disorders also commit crimes, and not all of those so afflicted do.

More important, despite the occasional assertion of psychiatrists or psychologists to the contrary, there is little empirical evidence that any specific personality trait is associated with deviant behavior. No consistent psychological differences of any kind have been found to differentiate identified deviants from nondeviants. An overwhelming number of studies have shown that criminals and delinquents, at least, do not differ from the normal population in such matters as intelligence, frequency of feeblemindedness, personality test scores, or neurosis and psychosis.

This accumulation of negative evidence does not surprise sociologists. The psychoanalytic approach, like the constitutional approach before it, is based on the same wrong assumption as are the popular understanding and the law: that deviants are different. *Prison populations* in the United States do differ significantly from the noninstitutionalized population. As a class, institutionalized criminals and delinquents are generally poorer and less educated than the rest of the population; they are less likely to be white, well educated, or from the middle or upper class. But these differences are largely reflections of police practice, the judicial process, and cultural definitions of deviance. As noted earlier, nearly everyone violates the law, but not everyone goes to prison for it.

*Sociological Theories of Deviant Behavior*

According to Tarvis Hirschi,

> Three fundamental perspectives on delinquency and deviant behavior dominate the current (sociological) scene. According to *strain* or motivational theories, legitimate desires that conformity cannot satisfy force a person into deviance. According to *control* or bond theories, a person is free to commit delinquent acts because his ties to the conventional order have somehow been broken. According to *cultural deviance* theories, the deviant conforms to a set of standards not accepted by a larger or more powerful society. Although most current theories of crime and delinquency contain elements of at least two and occasionally all three of these perspectives, reconciliation of their assumptions is very difficult.[22]

We will discuss each of these as types and describe some of the sociological approaches to deviance that exemplify them.

**Strain or Motivational Theories** Strain theories of deviance tend to concentrate on the moral order of society from Durkheim's perspective. Any society has a dominant normative order to which virtually all of its members are at least adequately exposed. Everyone internalizes essentially the same values and goals as a result of socialization. If conformity is taken for granted, how is nonconformity to be understood? The strain theorist's answer is, "the pressure of unfulfilled but legitimate desires."[23] Deviance occurs when people are prevented by some condition from fulfilling their learned expectations for themselves. Robert K. Merton, Richard Cloward, Lloyd Ohlin, and Albert K. Cohen are leading exponents of strain theory.

*Anomie* The word *anomie* was brought into sociology by Durkheim. It means, literally, *without norms,* and Durkheim used it to describe a *social context in which the moral order had broken down for an individual or group, a situation in which normal social structural constraints on behavior become inoperative.* Merton modified Durkheim's usage of the word and applied it explicitly to deviant behavior. He began by identifying two important and related elements in any society, *cultural goals* and *institutionalized means.* Cultural goals are the things a society's normative system defines as worth being and having. The institutionalized means are the ways a society accepts as legitimate for attaining the cultural goals. Anomie, in Merton's usage, arises when individuals are unable to obtain the goals they have been taught to strive for with the means that the society puts at their disposal. In Merton's view, a common reaction to this situation is to engage in deviant behavior.

In his original statement of anomie theory,[24] Merton used the example of material success in American society. The possession of money and all it will buy is an important goal for all Americans. For many it is the most important goal they have, not because they are necessarily "money mad," but because Americans judge each other as successful *people* according to their material acquisitions. Those who can't make it materially don't make it socially either. In an enormous variety of ways, all of our lives, we are taught that to succeed is crucial. For most of us, our very sense of self comes from the success we have made in society. The society also offers and defines hard work, education, thrift, and so forth as acceptable means for the attainment of success.

But because of accidents of social position, race or ethnicity, or other factors, some people are unable to use the socially acceptable means of goal attainment effectively or have their access to them blocked. The poor, for example, do not usually have access to the kind of education that may lead to success. Nonwhites may be denied success no matter how hard they work or even how educated they become. Such situations Merton defined as conditions of anomie.

Merton described five "modes of adaptation" to the means/goals problem. The first is the "normal" or conventional one that most people in any society more or less follow most of the time: *conformity.* They adopt the cultural goals offered them as appropriate things to strive for and the approved institutionalized means as the proper way to go about striving. The other four adaptations—innovation, ritualism, retreatism, and rebellion—are anomic reactions to social structural situations by individuals for whom the means don't work or for whom access to them is blocked.

Those who believe in the legitimacy of the goal of accumulating money and material success but are either unwilling or unable to use the socially approved means to achieve it Merton calls *innovators.* The legitimate means may have been blocked for them; perhaps they were denied educational opportunities or entry to the skilled trades because of their race. But innovators still want to attain the goal, so they use forbidden means to achieve it. They violate norms and may break the law. This, Merton believed, explained high crime rates among the poor.

People who lose sight of the goal while slavishly adhering to the means are *ritualists.* Some civil service bureaucrats fall into this category. Ritualistic bureaucrats pay little attention to the real needs of their clients, but instead busy themselves amassing forms, sorting, stamping, and processing them, having the client "stand behind the yellow line," and so forth. Ritualists concentrate on obeying all the rules of the system rigidly and without question.

Rejecting both cultural goals and the institutionalized means for their achievement, *retreatists* are the bohemians, beatniks, hippies, alcoholics, and drug addicts—alienated from society. Unwilling or unable to compete, retreatists decide that "the game's not worth the candle" and drop out entirely.

**Retreatism. Her home is the street.**

*Rebels* reject both conventional goals and approved means. They want a new normative structure . . . after their own revolution. The student radicals of the 1960s are excellent cases in point.

Anomie theory helps us understand the relationship between poverty and crime. In other societies, the demand for financial success is not the same for all social classes. All are not created equal in India, Italy, or England. In most of the world, children of the ghetto are not expected to "rise above," but rather to make do as best they can with what is available to them. In America, as we know, all men and women are supposed to be equal, and thus all Americans are expected to gain economic affluence. We are held personally responsible if we do not. The goal is the same for all, despite the overt and covert class structures that exist. Thus, if money can't be made through legitimate means, nonlegitimate means often come to be used.

*Delinquency and Differential Opportunity*
Richard Cloward and Lloyd Ohlin suggest some further refinements of Merton's anomie theory. They point out that having access to the legitimate "means," in Merton's terms, is not

the only problem. Other obstacles stand in the way of easy access to the *illegitimate* opportunity structure.[25] For example, lower-class boys generally share the same success ethic as middle-class boys. This ethic is measured primarily through material gain. Middle-class boys have access to legitimate means of attaining material gain, or at least are within reach of upward mobility. Lower-class boys, however, very soon recognize the gap between their level of aspiration and the expectation that they will realize it. Thus, they turn to whatever illegitimate opportunities are available in the neighborhood.

If illegal means are not easily available, adolescents do not develop a criminal subculture. Only those with ready access to illegal and violent means are likely to become criminals. In other words, differences in the social structure strongly influence an adolescent's choice of legitimate or illegitimate means to attain their goals.

*Delinquency as Strain-Reducing Behavior*
Albert Cohen studied lower-class adolescent male delinquency, which he describes an nonutilitarian, malicious, versatile, and negativistic.[26] This delinquency is not, however, without purpose, according to Cohen. The purpose is to solve problems or reduce strain. Cohen believes that all human activity is related to problem solving of one kind or another and that all problem solving basically involves two variables: the situation and the frame of reference.

The *situation* refers to the social and physical setting of the action and the *frame of reference* refers to the way in which the actor perceives it. When confronted with a problem, the actor may solve it by changing either the situation that produces it or the frame of reference. Cohen uses the example of a boy who is receiving a failing grade in a particular class in school. If he held a positive attitude toward the class and wanted to succeed, he could change the situation by working harder to pass. He could, however, change his frame of reference toward the class by convincing himself that it was not worth the bother. Either solution resolves the original emotional strain. If, in addition, the boy becomes convinced that a failing grade will enhance his reputation in the eyes of his peers, failure becomes a positive value.

Lower-class male delinquency, in Cohen's view, is a response to this kind of strain in

American society. Social aspirations may be more or less the same in all strata, but opportunity is not. Poverty, race, and ethnicity affect life chances, as we saw in Chapters 7 and 8. The lower-class boy has a problem. Television and the school have taught him middle-class aspirations and values, but his life situation gives him little chance of realizing them. That situation is the product of his society; he cannot alter it.

According to Cohen, the boy's psychological reaction to this dilemma "inverts" the frustrating middle-class value system. The characteristics of lower-class male delinquency (nonutilitarianism, maliciousness, and so on) represent psychological reversals or mirror images of middle-class values. In time, these become a new value system, which, being attainable, creates a reward structure within the framework of the delinquent gang. Actions for which the boy would be punished by middle-class society are rewarded by the gang. Failure according to middle-class standard becomes success according to gang norms.

**Control or Bond Theories** Strain theories assume that conformity is the normal mode of human behavior (in effect that people are generally moral); they thus see deviance as the phenomenon to be explained. Control theories take the opposite view. Control theories see human nature as neither intrinsically moral nor immoral and focus on the question of why people conform. The possibility of deviance is taken for granted; it is conformity that must be explained. Contrary to the popular saying, crime often *does* pay; why, then, do we not engage in it more often?

*Control Theory* Travis Hirschi, who coined the name "control theory," starts with Durkheim's assumption that deviant acts may result when an individual's *bond* to society is weak or broken. The elements of that bond consist of (1) *attachment* to other individuals, (2) *commitment* to specific social roles and activities with values and consequences for the future, (3) *involvement* in various life activities and interactions with others, and (4) *beliefs* concerning moral values, cultural norms, and so forth.

Depending upon the nature and quality of each of these four elements in a particular case, they produce either conforming or noncon-

forming behavior. Hirschi believes that it is not surprising that the four sometimes conjoin to produce deviance. If one has few attachments to others who might be supportive of conventional behavior (close ties to conventional parents, for example), the probability of deviant behavior is increased. Similarly, people committed to roles and activities in which conventionality can reasonably be seen to maximize the chance of attaining desired goals are likely to conform. But the absence of such commitments reduces the need to conform, as does the absence of active involvement in such roles and activities. Finally, there is variation in the strength with which people accept moral beliefs. If one strongly believes that it is wrong to engage in a particular behavior, one is unlikely to do so, but if the belief is only weakly held, it operates with reduced effectiveness. "The meaning and efficacy of such beliefs," Hirschi says, "are contingent upon other beliefs and, indeed, on the strengths of other ties to the conventional order."[27]

*Delinquency as Normative Conformity* Gresham M. Sykes and David Matza believe that delinquents rarely see themselves in opposition to the moral imperatives of middle-class society. They devise methods to neutralize the emotional consequences of their behavior in advance and thus escape the pressures to conform.[28] Instead of creating new norms, delinquents rationalize their behavior within the existing normative framework. This involves five major **techniques of neutralization:** (1) denial of responsibility, (2) denial of injury, (3) denial of the victim, (4) condemnation of the condemners, and (5) appeal to higher loyalties.

Delinquents who *deny responsibility* see themselves as billiard balls, helplessly propelled in various directions by factors beyond their control. These factors might be a ghetto environment, a broken home, bad companions, low income, and so on. By viewing themselves as more acted upon than acting, delinquents pave the way for deviance from norms without attacking the norms themselves. They simply refuse to be blamed for violating them.

*Denial of injury* is a matter of redefining deviant behavior in order to make it more acceptable. Vandalism becomes "mischief," auto theft is "borrowing." After all, "the insurance company will pay the injured party,'' reasons the delinquent. A gang fight is a private quarrel and should not cause the community any concern.

*Denial of the victim* involves either reconstructing the situation so that the victim is perceived as being punished for some transgression (thus deserving injury) or denying that there was any injury. Vandalism can be defined as revenge on an unfair school official or a

**techniques of neutralization:** psychological rationalizations or justifications for behavior. In the Sykes and Matza theory of delinquency these involve (1) denial of responsibility; (2) denial of injury; (3) denial of the victim; (4) condemnation of the condemner; (5) appeal to higher loyalties.

crooked store owner. The delinquent becomes a sort of Robin Hood working to right wrongs more quickly than the slow processes of the law.

*Condemnation of the condemners* involves a redefinition of the accuser as a deviant in disguise, a hypocrite. Police become ''pigs,'' teachers show favoritism, and parents ''don't know where it's at.'' The moral right of others to judge is thus denied. All of these neutralization techniques serve to deflect negative sanctions that would otherwise be associated with deviant acts.

In an *appeal to higher loyalties,* the norms of the legitimate society are implicitly accepted, but other norms are given precedence for the sake of the subgroup, the peer culture. Choosing between the claims of the law and the claims of loyalty to friends is a classic problem. The delinquent chooses the friends, believing this to be the only truly moral choice open to him.

*Containment Theory* Walter Reckless holds that group membership and social interaction determine how individuals act in particular life situations. He focuses on the elements in group life that tend to prevent an individual from being ''pulled into'' a deviant or criminal pattern.[29] In this view, deviance is explained by the failure of normal behavioral constraints to operate in specific individuals because of their social positions. Reckless argues that it is more useful to understand the social and psychological ''buffers'' *against* deviant behavior than to study deviance-provoking processes. Since most people are nondeviant most of the time, we must understand deviance as a failure of the normal rather than as something special or abnormal in itself.

There are two kinds of buffers or containments: (1) the external social structure and organization of society and the groups to which the individual belongs; and (2) the internal, psy-

**''Zoot-suiters'' were considered ''weird'' by most people in the 1940s. Among their own subgroups, they were ''cool.''**

chological controls that one imposes on oneself. The external constraint is the informal social control a group exerts on its members: role expectations, values, and so forth—all of the conscious and unconscious rules and values about how "people like us" are supposed to behave. The internal constraints are the components of "self" that give the individual the strength and motive to resist the deviant impulses that we all experience at one time or another. Normally, the combination of external and internal controls operates to keep us from acting in deviant ways. Internal controls direct us toward goals that are socially approved and give us a favorable concept of self. We thus become able to react to frustration with tolerance and we derive a strong tendency to identify with the nondeviant norms in the society. When these controls fail to operate for an individual because of such things as extreme poverty or severe racial discrimination, deviance follows the breakdown of the usual controls.

**Cultural Deviance Theories** Cultural deviance theories are rooted in two inarguable facts, (1) the diversity or heterogeneity of modern industrial societies, and (2) the generality of the socialization process. Sociologists working in this tradition argue that people learn the culture of the group around them, accepting a specific set of norms and values as normal simply because they are the ones present to be learned in the immediate environment. Since a heterogeneous society like that of the United States offers a multiplicity of environments widely differentiated by region, social class, race, religion, ethnicity, and so forth, inevitably some of the norms and values of one subculture clash with those of another, thus making individuals who adhere to one set of learned values appear "deviant" in the eyes of those socialized to another. Some extremists even deny the legitimacy of any definition of deviance at all (a matter of "middle-class hang-ups," or perceive urban criminals as guerrilla freedom fighters). A natural consequence of the position is to focus attention not on the "deviant" actor, but on the people and processes that define him or her as deviant. If deviance is in the eyes of the beholder, then to understand it we must study the beholder and the process of beholding, not the persons or acts beheld. The cultural deviance position was first stated by Edwin H. Sutherland, and is now advocated by Howard S. Beck-

er, Edwin Lemmert, and the "new criminologists."

*Differential Association* Edwin H. Sutherland, the dean of American midcentury criminologists, proposed the theory of differential association to explain criminal behavior.[30] Its basic assumption is that criminal behavior, like any other social behavior, is learned through association with others. It is neither physiological nor inherited, nor the product of warped psychology.

If criminal behavior is learned as any other behavior is learned, then it is learned through association with others, especially interaction within intimate personal groups. Throughout our lives, association and interaction with others teach us motives, attitudes, values, and rationalizations. The specific direction that these will take—law-abiding or law-violative—will depend on from whom we learn our behavior. Thus, differential association—differences in with whom we associate—in large part determines how we behave.

In every social group, there are individuals who define adherence to the law as acceptable, natural, and not really open to question, as well as people who are otherwise inclined. Often, in our culture, there is a mix. That is, most of us would not think seriously of robbery, yet using the company postage meter to mail our Christmas cards can be justified by saying "everybody does it." If everybody does it, then those "everybodys" are, in a sense, favorably defining the theft of postage from the company. Others would not engage in even this relatively minor form of law violation. In our mobile and complex society, we have the opportunity to mingle with both types.

Sutherland concludes, therefore, that people may become delinquent (deviant) to the degree that they associate and interact with others who favor law violation more commonly than they oppose it. Such association varies in frequency, duration, intensity, and priority, and these variables determine what individuals learn or how well they learn it. Further, while criminal behavior is an expression of general needs and values in the psychoanalytic sense, it cannot be *explained* by such things ("aggressiveness" for example), because noncriminal behavior is an expression of the same needs and values. It is not "need for money" that explains criminality, but the choices that an individual makes to fulfill that need. Such choices are the product of life-long learning and interaction with others.

*Labeling* The labeling theory of deviant behavior is primarily associated with Howard S. Becker.[31] It seeks to understand how an individual or a group interacts with others in a way that results in their becoming defined — labeled — as deviant. The argument is simple: Out of the enormous diversity of human behaviors, only certain ones are selected by societies or groups within them for definition as deviant. Judgments about what acts are deviant are highly relative and not by any means logically consistent. Not everyone who performs a given act will be called deviant for doing so, and the same act may or may not be called deviant at all times. Ingesting chemicals with the intent of altering our mental or physical condition may or may not be "drug abuse." It is sometimes a "headache remedy."

In labeling theory, the focus of attention turns to the "normals" who do the labeling, as opposed to the deviant and the deviant act. The labeling theorist studies how a particular behavior comes to be labeled as deviant. Society is an active partner in the creation of the deviant. "Nuts," "sluts," and "perverts" are not part of the natural world like rocks, rivers, and roosters. The first three are human creations. Our reaction to them plays a critical role in their behavior and our definition of it. Deviance is not an inherent quality of any act, but is conferred by the label.

An interesting refinement of labeling theory was introduced in 1964 by Erving Goffman. He referred to people with "spoiled" or somehow marred identities as people with a "stigma" attached to them.[32] People react differently to those so stigmatized, and more often than not, the reaction has no basis in logic. Thus we tend to speak louder to the blind, to be overly courteous to parents of mentally retarded children, and to avoid those with visible physical impairments. Goffman argued that we view such people as "stigmatized," or deviant. Deviance is not a term reserved only for those who commit crimes.

*Secondary Deviance* Edwin Lemert used the term **secondary deviance** to describe the behavior deviants develop as a result of having been labeled deviant in the first place.[33] For example, we label drug addicts as deviant and criminal

> **secondary deviance:** deviant behavior developed or exhibited by an individual as a consequence of having been labeled as deviant in the first place.

and ignore their physiological need for drugs. As a consequence of the application of these labels, the "normal" society represses the addict in many ways. The society claims that addiction is somehow tied to a lack of will power and, in order to strengthen the addict's will, makes it impossible to get drugs legally.

This method of "curing" deviance places addicts in a position where they must resort to crime to get the drugs they must have to survive. Their crimes are a direct consequence of the public reaction to the primary label (drug addict, deviant) and are not the result of the actual physical ingestion of the drug. A secondary deviant is a person whose life and identity are organized around the facts of deviance, someone forced by others to "live up to" the deviant label or identity.

*The New Criminology* The work of Richard Quinney represents what has become known as the "new criminology," a development of the conflict perspective in sociology. Quinney argues that current theories of crime and what should be done about crime have a single purpose, the maintenance of the current social system. Whatever social order is currently in vogue is to be maintained and anything threatening the stability of that order is subject to investigation, harassment, or whatever it takes to abort it.

Social scientists, this position asserts, have consistently focused on the criminals. "What made them do it?" is the question. Having supplied an answer, however unsatisfactory, they next "rehabilitate" the offender." The sources of crime are believed to be located in the person who violates the law rather than in the authority that defines behavior as criminal."[34] In this view crime is a product of corruption in the capitalist state. It is, therefore, inevitable, given the present structure of the political system. "Law is the tool of the ruling class," says Quinney. "Criminal law in particular is a device made and used by the ruling class to preserve the existing order. In the United States, the state — and its legal system — exists to secure and perpetuate the capitalist interests of the ruling class."[35]

## SUMMARY

The inability of mental health professionals to distinguish the "sane" from the "insane" gives rise to the question, What do we mean by deviance and how is it to be recognized? In one sense, neither the popular understanding of the phenomenon nor the law really do know what the concept means. This is because both assume that deviant people and deviant behavior are different from other people and other behavior and are distinguishable as such. But the facts do not support these beliefs. Deviance is not a quality inherent in either persons or behavior; it is a judgment that an individual is engaging in behavior that violates social or legal norms. Since judgments are made by someone, deviants themselves or others, they are relative to the normative system of the society in which they are made, the time, the place, the social status of the actor and victim (if any), and the consequences the act is perceived to have.

Deviant behavior, or the definition of a behavior as deviant, is inseparable from social control. The processes of social control (socialization, social organization, and social structure) not only define deviance through articulating what is right or proper, but also act to inhibit it through sanctions. In one sense, then, social control creates deviance because a statement of "right" necessarily implies a definition of "wrong."

Consideration of the varieties of deviant behavior, violations of law, custom, or manners and civility, give us some insights into its nature. The law makes a distinction between acts *mala in se* and *mala prohibita*—acts that are evil or wrong in themselves and acts that are wrong merely because they are forbidden. What may be considered "wrong in itself," of course, is culturally relative, as is what is merely forbidden; but either conception may be the cause of the judgment that an action is deviant. Thus the law sometimes forbids acts that members of the society do not consider normatively wrong, and some acts generally accepted as deeply wrong are not illegal. This phenomenon is responsible for much of the confusion and difficulty in the study of deviant behavior. It also accounts for the "special" character of crime and delinquency when considered as a category of deviance. The study of crime and delinquency is further complicated by such matters as victimless and white-collar crime, the unreliability of official statistics, and the confusion surrounding punishment and its effects.

In general, the nonsociological approaches to the study of deviance have been theoretical failures due to their acceptance of the assumption that deviants are different from other people. Sociological approaches fall into one of three categories, strain or motivational theories, control or bond theories, and cultural deviance theories. According to strain theories, the pressures for conformity are sufficiently great that deviance must be a kind of faulty attempt to conform to social norms. Control theories assume that human behavior is so various it is "normalized" or regulated only by mechanisms of social organization and control so that deviance represents a failure of these to operate in individual cases. Cultural deviance theories assume that deviants in general are conforming to learned expectations in "normal" ways, but they point to the heterogeneity of modern life as a source of multiple norm systems, some of which are inconsistent with others. Understanding deviance, then, becomes a matter of understanding how some groups acquire the social power to impose their standards on others.

## SUGGESTED READINGS

CAVAN, SHERRY. *Liquor License: An Ethnography of Bar Behavior*. Chicago: Aldine, 1966. Describes a survey of drinking and bar behavior conducted through participant observation and interviews in the San Francisco area. By analyzing who talks to whom, how pickups are arranged, how drinks are bought for others, the four main types of bar (home territory, convenience, sexual, night spots) and the "rules" of public drinking behavior are discovered.

CONKLIN, JOHN E. *"Illegal but Not Criminal: Business Crime in America*. Englewood Cliffs, N.J.: Prentice-Hall, 1977. A survey of both professional and popular literature on white-collar crime concentrating on its costs, frequency, motives, and *modus operandi*. Supports Sutherland's original contention that major corporations are habitual criminals.

DOUGLAS, JACK D. *The Nude Beach*. Beverly Hills, Calif.: Sage Publications, *Sociological Observations* vol. 1,

1977. An ethnography of behavior based on nine years' observation of a particular nude beach in California. It gives history of the practice in California, processes of entry and socialization, body code and language, and beach activities.

ERICKSON, KAI T. *Wayward Puritans: A Study in the Sociology of Deviance* New York: Wiley, 1966. Puts forth a theory of deviance as a resource a society utilizes to maintain its social order. Using historical materials from the Puritan Massachusetts Bay Colony in the seventeenth century, Erickson describes three "crime waves" the colony experienced and suggests that the styles of deviance a community experiences are the consequence of the way it perceives the boundaries of its cultural universe.

LOVE, EDMUND G. *Subways are for Sleeping.* New York: New American Library, 1956. A collection of brief biographical accounts of urban dwellers who survive without employment through such stratagems as living in Grand Central Station or utilizing subway trains to sleep, remaining in a hotel without payment by going naked to avoid eviction, etc.

THOMPSON, HUNTER S. *Hell's Angels: The Strange and Terrible Saga of the Outlaw Motorcycle Gangs.* New York: Ballantine, 1967. A first-person participant-observer account of a year in the original Hell's Angels by an author who later was very popular with college students.

# Chapter 17
# Collective Behavior and Social Movements

During the time this chapter was being written, a number of events occurred which readers may recall and, at the time, perhaps watched on television or read about in the newspaper. Several times Japanese leftist students created major riots attempting to halt the completion of an immense new airport near Tokyo. There was a revolution in Iran in which its former ruler, who had enjoyed the support of modern, well-armed forces, was driven from office in large part by the moral force of crowds of thousands marching in the streets in demonstrations against his rule. In Israel, the Arab minority demonstrated repeatedly concerning various matters connected with the peace treaty with Egypt, and Israelis fought with their own police and armed forces about the abandonment of settlements required by the treaty. More recently a crowd of several thousand people rioted in San Francisco in protest against the jury's verdict on the man who had shot a homosexual city official.

The study of collective behavior and social movements is concerned with events like those described above. People often react to such occurrences as bizarre or unusual and regard them as having little to do with ordinary life. Those who participate in them may be perceived as weird or irrational by others who become aware of them only through the mass media. "Why," we ask ourselves as we read of assassinations in Spain or revolutionary combat in Nicaragua, "do people have to behave like that? Why can't they just handle things normally, like the rest of us?"

We will discover in this chapter that judgments of this kind are often incorrect. Collective behavior and social movements are far more common than we may ordinarily think. Numerous masses and publics exist in our society at all times and crowds form every day in response to such ordinary occurences as fires or auto accidents. Social movements are merely group efforts to bring about change. They occur because the existing social or political structure is not receptive to group needs and provide alternative means of producing change.

Much about both collective behavior and social movements is understandable and rational. Human collectivities, whether rioting over a political issue or watching a musical performance, have common organizational and structural characteristics and behave in predictable ways. A panic in a crowded nightclub is not an incomprehensible act of God and a revolutionary organization is not much different from one devoted to ending environmental pollution. In the following pages we will examine such phenomena sociologically and learn how comprehensible, even ordinary, they really are.

## COLLECTIVE BEHAVIOR

The study of collective behavior involves such subjects as crowds, fads, mass behavior, and rumor. These topics have three characteristics in common. They deal with behavior which is relatively (1) spontaneous, (2) transitory, and (3) loosely structured. When auto accidents occur, for example, people often spontaneously assemble to help the injured or to watch others provide assistance and discuss how it happened. They do not remain together for very long, however. Once the disabled vehicles and the injured people have been removed, the bystanders usually disperse. Thus the life span of the crowd is short. It is transitory. During its existence, the crowd is likely to be loosely structured, so that few norms exist regarding its behavior; relationships between the crowd members are not well defined; the only leaders are those who have emerged from the crowd itself.

The fact that collective behavior is spontaneous, transitory, and unstructured places it in contrast with most of the forms of behavior we experience during our day-to-day activities. Much of our lives are spent doing familiar routines in structured settings. We awaken, eat, perform our jobs, and retire at remarkably consistent times of the day. Similarily, the roles we play during the course of any day are normally quite structured, nonspontaneous, and stable. We assume such familiar roles as those of student, employee, or spouse with great ease and perform them for hours at a time. Further, these roles are performed in group or organizational settings in conjunction with stable roles performed by others.

Collective behavior differs from these other "conventional" forms of behavior in being an adaptation to situations that are out of the ordinary. When people are confronted by an auto accident or fire, for example, they must react to a situation with which they are usually unfamiliar. The behavior in which they engage is spontaneous and unstructured because they have little preparation, in the form of roles, norms, and attitudes, for reacting to it. (By contrast, the members of the rescue squad which reacts to an accident are behaving according to well-defined roles and norms). Panics, riots, stock market crashes or booms, and even fads and crazes, can all be seen as collective responses to unusual circumstances. If there were no unusual circumstances confronting people, there would be no collective behavior. Instead, all our behavior would be governed by the traditional roles in the society.

Every society, however, occasionally experiences unanticipated or extraordinary events. Floods, tornadoes, and other natural disasters are examples; flagrant violations of societal mores, such as murders or kidnappings are other examples, as are rapid changes in the economy or the political system, such as bank closings, rapid price increases, or political assassinations. Such events are also sufficiently unanticipated and disruptive to produce one or more forms of collective behavior.

### Types of Collective Behavior

The examples of collective behavior mentioned so far can be divided into two categories. One consists of situations in which the people who constitute the collectivity in question are all located in the same place. Such individuals are said to be *spatially proximate*. Crowds, audiences, and lines are examples of spatially proximate collectivities. The second category consists of *diffuse collectivities*, or masses and publics. As the name implies, diffuse collectivities are characterized by the dispersion of their members over a large geographic area, so that there is little or no face-to-face interaction. As we shall see, the absence of face-to-face interaction does not mean that there is no communication; often there is a considerable amount. The

dispersion of individuals in masses and publics does, however, mean that the spread of ideas and sentiments may occur more slowly than in crowds or audiences.

### Diffuse Collectivities: Masses and Publics

A **mass** is *a category of geographically dispersed individuals who are participating in some event either cognitively or physically*. The millions of persons who annually watch the Rose Bowl football game on television constitute a mass. Although they are not physically present, they become *cognitively* (mentally) involved. By contrast, the people who moved to Alaska to benefit from the oil pipeline construction there constituted a mass by virtue of their actual physical involvement. If you consider the large number of events occurring throughout this society at any time and the number of persons who somehow become involved in them, you can see that hundreds of masses exist at any one time. Examples of masses include people who have seen the movie *Star Wars*, watched the Watergate trials, and followed the New York Yankees during their season.

The members of a mass are comparatively anonymous.[1] The only persons with whom they are likely to talk about the issue at hand are their immediate friends and family. Despite their dispersion and anonymity, however, those individuals who are part of a mass act in awareness of their mass membership. That is, they act and feel the way they do because they are conscious of the existence of thousands or millions of other persons who are also following the event. For example, investors in the stock market often buy or sell stocks not so much because of the actual economic conditions in the society, but because they are conscious of the presence of a large number of other investors and they anticipate how these others will react.

The comparatively recent development of the mass media, especially television and radio, has facilitated mass behavior by sending out large amounts of information in short time spans. For example, within 5½ hours of the time President Kennedy was shot, 99.8 percent of all Americans had learned of his death.[2] The scope and nature of the mass reaction to the assassination would have been much different had it not been for TV and radio.

Informal communication processes also play a part in mass behavior. For example, about half

> **mass:** a category of spatially dispersed persons participating in some event physically or cognitively, e.g., the television audience for a particular program.

of those who learned of President Kennedy's death got their information from friends in face-to-face interactions or over the telephone, rather than from radio or TV. So, while the media facilitated the communication, informal communication channels, such as friendship networks, were also important.

Friendship networks also help shape our reactions to such phenomena as TV programs, movies, and political events. Since we often experience these in a group context, our reactions are partly based upon the interpersonal influences operating within the group. If our friends like a movie, the chances are good that they will induce us to like it as well. Even when we experience some event by ourselves, there is a good possibility that we will look to our friends for their reactions to it. High-speed transportation and communication facilitate such interaction, even over long distances.

The individual members of masses are sometimes influenced by another source of information, the opinion leader. **Opinion leaders** are informal experts who are regularly consulted for their views on some subject. Such persons

President Kennedy's assassination. Within 5½ hours of this instant in 1963, 99.8% of all Americans had learned of it.

serve as intermediaries in a communication process that often begins with mass media sources, such as TV news broadcasts, and ends with individual members of the society. Opinion leaders in effect monitor news sources for information on issues; they interpret the information, and then convey all of this to their friends. This process is called the *two-step flow of communication*.

The impact of opinion leaders upon peoples' opinions was first identified in a study of voting behavior by Lazarsfeld and others.[3] They found that informal leaders and interpersonal influence played a greater role in influencing voting choices than did the media. Subsequent studies found similar results for fashion, movie attendance, and marketing. The opinion leadership studies found that such leaders were not concentrated in the upper levels of society but existed in every stratum and that people in any group or stratum looked to others "like themselves" for opinion leadership.[4]

Recognition of the existence and function of such communication intermediaries as opinion leaders is important because it points out that information does not necessarily flow simply and directly from media to populace. Other paths of communication also exist.

*Types of Mass Behavior* Several types of mass behavior can be identified. Fads, such as hoola hoops, skateboards, strobe lights, watching old Humphrey Bogart movies, dune buggies, and water beds are one type. **Fads** are *short-lived, frivolous forms of behavior engaged in by a number of persons.*[5] **Crazes** are even more *extreme forms of behavior, with an even shorter life span.* Goldfish swallowing in the 1920s and streaking in the mid-1970s are examples of this form of mass behavior. **Fashions** are a third form of mass behavior, closely related to fads. These are *the standards of dress that operate at a given time in the society.* Compared with fads, fashions tend to be less adventurous. Sandals, bell-bottomed pants, miniskirts, cotton madras shirts, long hair on men, and short

---

## THE WAR OF THE WORLDS

On the evening of October 30, 1938, a weekly radio program called the Mercury Theater broadcast a dramatization of H. G. Wells's "War of the Worlds." The theme of the story was that the earth was being invaded by beings from another planet. What was unusual about the radio broadcast was that it was made to appear as real as the circumstances would allow, as a Halloween prank. The producers of the broadcast were much more successful in frightening people than they actually intended. It is estimated that of the over six million people who heard the broadcast, at least one million were frightened or disturbed. Thousands of persons fled from the area where the invaders were supposed to be landing. The switchboards of police departments and military installations were inundated with frantic callers.

The millions who tuned in to the "War of the Worlds" broadcast constituted a mass. The frightened or disturbed reaction of some of the listeners was an hysteria. Hadley Cantril and others who studied the aftermath of the incident asked, "What factors contributed to the mass hysteria"?[6] The most important factor

was the realism of the broadcast. In the 1930s, radio was an important instrument for receiving news announcements. Only a few weeks earlier, millions of people had learned of the possibilities of a European War on their radios.

The "War of the Worlds" broadcast used a series of special "news bulletins" in the style of real news bulletins to which listeners had become accustomed. Actors assumed the roles of scientific and military experts and posed as "witnesses" to the events that were supposedly taking place. The details given by the "witnesses" were very specific ("Smoke is now spreading over Raymond Blvd!"). The "witnesses" used common expressions to describe what they "saw."

An important factor in an individual listener's becoming part of the mass hysteria was tuning in late to the radio program. Despite the realism of the broadcast, if a person heard it from the very beginning, it was unlikely that he or she would take it seriously. But a CBS poll of 920 persons indicated that 42 percent of the audience did tune in late.

hair on women are all examples of fashion.

Two other forms of mass behavior are booms and busts. **Booms** are said to occur *when large numbers of people simultaneously try to obtain or achieve something.* Thus land booms occur when people rush to buy up the available land in an area. Booms occur with some regularity in the investment world. A **bust** is the exact opposite of a boom, *a large-scale attempt of persons to simultaneously get rid of something.* The sudden widespread sales of a stock or withdrawal of savings from banks are examples of busts.

Another type of mass behavior is hysteria. **Mass hysterias,** like booms or busts, simultaneously involve many people in frenzied activities. In the case of hysterias, however, the objects of attention tend to be social rather than economic. During the 1950s millions of persons were afraid to express unpopular political views for fear of being labeled communists. The McCarthy Era, as it was called, was a period of mass hysteria. A classic example of mass hysteria was Orsen Wells' 1938 "War of the Worlds" broadcast.

*Publics* A **public** is a collection of persons confronted by some issue, divided in their opinions regarding it, and engaged in discussion about it.[7] Abortion, for example, is an issue around which a public has formed. Many people strongly feel that abortion is an important option for pregnant women to have. Such persons often have well-developed, logical arguments in support of their views. Others, however, feel that abortion is wrong. They too have well-developed arguments. Taken together, these so-called prochoice and prolife people constitute a public.

Publics are not usually physically located in one place. They are distributed over a wide area. Numerous publics exist in our society at the same time. Issues around which publics have formed in the past include the Vietnam War, ecology, marijuana, the Equal Rights Amendment, capital punishment, and gun control. Formal organizations also tend to become involved in the issues around which publics form. These organizations should not be confused with publics, which are unorganized collections of persons. Publics, however, may provide the basis for starting up new organizations or for supporting existing ones.

Since each individual in a society may simul-

**opinion leaders:** persons who are considered "expert" in some area to the extent that others seek their views and are influenced by them. Such figures are important interpreters in the "two-step flow" of information from the mass media to the mass audience.

**fad:** short-lived, frivolous forms of mass behavior engaged in by large numbers of people.

**craze:** an extreme, and extremely transitory, fad.

**fashion:** the standard of dress existing in a given society at a particular time.

**boom:** a situation in which large numbers of people attempt to obtain or achieve the same thing at the same time. Examples are demand in 1976–77 for CB radios and snowmobiles.

**bust:** a situation in which large numbers of people attempt to divest themselves of the same thing at the same time. A "run" on a bank would be an example.

Hysteria. Youngsters during a Peter Frampton concert.

taneously be a member of several publics, it is possible for a large number of persons to take similar sides on several important issues. Thus millions of persons might each be against abortion, marijuana reform, and gun-control legislation, while being for capital punishment. Often such clusters of viewpoints become incorporated in the platforms of political parties or as part of the ideologies of social movements. The cluster of views just identified is associated with conservative political parties and right-of-center social movements. In another example, the formation of a new political party in Canada, the *Parti Quebecois,* was the result of the alignment of French-speaking Canadians on several issues, such as the adoption of French as the official language of the province, and political independence from the national government in Ottawa. English-speaking Canadians tended to take the opposite side on these issues. In this instance the result has been tension, protest activities, and some rioting.

**Spatially Proximate Collectivities** Unlike masses and publics, some types of collectivities are *located within a small geographic area,* such as a street, an auditorium, or a hallway. These are called *spatially proximate collectivities,* and consist of aggregates, lines, and crowds. An **aggregate** is simply a collection of persons who are temporarily located in the same area. There is minimal organization and little or no interaction among the members of an aggregate. They are even likely to be gathered together for different reasons, perhaps enroute to entirely different destinations. Persons located in the foyer of an airline terminal, standing in an elevator, or waiting to cross a street at a stoplight, constitute aggregates. Much of the coldness and impersonality associated with contemporary urban life can be traced to the frequency with which we find ourselves members of such aggregates.

Upon occasion individuals join a different type of collectivity, called a line, or queue. **Lines** are simply collections of persons who are arranged according to some priority, usually their time of arrival, and who have some common objective or destination.[8] Examples include lines at movie theaters, bus depots, and athletic events. Compared with aggregates, lines possess slightly higher levels of organization. (In some instances the organization imparted to a line is the result of activity by persons with special occupational roles which include responsibilities for the formation and maintenance of lines, eg. movie theater ushers).

**Audiences,** sometimes called "conventionalized crowds," are collections of persons who have assembled together, usually at a prespecified location and date, and remain together for a predetermined length of time. The forms of behavior expected of audience members also tend to be prespecified. Spectators at a baseball game, for example, are expected to cheer the home team, boo the visiting team and the umpires, and take a seventh inning stretch. Persons assembled together for religious services, college lectures, and political conventions also constitute audiences because of the conventionalized settings and behaviors associated with them.

Aggregates, lines, and audiences are similar in that the individuals comprising them have little organization and are gathered together for a comparatively short period of time. Furthermore, there is generally little sense of urgency or importance associated with these collectivities. Occasionally, however, people who are assembled together are confronted with some new problem or condition. The changed circumstances surrounding the collectivity require that the individuals look to one another to interpret the situation and give meaning to it. When this occurs, the aggregate, line, or audience has become transformed into a *crowd.* A serious automobile accident in a downtown

Conventional audience.

intersection, for example, may come as an unexpected shock to the aggregate of people who are waiting to cross the street at a traffic light. Many of the people may turn to one another and ask: "How did the accident happen?" "Have the police been notified?" "How are the victims?" The intense interaction of persons who only moments earlier took no notice of one another is characteristic of their transformation from an aggregate to a crowd. Or members of an audience in a movie theater may find themselves confronted by a fire. In such a situation they will look to one another to see how everyone else is reacting. If some people are observed running for the exits, the remainder may interpret the situation similarly and also begin running.

**Crowds,** then, are collections of individuals who are spatially proximate, experience some unexpected or unusual situation, look to one another for the meaning of the situation, and then behave according to their interpretation of it. Some crowds consist of individuals who believe they must accomplish a specific goal. A lynch mob is an example of this, as is a collection of persons barricading a street during a riot. Members of such crowds often develop comparatively great interaction and organization. Other crowds are characterized more by the expression of favorable or unfavorable "feelings" over some issue than by any specific goal. The convergence of thousands of people in the streets of downtown Pittsburgh to celebrate the World Series victory of the Pittsburgh Pirates in 1971 was an example of this.

**Crowd Behavior** Four models are commonly used to describe crowd behavior: contagion, convergence, emergent norm, and gaming. Several of them can often be applied to the same incident of crowd behavior, because each makes some contribution to our understanding of the subject. The oldest is the *contagion* model. This focuses upon highly visible activities that occur in some crowds. Running, applause, standing, and even speaking are among the body movements that are identifiable, as well as panics, fainting episodes, hostile outbreaks, and some collective religious experiences. Two mechanisms account for the spread or contagion of behavior. Le Bon emphasized the importance of suggestion. Individuals, Le Bon argued, become more suggestible to outside

**mass hysteria:** the simultaneous involvement of large numbers of people in frenzied activity concerning some social object or phenomenon. The witch hysteria in seventeenth-century Massachusetts and the anticommunism of the McCarthy era are American examples.

**public:** a spatially diffused, unorganized population concerned or engaged in an issue of discussion and divided in opinion about it.

**aggregate:** a minimally organized collection of persons temporarily in the same geographic area with little interaction among them. The people leaving a football stadium after a game are an example.

**line** or **queue:** a collection of persons arranged in linear pattern and having some common objective or destination, such as purchasing tickets at a box office. Characterized by some minor organization but little interaction.

**audience** or **conventionalized crowd:** collections of persons assembled together, usually at a prespecified location and time, to observe or participate in some event. Characterized by considerable conventional organization, but little interaction.

**crowd:** a spatially proximate collection of persons with a central focus of attention and considerable individual interaction but little organization.

influences when they are assembled together in large numbers. The sheer physical presence of large numbers of other persons reduces the normal constraints which operate on individuals. Once these constraints are reduced, unconscious desires are released and people consequently act in an uninhibited manner.[9] While many theorists today do not take as psychological an approach as Le Bon, they do acknowledge the usefulness of the concept of suggestibility and the reciprocal effects that large numbers of persons assembled together may have on one another.

The second mechanism to account for contagion is called *circular reaction.* According to Herbert Blumer, individuals who are gathered together in crowds transmit their feelings to one another in a circular fashion, such that the excitement or alarm of one person is conveyed to another who, in turn, transmits back these same feelings.[10] The fact that others in the crowd express similar reactions to the situation helps to validate the original feelings and thus intensifies the emotions of all. A person who shouts "fire" in a crowded auditorium and then hears others also shout "fire," is likely to go on shouting even louder.

The contagion model describes processes that occur during the actual crowd activities. The *convergence* model of crowd behavior emphasizes the shared characteristics of the individuals who happen to "converge" upon an area to form a crowd.[11] The characteristics may be dormant or hidden, or they may be apparent. Because of their similarity, however, once the individuals are assembled, only some "spark" or precipitating factor is needed to trigger a common reaction. The convergence model requires that the researcher identify what those characteristics are. Dollard, for example, attributed the lynching of southern blacks to the

economic frustration experienced by groups of whites when cotton prices were low.[12]

In many cases, crowds are composed of individuals with several social and psychological characteristics in common. Each of the groups that rioted in the 1960s and early 1970s was remarkably homogeneous—students, blacks living in the inner cities, and prisoners. The similar socioeconomic status, backgrounds, and life experiences of the members of each of these groups, combined with their close living quarters, contributed to the ease with which crowds developed within them, according to the convergence model.

The *emergent norm* model of crowds is based on the observation that when a collection of persons is confronted by some unusual problem or condition, they look to one another for answers. Examples of unusual conditions include natural disasters, race riots, and even such frequent occurrences as auto accidents and fires. The disruption produced by such events promotes interaction among the people involved. This interaction may in turn lead to the "emergence" of a set of norms that specify what

**Emergent norm. Long lines of volunteers trying to hold back the flood in St. Louis, 1973.**

people should expect and how they should behave under the circumstances at hand.[13]

The norms that emerge within crowds are not necessarily original. They may simply be new to the persons assembled together, as in the case of a crowd of people who gather to watch a fire and then decide to organize and help put it out. While there is nothing unique about working together to extinguish a fire, the transformation of a collection of strangers into a team of fire fighters requires the establishment of a "new" set of norms. Of course, not all collections of people who are assembled together develop new sets of norms. Often the people confronted by the unusual circumstances will interact but will fail to develop consensus regarding how to behave.

The emergent norm model accounts for the development of distinctive forms of behavior among crowd members without requiring the assumption that all of the members think and feel the same things. According to the model, a common understanding develops regarding what sort of behavior is expected. This shared understanding is based on the emergent norm. The understanding encourages behavior which is consistent with the norm, inhibits behavior contrary to the norm, and justifies restraints initiated against persons who openly oppose it. Consequently, although many crowd members may not personally support the norm, they behave *as if* they supported it in order not to be punished by the norm supporters.[14]

The *gaming* model is based upon principles and assumptions derived from social psychological research begun in the 1950s. At the heart of this approach is the assumption that individuals try to solve their problems in rational ways. Rational behavior is such that rewards are maximized and costs are minimized. The rational individual, in other words, is one who can size up a situation and modify behavior to best meet objectives. In crowds, the rewards sought by individuals may include such things as gaining new information, demonstrating for or against something, recounting earlier crowd activities to newcomers, shouting, or destroying the symbols of some person or group. Costs to the crowd members include personal injury, arrest, and in some instances, identification by friends and relatives. When the costs and rewards to an individual are assessed, it is possible to predict the person's behavior. Richard

**panic:** uncoordinated flight from perceived danger.

Berk has provided a simple model which illustrates the applicability of "gaming" to crowd behavior.[15] The probability that a person will initiate some action, say looting, is dependent upon his or her assessment of three factors: the expected payoffs for acting; the expected payoffs for not acting; and the likelihood that others will support the behavior. This last factor, the likelihood of support by others, is important because support not only makes the behavior less dangerous (costly) but also signifies approval (reward) by others.

*Panic* **Panic** is *uncoordinated flight from some situation or object.*[16] The objective of persons in panic is to place distance between themselves and a perceived source of danger. Fires, battlefield operations, and natural disasters are situations in which panic behavior sometimes occurs. Contrary to popular belief, people are not easily induced to panic. In order for panic to develop four conditions are necessary:

1. Feeling of entrapment, that is, awareness of only one or a very limited number of escape routes.
2. Perceived threat, either physical or psychological, and usually the feeling that there is no time to do anything about it except escape.

Panic. South Vietnam, April 4, 1975: An American official punches a man who is trying to climb aboard the already overcrowded evacuation plane.

3. Blocked, inaccessible, or overlooked escape route.

4. Failure to communicate between front and rear. People at the rear assume that the exit is still open and push and shove those in front in their efforts to escape.[17]

*Rioting* **Rioting** may be defined as a form of crowd behavior in which *members of one social group indiscriminately attack the members and property of another.* Violence is common. Often, however, the intense feelings unleashed during riots are directed against symbols of the disliked group rather than group members themselves. Thus buildings may be burned and property looted or otherwise destroyed. Characteristic of rioting is a lack of discrimination when choosing which objects or persons to attack and a lack of overall coordination among riot participants. Rioters are likely to assault any member of the outgroup in question or any property of an outgroup member.

During the 1960s a number of race riots occurred across the country, from the Watts area of Los Angeles to New York's Harlem. The riots prompted numerous efforts to discover what caused them, who participated in them, and their characteristics. Lieberson and Silverman examined newspaper and magazine accounts of 76 white and black riots occurring between 1918 and 1963.[18] Their analysis indicates two factors which were frequently present when riots started: (1) real or alleged crimes against persons rather than property, particularly crimes such as murder or rape, and (2) real or alleged norm violations directed toward members of a different racial group, such as an assault on a black youth by a white police officer.

While the immediate precipitants of riots are relatively easy to identify, the underlying conditions conducive to them are less clear. In comparing cities that experienced riots with similar cities that did not, Lieberson and Silverman found few important differences. Population increases, high black unemployment, and high white unemployment did not distinguish riot from nonriot cities. Cities experiencing riots tended to have smaller occupational differences between whites and blacks, and tended to have lower white income levels than did nonriot cities. These findings suggest that rioting among whites is in part due to the eco-

nomic threat blacks are often perceived as posing to low-status whites. Finally, slightly more nonriot cities had higher proportions of black police and city council members than did the riot cities. Thus faith in the fairness and representativeness of government and agencies of social control also appears to be a deterrent.

Research on racial riots has helped eliminate many popular stereotypes. Perhaps the most common of these has been that all riots are similar. While some patterns are observable, there are considerable variations. The National Advisory Commission on Civil Disorders classified 164 racial riots in 128 cities in 1967 into three categories of severity—major, serious, and minor.[19] Only 8 were classified as major, those that lasted more than two days, with many fires, and widespread looting and violence. Cities of all sizes experienced riots, with 25 percent having two or more. However, the total number was highest in cities of 500,000 or less, while most of the major disorders occurred in cities of 250,000 or more. Retail businesses suffered the greatest loss, with liquor, clothing, and retail stores the usual targets. Comparatively little damage was done to public buildings, industrial property, and private residences.

The commission found the rioting to be associated with such background conditions as discrimination, prejudice, severely disadvantaged living conditions, and frustration over the inability to enact change. The incident that triggered the rioting was often relatively trivial, such as a routine traffic arrest. There was, however, a disturbed atmosphere throughout the community at the time of the precipitating incident, and typically a series of previous incidents had occurred in the weeks or months before the riot. The incidents, whether precipitating or occurring previously, commonly involved protest activities, white racist activities, police actions, or other official actions. The precipitating incident was frequently the same type as one or more of the previous incidents.

Once violence occurred there was no consistent pattern in the rioting. Some situational trends were noted, however. The incident that precipitated the riot generally occurred at locations and hours when many people were present; usually in the streets between 7:00 P.M. and 12:30 A.M. Violence tended to erupt in the evenings. The temperature on the days that violence first erupted was high (suggesting that people had gone outside to escape the heat of unair-conditioned apartments). Rioting activities were often repeated in a 24-hour cycle, with the transition from the relative quiet of the day to the evening's disorder typically occurring within a one- or two-hour period.[20]

A study of the Los Angeles Watts riot of 1965 indicated considerable variety in rioting behavior. The researchers identified 1,878 incidents of behavior in the riot and classified the incidents into five categories: reported fires (926); looting (555); throwing rocks or other objects (174); false alarms (138); and crowd-gathering incidents (85). The Watts area was divided into geographic areas called census tracts to allow the researchers to study the patterns of riot behavior occurring in the various areas. They found that generally riot behavior varied from one census tract to the next and that the rioting was not predictable from one area of Watts to the next. Relatively few of the tracts had no rioting at all. Thus, while rioting was widespread, it was diverse in its forms. The actual spread of the riot was almost random.

## Determinants of Collective Behavior

Many social scientists have tried to organize the various phenomena associated with collective behavior into a single, comprehensive framework. Many people feel that the framework proposed by Neil Smelser is the best to date.[21] It identifies six determinants that influence the type of collective behavior that will occur.

**Structural Conduciveness** Some social structures help to make certain types of collective behavior possible or likely. For example, prisoners are denied control over many aspects of their lives and prison authorities have that control in the form of a structural arrangement. This is conducive to the development of prison riots and prison reform movements. Furthermore, certain physical structures are more conducive to collective behavior than others. The confined living quarters of a prison facilitate high interaction among prisoners, a necessary element of crowd behavior. Conducive physical and social structures are necessary for collective behavior to occur. Structural conduciveness does not guarantee that an episode of collective

> **riot:** crowd behavior in which members of one group indiscriminately attack the persons or property of the members of another group.

behavior is forthcoming, however. Each of the remaining determinants must also be present for that to happen.

**Structural Strain** The dissatisfactions, anxieties, and tensions that people experience as a result of some structural condition is known as structural strain. Loss of jobs, loss of life, and economic uncertainty are all strain-producing situations resulting from some structure. Strains in prison frequently result from overcrowding, fear of assault by other prisoners, and the general absence of control over one's life.

**Generalized Belief** When people experience strain, it is possible although not automatic for them to develop a belief regarding the *cause* of their strain, its nature, and its remedy. In some situations, this belief is an accurate analysis of the problems. At other times, the beliefs may be inaccurate. In either case, however, members of the collectivity will act or not act on the basis of their generalized beliefs.

Four sources of strain can be identified by such generalized beliefs: situational facilities, roles, norms, and values. Panics and crazes occur when people try to move away from or toward various situations or objects. Hostile outbursts, such as mobs and riots, occur when

**Stores burn in Watts riot area in Los Angeles, August 13, 1965.**

people believe that their strain is caused by improperly played roles. Reform movements develop in response to a belief that norms need changing. Revolutionary movements occur when people believe that values need changing.

**Precipitating Factors** The existence of structural conduciveness, strain, and generalized beliefs does not automatically produce an episode of collective behavior. Usually some observable event is necessary to precipitate activity. Precipitating factors are events that are seen as confirming the previous interpretation of the situation, as it has been identified in the generalized belief. Thus, if the generalized belief states that the prison warden is insensitive to the needs of prisoners and if a prisoner dies because of apparent negligence by prison personnel, this event could precipitate an episode of collective behavior.

**Mobilization of Participants** The actual collective behavior (or social movement) results when the participants are mobilized by the precipitating factor. As mentioned earlier, four general types of behavior are distinguished: crazes and panics; hostile outbursts (mobs and riots); norm-oriented or reform movements; and value-oriented or revolutionary movements. In our hypothetical prison situation, mobilization of participants would refer to the outbreak of the riot.

How do authorities react to collective outbursts? Kent State, 1970.

**Application of Social Controls** Persons in positions of authority can influence the precipitation and outcome of collective behavior through their own action or inaction. State police and national guardsmen are brought to prisons to control riot behavior after it has begun. Promises to form panels to listen to prisoner grievances are also a form of social control applied after the fact. The formation of permanent grievance boards in prisons may help prevent future episodes of collective behavior by giving prisoners a chance to blow off steam and by actually helping to promote changes and thus eliminate the sources of strain.

### Rumor: A Collective Behavior Process

Communication within crowds is often based on unsubstantiated information. Persons gathered at the scene of a tornado, or during racial conflicts, or at an auto accident have a need to interact with one another and pool what available information they have. This communication is known as rumor. **Rumor,** then, is *a form of communication occurring in ambiguous situations for the purpose of constructing a meaningful interpretation.*[22] Unlike gossip, rumor deals with events that are important to people.

Shibutani notes that rumor is a *collective* process involving a division of labor among participants. The contribution of each person varies with the way in which he or she is involved in the situation and the relationship of that individual to others. Some people play messenger and bring information to the collectivity. Others may assume roles of interpreter, skeptic, decision maker, protagonist (sponsoring one perspective or plan over others), or audience. These roles can help shape the final content of the rumor.[23]

The speed of rumor construction depends on how excited people are and how much access they have to communication channels. When they are not greatly excited, rumors tend to develop at a moderate rate because people do not normally interact readily with strangers. When collective excitement is high, however, the speed of rumor transmission is limited only by the availability of communication channels.[24]

The actual content of rumor, whether plausible or "far-fetched," is influenced by four factors: the urgency of demand for news, how excited people are, whether or not rumor construction takes place in informal communication networks, like friendship groups, and whether or not critical deliberation is possible. When the demand for news is moderate, collective excitement is mild, informal communication channels are used, and critical deliberation is possible, the content of rumor tends to be plausible. The toilet paper "scare" of 1973–1974 is an example of the operation of such a rumor (see box). Because this was not viewed as a very serious condition, the demand for news was not excessive nor was the collective excitement. People could discuss the rumor with friends

> **rumor:** collective communication occurring in an ambiguous situation for the purpose of establishing meaning or certainty.

and had time to deliberate over it. By contrast, rumors regarding flying saucers or miracles tend to spread under a different set of circumstances. Rumors that are inconsistent with our cultural beliefs generally arise when the demand for news greatly exceeds the available supply, collective excitement is high, spontaneously formed communication channels are used, and people do not have time to carefully examine the content of the rumor.[25]

---

## THE "SHORTAGE" OF BATHROOM TISSUE: A CLASSIC STUDY IN RUMOR

**by Andrew H. Malcolm**
*New York Times*, February 31, 1974, p. 29.

Chester, Pa., Feb. 2—"You know, we've got all sorts of shortages these days," Johnny Carson told his faithful late-night television audience. "But have you heard the latest? I'm not kidding. I saw it in the paper. There's a shortage of toilet paper."

Thus began, on the night of last Dec. 19, the second chapter in what may go down in history as one of the nation's most unusual crises— The Toilet Paper Shortage—a phenomenon that saw millions of Americans strip every roll of bathroom tissue from thousands of grocery shelves.

It was a shortage full of humor, misunderstanding and fear. It was a shortage involving government officials, a TV personality, a well-meaning Wisconsin Congressman, eager reporters, industrial executives and ordinary consumers.

And it was a shortage that need never have been. For the toilet paper shortage was a rumor run wild in a nation that has recently become geared to expect shortages in items considered absolute necessities. . .

Fears of a possible bathroom tissue shortage, which continue in some areas as the result of abnormal buying and hoarding, seem to have sprouted last November, when news agencies carried articles about a shortage in Japan.

Meanwhile, in Washington, Representative

Harold V. Froehlich, a 41-year-old Republican from Wisconsin's heavily forested Eighth District, was getting considerable complaints from his constituents of a shortage of pulp paper, allegedly caused by companies that increased paper exports to avoid Federal price controls.

On Nov. 16, Mr. Froehlich issued a news release that began, "The Government Printing Office is facing a serious shortage of paper." Like most other news releases from such sources, it was virtually ignored.

Then Mr. Froehlich discovered that the Federal Government's National Buying Center had fallen 50 percent short in obtaining bids to provide 182,050 boxes of toilet tissue, a four-month's supply for the country's bureaucrats and soldiers.

On Dec. 11, a day now etched in the minds of Mr. Froehlich's staff, he issued another news release. It began:

"The United States may face a serious shortage of toilet paper within a few months. . . . I hope we don't have to ration toilet tissue. . . . A toilet paper shortage is no laughing matter. It is a problem that will touch every American."

"It got more attention than we ever dreamed of," one aide said of the release. The wire services picked it up. So did television networks.

Radio stations called to talk. German and Japanese correspondents lined up for interviews. In some reports, however, qualifying words like "potential" somehow disappeared.

In Philadelphia, reporters called the headquarters of the Scott Paper Company, one of the nation's 10 largest paper manufacturers. Television crews then filmed supermarkets and toilet paper streaming from machines in Scott's suburban plant here.

Company officers went on television to urge calm, saying there was no shortage if people bought normally.

### MANY CREDIBILITY GAPS

Some consumers may have believed those remarks—until they saw other shoppers wheeling cases of toilet tissue from some stores or signs of rationing each buyer to two rolls each. "There are so many credibility gaps today," said one paper executive, "and we fell into one."

Wire service reporters and broadcast newsmen passed the self-fulfilling shortage reports on to their readers and audiences, one of whom included Johnny Carson, a television talk show host whose nightly program is often geared to current events.

On Dec. 20, the day after his comments, the toilet-paper-buying binge began nationally.

In the Bronx, Jimmy Detrain, manager of the Food Cart Store on Lydig Avenue, watched customers check out with $20 in toilet paper purchases.

"I heard about it on the news," said Mrs. Paul McCoy of Houston, "so I bought an extra 15 rolls."

In Seattle, one store owner ordered an extra 21 cases of toilet paper. When he received only three cases, he became worried and rationed his supply. That prompted more buying, even at increased prices.

When Mrs. Clare Clark of Jenkintown, Pa., gave a party, guests asked what they could bring. "I told them toilet paper," she said.

Here in Chester, at Scott's plant, the world's largest such facility (capable of producing 7,500 miles of tissue every day), production continued at full capacity.

Although paper industry officials say The Toilet Paper Shortage was hard to believe, Steuart Henderson Britt, a professor of marketing at Northwestern University, regards the shortage as a classic study in rumor.

## SOCIAL MOVEMENTS

A **social movement** is *a collective venture extending beyond a local community or single event and involving a systematic effort to bring about changes in the way people think and behave.*[26] Consider the elements of this definition. First, *a social movement is a collective venture*; a considerable number of persons must be involved in an activity for it to be considered a social movement. Second, *movements are change-oriented.* They have as their objective some form of change in the way people think, in what they believe, and in their behavior. These changes may be attempts at instituting new norms or values in the society. For example, the women's movement has sought and achieved new laws (norms) which prohibit sex discrimination in employment. Some movements, however, have as their objectives the protection of existing values and norms which appear to be threatened. The Ku Klux Klan revival in the 1950s and 1960s was an attempt to preserve norms that allowed racial segregation. Still other social movements attempt to restore norms and values that have fallen into disuse. Groups that reject urban life and technology for communal life in harmony with nature exemplify this type of change.

Third, *movements extend beyond a single event or community.* Local activities by themselves are not movements. Only when they have spread across several communities and events are they movements. Fourth, *movements involve systematic effort;* that is, they are coordinated activities rather than random ones. Thus they have one or more organizations associated with them. These organizations may be highly formalized, as is the National Organization of Women, or they may be very loosely arranged, as was CORE, the Congress of Racial Equality.

*Social Movements, Collective Behavior, and Social Change*

Unlike collective behavior, which tends to have relatively little structure and to exist for comparatively short periods of time, social move-

Social movements are change oriented.

ments have structure, tend to last relatively long, and have continuity in goals, methods, and membership. Members of movements identify themselves more completely with the movements than do members of collectivities. Nevertheless, there is an important relationship between the two. Social movements have several types of collectivities and forms of collective behavior associated with them. Movements often publicize their goals by means of rallies and marches. Audiences assemble to observe the movement's activities. Occasionally these audiences become transformed into crowds. Masses and publics are also often associated with movements. They provide important sources of new contributors and members.

Millions of persons followed the activities of civil rights workers from CORE and SNCC (Student NonViolent Coordinating Committee) during their attempts to integrate interstate transportation facilities in the South in 1961. (These activities became known as the Freedom Rides.) The persons who followed the news stories constituted a mass. At the same time, many

**social movement:** a collective venture extending over time and space in a systematic effort to produce change.

people took sides over the issue of racial integration, some favoring segregation and others favoring integration. These persons constituted a public. As a result, both CORE and SNCC experienced great increases in financial donations and membership recruits.

This illustrates the interplay between collective behavior and organizational behavior in social movements. A complete picture or model of a social movement would include one or more organizations, various forms of mass and public behavior, and probably several forms of crowd behavior (see Figure 17.1). Social movements are thus difficult to describe or define in simple terms because of the different social forms that constitute them.

Movements differ from other organized attempts to change society. The methods used by a movement lie outside the normal institutional processes of the society. For example, rather

**FIGURE 17.1 One common social movement model**

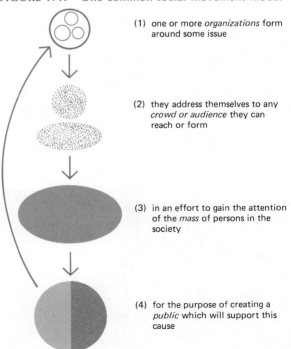

(1) one or more *organizations* form around some issue

(2) they address themselves to any *crowd or audience* they can reach or form

(3) in an effort to gain the attention of the *mass* of persons in the society

(4) for the purpose of creating a *public* which will support this cause

than attempting to change the laws by writing to political officials, lobbying, and backing candidates favorable to the changes, people involved in social movements might hold demonstrations or marches, engage in acts of civil disobedience, or even use violence. Groups that rely solely on political lobbying to achieve their goals, and use other established institutional processes, are called "interest groups" rather than movement organizations. The distinction between the two is not always easy to make, however, because movement organizations often utilize both types of methods. For example, the women's movement of the late 1960s and 1970s uses the political system to promote change but also goes outside the institutionalized political arrangements. Marches, rallies, consciousness-raising sessions, rape crisis centers, self-help groups, and activist organizations all promote women's interests with little or no assistance from political groups or the government.

Since movements employ noninstitutionalized methods to promote change, they can provide important functions for society. They can act as mechanisms to allow needed changes to occur when existing institutions are not responsive to the needs of various groups of people. The civil rights movement, the women's movement, the labor movement, the French Revolution, and the American Revolution are all examples of social movements which helped meet needs that were not being met by existing institutions. Social movements don't always serve this function, however. A large number of movements fail to eliminate the problems facing

their supporters. Sometimes this is because the supporters are not well organized, and sometimes the opposition is overwhelming. It is also possible for groups to incorrectly identify the source of their problems or to select impractical techniques to overcome them. For example, Roberta Ash notes that while Indians who practiced the Ghost Dance correctly identified whites as the source of their problems, they erroneously relied upon magical techniques to deal with them.[27]

### Determinants of Social Movements

Social movements may be seen as shaped by Smelser's six determinants that influence whether episodes of collective behavior will occur. The first, you will recall, is structural conduciveness, that is, whether or not existing structures allow movements to occur. Next is structural strain; people must experience some tension before they can be motivated to participate in a movement. This is followed by the creation of a generalized belief, the ideas regarding the source of the strains experienced and what should be done to remedy them. Movements occur, according to Smelser, only if the generalized belief identifies the source of strain as due to improper values or norms in the society. If some consensus develops regarding the need for one or more values to be changed before the society can function properly, then the groundwork is laid for a "value-oriented" movement. These are commonly called revolutions. Alternatively, if people believe that the societal values are acceptable but the rules of behavior or norms need to be changed, then there is a possibility for a "norm-oriented" movement to develop. These are usually referred to as reform movements.

If structural conduciveness, strain, and generalized beliefs regarding the need for changes in values or norms exist, then the circumstances are ripe for a social movement. What is still needed is a "spark," or precipitating factor, to bring things to a head. A precipitating factor is an incident of behavior that serves to confirm what people already believe and induces them to act. The fifth determinant is the actual social movement activity that finally occurs, the mobilization of participants. The last determinant of a movement is the application of social controls. Persons in positions of authority may try to

Social movements employ noninstitutionalized methods to promote change. A "die-in" in front of the Pacific Gas and Electric Company in San Francisco in a protest against nuclear power plants.

stop movement activities by outlawing movement organizations, arresting members, or stopping marches, rallies, or newspaper publicity. In many cases the application of social controls only succeeds in temporarily slowing down the development of a movement, and may precipitate additional movement activities. The unsuccessful attempt of the Shah of Iran to stifle opposition is an example.

Smelser's framework focuses upon important factors that affect how movements develop and it shows how these factors are interrelated. It also shows how movements and collective behavior are similar—they are influenced by the same general set of determinants—and how they differ—the sources of strain identified by the beliefs are different for the two. The framework is only able to treat the interrelations at an abstract level, however. Some critics feel that it is too abstract. Furthermore, the framework is only a way of looking at movements; it does not explain why any particular movement occurred.

Marcus Garvey on his way to a Madison Square Garden rally for the Universal Negro Improvement Association, 1922.

Nor can it be used to predict the development of movements in the distant future.

The origins of the Marcus Garvey movement in the United States illustrate how Smelser's framework is applied.[28] In 1918 in New York City, Marcus Garvey, a black immigrant from Jamaica, founded an organization to improve the social and economic conditions of blacks throughout the world. The organization was called the Universal Negro Improvement Association, or UNIA, although Garvey's efforts were largely confined to the United States. Millions of working- and lower-class blacks supported Garvey. It was the first major black organization to emphasize black pride and power. Grocery stores, a restaurant, a millinery store, a publishing house, and even a steamship line were started by Garvey for the movement. Considerable emphasis was placed on returning to Africa and reclaiming it for its rightful owners, the blacks of the world. The movement flourished for several years and then rapidly declined after Garvey's imprisonment for stock fraud in 1925. It did not entirely cease until the 1940s.

Several aspects of the American social structure were *conducive* to the development of a movement such as Garvey's. Denied access to educational and occupational opportunities because of formal and informal rules operating in the society, large numbers of blacks lived in ghettos. This facilitated *interaction.* Although organizations like the National Association for the Advancement of Colored People (NAACP) and the Urban League were already in existence, these were mostly composed of middle-class persons who did not address working- and lower-class blacks on their own terms. Blacks, especially those in the lower class, also experienced the structurally produced *strains* brought about by economic hardship. Some blacks identified the values held by whites as the source of their problems. They concluded that blacks should form their own political, economic, and social institutions. Marcus Garvey was one of those who held and helped spread this belief. He was a powerful and dynamic speaker whose speeches were a *precipitating factor* in the decision of many people to join the movement. Thousands of blacks were thus *mobilized* to join or support his organization. Finally, several *social controls* were applied to the UNIA and to Garvey as its leader. Garvey was arrested several times for rather minor infractions of the law and finally jailed. Although President Coolidge commuted Garvey's sentence after only part of it had been served, Garvey was required to leave the country. His departure signaled the decline of the UNIA.

### Revolutionary and Reform Movements

The Garvey movement is called a "value-oriented" movement because it sought to reorganize behavior on the basis of a new set of values. Such endeavors are also called revolutionary movements. Revolutionary movements have two characteristics which distinguish them from norm-oriented, or "reform" movements. First, they have goals that involve substantial changes in the social structure of the society. New economic, political, or educational arrangements are typical of the goals of revolutionary movements.

By contrast, reform movements seek to make less far-reaching changes in social structure. Typically these involve changes of law. Reform movements not only support the existing values of the society but often attempt to show how their goals are consistent with such values. Because revolutionary movements advocate substantial change, they are often looked upon with disdain or fear by those who desire to keep things as they are. Since people in positions of power in the society often have vested interests in holding their positions, they are likely to use whatever resources they have to oppose revolutionary movements.

Revolutionary movements often advocate or use illegal methods. Garvey, for example, advocated regaining control of Africa by whatever means possible. In part, revolutionary groups use the methods they do because more conventional, legal, methods would be ineffective. Often such groups perceive themselves as driven to use illegal methods since they are not allowed to exist peacefully in the society. For example, much of the violence attributed to the Black Panther party can be viewed as a response to great pressures placed on them by law enforcement agencies.

Reform movements differ from revolutionary movements in employing methods that are almost always legal. Reform groups work within established channels to achieve their goals. The work of the NAACP, from its inception to the present, illustrates how reform groups oper-

ate. Voter registration and education campaigns as well as court cases and political lobbying are among the tactics successfully employed by this organization.

### The Life Cycle of Social Movements

Many movements undergo a series of changes which, taken together, may be said to constitute a life cycle. Dawson and Gettys have identified four stages in this cycle.[29] First is a period of unrest. Some segment of the population experiences strains, tension, and uncertainty, but nothing is done about them. Next comes a period of popular excitement. People begin to speak out, demonstrations and rebellions occur, and property may be destroyed. These activities are uncoordinated, however. The third stage consists of the development of formal organizations. Formal leaders are identified, goals are established, and strategies for achieving them are devised. The beliefs on which the movement was founded and the rationale for actions taken become codified into an **ideology.** Fourth, as the movement increases in size, the organizations become increasingly bureaucratic. The original unpaid volunteers are replaced by professional staff members. And the movement itself becomes an accepted part of the society.

These stages are idealized. Not all movements go through all of them. Some show little evidence of the "unrest" and "popular excitement" stages. And very few reach the last stage. Nevertheless, the life-cycle approach is useful because it shows how many of the characteristics associated with movements are connected with one another over the course of time.

Another function of the life-cycle approach is that it calls attention to two complementary perspectives which may be applied to social movements: the individual and the organizational. Much of the behavior associated with the early stages of a movement's life cycle can best be understood by taking a perspective which focuses on the individuals who participate in them. Writers who take this approach ask such questions as, "Under what conditions are people most likely to join movements?" and "What types of people are likely to join?" As movements become increasingly organized, a second perspective takes on increasing importance, one which focuses on the nature of the movement organization. Writers who take this approach ask, "How do movement organizations differ from other types of organizations?" and "What organizational characteristics are associated with goal attainment?" Researchers in this field have analyzed social movements by taking either an individual or an organizational perspective.

**Approaches Focusing on Individuals**
Anthony Wallace has suggested that social movements can be viewed as attempts by local populations to change the images or models they have of how their culture operates.[30] These images identify the important elements of the culture and show how they are interrelated. Laws, institutions, customs, other groups, and even the individual's own self-image are among the elements included in the model. Individuals use these models to solve their day-to-day problems and satisfy their needs. Sometimes, however, the members of society find that the components of their culture are not properly interrelated, that is, their models are unsatisfactory. This produces stress. The people then become motivated to change their model of how the society operates. When large numbers of people become so motivated, "revitalization movements" are said to occur. The society then undergoes a massive restructuring in which major social and cultural elements are changed. The result is a more harmonious relationship among the cultural elements, that is, a more satisfying model.

Another approach that looks at social movements in terms of the individuals who participate in them is Frantz Fanon's. Fanon was concerned about the social harm caused by colonialism, especially in Africa. Under that system, people and material resources were exploited. People were made to feel inferior, and consequently lost their self-respect. Fanon saw violence as a device for gaining freedom.[31] As such, violence had several positive functions. For individuals, it could act as a cleansing force and purge feelings of inferiority and despair. For the "revolution," violence could invest people with a feeling of purpose and overcome the regionalism and tribalism that historically kept natives from organizing against the colonials. The common hatred of the colonials could displace or subdue the old hatreds and distrust of prior years.

Many of those who write about social movements, such as Fanon, are generally sympathetic to social change. Other writers, such as Eric Hoffer, however, are less sympathetic. Hoffer argues that different types of mass movements, such as large-scale religious and nationalistic movements, tend to be supported by the same types of people.[32] Often, the members of these movements are persons who have been rejected by others in the society. Potential converts are frustrated persons. Their frustration is due to their consciousness of a blemished self which cannot be improved. Because of their frustration they wish to escape that self, and participating in social movements provides an opportunity for that escape. Participation gives people a feeling of direction, togetherness, and redemption. Consequently, the people who make up the membership of these movements are likely to follow their leaders blindly, they are "true believers," according to Hoffer.

Many writers question the accuracy of Hoffer's descriptions. They argue that people who join movements may do so for a variety of reasons, ranging from personal benefit to purely altruistic and selfless reasons. An interpretation such as Hoffer's suggests that most participants join movements because of some personal problem they experience rather than for "legitimate" reasons. While Hoffer probably does overstate his case, he contributes to our overall perspective on movements by showing that some participation may be for reasons unrelated to the actual movement goals.

Ted Gurr attempts to account for political violence, including guerrilla wars and rebellions.[33] Two questions underlie his research: "What are the psychological and social sources of the potential for violence?" and "What determines the extent to which that potential is focused on the political system?" The major concept used to account for the sources of political violence is **relative deprivation.** This refers to the extent that a person perceives a discrepancy between those goods or life conditions he or she feels

> **ideology:** a doctrine or way of thinking. A social or political ideology is a rationalization and justification for a set of practices or program.
>
> **relative deprivation:** the perceived discrepancy between the goods or life conditions one feels entitled to and those felt possible of attainment.

*entitled to* and those that he or she feels it *possible to attain.* Thus persons feeling entitled to things that are unlikely to be forthcoming are likely to feel deprived. This deprivation is relative in the sense that a person does not need to be destitute or under political tyranny to feel deprived. All that is required is an imbalance between what people feel they deserve and what they feel they will actually obtain.

When people become frustrated over some deprived condition, one of the options they sometimes choose is to act aggressively toward the condition or person they regard as responsible for it. This frustration-aggression mechanism is important to Gurr's perspective on collective violence because the frustration people feel as a result of relative deprivation may be channeled into aggressive behavior. If people perceive the political system as responsible for their deprivations, they may correspondingly act aggressively, or violently, toward that system.

### Approaches Focusing on Organizations

Luther Gerlach and Virginia Hine identify the

**Walking in the rain to register to vote in Selma, Alabama, 1965:** *(left to right)* **the Reverends Martin Luther King, Jr., Ralph Abernathy, and Andrew Young.**

characteristics commonly associated with social movement organizations.[34] First, they note that power and leadership tend to be *decentralized* in social movements, as, for example, in the Pentecostal and Black Power movements. Rather than a single person holding power, it is dispersed among several leadership positions. In the Black Power movement, several leaders existed, none of whom could claim to speak for all blacks. These included Floyd McKissick, Bobby Seale, and Stokely Carmichael. Second, Gerlach and Hine observed that the actual organizational structures of movements tend to be dispersed. This is referred to as *segmentation.* Several organizations usually exist within any movement, and each organization is likely to be divided into smaller units such as regional branches, chapters, and cells. Finally, although movement organizations are segmented, the parts are interconnected through various informal and formal relations. This interconnectedness is called *reticulation.* Thus, while several separate Black Power organizations existed, the leaders frequently met with one another, people often were members of more than one organization, and members of different organizations exchanged ideas and developed friendships at rallies or demonstrations.

These organizational characteristics provide useful functions for social movements. Generally speaking, they help to promote the growth of the movement and to prevent suppression. For example, because movements tend to have several organizations and leaders, it is easier to maintain security against infiltration by members of other groups, including governmental agencies. The segmentation of movement organizations also promotes penetration of the movement into more than one sector of the society. Chapters might thus be formed among several different classes or ethnic groups. Also, innovation within the movement is promoted by the presence of several organizations and a lack of centralized leadership. When more than one organization exists in the same movement, some competition is likely. This forces the organizational leadership to try different goals, methods, and appeals. The result can lead to important gains for the movement as a whole. Finally, through such competition and innovation, the movement is less likely to fail.

Mayer Zald and Roberta Ash discuss some of the ways in which social movement organizations differ from other types of organizations, such as businesses.[35] Two such differences are that movement organizations aim to change the society, and they must generally rely on non-material rewards to attract and hold their members. Zald and Ash argue that the rather unique combination of characteristics of movement organizations means that as time passes they may not necessarily become increasingly bureaucratic and rigid, as do most conventional types of organizations. (This contradicts one element in the life-cycle framework of Dawson and Gettys.)

Most other types of organizations become increasingly conservative, self-serving and oligarchic, as they get older. Zald and Ash argue that these processes do not necessarily occur in movement organizations. It is possible for such organizations to change in other ways. Thus it is not uncommon for movement organizations to split into factions, become increasingly radical, or even simply to disappear. These are all types of changes that significantly depart from the expected trend toward bureaucratization and rigidity.

## SUMMARY

Many conventional views about collective behavior are often in error. First, collective behavior is much more common than we ordinarily think. Numerous masses and publics exist across our society at any given time; and crowds form in response to such everyday occurrences as fires and auto accidents. Second, collective behavior is more comprehensible than is commonly thought. It is formed as a reaction to unanticipated or unusual events, a collective effort on the part of the individuals involved to give meaning to their experiences. As such, it is understandable and quite rational.

Several models or approaches help to organize our thinking regarding collective behavior, especially regarding crowds. Writers have focused upon the contagion of sentiments within crowds, the social or psychological characteristics of people who converge to form a crowd, the importance of norms that have emerged in crowds, and the calculations and general rationality of individuals in crowds. While the descriptions of crowd activities given by these models differ from one another, they all help to make crowd behavior less mysterious.

Social movements are group efforts at

bringing about social changes. When the changes are relatively small and the movement members use legal and generally peaceful methods, the movements are called reforms. Alternatively, when the changes sought are major, involving the restructuring of entire institutions, and the methods employed are illegal or violent, the movements are called revolutions. In either case, movements include the presence of one or more organizations and various types of collectivities, such as masses and crowds.

Many movements occur because the existing political or social structure is not receptive to the needs of groups in the society. They provide an alternative way of accomplishing changes, outside of the existing political or social system.

Smelser's approach to social movements helps to show how they are related to other aspects of the society. They only occur when the structure of the society is conducive to them and when people experience strains because of the structure. Despite the importance of structure, movements will not occur unless people also come to believe that something is wrong in the society and that they are capable of remedying the condition.

## SUGGESTED READINGS

FANON, FRANTZ. *The Wretched of the Earth*. New York: Grove, 1968. Provides an analysis of the evils of colonialism and how native populations overthrow colonial rule.

FREEMAN, JO. *The Politics of Women's Liberation*. New York: McKay, 1975. Discusses the origins and nature of the contemporary women's movement in the United States.

GUSFIELD, JOSEPH R. *Symbolic Crusade*. Urbana: University of Illinois Press, 1969. A history and analysis of the movement to stop alcoholic consumption in the United States.

HOFFER, ERIC. *The True Believer,* New York: HARPER & ROW, 1951. A classic work which analyzes mass movements in terms of the individuals who participate in them.

MALCOLM X, *Autobiography of Malcolm X.* New York: Grove, 1966. An insightful description of how Malcolm X came to join the Black Muslims and the nature of that organization.

STONER CARROLL, AND JO ANNE PARKE. *All Gods Children.* New York: Penguin, 1979. A detailed and rather critical account of contemporary cults, including "Moonies," "Divine Light," "Scientology," and the "Krishna" cult.

WOLFE, TOM. *The Electric Kool-Aid Acid Test.* New York: Farrar Straus, 1968. A description of the personalities and events which shaped the "hippie" phenomenon in the United States.

# Chapter 18
# Social and Cultural Change

In 1902 a cast-iron cookstove like the one in our illustration would have been found in almost any home in the United States. Such stoves are still in use in a few remote regions, and until recently, at least, were used for cooking in railroad dining cars. But in the course of one generation, or at the most two, they have almost completely disappeared, not only from everyday life but from cultural awareness.

The rapidity and scope of social and cultural change in this century are impressive. How do we account for such a rapid rate of social and cultural change, and what are its effects? When the household tools of only yesterday are incomprehensible to us and we are already fearful or quarrelsome about the future, it is clear that sociocultural change has an overwhelming impact on us. We contend with it all our lives, and we may, before we are very old, see our grandchildren look back on today's artifacts uncomprehendingly as we now look on this one. This accelerating rate of change holds profound implications for the future. What are the sources of change in any society? What factors influence acceptance of, or resistance to, change? What role does technology play in change? What are the major social theories of change and the relation between change and societal disorganization? Finally, to what extent is it possible for a society to plan change?

Throughout the chapter, we will treat social and cultural changes together. We do this because social and cultural changes occur together and influence each other, although conceptually we may distinguish between them. *Cultural change* is a change in normative, cognitive, or material culture (the change from the wood-burning stove to the modern gas stove or microwave oven). *Social change* involves transformations in social organization or activity, such as a change in fertility rates or family structure. In most cases, however, cultural and social changes are so intertwined with each other that it is difficult to separate them completely. (The change in stoves, for instance, involves changes in family life: No longer does the family have to haul in wood or coal for the stove, for example, or worry about keeping the fire going, to mention just one connection.) For this reason, we will often refer simply to the phenomenon of change.

509

## SOURCES OF CHANGE

What prompts change? How does it begin in the first place? This is one of the most fundamental and challenging questions we can ask. *Change may result from internally induced actions.* Such indigenous or home-inspired transformations (discoveries or inventions) are called **innovations.** Change may also result from the incorporation of diverging patterns practiced by others; this is called **diffusion.** Diffusion accounts for a much greater share of change than innovation. *Crises* and *conflicts* are also significant precipitants of change. Although change is often the result of these social conditions, it may also produce these states in turn.

### Innovation

In ancient Mexico, nomadic hunters and gatherers used to discard at their campsites the cobs from the wild corn they gathered. The corn plants that later grew at these locations yielded larger plants with bigger ears of corn. This observation led to the domestication and hybridization of corn and other plants, a cultural development that was to be critical for the rise of Mesoamerican culture and the eventual establishment of urban settlement patterns. Thus the innovation of developing and cross-fertilizing maize seeds had a far-reaching impact on the lives of the people of ancient Mexico and, in time, the world.

Innovations can come about through the discovery of new materials in the environment as they did for the ancient Mesoamericans. On other occasions innovations result from putting already known materials to new uses. For example, gunpowder was widely used in ancient China for amusement and recreation. Eventually it was adapted for defense against enemies. Innovations are also made by recombining elements into new complexes or by inventing new processes or new ways of doing things. For example, given the existence of the glider and the internal combustion engine, the invention of the airplane was almost inevitable. Such simple extensions and new applications often produce profound cultural changes, such as those that accompanied the development of air transport.

If the new element is truly new, it may be called a *discovery;* if it involves a new combination or use of cultural elements already known, it will probably be called an *invention.* Einstein's theory of relativity and the germ theory of disease were discoveries; the automobile and the computer were inventions. Both inventions and discoveries can be either material or nonmaterial. The discovery of the New World by European explorers was a true discovery, and cafeterias and coeducation were true inventions.

Innovation is the result of a cumulative process. For example, the invention of a practical steam engine by James Watt would not have been possible without the metallurgical techniques that were available at the time it was produced. Watt's invention built on the work of the ancient Greeks, who first applied steam power to driving toys and other mystifying devices, as well as on late seventeenth century steam engines that were used for pumping water from houses and mines, and on Thomas NewComen's "atmospheric engine" that utilized low steam pressure.[1]

The sociological accuracy of the old saying, "necessity is the mother of invention," must be doubted. During World War II, for example, the Japanese "needed" an atom bomb no less than did their American opponents. Yet, in the early 1940s, only the United States and Britain possessed the technology and the trained personnel to build a workable nuclear bomb.

Inventions are often stumbled upon accidentally. Such **serendipitous** revelations of new and valuable things are not at all uncommon. The discovery of X rays, the vulcanization of rubber, penicillin and dynamite, among numerous other indispensable cornerstones of modern industrial society, all arose unexpectedly, most only minimally in response to the pressures of "necessity."

Innovative behavior or creativity continues to fascinate social scientists. Psychologists focus upon the perceptual, cognitive, and intellectual capacities of men and women of "genius." Social psychologists pay greater attention to the social networks and milieus associated with innovative actions. This approach is more akin to sociological investigations of the subject that have highlighted the social conditions and cultural elements available for the working inventor.

## Diffusion

Another source of change is *diffusion—the spread of cultural traits from one society to another*. In the United States, with its great stress on individualism, rationality, and science, we tend to regard innovation as the most fundamental dynamic force in change. But diffusion is far more influential than most people acknowledge. In his portrait of the "100 percent American," Ralph Linton estimated that no more than 10 percent of the material objects used by any people represent its own innovations.[2] Linton states that diffusion is responsible for the vast majority of the things we do, use, and think.

In preindustrial and preliterate societies the diffusion of cultural patterns requires some kind of physical contact among people. Diffusion in earlier societies must have occurred predominately through migration, trading, predatory relationships, and occupancy of con-

**cultural change:** change in normative, cognitive, or material culture.

**social change:** alteration in patterns of social organization or activity.

**innovation:** a discovery or invention, or the process of discovery or invention.

**diffusion:** the transmission of traits from one culture to another.

**serendipitous:** of or relating to *serendipity*, the accidental discovery of something of value while doing or looking for something else.

**Cultural diffusion.**

tiguous territory. With the development of writing and mass communications, large numbers of people greatly removed from one another in time and place, and holding sharply diverging ideas and values, could conceivably come to change and influence each other.

In assessing modern communications, Marshall McLuhan envisioned the development of "a global village."[3] It certainly seems that his prophesy is about to become a reality. The nations of the Western world are already extensively interconnected with everything from telephone lines to satellites, and it should not be much longer, perhaps two generations, before the entire world is truly interconnected and interdependent.

Although the mass media present a profound potential for greater cultural homogenization, how much can people's ideas and patterns be changed by it, if at all? An abundance of social science research has been done on the effects of the communication media. The findings are by no means clear-cut or mutually supportive. Perhaps the most important conclusion we can draw from these studies is that media effects are complex and varied.

Yet certain tends have emerged. Paul Lazarsfeld, Joseph Klapper, and others have found that the audience is not a unitary body, but is composed of diverging publics who selectively expose themselves to the media.[4] Usually people subject themselves to media content consistent with their ideological and social perspectives. Moreover, members of an audience selectively perceive the elements of the messages they get and selectively retain those ideas that support their original values and biases. A great deal of evidence demonstrates that the media can do more to disseminate facts than to modify attitudes. This may lead us to wonder whether the media ever play a decisive role in bringing about closer participation and rapprochement among the world's people.

Some studies conducted in developing countries[5] suggest that media exposure by itself may promote more secular, scientific, and rational orientations among its recipients. Thus in some way the media may ultimately come to engender more common perspectives among the world's inhabitants.

How are cultural patterns transmitted from one society to another? Everett Rogers,[6] summarizing the results of many diffusion studies found that traits spread more rapidly when they (1) offer relative advantages over those they supersede, (2) are compatible with existing values and experiences of the adopters, (3) are simple enough for ready understanding and application, (4) are divisible and can be tried on a limited basis, and (5) are readily observed and communicated.

Material culture traits diffuse more readily than nonmaterial ones. People more easily adopt a new farming implement than a new religion. Homer Barnett suggests several reasons why this is so.[7] First, language differences between cultures impede the flow of ideas more than things. Second, the advantages of a readily observable cultural form, such as a steel knife, are more easily demonstrated than those of a new organizational form, such as participatory democracy. Finally, an individual's adoption of a physical object is less likely to involve other members of the group. There are likely to be fewer opponents because the consequences for the group are less foreseeable from physical objects than from nonmaterial ones. It is easier for missionaries to distribute Bibles than to alter ritual patterns.

As cultural traits spread from one culture to another, they are not simply accepted or rejected, but are often revised or reinterpreted. A colorful mask originally used as a fertility symbol by a South American tribe may hang on your wall as a decorative object; when Europeans adopted the use of tobacco from native Americans, they transformed it from a ceremonial ritual to a source of personal gratification. As variations on the pipe, they developed cigarettes, chewing tobacco, and snuff. Such modifications are common as cultural traits circulated among and within cultures.

## Crises and Conflicts

In addition to innovation and diffusion, *crisis* and *conflict* may cause change because they alter social structures and relationships and require adaptation to new conditions.

The 1954 Supreme Court decision in *Brown* v. *Board of Education* exerted a far-reaching impact upon American society generally. The historic ruling—denying the constitutionality of separate educational facilities for blacks and whites—helped produce an unending cycle of change, conflict, and further change. The conflict over educational opportunity helped launch the civil rights movement, which in turn gave rise to "white backlash." Still later, civil rights advocacy developed into the more militant black protest movement, an increase in black pride, urban rioting, and black separatism. Although the historical record is clear, the chain of cause and effect is blurred because of the many changes and conflicts that followed in the wake of the initial Supreme Court decision.

An increasing number of civil rights laws have been enacted, including affirmative action legislation. Public schools in the South have been desegregated to a significant extent. Although racial conflict is far from resolved, a

**James Meredith goes to class at the University of Mississippi, 1962. Federal marshals no longer required to enroll black students in American universities; the crisis brought about change.**

more conciliatory mood appears to have replaced the intense and turbulent racial conflict that prevailed during the late sixties. Now a former segregationist leader such as George Wallace reaches out for rapprochement with the black community, when twenty years earlier he vowed that he would never accede to desegregation. Blacks have made gains in the political arena. The cycle of conflict and change persists but, more than ever before, within the legitimated framework of electoral politics.

On a smaller scale, consider the crisis several years ago caused by a fire in a telephone switching center in New York City that interrupted the use of approximately 170,000 telephones for nearly three weeks—the most serious telephone failure in the company's history. Following the shutdown, most of the businesses in the affected areas suffered serious production problems and losses of sales. Some businesses, however, were unimpeded, and a few thrived—messenger services, for example. Residents of the affected area who had never mingled with their neighbors now found occasion to get acquainted; letter writing increased. Habits and patterns were temporarily changed by the brief crisis of the telephone company. Had it gone on for a longer period, more enduring changes would undoubtedly have resulted.

According to William F. Whyte, interpersonal conflict is likely to result in greater bureaucratization.[8] Whyte observed considerable conflict between restaurant waitresses and higher-status male cooks and bartenders, who resented taking orders from those of lower status. This status discrepancy often led to emotional outbursts, especially during busy periods. Such status conflict can be reduced by the use of written orders and by creating physical barriers like counters and pass-throughs between the waitresses and the male kitchen staff. Thus more elaborate rules of procedure may arise to remedy situations of interpersonal conflict.

### Crisis and Conflict Arising from Change

Crisis and conflict often initiate change, but it is also true that change can promote or intensify crisis and conflict. Change often makes people uneasy; it uproots us from familiar surroundings, meanings, habits, and relationships, creating fear and anxiety. The psychologically disruptive potential of change is greatly influenced by the conditions under which change arises,

the values shared in different societies, and the outlooks common to different groups. Even when members of a society welcome change, when novelty is generally viewed as a blessing, change can bring about massive social upheaval. W. F. Cottrell's classic study of Caliente, a railroad town in the American Southwest, demonstrates the crisis potential of change.[9]

Caliente was a one-industry town that thrived on servicing steam locomotives. It was a stop on the railroad where crews changed, engines were repaired, and trains took on fuel and water. With the development of the diesel engine, which required less frequent stops for fuel, water, and servicing, Caliente became superfluous. When the railroad closed its facilities, there was no need for the hotel, clubhouse, and associated buildings. The town lost not only its major industry, but also the major source of its tax revenues. Many inhabitants were forced to leave and search for employment elsewhere. Merchants lost their clientele, churches their congregations; homeowners faced a continuing decline in property values. The town's search for a new industrial base was not successful. Without the railroad industry, Caliente became a sociocultural dinosaur.

The disruptive consequences of change are manifold. Introducing new elements into a culture—whether they be social, physical, or ideational—often promotes or intensifies social conflict. As so many American western films have shown, the westward migrations of European settlers across the continent generated conflict between the settlers and the native

Caliente did not suffer the fate of this nineteenth century ghost town, but the cause of its decline (failure of a single technology) was the same.

*"Are there any new fads your mother and I should be picking up on, dear?"*

Reprinted by permission of Newspaper Enterprise Association.

**Most urban-industrial societies view change positively.**

Americans, among the cattle-ranchers, the sheepherders, and the farmers, between the early migrant frontier types and the later-arriving homesteaders. A contemporary analogue of this earlier conflict may be found in the increasing discord between industrial interests on the one hand and environmentalists on the other.

Whenever technical innovation is introduced, it tends to arouse discord between those who stand to profit from it and those who are likely to sustain losses. The viewpoints people hold are not likely to be exclusively economic, however; they often have moral and other dimensions as well. Consider, for example, the development of a new product for crowd control—a gas that quells collective behavior better than other existing products. Its supporters are likely to be found among law-and-order advocates, the police, and paramilitary interests; its detractors are likely to be civil libertarians, proponents of participatory democracy, and members of the youth movement.

Societies are often factionalized. The interests and actions of some subgroups are seen as diametrically opposing those of others. In peasant societies, people who advocate change often experience rejection and hostility after initially

being accepted by certain members of the community. As George Foster puts it, "Establishing friendship with a person identifies the outsider with that person's group or faction, and by implication, he assumes the villagers' hostility to rival groups and factions."[10] In this sociocultural climate, change advocated by one group almost invariably produces opposition among the others; here change is likely to intensify conflict.

## FACTORS INFLUENCING THE RESPONSE TO CHANGE

In different societies, the socially shared responses to novelty vary considerably. At some times change is readily accepted; on other occasions, it is greatly resisted. What accounts for these differences in societal responses to change?

### Beliefs, Attitudes, Values, Traditions, and Habits

Most urban-industrial societies view change positively. Many Americans, for instance, are enthusiastic about the latest ideas, fashions, and fads. Three of their central values that encourage and approve of innovation are particularly influential: the emphasis on science and experimentation, the preoccupation with progress, and the significance accorded to individual achievement. In the urban-industrial world, not only is change normal, it represents the fulfillment of the cultural ideal. Groups that represent these values not only enhance the acceptance of change, they are likely to be influential in spurring further novelty and revision.

In contrast, in nonindustrialized parts of the world, novelty and change are far less appealing. People venerate the past, worship their ancestors, conform to the expectations of their elders, and make every effort to preserve the *status quo*. The individual is conditioned to view new things with skepticism and not to deviate from past practice. In societies where tradition is revered to this degree, change is likely to be strenuously resisted and, consequently, far less common than in industrial societies.

Aside from general attitudes toward change, members of different societies hold specific attitudes and beliefs that affect the acceptance of new patterns. Suppose, for example, that a new factory is set up in a traditional peasant community. Although the employer offers higher wages than those that prevail in the community, it is difficult to attract employees. Absenteeism is high, and many workers never return to work after their first payday. The peasants in this community are not lazy: We may observe them diligently working long hours elsewhere in the community. What, then, accounts for this seemingly erratic behavior?

This community may have a strong extended family orientation, where people are used to working with kin and being paid not with money but with some kind of barter—food or help with tasks that require several people. An impersonal, cash-based factory system would be at variance with the work attitudes of such a group, because in the factory, people would not be employed in kin-structured work groups and money would not have the traditional symbolic values of ritual reciprocal obligation and status reinforcement.

Of course, peasants are not the only ones whose attitudes and beliefs may resist change; members of developed societies often are fixed in their ways. For example, many people, even in the United States, go hungry or suffer serious protein deficiencies. Yet many nutritious food sources are totally ignored: horsemeat, insects, and so-called trash fish, like squid, shark, and sea robin. These foods are considered suitable only for consumption by pets, if at all, although in other cultures, many of them are not only acceptable but considered delicacies.

Consider also the inefficient and wasteful loss of protein that results from the American penchant for eating meat. Approximately half of the United States' total agricultural produce is used to feed livestock—as much grain as it would take to feed all the people of China and India for a year. The protein content of the average steer involves the conversion of about twenty-one pounds of crops into one pound of expensive steaks and roasts.[11] Contrary to popular opinion, most nutritionists find that a higher consumption of agricultural produce would offer a healthier diet than the present one. A considerable part of the world's current food shortage could be reduced by changing American eating habits.

Value shifts may also have profound effects

**FIGURE 18.1   Increase in persons living as primary individuals, in the United States; 1960–1970**

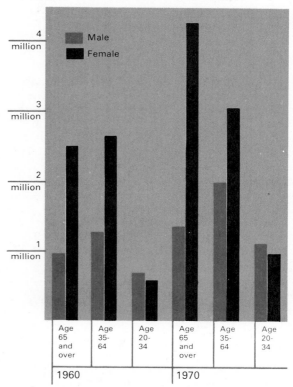

Value changes like the one shown here may radically alter a society. While these figures reflect mortality and health factors to some degree, they show alteration in values and habit patterns even more. In previous years, more older people were cared for in the homes of their children, and fewer younger people lived alone or with persons to whom they were not related.

on a society. Figure 18.1 shows that the number of elderly people living alone has increased significantly in the United States in recent years, as has the number in the age group from thirty-five to sixty-four. More younger people also lived as primary individuals in 1970. Although demographic factors have something to do with this pattern, changing American values toward marriage and living together are unquestionably significant. Those who do not conform to the cultural ideal of the happily married couple living together with their children, such as divorced people, childless couples, couples living together outside of marriage, members of a commune, and other adherents of divergent family life styles, all enjoy increasing acceptance and tolerance in today's more liberated, secular, and urbane society.

### Perceived Need and Demonstrability

When a need is widely perceived, innovations are more readily accepted. Inventions and discoveries that satisfy no need are often ignored until a need for them emerges. Leeuwenhoek invented a microscope in 1674, but it was not until the germ theory of disease had been established—so that the need to identify microorgansims arose—that the value of the microscope to medicine and biology became established.

Perceived needs provide a climate for the acceptance of innovation, but in and of themselves, they are insufficient to generate it. Al-

though we urgently need a cancer cure, safe and abundant energy resources, and cheap, effective birth control techniques, these perceived needs are no guarantee that the invention or discovery will be made. Necessity, in other words, is the mother only of acceptability.

Before an innovation can be accepted and approved by a group, members must be convinced not only that they need it, but that its present form truly satisfies their need. Unless an invention is actually useful, it will not be adopted. The typewriter and the automobile are good examples of this. When the typewriter was first invented, many people questioned the value of paying a great deal of money for a machine that would do the same work as the one-cent pen. There were also doubts as to whether women—the potential users of the new machine—could endure the "strenuous" course of study necessary to acquire typing pro-

---

### FRISBEES ARE TOSSED INTO THE SMITHSONIAN

Washington, June 30—The Smithsonian Institution opened an exhibition of Frisbees today.

The Frisbee's prototype—an ordinary, unshined, 10-inch metal pie tin from the Frisbie (sic) Pie Company of Bridgeport, Conn.—has been placed next to a colorful collection of more modern Wham-o Company disks that bear the Frisbee trademark.

The National Air and Space Museum put the throwing disks in a gallery devoted to flight for amusement.

It is widely believed by experts that the Frisbee was born when Yale students decided to forfeit their 5-cent deposits and throw the pie tins, crying "Frisbie!" the way golfers cry "Fore!"

#### TRACED TO ANCIENT GREEKS

The Frisbee's pedigree has been traced to the pie tin in a treatise by Dr. Stancil E. D. Johnson, a psychiatrist in Carmel, Calif. He investigated the now defunct pie company, which sold 80,000 pies daily as recently as 1956, and discovered that the lid of the company's cookie tin also flew fairly well and might have been a real forerunner.

But some who play with the Frisbee give the credit for its origin to the ancient Greeks. The statue of Discobolus, the discus thrower, is thought by some to represent a Frisbee

champion attempting a tricky overhand wrist flip.

The pie tin on display was borrowed from Victor Malafronte, a Frisbee champion from Berkeley, Calif., who is known as "superwhiz."

The newer curve-lipped plastic models, developed by W. Frederick Morrison in 1948, are accompanied by photographs of their many uses: the thumb grip, the pancake catch, the behind-the-back catch and assorted tosses. There are also photographs of a "tipping and nail delay" artist who seems to be spinning the disk on his forefinger to demonstrate a solitaire form of play.

When Frisbee players are more sociable, they line up on two seven-person teams opposite each other. Each player tries to stop running within three steps after the catch and return the toss to a fellow team member as close to a 60-yard goal line as possible without the disk's being intercepted. The plastic Frisbees presumably make the game less painful than if played with pie tins.

The Smithsonian sponsors a Frisbee Festival each September, and last year 5,000 people showed up to throw Frisbees at one another.

ficiency. It was not until these obstacles were surmounted that the typewriter was widely adopted.

In the case of the automobile, early models ran so erratically and required so many adjustments and repairs, that the derisive advice, "Get a horse" became a byword. Moreover, the first automobiles were so expensive, they were regarded as rich men's toys. Only after the cars had been mechanically improved, particularly by the development of the self-starter, and after assembly-line production greatly lowered costs, did the automobile gain widespread acceptance.

## The Cultural Base

The total accumulation of available knowledge and technique has a great deal to do with both the quantity and the kind of innovations that are devised. This cultural repository limits the range of all inventions. In the late fifteenth century, Leonardo da Vinci sketched many machines—the airplane, helicopter, and submarine, among others—that were workable in principle, but the technology of his day was inadequate to build them.

Acceptance of the automobile was delayed by the lack of auxiliary services. There were few fuel and repair facilities, inadequate and insufficient highways, and overnight accommodations for travelers were not widely available. Sidney Aronson contends that the development of the bicycle inadvertently played a crucial role in increasing the use of the automobile.[12] He maintains that the popularity of cycling led to expansion and improvement of the nation's roadways and other supportive facilities which later were readily converted from serving cyclists to catering to motorists. Without such a network of facilitative apparatus, the automobile never would have been feasible. Thus, inventions tend to stimulate still more inventions.

As the culture base expands, *rates* of change are also likely to increase. The greater the number of elements in a given culture, the greater the number of possible combinations and recombinations. For example, glass makes possible costume jewelry, drinking goblets, window panes, test tubes, electric light bulbs, radio and television tubes, lenses, and many other products. Lenses in turn bring on eyeglasses, magnifying glasses, telescopes, microscopes, cameras, range finders, searchlights, and the like. Thus, as cultures become more diverse and complex, rates of change accelerate.

## Costs and Vested Interests

Costs also influence the willingness to accept change. The motoring age was postponed until Henry Ford developed the assembly line, which brought the automobile within the economic range of the majority of consumers. Early television receivers had a very limited appeal because of their extremely high cost. For an innovation to gain wide public acceptance, it must be reasonably priced.

Costs are not exclusively economic, however. The liabilities of change also include social and cultural dislocations that may be taxing and unsettling. In 1932, August Dvorak developed a new keyboard for the typewriter, placing all the vowels and frequently used letters in closer proximity to one another. Dvorak's system is vastly superior to the conventional keyboard, called "qwerty" after the first six letters on the top row. Typists trained on Dvorak machines often double their typing speed and make fewer errors and report less fatigue than typists using "qwerty." Typewriter manufacturers have not been unwilling to produce Dvorak keyboards; most offer it for a slight additional charge. Yet this much more efficient system remains virtually unaccepted because users—typists, industries, and schools—are committed to "qwerty" and agonize at the prospect of readjustment.[13] Exactly the same kind of resistance continues to leave the United States virtually the only nation in the world not utilizing the metric system.

Change affects people differently. Those who benefit from the *status quo* have a vested interest in maintaining it and are likely to mount considerable opposition to change when it threatens to diminish their power, rewards, and esteem. In traditional peasant societies, for example, native medical curers and midwives are likely to resent modern medical programs; landlords are likely to oppose too much education for peasants for fear that their workers may become dissatisfied with menial jobs and demand drastically improved conditions; moneylenders are likely to oppose low-interest government credit programs. The more we benefit from the *status quo*, the more likely we are to oppose change.

Despite the proven workability of socialized medicine in many industrial societies, the American Medical Association (AMA) has consistently opposed its adoption in the United States. The AMA claims that individuals would lose the right to select physicians, and the quality of health care and progress in medical science would decline if administered by a gigantic, impersonal, and inefficient bureaucracy. The vested interests of the medical profession fail to mention that physicians may lose income through socialized practice, that government agencies may exert more control over them, and that, as salaried employees, physicians may find their social status diminishing.

Usually, vested interests like the AMA are not entirely hypocritical; they hold strong convictions and earnestly believe that the society would be irreparably harmed by the innovations they oppose. They are deeply committed to the norms and social structures in which they participate and they often effectively mobilize to retard change or suppress it altogether. An example is the National Rifle Association's ex-

Isolated societies are resistant to change. However, when they are located near other societies, as the Pennsylvania Amish are, they become vulnerable to intrusion. This Amish mother contrasts strangely with the modern new world of merchandising; she is shopping for toys for her children.

tensive propaganda campaign to prevent the passage of legislation to restrict the use of handguns. The NRA is in part supported by arms manufacturers, but undoubtedly many NRA sympathizers genuinely fear the results of restrictive legislation.

When change is perceived as enhancing rewards, of course, vested interests are likely to embrace it. American automakers, for example, resist strenuously most federal requirements for auto safety devices, which they perceive as increasing the price of cars without increasing the public's desire to buy them. But they welcomed such innovations as air conditioning, tape decks, mag wheels, and racing stripes, because buyers are eager to pay for these accessories.

### Isolation and Contact

Because most cultural patterns are transmitted by diffusion, those societies in closest contact with others are most likely to change. Thus geographical factors may facilitate or retard innovation. A society that is cut off from others by mountains, an impassable body of water, a desert, or a jungle, or a population dispersed in isolated settlements, is likely to be highly stable and quite resistant to change. For example, in research on American Anabaptist groups—the Amish and the Hutterites—William Pratt observes that the more isolated and scattered Hutterites, living in southwestern Canada, South Dakota, and Montana, have maintained close adherence to their Anabaptist ideal of unlimited procreation (the median number of children per Hutterite family is 10.4).[14] There appear to be few defectors from these groups to the mainstream culture. By contrast, the more highly concentrated Amish, living in more populous areas in Pennsylvania and Ohio, have fewer children per family (6.7), and more defectors to the dominant culture.

Groups that are adjacent to one another are more likely to share cultural traits. If their basic cultures are similar, the likelihood of mutual influence is increased even more; but if language barriers exist and cultural patterns sharply diverge, the tendency to accept innovation is diminished. The English-speaking provinces of Canada, for example, are more "Americanized" than French-speaking Quebec.

Societies located at world crossroads are likely to be centers of change. This results from their great exposure to new elements and an attempt to integrate these new patterns into their own sociocultural systems. We noted earlier that as the cultural base is enlarged, the combinations and possibilities for change increase dramatically. This may account for the remarkably high volume of change found in capital cities and great seaports such as Paris, New York, London, Tokyo, Rio de Janeiro, Athens, and Cairo, which exhibit an interest in change very different from the attitudes prevalent in their surrounding countrysides.

During the twentieth century, isolation between cultures has been drastically reduced by spectacular innovations in transportation and communication. These have vastly extended and intensified the transcultural flow of ideas. Soon it will no longer be possible for cultures to enjoy the relative seclusion and isolation that existed throughout most of history. The infinite possibilities for sharing knowledge among cultures also hold the frightening prospects of destroying cultural diversity and promoting the dominance of some cultures over others.

### Environment and Population

The environment is the underpinning of cultures. When the environment changes, it can have profound repercussions on culture. An earthquake, a volcanic eruption, or a hurricane can obviously have immensely adverse consequences for social life, but even minor changes can pose serious threats. For example, a few years ago several ocean currents changed direction, and as a result the Humboldt Current no longer brought the usual great quantities of anchovies to the Peruvian coast. Peruvian production of fish meal, used in making animal feed — one of the economy's fundamental industries — declined tremendously. The resulting losses in foreign exchange were drastic, precipitating an economic castastrope.

Similarly, pollution, drought, soil erosion, and abnormally cold temperatures can produce far-reaching economic and social consequences. When a society depends heavily on one crop or industry, these consequences are likely to be compounded. The San Bernardino Valley of California, for instance, was once the heart of the American citrus industry, but air pollution has now made citrus trees there almost extinct.

Population changes, themselves social changes, are likely to produce still further changes in culture and social structure. The influx of a large group bearing a divergent culture must influence those whose ranks they join. In turn they are likely to be affected by their newly adopted culture. In addition, the culture they left is likely to undergo change as a result of their absence. Joseph Lopreato attributes the sharp surge of economic development in southern Italy since the end of World War II to the outmigration of large numbers of its inhabitants. For many years, southern Italian society was economically depressed, one of the last cultural backwaters of Europe. According to Lopreato, too many people attempted to provide for their existence in a fundamentally inhospitable environment characterized by low-grade soils, rocky terrain, and semiarid climate. It was only after large-scale migrations took place

**Environment — and its deterioration — can have far-reaching effects on culture.**

that the economy could sustain the remaining population and absorb the innovative ideas and new capital that the emigrants sent back to their homeland.[15]

Internal population changes, such as fluctuations in birth and death rates are also likely to produce social and cultural changes. As a consequence of fertility and mortality changes, some classes or kinship groups are likely to expand and others to contract. A population increase among a ruling elite could lead to political competition and conflict between people vying for leadership positions. By contrast, a decrease in an elite population could create vacancies at the top, facilitating social mobility and alleviating social discord and unrest. The declining birthrate among the Roman nobility in the last days of the empire—apparently caused, interestingly enough, by lead poisoning from cooking utensils, which were most definitely "in" at the time—may well have contributed to the political fluidity of the period.

As we saw in Chapter 10, demographic change inevitably results in altering the age composition of a group. A disproportionate increase of a particular age segment is likely to influence the values, beliefs, and attitudes of the whole group. It is conceivable that a swelling of the ranks of youth could result in greater receptivity to some types of change. For example, many social analysts have noted that some profound changes and the social turbulence of the 1960s in the United States coincided with the coming of age of the post-World War II "baby boom" population.

Increasing population also produces profound effects on a society, including an increase in impersonal relationships, the expansion of secondary groups, and greater institutional differentiation and specialization. Generally, social life becomes more complex in very large societies. The economy of the society must yield higher productivity if the expanded membership of the society is to be sustained. But when population growth is very high, as it is in many developing nations, the possibilities for increasing productivity and economic growth are diminished. As we saw in Chapter 10, rapidly expanding populations are likely to have unusually large proportions of youthful members who can contribute very little to productivity and who are economically dependent.

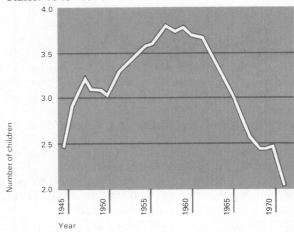

**FIGURE 18.2  Children per family in the United States: 1945–1970**

Year

Number of children

As the birth rate declines, the proportion of younger people in the population will also decline. By the year 2000, a significant segment of the American population will be elderly (the boom births of the 1950–1960 period), and will require very different social services than a population relatively young.

In both Costa Rica and Mexico, for example, approximately half the population is under fifteen years of age. This imposes inescapable burdens on the economy.

In the developed world, by contrast, low-population growth and advancing medical technology have created unprecedented possibilities for *gerontocratic* societies, those ruled or dominated by the elderly. Figure 18.2 permits us to estimate how soon the United States may become a gerontocratic society. Projected into the late 1970s, it suggests a society of less-than-middle-aged people who are decreasingly inclined to have children. But young swingers, inevitably, will become old. Add forty years to this chart and, assuming that the trend toward small families continues, we will see a society dominated by old people with relatively few young people to replace them. How society's values, norms, and behavior patterns will be altered by this change remains to be seen.

*Social Relations Networks*

Another factor affecting the acceptance or rejection of change is the involvement in social relations networks of the individuals and organizations who introduce it. Research on the diffusion of medical technology, farming techniques, and political attitudes suggests a "two-step flow" in the adoption of many innovations.[16] First, the mass media serve as informing devices. They are most influential among early adopters of an innovation. In turn, these individuals serve as opinion leaders, influencing the adoption of new patterns among wider social segments. Early adopters provide the prestige, continuity, positive effect, and visible proof of the utility of new patterns that are often indispensiable for widespread acceptance.

Research on the acceptance of family planning in developing countries shows successful results obtained by paraprofessional field workers drawn from the ranks of former midwives.[17] Change is more often accepted when those who advocate it are known to be trustworthy and capable. Former midwives have just these qualities. As indigenous members of the community they are generally respected among their potential clients and can readily communicate with them. Most important from the standpoint of family planning, midwives are acknowledged as those most competent and knowledgeable in matters of fertility and contraception. Thus they are recognized as culturally appropriate opinion leaders without whose support and participation the desired social change would be difficult, if not impossible, to achieve.

## Change Agents

Change is often introduced by individuals who may be called **change agents.** They may be government officials, technical assistance workers, agricultural, industrial, or management specialists, public health officials, or school administrators. Or they may represent religious interests (missionaries), social reform groups, political concerns, or commercial interests. Usually, change agents are strongly committed to the ideas they advocate; they are convinced that the adoption of their measures will improve life experiences. Of course, this is not always true. How much success they have in promoting change has a great deal to do with how they conduct their activities, the social situation in which they attempt to introduce change, and their own positions in the social structure.

> **change agent:** a person who initiates, causes, or introduces social or cultural change. Traders and missionaries are often change agents and the U.S. Peace Corps was established for that purpose.

Generally, the greater the prestige of the change agent, the more likely the proposed innovation is to be accepted. Once innovations are adopted by those at the pinnacles of power and prestige, they tend to diffuse rapidly throughout the entire social structure. For example, after Betty Ford and Happy Rockefeller had well-publicized breast surgery, American women became especially concerned about breast cancer and produced an unprecedented demand for breast cancer examinations.

Under some circumstances, the prestige of

**Change agent.** A Peace Corps volunteer teaches the women of a village in the British Honduras how to grind corn with a hand mill.

the change agent may retard acceptance. Ozzie Simmons reports that high-status physicians in a health program in Chile tended to get terse and uncommunicative responses from their lower-status patients. These clients found it difficult to talk freely about their health and confide in the doctor, viewing such talk as bordering on impertinence. Yet the patients would readily tell their problems to nurses, whom they considered closer to them in status.[18]

This leads us to consider perhaps the most powerful factor in spreading change: change agents must be thoroughly familiar with the values, cultural patterns, and interpersonal relationships of those with whom they work. Allan Homberg observed that giving domestic fowl to the Stone Age Siriono tribe in Bolivia produced some unanticipated and undesirable consequences to intrafamily and interfamily patterns. Some who were previously not recognized as authority figures now assumed dominant positions, and the tribe had to evolve new shared understandings for the distribution and use of the fowl. Nomadic habits were also dislocated, as the people adjusted to the necessities of the birds. The same kinds of major dislocations also accompanied the introduction of the steel ax to the Siriono.[19] Along this same line George Foster reports:

> In village India, cooking is traditionally done over an open dung fire in the kitchen. There is no chimney and there are few windows, so the room fills with cooking smoke, which gradually filters through the thatch roof. Cooking is unpleasant under such conditions, and respiratory and eye ailments are common. The Community Development Programme has recognized this situation as a serious threat to health and has developed an inexpensive pottery stove, "a smokeless chula," which maximizes the efficiency of fuel and draws smoke off through a chimney. It is sold at very low cost to villagers. Yet the smokeless chula has had limited success. In much of India wood boring white ants infest roofs; if they are not suppressed they ruin a roof in a very short time. The continual presence of smoke in the roof accomplishes this end. If smoke is eliminated roofs must be replaced far more often, and the expense is greater than farmers are able to support. So the problem of introducing the smokeless chula—at least in many areas—lies not in the villager's addiction to smoke irritated eyes, nor his love of tradition, nor his inability to understand the cooking advantages of the new stove, nor in the direct cost of the stove itself. He has considered the trade-off alternatives and decided that the disadvantages of the new stove outweigh the advantages.[20]

If change agents are to succeed in advancing their aims and satisfying the needs of those they serve, they must be mindful of the consequences. They should exert every effort to anticipate all possible results of change. It is especially advisable to include the clientele in planning and implementing change, if possible. Consider the attempt to introduce a new farming technique to the Papago tribe of the American Southwest. The new technique, called the bolsa system, was supposed to increase the agricultural productivity of the Papago. The plan involved diverting flood waters into a specified area, the bolsa, or pocket, that subsequently was to be cultivated. The Bureau of Indian Affairs developed the plan and the Civilian Conservation Corps provided for the necessary construction.

Despite the sizable investment of energy and capital, the project was a dismal failure. Subsequent investigation revealed that the bolsa was poorly engineered and constructed, the climate on the reservation was unsuitable, and the water supply was insufficient. Although the Papago were generally receptive to Anglo innovation, they recognized the weaknesses of the plan and reverted to their old agricultural practices. As Garth Jones commented:

> The attempt failed because the administrators did not master the technique they borrowed before introducing it. . . . They did not bring the people into the planning. . . . with the result that further technical difficulties developed which could have been avoided.[21]

Had the planners seriously consulted with the Papago and heeded their advice, they would have known about the real availability of water in the region. As a result they might have been able to adapt the plan or to abandon it in favor of a more viable alternative. These mistakes were further compounded by other unforseen conditions and the fact that the agents of change did not share the clients' culture.

### Technology and Cultural Lag

Economy and technology have a far-reaching impact on social and cultural life, affecting how people organize their activities, how they coordinate their relationships, and how they conceptualize and evaluate their experiences. The way people earn their living is likely to affect their family life, their religious beliefs, their

Technology often exerts a dominating influence on change. A turn-of-the-century blacksmith and his nemesis, the automobile.

whether they personify the earth—which might mean they would not use a blade to cut it for plowing—and an endless range of other items, are all likely to be affected by technology.

Technology often influences the direction and extent of change. Consider what happened when the automobile replaced horse-drawn transportation in the United States: the demise of the blacksmith, the buggy maker, and the liveryman; the development of the massive car-producing industry, plus the birth of all the industries connected with automobile use—motels, drive-ins, filling stations, parking lots, and so on and on. The automobile brought with it industrial expansion and decentralization; it greatly increased government functions and control: highway and bridge maintenance, automobile and fuel taxes, drivers' licenses, and motor vehicle registration. It increased some old health problems—emphysema and other lung diseases—and caused some new ones—automobile fatalities and injuries. It led to the development of suburban living patterns, the diminution of extended family life, changing courtship patterns, and increasing premarital sexual activity.[22] When technology changes, it often brings with it changes in a variety of other realms.

In today's world, rapid advances in technology often far outstrip change in the nonmaterial parts of culture—customs, values, beliefs, and laws. This imbalance leads to the phenomenon of cultural lag we first discussed in Chapter 3. The development of nuclear weapons and many other technical improvements in weaponry and warfare have far surpassed techniques in diplomacy and statesmanship. Our increasingly mechanized industry needs fewer workers with great physical strength and thus can easily accommodate many females in the work force, but these changes in technology have far outstripped society's conceptions of the rights and roles of women. The women's movement is, in part, a response to this condition.

Recent technological advances in medical science demonstrate the principle of cultural lag. Vastly extended life expectancy has resulted in a potentially catastrophic population explosion because of a lag in accepting and developing suitable birth control methods. In those industrial societies where longevity has increased most, aging is becoming a social problem. Elderly members of most industrial societies are often denied meaningful social roles, have in-

political convictions, their ideas about education, and many other important social dimensions. Whether families are large or small, close-knit or widely dispersed, whether the people revere rainfall and to what degree, even

History's first atomic artillery shell, fired from a 280-mm artillery gun. Will the lag in social-institutional reaction to nuclear weapons make humans obsolete?

sufficient material and physical resources, and inadequate social services. The delivery of health care is fraught with gaps and lags. Who will benefit from medical progress, what kinds of medical research should have higher priorities than others, when should life-extending facilities be used? These questions have not received as much emphasis as those pertaining to technical matters. To a great extent, these issues and problems have been a result of medical technical developments.

In a rapidly changing society, cultural lags are inevitable, and within varying lengths of time, they are ordinarily accommodated by the culture. But some cultural lags can be very disruptive. They can conceivably endanger the long-term survival of humankind. The atom bomb is one obvious example. The Pill, with its influence on sexual behavior, childbearing, and family life may prove even more disruptive.

Other obvious examples of cultural lag with potentially disasterous consequences include the effect of industrial pollution on the biosphere, the decimation of oceanic life, the possible effect on the ozone layer by the use of aerosol sprays, and the inability of human political systems to deal with the technological possibilities now in the hands of individuals and available for assassination, terrorism, and blackmail. Lastly, consider the individual's helplessness in the face of the technological assaults of government agencies through bugs, taps, long-distance recording equipment, sophisticated cameras, and listening devices.

## Modernization

In the process of modernization peasant agricultural societies develop into advanced urban-industrial ones. Revolutionary changes in communication and transportation have created unprecedented possibilities for economic and cultural contact between ever-increasing numbers of people throughout the world. People in formerly peasant villages are beginning to hunger for change and for the material benefits available in urban-industrial societies. Similarly, in order to sustain high living standards, the developed societies rely increasingly on the natural resources, markets, and labor supplies of developing countries. Thus, the paths of the developed and developing societies of the world appear to be converging. As both worlds increasingly intersect, modernization appears to be encouraged.

Modernization involves comprehensive change throughout most of a society's major institutions. The key element is industrialization. With it comes increasing economic productivity, equalization of incomes, and expanded opportunities for social mobility. Cities grow. The mass media expand. Literacy and educational opportunities increase. Living standards rise, with advances in health care, sanitation, housing, and other consumer advantages. The institutions of government, religion, and the family are also affected. Modernization consolidates power in society and encourages development of a centralized state bureaucracy. Activities and allegiances that were once coordinated on a local village level by tribal chiefs, priests, and village elders come increasingly under the jurisdiction of provincial and national government officials. Religion, once a dominant social institution, becomes secularized and subordinated to the state and the economy. Large extended families are replaced by smaller nuclear structures, and kinship itself begins to assume a diminished role in social affairs. Outlooks, values, and psychological orientations also change. People become more ambitious, worldly, open to new experiences, and eager to exert an influence on the world beyond their villages. Tribal and familial loyalties, and the acceptant, fatalistic, and unthinking adherence to traditional norms give way to restless, assertive, and forward-looking attitudes.

Such thoroughgoing change is capable of producing massive social dislocations. In western Europe and North America, where modernization took place over a relatively long time, social institutions were able to adapt gradually and with few disruptive consequences. But among the emerging nations today, change has come about much more rapidly and with far greater danger of social disorganization. In many of these societies, sharp social cleavages have appeared between the would-be modernizers and the more traditionally inclined. Thus the frequent political instability—riots, revolutions, *coups d'e'tat*, and millennial religious movements—characteristic of so many developing countries becomes more readily understood.

Yet despite its potentially upsetting qualities, modernization sparks the hopes of increasing numbers in the world's emerging nations. How can it be promoted? Robert Heilbroner suggests that the expansion of agricultural productivity is usually the beginning of economic development. Often in developing countries an inefficient organization of productive resources retards progress. Many acres of land owned by the wealthy may be less than fully utilized. Peasants may have to travel great distances to work their small farm plots. Land reform may be necessary to attain greater agricultural productivity. Greater worker-producer control over the land may replace land tenancy and sharecropping to enhance worker motivation.

According to Heilbroner, development can succeed only if the increased agricultural productivity is not consumed, but is used to develop capital. Capital is necessary to build new roads, buy equipment, and construct dams, factories, schools, etc. Sacrifices are needed to acquire the capital that will eventually generate even greater productivity. Ultimately fewer people engage in agricultural labor, making more people available to build roads, work in factories, and develop the industrial sector. To spur economic development, emerging nations also need foreign aid—grants and loans, skilled technical and managerial personnel—to initiate and carry forward developmental plans. Many analysts maintain that political stability is most important for encouraging modernization. Such stability helps fuel nationalistic sentiments—essential for inspiring personal sacrifices—and is likely to attract vitally needed foreign investment capital. For Heilbroner, population growth is a negative factor in the growth equation. When population growth is high it forecloses economic growth by curtailing investments.

Other scholars stress social and social psychological elements in promoting modernization. Alex Inkeles finds that education is important in making people modern, giving them modern attitudes and diminishing their traditional loyalties. Occupational experiences in large-scale organizations, especially factory work, help to teach and engender modern attitudes.[23] Daniel Lerner suggests that exposure to the mass media enhances psychic mobility or the capacity to empathize which is fundamental to a modern outlook.[24] Other researchers emphasize needs for achievement and ambition,[25] downward mobility,[26] and alienation from traditional institutions.[27] These are but a few of the many factors in advancing modernization.

## THEORIES OF CHANGE

Theoretical speculation not only deepens our understanding of the causes and consequences of change, it enhances our apprehension of when, where, and under what social conditions change is likely to occur and when it is likely to be extreme.

### *Evolutionary and Neo-evolutionary Theory*

In the late nineteenth century, there was considerable interest in the *evolutionary theory of change*. Early evolutionary theorists shared the basic assumptions that (1) change tends to be cumulative, (2) it brings about increasing social and cultural differentiation and complexity, and (3) it enhances adaptation, thereby promoting progress. Most contemporary sociologists probably would agree with the first two assumptions but would be somewhat doubtful about the third.

The early thinkers were convinced that change inevitably brought about improvement. For Lewis H. Morgan, change meant the passage from savagery to barbarism and ultimately to civilization. For Herbert Spencer, it meant the replacement of military-religious societies by industrial orders. For Auguste Comte, change meant the passage from what he called the theological stage of social organization to a scientific stage. Latter-day sociologists regard these theories as unscientific because most of the early thinkers offered very limited, highly selective, and sometimes inaccurate evidence to substantiate their claims.

But contemporary social scientists still find useful the theories of Emile Durkheim and Ferdinand Tönnies. Not only are their procedures more consistent with contemporary scientific practice, but their viewpoints describe rather well the trends observed in today's complex societies. Durkheim, you will recall, argued that change tends to transform the basis of social cohesion in society from the mechanical solidarity characteristic of so-called primitive societies, to the organic solidarity found in complex industrial societies. Durkheim held that technical progress tends to weaken the relational bonds among members of society. This, of course, is exactly what we have seen in our discussions of the increasing specialization and diversification of social institutions.

Tönnies' theory is consistent with Durkheim's view. His distinction between *Gemeinschaft* and *Gesellschaft* parallels Durkheim's distinction between mechanical and organic solidarity. Tönnies felt that the individualism and struggle for power characteristic of urban societies could result in cultural disintegration: as people become more socially fragmented, isolated, and independent of communal and institutional bonding, the integration and stability of traditional society weakens. For both Durkheim and Tönnies, change did not inevitably bring progress; it had varied consequences, some positive and some negative.

Notwithstanding these perceptive insights, during the early twentieth century, evolutionary theories were subject to increasing criticism. Since World War II, however, there has been a resurgence of interest in evolutionary thought among sociologists and anthropologists, frequently called *neo-evolutionism.*

**Neo-evolutionism**   Early evolutionary theorists looked upon progress as an all-pervasive phenomenon taking place throughout social and cultural life, including the moral realm.

Most contemporary evolutionists have been reluctant to apply the notion of progress to all aspects of social and cultural affairs, confining the idea of increasing adaptation more or less exclusively to the technical sphere and to social-organizational complexity.

Leslie White was one of the first to revitalize evolutionary theory. Like some of his predecessors, White maintained that it is not populations which evolve, but culture. Although local conditions can affect particular lines of cultural development for limited time periods, an overall evolution of culture exists as a distinctive and unique entity. White's general neo-evolutionary view holds that as culture evolves, there is a progressive increase in the amount of energy placed under human control. In this conception, the idea of progress is confined to greater mastery of the environment.[28]

Elman Service, another neo-evolutionary theorist, sees progressive developments in social organization. According to Service, the earliest societies, usually hunting and gathering economies, are characterized by the *band form.* The band is a small group whose members live in nuclear or extended families in close proximity to each other, most often regarding each other as social equals.

With the domestication of plants and animals, the group is able to sustain a larger membership and consequently is likely to evolve into a *tribal society.* Tribes, composed of several clans, embrace groups of related, more or less equal families. Leadership in both tribes and bands is usually charismatic, based on the talents or spiritual powers of the leader. The success of the tribe depends on the ability of its various components to cooperate and to defend themselves against would-be invaders.

As horticultural economies become more proficient and capable of sustaining larger populations, differentiation and specialization of functions continue, and the tribe is likely to evolve into a *chiefdom.* The chiefdom is characterized by the development of the (usually hereditary) position of chief. The chief coordinates the group's more highly specialized functions, usually by developing a corps of specialized retainers, often kinsmen, thus creating an aristocratic hierarchy of authority. The invention of such a hierarchy differentiates the chiefdom from all previous social organizational forms.

The *state* is the last stage of social organizational development, characteristic of industrial societies. The distinguishing characteristic of the state is more effective control by the leadership over the members of the society. The state contains a police force or military body, the only group legitimately empowered to exercise force. (A tribal chief's advantage of force differs from the monopoly of force available to leadership in the state.)[29]

Another variant of neo-evolutionary theory is found in Robert Redfield's work on "folk-urban drift." Redfield built his conceptual scheme on the pioneering work of Durkheim, Tönnies, and others. After studying several communities in Yucatán, Mexico, Redfield concluded that social change tends to result in a gradual shift away from the "folk," or traditional, community to an urban society, where the values, quality of life, and social organization sharply diverge from traditional forms. Urban society contrasts fundamentally with its folk antecedents.[30]

## Conflict Theory

Another perspective on social change is *conflict theory*, originally formulated by Karl Marx (see Chapter 2). Marx and Engels maintained that "the history of all hitherto existing society is a history of class struggle," implying that all the noteworthy events of history were products of class struggles and conflicts. As groups become ascendant over each other, society changes, and change persists as these rivalries and conflicts endure. The American Civil War, for example, was caused to a large degree by the conflict between two divergent economic interests. On the one hand was the industrial North, with its emerging factories and offices, which were best sustained by a wage-labor system in which workers could be hired or fired as needs changed. On the other hand was the agrarian South, with its plantation economy and its need for cheap labor. The war itself was produced by the conflict between these contending interests, and once it was over, further dramatic changes took place, particularly in the South, which was obliged to renounce its former economic and social institutions.

In general, conflict theorists maintain that the competition between groups inevitably produces divergence, opposition, and conflict. The enduring struggle makes for continuing

change. Although much conflict is not necessarily turbulent, and may in fact be well organized (collective bargaining, for example), occasional eruptions of violence do indeed flare up between contending groups. As rulers succeed one another, those in power attempt to implement their ideas and impose their values on the rest of their society. Those subjected to their domination, in turn, inevitably rise up and oppose those in power. Once the formerly subordinated groups assume control, they are likely to be opposed by the vanquished, thus completing the dialectical cycle of conflict and change. Many modern conflict theorists follow Marx in maintaining that changes tend to generate increasing polarization between opposing forces which finally clash, producing conflict and possibly warfare or revolution, out of which arises a new social order.

Some recent theorists have attempted to revise Marxism in the light of postcapitalistic conditions. Ralf Dahrendorf, for instance, points to authority relationships, rather than economic interests, as the fundamental point of cleavage in contemporary industrial society. Dahrendorf sees conflict arising between those who seek to maintain the *status quo* and those who attempt to expand their powers.[31] Other conflict theorists apply the dialectic in still a different way, conceiving of revolution as a rejuvenating response, promoting renovation and renewal of an otherwise decadent and perverted social order that has overextended its ideals and authority.[32]

## Equilibrium Theory

The notion of equilibrium (balance) was borrowed originally from mechanics and the biological sciences. The fundamental assumption of *equilibrium theory* is that when a change takes place in any one component in a system, it tends to spur further change in the other elements, which accommodate the new element and integrate it within the entire structure.

In general, systems strive toward equilibrium. For example, the development of jet engines during World War II revolutionized air transport and led to a number of further changes. New airports had to be built at the outskirts of existing cities because they required large amounts of land. The city had to change to accommodate them. The distances

The jet aircraft initiated a whole complex of changes as our culture adapted to its requirements and possibilities.

involved, in turn, spun off a host of other features: helicopter commuter flights, great airport complexes, and so forth. While each new development of this kind has tended to create problems of its own, equilibrium theorists see in this history of events the kinds of adjustive responses that societies make to incorporate change and keep a social order "in balance."

**Structural Functionalism** Perhaps the best-known equilibrium theory is the *structural functionalist* viewpoint, which we first met in Chapter 2. According to Talcott Parsons, society is a system composed of a set of interrelated parts or structures that function so as to promote social stability. Every society must provide for five basic needs if it is to endure: (1) member replacement, (2) member socialization, (3) production of goods and services, (4) preservation of order, and (5) provision and maintenance of a sense of purpose. These needs tend to give rise to a set of accommodating structures. The family provides for replacement, the educational system for socialization, and so on.

In primitive societies, these structures typically are fused. Kinship institutions, for example, ordinarily provide for replacement, socialization, and economic and religious needs, and may even sustain political ones. But as societies evolve—there is an evolutionary element to Parson's view—differentiation leads to further structural elaborations; institutions evolve to integrate the now more diverse structures. For example, as industrialization proceeded, schools began to assume a more dominant position in training younger members of society to fulfill adult social roles. Thus the family lost some of its former socializing functions and became more specialized in its remaining activities. Yet, within the school, a number of integrative facilities, such as parent-teacher associations, guidance counselors, and school psychiatrists, enlarge the educational function beyond merely imparting subject matter and skills, to serve the whole person, and to coordinate the schools with social institutions, such as the family, the church and the business community. When change occurs in any one part of the social system, it tends to have reverberations among the others, whose overall thrust promotes adaptation, equilibrium, and social stability.[33]

During the 1940s and 1950s, equilibrium theories and structural functionalism in particular were popular in American sociology. In recent years, however, this perspective has come under increasing criticism. Many charge that it tends to minimize the importance of social change. Change is seen as an alien element, something that occurs outside the social system, unlikely to arise within the system itself. Others claim that structural functionalism has a conservative bias, tending to overestimate the amount of consensus in society and failing to take adequate account of social conflicts and their potential for change.

## Cyclic (Rise-and-Fall) Theories

*Cyclic (rise-and-fall) theories of change* do not envision long-run trends in change. They see societies as undergoing periods of growth and decline or as swinging back and forth between extremes along several important dimensions. A number of these theories compare societies to living organisms, viewing the pattern of change in society as following the stages of the life cycle: birth, growth, maturity, and old age.

**Oswald Spengler** Oswald Spengler conceived of cultures as relatively autonomous and distinctive systems, each with its own style and unique destiny. All cultures pass through childhood, youth, maturity, and old age (see Figure

**FIGURE 18.3** **Spengler's model of cyclic change**

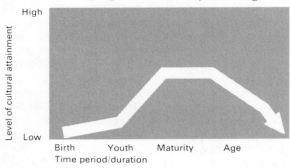

18.3). Civilization is the final stage in the life of a culture. The usual life span of a culture is approximately a thousand years. In the generally gloomy mood that followed World War I, Spengler prophesied the end of Western civilization.[34]

**Arnold Toynbee** Arnold Toynbee hypothesized that civilizations arise in response to some challenge from the social or physical environment (see Figure 18.4).[35] If the challenge is insufficient, or if it is too overwhelming, there will be a lack of effective drive toward attaining civilization. For example, the frigid climate and scarce resources of the Arctic have greatly limited the cultural response and development of Eskimo peoples. Conversely, the vast abundance of assets and good weather of the South Pacific islands have effectively reduced initiative among the Polynesians. But when the challenge is powerful enough to stimulate without being too overwhelming, as it was in the Nile River basin, an elaborate and complex civilization can develop.

Toynbee thought that twenty-one peoples in human history have attained civilization. Four or possibly five of these civilizations were original rather than derived from others. The original civilizations arose in Egypt, Sumer, and China, among the Mayans, and possibly in India—all others are derivative.

The presence of a creative minority is necessary in order to launch a civilization, Toynbee thought. Through its leadership, ingeniousness, and inspiration, a society is able fully to realize its potential. Eventually, this creative minority fails to take the appropriate measures, thus bringing about its own downfall and the

death of the civilization. In the terminal stages of a civilization, internal discord prevails, and the ruling elite imposes itself by brute force, resulting in widespread opposition among the majority. The vitality of a civilization endures as long as its elite makes the correct adaptive responses to sustain it.

**Pitirim Sorokin** Pitirim Sorokin contended that cultures tend to be characterized by one of two dominant themes: *Sensate cultures* stress values based on sensory experience, while *ideational cultures* give priority to spiritual and metaphysical values.[36] Once a culture emphasizes either extreme, it begins to revert back to its

**FIGURE 18.4** **Toynbee's model of cyclic change**

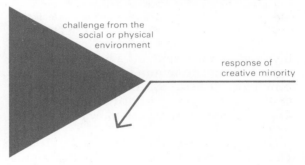

Case I: The challenge is too overwhelming and the culture fails or remains marginal, e.g. the Eskimo

Case II: The challenge is too easily overcome, the culture is not adequately stimulated, and it fails or remains marginal, e.g., Polynesia

Case III: The challenge is powerful enough to stimulate without being overwhelming, e.g. Egypt, and the culture becomes a true civilization

**FIGURE 18.5** Sorokin's model of cyclic change

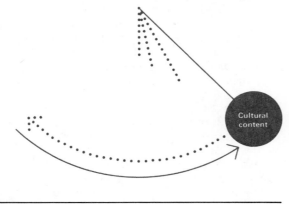

| Ideational themes | Idealistic themes | Sensate themes |

**As a culture approaches either extreme, it begins to swing back toward the opposite extreme. In the intermediate period, which Sorokin called "idealistic," a mixture of ideational and sensate themes prevails.**

polar opposite. As a culture swings back and forth between these two themes, it reaches an *idealistic* point, where a mixture of both sensate and ideational values prevail (see Figure 18.5).

Sorokin believed that one could identify which themes take precedence by surveying the artistic product of a given culture. He contended that Ancient Greece was an ideational culture that became idealistic during the Golden Age. Roman civilization marked a swing toward sensate life. During the Middle Ages, an ideational culture returned. The Renaissance was characterized by an idealistic synthesis.[37] Since the Renaissance, we have been heading in the direction of a more sensate culture. If the revival of religion among many of those committed to communal life styles reflects the latest trends, possibly we may anticipate a resurgence of the ideational theme.

**Max Weber** Weber's work demonstrated how religious ideology was influential in stimulating the growth of capitalist enterprise. He placed great emphasis upon the role of knowledge and ideology in stimulating change toward *rationalization*. Bureaucracy and rational legal authority everywhere supplant the more personal and informal features of traditional domination. Thus science, relation by contract, and the law—with their impersonal, formal-ized, and rational characteristics—continue to erode the time-honored, spontaneous, and unreasoning features of formerly traditional societies. This seems like an evolutionary theory. Yet there are dimensions to Weber's thinking that show leanings toward a rise-and-fall theoretical scheme.

In Weber's theory, there is always the possibility of the emergence of a charismatic leader. No one can anticipate with certainty when such a leader will appear, although the social conditions receptive to it are generally known. When such leadership does arise it is capable of exerting a far-reaching impact on society. Consider the changes effected by such charismatic leaders as Jesus, Mahatma Gandhi, Mao Tse Tung, Fidel Castro, Adolph Hitler, Franklin D. Roosevelt, and others. Charismatic leadership is capable of inspiring great devotion and inducing significant change in society.

Yet Weber noted that charismatic leadership possesses numerous limitations. The authority vested in the charismatic leader is inherently unstable and transitory. It is often difficult to extend the authority beyond those who have direct contact with the leader. Moreover, when the leader dies or leaves there is a succession problem. The charisma is apt to depart with the leader. Thus charismatic leadership is likely to be transformed into the more stable forms of either traditional or rational legal authority.

## CHANGE AND SOCIETAL DISORGANIZATION

One of the themes we have emphasized in this chapter is the disruptive potential of change. Change can usher in a host of social problems, and it may even cause social and cultural disorganization as in the disintegration of Caliente brought about by the introduction of the diesel engine. Nuclear power may yet destroy us and perhaps all life on earth as well.

Technological innovation is not, of course, the only cause of social and cultural dislocations. The historical record is filled with instances where the migration of groups or the diffusion of ideas and beliefs from one society to another resulted in increasing social problems and social disorganization. The contemporary plight of the native American is ample testimony to the personal and social disorganization—pauperization, alcoholism, and suicide, among others—that can arise as a result of exposure to new cultural elements.

Aboriginal peoples and peasants are not the only victims of the hardships and problems that change often brings. People in complex industrial societies have not gone unscathed by change. The automobile has brought alarming increases in health and environmental problems that seriously threaten human life, not to mention an appalling death toll from highway accidents. Sharp conflicts have developed between automobile interests and conservationists. But the foundation of the American economy is the automobile, with one out of every six workers directly or indirectly engaged in its production and maintenance.

In addition to the dependence of the American economy on the automobile, the entire society seems to have been built to accommodate cars. In cities and suburbs largely laid out since World War I, builders and planners plainly assumed that the universal form of transportation would be the privately operated automobile. Cities abandoned or never built adequate public transportation systems; suburban streets wind for miles without a sidewalk; great parking plazas surround immense shopping centers miles from residential areas, freeways twine through and around the central cities to permit access to suburban population centers. What would happen to the contemporary American city if gasoline became unavailable? Los Angeles might have to be either demolished and rebuilt or else abandoned.

Changes in ideas and other forms of nonmaterial culture also threaten the stability of modern society. Not long after *Brown* v. *Board of Education* in 1954, a massive upsurge of racial conflict occurred in many American cities. In part, those outbreaks owe their origins to the rising expectations of blacks inspired by legal affirmations of equality that were not matched in black experience. Violent racial outbursts quieted in the later 1970s, but could recur if black aspirations were again perceived as unachievable.

Nuclear power plant. If planned change is to be successful, it requires the cooperation of those planned for; this is often ignored by proponents of nuclear power.

## IS PLANNED CHANGE POSSIBLE?

Today many people feel that the range and intensity of problems and the complexity of the forces surrounding human action are so immense that we can only blunder along, following the currents of change wherever they may take us. Others remain optimistic, believing that the course of change can be directed, that we can control our destiny. One of the guiding principles of science is that the systematic knowledge it develops can be applied to human experience to help direct the course of change. Admittedly, the results obtained thus far in social science have been less impressive than those derived from physical science. Yet increasing numbers of social scientists remain confident that their work will contribute to social changes that will help sustain humanity and improve the quality of life on this planet.

It is vitally important to involve those planned for in the planning process. If planned change is to be successful, it requires the support and participation of those who will be affected by it. Many studies have confirmed this principle.[38]

Elite direction of social planning is the prevailing mode in communist societies. Yet throughout history, in all societies following communist precepts, adherence to the authoritarian model has been far from complete. There has always been some measure of grass roots involvement in planning in most communist societies, and it seems to have been the Russian experience that plans involving the planned-for work better than those created autocratically in Moscow.

Individuals reared in democratic capitalist societies sometimes find the idea of state management and control unappealing and contrary to the values of individual freedom and self-determination. But the democratic approach is not necessarily the only way or the most rapid way to effect change. In many developing nations, elite-led social and economic planning may be the only effective way of dealing with the massive problems these societies encounter, despite serious dislocations for individuals.

According to Robert Heilbroner's examination of economic underdevelopment, an uncoordinated free market system is unlikely to inspire the necessary postponements in consumption that will be required to generate investment capital for growth. Heilbroner holds that only in a planned economy is it possible to coordinate all the measures necessary to introduce and sustain economic development.[39] Only a planned economy can undertake the necessary massive land reforms, to move workers and capital in a coordinated way, to diversify the production process if need be, and to generate the sacrifices needed to spur development. Moreover, in some societies, peasants may expect authoritarian leadership by government officials; they may find democratic efforts at change confusing and inappropriate.

Communist China and Cuba offer good examples of the success of planned change in peasant societies. Although economic statistics are sparse and not altogether reliable, Western social scientists have been generally impressed with the achievements in food production, housing, and health care in both countries. Both governments have succeeded in virtually eliminating starvation and in bringing about dramatically improved living conditions, where in the past hunger and poverty perennially plagued large numbers of their citizens. Al-

though some of the gains have been the result of redistributing societal resources, without the substantial economic gains that have been achieved, these improvements would never have been possible. Such achievements might be regarded as particularly noteworthy when we consider the relatively short time in which they have been attained, the extent of China's technological backwardness and its vast population, and Cuba's former extreme dependence upon the American economy. However much we may value the democratic approach to change, it is not necessarily the most effective for all cultures, in all situations.

Planning can be greatly facilitated by modern computer technology. We can now project far into the future the long-range consequences of every conceivable activity: agricultural and population policy making, industrial expansion and market practice, investment and construction, among others.

Handling this multilayer circuit board is touchy business for this operator at Honeywell's Phoenix Computer Operations. There are a lot of computers in our future. Will they create a society presently unimaginable?

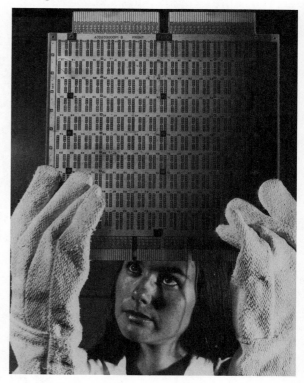

The computer revolution marks a major technological change, the total impact of which we have yet to experience. (It is not uncommonly believed, for example, that contemporary Americans may live to see money as such become obsolete, with all financial transactions taking place via credit card and computer. Such an idea was the stuff of science fiction only ten years ago.) But computers do not really think as human beings do, and they are utterly dependent for their seemingly miraculous abilities on the kind and quality of data fed them. ("Garbage in—garbage out," the programmers say.) Computers offer the possibility of facilitating planned change, but they cannot accomplish it for us. If modern society is to survive future shock, it remains for human beings to use computers well and to plan wisely and effectively, in ways no machine can do.

## CHANGE AND THE FUTURE

Many current analysts think that we have entered a new era of unprecedented and accelerated change. Alvin Toffler contends that the rate of change in today's society is so high it presents us with a problem of **future shock,** resulting from our inability to adjust to a pace that, in effect, makes us live in our own futures.[40] Future shock is akin to *culture shock*—the sense of bewilderment, frustration, and disorientation that people experience when they confront an unfamiliar culture. While many may not share Toffler's view that today's high rate of change is inherently problematical, others see that it has produced qualitatively different social conditions. Margaret Mead contends that we have shifted from a "postfigurative" culture, in which the young learned from the old, to one that is "configurative," in which both children and adults learn chiefly from their peers.

What will be the ultimate consequences of today's change-oriented society on the days and years ahead? Viewpoints vary considerably. While some, such as Paul Ehrlich, envision an "eco-catastrophe" where the environment may

**future shock:** the sense of bewilderment, frustration, and disorientation sometimes produced in people by very rapid social change. Future shock can be conceived of as resulting from inability to adjust to the pace of change.

be rendered useless because of overexploitation and where worldwide plague and thermonuclear war are probable as population growth continues unchecked, others, such as Olaf Helmer, are more optimistic, predicting that technology will solve many of the problems that now confront us, ushering in a new era of unprecedented affluence, ready communication, drug-induced pleasure, and longevity. Some like Toffler, envision a future society that will offer increasing potentialities for democratic governance; others, such as George Orwell, foresee an increasingly totalitarian world.

And what does the future portend for the developing countries? Are they likely to follow the patterns that prevail in developed societies? M. S. Iyengar contends that the developing nations could move into the future directly, bypassing the whole stage of industrialism, leaving the rich and so-called advanced nations behind. If the future society is one where work is no longer a central feature of people's social activities and if iron and steel dominated industrial systems become impediments to change, rather than assets, it may well be that developing societies may have distinctive advantages over developed ones and thus be more adaptable.

The immense magnitude of contemporary change has given rise to a new field of study devoted to the future and our adjustment to it: *futurology.* Futurologists come from a variety of disciplines—social and physical scientists, social planners, theologians, business leaders, technologists, science fiction writers, and others. Sharing a common fascination with our unknown futures, these thinkers hope to identify the directions of change in the years ahead.

## SUMMARY

Social change (changes in social organization or activities in society) differs from cultural change (alterations of norms, beliefs, and material culture) but they usually are inseparably linked.

Three basic causes of change are innovation, diffusion, and crises and conflicts.

Many factors influence whether changes will be accepted or resisted by members of society. They include: the beliefs, attitudes, values, traditions, and habits of the group, the perceived needs for change, the ready demonstrability of the new pattern, the cultural base, costs and vested interests. Any or all of these factors influence whether group members welcome change or resist it. This, in turn, affects the rates at which change occurs in given situations.

Still other factors govern the response to change. Geography can impede or facilate change by isolating or permitting ready contact between groups. Environmental and population changes are also important. As an earthquake or drought would obviously effect change, so too may an alteration in the pattern of population growth and migration. Similarly, societies with particular kinds of population growth patterns may be encouraged or discouraged from changing. For example, those with high birth and death rates and a large proportion of children would be likely to have great difficulty industrializing. Finally, social relations networks, the presence or absence of change agents, and the way change agents conform to the group's cultural traditions will have much impact upon whether changes are accepted or rejected.

Technology usually influences the direction and extent of change. Yet cultural lags inevitably arise when changes in the material or technical realm surpass those occurring in adaptive responses. Sometimes cultural lags produce serious social dislocation, impairing the continuing survival of the group. The modernization of peasant agricultural societies into urban-industrial ones is an important social trend in today's world. It can be promoted by increasing agricultural productivity, land reform, expanded domestic and foreign investments, increased educational participation, and mass media exposure.

There are four major conceptions of the process of social change. Evolutionary and neo-evolutionary theories emphasize the cumulative growth and developments of change. Conflict theories view change as the product of competition among various contending groups or social classes. Equilibrium theories see change in any one component of a social structure as initiating changes in all other components to restore "balance." Cyclic theories view change either as following a pattern of alternation between polar social types or else as following a growth-and-decay pattern based on an organic model.

We have emphasized the potentially disorganizing consequences of change. Many aboriginal and peasant cultures have been destroyed by contact with and domination by technologically developed societies. Developed societies, too, face serious obstacles in sustaining themselves from the ever-present challenges of change. Thus the need for effectively planned change assumes ever-increasing dimensions today. Successfully planned change requires grass roots support—involvement of those planned for—if optimum adaptations are to be encouraged. Yet, in dealing with the enormous challenge of economic underdevelopment there is some evidence from Cuba and China that elite-led change can yield adaptive consequences, as well.

Looking ahead in developed societies some scholars feel that the pace of contemporary change is so rapid that it produces disorientation and bewilderment for many. Much disagreement exists among scholars today on the ultimate consequences of change. Some see imminent doom while others envision an era of unprecedented affluence and social harmony. Futurology, a new field of study, has emerged to anticipate our unknown futures.

## CONCLUDING REMARKS: CONTEMPORARY TRENDS

As you have seen from this introduction to our field, the sociological vision is extremely broad, embracing all human interaction. As we try to understand social reality, we see a kalidescope of events that defy coherent comprehension.

Our social activities, historical records, daily newspapers, reports of government bureaus, and the like reveal a welter of such enormity, complexity, and diversity that the task of ordering this into meaningful patterns seems beyond the scope of any disciplined group effort. Yet the sociological method offers us some rational and feasible way to catalogue all this data and to discern patterns and uniformities among all the changes.

We are beginning to develop sociological perspectives, putting the apparent chaos of change into meaningful and testable patterns. Some of our understandings are narrow. We are becoming aware, for example, that with industrialization our families are growing smaller. We are also learning that with time our economic organizations are growing in size, becoming global in their influence and more and more centralized. We are also beginning to put such narrower patterns together into larger and more all-encompassing social trends.

We observe a trend toward ever greater bureaucratization. With industrialization we have seen a phenomenal growth of cities and with this a transformation from informal, intimate, spontaneous, and primary relationships to more formal, rational, deliberate, and impersonal ones. With scientific advance and technological development we have seen a trend to ever greater specialization, differentiation, and individualization. With the coming of cities we have seen the emergence of mass societies, where people's relationships have become increasingly commercialized and where feelings of close kinship have been narrowed to their apparent ultimate point — the nuclear family. No longer is social status a mostly inherited and enduring quality assigned to persons. Social advancement and the possibilities for determining one's own goals and occupation in life are increasingly matters of individual choice. Amidst overall improvements in our material well-being, we seem to have more fragmented and transitory social relationships. We know our political leaders less well personally, but we seem to participate in politics to a greater extent than ever before. While some of our older social problems have faded, new ones are appearing, and some minor social problems have become major ones. We are still learning that a great many other patterns are associated with this process of urban, industrial, and scientific growth.

These trends that we are referring to are not merely characteristic of our society and its Western European forebears. They represent global trends found in every emerging nation, irrespective of differences in religious and philosophical viewpoints. They are part of this tranformation we have called modernization. Thus, the patterns of Muncie, Indiana, are also the patterns of Nairobi, Kenya, and Puno, Peru.

At present, our postindustrial futures seem unclear. We will require many fresh sociological insights if our knowledge is to be extended beyond the historical record and if the predictive goals of our discipline are to be more fully realized. The challenge of change must inevitably stir our sociological imaginations: our continuing survival may depend upon it.

## SUGGESTED READINGS

APPLEBAUM, RICHARD, *Theories of Social Change*. Chicago: Markham, 1970. In this concise and clear text the author systematically reviews many of the leading sociological theories of social change. This is a worthwhile primer for more serious students of social change.

ETZIONI, AMATAI, and EVA ETZIONI-HALEVY, eds. *Social Change: Sources, Patterns and Consequences*. New York: Basic, 1973. In this compendium of essays the editors offer a broad-ranging array of perspectives on social change. Readings cover both leading classical and current theories of change, besides examining the dimensions of change in developing and developed societies.

FOSTER, GEORGE. *Tzintzuntzan: Mexican Peasants in a Changing World*. Boston: Little, Brown, 1967. Focusing upon a particular peasant community, the author examines the mutually supportive characteristics that serve to retard social change. Emphasis is also directed to the kinds of things that may be done that may facilitate change in such communities, obtaining peasant participation and involvement in change efforts.

LERNER, DANIEL. *The Passing of Traditional Society*. New York: Free Press, 1958. Focusing upon Middle Eastern societies the author offers a theory of the modernization process in developing societies. Great emphasis is accorded to the media of communication in facilitating modernization.

TOFFLER, ALVIN. *Future Shock*. New York: Random, 1970. In this very lively and readable former bestseller, the author discusses the high rates of change in today's industrial societies. Very perceptively the author examines the disruptive potential that change may bring to industrial peoples.

TURNBULL, COLIN. *The Mountain People*. New York:

Simon and Schuster, 1972. This book focuses upon the Ik, an African group of nomadic hunters, whose culture has been attenuated by the change processes of colonialism and nationalism. A once unified and prosperous people, the Ik have turned into scattered bands of hostile people whose singular goal is survival. In this fascinating account Turnbull's analysis portrays the vulnerability of social structures to the ravages of change.

# Chapter 19
# Social
# Research
# Methods

The officials gazed somberly into the faces of the overflow crowd of citizens. The crowd had gathered to hear the Council's decision on an important matter, and they were tense with anticipation. What could have stirred so much public interest? A new tax increase perhaps? A confession of wrongdoing in high places? A law banning the ownership of dogs? No, it is none of these. It is a decision to permit a group of laboratory scientists to continue their experiments with deoxyribonucleic acid—DNA.

This is not a scene from a science fiction fantasy. The meeting described actually took place in Cambridge, Massachusetts, in July 1976. It illustrates how activities formerly regarded as "purely scientific," and therefore outside the realm of politics, increasingly have become matters of keen public concern. The DNA experiments involve recombining or "splicing" tiny pieces of genetic material to create new forms of life. The technique for doing this was discovered in 1973, and since that time, both scientists and ordinary citizens have been caught up in an emotional debate over where such experiments in genetic engineering may lead. No one can predict what new creatures may be created as genes from different living organisms are spliced together. And many people fear that a pathogen (a "killer bug") might escape from the laboratory and ravage the population of the entire world.

The fear of worldwide epidemics did not spring entirely from the fevered imaginations of scientifically ignorant laymen. The first warnings were issued by scientists themselves. In 1976 the National Institutes of Health (NIH) issued guidelines concerning gene-splicing. Since then several proposals have been put forward in Congress to bring recombinant DNA research under government control.

Although no one can be certain, it now appears that there is little chance that a global epidemic will be created by gene-splicing research. Nevertheless, the argument over regulation continues because genetic engineering raises moral and legal questions as well as biological ones. Do scientists have the right to tinker with the basic mechanisms of life? Suppose new life forms are created, who is responsible for them? This question has special force as experiments in genetic engineering move from bacteria and viruses to human beings. The world's first test tube baby was born in England during August 1978; and in that same month a woman in New York won a court case against a scientist who had interrupted her test tube pregnancy. Also during 1978, a book appeared in which the author claimed the first human clone had been born. What effects will such developments have on the meaning and dignity of human life, as well as on the prospects for human survival? Even if laymen do not understand the techniques or methods of the scientist, they do recognize that scientific activity can have a powerful effect on the quality of their lives; and they feel they should have some say in how such activities are conducted.

The contemporary skepticism of scientific research is nothing new to sociologists. The genuine dangers of social research have always been more visible to people — who after all are the subjects of such research — than have those of natural and physical research. But the issue has been greatly sharpened as social researchers have moved in the direction of adapting scientific ideas and methods to the study of human beings. Social research skills may be abused, for example, to invade the privacy of others or even to manipulate another's thoughts and actions. Such a possibility was dramatized during the 1950s, when the Chinese Communist forces in Korea performed brainwashing experiments on American prisoners of war

**American prisoners of the Chinese in Korea.**

Many people doubt that social researchers can actually apply scientific reasoning to the study of human beings. Nevertheless, much work along this line has taken place, and the results of these efforts deserve thoughtful consideration.

Even if social research methods are not truly scientific, they may nonetheless increase our understanding of why human beings behave as they do; and this understanding may or may not contribute to human welfare. The second overarching question of interest to us, therefore, is, "How can social research be conducted with due regard for such sensitive matters as privacy, the use of deception, and the welfare of those who participate in social research?"

There is little doubt that we desperately need the kind of accurate and useful information that a scientific sociology might provide; but social scientists, as well as the general public, have become increasingly aware that the effort to gain such knowledge inevitably involves ethical risks. Clearly, some kind of balance is required between the need for ethical safeguards and the needs of society for knowledge about itself.

leading many previously loyal Americans to radically change their political convictions and behavior toward each other. These experiments also led indirectly to the death of some of the prisoners.

These considerations suggest two overarching questions—one technical, the other ethical—around which this chapter will revolve. First, "To what extent is it possible for social researchers to use the methods that apply to the natural and physical worlds to study the social world?"

## PLANNING FOR RESEARCH

Sociologists have devised ways to apply the scientific method to the study of human groups. Indeed, most sociologists today think of themselves as scientists and of the scientific method as their principal intellectual tool. But this apparent consensus on purposes and methods conceals a tremendous diversity of opinion about how the social sciences compare with the physical sciences and on the procedures that are appropriate for gaining a scientific knowledge of human beings.

Ideally speaking, scientific inquiry begins with an hypothesis which, also ideally, is de-

rived from a theory. An **hypothesis** is a *precise statement of what the researcher expects to find;* a **theory** is *a more general statement (or set of statements) that explains many different facts by reference to underlying principles and relationships.* The hypothesis that married people are less likely to commit suicide than unmarried people, for example, may be derived from Emile Durkheim's theory that membership in strong or cohesive groups gives meaning to life and therefore helps to prevent suicide.[1] Although the term *theory* frequently occurs in everyday, as well as scientific, language, its scientific and commonsense meanings differ markedly. In commonsense thought, *theory* is often regarded as inferior, or even opposed, to *fact*. It is commonly believed that theories are merely vague statements of possible truth. But among scientists, theory is regarded as preceding and assisting in the discovery of fact and as giving meaning to facts. While theories must be submitted to the test of facts and may be modified by them, it is pointless to gather random pieces of information without having a theory to organize and direct the search. To summarize the relationship of theory and fact, theory without fact is empty; fact without theory is blind.

On the basis of hypotheses and theories, a researcher may proceed to plan concrete studies. Planning ideally includes a careful consideration of how the research will be designed, how the data will be gathered and analyzed, and how the results will be interpreted. In reality, however, the process is much more complex and disorderly than this and a great deal of significant research has been accomplished without proceeding in the order given.

Many exciting research ideas are not derived from existing social theories. They may be based on personal experiences, observations, and "hunches." S. M. Lipset, for instance, had the idea of conducting a study of the International Typographical Union (ITU) partly because his father had been a member of the union.[2] The young Lipset had heard conversations about the union and had attended meetings. Years later, he recognized that the ITU differed in some important ways from most other labor unions so that a study of it could be of theoretical significance.

Frequently researchers will gather information concerning a topic of interest but will not hit upon their main hypothesis until they begin to understand what the evidence means. According to Robert Bellah, for example,

> The usual textbook notion of social research is that one forms a hypothesis and then proceeds to gather data to confirm or negate it. . . . The researcher often finds himself with an abundance of data, and the problem is how to make sense of it.[3]

A social research project, then, may begin with or without an hypothesis, and the hypothesis may or may not actually be derived from an existing theory, although theories and hypotheses are considered the best starting places

**hypothesis:** a statement of presumed or alleged fact, worded in such a way as to permit or invite test and made for that purpose.

**theory:** an at least partially verified statement of apparent relationships and underlying principles concerning observed phenomena.

New Yorker, January 28, 1974. Drawing by Dedini; © 1974 The New Yorker Magazine, Inc.

**Most research begins with an hypothesis, which may be no more than an inspired guess.**

for research. Although the studies by Lipset and Bellah were not conducted in exact accord with the ideal sequence of scientific inquiry, both scholars were deeply immersed in the literature of their respective fields and had a thorough acquaintance with many theories and hypotheses bearing on their research. Each of them had a well-defined focus of study to guide his work. Lipset wanted to know why the ITU had been able to maintain a democratic system of government while most labor unions became "oligarchic." Bellah wanted to know how Japan, a product of non-Western history, developed into an industrialized nation. It was therefore likely that their research would be significant even though they did not follow the ideal pattern of study.

Although there is no formula or recipe for having good ideas—they may just pop into one's head or seem to be intuitive—one should be acquainted with the theories and works of others before starting to collect facts. And, in general, it is helpful to have a clearly stated hypothesis whether it is derived from theory or not. Such an hypothesis not only tells us *what* facts should be gathered, it gives us clues about *where* and *how* to gather them. A research question is intimately connected with both its research design and its data-gathering methods.

## RESEARCH DESIGN

Once a topic has been chosen or an hypothesis has been stated, we must consider various ways to learn what we wish to know. Consider, for instance, some questions to be answered before conducting a study of underemployed black men. Should we focus on all such men in the United States? Or only on those in certain states, countries, cities, or neighborhoods? Should we study only underemployed black men, or should we compare them with black men who are full-time workers? Or should we perhaps compare them with underemployed whites? The answers to these questions would tell us some vital things about which methods of data gathering should be used. If we wished to study the entire United States, for example, we would almost certainly need to use information gathered by the Bureau of the Census and other agencies of the federal and state governments.

But the problem need not be tackled in this way at all. In an influential study of underemployed black men, Elliot Liebow focused on a small group of men who lived in a specific neighborhood in Washington, D.C.[4] He started with no specific hypotheses, deciding to describe the lives of the men as fully and in as much detail as possible, by living among the men and getting to know them as well as he could. Each of these decisions had a marked effect on the design of Liebow's study and on the techniques of gathering data that were of value to him.

Because of the wide range of interests among sociologists and the many methods they may

Street corner surveying.

use, we will limit our discussion to a few of the most prominent research designs, survey research, the comparative historical study, the case study, and the social experiment.

### Survey Research

The most common type of sociological research is the **survey.** You are probably already familiar with surveys in some form. The results of public opinion polls are reported frequently in newspapers and magazines. Business firms undertake surveys to discover how consumers react to packaging or commercials. Political candidates commission polls to discover how well they are known or which issues are important to voters.

Three essential elements distinguish the survey from other forms of research. First, paper-and-pencil instruments of some kind are used, such as questionnaires or interviews. Second, these are administered in the field, that is, in natural situations—homes, offices, street corners, and so on. Third, a sample of the population is questioned in order to obtain an estimate of the characteristics of the entire population concerned. Survey researchers go to a sample of the people they wish to study and ask questions. The answers they receive are assumed to be representative of the whole population the sample is drawn from.

The methods employed by different kinds of survey researchers have many points in common. The principal difference between the sociological survey and the types with which you may be more familiar is this: Since sociologists are usually interested in testing or exploring hypotheses and theories, they frequently wish to do more than describe differences among groups.[5] They also make **causal inferences** — determine whether cause-and-effect relationships exist among the different factors under study.

To illustrate, sociologists have found that people of high education appear to have less prejudice toward minorities than do people of low education.[6] Does this mean that high education leads to or causes lower levels of prejudice? That is what most of us assume, and it is certainly a plausible interpretation; but consider this possibility: Suppose that people without ethnic prejudices are more likely to do well in school. If this were true, it would be correct to say that high prejudice reduces education. Or suppose that people of high education are more likely to be embarrassed by their prejudices and are therefore more guarded in their answers to survey questions. They may give answers to make themselves appear less prejudiced than they really are. Suppose, finally, that education and prejudice may actually change together through time but that some other fact is responsible. For example, if some preschool children develop greater social skill than others, those who have greater social skill are likely both to enjoy school and to become more tolerant of others. Under these circumstances the connection between high education and low prejudice would be accounted for by differences in social skills. Such *alternative interpretations* should always be considered when we attempt to interpret the meaning of survey findings.

Sociologists usually study the interrelationships among various factors and attempt to choose sensibly among competing alternative

**survey research:** social research involving the use of paper and pencil instruments (typically interviews and questionnaires) administered "in the field" to samples of relevant populations.

**causal inference:** the process of drawing conclusions about cause and effect relationships from research data.

**selection control:** careful selection of the units to be studied to insure the best possible approximation of that which is to be investigated; finding the purest possible examples of the phenomenon under investigation.

interpretations. The design of a survey is an important tool in this effort. To show how a survey may be designed to strengthen or rule out certain interpretations, let us summarize briefly some research on health care behavior.

Several studies have shown that mothers of high socioeconomic status are more likely to use preventive health care services for themselves and their children than are mothers of low socioeconomic status.[7] To explore further the relationship between status and health care behavior, Bonnie Bullough reasoned as follows: Since we know that people of high socioeconomic status are more likely to use preventive health care services than people of low socioeconomic status, it should be useful to learn whether people at the same level differ from each other very much in their use of such services. If so, some factor or factors besides the socioeconomic one must be involved. Bullough decided to survey a sample of people living in three poverty neighborhoods in Los Angeles. Since only people of low socioeconomic status were selected for study, Bullough hoped they would all be roughly alike in this respect and that differences in socioeconomic status would therefore be eliminated (or "controlled") as an explanatory factor. Thus the design of the study included a consideration of the causal inferences to be made from it.

To be sure that the members of a survey sample will resemble one another in more than one way, a researcher can extend **selection control** to include some additional factors. Bullough, for example, restricted her sample to include only women who had recently given birth to babies. Thus the people in her sample not only had similar socioeconomic status, but also were all of the same sex and would all have reason to use preventive health care services.

What about socioeconomic status? Restricting the sample to poverty neighborhoods narrowed income differences, but rather large gaps in income still remained. Some sample participants had monthly incomes greater than $900 while others had monthly incomes lower than $200. Were these socioeconomic differences large enough to explain whatever differences there were in preventive health care behavior?

The answer was "yes." Not only does the broad range of socioeconomic statuses to be found in most communities appear to influence preventive health care behavior, the much narrower range to be found within poverty neighborhoods also seems to have an effect. Whenever selection control is only partially successful in removing the influence of a particular factor, the researcher may attempt to eliminate the remaining influence of the factor by the method of **internal comparison.** Bullough did this by dividing her sample into two groups, one above and one below the poverty line established by the Social Security Administration. She was then able to compare the health practices of the two groups.

Thus Bullough selected and continued to refine her sample population. She concluded that poverty and lack of education did contribute to the neglect of preventive care, but that the effects of these factors were reinforced by "the culture of poverty," which includes feelings of powerlessness, hopelessness, and social isolation—what sociologists often call alienation, Marx's term. Bullough also found that identification as a black or Chicano contributed to alienation. The form of preventive health care most affected by alienation was family planning, although all others except dental care (which was largely related to income) were also affected.

There are two main ethical questions in survey research. First, most survey researchers promise to keep all or portions of their findings confidential and to report in such a way that individuals cannot be identified. When such promises are made, the researcher must make every effort to protect those who have assisted him or her. Whether investigators have the right to keep their sources and records confidential in this way is the subject of several court

cases at this time. Second, the researcher must consider how the information gained will be used and for whose benefit. Some sociologists maintain that unless research information has direct benefits for those who participate, a study is unjustified. Most sociologists probably would agree that at the very least they should do everything in their power to prevent the participants from being injured by the findings.

### The Comparative Historical Study

Some of the most influential sociological researches are **comparative historical studies,** investigations using historical material as research data. These studies offer no possibility of direct control over the study materials. Nevertheless, the researcher attempts to control the data as much as possible. Let us examine briefly how some of the ideas we have been discussing were used by Durkheim in his work *Suicide,* discussed briefly in Chapter 2.

By focusing on differences in rates of suicide (such as the number of suicides per 100,000 people in a given group per year), Durkheim was able to investigate variations in the occurrence of suicide among the different groups. For example, he found that there were religious differences in the rates of suicide. He used this fact to discuss an idea that many people accept, namely, that people who commit suicide are mentally unbalanced. If Protestants, Catholics, and Jews show different rates of suicide and if insanity is an important cause of suicide, then those groups with higher rates of insanity should also have correspondingly higher rates of suicide. Even in this brief form of the argument, you will notice some of the elements of the logic we have been discussing. The researcher wishes to see whether the presence of one thing, such as Protestant belief, is regularly connected with another thing, in this case, insanity. In this particular study, of course, he cannot eliminate or control all of the many factors that might enter into and affect such a relationship. He can, however, compare different groups that are similar or different in theoretically important ways. If satisfactory information is available, the researcher can reach back into history or across national borders to discover groups that may be matched in order to eliminate certain alternative interpretations.

Using comparative historical materials, Durkheim concluded that suicide expressed the nature and degree of social bonding.

By proceeding in this way, Durkheim found that although Jews were more likely to suffer mental illness than were Protestants and Catholics, they were less likely to commit suicide. From such evidence he concluded that group differences in rates of mental illness could not adequately explain group differences in rates of suicide. Similarly, Durkheim argued against the role of alcoholism, nationality, climate, and other factors as causes of suicide. His preferred explanation was that different social environments influence the probability that a person will commit suicide. Those who are freed from group controls are more likely to commit suicide than are those protected by group affiliations. Thus the married commit suicide less

**internal comparison:** the internal division into two or more categories for comparative purposes of data already refined by selection control.

**comparative historical study:** social research utilizing historical materials as data.

**case study:** social research utilizing intensive study of a single instance of a social phenomenon as data, e.g., a riot, work group, church congregation, and so on.

frequently than the unmarried, and people kill themselves more frequently in peacetime than in wartime (when the bonds of social cohesion are strengthened by an external threat).

Comparative historical studies are quite different from surveys. For one thing the researcher relies on preexisting information instead of going directly to the people involved. For another, many of the ethical questions that may appear in a survey do not appear here. However, as in a survey, comparative historical research should be designed to exert as much control as possible over the data.

### The Case Study

The **case study** is an intensive examination of a single instance of a social phenomenon or group. Any social unit or event can be the focus of analysis. The case study design is usually selected when the researcher wants to understand in the richest possible detail the inner workings of a specific social group or the exact circumstances associated with an event. A thorough immersion in a single case may suggest many tentative generalizations and hypotheses to be tested in other types of studies.

The case study method may also be extremely useful as a type of test for certain kinds of hypotheses. For example, Lipset's study of the ITU gained in importance because the ITU was what is called a "deviant" case—it was an exception to the rule that labor unions tend toward an oligarchic form of government. By selecting a deviant case for analysis, Lipset hoped to show in a detailed way why this particular union departed from the "normal" development of union government. An understanding of the "deviant" case, of course, contributes to our understanding of the "normal" course of events.

Sometimes a researcher undertakes the analysis and comparison of two or more cases. This study design, although time-consuming, enables the researcher to combine the insight and depth afforded by the case study with the ability to generalize somewhat more freely from the results. We will describe later an actual example of this type of study conducted by Peter Blau.

Some case studies rely on a close personal involvement of the researcher with those being studied, while others may be conducted entirely on the basis of published reports and official records. The ethical problems arising in these situations differ substantially. Whenever researchers develop personal relationships with those under study, they may be torn by the conflicting rules of objective reporting, on the one hand, and the expectations of friends, on the other. When this dilemma arises, the researcher must weigh carefully the costs and benefits of the research findings. The choice will be easier if there has been complete honesty from the beginning.[8]

### The Social Experiment

The ideal sequence of social research begins with an hypothesis derived from a theory, and then attempts to obtain facts that would feedback and strengthen or weaken the theory in question. This ideal is based upon the classical laboratory experiment.

In its ideal form, the classical experiment enables the researcher to manipulate a single **independent variable** (X) to see what effect, if any, it produces in a single **dependent variable** (Y), while all other variables are controlled. Through this type of study, scientists may show (1) that as X changes Y also changes and (2) that only changes in X affect Y. These points are illustrated in Figure 19.1.

Obviously, there are many obstacles to the direct use of classical experiments in the social sciences. Some of these are technical in nature. It is often very difficult, if not impossible, for the social researcher actually to alter a social condition to see what effect the alteration would have. Even if such as alteration is possible, it may be impossible to prove that the subsequent effect is the consequence of the alteration rather than the consequence of something

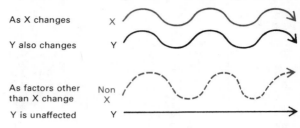

**FIGURE 19.1** **The logic of the classical experiment**

Therefore, changes in X lead to or cause changes in Y

else that also occurred. In short, the degree of control over experimental variables demanded by the classical experiment is usually impossible in social research. The precise measurement of changes is also a problem. Even more important is the problem of the ethics of manipulating human subjects in the ways required by the classical experiment.

The *laboratory social experiment* is a modification of the classical experiment. In it, the social researcher applies as much of the logic and rigor of the classical experiment as possible, given the difficulties and ethical problems involved in studying human behavior. Carl Hovland, for example, used an experimental design to study this question: When a controversial subject is being presented, does it matter which side is presented first?[9] Many people have expressed the fear that first impressions are lasting and that, therefore, in many practical matters people are unduly swayed by the first argument they hear. Hovland's review of previous studies found some support for this fear; but he also found some negative evidence. On the basis of previous research, he designed a complex experiment in which two persuasive arguments were presented to different groups of people. Some of the people heard the "pro" side first while others heard the "con" side first. All the participants answered questionnaires about their beliefs before the experiments were conducted; but some people also received the belief questionnaire in between the reading of the arguments, while others received it only after both sides of the argument had been read. In this way Hovland was able to compare a number of groups who had heard different arguments in different orders and with different instructions on the belief questionnaire. On the basis of this experiment, Hovland concluded that under some conditions, the first argument may indeed have an advantage; however, in many of the most important practical situations, such as legal trials and political campaigns, people are not necessarily swayed by the first argument.

Another type of social experiment is the *natural experiment*. Natural experiments study existing situations, things going on in the real world, that may constitute a test of some kind. To conduct a natural experiment, a sociologist might seek an existing situation in which two or more groups of people are similar in important respects but have undergone, or are about to undergo, different experiences. For example, Morton Deutsch and Mary Collins compared four public housing projects in which there were both white and black residents.[10] In two settings, the residents were racially segregated within the project. In the other two settings, white and black residents were assigned apartments without regard to race. This created an opportunity for a study of the reactions of the tenants to two situations that were very similar except that the members of the two races were physically closer in one project than in the other. The researchers found that white housewives who lived in the two integrated projects had more neighborly relations with blacks than did the white housewives in the two segregated projects. The study also showed that the longer the white housewives lived in the projects—segregated as well as integregated—the more favorable their attitudes toward black people became. By taking advantage of a naturally occurring process—the assignment of people to segregated and integrated housing projects—Deutsch and Collins were able to simulate experimental conditions. Although the researchers did not have the power to place people in one or another type of social setting to see what effects this would have, they were able to study the effects *as if* such an experiment had been arranged.

## DATA-GATHERING METHODS

The above discussion has been concerned primarily with the overall design of research projects. Although we have referred to various data-gathering methods, we have not explained

**independent variable:** the variable manipulated in order to determine its influence on other (dependent) variables.

**dependent variable:** the variable permitted to vary in order to determine whether it is influenced by another (independent) variable; the variable left unmanipulated by the experimenter.

what these methods are. Such methods as observation, interviews, and questionnaires, through which the data to be studied are *created*, are called primary sources. *Existing* records, such as the United States Census of Population or published vital statistics, are called secondary sources.

### Observation

The advantage of the trained sociological observer over any other person usually does not lie in the keenness of the sociologist's observations. Very few sociologists are trained like Sherlock Holmes to reach nearly miraculous conclusions concerning people's backgrounds, occupations, and hobbies merely by glancing at their clothes, their posture, the signs of wear on their shoes, and the stains on their forefingers. If we may presume that the great Holmes was trained to notice everything, we may say in contrast that sociologists are trained to notice primarily those things that are important to the hypothesis they are testing. They are trained to exclude from their vision many things that may be of interest to other observers. They are deliberately selective in their observation.

To gather data by direct observation the sociologist must first decide what to observe. Suppose we have the opportunity to observe, for purposes of a research study, a work group in a factory or a crowd of people who have assembled to protest a government action. Which group we choose will depend on the question guiding the study. If the question is, "Why do some groups have high morale and work together cooperatively?" we will probably prefer the factory work group to the crowd. But if the question is, "Why are some approaches to social change more effective than others?" observing the crowd of protesters will probably be more instructive.

The process of selective observation does not end with deciding which group to observe. The next question is what specifically *about* a given group should be observed. If we were observing the factory group, we would have little interest in the relative strengths of two different building materials the workers were using, but we would be interested in observing matters that bear on the guiding question, such as the social statuses represented in the group, the differences in prestige accorded to various individuals, and the amount of authority exerted by different members of the group.

Having decided what to observe, we must decide how active to be in the process. For instance, we might simply watch the people who are being studied but attempt not to disturb them; or we might ask questions to discover how the participants interpret various events; or we might become members of the group, participating fully in its activities while continuing to observe. It is also possible to move about among these different roles during the course of a study.

The role of observer, especially the role of **participant observer,** involves many issues of method and ethics. To what extent do people alter their behavior when the observer is present? When we ask questions, will they tell the truth? How can we record our observations so they will not be forgotten or distorted? Should we explain to those being studied the details of the research? If people confide in the researcher, will they be injured in some way?

In a study of two government agencies, Peter Blau wanted to learn more about the relationship between the formal and informal social organizations that exist within bureaucracies.[11] He obtained permission to study a state employment agency (which he called Department X) and a federal law-enforcement agency (called Department Y).

He began to encounter difficulties soon after entering the first agency. For instance, he spent about two weeks becoming familiar with the agency and its operations before beginning his formal observations. He then explained to the agents who he was and what he wanted to do. But this delay, he learned, was an error. During the two weeks Blau was becoming familiar with the setting, the *agents* were observing *him*, and various rumors about his presence were circulating. Since he had been brought in by management, he was suspected of being a "company spy." In his study of Department X, Blau corrected this error by explaining his purpose the day he arrived.

During his first week of observation in Department Y, Blau spent most of his time getting acquainted with the agents, asking about their work, and so on. But then he made another mistake. Before he had fully won the confidence of the group, he began to make notes. This change in this behavior aroused the agents' suspicions. Despite his explanations, some of the agents believed he was an efficiency expert checking up on them—a view which interfered with the progress of his study.

Blau noted some other difficulties in his role as observer. He had to decide, for instance, to what extent and in what ways professional ethics required him to be candid with those he was studying. Blau's resolution of the problem was to be quite open in revealing everything except his hypotheses. In his words, "My trump card in establishing rapport . . . was actually being what I pretended to be. . . ."[12] He also had to take precautions in publishing his findings not to include information that would make it possible for someone to identify the agency (and perhaps individual agents) he had studied. He had guaranteed the anonymity of his informants and was ethically bound to live up to that promise.

Despite the practical difficulties, Blau was

Direct observation is the traditional research method of the cultural anthropologist. Margaret Mead is shown among a group of the natives she studied.

able to complete the studies by acknowledging his errors and taking steps to correct them. The completed studies have been widely praised as examples of imaginative and careful social research.

Blau was an active observer, not only watching but questioning people as well. He was not, however, a member of the groups he observed. A participant observer becomes an active member of the group under study, simultaneously participating and observing. Participant observations have the advantage of giving an ''inside'' view of the workings of a group. They usually are rich in character portrayal and show the human side of group life in a dynamic, detailed way. William F. Whyte's study of Italian ''cornermen'' in Boston is a notable example of this type of observation procedure.[13]

### Interviews and Questionnaires

Like observation, **interviews** and **questionnaires** generally are used to gather information directly from the individuals under study. But unlike observation, interviews and questionnaires are designed to ask people about their attitudes and behaviors instead of watching their activities directly. An interview is a prepared list of questions that an interviewer asks

**participant observation:** a modification of the observation method of social research in which the observer not only watches and records, but actually becomes a participant or actor in the events observed. Participant observation may be overt or covert, i.e., the observer may or may not let his actual role be known to the others with whom he is interacting.

**interview:** a prepared list of questions asked of a subject (or respondent) in a face-to-face encounter.

**questionnaire:** a written list of questions filled out or answered in writing by a respondent as a data-gathering technique in social research.

a subject in a face-to-face encounter, either remembering the answers or recording them in some way (see Figure 19.2). A questionnaire is also a prepared list of questions, but it is ad-

**FIGURE 19.2   Survey conducted through interviews by National Opinion Research Center**

```
                    -2-                      BEGIN DECK 01

We are faced with many problems in this country, none of which can be solved
easily or inexpensively.  I'm going to name some of these problems, and for each
one I'd like you to tell me whether you think we're spending too much money on it,
too little money, or about the right amount.  First (READ ITEM A) . . . are we
spending too much, too little, or about the right amount on (ITEM)?
READ EACH ITEM; CODE ONE FOR EACH.
```

|   |   | Too much | Too little | About right | Don't know |   |
|---|---|---|---|---|---|---|
| A. | Space exploration program | 3 | 1 | 2 | 8 | 06/9 |
| B. | Improving and protecting the environment | 3 | 1 | 2 | 8 | 07/9 |
| C. | Improving and protecting the nation's health | 3 | 1 | 2 | 8 | 08/9 |
| D. | Solving the problems of the big cities | 3 | 1 | 2 | 8 | 09/9 |
| E. | Halting the rising crime rate | 3 | 1 | 2 | 8 | 10/9 |
| F. | Dealing with drug addiction | 3 | 1 | 2 | 8 | 11/9 |
| G. | Improving the nation's education system | 3 | 1 | 2 | 8 | 12/9 |
| H. | Improving the conditions of Blacks | 3 | 1 | 2 | 8 | 13/9 |
| I. | The military, armaments and defense | 3 | 1 | 2 | 8 | 14/9 |
| J. | Foreign aid | 3 | 1 | 2 | 8 | 15/9 |
| K. | Welfare | 3 | 1 | 2 | 8 | 16/9 |

**FIGURE 19.3   Self-administered survey conducted by a U.S. Congressman**

**CONGRESSMAN TIM HALL'S 1976 QUESTIONNAIRE**

|  | CONSTITUENT 1 YES NO | CONSTITUENT 2 YES NO |
|---|---|---|
| **THE ECONOMY** | | |
| 1. Do you consider unemployment a more serious economic problem than inflation? | ☐ ☐ | ☐ ☐ |
| 2. Do you support Congressional efforts to reduce unemployment by providing public service jobs? | ☐ ☐ | ☐ ☐ |
| 3. Should revenue sharing, a program which returns some $6 billion a year in federal taxes back to local and state government, be continued? | ☐ ☐ | ☐ ☐ |
| 4. Do you support my efforts to increase the federal estate tax exemption from $60,000 to $200,000 in order to assist family farms and small business owners? | ☐ ☐ | ☐ ☐ |
| 5. During the past year, has your family's standard of living . . . improved? | ☐ | ☐ |
|    remained about the same? | ☐ | ☐ |
|    declined? | ☐ | ☐ |
| **FOREIGN POLICY** | | |
| 6. Do you generally agree with the foreign policy being conducted by President Ford and Secretary Kissinger? | ☐ ☐ | ☐ ☐ |
| 7. Do you think the U.S. should restore economic relations with Cuba? | ☐ ☐ | ☐ ☐ |
| 8. Should the U.S. renegotiate our treaty with Panama? | ☐ ☐ | ☐ ☐ |
| 9. Do you favor the resumption of military aid to Turkey? | ☐ ☐ | ☐ ☐ |
| 10. Do you favor a larger Congressional role in foreign policy? | ☐ ☐ | ☐ ☐ |
| **ENERGY AND ENVIRONMENT** | | |
| 11. Which of the following action or actions do you favor to help reduce U.S. dependence on foreign oil? | | |
|    a) do you favor the construction of nuclear power plants? | ☐ ☐ | ☐ ☐ |
|    b) do you support additional federal research in solar energy? | ☐ ☐ | ☐ ☐ |
|    c) do you support deregulation of oil and gas prices? | ☐ ☐ | ☐ ☐ |
| 12. Do you think the criticism leveled at the major oil companies has been justified? | ☐ ☐ | ☐ ☐ |
| 13. Do you favor the break-up of the major oil companies? | ☐ ☐ | ☐ ☐ |
| **CRIME** | | |
| 14. Should persons convicted of crimes involving firearms receive mandatory prison sentences? | ☐ ☐ | ☐ ☐ |
| 15. Do you support the reimposition of the death penalty for certain crimes? | ☐ ☐ | ☐ ☐ |
| 16. Do you favor the decriminalization of the use of marijuana? | ☐ ☐ | ☐ ☐ |
| 17. Do you favor the banning of cheap, small firearms, commonly called Saturday night specials? | ☐ ☐ | ☐ ☐ |
| **MISCELLANEOUS** | | |
| 18. Do you support my efforts to keep the Postal Service from closing small rural post offices? | ☐ ☐ | ☐ ☐ |
| 19. Do you support subsidizing the Postal Service from additional money from the general treasury? | ☐ ☐ | ☐ ☐ |
| 20. Which of the following actions do you support in order to maintain the soundness of the social security system? | | |
|    a) increase social security taxes | ☐ ☐ | ☐ ☐ |
|    b) provide funds from the general treasury | ☐ ☐ | ☐ ☐ |
|    c) do not provide cost-of-living benefit increases | ☐ ☐ | ☐ ☐ |
| 21. Do you support a national catastrophic health insurance system to cover extraordinary medical expenses? | ☐ ☐ | ☐ ☐ |
| 22. Do you favor a Constitutional amendment restricting the Supreme Court's ruling on abortion? | ☐ ☐ | ☐ ☐ |
| 23. Do you approve of a federal/state grain inspection system in order to eliminate present abuses and fraud? | ☐ ☐ | ☐ ☐ |

Other comments _____

(please print)   NAME _____ ADDRESS _____ CITY _____ ZIP _____

FIGURE 19.4  Bullough's hopelessness scale

1. Sometimes I feel that life is not worth living.
2. It is possible to get ahead if a person tries hard enough.
3. I have always been optimistic about my own future.
4. I think that education pays off in the long run.
5. I feel hopeful.
6. I do not think I will ever really be successful.
7. In spite of what some people say, the lot of the average man is getting worse.
8. It's hardly fair to bring children into the world with the way things look for the future.

strongly agree
agree
uncertain
disagree
strongly disagree

The respondent is asked to pick one of the five possible answers to each question, from strongly agree to strongly disagree. The responses are assigned numbers, five for strongly agree down to one for strongly disagree. Note that not all of the items are in the same direction—some are optimistic, some pessimistic in tone. If a respondent consistently indicated strong agreement with pessimistic items and strong disagreement with optimistic items, we would probably be quite safe in assuming that he truly did have hopeless feelings about life.

ministered by giving the list to the respondents and asking them to fill it out in written form themselves (see Figure 19.3).

Interviews and questionnaires often contain **attitude scales.** An attitude scale is a list of statements with several possible responses to each. Respondents are asked to reply by checking the answer that most closely indicates the strength of their agreement or disagreement with the statements. A good example of an attitude scale is the one Bullough used in her study of health care behavior to measure feelings of hopelessness (see Figure 19.4).

Attitude scaling offers several advantages. First, researchers have learned that many people are more willing and better able to respond to a particular subject if it is presented to them in several specific statements than if they are asked one general question. The attitude scale breaks a complicated question into several definite parts. Another obvious advantage is that the researcher can assign numbers to different levels of intensity of attitudes. Using these numbers, the researcher can estimate the intensity of a given attitude held by a particular per-

son in comparison to others who have responded to the same statements. Even though the numbers are not exact representations, they nonetheless facilitate the task of estimating the strength or weakness of a respondent's attitude.

### Secondary Sources

Social researchers often get information from **secondary sources of data.** These bodies of information amassed by other people are often extremely important to sociologists. The United States Bureau of the Census, for instance, gathers quantities of information that may constitute part or all of the data used in a social research project. Many other federal agencies, such as the Bureau of Labor Statistics, the National Center for Health Statistics, and the Federal Bureau of Investigation, gather and publish various kinds of valuable reports. The list of official sources may be extended to include the publications of numerous agencies of the United Nations, state and local agencies within the United States, and national agencies throughout the world. Many social research questions can be answered more easily by drawing on the resources of a library than by undertaking special field research.

## PROBLEMS IN SOCIAL RESEARCH

We have noted in passing certain kinds of problems faced by sociologists as they engage in research work. Three fundamental problems, validity, reliability, and representativeness concern the nature of knowledge itself and thus span all methods of gathering information.

### Validity and Reliability

Simply stated, **validity** is a matter of truth; **reliability** is a matter of consistency. For example, if a measurement technique produces data that truly represent the thing being studied, it is valid; and if the technique gives consistent findings in different studies, it is reliable. In general, it is simpler to show that a measurement technique is reliable than to show it is valid; but both problems require the researcher's careful attention.

To illustrate, let us refer again to the hopelessness scale used by Bullough. Tests of the validity of this attitude measure might include an inspection of the content of the statements **(face validity)** and comparisons of a person's hopelessness score with some related item of behavior **(criterion validity),** such as enrolling in college to work toward a degree.

The attempt to establish face validity is really a commonsense procedure. A statement such as "I have always been optimistic about my own future" appears to most people, "on its face," to refer to how hopeful a person feels. But a person who feels hopeful, we may reason, then should engage in some behavior that reflects that feeling. Such a person might, for example, show great enthusiasm for work and undertake various projects that can only be completed after a long and sustained effort. Consequently, if most of those who appear to feel hopeless on the basis of their agreement with the hopelessness statements act in ways that are consistent with their stated feelings, then we have some evidence—criterion validity—beyond face validity that the answers given are true and refer to real differences in the respondents' attitudes.

Similar reasoning is involved in discussions of reliability. Consider a situation in which many of those who feel comparatively hopeless, as judged by their answers to seven of the eight items in a scale, give answers to the eighth item indicating feelings of hope. This contradiction may lead us to reject the eighth item as unreliable. Or we might measure feelings of hopelessness in a particular group at one time and then repeat the measurement at a later time to see whether the results are similar. If they are not and if there is no compelling reason to believe an actual change has occurred in the attitudes of the study participants, then we might dismiss the scale as unreliable.

*Representativeness*

The problem of **representativeness** is a matter of *typicality*. To continue with the example of Bullough's health care survey, remember that she did not interview all of the mothers in Los Angeles who reasonably could have been included in her study. She interviewed only some of these mothers. Therefore, the validity and reliability of her study rest also on the extent to which the selected samples stand for or represent the total population from which they were drawn. If the samples are in fact represen-

**attitude scale:** a device used in questionnaires and interviews to measure the degree to which a respondent holds a given attitude toward something. Such scales commonly state an attitude or preference, such as "I think we ought to bomb Sardonia back to the Stone Age," and then ask the respondent to indicate the degree to which he or she agrees or disagrees with the stated opinion.

**secondary sources of data:** data banks or archives of information originally gathered for other purposes which may be utilized for social research, e.g., a census, vital statistics, arrest records, and so on.

**validity:** a quality attributed to propositions or measures to the degree to which they conform to established knowledge or truth. An attitude scale is considered valid, for example, to the degree to which its results conform to other measures of possession of the attitude.

**reliability:** a quality attributed to propositions or measures to the degree to which they produce consistent results. An attitude scale is considered reliable, for example, to the degree to which the same respondents, or very similar respondents, receive the same or very similar scores upon repeated testing.

**face validity:** an essentially commonsense test of validity; the assertion that it "makes sense" to believe that a given measure is valid for some reason.

**criterion validity:** the establishment of validity of a measure by checking its results against those of another measure of the same phenomenon.

**representativeness:** a quality attributed to sample data when they are typical of the larger population from which they are drawn.

tative, then whatever is true for them is true also for the larger population. If the data are unrepresentative, that is, atypical, then all we can know is what is true for these particular samples.

The main method social researchers use to obtain representative samples is the **probability sample,** a sample drawn so that each individual or unit in a population has an equal chance to be included. The most widely known and used (but frequently misunderstood) type of probability sample is the **random sample.** News sources commonly report the results of small surveys of a supposedly random sample of people. In the vast majority of such surveys, the reporters either select as participants people presumed to have some knowledge of the news event in question, or they stand on a street corner and question whoever walks by. Usually, of course, reporters try to interview a cross section of the population—they question men as well as women, old people as well as young, upper-class as well as lower-class people.

But samples of those with special knowledge, those who happen to be walking by, or those who in commonsense terms seem to represent a cross section of the population, are not random samples. A sidewalk sample selected by chance by our hypothetical reporter might well be chosen without deliberate bias, yet it might still be totally unrepresentative of the community as a whole.

To draw a random sample or some other probability sample one must (1) define exactly which people constitute the population to be sampled—for instance, all of the people listed in a particular city directory; and (2) select people for inclusion in the sample by a procedure that gives each person an equal or known chance to be included. One way to approximate the condition that every person in the list will have an equal opportunity to be selected is (1) to number in order the names in the list, (2) to decide how large the final sample is to be, and (3) to use a table of random numbers or some other mechanical procedure to select the desired number of individuals. The third step ideally eliminates the researcher's preferences or biases. Obviously most samples that are selected are "convenience" samples, rather than random or other probability samples. To achieve simple randomness is not always a simple matter.

But even if a sample is random, what assurance have we that it is also representative? Would it not be possible to draw a random sample that *by chance* gives a disproportionately heavy weighting to a particular viewpoint? The answer is "yes." But, happily, the *probability* of drawing an unrepresentative sample by random means is known and, therefore, can act as a guide to the researcher's effort to deter-

If a sample is not representative, erroneous conclusions may be drawn.

mine what the results mean. The chance is comparatively small that one will randomly draw a highly unrepresentative sample.

## DATA ANALYSIS

We now turn to what one does with social research information after it has been collected. In many studies, the researcher plans much of this phase before preparing questionnaires or other data-gathering devices and before selecting a sample and spending time, energy, and money to get in touch with each person in the sample. Once the data have been gathered, many different techniques of analysis may be used. Some of the most useful are very simple and easily learned.

## Frequency Counts

Suppose a researcher wants to know, "How many people favor or oppose elective abortion?" and has gathered some data on a small sample of people. Suppose also that a person who is most favorable toward elective abortion is given a score of 5, while one who is least favorable is given a score of 0. All those who are in between, of course, are scored 1, 2, 3, or 4, depending on how favorable they are. Now, all that is necessary to answer the question is to count the number of times each score was received. A convenient way to do this is to write down the six score numbers (0-5) and place tally marks beside them while going through the data. The total number of tally marks beside each score number is the **frequency count.** As we shall see, this simple procedure (which you probably already know) is an extremely useful tool of sociological analysis.

**Grouping the Data** We seldom are satisfied simply to know whether a number of people hold a particular opinion. We usually wish to relate the opinion under study to certain other facts about the people in the sample. For instance, we may wonder, "Do men and women agree concerning elective abortion?" To answer this question we would examine the results of the study, noting each person's sex and opinion score. These two characteristics may be represented by a single tally mark in one "cell" (See Table 19.1). If a woman has an opinion score of 3, we put one tally mark in cell

**probability sample:** a sample drawn in such a way that every unit in the population being sampled has the same statistical chance (probability) of being selected for inclusion.

**random sample:** a probability sample that insures each member of the population sampled an equal chance of being drawn through some essentially mechanical procedure: blind drawing, use of a table of random numbers, and so on. The random sample is the simplest and most common form of probability sample.

**frequency count:** a tabulation of the frequency with which an event or phenomenon appears.

**cross-tabulation:** the procedure of counting cases possessing one characteristic which also possess another, and representing them with a single tally, for example, the number of males in your Soc class who also got an "A" on the first quiz.

b; a man with a score of 2 gets a mark in cell c. This procedure, called **cross-tabulation,** is continued until each person's score has been examined.

We are now almost ready to decide whether men and women agree on elective abortion. Only two small steps remain. First, we count the tally marks in the cells of our table. Second, we express the resulting frequency counts as percents. If roughly the same percent of men and women are found in cells a and b (that is, are favorable), then the sexes agree on elective abortion. If there is a substantially higher (or lower) percent of the men in cell a than women in cell b, they disagree. In this case we may state the result by saying that there *is* an association, or **correlation,** between people's sex and their opinions of elective abortion. That is, the two things are related in some way.

These same methods can be used to expand the analysis. For instance, suppose we find that women are more favorable toward elective abortion than men. Suppose, too, that we are uncertain about this finding. Could it be that the women in our sample are on average younger than the men and that younger people are more favorable toward elective abortion? If

TABLE 19.1    Men and Women's Options about Elective Abortion

| Opinion | Men | Women |
|---|---|---|
| Favorable (3, 4, 5) | a | b |
| Unfavorable (0, 1, 2) | c | d |

so, our findings may reflect the fact that the men and women in our sample differ in age. To test this idea, we need only to construct two tables similar to Table 19.1—one for the men and one for the women. In each of these tables, we would cross-tabulate each person's age and opinion score. If there is no difference between the opinions of older and younger people, then we may assume age has little to do with opinions on elective abortion.

These examples show you how to use simple techniques to continue an analysis from one question to another and thereby test a tentative conclusion. Of course, many methods of analyzing data are far more complex than those described but the basic ideas are similar to those outlined here.

### Unstructured Data and Content Analysis

Some information easily lends itself to counting and tabulation, but some researchers do not use highly structured interview or questionnaire forms. They prefer to talk to people about problems and record the conversations in shorthand, in note form, or afterward from memory. Sometimes a researcher requests permission to tape-record an entire conversation and then transcribe the tape for analysis.

These approaches have the obvious advantage of providing a more complete record than the standard interview or questionnaire. They also may create a greater sense of freedom and congeniality between the researcher and the study participants and thus lead to richer and perhaps more candid study results. The disadvantages of these approaches include longer and more expensive interviews, problems in gathering strictly comparable information from each study participant, and the sheer volume of the information accumulated.

In any event, the processes of analysis described above can be adapted to analyze the content of **unstructured data.** For example, we may examine the notes or tape recordings for each participant to determine whether certain traits or characteristics are present or absent. Perhaps we are interested in whether people are concerned about the industrial pollution of a particular lake and we have asked them to tell about some of the main problems of their community. If a person spontaneously mentions as a problem the fact that the Scrappo Corporation

is dumping wastes into Lake Lovely, then we may tabulate this point. If a large number of people mention the same problem, we may attempt to decide which of the study participants feel strongly about this issue. Or we may wish to determine which participants are in favor of the existing practices and which oppose it. In this way, we may develop tabulations and cross-tabulations by analyzing the content of the data.

**Content analysis** may also be applied to written materials, especially published materials.[14] The themes of popular novels, science fiction, and comic strips have all been subjected to content analysis by sociologists to determine what "messages" they carry in addition to their apparent content. One analysis found that the "Little Orphan Annie" comic strip had a bias against the poor and the nonwhite, reflected principally in the negative ways in which such people were portrayed.[15] According to another study, much science fiction has a promilitary, proaction, antiintellectual bias.[16]

## INTERPRETATION

We have already mentioned certain problems relating to the interpretation of the results of a social study. We noted the importance of considering more than a single explanation of any correlation that may be discovered and of determining, or at least assessing plausibly, the sequence in which different factors affect one another. We have also implied that an interpretation may confirm or question the validity of some information and thus determine whether a conclusion is supported or overthrown. And we have touched upon the problem of estimating whether the findings of a particular study apply to the larger population that is assumed to be represented by the sample chosen for study. We now amplify these points through a brief consideration of some common errors of interpretation.

### Connections and Causes

We have seen that the idea of a connection or correlation between events is basic to any analysis that tries to explain why or how things happen the way they do. But we must guard against the easy assumption that a correlation means that one of the factors is a *cause* of the other. To prove that a correlation represents a cause-and-effect relation, certain minimum standards must be met. For example, it is generally held that the cause must appear before the effect. If a window is suddenly shattered, we try to find the cause in events that occurred before the window was broken. Similarly, if riots occur in a city, we search for causes in the events preceding the outburst. Mistakes made in the time ordering of events may result in errors of interpretation.

Suppose you are unfamiliar with the United States, and you noticed that divorces are granted very frequently to persons who recently have moved to the state of Nevada. You might conclude that moving to Nevada is a cause of marital discord and divorce. Anyone familiar with this situation would be able to explain that this correlation arises because many people who wish to divorce move to Nevada (at least temporarily) to take advantage of that state's lenient divorce laws. In this case, we would dismiss the conclusion that moving to Nevada causes divorces because it confuses the independent and dependent variables—the cause and the effect. Clearly, in this instance we cannot correctly interpret the correlation until we discover the true time sequence.

Once the time sequence between correlated factors has been established, we still may wonder whether the earlier factor has any causal significance for the later one. For instance, roosters crow and *then* the sun rises; the leaves begin to fall and *then* winter comes. In order to show that an earlier factor is genuinely connected to a later factor, we must construct an explanation of the connection that outlines in detail how the first factor gives rise to the second. We would not, for example, be able to construct a satisfactory explanation to show that the crowing of the roosters causes the sun to rise. We would not be able to show how the crowing leads to the sun's rising, and we *would* be able to show that the sun rises whether or not the roosters crow.

It is easy to see in the examples just given that the first event probably is not causally connected to the second. But in most of the questions of interest to sociologists, the matter is much more complicated. Does marital instability lead to juvenile delinquency? Does an influx of black people lead to increased racial tension?

**correlation:** a numerical expression of the degree of association between two variables; specifically, the degree to which variation in one is associated with variation in the other. Correlation is expressed as varying between +1.00 and −1.00 and may be either positive (direct) or negative (inverse). For example, in almost any human population, there will be a positive, or direct, correlation between measured height and weight; as one goes up, so will the other.

**unstructured data:** social research data not preorganized by questionnaires, interview schedules, frequency counts, and so on. Examples might include unguided conversations, diaries, records originally kept for one purpose but now checked for another, and so on.

**content analysis:** the procedure for structuring or organizing unstructured data by identifying and counting themes, classifying content, and so on.

Do economic depressions lead to increased alcoholism? The complex issues raised by such questions require the sociologist to exercise

Does visiting Nevada cause divorce?

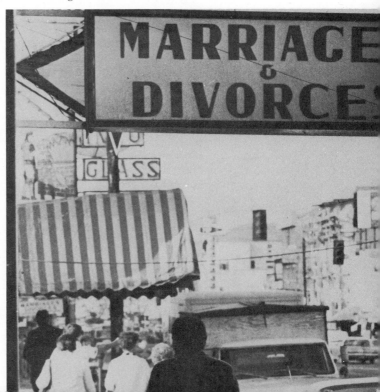

great caution in interpreting correlations, even when the time sequence has been reasonably well established.[17]

## Types of Group Differences

Another error of interpretation arises because people do not recognize the base of comparison on which a generalization rests. Consider the following statement: "Working-class people contract tuberculosis more frequently than do middle-class people." When confronted by such a generalization, we must wonder not only "Is it true?" but also "If it is true, in what sense is it true?" Suppose we assume the statement means nearly all working-class people contract tuberculosis and almost no middle-class people do. This is an extreme interpretation, to be sure, but it does not contradict the generalization. Another, more plausible, interpretation might be that although tuberculosis is no longer a common disease, it occurs somewhat more frequently among the working class than the middle class.

Obviously, interpretation would be easier if the generalization had been more specific in the first place. Regrettably, we are frequently faced with such unspecific generalizations and are left to wonder whether they rest on one type of group comparison (such as very large versus very small) or some other type (such as small versus smaller).

Some generalizations involve another type of group differences, *overlapping distributions*. An example is: "Women are shorter than men." In this case, we immediately recognize that the generalization refers to averages, not to all women and all men. We know that in large populations, many women will be taller than the average man and many men will be shorter than the average woman. But many other kinds of group differences are not so easily understood, especially if the comparisons involve a possible implication of group superiority or inferiority. For example, such qualities as intelligence and honesty are of this form, but people sometimes do not interpret them in this way. Whether you are interpreting the findings of others concerning group differences or are presenting conclusions of your own, it is crucial to determine the type of group differences involved.

## Lying with Statistics

One final problem of interpretation is that statistical presentations may inadvertently (if not deliberately) create false impressions. This is presumably what prompted Disraeli's famous statement, "There are three kinds of lies: lies, damned lies, and statistics." No doubt you are already familiar with many questionable statistical techniques used by advertisers, political campaign managers, newspapers, and others who wish to persuade. For example, claims about percentage increases may be made in which no basis for comparison is given: "Our product cleans 18 percent faster"; or "Save 30 percent!" Reference may be made to a "government report" or a study by "an independent laboratory" that "proves" that Perfumo is superior to all other deodorants tested. But what if the report actually says that although there were small differences among the products, none of them were really effective?

These and many other abuses of statistical data have been discussed in an instructive and entertaining book by Darrell Huff entitled *How to Lie with Statistics*.[18] Huff explains how newspapers may create the impression that there is a crime wave, how samples may be selected with particular biases, how graphs may be constructed to emphasize or deemphasize certain trends, how irrelevant information may be presented as if it were relevant, and so on.

Scholars, of course, are trained to avoid presenting their findings in ways that intentionally invite misinterpretations, especially misinterpretations that are favorable to the argument they support. They are trained instead to interpret their findings with as little bias as is humanly possible. Nevertheless, even accurate and conscientious displays of numbers may be misinterpreted. A good example of this point is what Huff refers to as "The Well-Chosen Average."

Everyone is familiar with some concept of an average. Frequent references are made to the "average person" or the "average family." Yet it is not always clear what is meant by such references. We may safely assume that most of the time people have in mind the average that results when a series of numbers is added and the resulting sum is then divided by the total number of units in the series. This kind of average is called the **arithmetic mean** or, simply, the mean.

Suppose we wish to know the average income of families in the United States. The mean may be calculated by listing all of the pertinent incomes and dividing by the number of incomes. Now in a real sense no statistical "lie" has been told in this instance; but the resulting calculation, though perfectly correct, would include a number of extremely high incomes that would cause the average to be much higher than most of us might expect. To understand how extreme numbers, either high or low, may seem to exaggerate an arithmetic mean, consider the following simple example: (1) add the numbers 8, 8, 10, 14, and 40; (2) divide the resulting sum of 80 by 5; (3) notice that the average of 16 is larger than four of the five numbers on which it is based. In this way an arithmetic mean of incomes, though absolutely correct, may create the impression that more people earn the average amount than actually is the case.

A different kind of average, the **median,** is

**arithmetic mean:** the common "average." Arithmetically, the sum resulting when a series of numbers are summed and then divided by the total number of units in the series. Sometimes called simply "the mean." The mode and median are also averages of different kinds.

**median:** the value in a distribution that represents the midpoint in the number of units in the arrayed distribution; the value that divides the distribution in half in terms of its size; a form of average.

more serviceable in this particular respect. The median is the number that divides a series of numbers into two equal parts; half the numbers lie above the median and half below it. In our simple example above, the number 10 is the median because two numbers lie above it and two lie below it. Notice that the number 10, though no more "correct" an "average" than the number 16, may, for the purpose of assess-

---

## HOW TO LIE WITH STATISTICS

In the summer of 1976 a large American oil company published widely an advertisement illustrated by two pies. The uncut one was labeled *a monopoly,* and the other, cut into many pieces of various sizes, was labeled *not a monopoly.* The advertisement was a response to proposed federal legislation intended to prevent control by any single firm over the entire petroleum production process, from oil well to gasoline pump. This kind of control is common in the industry today.

The thrust of the ad was, "We're not a monopoly." Why not? Because, the reader was told, more than sixteen thousand companies in fact share a piece of the pie, and that could not be monopolistic.

But did the ad in fact tell us everything we need to know in order to understand the situation? Probably not. First, it referred only to U.S. oil companies. That leaves out of consideration several of the largest companies in the world, which do a large amount of business here but are owned elsewhere. Then it claimed that "not one *American* oil company accounts

for more than 8½ percent of the oil *produced in this country"* (italics added) and concluded that no monopoly was possible. What about all the oil produced abroad but owned by these same firms? The volume that accounts for is a significant share of all of the oil consumed in the United States in 1976.

Finally, the ad leads us to believe that it is depicting more than sixteen thousand separate, independent firms. Is that true? Or are some of them, in fact, owned and controlled by others while being depicted as independent? We cannot answer that question from anything in the ad, and it might prove extremely difficult to answer at all. (It is sometimes a problem to both the Federal Trade Commission and the Internal Revenue Service as well.) We do, however, have one clue. Turn over any gasoline company credit card and see what other companies also honor the card. Some such arrangements are undoubtedly genuine trade-offs of service between independent firms for the sake of customer convenience. But are they all?

ing incomes, be more nearly representative of the series of numbers than the mean.

A third type of average refers to whatever is most frequent, common, or typical. A person might say in regard to incomes that "the average person earns less than $10,000 per year." Even if the mean and the median are above $10,000, the income that occurs most frequently—and therefore the one that many people consider the average—may be lower than $10,000. The num-

ber that occurs most frequently in a series is called the *mode*. In the example above, the number 8 is the mode, because it occurs twice and the other numbers occur only once each.

Thus a person may select the mean, the median, or the mode—each a correct average—to represent a series of numbers. Which of these averages is to be preferred depends upon the researcher's purposes. Anybody who wishes to interpret the findings correctly must be aware of the different emphases implied by these averages. Although the statistics may not lie, the interpreter may convert them into lies by reading into them a meaning that is unwarranted. In order to overcome this problem, researchers will often report more than one of the averages discussed here.

### Implications for Theory

Suppose that a research project has moved through all the stages of research outlined in this chapter, that the results of the study have been carefully examined for errors of interpretation, and that the researcher has decided whether, or to what extent, the initial study hypothesis was correct. For many practical purposes, the researcher's job is done; but in the ideal sequence which we have referred to, one last and very important step in the process of interpretation remains. On the assumption that the study's hypothesis was derived from theory, the researcher now must consider how the results "feed back" onto, and affect, the parent theory. In this way, specific study results help the sociologist evaluate, sharpen, or reformulate existing theory. The theory then may be of greater service to those who wish to generate new hypotheses to guide subsequent studies. The entire sequence of stages we have discussed is outlined in Figure 19.5.

### SCIENTIFIC METHOD IN SOCIOLOGY

Earlier we noted that most sociologists think of themselves as scientists but that this apparent consensus masks numerous important differences concerning the nature of scientific sociology. Many of the lines of division here have been described in Chapter 2: functionalists versus conflict theorists versus symbolic interac-

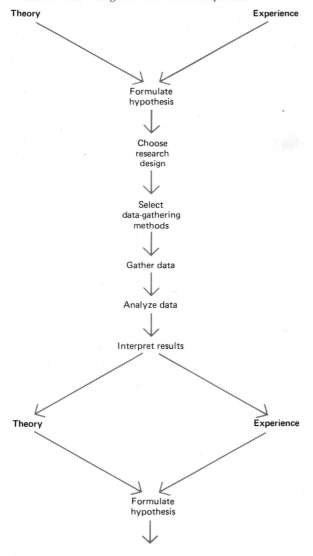

FIGURE 19.5    Stages in the research process

tionists versus ethnomethodologists versus radical theorists, and so on. These divisions are so broad and complex that any effort to simplify them must necessarily gloss over various points that many sociologists consider paramount. At a very general level, however, we may discern one line of division that seems to encompass many smaller ones. Although most sociologists cannot easily be labeled or categorized, there are some significant, if blurred, distinctions between objectivists and subjectivists.

*Objectivists* stress the importance of an "outside" view of the social world. They doubt that the participants in a social setting are likely to possess an objective understanding of why things are as they are. Only the scientist, viewing the situation in a neutral, factual, and, if possible, quantitative way, can explain what is going on. Sociologists who lean toward this view tend to think of sociology as a science resembling physics or chemistry. Social reality exists "out there," waiting to be discovered by the scientist. Objectivists prefer tightly designed research focusing on sharply defined and precisely measured variables. Survey research, social experiments, and secondary analyses of census data are among their favorite research designs and methods. Accurate prediction is generally considered the primary goal of research, and Durkheim's insistence on the reality of social facts is an important point of departure.

*Subjectivists,* in contrast, stress an "inside view" of the social world. Sociologists who prefer this view usually believe that social science cannot, and should not attempt to, copy the thinking and methods of the physical sciences. They believe that researchers must learn to take the role of the other—to approach as nearly as possible in imagination the act of "getting inside the skin" of the person being studied. Variations in people's perceptions and social definitions of reality are of the utmost importance. The outsider, from this perspective, can never fully grasp the meaning or significance of a social situation. Subjectivists prefer research reports that are qualitative and rich in detail, giving the reader the "feel" of the social groups and situations under study. The symbolic side of social life is thought to be of the highest importance. Case studies and observation are among their favorite research designs and

methods. Understanding *(verstehen)* is generally cited as the primary goal of research, and Weber's emphasis on the significance of social definitions is applauded.

To repeat, a majority of sociologists trace their intellectual heritage in some respects to *both* of these great schools of thought. There is nevertheless a genuine tension between the two positions—a tension that has a powerful effect on the way different sociologists think of social scientific endeavor and on the kinds of research methods they choose.

## ETHICS IN SOCIAL RESEARCH

Throughout this chapter, we have observed the importance of ethical considerations in social research. So far, however, we have been content to refer to these problems in a rather general way. Now we must describe briefly two highly publicized studies that brought into sharp focus the conflict between the social scientist's right to pursue knowledge freely and other people's rights to privacy and protection against deception. The first study was a study of jury deliberations. The second was a study of impersonal homosexual acts in public restrooms.

The Wichita Jury Study was a part of an extensive set of projects conducted by faculty members of the University of Chicago School of Law.[19] The study included questionnaires given to state and federal judges, a survey comparing the attitudes of persons who had and had not served on juries, interviews with people who had just served on juries, and observations of jury trials. None of these methods created any unusual ethical problems. However, with the guarded consent of a federal appeals judge, a number of secret tape recordings were made of the proceedings of the juries in six civil cases.

The secret bugging of the jury room was revealed over one year later at a judicial conference, sparking a controversy that led rapidly to hearings before the United States Senate's Internal Security Subcommittee and to the passage of a federal law prohibiting such recordings under any circumstances.

Although the responses of the federal government focused mainly on the question of the regulation of social research, the ethical issue—unrestricted scientific inquiry versus the privacy and sanctity of jury deliberations—has continued to attract interest and discussion. The defenders of the secret recordings insisted there was no intention to undermine or discredit the jury system. They said, rather, that the knowledge gained about what actually goes on in jury rooms—as opposed to what people claim after the fact—could be used to strengthen this pillar of the American judicial system. Any effective reform of the system, indeed, will require accurate information of this type.

Critics of the Wichita Jury Study argue that nothing, including the need for scientific knowledge, can justify the breach of confidence permitted in this study. Just because scientists think gaining knowledge is the most important thing does not mean the society must accept this view in all cases. This episode reveals that there are competing values in society (as in the DNA controversy) and that no one value perspective has an unchallengable claim to superiority.

The second study, conducted by Laud Humphreys, was based primarily on direct observations of homosexual acts between men in public restrooms (called "tearooms") and on interviews with a sample of the participants in these acts.[20] Since men who engage in impersonal sex in tearooms are afraid of being caught and are very suspicious of other people who are present, a lookout frequently is posted. The "watch queen" is expected to signal if a police car or a stranger approaches.

Humphreys learned the "watch queen" role and thus was able to observe hundreds of homosexual encounters. He also became acquainted with some of the participants and was able to obtain extensive interviews with them.

But the study had a second part that took place over a year after the observation phase, and this is the part that has aroused the most controversy. Although Humphreys was keenly aware of his ethical responsibility to the men he had studied, he traced some of them to their homes, disguised himself, and interviewed them in the privacy of their homes. His "cover" was that he was conducting a social health survey (which he was). In this way, he interviewed fifty of the tearoom participants without their knowing he had observed their illegal sexual acts; and he did so under conditions that might

---

**FIGURE 19.6  Some Ethical Rules for Sociologists**

The sociologist must—
1. maintain scientific objectivity
2. decline research beyond his or her competence
3. respect the research subject's rights to privacy and dignity
4. avoid causing personal harm to research subjects
5. protect the confidentiality of information as far as legally possible.
6. present research findings honestly and without distortion
7. use his or her role only to obtain information for professional purposes
8. acknowledge the assistance of all persons who collaborate in research
9. report fully all sources of financial support
10. dissociate himself or herself from research that is likely to violate the above principles

---

have revealed this fact to other members of their families.

Nicholas von Hoffman objected that Humphreys had "collected information that could be used for blackmail, extortion, and the worst kind of mischief without the knowledge of the people involved." He went on to say that Humphreys' claim to have had pure motives is no different from the claims of FBI agents who justify wiretapping as being in a good cause. He concluded that no information is so valuable that it should be obtained "by nipping away at personal liberty. . . ."[21]

The issues of method and ethics raised by Humphreys' research are still with us; and, for the most part, we still rely mainly on the integrity and professional discipline of researchers as the first line of defense. Nevertheless, two important responses to the ethical issue may be mentioned.

First, in 1975 the federal government established a commission to oversee all research having to do with human subjects. To help assure the protection of all human beings under study, the commission has published guidelines to regulate research. In response to these guidelines, universities have appointed committees on the use of human subjects. All research proposals using humans as research subjects must be referred to these committees for approval before the research may be conducted.

In addition, the American Sociological Association (like other professional associations) has created its own code of professional ethics and its own committee to review sociological research. The code of ethics tells investigators how they must conduct their research in order to safeguard the rights of subjects.[22] The committee acts as a referee for questions concerning ethical practices.

It is not yet possible to say whether these steps have gone far enough in balancing the claims of scientific investigation and the rights of others. Some professional observers believe that they have gone too far. In any event, there clearly are no easy answers in this matter. Both sets of values are strongly embedded in American history and civilization; and both are essential to the maintenance and strengthening of American institutions.

## SUMMARY

Although it is seldom possible to define and measure social properties (for example, social cohesion) as precisely as physical properties (for example, length or width), it is nevertheless useful to think about social properties as if they were subject to exact treatment. Sociologists may view complex social phenomena as if they consisted of different variables or forces acting on and interacting with one another, even though the measurement of these variables may be nothing more than noting whether a characteristic is present or absent. By working with the intellectual tools of the laboratory scientist (even without their direct control of the factors entering the study situation), social researchers may discover correlations and attempt to unravel the criss-crossing patterns of cause and effect in the complex world of human social activities.

To be useful, the process of defining and measuring variables must have some direction; it must focus on certain aspects of social reality and ignore others. Although a research focus may originate in a number of ways, the approach approved by most sociologists is to derive guiding hypotheses from existing theories. Ideally this approach assists individual researchers to build on the work of others and to contribute to the accumulation of related discoveries. A theoretically relevant focus helps the researcher plan a given piece of research and anticipate more clearly the problems to be faced in its later stages. The intellectual discipline imposed on the researcher by the scientific point of view is vital to the attempt to gain valid knowledge about human problems. Whether the sociologist is an objectivist or a subjectivist, the broad rules of scientific proof are of value. We have stressed, however, that the different assumptions of sociologists within these two large schools of research lead the objectivists to prefer surveys and social experiments and the use of highly structured interviews and questionnaires, while subjectivists tend to prefer case studies and observational methods. No matter how the data are collected, a convincing, logical case must be made for the validity, reliability, and representativeness of the data if conclusions based on them are to considered sound.

To say that the scientific frame of reference may be useful to social researchers, however, is not to say that their concerns end with such technical matters as research design, data analysis, and interpretation. Social research involves human beings, and, as such, it inevitably involves ethical questions as well. By conducting surveys or observing people's behavior, the researcher may make discoveries that are potentially harmful not only to those studied but to the entire society. And if data are gathered secretly or through deception, both moral and democratic principles may be affronted. These possibilities place a heavy burden on the organized body of social researchers as well as on the individual researcher. Those who undertake these tasks need a keen appreciation of the potentials—for good or evil—of the research process and of the knowledge that may be gained from it.

Sociologists can make no claim that their professional efforts to strike the proper balance in these sensitive matters have been completely successful. But the problems are being confronted, and many safeguards already have been constructed. There is good reason to believe that a cumulative, valid knowledge of human social behavior may be gained without sacrificing other values that are at least as important as the quest for knowledge. If so, then the fruits of social research may well make their own distinctive contribution to the construction of a more democratic society.

## SUGGESTED READINGS

HAMMOND, PHILLIP E., ed. *Sociologists at Work*. New York: Basic, 1964. The standard work on the actual course of the research process. Contains brief descriptions of several important studies, by their authors.

HOLLINGSHEAD, AUGUST B. *Elmtown's Youth*. New York: Wiley, 1949. An engaging account of the way differences in social class placement affect adolescents. Fine illustration of different techniques social researchers may employ in a community study.

HUFF, DARRELL. *How to Lie With Statistics*. New York: Norton, 1954. An excellent, entertaining discussion of the various problems and pitfalls of statistical presentations.

MADGE, JOHN. *The Origins of Scientific Sociology*. New York: Free Press, 1962. Briefly describes twelve important studies that have contributed to the development of the scientific perspective in sociology. Valuable both as an account of scientific development and as an introduction to the substance of some famous sociological research.

WHYTE, WILLIAM F. *Street Corner Society*. Chicago: The University of Chicago Press, 1943. Probably the most famous and generally admired example of participant observation research. Exceptionally well-written account of the lives of the men in a street corner gang.

ZEISEL, HANS. *Say It with Figures*, 4th rev. ed. New York: Harper & Row, 1957. A very clear, readable presentation of the simplest forms of quantitative analysis. It includes an outstanding discussion of cross-tabulation.

# Notes

## CHAPTER 1

1. Frank E. Manuel, *The Prophets of Paris* (New York: Harper Torchbooks, 1965).

## CHAPTER 2

1. These materials are drawn from David McLellan, *Marx before Marxism* (New York: Harper Torchbooks, 1971); and Maximilien Rubel and Margaret Manale, *Marx without Myth* (New York: Harper Torchbooks, 1976).

2. These materials are drawn from Steven Lukes, *Emile Durkheim: His Life and Work* (Baltimore: Penguin Books, 1973); and Geoffrey Hawthron, *Enlightenment and Despair: A History of Sociology* (Cambridge: Cambridge University Press, 1976), pp. 16–36.

3. Hawthron p. 117.

4. Emile Durkheim, *Suicide* (London: Routledge, 1970).

5. These materials are drawn from H. H. Gerth and C. Wright Mills, *From Max Weber: Essays in Sociology* (New York: Oxford University Press, 1958), pp. 3–31.

6. Gerth and Wright, pp. 17–18.

7. See Irving M. Zeitlin, *Rethinking Sociology* (New York: Appleton-Century Crofts 1973), pp. 123–136.

8. For example see Amitai Etzioni, *The Active Society* (New York: Free Press, 1968).

9. See Lewis A. Coser, *The Functions of Social Conflict* (New York: Free Press, 1956); and *Continuities in the Study of Social Conflicts* (New York: Free Press, 1967).

10. Jonathan H. Turner, *The Structure of Sociological Theory* (Homewood, Ill.: Dorsey Press, 1974), pp. 114–117.

11. The notes for these lectures were collected after Mead's death and published. The best known is *Mind, Self and Society* (Chicago: University of Chicago Press, 1934).

12. See Howard Becker, "Whose Side Are We On?" *Social Problems* 14 (Winter 1967) pp. 239–47.

13. Peter L. Berger and Thomas Luckmann, *The Social Construction of Reality* (Garden City, N.Y.: Anchor Books, 1967).

14. Hans Gerth and C. Wright Mills, *Character and Social Structure* (New York: Harcourt, 1953).

15. New York: Academic Press, Inc., 1974.

16. New York: Oxford University Press, 1959.

17. Charles H. Anderson, *The Political Economy of Social Class* (Englewood Cliffs, N.J.: Prentice Hall, 1974).

18. See, for example, Dusky Lee Smith, "The Sunshine Boys: Toward a Sociology of Happiness." in J. David Colfax and Jack L. Roach (eds.) *Radical Sociology* (New York: Basic Books, Inc., 1971).

19. Jürgen Habermas, *Legitimation Crisis* (Boston: Beacon Press, 1975).

## CHAPTER 3

1. Clifford Geertz, *The Interpretation of Cultures* (New York: Basic Books, 1973), p. 36.

2. Edward B. Tylor, *Primitive Culture* (London: Murry, 1871), p. 1.

3. Clyde Kluckhohn and William Kelly, "The Concept of Culture," in Ralph Linton (ed.), *The Science of Man in the World Crisis* (New York: Columbia University Press, 1945).

4. W. G. Sumner, *Folkways* (New York: New American Library, 1907).

5. O. Michael Watson, *Proxemic Behavior: A Cross-cultural Study* (The Hague: Mouton, 1970).

6. Robin Williams, Jr., *American Society: A Sociological Interpretation* (New York: Knopf, 1960).

7. Carlos Castaneda, *The Teachings of Don Juan: A Yaqui Way of Knowledge* (Berkeley and Los Angeles: University of California Press, 1968); Castaneda, *A Separate Reality: Further Conversations with Don Juan* (New York: Simon and Schuster, 1971); Castaneda, *Journey to Ixlan* (New York: Simon and Schuster, 1972); and Castaneda, *Tales of Power* (New York: Simon and Schuster, 1974).

8. David Bidney, "Cultural Relativism", in David Sills (ed.), *International Encyclopedia of the Social Sciences* (New York: Macmillan and Free Press, 1968), vol. 3, p. 543.

9. Philip L. Newman, *Knowing the Gururumba* (New York: Holt, Rinehart and Winston, 1965), p. 104.

10. Kluckhohn and Kelly, *ibid.*

11. P. Ekman and W. Friesen, "Constants across Cultures in the Face and Emotion," *Journal of Personality and Social Psychology* 17 (February 1971), pp. 124–129.

12. J. Itani, "The Society of Japanese Monkeys," *Japan Quarterly* 8 (October–December 1961), pp. 421–430.

13. Harlan Lane, *The Wild Boy of Aveyron* (Cambridge, Mass.: Harvard University Press, 1976).

14. Geertz, pp. 33–54.

15. Leslie White, with B. Dillingham, *The Concept of Culture* (Minneapolis: Burgess, 1973) p. 1.

16. W. N. Kellogg and L. Kellogg, *The Ape and the Child: A Study of Environmental Influence upon Early Behavior* (New York: McGraw-Hill, 1933).

17. K. J. Hayes and C. Hayes, "Imitation in a Home-Raised Chimpanzee," *Journal of Comparative Physiological Psychology* 45 (October 1952), pp. 450–459.

18. Sarel Eimerl, Irven DeVore, and the Editors of Time-Life Books, *The Primates* (New York: Time-Life Books, 1965).

19. R. A. Gardner and B. J. Gardner, "Teaching Sign Language to a Chimpanzee," *Science* 165 (1969), pp. 664–672.

20. Eugene Linden, *Apes, Men and Language* (New York: Penguin, 1976).

21. David Premack, "The Assessment of Language Competence in the Chimpanzee," in A. Schrier and F. Stollnitz (eds.), *Behavior of Nonhuman Primates* (New York: Academic Press, 1971).

## CHAPTER 4

1. Dennis Coon, *Introduction to Psychology* (New York: West Publishing Company, 1977), p. 432.

2. Nevit Sanford, "Personality" in David L. Sills, ed., *International Encyclopedia of the Social Sciences*, XI (New York: Macmillan and Free Press, 1968), pp. 587–606.

3. Stanley Milgram, *Obedience to Authority* (New York: Harper Row, 1974).

4. Edward Wilson, *Sociobiology, The New Synthesis* (Cambridge, Mass.: Harvard University Press, 1975).

5. Edward Wilson, *On Human Nature* (Cambridge, Mass.: Harvard University Press, 1978).

6. Theodosius Dobzhansky, "Differences Are Not Deficits," *Psychology Today*, December 1973, pp. 96–101.

7. Otto Klineberg, "What Psychological Tests Show," in Bernard J. Stern and Allain Locke (eds.), *When People Meet* (New York: Progressive Education Association, 1942).

8. Arthur Jensen, "How Much Can We Boost I.Q. and Scholastic Achievement?" *Harvard Educational Review* **39** (Winter 1969), pp. 1–123.

9. Eleanor Maccoby and Carol Jacklin, *The Psychology of Sex Differences* (Stanford, Calif.: Stanford University Press, 1974).

10. Margaret Mead, *Sex and Temperament in Three Primitive Societies* (New York: William Morrow, 1935).

11. Carol Tavris and Carole Offir, *The Longest War* (New York: Harcourt Brace Jovanovich, 1977), pp. 93–130.

12. John Money and A. A. Ehrhardt, *Man and Woman, Boy and Girl* (Baltimore: Johns Hopkins Press, 1972).

13. William Sewell, "Infant Training and the Personality of the Child," *American Journal of Sociology* **58** (September 1952), pp. 150–159.

14. B. F. Skinner, *Beyond Freedom and Dignity* (New York: Knopf, 1972), p. 18.

15. The discussion of Mead's three stages is largely taken from Reece McGee, *Points of Departure*, 2d ed. (Hinsdale, Ill.: Dryden Press, 1975).

16. Harry Harlow and M. K. Harlow, "Social Deprivation in Monkeys," *Scientific American*, November 1962, pp. 136–146.

17. Kingsley Davis, "Final Note on a Case of Extreme Isolation," *American Journal of Sociology* **52** (March 1947), pp. 432–437.

18. Albert Bandura, Dorthea Ross, and Sheila Ross, "A Comparative Test of the Status Envy, Social Power, and Secondary Reinforcement Theories of Identificatory Learning," *Journal of Abnormal and Social Psychology* **67** (December 1963), pp. 527–534.

19. Brian Sutton-Smith and B. G. Rosenberg, *The Sibling* (New York: Holt, Rinehart and Winston, 1970).

20. Surgeon General's Scientific Advisory Committee on Television and Social Behavior, *Television and Growing Up: The Impact of Televised Violence*, U.S. Department of Health Education, and Welfare (Washington, D.C.: U.S. Government Printing Office, 1971).

21. Alfred Kinsey, Wardell Pomery and Clyde Martin, *Sexual Behavior in the Human Male* (Philadelphia: Saunders, 1948).

22. William Masters and Virginia Johnson, *Human Sexual Behavior* (Boston: Little, Brown, 1966).

23. This discussion of Goffman's work is drawn primarily from Erving Goffman, *The Presentation of Self In Everyday Life* (Garden City, N.Y.: Doubleday, 1959) and Goffman, *Interaction Ritual* (Garden City, N.Y.: Doubleday, 1967).

24. Erving Goffman, *The Presentation of Self In Everyday Life* (Garden City, N.Y.: Doubleday, 1959), p. 252.

25. Erving Goffman, *Asylums* (Garden City, N.Y.: Doubleday, 1961).

26. Robert Scott, *The Making of Blind Men* (New York: Russell Sage, 1969).

## CHAPTER 5

1. A. H. Maslow, *Motivation and Personality* (New York: Harper Row, 1970).

2. George C. Homans, *Social Behavior* (New York: Harcourt Brace and World, 1961), p. 13.

3. Peter M. Blau, *Exchange and Power in Social Life* (New York: Wiley, 1964), p. 91.

4. Marvin E. Olsen, *The Process of Social Organization*, 2nd ed. (New York: Holt, Rinehart and Winston, 1978), p. 91.

5. Blau, pp. 89–98.

6. The following discussion follows Olsen, p. 35.

7. Raymond W. Mack and Richard C. Snyder, "The Analysis of Social Conflict—Toward and Overview and Synthesis," *Journal of Conflict Resolution*, **1** (2) (June 1957), pp. 212–248.

8. Robert A. Nisbet, *The Social Bond* (New York: Knopf, 1970), p. 66.

9. Michel Crozier, *The Bureaucratic Phenomenon* (Chicago: University of Chicago Press, 1964).

10. Olsen, pp. 212–213.

11. S. Stansfield Sargent, "Conceptions of Roles and Ego in Contemporary Psychology," in John H. Rohrer and Muzafer Sherif, (eds.), *Social Psychology at the Crossroads* (New York: Harper & Row, 1951), pp. 355–370.

12. Ralph H. Turner, "Role-Taking: Process Versus Conformity," in Arnold M. Rose, (ed.), *Human Behavior and Social Process* (Boston: Houghton Mifflan, 1962), pp. 20–40.

13. William J. Goode, "A Theory of Role Strain," *American Sociological Review*, **25** (4) (August 1960), pp. 483–496.

14. Goode, p. 485.

15. Marvin E. Olsen, "A Conceptual Analysis of Role Conflict, unpublished manuscript, 1978.

16. Jackson Toby, "Some Variables in Role Conflict Analysis," *Social Forces*, **52**, pp. 323–327.

## CHAPTER 6

1. Thomas Hobbes, *Leviathan* (Oxford, England: James Thornton, 1881), p. 94.

2. Emile Durkheim, *The Rule of Sociological Method*, translated by Sarah A. Solovay and John H. Mueller (New York: Free Press, 1933).

3. Robert F. Bales, *Interaction Process Analysis* (Reading, Mass.,: Addison-Wesley, 1949).

4. Floyd Hunter, *Community Power Structure* (Chapel Hill: The University of North Carolina Press, 1953).

5. Amos H. Hawley, "Community Power and Urban Renewal Success," *American Journal of Sociology*, **68** (January 1963), pp. 422–431.

6. James Coleman, *Community Conflict* (New York: Free Press, 1957), pp. 10–14.

7. Emile Durkheim, *The Division of Labor in Society*, translated by George Simpson, (New York: Free Press, 1951).

8. William F. Whyte, *Street Corner Society* (Chicago: University of Chicago Press, 1943).

9. Peter Blau, and W. Richard Scott, *Formal Organizations* (San Francisco: Chandler Publishing Co., 1962), pp. 45–67.

10. Mayer Zald, ed., *Social Welfare Institutions* (New York: Wiley, 1965).

11. David L. Sills, *The Volunteers* (New York: Free Press, 1958).

12. Philip Selznick, *TVA and the Grass Roots* (Berkeley: University of California Press, 1949).

13. Karl von Clausewitz, *On War*, trans. by O. J. Maathijs Jolles (New York: Harper & Row, 1956).

14. Ferdinand Tonnies, *Community and Society: Gemeinschaft and Gesellschaft*, trans. and ed. by Charles P. Loomis (New York: Harper & Row, 1957).

15. Max Weber, *The Theory of Social and Economic Organization*, translated by A. M. Henderson and Talcott Parsons (New York: Free Press, 1947).

16. Robert Michels, *Political Parties*, translated by Eden and Adar Paul (New York: Free Press, 1966), p. 265.

## CHAPTER 7

1. *The Little Engine That Could*, Retold by Watty Piper (New York: Platt and Munk, 1961).

2. Celia S. Heller (ed.), *Structured Social Inequality* (New York: Macmillan, 1969), pp. 51–62.

3. Henry Orenstein, *Gaon: Conflict and Cohesion in an Indian Village* (Princeton, New Jersey: Princeton University Press, 1965), pp. 154–55.

4. Orenstein, p. 150.

5. H. H. Gerth and C. Wright Mills, *From Max Weber: Essays in Sociology* (New York: Oxford University Press, 1958), pp. 188–89.

6. Gerald D. Berreman, *Caste in the Modern World* (Morristown: N.J.: General Learning Press, 1973), pp. 2–11.

7. Martin Luther King, Jr., *Stride Toward Freedom: The Montgomery Story* (London: Gollancz, 1959), p. 64.

8. Eric R. Wolf and Edward C. Hansen, *The Human Condition in Latin America* (New York: Oxford University Press, 1972), p. 147.

9. Kingsley Davis and Wilbert T. Moore, "Some Principles of Stratification," *American Sociological Review* 10 (April 1945), pp. 242–249.

10. Karl Marx and Friedrich Engels, *The Communist Manifesto*, trans. Samuel Moore and ed. Joseph Katz (New York: Washington Square Press, 1964), p. 95.

11. See Holger Stub, *Status Communities in Modern Society* (Hinsdale, Ill.: Dryden Press, 1972).

12. Thorstein Veblen, *The Theory of the Leisure Class* (New York: Macmillan, Copyright 1899, 1912).

13. "What's In, What's Out: The Search for Status," *U.S. News and World Report* (Feb. 14, 1977), pp. 38–40.

14. See W. Lloyd Warner, J. O. Low, Paul S. Lunt and Leo Srole, *Yankee City* (New Haven, Conn.: Yale University Press, 1963) and W. Lloyd Warner and Associates, *Democracy in Jonesville* (New York: Harper & Row, 1949).

15. W. Lloyd Warner, with Marchia Meeker and Kenneth Eells, *Social Class in America* (New York: Harper Torchbooks, 1960).

16. Frank Parkin, *Class Inequality and Political Order* (New York: Praeger, 1971), p. 46.

17. William McCord and Arline McCord, *Power and Equity* (New York: Praeger, 1977), p. 124.

18. G. William Domhoff, *Who Rules America?* (Englewood Cliffs, N.J.: Prentice-Hall, 1967), p. 5.

19. Donald R. Matthews, *U.S. Senators and Their World* (Chapel Hill: University of North Carolina Press, 1960).

20. See McCord and McCord, p. 120.

21. See Robert W. Hodge, Paul M. Siegel and Peter H. Rossi, "Occupational Prestige in the United States, 1925–63," *American Journal of Sociology* 70 (November 1964), pp. 286–302.

22. U.S. Bureau of the Census, Table No. 227. "Lifetime and Mean Income of Males in Current and Constant (1972 dollars), by Years of School Completed: 1967 to 1972," *Statistical Abstract of the United States: 1977*. (98th edition) Washington, D.C., 1977, p. 141.

23. U.S. Department of Labor, Bureau of Labor Statistics, *Monthly Labor Review* (June 1977), p. 39.

24. U.S. Bureau of the Census, Table No. 224, "Years of School Completed by Major Occupation Group of Employed Persons, by Sex and Race: 1959 to 1976," *Statistical Abstract of the United States: 1977* (98th edition.) (Washington, D.C.: U.S. Government Printing Office 1977), p. 140.

25. U.S. Bureau of the Census, Census of Population, *1970 Subject Reports*, Final Report PC (2)—7A, *Occupational Characteristics* (Washington, D.C.: U.S. Government Printing Office, 1973), Table 1.

26. S. M. Miller and Pamela A. Roby, *The Future of Inequality* (New York: Basic Books, 1970), pp. 91–97 and U.S. Department of Commerce. Office of Federal Statistics Policy and Standards. Bureau of the Census, *Social Indicators: 1976* (Washington, D.C.: U.S. Government Printing Office, 1977), p. 175.

27. Oscar Ornati, *Poverty amid Affluence* (New York: Twentieth Century Fund, 1966), pp. 73, 184.

28. Miller and Roby, pp. 92–93.

29. Richard Centers, *The Psychology of Social Classes* (Princeton, N.J.: Princeton University Press, 1949).

30. Herman M. Case, "An independent Test of the Interest-Group Theory of Social Class," *American Sociological Review* 17 (December 1952), pp. 751–755.

31. See, for example, Floyd Dotson, "Patterns of Voluntary Association among Urban Working Class Families," *American Sociological Review* 16 (October 1951), pp. 687–693; W. Lloyd Warner and Paul S. Lunt, *The Social Life of a Modern Community* (New Haven, Conn.: Yale University Press, 1941); and Murray Hausknecht, *The Joiners* (New York: Bedminster Press, 1962).

32. Herbert H. Hyman and Charles R. Wright, "Trends in Voluntary Association Memberships of American Adults: Replication Based on Secondary Analysis of National Sample Surveys," *American Sociological Review* 36 (April 1971), pp. 191–206; and James Curtis, "Voluntary Association Joining: A Cross-National Comparative Note," *American Sociological Review* 36 (October 1971), pp. 872–880.

33. U.S. Department of Commerce. Office of Federal Statistics Policy and Standards. Bureau of the Census. *Social Indicators: 1976*. (Washington, D.C.: U.S. Government Printing Office. Issued December 1977), p. 496.

34. Herbert J. Gans, *The Urban Villagers;* (New York: Free Press, 1962); Albert K. Cohen and Harold M. Hodges, Jr., "Characteristics of the Lower-Blue-Collar Class," *Social Problems* 10 (Spring 1963), pp. 303–334; and Elliot Liebow, *Tally's Corner* (Boston: Little, Brown, 1967).

35. Mirra Komarovsky, *Blue-Collar Marriage* (New York: Random House 1962).

36. Melvin L. Kohn, *Class and Conformity: A Study in Values* (Homewood, Ill.: Dorsey Press, 1969), pp. 105–106.

37. Joseph A. Kahl, *The American Class Structure* (New York: Holt, Rinehart and Winston, 1957), pp. 187–220.

38. S. M. Miller and Frank Riessman, "The Working Class Subculture: A New View," *Social Problems* 9 (Summer 1961), pp. 86–97.

39. U.S. Department of Labor, Bureau of Labor Statistics, *Monthly Labor Review* (October 1977), p. 6.

40. Valerie Kincade Oppenheimer, "Demographic Influence on Female Employment and the Status of Women," *American Journal of Sociology* 78 (January 1973), pp. 946–948.

41. U.S. Department of Labor, Bureau of Labor Statistics, *Monthly Labor Review* (October 1977), p. 4.

42. U.S. Department of Labor, Manpower Research Monograph No. 21, *Dual Careers*, vol. 1, pp. 173–74.

43. Carol A. Whitehurst, *Women in America: The Op-*

*pressed Majority* (Santa Monica, Calif.: Goodyear Publishing Company, Inc., 1977), p. 59.

44. U.S. Department of Labor, Bureau of Labor Statistics, *Monthly Labor Review* (June 1977), p. 37.

45. U.S. Department of Labor, Bureau of Labor Statistics, *Monthly Labor Review* (June 1977), pp. 38–39.

46. U.S. Department of Labor, Employment Standards Administration, Women's Bureau, *The Earnings Gap Between Women and Men*, 1976, p. 9.

47. Larry E. Suter and Herman P. Miller, "Income Differences between Men and Career Women," *American Journal of Sociology* **78** (January 1973). The method used by Suter and Miller somewhat overestimates the work experience of women (see p. 964).

48. U.S. Department of Labor, Employment Standards Administration, Women's Bureau, *The Earnings Gap Between Women and Men*, 1976, p. 3.

49. The following discussion is based on Patricia Ruth Jette, "The Contemporary Status of Women in American Society," unpublished manuscript.

50. William H. Sewell and Vimal P. Shah, "Socioeconomic Status, Intelligence, and the Attainment of Higher Education," *Sociology of Education* **40** (Winter 1967), pp. 1–23.

51. Oscar Lewis, "The Culture of Poverty," *Scientific American,* October 1966, pp. 19–25.

52. Pitirim A. Sorokin, *Social and Cultural Mobility* (New York: Free Press, 1959).

53. Hodge, Siegel, and Rossi, "Occupational Prestige in the United States, 1925–63."

54. Jack P. Gibbs and Walter T. Martin, *Status Integration and Suicide: A Sociological Study* (Eugene: University of Oregon Books, 1964).

55. Seymour Martin Lipset and Reinhard Bendix, *Social Mobility in Industrial Society* (Berkeley and Los Angeles: University of California Press, 1959.

56. S. M. Miller, "Comparative Social Mobility: A Trend Report," *Current Sociology* **9** (1960), pp. 1–89.

57. Peter M. Blau and Otis Dudley Duncan, *The American Occupational Structure* (New York: Wiley, 1967), pp. 23–80.

58. See Lipset and Bendix, *Social Mobility in Industrial Society*, pp. 227–229; and Harry J. Crockett, Jr., "The Achievement Motive and Differential Occupational Mobility in the United States," *American Sociological Review* **27** (April 1962), pp. 191–204.

59. Joseph A. Kahl, "Educational and Occupational Aspirations of 'Common Man' Boys," *Harvard Educational Review* **23** (Summer 1953), pp. 186–203.

60. William H. Sewell, "Inequality of Opportunity for Higher Education," *American Sociological Review* **36** (October 1971), p. 800.


CHAPTER 8

1. William Meyer, *Native American* (New York: International Publishers, 1971), p. 32, quoted in Joe R. Feagin, *Racial and Ethnic Minorities* (Englewood Cliffs, N.J.: Prentice-Hall, 1978), p. 197.

2. Eliot Lord, John J. D. Trenor, and Samuel J. Barrows, *The Italian in America* (San Francisco: R. and E. Associates, 1970), pp. 17–18, quoted in Feagin, p. 119.

3. Charles F. Marden and Gladys Meyer, *Minorities in American Society*, 5th ed. (New York: Van Nostrand, 1978), p. 124.

4. "Judge Censured for Anti-Latin Remarks," *Los Angeles Times,* June 11, 1970.

5. See Marden and Meyer, p. 4; Norman R. Yetman and C. Moy Steele, eds., *Majority and Minority* (Boston, Mass.: Allyn and Bacon, 1971), p. 3; and Feagin, pp. 10–11.

6. See Marden and Meyer, pp. 27–28, and Feagin, pp. 50–76. Feagin reviews the literature on the source of dominance of white Anglo-Saxon Protestants.

7. Feagin, pp. 50–76.

8. See John Porter, *The Vertical Mosaic* (Toronto: University of Toronto Press, 1968); Howard Roseborough and Raymond Breton, "Perceptions of the Relative Economic and Political Advantages of Ethnic Groups in Canada," in *Canadian Society,* edited by B. R. Blishen, Frank E. Jones, Kaspar D. Naegele, and John Porter, 3rd ed. (Toronto: Macmillan of Canada, 1968).

9. See Sammy Smooha, "Black Panthers: The Ethnic Dilemma"; and Mark Iris and Avraham Shama, "Black Panthers: The Movement," *Society* (May, 1972), pp. 31–44; and Leonard Weller, "Interethnic Relations," *Sociology in Israel* (Westport, Conn.: Greenwood Press, 1974), pp. 124–142.

10. "Liberia: The Passing of Uncle Shad," *Newsweek* (August 2, 1971), p. 33.

11. Gordon Allport, *The Nature of Prejudice* (New York: Doubleday Anchor Books, 1958), pp. 6–7.

12. This quote was first seen in Paul Jacobs, "Guess Who's Coming to Dinner?" *Los Angeles Free Press,* May 3, 1968. The quote is from an article written by the New York City Police Commissioner Bingham, in an article the latter wrote in *The North American Review,* 1908. The quotation was repeated in a *New York Times* article, September 17, 1908, "Wrong about Jews, Bingham Admits." See The New York Times, *Ethnic Groups in American Life* (New York: Arno Press, 1978) p. 346.

13. "Head of Joint Chiefs Criticizes Jewish Influence in the U.S.," *The Washington Post,* November 13, 1974.

14. Arnold Forster, "The Banks and the Press," Memorandum, December 2, 1974, Anti-Defamation League, 315 Lexington Avenue, New York, N.Y. 10016; and Stephen D. Isaacs, *Jews and American Politics* (Garden City, New York: Doubleday, 1974); and Stephen D. Isaacs, Editorial *Washington Post,* November 21, 1974.

15. Robin Williams, Jr., "The Reduction of Intergroup Tensions," *Social Science Research Council,* 1947, p. 39.

16. Edward Sagarin, ed., *The Other Minorities* (Xerox College Publishing: Waltham, Mass., 1971).

17. U.S. Bureau of the Census, *Statistical Abstracts,* 1977 (Washington, D.C.: U.S. Government Printing Office) p. 406, No. 660.

18. Ibid, page 452, No. 730.

19. Larry E. Suter and Herman P. Miller, "Income Differences Between Men and Career Women," *American Journal of Sociology* **78** (January, 1973), p. 965.

20. Edward Sagarin, *The Other Minorities,* (New York: Wiley, 1971), pp. 34–35.

21. Theodosius Dobzhansky, *Mankind Evolving: The Evolution of the Human Species* (New Haven, Conn.: Yale University Press, 1962), p. 228.

22. Robert Blauner, *Racial Oppression in America* (New York: Harper & Row, 1972), pp. 51–81.

23. Robert K. Merton, "The Self-Fulfilling Prophesy," *Social Theory and Social Structure,* revised and enlarged ed. (Glencoe, Ill.: Free Press, 1957), pp. 421–36.

24. Charles Wagley and Marvin Harris, *Minorities in the New World* (New York: Columbia University Press, 1958), pp. 241–42.

25. George E. Simpson and J. Milton Yinger, *Racial and Cultural Minorities,* 4th ed. (New York: Harper & Row, 1972), pp. 17–23.

26. Milton M. Gordon, *Assimilation in American Life* (New York: Oxford University Press, 1964), p. 88.

27. Marden and Meyer, p. 379.

28. Pierre L. van den Berghe, *Race and Racism* (Wiley, 1967), p. 14.

29. Simpson and Yinger, p. 23.

30. Louis Wirth, "The Problem of Minority Groups," in Ralph Linton, ed., *The Science of Man in the World Crisis* (New York: Columbia University Press, 1945).

31. Hobert F. Spencer et al., *The Native Americans* (New York: Harper & Row, 1965), p. 500.

32. Harold E. Fey and D'Arcy McNickle, *Indians and Other Americans* (New York: Harper & Row, 1970), p. 63.

33. Spencer et al., *op cit*, p. 500.

34. Stan Steiner, *The New Indian* (New York: Harper & Row, 1968), p. 163.

35. Ibid., p. 162.

36. Wendell H. Oswalt, *This Land Was Theirs* (New York: Wiley, 1973), p. 587.

37. *A Study of Socio-Economic Characteristics of Ethnic Minorities Based on the 1970 Census*, vol. 3, *American Indians*, HEW Publication N (OS), 75–122, July 1974.

38. Ibid.

39. Steiner, Chapter 15.

40. John Hope Franklin, *From Slavery to Freedom* (New York: Knopf, 1948), p. 465.

41. Gilbert Osofsky, "Harlem: The Making of a Ghetto" (Ph.D. diss., Columbia University, 1963); and Allan Spear, *Black Chicago: The Making of a Negro Ghetto, 1890–1920* (Chicago: University of Chicago Press, 1967).

42. Alphonso Pinkney, *Black Americans*, (Englewood Cliffs, N.J.: Prentice-Hall, 1969), p. 330.

43. August Meier and Elliott Rudwick, *From Plantation to Ghetto* (New York: Hill and Wang, 1966), p. 213.

44. U.S. Bureau of the Census, *Statistical Abstract of the United States, 1978* (Washington, D.C.: U.S. Government Printing Office, 1978), p. 440 and p. 780.

45. Ibid.

46. U.S. Bureau of the Census, *Statistical Abstracts, 1977* (Washington, D.C.: U.S. Government Printing Office), p. 407.

47. Ibid., p. 389.

48. Ibid., p. 445.

49. Ibid., p. 454.

50. Stanford Lyman, *Chinese Americans* (New York: Random House, 1974), p. 63.

51. Wen Lang Li, "Chinese Americans: Exclusion from The Melting Pot," in Anthony G. Dworkin and Rosalind J. Dworkin, editors, *The Minority Report* (New York: Praeger Publishers, 1976), pp. 307–08.

52. U.S. Bureau of the Census, 1970, Subject Reports: Final Report PC (2)-1 G, *Japanese, Chinese, and Filipinos in the United States* (Washington, D.C.: U.S. Government Printing Office, 1973), p. 68.

53. U.S. Bureau of the Census, *Census of Population, 1970* (Washington, D.C.: U.S. Government Printing Office, 1972), Tables 6, 13.

54. Wen Lang Li, pp. 312–15.

55. Ibid., pp. 314–16.

56. Ibid., pp. 316–22.

57. Albert H. Yee, "Myopic Perceptions and Textbooks: Chinese-American Search for Identity," *Journal of Social Issues* **29** (1973): 105, quoted in Wen Lang Li, p. 318.

58. George E. Simpson and J. Milton Yinger, *Racial and Cultural Minorities*, 3d ed. (New York: Harper & Row, 1965), p. 94.

59. Joe Yamamoto and Mamoru Iga, "Japanese Enterprise and American Middle Class Values," *The American Journal of Psychiatry*, **131** (May 1974), p. 578.

60. U.S. Department of Health, Education, and Welfare, *A Study of Selected Socio-Economic Characteristics of Ethnic Minorities Based on the 1970 Census* (Washington, D.C.: U.S. Government Printing Office, 1974), pp. 70 ff.

61. Ibid.

62. Ibid., pp. 105–08. See also Gene N. Levine and Daniel M. Montero, "Socioeconomic Mobility Among Three Generations of Japanese Americans," *Journal of Social Issues* **29** (1973), 33 ff.

63. Joe R. Feagin, pp. 355–60.

64. Carey McWilliams, *North from Mexico* (New York: Greenwood Press, 1968), p. 267.

65. Joan W. Moore, *Mexican Americans*, 2d ed. (Englewood Cliffs, N.J., 1976: Prentice-Hall), p. 50. These statements are based on statistics taken from the *U.S. Immigration and Naturalization Service* from material in *Review of Hearings Before the House Committee on the Judiciary, Subcommittee No. 1, Immigration and Nationality* (Washington, D.C.: February, 1973). The figures are based upon the federal fiscal year, July 1 to June 30.

66. *Time*, **2** (February 19, 1979), p. 13.

67. Ibid.

68. U.S. Bureau of the Census, *Statistical Abstracts of the United States, 1977* (Washington, D.C.: U.S. Government Printing Office), p. 30.

69. Ibid., p. 137.

70. Ibid., p. 30.

71. Ibid., p. 450.

72. Ibid., p. 457 and p. 460.

73. Oscar Lewis, "The Culture of Poverty," *Scientific American*, October 1966, pp. 19–25.

74. *Statistical Abstracts of the U.S., 1977*, p. 30.

75. Ibid., p. 137.

76. Ibid., p. 30.

77. Ibid., p. 460.

78. Leon J. Kamin, *The Science and Politics of I. Q.* (New York: Wiley, 1974), pp. 15–19.

79. Eliot Lord, John J. D. Trevor, and Samuel J. Barrows, *The Italian in America* (San Francisco: R. and E. Associates, 1970) pp. 17–18, quoted in Joe R. Feigin, *Racial and Ethnic Relations* (Englewood Cliffs, N.J.: Prentice-Hall, 1978), p. 119.

80. Michael Krause, *Immigration: The American Mosaic* (New York: Van Nostrand, 1966), p. 93.

81. See William Shannon, *The American Irish* (New York: Crowell-Collier and Macmillan, 1963); and John Higham, *Strangers in the Land* (New York: Atheneum, 1971).

82. H. M. Sachar, *The Course of Modern Jewish History* (New York: World, 1958).

83. W. I. Thomas and Florian Znaniecki, *The Polish Peasant in Europe and America*, 2d ed. (New York: Knopf, 1927).

84. Erich Fromm, *Escape from Freedom* (New York: Holt, Rinehart and Winston, 1941), pp. 19–20.

85. E. Digby Baltzell, *The Protestant Establishment: Aristocracy and Caste in America* (New York: Vintage Books, 1964) p. 321.

86. Thomas R. Dye, *Who's Running America?* (Englewood Cliffs, N.J.: Prentice-Hall, 1976), pp. 3–8 and 150–153, quoted in Joe Feagin, *Racial and Ethnic Relations*, p. 74.

87. Feagin, p. 74.

88. Horace Kallen, *Americanism and Its Makers* (Bureau of Jewish Education, 1944), pp. 13–14.

89. Harold Cruse, *Rebellion or Revolution* (New York: Morrow, 1969), p. 106.

## CHAPTER 9

1. Kingsley Davis (ed.), *Cities: Their Origin, Growth, and Human Impact* (San Francisco: Freeman, 1973), pp. 1–6.

2. John J. Palen, *The Urban World* (New York: McGraw-Hill, 1975), pp. 67–69.

3. United Nations, *Growth of the World's Urban and Rural Population, 1920–2000, Population Studies, No. 44* (New York: Department of Economic and Social Affairs, 1969), p. 19.

4. Kingsley Davis, *World Urbanization 1950–1970*, vol. 1 of *Basic Data for Cities, Countries and Regions, Population Monograph Series, No. 4* (Berkeley, Calif.: University of California, Institute of International Studies, 1969), p. 18.

5. Amos H. Hawley, *Urban Society: An Ecological Approach* (New York, Ronald, 1971), p. 6.

6. Louis Wirth, "Urbanism as a Way of Life," *American Journal of Sociology* 44 (July 1938), pp. 3–24.

7. George Simmel, "The Metropolis and Mental Life," in R. Sennett (ed.), *Classic Essays in the Culture of Cities* (New York: Appleton-Century-Crofts, 1969), pp. 47–60; and Stanley Milgram, "The Experience of Living in Cities," *Science* 167 (March 1970), pp. 1461–1468.

8. Palen, p. 112.

9. Palen, p. 11.

10. See David Rodnick, *An Introduction to Man and His Development* (New York: Appleton, 1966).

11. Palen, p. 15.

12. Gideon Sjoberg, "The Origin and Evolution of Cities," in Kingsley Davis (ed.), *Cities: Their Origin, Growth, and Human Impact* (San Francisco: Freeman, 1973), p. 20.

13. Kingsley Davis, "The Origin and Growth of Urbanization in the World," *American Journal of Sociology* 60 (March 1955), p. 430.

14. Sjoberg, pp. 22–23; see also V. Gordon Childe, "The Urban Revolution," *Town Planning Review* 21 (April 1951), pp. 3–17; and Gideon Sjoberg, *The Preindustrial City* (Glencos, Ill., Free Press, 1960).

15. See Palen, pp. 25–31.

16. Henri Pirenne, *Economic and Social History of Medieval Europe* (New York: Harcourt, 1936), p. 173, cited in Palen, p. 29.

17. John V. Grauman, "Orders of Magnitude of the World's Urban Population in History," *Population Bulletin of the United Nations, No. 8, 1976* (New York: Department of Economic and Social Affairs, 1977).

18. Noel P. Gist and Sylvia Heis Fava, *Urban Society*, 6th ed. (New York: Crowell, 1974), pp. 30–31.

19. United Nations, "Growth of the World's Urban and Rural Population, 1920–2000."

20. W. Parker Frisbie, "The Scale and Growth of World Urbanization," in John Walton and Donald E. Carns (ed.), *Cities in Change: Studies of the Urban Condition*, 2d ed., (Boston: Allyn and Bacon, 1977), pp. 44–58.

21. Wirth, summarized in Palen, p. 36.

22. Gist and Fava, pp 149–180; see also Kent Schwirian, ed., *Comparative Urban Structure: Studies in the Ecology of Cities* (Lexington, Mass.: Heath, 1974); and Brian J. L. Berry and John D. Kasarda, *Contemporary Urban Ecology* (New York: Macmillan, 1977).

23. Robert E. Park, "The City: Suggestions for the Investigation of Human Behavior in an Urban Environment," *American Journal of Sociology* 20 (March 1915), pp. 577–612; see also Robert E. Park and Ernest W. Burgess, *The City* (Chicago: University of Chicago Press, 1925).

24. Jonathan H. Turner, *American Society: Problems of Structure* (New York: Harper & Row, 1972).

25. Ernest W. Burgess, "The Growth of the City," in Park and Burgess, pp. 47–62.

26. Homer Hoyt, *The Structure of Residential Neighborhoods in American Cities* (Washington, D.C.: Federal Housing Administration, 1939).

27. See Chauncy Harris and Edward L. Ullman, "The Nature of Cities," *Annuals of the American Academy of Political and Social Science* 242 (November 1945), pp. 7–17.

28. For example, Otis Dudley Duncan and Beverly Duncan, *The Negro Population of Chicago: A Study of Residential Succession* (Chicago: University of Chicago Press, 1957); Stanley Lieberson, *Ethnic Patterns in American Cities* (New York: Free Press, 1963); Leo F. Schnore and Philip C. Evenson, "Segregation in Southern Cities," *American Journal of Sociology* 72 (July 1966), pp. 58–67; Karl E. Taeuber and Alma F. Taeuber, *Negroes in Cities: Residential Succession and Neighborhood Change* (New York: Atheneum, 1969); Nathan Kantrowitz, "Ethnic and Racial Segregation in the New York Metropolis," *American Journal of Sociology* 74 (May 1969), pp. 685–696; John Fine, Dorval D. Glenn, and J. Kenneth Monts, "The Residential Segregation of Occupational Groups in Central Cities and Suburbs," *Demography* 8 (February 1971), pp. 91–101; Annette Sorenson, Karl E. Taueber, and Leslie J. Hollinsworth, Jr., "Indexes of Racial Residential Segregation for 109 Cities in the United States: 1950 to 1970," *Sociological Focus* 8 (April 1975), pp 125–142; Avery M. Guest and James A. Weed, "Ethnic Residential Segregation: Patterns of Change," *American Journal of Sociology* 81 (March 1976), pp. 1088–1111; Thomas L. Van Valey, Wade Clark Roof, and Jerome E. Wilcox, "Trends in Residential Segregation: 1960–1970," *American Journal of Sociology* 82 (January 1977), pp. 826–844; and Alber A. Simkus, "Residential Segregation by Occupation and Race in Ten Urbanized Areas, 1950–1970," *American Sociological Review* 43 (February 1978), pp. 81–93.

29. See Taueber and Taueber.

30. See Guest and Weed; Van Valey et al.; and Simkus.

31. See Leo F. Schnore, "The Socioeconomic Status of Cities and Suburbs," *American Sociological Review* 28 (February 1963), pp. 76–85; "Urban Structure and Suburban Selectivity," *Demography* 1 (1) (1964) pp. 164–176; and "Measuring City-Suburban Status Differentials," *Urban Affairs Quarterly* 3 (September 1967), pp. 95–108; J. John Palen and Leo F. Schnore, "Color Composition and City Suburban Status Differentials: A Replication and Extension," *Land Economics* 41 (February 1965), pp. 87–91; James R. Pinkerton, "City-Suburban Residential Patterns by Social Class: A Review of the Literature," *Urban Affairs Quarterly* 4 (June 1969), pp. 499–519; and Leo F. Schnore and Joy K. O. Jones, "The Evolution of City-Suburban Types in the Course of a Decade," *Urban Affairs Quarterly* 4 (June 1969), pp. 421–423.

32. U.S. Bureau of the Census, *Annual Housing Survey: 1976, Current Housing Reports: Series H-150-76:* Table D.

33. Edward C. Burks, "Population Falling in Older U.S. Cities," *The New York Times*, December 7, 1978, p. A20.

34. United States Bureau of the Census, 1978.

35. Gist and Fava, p. 273.

36. John D. Kasarda, "Urbanization, Community, and the Metropolitan Problem," in David Street and Associates, *Handbook of Contemporary Urban Life* (San Francisco: Jossey-Bass, 1978), p. 37.

37. Gist and Fava, p. 269.

38. Gist and Fava, pp. 264–266.

39. Hawley, p. 227.

40. Wirth.

41. See Sidney M. Greenfield, "Industrialization and the Family in Sociological Theory," *American Journal of Sociology* **67** (November 1961), pp. 312–322; and William J. Goode, *World Revolution and Family Patterns*, (New York: Free Press, 1963).

42. Rudy Ray Seward, *The American Family: A Demographic History* (Beverly Hills, Cal.: University of California Press, 1978), pp. 21–27.

43. See F. Kobrin, "The Fall of Household Size and the Rise of the Primary Individual in the United States," *Demography* **13** (February 1976), pp. 127–238.

44. Paul C. Glick and Arthur J. Norton, "Marrying, Divorcing, and Living Together in the U.S. Today," *Population Bulletin* **32** (October 1977) pp. 1–39; and Shirley Harkess, "Family and Sex Roles in Urban Society," in David Street and Associates, *Handbook of Contemporary Urban Life* (San Francisco: Jossey-Bass, 1978), pp. 163–201.

45. Seward, pp. 111–158.

46. Claude S. Fischer, *The Urban Experience* (New York: Harcourt Brace Jovanovich, 1976), pp. 143–148.

47. Fischer, p. 145.

48. Hawley, pp. 120–122; and Gist and Fava, pp. 384–386.

49. See William Kornhauser, *The Politics of Mass Society* (Glencoe, Ill.: The Free Press, 1959).

50. Gist and Fava, pp. 354–355.

51. See Herbert Hyman and Charles Wright, "Trends in Voluntary Association Memberships among American Adults: Replication Based on Secondary Analysis of National Sample Surveys,: *American Sociological Review* **36** (April 1971), pp. 191–206.

52. See Stephen J. Cutler, "Voluntary Association Membership and the Theory of Mass Society," in Edward O. Laumann, *Bonds of Pluralism: The Form and Substance of Urban Social Networks* (New York: Wiley, 1973), pp. 133–159; and Claude S. Fischer, "The Study of Urban Community and Personality," in Alex Inkeles, James Coleman, and Neil Smelser (eds.) *Annual Review of Sociology*, vol. 1 (Palo Alto, Cal.: Annual Reviews, Inc., 1975), pp. 67–90; and David Horton Smith, "Voluntary Action and Voluntary Groups," in Inkeles, Coleman, and Smelser, pp. 247–270.

53. James S. Coleman, "Community Disorganization and Urban Problems," in Robert K. Merton and Robert Nisbet (eds.), *Contemporary Social Problems*, 4th ed. (New York: Harcourt Brace Jovanovich, 1976), pp. 557–601; and James S. Coleman, and Sara D. Kelly, "Education," William Gorham and Nathan Glazer (eds.), in *The Urban Predicament* (Washington, D.C.: The Urban Institute, 1976), pp. 231–280.

54. Stanley H. Udy, *Work in Traditional and Modern Society* (Englewood Cliffs, N.J.: Prentice-Hall, 1970), p. 87.

55. United States Bureau of the Census, 1978, Table N.

56. But see Scott Greer, *Metropolitics: A Study of Urban Culture* (New York: Wiley, 1963), and *The Urbane View: Life and Politics in Metropolitan America* (New York: Oxford University Press, 1972); and John C. Bollens and Henry J. Schmandt, *The Metropolis* (New York: Harper & Row, 1965).

57. See John D. Kasarda, "Structural Implications of System Size," *American Sociological Review* **39** (February 1974), pp. 1928.

58. George E. Peterson, "Finance," in William Gorham and Nathan Glazer (eds.), *The Urban Predicament* (Washington, D.C.: The Urban Institute, 1976), pp. 35–118.

59. David Street and Jeffrey L. Davidson, "Community and Politics in City and Suburb," in David Street and Associates, *Handbook of Contemporary Urban Life* (San Francisco: Jossey-Bass, 1978), pp. 473–474.

60. Edward C. Banfield, *Political Influence* (New York: Free Press, 1961), p. 235.

61. Coleman, p. 569.

62. Hawley, p. 248.

63. Charles Abrams, *The City is the Frontier* (New York: Harper & Row, 1965), pp. 26–27.

64. Alvin L. Schoer, *Slums and Social Insecurity* (Washington, D.C.: Department of Health, Education, and Welfare, 1963).

65. Frank deLeeuw, Ann B. Schnare, and Raymond J. Stroyk, "Housing," in William Gorham and Nathan Glazer (eds.), *The Urban Predicament* (Washington, D.C.: The Urban Institute, 1976), p. 122.

66. Abrams, pp. 155–183.

67. See Martin Anderson, *The Federal Bulldozer* (Cambridge, Mass.: The MIT Press, 1964); Herbert J. Gans, "The Failure of Urban Renewal: A Critique and Some Proposals," *Commentary* **39** (April 1965), pp. 29–37; and Scott Greer, *Urban Renewal and American Cities: The Dilemma of Democratic Intervention* (Indianapolis: Bobbs-Merrill, 1966).

68. Hawley, p. 258; see also Chester Hartman, "Displaced Families," *Society* **9** (July/August 1972), pp. 53–65.

69. Gist and Fava, p. 654.

70. Michael Kemp and Melvyn D. Cheslow, "Transportation," in William Gorham and Nathan Glazer (eds.), *The Urban Predicament* (Washington, D.C.: The Urban Institute, 1976), p. 281.

71. Kemp and Cheslow, p. 240.

72. Wilfred Owen with the assistance of Inai Bradfield, *The Accessible City* (Washington, D.C.: The Brookings Institution, 1972), p. 5.

73. United States Bureau of the Census, *Selected Characteristics of Travel to Work in 20 Metropolitan Areas: 1976. Current Population Reports: Special Studies*, Series P-23, No. 72, 1978b.

74. Kemp and Cheslow, p. 325.

75. Hawley, p. 242.

76. Owen, pp. 34–39.

77. Kemp and Cheslow, pp. 296–299.

78. Lewis Mumford, *The Highway and the City* (New York: Mentor Books, 1964), p. 248.

79. Gist and Fava, p. 333.

80. Michael Harrington, *The Other America* (New York: Macmillan, 1962).

81. Elmer H. Johnson, *Social Problems of Urban Man* (Homewood, Ill.: Dorsey Press, 1973), pp. 143–144.

82. United States Bureau of the Census, *Social and Economic Characteristics of the Metropolitan and Nonmetropolitan Population, 1967–1970, Current Population Reports: Special Studies*, Series P-23, No. 75, Table S, 1978c.

83. See Willis D. Hawley and James Sauna, *The Study of Community Power: A Bibliographic Review* (Santo Barbara, Calif.: Clio Press, Inc., 1972).

84. Floyd Hunter, *Community Power Structure* (Chapel Hill N. C.: University of North Carolina Press, 1953).

85. Robert A. Dahl, *Who Governs? Democracy and Power in an American City* (New Haven, Conn.: Yale University Press, 1961).

86. Thomas Fraser Pettigrew, "Race and Intergroup Relations," in Robert K. Merton and Robert Nisbet (ed.), *Contempo-*

*rary Social Problems,* 4th ed. (New York: Harcourt, 1976), pp. 469–482.

87. Johnson, p. 376.

88. J. D. Greenstone and P. E. Peterson, *Race and Authority in Urban Politics, Community Participation, and the War on Poverty* (New York: Russell Sage Foundation, 1973).

89. Pettigrew, p. 476.

90. Sidney Kronus, "Race, Ethnicity, and Community," in David Street and Associates, *Handbook of Contemporary Urban Life* (San Francisco: Jossey-Bass, 1976), p. 211.

91. Fischer, p. 95.

92. Edwin H. Sutherland and Donald R. Cressey, *Criminology* 9th ed. (New York: Lippincott, 1974) p. 176; and Gwynn Nettler, *Explaining Crime* (New York: McGraw-Hill, 1974), p. 132.

53. Fischer, p. 89.

54. Sutherland and Cressey, p. 197.

95. Fischer, p. 91.

96. Daniel Bell, *The End of Ideology* (Glencoe, Ill.: The Free Press, 1960), p. 137; and Theodore N. Ferdinand, "The Criminal Patterns of Boston since 1849," *American Journal of Sociology* **73** (July 1967), pp. 84–97.

97. Fischer, pp. 92–94.

98. See Herbert Blumer, *Symbolic Interactionism* (Englewood Cliffs, N.Y.: Prentice-Hall, Inc., 1969).

99. Ralph Thomlinson, *Population Dynamics: Causes and Consequences of World Demographic Change,* 2nd ed. (New York: Random House, 1976), pp. 313–314.

100. Fischer, p. 79.

101. Thomlinson, p. 322.

102. Robert M. Hauser and David L. Featherman, *The Process of Stratification: Trends and Analyses* (New York: Academic, 1977), p. 250.

103. See Otis Dudley Duncan and Albert J. Reiss, *Social Characteristics of Urban and Rural Communities, 1950* (New York: Wiley, 1956); and Schnore, 1963.

104. See Charles W. Mueller, "City Effects on Socioeconomic Achievements: The Case of Large Cities," *American Sociological Review* **39** (October 1974), pp. 653–667; and Hauser and Featherman.

105. Peter M. Blau and Otis Dudley Duncan, *The American Occupational Structure* (New York: Wiley, 1967); and Hauser and Featherman.

106. See Wirth, 1938.

107. Robin M. Williams, Jr., *American Society,* 3rd ed. (New York: Alfred A. Knopf, 1970), pp. 454–458.

108. Kingsley Davis, *Human Society* (New York: Macmillan, 1949), pp. 332–333.

109. See Ralph Turner, *The Social Context of Ambition* (San Francisco: Chandler, 1964).

110. David Matza and Henry Miller, "Poverty and the Proletariat," in Robert K. Merton and Robert Nisbet (eds.), *Contemporary Social Problems,* 4th ed. (New York: Harcourt, 1976), pp. 639–673.

111. See Philip M. Hauser, "The Chaotic Society: Product of the Social Morphological Revolution," *American Sociological Review* **34** (February 1969), pp. 1–18; Omar R. Galle, Walter R. Gove, and J. M. McPherson, "Population Density and Pathology: What are the Relationships for Man," *Science* **176** (April 1972), pp. 23–30; Amos H. Hawley, "Population Density and the City," *Demography* **9** (November 1972), pp. 521–529; Claude S. Fischer, Mark Baldassare, and Richard J. Ofshe, "Crowding Studies and Urban Life: A Critical Review," *Journal of the American Institute of Planners* **31** (November

1975), pp. 406–418; Jonathan L. Freedman, *Crowding and Behavior* (San Francisco: Wh. H. Freeman and Co., 1975); Mark Baldassare, "Human Spatial Behavior," in Ralph H. Turner, James Coleman, and Renée C. Fox (eds.), *Annual Review of Sociology,* vol. 4, (Palo Alto, Calif.: Annual Reviews, Inc. 1978) pp. 29–56; Harvey M. Choldin, "Urban Density and Pathology," in Turner, Coleman, and Fox, pp. 91–113; and Omar R. Galle, and Walter R. Gove, "Overcrowding, Isolation, and Human Behavior: Exploring the Extremes in Population Distribution," in Karl Taeuber and James Sweet (eds.), *Social Demography* (New York: Academic, 1978), pp. 95–132.

112. Hawley, p. 522.

113. See Choldin; and Galle and Gove.

114. Benjamin D. Zablocki and Rosabeth Moss Kanter, "The Differentiation of Life Styles," in Alex Inkels, James Coleman, and Neil Smelser (ed.), *Annual Review of Sociology,* vol. 2 (Palo Alto, Calif.: J. Annual Reviews, Inc., 1976), pp. 269–298.

115. Fischer, p. 197.

116. Howard S. Becker and Irving Louis Horowitz, "The Culture of Civility: San Francisco," in John Walton and Donald E. Carns, eds., *Cities in Change: Studies on the Urban Condition,* 2nd ed. (Boston: Allyn and Bacon, 1977), pp. 199–205.

117. Glick and Norton, 1977.

118. Rosabeth M. Kanter, *Commitment and the Community: Communes and Utopias in Sociological Perspective* (Cambridge, Mass.: Harvard University Press, 1972), p. 171.

119. Gist and Fava, pp. 430–454.

120. See Max Kaplan, *Leisure in America* (New York: John Wiley and Sons, 1960); and Rolf Meyerson, "Leisure," in Angus Campbell and Philip E. Converse (eds.), *The Human Meaning of Social Change* (New York: Russell Sage Foundation, 1972).

121. David H. Karp, Gregory P. Stone, and William C. Yoels, *Being Urban: A Social Psychological View of City Life* (Lexington, Mass.: Heath, 1977).

122. See Fischer, *The Urban Experience,* upon which this section draws heavily.

123. See Simmel; Wirth; and Milgram.

124. Fischer, 1976, p. 33.

125. Herbert J. Gans, *The Urban Villagers* (New York: The Free Press, 1962) and *The Levittowners* (New York: Vintage Books, 1967); and Oscar Lewis, "Further Observations on the Folk-Urban Continuum and Urbanization," in Philip M. Hauser and Leo F. Schnore (eds.), *The Study of Urbanization* (New York: Wiley, 1965).

126. Fischer, 1976, p. 34.

127. Claude S. Fischer, "Toward a Subcultural Theory of Urbanism," *American Journal of Sociology* **80** (May 1975), pp. 1319–1341.

128. Fischer, *The Urban Experience,* p. 36.

129. See Fischer, "Toward a Subcultural Theory of Urbanism."

130. Kornhauser.

131. See Melvin Seeman, "The Urban Alienations: Some Dubious Theses from Marx to Marcuse," *Journal of Personality and Social Psychology* **19** (August 1971), pp. 135–143; and "Alienation and Engagement," in Angus Campbell and Philip E. Converse (eds.), *The Human Meaning of Social Change* (New York: Russell Sage Foundation, 1972).

132. Fischer, *The Urban Experience,* p. 173; see also Fischer, "On Urban Alienations and Anomie: Powerlessness and Social Isolation," *American Sociological Review* **38** (June 1973), pp. 311–326.

133. See Galle and Gove.

134. See Mildren B. Kantor (ed.), *Mobility and Mental Health* Springfield, Ill.: Charles C Thomas, 1965).

135. See Dorothea Leighton, J. S. Harding, D. B. Macklin, A. M. MacMillan, and A. H. Leighton, *The Character of Danger* (New York: Basic Books, 1963).

136. See Leo Srole, Thomas S. Langner, Stanley T. Michael, Marvin K. Opler, and Thomas A. C. Rennie, *Mental Health in the Metropolis* (New York: McGraw-Hill, 1962); and Bruce P. Dohrenwend and Barbara S. Dohrenwend, "Psychiatric Disorders in Urban Settings," in Gerald Kaplan (ed.), *American Handbook of Psychiatry,* 2nd ed., vol. 2: *Child and Adolescent Psychiatry, Sociocultural and Community Psychiatry* (New York: Basic Books, 1974), pp. 424–447; and Warren B. Miller, "Psychological and Psychiatric Aspects of Population Problems," in David A. Hamburg and Keith H. Brodie (eds.), *American Handbook of Psychiatry,* 2nd ed., vol. 6: New Psychiatric Frontiers (New York: Basic Books, 1975), pp. 977–1019.

137. See Leo Srole, "Urbanization and Mental Health: Some Reformulations," *American Scientist* **60** (September/October 1972), pp. 576–583.

138. See Dohrenwend and Dohrenwend; and Miller.

139. John B. Calhoun, "Population Density and Social Pathology," *Scientific American* **206** (February 1962), pp. 139–148.

140. Fischer, *The Urban Experience,* p. 187.

141. Fischer, *The Urban Experience,* p. 188.

142. Park.

143. Robert W. Winslow and Virginia Winslow, *Deviant Reality: Alternative World Views* (Boston: Allyn and Bacon, 1974).

144. Kingsley Davis, *World Urbanization 1950–1970,* vol 2: *Analysis of Trends, Relationships and Developments. Population Monograph Series, No. 9* (Berkeley, Cal.: Institute of International Studies, University of California, 1972).

145. See Calvin L. Beale, *The Revival of Population Growth in Nonmetropolitan America, Economic Research Service Publication ERS-605* (Washington D.C.: U.S. Department of Agriculture, 1975); James L. Sundquist, *Dispersing Population: What Americans can Learn from Europe* (Washington, D.C.: Brookings Institution, 1975); and Calvin L. Beal and Glenn V. Fuguitt, "The New Pattern of Nonmetropolitan Population Change," in Karl E. Taeuber, Larry L. Bumpass, and James A. Sweet (eds.), *Social Demography* (New York: Academic, 1978), pp. 157–177.

146. See Beale and Fuguitt.

147. See Lester R. Brown, "The Urban Prospect: Reexamining Basic Assumptions," *Population and Development Review* **2** (June 1976), pp. 267–277.

148. See Lester R. Brown, *The Twenty-Ninth Day: Accomodating Human Needs and Numbers to the Earth's Resources* (New York: Norton, 1978).

149. See Brown, 1976.

150. See Barbara Ward, *The Home of Man,* (New York: Norton, 1976), pp. 234–257.

151. Brain J. L. Berry, *The Human Consequences of Urbanization,* (New York: St. Martins, 1973) p. 178.

152. Daniel P. Moynihan, "Toward a National Urban Policy," *The Public Interest* **17** (Fall 1969), pp. 3–20.

153. Gerald D. Suttles, "Changing Priorities for the Urban Heartland," in David Street and Associates, *Handbook of Contemporary Urban Life* (San Francisco: Jossey-Bass, 1978), pp. 519–547.

154. See Ward; and Brown, *The Twenty-Ninth Day.*

## CHAPTER 10

1. Lester R. Brown, *The Twenty-Ninth Day: Accommodating Human Needs and Numbers to the Earth's Resources* (New York: Norton, 1978), pp. 12–44.

2. United Nations, *The Determinants and Consequences of Population Trends: New Summary of Findings on Interaction of Demographic, Economic, and Social Factors,* vol. 1, Department of Economic and Social Affairs, Population Studies No. 50 (New York: United Nations, 1973), p. 2.

3. Thomas Robert Malthus in Gertrude Himmelfarb (ed.), *On Population,* ed. (New York: Modern Library, 1960).

4. See Roland Pressat, *Population* (Baltimore: Penguin, 1971), p. 112.

5. John C. Caldwell, "Toward a Restatement of Demographic Transition Theory," *Population and Development Review* **2** (September/December 1976), p. 352.

6. United Nations, *The Determinants and Consequences of Population Trends: New Summary of Findings on Interaction of Demographic, Economic, and Social Factors,* vol. 1, p. 31.

7. John D. Durand, "A Long-range View of World Population Growth," *Annals of the American Academy of Political and Social Science* **369** (January 1967), p. 7.

8. See Michael Micklin (ed.), *Population, Environment, and Social Organization: Current Issues in Human Ecology* (Hinsdale, Ill.: Dryden Press, 1973).

9. Shirley Foster Hartley, *Population: Quantity vs. Quality* (Englewood Cliffs, N.J.: Prentice-Hall, 1972), p. 87.

10. United Nations, *The Determinants and Consequences of Population Trends: New Summary of Findings on Interaction of Demographic, Economic, and Social Factors,* vol. 1, pp. 183 and 191.

11. Donald J. Bogue, *Principles of Demography* (New York: Wiley, 1969), p. 131; and U.S. Bureau of the Census, *Census of the Population,* vol. 1: *Characteristics of the Population* (Washington, D.C.: U.S. Government Printing Office, 1973), p. 42.

12. Philip M. Hauser, "The Chaotic Society: Product of the Social Morphological Revolution," *American Sociological Review* **34** (February 1969), pp. 1–19.

13. U.S. Bureau of the Census, *Population of the United States: Trends and Prospects, 1950–1990,* Current Population Reports, Series P-23, No. 49 (Washington, D.C.: U.S. Government Printing Office, 1974), p. 61.

14. Ibid.

15. J. C. Elizaga, "Internal Migrations for Latin America," *Milbank Memorial Fund Quarterly* **43** (1965), pp. 144–161.

16. S. H. Ominde, *Land and Population Movements in Kenya* (Evanston, Ill.: Northwestern University Press, 1968); and John C. Caldwell, *African Rural-Urban Migration: The Movement to Ghana's Towns* (New York: Columbia University Press, 1969).

17. United Nations, *The Determinants and Consequences of Population Trends: New Summary of Findings on Interaction of Demographic, Economic, and Social Factors,* vol. 1, p. 283.

18. Joseph J. Spengler, *Facing Zero Population Growth: Reactions and Interpretations, Past and Present* (Durham, N.C.: Duke University Press, 1978), p. 92.

19. Lester R. Brown, with Erik P. Eckholm, *By Bread Alone* (New York; Praeger, 1974), pp. 37–38.

20. Lester R. Brown, *Man, Land, and Food: Looking Ahead at World Food Needs,* Foreign Agricultural Economic Report No. 11 (Washington, D.C.: U.S. Government Printing Office, 1963), p. 31.

21. Brown and Eckholm, p. 60.

22. Ibid., p. 32.

**571**

23. See, for example, Robert F. Chandler, Jr., "The Scientific Basis for the Increased Yield Capacity of Rice and Wheat, and Its Present and Potential Impact on Food Production in the Developing Countries," in T. T. Poleman and D. K. Freebairn (eds.), *Food, Population, and Employment: The Impact of the Green Revolution* (New York: Praeger, 1973); Committee on Engineering Policy, *World Hunger: Approaches to Engineering Actions* (Washington, D.C.: National Research Council, 1975); and S. H. Wittwer, "Food Production: Technology and the Resource Base," *Science* **188** (May 9, 1975), pp. 579–584.

24. See Clifton R. Wharton, Jr., "The Green Revolution: Cornucopia or Pandora's Box?," *Foreign Affairs* **47** (April 1969), pp. 464–476; Lester R. Brown, *In the Human Interest* (New York: Norton, 1974), pp. 50–53; Brown and Eckholm, *By Bread Alone*, pp. 133–146; and Pierre R. Crossen, "Institutional Obstacles to Expansion of World Food Production," *Science* **188** (May 9, 1975), pp. 519–524.

25. Brown, *The Twenty-Ninth Day*.

26. Brown and Eckholm, *By Bread Alone*, p. 11.

27. Joseph L. Fisher and Neal Potter, "Natural Resource Adequacy for the United States and the World," in P. M. Hauser (ed.), *The Population Dilemma,* 2d ed. (Englewood Cliffs, N.J.: Prentice-Hall, 1969).

28. United Nations, *The Determinants and Consequences of Population Trends: New Summary of Findings on Interaction of Demographic, Economic, and Social Factors,* vol. 1, p. 377.

29. Joel Darmstadter, "Energy Consumption: Trends and Patterns," in Sam H. Schurr (ed.), *Energy, Economic Growth, and the Environment* (Baltimore: Johns Hopkins University Press, 1972).

30. Donella H. Meadows, Dennis L. Meadows, Jorgen Randers, and William W. Behrens, III, *The Limits to Growth: A Report of the Club of Rome's Project on the Predicament of Mankind* (New York: Universe Books, 1972), pp. 64–68.

31. Paul R. Ehrlich, Ann H. Ehrlich, and John P. Holdren, *Human Ecology: Problems and Solutions* (San Francisco: Freeman, 1973), p. 115.

32. I. G. Simmons, *The Ecology of Natural Resources* (London: Arnold, 1974), pp. 276–277.

33. Ibid., pp. 342–343.

34. Hartley, *Population: Quantity vs. Quality,* p. 181.

35. Lester R. Brown, *World without Borders* (New York: Random House, 1972), p. 42.

36. See Michael Micklin, "Demographic, Economic, and Social Change in Latin America: An Examination of Causes and Consequences," *Journal of Developing Areas* **4** (January 1970), pp. 173–197; and Brown, *In the Human Interest*, pp. 145–147.

37. Robert Heilbroner, *An Inquiry into the Human Prospect* (New York: Norton, 1974).

38. Lester R. Brown, Patricia L. McGrath, and Bruce Stokes, "Twenty-Two Dimensions of the Population Problem," *Worldwatch Paper* No. 5. (Washington, D.C.: Worldwatch Institute, March 1976), p. 57.

39. Dorothy Nortman, assisted by Ellen Hofstatter, "Population and Family Planning Programs: A Factbook," in *Reports on Population/Family Planning,* No. 2, 8th ed. (New York: The Population Council, October 1976).

40. Donald J. Bogue, "The End of the Population Explosion," *Public Interest* **7** (Spring 1967), p. 19.

41. Kingsley Davis, "Population Policy: Will Current Programs Suceed?," *Science* **158** (November 10, 1976), pp. 730–739.

42. Walter B. Watson and Robert J. Lapham (eds.), "Family Planning Programs: World Review, 1974," *Studies in Family Planning* **6** (August 1975), p. 219.

43. Joseph E. Potter, Myriam Ordonez G., and Anthony R. Meacham, "The Rapid Decline in Colombian Fertility," *Population and Development Review* **2** (September/December 1976), pp. 509–528.

44. K. S. Srikanton, *The Family Planning Program in the Socioeconomic Context* (New York: The Population Council, 1977), p. 232.

45. United Nations Economic and Social Council, Population Commission, *Report of the Ad Hoc Consultative Group of Experts on Population Policy* (C/CN, 9/267) (New York: United Nations, May 23, 1972), p. 6.

46. Nortman and Hofstatter, "Population and Family Planning Programs: A Factbook."

47. John S. Aird, "Fertility Decline and Birth Control in the People's Republic of China," *Population and Development Review* **4** (June 1978), p. 225.

48. Ibid., pp. 227 and 232; see also "Fertility Control and Public Health in Rural China: Unpublicized Problems," *Population and Development Review* **3** (December 1977), pp. 482–485.

## CHAPTER 11

1. Norman W. Bell and Ezra F. Vogel, "Toward a Framework for Functional Analysis of Family Behavior," in Bell and Vogel (eds.), *The Family* (New York: Free Press, 1968, rev. ed.), p. 2.

2. Morris Zelditch, "Family, Marriage, and Kinship," in R. E. L. Faris (ed.), *Handbook of Modern Sociology* (Chicago: Rand McNally, 1964), p. 681.

3. Ira L. Reiss, *The Family System in America* (New York: Holt, Rinehart and Winston, 1971), ch. 2. See also, Lucille Duberman, *Marriage and Other Alternatives* (New York: Praeger, 1977), pp. 8–10.

4. Ernest L. Schusky, *Manual for Kinship Analysis* (New York: Holt, Rinehart and Winston, 1965).

5. See, William J. Goode, *World Revolutions and Family Patterns* (New York: Free Press, 1970), pp. 10–18.

6. George P. Murdock, *Social Structure* (New York: Crowell-Collier and Macmillan, 1949).

7. Ira L. Reiss, *The Family System in America* (New York: Holt, Rinehart and Winston, 1976, rev. ed.), pp. 295–299.

8. See, Edmund S. Morgan, *The Puritan Family* (New York: Harper & Row, 1966); Mirra Komarovsky, *Blue-Collar Marriage* (New York: Vintage Press, 1967), pp. 222–25; Robert O. Blood, Jr. and Donald M. Wolfe, *Husbands and Wives* (New York: Free Press, 1965), pp. 22–24.

9. E. Franklin Frazier, *The Negro Family in the United States* (Chicago: University of Chicago Press, 1966); and Lee Rainwater and William L. Yancey, *The Moynihan Report and the Politics of Controversy* (Cambridge, Mass.: The M.I.T. Press, 1967).

10. William J. Goode, *The Family* (Englewood Cliffs, N.J.: Prentice-Hall, 1964), p. 14.

11. Edward Shorter, *The Making of the Modern Family* (New York: Harper & Row, 1977).

12. Bell and Vogel, p. 10.

13. Daniel Yankelovich, *The New Morality* (New York: McGraw-Hill, 1974).

14. See Bell and Vogel, pp. 20–30.

15. Lilian Breslow Rubin, *Worlds of Pain* (New York: Harper & Row, 1976).

16. Emile Durkheim, *Moral Education* (New York: Free Press, 1961).

17. Peter L. Berger and Brigitte Berger, "The Blueing of America," *New Republic* (April 13, 1971).

18. Talcott Parsons and Robert F. Bales, *Family, Socialization and Interaction Process* (New York: Free Press, 1955).

19. Ann Oakley, *Women's Work* (New York: Random House, 1976), pp. 222–241.

20. Mirra Komarovsky, *Dilemmas of Masculinity* (New York: Norton, 1976), pp. 54–59.

21. Murdock, *Social Structure;* and Robert F. Winch, *Mate-Selection* (New York: Harper & Row, 1958).

22. Andree Michel, *The Modernization of North African Families in the Paris Region* (The Hague: Mouton, 1974), p. 15.

23. Robin M. Williams, Jr., *American Society,* 3rd ed. (New York: Knopf, 1970), p. 56.

24. Talcott Parsons, *Social Structure and Personality* (New York: Free Press, 1964), p. 61.

25. Thomas J. Espenshade, "The Value and Cost of Children," *Population Bulletin,* Vol. 32, No. 1 (Population Reference Bureau, Inc., Washington, D.C.; 1977), pp. 4–5.

26. Blood and Wolfe, *Husbands and Wives,* p. 121.

27. Blood and Wolfe, p. 150.

28. Shorter, pp. 277–280.

29. Helena Z. Lopata, *Occupation: Housewife* (New York: Oxford University Press, 1974).

30. C. K. Yang, *The Chinese Family in the Communist Revolution* (Cambridge, Mass.: The M.I.T. Press, 1965), p. 81.

31. William J. Goode, *Women in Divorce* (New York: Free Press, 1965), pp. 43–55.

32. Paul C. Glick and Arthur J. Norton, "Marrying, Divorcing, and Living Together in the U.S. Today," *Population Bulletin,* Vol. 32, No. 5 (Population Reference Bureau, Inc., Washington, D.C., 1977), pp. 36–37.

33. Shorter, pp. 161–167; 245–254.

34. Glick and Norton, p. 37.

35. Yankelovich, *The New Morality,* p. 23.

## CHAPTER 12

1. Theodore M. Newcomb, *The Impact of College Upon Students* (San Francisco: Jossey-Bass, 1969).

2. Clifford Geertz, "The Impact of the Concept of Culture on the Concept of Man," in David H. Spain (ed.) *The Human Experience* (London: Dorsey, 1975), pp. 21–43.

3. Jack Douglas (ed.), *Introduction to Sociology: Situations and Structures* (Toronto: Free Press, 1973), p. 177.

4. Everett K. Wilson, *Sociology: Rules, Roles, Relationships* (Toronto: Dorsey Press, 1971).

5. Sarane Boocock, *An Introduction to the Sociology of Learning* (Boston: Houghton Mifflin 1972), pp. 11–13.

6. Ann P. Parelius and Robert J. Parelius, *The Sociology of Education* (Englewood Cliffs, N.J.: Prentics-Hall, 1978).

7. Emile Durkheim, *Education and Sociology,* trans. Sherwood D. Fox (Glencoe, Ill.: Free Press, 1956), pp. 70–75.

8. Emile Durkheim, *Moral Education,* trans. Everett K. Wilson and Herman Schaurer (New York: Free Press, 1961).

9. Parelius and Parelius, p. 7.

10. Durkheim, *Education and Sociology,* p. 71.

11. Talcott Parsons, "The School Class as a Social System," *Harvard Educational Review,* **29** (Fall 1959).

12. See, for example, Samuel Bowles, "Unequal Education and the Reproduction of the Social Division of Labor," in *Schooling in Corporate Society,* Martin Carnoy (ed.), (New York: McKay, 1972), p. 56; Michael B. Katz, *Class, Bureaucra-*

*cy, and Schools* (New York: Praeger, 1971), p. xviii; and Patricia Cayo Sexton, *Education and Income* (New York: Viking, 1961).

13. Willard Waller, *The Sociology of Teaching* (New York: Russell and Russell, 1961).

14. Waller, p. 10.

15. Edward F. Vacha, "Culture of Children's Play" (Ph.D. diss., University of California, Santa Barbara, 1976).

16. Samuel Bowles and Herbert Gintis, *Schooling in Capitalist America: Educational Reform and the Contradictions of Economic Life* (New York: Basic Books, 1976).

17. David K. Cohen and Bella H. Rosenberg, "Functions and Fantasies: Understanding Schools in Capitalist America," *History of Education Quarterly* (Summer 1977), pp. 113–168.

18. Bowles and Gintis, p. 262.

19. Robert K. Merton, *Social Theory and Social Structure,* 2nd ed. (New York: Free Press, 1968), pp. 73–138.

20. David Goslin, *The School in Contemporary Society* (Chicago: Scott, Foresman, 1965), p. 4.

21. Philip W. Jackson, *Life in Classrooms* (Holt, Rinehart and Winston, 1968).

22. Alvin Toffler, *Future Shock* (New York: Random House, 1970.)

23. Susan Jacoby, *Inside Soviet Schools* (New York: Hill and Wang, 1974), pp. 12–13.

24. Peter M. Blau and Otis D. Duncan, *The American Occupational Structure* (New York: Wiley, 1967).

25. Quoted in Joseph Lopreato and Lionel S. Lewis, *Social Stratification: A Reader* (New York: Harper & Row, 1974), p. 43.

26. Michael Harrington, *Socialism* (New York: Bantam Books, 1972), pp. 445–49.

27. Robert D. Reischauer, Robert W. Hartman, and Daniel J. Sullivan, *Reforming School Finances* (Washington, D.C.: Brookings Institution, 1973).

28. *Digest of Educational Statistics, 1977–78,* Table 31, p. 36.

29. *Digest of Educational Statistics, 1977–78,* Table 97, p. 94.

30. *Digest of Educational Statistics, 1977–78,* Table 90, p. 88.

31. *Digest of Educational Statistics, 1977–78,* Figure 9, p. 91.

32. *Digest of Educational Statistics, 1977–78,* p. 114.

33. *Digest of Educational Statistics, 1977–78,* p. 107.

34. James S. Coleman, *The Adolescent Society: The Social Life of the Teenager and its Impact on Education* (Glencoe, Ill.: Free Press, 1963).

35. This section draws mostly on Howard S. Becker, Blanche Geer, and Everett C. Hughes, *Making The Grade: The Academic Side of College Life* (New York: Wiley, 1968); and Jules Henry, *Culture Against Man* (New York: Random House, 1963).

36. Coleman, p. 3.

37. Parelius and Parelius, p. 176.

38. This section draws mostly from Theodore M. Newcomb, "Student Peer Group Influence," in Nevitt Sanford (ed.), *The American College* (New York: Wiley, 1962), pp. 469–488; and J. H. Bushnell, "Student Culture at Vassar," in N. Sanford (ed.) pp. 489–514.

39. Everett C. Hughes, et al., "Student Culture and Academic Effort," in Sanford (ed.), pp. 515–530.

40. Becker, et al.

41. For a good summary of the research, see Charles M. Bonjean and Reece McGee, "Undergraduate Scholastic Dishonesty: A Comparative Analysis of Deviance and Control Systems,"

*Southwestern Social Science Quarterly* (December 1965), pp. 289–296.

42. Bonjean and McGee, p. 290.

43. Parelius and Parelius, p. 285.

44. K. P. Cross, *Beyond the Open Door: New Students to Higher Education* (San Francisco: Jossey-Bass, 1971), p. 7.

45. Ernest Q. Campbell and C. Norman Alexander, Jr., ''Peer Influences on Adolescent Educational Aspirations and Attainments,'' *American Sociological Review* **29 (1)** (August 1964), pp. 58–75.

46. Boocock, p. 183.

47. James J. Coleman et al., *Equality of Educational Opportunity* (Washington, D.C.: U.S. Government Printing Office, 1966), p. 20.

48. Newsweek, August 7, 1978, p. 29.

49. This section is based on Richard A. Rehberg and Evelyn R. Rosenthal, *Class and Merit in the American High School* (New York: Longmans, 1978).

50. Parelius and Parelius, p. 287.

51. ''Puzzles and Paradoxes: Males Dominate in Educational Success,'' *The Education Digest* **41**, pp. 4–14.

52. Boocock, p. 87.

53. Walter Guzzardi, Jr., ''The Uncertain Passage from College to Job,'' *Fortune* (January 1976), p. 129.

54. Ivar Berg and Sherry Gorelick, *Education and Jobs: The Great Training Robbery* (New York: Praeger, 1970); and Randall Collins, ''A Conflict Theory of Sexual Stratification,'' *Social Problems* **19** (Summer 1972), pp. 9–12.

55. The following discussion is based largely on Thomas F. Pettigrew and Robert C. Green, ''School Desegregation in Large Cities: A Critique of the Coleman 'White Flight' Thesis,'' *Harvard Educational Review* **46 (1)** (1976), pp. 1–53.

56. Coleman, p. 3.

57. Coleman, p. 21.

58. George Gallup, ''Seventh Annual Gallup Poll of Public Attitudes Toward Education.'' *Phi Delta Kappan*, Dec., 1975, pp. 229–231.

59. David J. Armor, ''The Double Double Standard: A Reply,'' *Public Interest*, (Winter 1973), pp. 119–131; and Robert A. Dentler, et al. (eds.), *The Urban R's: Race Relations on the Problem in Urban Education* (New York: Praeger, 1967).

60. Morris Rosenberg and Roberta Simons, *Black and White Self-Esteem: The Urban School Child* (Washington, D.C.: Arnold M. Rose Monograph Series, American Sociological Association, 1971), pp. 24–26; and Nancy H. St. John, *Desegregation: School Outcomes for Children* (New York: Wiley, 1975), p. 119.

61. Thomas Sowell, ''Black Excellence: The Case of Dunbar High School,'' *The Public Interest* (Spring 1974), pp. 3–21.

62. Green and Pettigrew, p. 5.

63. Christopher Jencks and others, Inequality: A Reassessment of the Effect of Family and Schooling in America (New York: Basic Books, 1972), pp. 176–246

## CHAPTER 13

1. Mark Twain, *Letters from the Earth* (Greenwich, Conn.: Fawcett, 1968), pp. 179–180.

2. Emile Durkheim, *The Elementary Forms of the Religious Life* (New York: Free Press, 1965), p. 37.

3. See Ninian Smart, *The Religious Experience of Mankind* (New York: Scribner's Sons, 1976), pp. 27–53; and John B. Noss, *Man's Religions* (New York: Macmillan, 1971), pp. 4–33.

4. See Max Weber, *The Religion of China* (New York: Free Press, 1951); and C. K. Yang, *Religion in Chinese Society* (Berkeley, Calif.: University of California Press, 1961).

5. Sir Edward B. Taylor, *Primtive Culture* (New York: Harper and Row, 1958).

6. Ibid.

7. Ibid., p. 62.

8. Rudolf Otto, *The Idea of the Holy* (New York: Oxford University Press, 1958).

9. See Roland Robertson, *The Sociological Interpretatation of Religion* (New York: Schocken, 1972), pp. 113–149.

10. See Robert N. Bellah, *Beyond Belief* (New York: Harper & Row, 1970), pp. 29–44.

11. Bronislaw Malinowski, *Magic, Science, and Religion* (Garden City, N.Y.: Doubleday, 1948).

12. See Andrew Dickson White, *A History of the Warfare of Science and Theology in Christendom* (New York: Free Press, 1965).

13. Ludwig Feuerbach, *The Essence of Christianity* (New York: Harper & Row, 1957).

14. Karl Marx, *The Economic and Philosophic Manuscripts of 1844* (New York: International Publishers, 1964), pp. 170–174.

15. H. Richard Niebuhr, *The Social Sources of Denominationalism* (New York: Meridian Books, 1957).

16. N. J. Demerath, III, *Social Class in American Protestantism* (Chicago: Rand McNally, 1965).

17. Rodney Stark and Charles Y. Glock, *American Piety: The Nature of Religious Commitment* (Berkeley, Calif.: University of California Press, 1968).

18. Durkheim, *The Elementary Forms of the Religious Life*, pp. 28–29.

19. W. Lloyd Warner, *The Family of God* (New Haven, Conn.: Yale University Press, 1961).

20. Will Herberg, *Protestant-Catholic-Jew* (Garden City, N.Y.: Doubleday, 1960).

21. Robert N. Bellah, ''Civil Religion in America,'' *Daedalus* **96** (Winter 1967), pp. 1–21.

22. Max Weber, *The Protestant Ethic and the Spirit of Capitalism* (New York: Scribner's, 1958).

23. Robert K. Merton, *Social Theory and Social Structure* (New York: Free Press, 1968), pp. 628–660.

24. Gerhard Lenski, *The Religious Factor*, rev. ed. (Garden City, N.Y.: Doubleday, 1963).

25. Ernst Troeltsch, *The Social Teaching of the Christian Churches* (London: Allen & Unwin, 1931).

26. Liston Pope, *Millhands and Preachers* (New Haven, Conn.: Yale University Press, 1942).

27. J. Milton Yinger, *The Scientific Study of Religion* (New York: Crowell-Collier and Macmillan, 1970).

28. Peter L. Berger and Thomas Luckmann, *The Social Construction of Reality* (Garden City, N.Y.: Doubleday, 1966).

29. Peter L. Berger, *The Sacred Canopy* (Garden City, N.Y.: Doubleday, 1967).

30. Sidney E. Mead, *The Lively Experiment* (New York: Harper & Row, 1963).

31. See Seymour Martin Lipset, *The First New Nation* (New York: Basic Books, 1963).

32. Perry Miller, *Errand into the Wilderness* (New York: Harper & Row, 1964), p. 150.

33. Lipset, *The First New Nation*.

34. Quoted in Richard L. Tomasson, *Sweden: Prototype of Modern Society* (New York: Random House, 1970), p. 78.

35. Jeffrey K. Hadden, *The Gathering Storm in the Churches* (Garden City, N.Y.: Doubleday, 1969), p. 25.

36. Stark and Glock, *American Piety: The Nature of Religious Commitment*, pp. 141–162.

37. Talcott Parsons, *Sociological Theory and Modern Society* (New York: Free Press, 1967), pp. 385–421.

38. Quoted in Gene Brown (ed.), *Religion in America* (New York: Arno Press, 1977), pp. 412–413.

39. See David O. Moberg, *The Great Reversal: Evangelicalism Versus Social Concern* (New York: Lippincott, 1972).


## CHAPTER 14

1. Hans Gerth and C. Wright Mills, *From Max Weber: Essays in Sociology* (New York: Oxford University Press, 1946), p. 180.

2. See Edward W. Lehman, *Political Society: A Macrosociology of Politics* (New York: Columbia University Press, 1977), pp. 47–48.

3. See Max Weber, *The Theory of Social and Economic Organization* (New York: Oxford University Press, 1947), pp. 324–406.

4. Ibid., p. 328.

5. Gerth and Mills, p. 78.

6. Seymour M. Lipset, "Political Sociology," in Robert K. Merton, Leonard Broom, and Leonard Cottrell, Jr. (eds.), *Sociology Today* (New York: Basic Books, 1959), pp. 91–92.

7. C. Wright Mills, *The Power Elite* (New York: Oxford University Press, 1956).

8. See William C. Mitchell, "The shape of political theory to come: from political sociology to political economy," in S. M. Lipset (ed.), *Politics and the Social Sciences* (New York: Oxford University Press, 1969), pp. 101–136.

9. Edward Shils, *Political Development in the New States* (The Hague: Mouton, 1968), pp. 51–60.

10. For a discussion of this conceptualization of democratic society see Robert A. Dahl, *Modern Political Analysis* (Englewood Cliffs, N.J.: Prentice-Hall, 1963), chapter 2. Major studies of the relationships between social structure, culture, and politics include: Gabriel Almond and Sidney Verba, *The Civic Culture: Political Attitudes and Democracy in Five Nations* (Princeton, N.J.: Princeton University Press, 1963); Seymour Martin Lipset, *Political Man: The Social Bases of Politics* (Garden City, N.Y.: Doubleday and Co., 1960); Seymour Martin Lipset, *The First New Nation* (Garden City, N.Y.: Doubleday, 1963); Harry Eckstein, *Division and Cohesion in Democracy* (Princeton, N.J.: Princeton University Press, 1966); Barrington Moore, Jr., *Social Origins of Dictatorship and Democracy: Lord and Peasant in the Making of the Modern World* (Boston: Beacon Press, 1966).

11. Alexis de Tocqueville, *Democracy in America* 2 vols. (New York: Vintage Books, 1955).

12. Carl J. Friedrich and Zbigniew K. Brzezinski, *Totalitarian Dictatorship and Autocracy* (New York: Praeger. 2nd ed., 1966), chapter 2.

13. See Alfred G. Meyer, *Communism*, 3d ed. (New York: Random House, 1967).

14. Maurice Duverger, *Political Parties* (London: Methuen, 1954), p. 46.

15. This characterization of competitive party systems is based on Giovanni Sartori, *Parties and Party Systems* (Cambridge: Cambridge University Press, 1976).

16. *1977 Statistical Abstract of the United States* (Washington, D.C.: U.S. Department of Commerce, Bureau of the Census), p. 316.

17. *Historical Statistics of the United States* (Washington, D.C.: U.S. Department of Commerce, Bureau of the Census, 1976), pt. 2, p. 1100; *1977 Statistical Abstract of the United States*, p. 268.

18. See Robert Michels, *Political Parties: A Sociological Study of the Oligarchical Tendencies of Modern Democracy* (New York: Collier Books, 1962).

19. See Seymour M. Lipset, Martin Trow, and James Coleman, *Union Democracy* (New York: Free Press, 1956).

20. See David Snyder and Charles Tilly, "Hardship and Collective Violence in France, 1830 to 1860" *American Sociological Review*, **37**, **(5)** (October 1972), pp. 520–532.

21. Ted Robert Gurr, "Psychological factors in civil violence" *World Politics*, **20** (January 1968), pp. 245–278.

22. Sidney Verba and Norman Nie, *Participation in America: Political Democracy and Social Equality* (New York: Harper & Row, 1972).

23. *Ibid.*, p. 335.

24. See Seymour Martin Lipset, *Political Man: The Social Bases of Politics* (Garden City, N.Y.: Doubleday, 1963).

25. See Douglas P. Bwy, "Political Instability in Latin America: The Cross-Cultural Test of a Causal Model" *Latin American Research Review* 3 **(2)** (Spring 1968) pp. 17–66.

26. See Ted Robert Gurr, "A Causal Model of Civil Strife: A Comparative Analysis Using New Indices" *American Political Science Review* 62 (December 1968) pp. 1104–1124.

27. Irving Louis Horowitz and Martin Liebowitz, "Social Deviance and Political Marginality: Toward a Redefinition of the Relation Between Sociology and Politics" *Social Problems*, **15, (3)** (1968).

28. Michael Lewis, "The Negro Protest in Urban America," in Joseph R. Gusfield (ed.), *Protest, Reform and Revolt* (New York: Wiley, 1970), p. 156.

29. See Theodore Able, *Why Hitler Came to Power* (New York: Prentice-Hall, 1938).

30. Major studies of political socialization, upon which this section is based, include: David Easton and Jack Dennis, *Children in the Political System* (New York: McGraw-Hill, 1969); Fred I. Greenstein, *Children and Politics* (New Haven, Conn.: Yale University Press, 1965); Robert D. Hess and Judith V. Torney, *The Development of Political Attitudes in Children* (Chicago: Aldine, 1967); Dean Jaros, *Socialization to Politics* (New York: Praeger, 1973); M. Kent Jennings and Richard G. Niemi, *The Political Character of Adolescence* (Princeton, N.J.: Princeton University Press, 1974).

31. Robert N. Bellah, "Civil Religion in America," *Daedalus* (Winter 1967); Robert N. Bellah, *The Broken Covenant: American Civil Religion in the Time of Trial* (New York: Seabury, 1975).

32. Easton and Dennis, *Children in the Political System*, pp. 391–393.

33. Greenstein, *Children and Politics*, p. 42.

34. Jennings and Niemi, *The Political Character of Adolescence*, p. 271.

35. *National Task Force on Citizenship Education Report* (Washington, D.C.: U.S. Department of Health, Education and Welfare, 1978).

36. Two of the most influential studies of the relationship between industrialization and democracy are Gerhard E. Lenski, *Power and Privilege* (New York: McGraw-Hill, 1966) and Seymour Martin Lipset, *Political Man: The Social Bases of Politics* (Garden City, N.Y.: Doubleday and Co., 1960).

37. C. Wright Mills, *Power, Politics and People* (New York: Oxford University Press, 1963), p. 23.

38. Floyd Hunter, *Community Power Structure* (Chapel Hill, N.C.: University of North Carolina Press, 1953).

39. Mills, *The Power Elite,* p. 283.

40. Mills, *The Power Elite,* p. 308.

41. See William Domhoff, *Who Rules America?* (Englewood Cliffs, N.J.: Prentice-Hall, 1967) and William Domhoff *The Higher Circles* (New York: Vintage, 1970).

42. Robert A. Dahl, *Who Governs?* (New Haven, Conn.: Yale University Press, 1961).

43. Arnold M. Rose, *The Power Structure* (New York: Oxford University Press, 1967).

44. John Walton, "Substance and Artifact: The Current Status of Research on Community Power Structure," *American Journal of Sociology.* **72** (January 1966) pp. 430–438.

45. See Robert Perrucci and Marc Pilisuk, "Leaders and Community Elites: The Interorganizational Bases of Community Power" *American Sociological Review* **35** (December 1970), pp. 1040–1057.

46. See Edward Laumann, Peter Marsden, and John Galaskiewicz, "Community Elite Influence Structures: Extensions of a Network Analysis" *American Journal of Sociology* **83, (3)** (November 1977) pp. 594–631.

## CHAPTER 15

1. See Elman R. Service, *Profiles in Ethnology* (New York: Harper & Row, 1963), pp. 3–25.

2. Walter Goldschmidt, *Man's Way* (New York: Holt, Rinehart and Winston, 1959), pp. 193–194.

3. Ibid., p. 195.

4. Ibid., pp. 196–209, an excellent brief summary of the central characteristics of advanced agricultural societies.

5. See S. M. Lipset, *Political Man* (Garden City, N.Y.: Doubleday, 1959), pp. 48–75, for a detailed analysis of this issue.

6. See Joseph R. Strayer et al., *The Mainstream of Civilization* (New York: Harcourt Brace Jovanovich, 1969), pp. 577–591, for a good survey of some of the social effects of industrialization.

7. R. G. Lipsey and P. O. Steiner, *Economics* (New York: Harper & Row, 1975), p. 395.

8. Ralph Gray and John M. Peterson, *Economic Development of the United States* (Homewood, Ill.: Irwin, 1974), pp. 505–506.

9. "Labor: Long Way from Pittsburgh," *Time,* May 16, 1955, p. 27.

10. Ibid.

11. J. M. Kreps and Joseph J. Spengler, "The Leisure Component of Economic Growth," in H. R. Bowen and Garth L. Mangum (eds.), *Automation and Economic Progress* (Englewood Cliffs, N.J.: Prentice-Hall, 1966).

12. U.S. Bureau of the Census, *Statistical Abstract of the United States, 1977* (Washington, D.C.: U.S. Government Printing Office, 1975), p. 400, no. 654.

13. The data are from "Size Distribution of Income in 1963," *Survey of Current Business,* April 1964, Table 4. Figures for 1913 are very rough approximations.

14. U.S. Bureau of Census, *Statistical Abstracts of the United States, 1977* (Washington, D.C., U.S. Government Printing Office, 1977), no. 708.

15. Lipset, *Political Man,* p. 66.

16. U.S. Bureau of the Census, *Statistical Abstract of the United States, 1977* (Washington, D.C.: U.S. Government Printing Office, 1977), Table 660.

17. See Edward Fried et al., *Setting National Priorities: The 1974 Budget* (Washington, D.C.: Brookings Institution, 1973), p. 42.

18. Elizabeth K. Nottingham, *Religion and Society* (New York: Random House, 1964), pp. 19–26.

19. Thomas F. O'Dea, *The Sociology of Religion* (Englewood Cliffs, N.J.: Prentice-Hall, 1966), pp. 72–97.

20. *Statistical Abstract of the United States, 1974,* Table 1040, p. 614.

21. *Manpower Report of the President* (Washington, D.C.: U.S. Government Printing Office, April 1974), p. 268.

22. *U.S. Bureau of Census, Statistical Abstracts, 1977,* (Washington, D.C.: U.S. Government Printing Office, 1977), no. 625.

23. Ibid., No. 632.

24. Ibid., No. 730.

25. Larry E. Suter and Herman P. Miller, "Income Differences Between Men and Career Women," *American Journal of Sociology* **78** (January 1973), p. 965.

26. "Older Workers' Role Grows Smaller," *Los Angeles Times,* August 21, 1978, Part III, p. 10.

27. *The Chronicle of Higher Education,* July 31, 1978, p. 2.

28. A. A. Berle and G. C. Means, *The Modern Corporation and Private Property* (New York: Commerce Clearing House, 1932).

29. Paul A. Samuelson, *Economics,* 10th ed. (New York: McGraw-Hill, 1976), p. 113.

30. Ibid.

31. Ibid., p. 112.

32. Wilbert E. Moore, *The Conduct of the Corporation* (New York: Random House, 1966), p. 5.

33. See John Kenneth Galbraith, *The New Industrial State* (Boston: Houghton Mifflin, 1967), p. 320.

34. Williard F. Mueller, *A Primer on Monopoly and Competition* (New York: Random House, Inc., 1970), p. 80–81, and Robert Lekachman, *Economists at Bay: Why the Experts Will Never Solve Your Problem* (New York: McGraw-Hill, 1976), p. 164.

35. See Herbert J. Gans, "The New Egalitarianism," *Saturday Review* (May 6, 1972), p. 43.

36. Ronald Segal, "Everywhere at Home, Home Nowhere," *Center Magazine* **6, (3)** (May–June 1973), pp. 8–9.

37. Neil H. Jacoby, "The Multinational Corporation," *Center Magazine,* **3, (3)** (May 1970), pp. 37–55.

38. Lekachman, *Economists at Bay,* pp. 165–6.

39. *New York Times,* June 19, 1975, p. 35, cited in Lekachman, *Economists at Bay,* p. 165.

40. Lekachman, *Economists at Bay,* p. 165–6.

41. Anthony Sampson, *The Sovereign State of I.T.T.* (Greenwich, Conn.: Crest, 1973).

42. Sampson, p. 85, summarized in Lekachman, *Economists at Bay,* pp. 168–71.

43. Richard Barnet and Ronald Mueller, *Global Reach* (New York: Simon and Schuster, 1974), pp. 13–14, cited in Lekachman, *Economists at Bay,* p. 163.

44. *Statistical Abstracts of the United States, 1974,* Table 567.

45. See U.S. Department of Labor, *Handbook of Labor Bureau Statistics, 1977,* Table No. 137.

46. Daniel R. Fusfeld, *Economics* (Lexington, Mass.: Heath, 1976) p. 608.

47. Samuelson, *Economics,* pp. 132–133.

48. Fusfeld, *Economics,* p. 576.

49. Samuelson, *Economics,* p. 152.

50. Ibid., p. 48.

51. See Lipset, *Political Man,* pp. 285–309.

52. Seymour Melman, "Pentagon Capitalism," *The Military-Industrial Complex* (New York: Harper & Row, 1972), p. 287.

53. Donald McDonald, "Militarism in America," *Center*

Magazine, **3**, **(1)** (January–February 1970), pp. 14–15; Seymour Melman, *Pentagon Capitalism: The Political Economy of War* (New York: McGraw-Hill, 1970) pp. 177–179.

54. John K. Galbraith, *The New Industrial State* (New York: Signet Books, 1968), p. 317.

55. *Statistical Abstracts of the United States, 1977*, p. 359.

56. Stanley Lieberson, "An Empirical Study of Military-Industrial Linkages," *Industrial Complex: A Reassessment*, Sam S. Sarkesian (ed.), (Beverly Hills: Sage Publications, 1972), pp. 53–94.

57. Cited in Seymour Melman, *Pentagon Capitalism: The Political Economy of War* (New York: McGraw-Hill, 1970), p. 235.

58. For an excellent and brief overview of the development of economic thought see Neil J. Smelser, *The Sociology of Economic Life*, 2nd ed., (Englewood Cliffs, N.J.: Prentice-Hall, Inc., 1976), pp. 1–27.

59. Samuelson, *Economics*, p. 841.

60. Samuelson, *Economics*, p. 845.

61. *Statistical Abstracts of the United States, 1977*, p. 453–4, no. 733 and no. 735.

62. Ibid., p. 450, no. 726.

63. Ibid., p. 450, no. 726.

64. A Study of Socio-economic Characteristics of Ethnic Minorities Based on the 1970 Census, vol. 3, American Indians, H.E.W. Publications (OS) 75–122, July, 1974.

65. Ibid., 452, no. 730.

66. Ibid., p. 387, no. 625.

67. Ibid., p. 389, no. 629.

68. *Work in America:* Report of a Special Task Force to the Secretary of Health, Education, and Welfare. (Cambridge, Mass.: The M.I.T. Press, 1973).

69. *The Chronicle of Higher Education*, July 31, 1978, p. 2.

70. See Seymour Melman, *The Permanent War Economy* (New York: Simon and Schuster, 1974).

71. Paul R. Ehrlich and Anne H. Ehrlich, *The End of Affluence* (New York: Ballantine Books, 1974) p. 23.

72. "Poor Nations' Future Grim—World Bank," *Los Angeles Times*, August 16, 1978, Part III, p. 3.

73. Daniel Yankelovich, "The Meaning of Work," in Jerome M. Rosow (ed.), *The Worker and the Job* (Englewood Cliffs, N.J.: Prentice-Hall, 1974).

74. See Richard C. Wilcock and Walter H. Franke, *Unwanted Workers* (New York: Free Press, 1963).

75. Nancy C. Morse and Robert S. Weiss, "The Function and Meaning of Work and the Job," *American Sociological Review* **20** (April 1955).

76. H. C. Wilensky, "Work as a Social Problem," in Howard S. Becker (ed.), *Social Problems* (New York: Wiley, 1966), p. 143.

77. Ibid., p. 165.

78. Ibid., p. 148.

79. See for example, Daniel Bell, *The Coming of Post-Industrial Society* (New York: Basic Books, 1973), Bell (ed.), *Toward the Year 2000: Work in Progress* (Boston: Houghton Mifflin, 1968); Herman Kahn and Anthony J. Wiener, *The Year 2,000* (New York: Crowell-Collier and Macmillan, 1967); and Alvin Toffler, *Future Shock* (New York: Random House, 1970).

80. Kahn and Wiener, *The Year 2,000* p. 195.

81. Kreps and Spengler, "The Leisure Component of Economic Growth," p. 128.

82. *Statistical Abstract of the United States, 1977*, no. 654.

83. H. P. Miller, "The Distribution of Personal Income in the United States," in Dennis M. Wrong and Harry L. Gracey (eds.)

*Readings in Introductory Sociology* (New York: Crowell-Collier and Macmillan, 1972), p. 407.

84. *Statistical Abstract of the United States, 1977*, no. 708.

85. See Daniel Bell, "Notes on the Post-Industrial Society," *Public Interest* **1** (Winter 1967), and **2** (Spring 1967); and Bell, *The Coming of Postindustrial Society*, pp. 358–367.

86. Bell, *The Coming of Post-Industrial Society*, p. 362.

87. Charles Reich, "The New Property," *Public Interest* **3** (Spring 1966), p. 57.

88. John Maynard Keynes, "Economic Possibilities for Our Grandchildren," in Paul A. Samuelson, *Readings in Economics*, 7th ed. (New York: McGraw-Hill, 1973).

## CHAPTER 16

1. Howard S. Becker, *Outsiders: Studies in the Sociology of Deviance* (New York: Free Press, 1963), p. 26.

2. James S. Wallerstein and Clement J. Wylie, "Our Law-Abiding Law-Breakers," *Probation* **25** (April 1947), pp. 107–112.

3. Georg Simmel, *Conflict and the Web of Group Affiliation*, trans (New York: Free Press, 1955).

4. Emile Durkheim, *The Division of Labor in Society* (New York: Free Press, 1960).

5. Kai T. Erikson, *Wayward Puritans: A Study in the Sociology of Deviance*, (New York: Wiley, 1966), pp. 10–11.

6. Lewis Coser, *The Functions of Social Conflict* (New York: Free Press, 1956); and *Continuities in the Study of Social Conflict* (New York: Free Press, 1967).

7. Charles Winick and Paul Kinsie, *The Lively Commerce: Prostitution in the United States* (Chicago: Quadrangle Books, 1971).

8. Edwin H. Sutherland, "Differential Association," in Marvin E. Wolfgang, Leonard Savity, and Norman Johnston (eds.), *The Sociology of Crime and Delinquency* (New York: John Wiley, 1970).

9. President's Commission on Law Enforcement and the Administration of Justice, *The Challenge of Crime in a Free Society* (Washington, D.C.: U.S. Government Printing Office, 1967).

10. See, for example, Wallerstein and Wylie, "Our Law-Abiding Law-Breakers"; and Austin Porterfield, "Delinquency and Its Outcome in Court and College," *American Journal of Sociology* **49** (November 1943), pp. 199–208.

11. Jay R. Williams and Martin Gold, "From Delinquent Behavior to Official Delinquency," *Social Problems* **20** (Fall 1972), pp. 209–229.

12. Philip H. Ennis, "Crimes, Victims, and Police," *Transaction 4* (1967), pp. 36–44.

13. "Wide Disparities in Crime Totals Found in Sampling of 8 Cities," *The New York Times*, January 27, 1974, p. 34.

14. David Burnham, "New York is Found Safest of 13 Cities in Crime Study," *The New York Times*, April 15, 1974, p. 1.

15. James P. Levine, "The Potential for Crime Overreporting in Criminal Victimization Surveys," *Criminology* **14 (3)** (November 1976) pp. 307–330.

16. For a thoroughgoing review of the system and philosophy of Anglo-American penology, see Sue Titus Reid, *Crime and Criminology*, 2nd ed. (New York: Holt, Rinehart and Winston, 1979).

17. President's Commission on Law Enforcement and the Administration of Justice, *The Challenge of Crime in a Free Society*.

18. William H. Sheldon, *An Introduction to Constitutional Psychiatry* (New York: Harper & Bros., 1949).

19. Sheldon Glueck and Eleanor Glueck, *Unraveling Juvenile Delinquency* (New York: Harper & Bros., 1952).

20. George B. Vold, *Theoretical Criminology* (New York: Oxford University Press, 1958), p. 119.

21. National Commission on Law Observance and Enforcement, *Report on the Causes of Crime* (Washington, D.C.: U.S. Government Printing Office, 1931).

22. Travis Hirschi, *Causes of Delinquency* (Berkeley: University of California Press, 1971), pp. 3–4.

23. Ibid., p. 225.

24. Robert K. Merton, "Social Structure and Anomie," *American Sociological Review* **3** (October 1938), pp. 672–682.

25. Richard A. Cloward and Lloyd E. Ohlin, "Differential Opportunity Structure," in Wolfgang, Savitz, and Johnston (eds.), *The Sociology of Crime and Delinquency* (New York: Wiley, 1970).

26. Albert K. Cohen, *Delinquent Boys* (New York: Free Press, 1955).

27. Travis Hirschi, *Causes of Delinquency*, p. 26.

28. Gresham M. Sykes and David Matza, "Techniques of Neutralization," *American Sociological Review* **22** (December 1957), pp. 664–670.

29. Walter C. Reckless, *The Crime Problem* (New York: Appleton-Century-Crofts, 1961).

30. Sutherland, "Differential Association," in Wolfgang, Savity, and Johnston, eds., *The Sociology of Crime and Delinquency*.

31. Becker, *Outsiders: Studies in the Sociology of Deviance*.

32. Erving Goffman, *Stigma: Notes on the Management of Spoiled Identity* (Englewood Cliffs, N.J.: Prentice-Hall, 1964).

33. Edwin M. Lemert, *Human Deviance, Social Problems, and Social Control* (Englewood Cliffs, N.J.: Prentice-Hall, 1967).

34. Richard Quinney, ed., *Criminal Justice in America*, Boston: Little Brown, 1974) p. 13.

35. Ibid., p. 8.

## CHAPTER 17

1. Herbert Blumer, "Elementary Collective Groupings," in Alfred McClung Lee (ed.), *Principles of Sociology* (New York: Barnes & Noble, 1946, pp. 185–186.

2. Paul B. Sheatsley and Jacob J. Feldman, "The Assassination of President Kennedy: A Preliminary Report on Public Reactions and Behavior," *Public Opinion Quarterly* **28** (Summer 1964), p. 192.

3. Paul F. Lazarsfeld, Bernard Berelson, and Hazel Gaudet, *The People's Choice*, 3d ed. (New York: Columbia University Press, 1968).

4. See, Elihu Katz, "The Two-Step Flow of Communication: An Up-to-date Report on an Hypothesis," *Public Opinion Quarterly* **21** (Spring 1957), pp. 61–78, for a summary of the related research.

5. See Orrin E. Klapp, *Currents of Unrest* (New York: Holt, Rinehardt and Winston, Inc., 1972), p. 312 for a further description of fads.

6. Hadley Cantril et al., *The Invasion from Mars* (Princeton, N.J.: Princeton University Press, 1940.)

7. Blumer, "Elementary Collective Groupings," pp. 189–190.

8. Barry Schwartz, *Queuing and Waiting* (Chicago: University of Chicago Press, 1975.)

9. Gustave LeBon, *The Crowd* (New York: Ballantine Books, 1969), pp. 25–27.

10. Herbert Blumer, "Elementary Collective Behavior," in Alfred McClung Lee (ed.), *Principles of Sociology* (New York: Barnes & Noble, 1946), pp. 170–171.

11. Ralph H. Turner and Lewis M. Killian, *Collective Behavior*, 2nd ed. (Englewood Cliffs, N.J.: Prentice-Hall, 1972), pp. 18–21 and 94–95.

12. John Dollard et al., *Frustration and Aggression* (New Haven, Conn.: Yale University Press, 1939).

13. Turner and Killian, *Collective Behavior*, pp. 21–25.

14. Ibid.

15. Richard Berk, "A Gaming Approach to Crowd Behavior," *American Sociological Review* **39** (June 1974), pp. 355–372. For additional discussion on the gaming approach to crowds see, Richard Berk *Collective Behavior* (Dubuque, Iowa: Brown, 1974), pp. 54–75.

16. Turner and Killian, *Collective Behavior*, p. 81.

17. Irving L. Janis et al., "The Problem of Panic," in Duane P. Schultz (ed.), *Panic Behavior* (New York: Random House, 1964), p. 120.

18. Stanley Lieberson and Arnold R. Silverman, "The Precipitants and Underlying Conditions of Race Riots, *American Sociological Review* **30** (December 1965), pp. 887–898.

19. National Advisory Commission on Civil Disorders, *Report of the National Advisory Commission on Civil Disorders* (Washington, D.C.: U.S. Government Printing Office, 1968), pp. 112–116.

20. Ibid., pp. 117–124.

21. Neil J. Smelser, *Theory of Collective Behavior* (New York: Free Press, 1962).

22. Tomatsu Shibutani, *Improvised News* (Indianapolis: Bobbs-Merrill, 1966), p. 17.

23. Ibid., pp. 15–16.

24. Ibid., p. 165.

25. Ibid., pp. 165–166.

26. C. Wendell King, *Social Movements in the United States* (New York: Random House, 1956), p. 27.

27. Roberta Ash, *Social Movements in America* (Chicago: Markham, 1972), pp. 10, 142–147.

28. See David E. Cronon, *Black Moses* (Madison: The University of Wisconsin Press, 1969), for a discussion of the history of the Garvey movement.

29. Carl A. Dawson and Warner E. Gettys, *An Introduction to Sociology* (New York: Ronald, 1935).

30. Anthony Wallace, "Revitalization Movements," *American Anthropologist* **58** (April 1956), pp. 264–280.

31. Frantz Fanon, *The Wretched of the Earth* (New York: Grove 1963).

32. Eric Hoffer, *The True Believer* (New York: Harper & Row, 1959).

33. Ted Robert Gurr, *Why Men Rebel* (Princeton, N.J.: Princeton University Press, 1971).

34. Luther P. Gerlach and Virginia H. Hine, *People, Power, Change* (Indianapolis: Bobbs-Merrill 1970).

35. Mayer N. Zald and Roberta Ash, "Social Movement Organizations: Growth, Decay and Change" *Social Forces* **44** (March 1966), pp. 327–340.

## CHAPTER 18

1. Bryce Ryan, *Social and Cultural Change* (New York: Ronald Press, 1969), pp. 99–100.

2. Ralph Linton, *The Study of Man* (New York: Appleton, 1936), pp. 326–327.

3. Marshall McLuhan, *Understanding Media* (New York: McGraw-Hill, 1965).

4. E. Katz and P. Lazarsfeld, *Personal Influence* (New York: The Free Press, 1955); Joseph Klapper, *The Effects of Mass Communication* (New York: Free Press, 1960).

5. Daniel Lerner, *The Passing of Traditional Society* (New York: Free Press, 1958); Bryce Ryan, "The Ceylonese Village and the New Value System," *Rural Sociology*, **17** (1952), pp. 9–28.

6. Everett Rogers, *Diffusion of Innovations* (New York: Free Press, 1962).

7. Homer Barnett, *Innovation: The Basis of Cultural Change* (New York: McGraw-Hill, 1953), pp. 375–377.

8. William F. Whyte, "The Social Structure of the Restaurant" *American Journal of Sociology* **54** (January 1949), pp. 302–308.

9. W. F. Cottrell, "Death by Dieselization," *American Sociological Review* **16** (June 1951), pp. 358–365.

10. George Foster, *Traditional Societies and Technological Change* (New York: Harper & Row, 1973), p. 116.

11. Frances Moore Lappe, "Fantasies of Famine," *Harper's Magazine* (February 1975), pp. 51–54, 87–90.

12. Sidney Aronson, "The Sociology of the Bicycle," *Social Forces* **30** (1952), pp. 305–312.

13. Charles Lekberg, "The Tyranny of Querty," *Saturday Review* (September 30, 1972), pp. 37–40.

14. William Pratt, "The Anabaptist Explosion," *Natural History Magazine* (February 1969), pp. 8–23.

15. Joseph Lopreato, *Peasants No More* (San Francisco: Chandler, 1967).

16. See James Coleman, Elihu Katz, and Herbert Manzel, "The Diffusion of an Innovation among Physicians," *Sociometry* **29** (1957), pp. 253–270; Everett Rogers, *Diffusion of Innovations;* and Elihu Katz and Paul Lazarsfeld, *Personal Influence* (New York: Free Press, 1955).

17. Everett Rogers, *Communication Strategies for Family Planning* (New York: Free Press, 1973).

18. Ozzie Simmons, "The Clinical Team in a Chilean Health Center," in Benjamin Paul (ed.), *Health Culture and Community: Case Studies in Public Reactions to Health Problems* (New York: Russell Sage Foundation, 1955).

19. Allen Homberg, *Nomads of the Long Bow: The Siriono of Eastern Bolivia* (Garden City, N.Y.: Doubleday, 1969); and "Adentures in Culture Change," in Robert Spencer (ed.), *Method and Perspective in Anthropology* (Minneapolis: University of Minnesota Press, 1954).

20. Foster, *Traditional Societies and Technological Change,* p. 96.

21. Garth Jones, "Strategies and Tactics in Planned Organizational Change," *Human Organization* **24** (1965), pp. 192–200; see also Henry Dobyns, "Blunders with Bolsas," *Human Organization* **10** (Fall 1951), pp. 25–32.

22. See Francis Allen, "The Automobile," in Francis Allen, et al., *Technology and Social Change* (New York: Appleton, 1957).

23. Alex Inkeles, "Making Men Modern," *American Journal of Sociology,* **75 (2)** (September 1969), pp. 208–225.

24. Daniel Lerner, *The Passing of Traditional Society* (New York: Free Press, 1958).

25. McClelland, David, *The Achieving Society* (New York: D. Van Nostrand, 1961); Joseph Kahl, *The Measurement of Modernism* (Austin Texas: University of Texas Press, 1968).

26. Everett Hagen, *On The Theory of Social Change* (Homewood, Ill.: Dorsey, 1962).

27. William McCord, "Portrait of Transitional Man," in Irving L. Horowitz (ed.), *The New Sociology* (New York: Oxford Press, 1965).

28. Leslie White, *The Science of Culture* (New York: Grove, 1949).

29. Elman Service, *Primitive Social Organization* (New York: Random House, 1962).

30. Robert Redfield, *The Folk Culture of the Yucatan* (Chicago: University of Chicago Press, 1941).

31. Ralf Dahrendorf, *Class and Class Conflict in Industrial Society* (Stanford, Calif.: Stanford University Press, 1959).

32. See, for example, Herbert Marcuse, *One Dimensional Man* (Boston: Beacon, 1964); and Frantz Fanon, *The Wretched of the Earth* (New York: Grove Press, 1968).

33. See Talcott Parsons, *The Social System,* (New York: Free Press, 1951; and Parsons, *The System of Modern Societies,* (Englewood Cliffs, N.J.: Prentice-Hall, 1971).

34. Oswald Spengler, *The Decline of the West,* trans. Charles F. Atkinson (New York: Knopf, 1926–1928)

35. Arnold Toynbee, *A Study of History* (New York: Oxford University Press, 1935–1961).

36. Pitirim Sorokin, *Social and Cultural Dynamics* (New York: American, 1941).

37. Kenneth Clark, *Civilisation: A Personal View* (New York: Harper & Row, 1969), pp. 58–60.

38. See, for example, L. Coch and J. French, "Overcoming Resistence to Change, *Human Relations* **1** (1948), pp. 512–532; and Kurt Lewin, "Group Decision and Social Change," in E. Maccoby, T. Newcomb, and E. Hartley (eds.) *Readings in Social Psychology,* 3d ed. (New York: Holt, Rinehart and Winston, 1958).

39. Robert Heilbroner, *The Great Ascent* (New York: Harper & Row, 1963).

40. Alvin Toffler, *Future Shock* (New York: Random House, 1970) pp. 15–16.

## CHAPTER 19

1. Emile Durkheim, *Suicide: A Study in Sociology,* trans. John A. Spaulding and George Simpson (New York: Free Press, 1951).

2. Seymour Martin Lipset, "The Biography of a Research Project: *Union Democracy,*" in Phillip E. Hammond (ed.), *Sociologists at Work* (New York: Basic Books, 1964), pp. 96–120.

3. Robert N. Bellah, "Research Chronicle: *Tokugawa Religion,*" in Phillip E. Hammond (ed.), *Sociologists at Work* (New York: Basic Books, 1964), pp. 142–159.

4. Elliot Liebow, *Tally's Corner* (Boston: Little, Brown, 1967).

5. Sociologists nevertheless do a great deal of descriptive work to answer questions about how many people there are in different places, how many people are of certain ages and which sex, what is happening to the birth, death, and divorce rates, and so on.

6. See for example Bernard Berelson and Gary A. Steiner, *Human Behavior: An Inventory of Scientific Findings* (New York: Harcourt, 1964), p. 515.

7. Bonnie Bullough, "Poverty, Ethnic Identity, and Preventive Health Care, "*Journal of Health and Social Behavior* **13** (December 1972), pp. 347–359; David Coburn and Clyde R. Pope," "Socioeconomic Status and Preventive Health Behavior," *Journal of Health and Social Behavior* **15** (June 1974), pp. 67–78; and L. C. Deasy, "Socio-economic Status and Participation in the Poliomyelitis Vaccine Trial," *American Sociological Review* **21** (April 1956), pp. 185–191.

8. For perceptive discussions of this and other ethical dilemmas see Myron Glazer, *The Research Adventure* (New York: Random House, 1972).

9. Carl I. Hovland, "The Role of Primacy and Recency in Persuasive Communication," in Eleanor E. Maccoby, Theodore M. Newcomb, and Eugene L. Hartley (eds.), *Readings in Social Psychology*, 3rd ed. (New York: Holt, Rinehart and Winston, 1958), pp. 137–149.

10. Morton Deutsch and Mary Evans Collins, "Interracial Housing," in William Petersen (ed.), *American Social Patterns* (New York: Doubleday Anchor Books, 1956), pp. 7–61.

11. Peter M. Blau, "The Research Process in the *Study of The Dynamics of Bureaucracy*," in Phillip E. Hammond (ed.), *Sociologists at Work* (New York: Basic Books, 1964), pp. 16–49.

12. Blau, "The Research Process in the *Study of The Dynamics of Bureaucracy*," p. 29.

13. William Foote Whyte, *Street Corner Society* (Chicago: University of Chicago Press, 1943).

14. For a discussion of the broader uses of content analysis, see Bernard Berelson, *Content Analysis in Communication Research* (New York: Free Press, 1952).

15. Donald Auster, "A Content Analysis of Little Orphan Annie," *Social Problems* 2 (July 1954), pp. 26–33.

16. Walter Hirsch, "The Image of the Scientist in Science Fiction," in Bernard Barber and Walter Hirsch (eds.), *The Sociology of Science* (New York: Free Press, 1962).

17. For an excellent brief treatment of the scientific criteria for establishing causality, see Sanford Labovitz and Robert Hagedorn, *Introduction to Social Research* (New York: McGraw-Hill, 1971), pp. 3–12.

18. Darrell Huff, *How to Lie with Statistics* (New York: Norton, 1954).

19. This brief summary relies on the excellent discussions in Glazer, *The Research Adventure*, pp. 102–107 and Ted R. Vaughn, "Governmental Intervention in Social Research: Political and Ethical Dimensions in the Wichita Jury Recordings," in Gideon Sjoberg (ed.), *Ethics, Politics, and Social Research* (Cambridge, Mass.: Schenkman, 1967), pp. 50–77.

20. This brief summary relies on the excellent discussion in Glazer, *The Research Adventurer*, pp. 107–116 and on Laud Humphreys, "Tearoom Trade: Impersonal Sex in Public Places," Laud Humphreys, "The Sociologist as Voyeur," and Nicholas van Hoffman, "Sociological Snoopers," all in George Ritzer (ed.), *Social Realities* (Boston: Allyn and Bacon, Inc., 1974), pp. 22–48.

21. von Hoffman, "Sociological Snoopers," p. 47–48.

22. Everett K. Wilson, *Sociology: Roles, Rules, and Relationships* (Homewood, Ill.: Dorsey Press, 1971).

# Credits

(continued from p. iv)

**Chapter 2**
**p. 24,** The Bettmann Archive; **p. 26,** Culver Pictures; **p. 27,** The Bettmann Archive; **p. 28** (top), Environmental Protection Agency, EPA-Documerica, Charles O'Rear; **p. 28** (bottom), ACTION Peace Corps; **p. 30,** The Bettmann Archive; **p. 32,** © M. E. Warren, 1972, Photo Researchers; **p. 37,** Roger Malloch, Magnum; **p. 38,** UPI; **p. 39,** © Alice Kandell, Rapho/Photo Researchers.

**p. 46,** Featherkill Studios, Burnsville, Minn.

**Chapter 3**
**p. 50,** James H. Karales, © Peter Arnold; **p. 52** (right), Mary McCarthy, © Peter Arnold; **p. 55** Santi Visalli; **p. 60,** UPI; **p. 61,** Culver Pictures; **p. 64,** B. T. and R. A. Gardner; **p. 66,** © Betty Lane, Photo Researchers.

**Chapter 4**
**p. 78,** John Rees, Black Star; **p. 81,** TASS from SOVFOTO; **p. 84,** © Helen Hammid, Rapho/Photo Researchers; **p. 87,** Sybil Shelton, Monkmeyer Press Photo Service; **p. 90,** H. F. Harlow, University of Wisconsin Primate Library; **p. 91,** Vivienne, Photo Researchers; **p. 92,** © Erika Stone 1979; **p. 94,** © Susanne Anderson, Photo Researchers; **p. 96,** Magnum Photo Library; **p. 98,** © Sepp Seitz, Magnum.

**Chapter 5**
**p. 105,** Marion Bernstein, Editorial Photocolor Archives; **p. 107,** Andrew Sacks, Editorial Photocolor Archives; **p. 108,** UPI; **p. 109,** © Jan Lukas, Rapho/Photo Researchers; **p. 111,** Elliott Erwitt, Magnum; **p. 115,** © Jan Lukas, Photo Researchers; **p. 116,** James Carroll, Editorial Photocolor Archives.

**Chapter 6**
**p. 124,** © Jan Lukas, Photo Researchers; **p. 127,** © Ray Ellis, Photo Researchers; **p. 128,** UPI; **p. 130,** © Paul Sequeira, Rapho/Photo Researchers; **p. 131,** © Robert A. Isaacs, 1975, Photo Researchers; **p. 134** (left), United Nations; **p. 134** (right), Andrew Sacks, Editorial Photocolor Archives; **p. 136** (top), Stephen Rapley; **p. 136** (bottom) Esther Silber; **p. 139,** © Jan Lukas, Rapho/Photo Researchers; **p. 141,** ACTION VISTA; **p. 142,** UPI; **p. 144** (left), The Bettmann Archive; **p. 144** (right), Cary Wolinsky, Stock, Boston; **p. 145** (top) The Bettmann Archive; **p. 145** (bottom), Hiroyuki Matsumoto, Black Star; **p. 150,** Jo-Anne Naples. **p. 154,** © Rhoda Galyn.

**Chapter 7**
**p. 158,** The New York Times; **p. 160** (left), J. Issac/United Nations; **p. 160** (right), UPI; **p. 164,** The Bettmann Archive; **p. 165,** The Bettman Archive; Table 7.2, **p. 166,** from Theodore Caplow, *The Sociology of Work,* University of Minnesota Press: Minniapolis, Copyright 1954. Reprinted by permission. Originally from Monsanto Chemical Company; **p. 170,** Burt Glinn, Magnum; **p. 172,** Michael Abramson, Black Star, **p. 175,** © Charles Gatewood; **p. 178,** Andrew Sacks, Editorial Photocolor Archives; **p. 183,** UPI; Table 7.3, **p. 170,** based on data taken from U.S. Bureau of the Census, Table No. 663, "Median Annual Earnings of Workers, by Sex and Occupation: 1975 and 1976," *Statistical Abstract of the United States: 1977* (98th ed.). (Washington, D.C., 1977), p. 411; Figure 7.3, **p. 171,** based on data taken from U.S. Bureau of the Census, Table No. 730, "Median Money Income of Year-Round Full-Time Workers with Income by Age, Sex and, Educational Attainment: 1965 to 1976," *Statistical Abstract of the United States: 1977* (98th ed.) (Washington, D.C., 1977), p. 452; Table 7.4, **p. 171,** based on data taken from U.S. Bureau of the Census, Table No. 224, "Years of School Completed by Major Occupation Group of Employed Persons, by Sex and Race: 1959 to 1976," *Statistical Abstract of the United States: 1977* (98th ed.) (Washington, D.C., 1977), p. 140. Table 7.5, **p. 173,** based on data taken from U.S. Bureau of the Census, Table 83, "Children Ever Born to Women 35 to 44 Years Old, by Marital Status and Selected Characteristics: 1950 to 1976, "*Statistical Abstract of the United States: 1977* (98th ed.) (Washington, D.C., 1977), p. 59; Figure 7.5, **p. 174,** adapted from U.S. Department of Commerce. Office of Federal Statistics Policy and Standards. Bureau of the Census. *Social Indicators: 1976* (Washington, D.C., 1977), p. 493; Figure 7.6, **p. 177,** from U.S. Department of Labor, Bureau of Labor Statistics, *Monthly Labor Review* (Washington, D.C.,

October 1977), p. 7; Figure 7.7, **p. 178,** from the Women's Bureau, Employment Standards Administration, from April 1973 data published by the U.S. Department of Labor, Bureau of Labor Statistics; Figure 7.9, **p. 182,** from U.S. Department of Commerce, *Social Indicators: 1976.* (Washington, D.C., 1977), p. 270; Table 7.6, **p. 182,** adapted from William H. Sewell and Vimel P. Shah, "Socioeconomic Status, Intelligence, and the Attainment of Higher Education," *Sociology of Education* 40 (1967), p. 15; Figure 7.9, **p. 182,** from U.S. Department of Commerce, *Social Indicators: 1976* (Washington, D.C.), p. 427; Table 7.7, **p. 185,** adapted from U.S. Bureau of the Census, Table No. 713, "Money Income of Families—Percent of Aggregate Income Received by Each Fifth and Highest 5 Percent: 1950 to 1976," *Statistical Abstract of the United States: 1977* (98th ed.) (Washington, D.C., 1977), p. 443; Figure 7.10, **p. 186,** from U.S. Department of Commerce, *Social Indicators: 1976* (Washington, D.C., 1977), p. 427.

**Chapter 8**
**p. 193,** Penny Weaver, Poverty Law Report, Southern Poverty Law Center; **p. 195,** The Bettmann Archive; **p. 197,** UPI; **p. 201,** UPI; **p. 203;** UPI; **p. 206,** Henri Cartier-Bresson, Magnum; **p. 207,** The New York Public Library Picture Collection; **p. 208,** UPI; Table 8.2, **p. 209,** U.S. Bureau of the Census, *Statistical Abstracts* (Washington, D.C., 1977), p. 407; **p. 210,** The Bettmann Archive; **p. 212,** UPI; **p. 213,** © Rafael Marcia, Photo Researchers; **p. 215,** New York Public Library Picture Collection; Table 8.3, **p. 216,** and Table 8.4, **p. 217,** adapted from Andrew M. Greeley, *Ethnicity in the United States* (New York: John Wiley and Sons, 1974). Reprinted by permission of John Wiley and Sons; **p. 219,** New York Convention and Visitor's Bureau.

**Chapter 9**
**p. 222,** Erich Hartmann, Magnum; **p. 224** (top), Alain Keler, Editorial Photocolor Archives; Figure 9.1, **p. 225,** from U.S. Office of Management and Budget Statistical Policy Division, *Standard Metropolitan Statistical Areas, 1975* (rev. ed.) (Washington, D.C., 1975); **p. 228,** Jericho Excavation Fund; **p. 229,** Cie. des Arts Photomécaniques, Paris; Figure 9.2, **p. 231,** from *Annals,* 242 (Nov. 1945), pp. 7-17; **p. 232,** Tony Linck; Table 9.1, **p. 233,** U.S. Bureau of the Census, as reported in Burks (1978); Table 9.2, **p. 234,** U.S. Bureau of the Census (1978c), Tables J, K, 6, and 7; **p. 235** (top) Grete Mannheim, Photo Researchers; Table 9.3, **p. 236,** adapted from Curtis (1971), Table 3; Table 9.4, **p. 236,** adapted from U.S. Bureau of the Census (1978), Table M; Table 9.5, **p. 238,** from U.S. Bureau of the Census (1978), Table O; **p. 239,** Wide World; Table 9.6, **p. 240,** adapted from U.S. Bureau of the Census (1978a), Table A-4; **p. 241,** Editorial Photocolor Archives; Table 9.8, **p. 242,** adapted from U.S. Bureau of the Census (1978c), Table 20; **p. 244,** © Rhoda Galyn; **p. 246,** Jan Lukas, Editorial Photocolor Archives; Table 9.9, **p. 247,** adapted from U.S. Bureau of the Census (1978a), Table A-1; **p. 248,** © Rhoda Galyn; **p. 249,** Daniel S. Brody, Editorial Photocolor Archives; Figure 9.3, **p. 250,** after "Living Space: Troubled Cities Need More Green Space," *National Wildlife,* October/November 1971. Copyright 1971 by the National Wildlife Federation. Reprinted by permission.

**Chapter 10**
Figure, **p. 256,** computed from various sources; Figure 10.1, **p. 259,** National Research Council, Panel on Decennial Census Plans, *Counting the People in 1980: An Appraisal of Census Plans* (Washington, D.C.: National Academy of Sciences, 1978), p. 143; Table 10.1, **p. 258,** from Donald J. Bogue, *Principles of Demography* (New York: Wiley, 1969), p. 102. Reprinted by permission; **p. 262,** UPI; Figure 10.2, **p. 264,** reprinted by permission from Ralph Thomlinson, *Population Dynamics* (New York: Random House, 1965), **p. 266,** UPI; Table 10.3, **p. 266,** data prior to 1978 from United Nations, *The Determinants and Consequences of Population Trends: New Summary of Findings on Interaction of Demographic, Economic and Social Factors,* vol. 1, Population Studies No. 50 (New York: United Nations, 1973), p. 10, Table II-2; 1978 data from Wilson Prichett, III, *1978 World Population Estimates* (Washington, D.C.: The Environmental Fund, 1978); **p. 268,** U.S. Environmental Pro-

tection Agency; Table 10-4, **p. 268,** calculated from United Nations, *Demographic Yearbook, 1976* (New York: United Nations, 1976), pp. 116–117, Table 2; Table 10.5, **p. 269,** compiled from United Nations, *Demographic Yearbook, 1970* (New York: United Nations, 1970), p. 105, Table 1. Also from Wilson Prichett, III, *1978 World Population Estimates* (Washington, D.C.: The Environmental Fund, 1978) and United Nations Secretariat, Population Division of the Department of Economic and Social Affairs, *Selected World Demographic Indicators by Region and Country or Area, 1970–1975.* (Based on medium variant projections.); Table 10.6, **p. 270,** unpublished data complied by the Population Division, Department of Economic and Social Affairs, United Nations, January 1979; Table 10.7, **p. 270,** sources: figures for 1920 taken from United Nations, *Growth of the World's Urban and Rural Population, 1920–2000*, Population Studies No. 44 (New York: United Nations, 1969). Figures for later years compiled from United Nations Secretariat, "Demographic Trends in the World in its Major Regions, 1950–1970," background paper for World Population Conference, 16 April 1974, E/CONF. 60/CBP/14; Population Division, Department of Economic and Social Affairs of the United Nations Secretariat, "Trends and Prospects in the Populations of Urban Agglomerations, 1950–2000, as Assessed in 1973–1975," 21 November 1975, ESA/P/WP.58; and United Nations, Department of Economic and Social Affairs Statistical Office (New York: United Nations, 1976), pp. 39–40, Table 3; Figure 10.4, **p. 271,** from Haupt, Arthu, and Thomas T. Kane, *Population Handbook* (Washington, D.C.: Population Reference Bureau, 1976), p. 14; Table 10.8, **p. 274,** source: United Nations Secretariat, Population Division of the Department of Economic and Social Affairs, *Selected World Demographic Indicators by Region and Country or Area, 1970–1975* (Based on medium variant projections); Table 10.9, **p. 275,** calculated from United Nations, *Demographic Yearbook, 1976* (New York: United Nations, 1976), pp. 116–117, Table 2; **p. 277,** Sepp Seitz, Magnum, **p. 279,** U.S. Agency for International Development; **p. 280,** UPI; **p. 281,** U.S. Environmental Protection Agency; **p. 282,** Eric Kroll; **p. 283,** Editorial Photocolor Archives; **p. 284,** United Nations, **p. 286,** Zero Population Growth.

**p. 292,** Charles Gatewood

### Chapter 11

**p. 292,** Raimondo Borea, Editorial Photocolor Archives; **p. 294,** Museum of the American Indian. Heye Foundation; **p.296,** © Erika Stone 1978; Figure 11.1, **p. 297,** after p. 151 of *The Study of Society,* 2d ed. Copyright © 1977 The Dushkin Publishing Group, Sluice Dock, Guilford, Ct. 06437; Figure 11.3, **p. 299,** U.S. Department of Commerce, *Social Indicators: 1976* (Washington, D.C., 1977), p. 46; Figure 11.4, **p. 300,** *Social Indicators: 1976* (Washington, D.C., 1977), p. 46; **p. 302,** (top) The Bettmann Archive; **p. 302** (bottom), Bill Owens, Magnum; Figure 11.5, **p. 303,** *Social Indicators: 1976* (Washington, D.C., 1977), p. 61; Table 11.1, **p. 304,** *Statistical Abstract of the United States: 1978* (Washington, D.C., 1978), p. 69; Figure 11.6, **p. 304,** from Norman W. Bell and Ezra F. Vogel, *A Modern Introduction to the Family* (New York: The Free Press, rev. ed., 1968), p. 10. Reprinted by permission; **p. 305,** UPI; **p. 307,** UPI, **p. 309,** © Georg Gerster, Rapho/Photo Researchers; Table 11.2, **p. 309,** Thomas J. Espenshade, "The Value and Cost of Children," *Population Bulletin,* 32 (1) (Washington, D.C.: Population Reference Bureau, 1977), p. 24; Table 11.3, **p. 309,** Espenshade (see Table 11.2), **p. 25;** Figure **p. 310,** Christy Park from Monkmeyer Press Photo Service; **p. 313** (left) Christa Armstrong, © 1976, Photo Researchers; **p. 313** (right) Michael Abramson, Black Star; Figure 11.7, **p. 315,** *Social Indicators: 1976* (Washington, D.C., 1977); **p. 316,** Linda Rogers, Editorial Photocolor Archives; **p. 317,** Ann Chwatsky, Editorial Photocolor Archives; **p. 319,** UPI; Figure 11.8, **p. 320,** Paul C. Glick and Arthur J. Norton, "Marrying, Divorcing, and Living Together in the U.S. Today," *Population Bulletin* 32 (5) Washington, D.C.: Population Reference Bureau, Inc., 1977), p. 5; Figure 11.9, **p. 320,** *Social Indicators: 1976* (Washington, D.C., 1977), p. 58; Figure 11.10, **p. 320,** *Social Indicators: 1976* (Washington, D.C., 1977), p. 57; Figure 11.11, **p. 321,** *Social Indicators: 1976* (Washington, D.C., 1977), p. 58; Table 11.4, **p. 321,** sources: U.S. Bureau of the Census, *Census of Population,* 1960, vol. 11, 4B, *Persons by Family Characteristcs,* Table 11, and unpublished *Current Population Survey Data, 1977.* Table in Glick and Norton, (see Figure 11.8 above), p. 33; Table 11.5, **p. 322,** source, unpublished *Current Population Survey* data, 1977. Table in Glick and Norton (see Figure 11.8 above), p. 33; Table 11.6, **p. 323,** sources: Live births: U.S. National Center for Health Statistics. *Monthly Vital Statistics Report Advance Report. Final Natality Statistics. 1975.* Vol 25, No. 10 Supplement. Tables 1 and 12 *and 1974.* Vol 24, No. 11 Supplement 2. Table 11, and *Vital Statistics of the United States, 1973.* Vol 1. *Natality.* Tables 1-1 and 1-29. Legal abortions Ellen

Sullivan, Christopher Tietze and Joy G. Dryloos. "Legal Abortion in the United States 1975-1976." *Family Planning Perspectives.* Vol 9. No. 3 (May/June 1977) pp. 116-129, especially p. 121. Illegal abortions: Estimated by method described by Willard Cates. Jr., and Roger W. Rochat. "Illegal Abortions in the United States 1972-1974." *Family Planning Perspectives.* Vol. 8. No. 2 (March/April 1976) pp. 86-92, especially p. 92. Spontaneous abortions and stillbirths: on advice of Christopher Tietze, assumed to be 30 percent as numerous as live births plus 15 percent as numerous as induced abortions. Table in Glick and Norton (see Figure 11.8 above), p. 24.

### Chapter 12

**p. 331,** Leonard Freed, Magnum; **p. 332,** Dan O'Neil, Editorial Photocolor Archives; **p. 333,** from Layfayette (Indiana) Journal and Courier, March 6, 1975. Reprinted by permission; **p. 335,** Daniel S. Brody, Editorial Photocolor Archives; Table 12.1, **p. 338,** U.S. Department of the Army, Office of the Surgeon General, *Summary of Registrant Examinations for Induction;* Figure 12.4, **p. 339,** Digest of Educational Statistics, 1977–1978, Figure 3, p. 22; **p. 340,** Tom Shetterly, Editorial Photocolor Archives; Table 12.2, **p. 341,** U.S. Department of Health, Education and Welfare. National Center for Education Statistics, unpublished data derived from *Education Directory: Colleges and Universities, 1976–1977;* Table 12.3, **p. 342,** Cooperative Institutional Research Program. *The American Freshman: National Norms for Fall 1976;* **p. 343,** Martha Cooper; Figure 12.5, **p. 344,** *Digest of Educational Statistics, 1977–1978, pp. 102–103;* **p. 346,** © 1976 Ed. Lettau, Photo Researchers; Figure 12.6, **p. 345,** *Digest of Higher Educational Statistics, 1977–1978,* p. 107; Figure 12.7, **p. 346,** Sarane Boocock, *An Introduction to the Sociology of Learning,* (Boston: Houghton Mifflin Company, 1972), p. 213. By permission; **p. 347,** Wide World; Figure 12.4, **p. 350,** from Daniel W. Rossides, *The American Class System: An Introduction to Social Stratification* (Boston: Houghton Mifflin Co., 1976), p. 211; Table 12.5, **p. 350,** adapted from K. P. Cross, *Beyond the Open Door: New Students to Higher Education* (San Francisco: Jossey-Bass, Inc., 1971), p. 7; Table 12.6, **p. 351,** James J. Coleman et al., *Equality of Educational Opportunity* (Washington, D.C., 1960), p. 20; **p. 352** Bruce Anspach/EPA Newsphotos; Figure 12.9, **p. 353,** Walter Guzzardi, Jr., "The Uncertain Passage from College to Job," *Fortune* (January 1976) p. 129, by permission; Table 12.7, **p. 354,** U.S. Department of Commerce, Bureau of Census, Current Population Reports, Series P–60, No. 105, March 1976, Table 173; **p. 356,** UPI.

### Chapter 13

Table 13.1, **p. 363,** *1977 Encyclopedia Britannica Book of the Year* (Chicago: Encyclopedia Britannica, 1978); **p. 365,** Ian Berry, Magnum; **p. 367.** Karega kofi Moyo **p. 369,** UPI; Table 13.2, **p. 370,** N. J. Demerath, III, *Social Class in American Protestantism* (Chicago: Rand McNally, 1965), p. 2. By permission; **p. 372** (left), Editorial Photocolor Archives; **p. 372** (right), SCALA/New York/France, Editorial Photocolor Archives; **p. 373,** The Bettmann Archive; **p. 374,** Martin Adler Levick, Black Star; **p. 375,** Jo-Anne Naples; **p. 371,** Richard Stromberg, Media House, Chicago; **p. 380** (left), Editorial Photocolor Archives; **p. 380** (right: top and bottom) Michael Weisbrot and Family; **p. 381,** Table 13.3, Constant Jacquet, Jr., *Yearbook of American and Canadian Churches,* (Nashville, Tenn.: Abingdon Press, 1978). Figure 13.1, **p. 382,** from Gallup Poll, *New York Times,* December 22, 1968. Reprinted by permission of The Gallup Poll (The American Institute of Public Opinion) © 1968 by The New York Times Company. Reprinted by permission; Table 13.4, **p. 382,** George H. Gallup, *The Gallup Poll,* vol. 3, 1959–1971 (New York: Random House, 1972), p. 2174. Reprinted by permission; Figure 13.2, **p. 383,** *Social Indicators: 1976* (Washington, D.C., 1977), p. 544; **p. 383** (bottom), Bruce Davidson, Magnum; Figure 13.3, **p. 385,** *Social Indicators: 1976* (Washington, D.C., 1977), p. 543; Figure 13.4, **p. 386,** *Social Indicators: 1976* (Washington, D.C., 1977), p. 537; Figure 13.5, **p. 387,** *Social Indicators: 1976* (Washington, D.C., 1977), p. 538; **p. 388,** Robert Burroughs, Black Star.

### Chapter 14

**p. 394,** UPI; p. 396 (left), The Bettmann Archives; **p. 396** (right), UPI; **p. 396** (bottom), UPI; **p. 400,** UPI; **p. 403,** The Bettmann Archives; **p. 406** (left), The Bettmann Archives; **p. 406** (right), UPI; **p. 406** (bottom), UPI; **p. 408,** The Bettmann Archives; Table 14.1, **p. 409,** adapted from Sidney Verba and Norman Nie, *Participation in America: Political Democracy and Social Equality* (New York: Harper & Row, 1972); **p. 409,** © Alex Webb, Magnum; Figure 14.1, **p. 410,** adapted from Lester Milbrath, *Political Participation* (Chicago: Rand McNally, 1965); **p. 412,** UPI; **p. 413,** Peter Simon, Stock, Boston; **p. 417** (left), Wide World; **p. 417** (right), UPI; **p. 418,** UPI.

**Chapter 15**
**p. 426** The Bettmann Archive; **p. 427,** The Bettmann Archive; Figure 16-1, **p. 428,** data for 1950 and 1960 from U.S. Bureau of the Census, Census of Population; for 1965 from U.S. Bureau of Census, *Statistical Abstract of the United States, 1966* (Washington, D.C.: U.S. Government Printing Office, 1966), Tables 307 and 314; for 1970 from U.S. Department of Labor, *Yearbook of Labor Statistics* (Washington, D.C., 1970), p. 171. Appeared in Eshref Shevky and Marilyn Williams, *The Social Areas of Los Angeles* (Los Angeles and Berkeley: University of California Press, 1949), p. 4. Reprinted by permission. Also in Leonard Broom and Philip Seiznick, *Sociology,* 5th ed. (New York: Harper & Row, 1973), p. 549. Reprinted by permission; Table 15-1, **p. 428,** from U.S. Bureau of the Census, *Historical Statistics of the United States: Colonial Times to 1957* (Washington, D.C., 1961); U.S. Bureau of the Census, *Statistical Abstract of the United States, 1950* (Washington, D.C., 1950), p. 107; U.S. Bureau of the Census, *Current Population Reports,* Series P-25 No. 365, May 5, 1967, and Series P-20, No. 222, June 28, 1971. The 1975 data were obtained from the *Statistical Abstracts of the U.S., 1977* (Washington, D.C., 1977), p. 128, Table No. 200; Figure 15-2, **p. 429,** based on Seymour M. Lipset, "Political Sociology," in *Sociology,* ed. N. J. Smelser (New York: Wiley, 1973), p. 410. Reprinted by permission; **p. 430,** reproduced from the collection of the Library of Congress. **p. 431,** Susanne Szasz; **p. 433,** Charles Moore, Black Star; Table 15-2, **p. 435,** Census Bureau, *Historical Statistics of the United States, Colonial Times to 1957,* p. 74 (for data before 1950); Census Bureau, 1976, p. 372. Data beginning 1950 is not totally comparable with previous years due to a reclassification of occupations. Data for 1977 from *Statistical Abstracts of the U.S.* (Washington, D.C., 1977), No. 660; Table 15.3, **p. 436,** U.S. Bureau of the Census, *Census of Manufacturers,* vol. 1, (Washington, D.C., 1971) pp. SR2–6 to SR2–46; Table 15.4, **p. 438,** *The World Almanac, 1976,* pp. 84 and 681–682; and *Moody's Handbook of Common Stocks,* Summer, 1976; **p. 438,** Elliott Erwitt, Magnum; Table 15-5, **p. 439,** *Statistical Abstracts of the U.S., 1977,* No. 682; Tables 15.6, **p. 441,** from the United Nations, with updating from *Economics* by Paul A. Samuelson. Copyright © 1976 by McGraw-Hill, Inc. Used with permission of McGraw-Hill Book Company; **p. 442,** The Bettmann Archive; Table 15.7, **p. 442,** from *The Common Cause Report from Washington 1* (Spring 1975), pp. 7, 8. Reprinted by permission; Table 5.8, **p. 442,** from *The Common Cause Report from Washinton 7* (Spring 1976), pp. 7, 8. Reprinted by permission; **p. 446,** Andrew Souks, *Editorial Photocolor Archives;* Table 15.9, **p. 447,** from H. L. Wilensky, "Work as a Social Problem," in *Social Problems: A Modern Approach,* ed. Howard S. Becker (New York: Wiley, 1966), p. 134. Reprinted by permission. Data from H. L. Wilensky, "The Uneven Distribution of Leisure," *Social Problems 9* (Summer 1961), pp. 32–56. Reprinted by permission. Table 15.10, **p. 449,** reprinted by permission from Daniel Bell, *The Coming of Post-industrial Society: A Venture in Social Forecast-ing* (New York: Basic Books, 1973); p. 359; **p. 449,** by Henri Dauman, Time-Life Picture Agency, Time, Inc.

**p. 454,** Jane Hamilton-Merritt

**Chapter 16**
**p. 459** (bottom), Richard Stromberg, Media House, Chicago; **p. 461** (top), Karega Kofi Moyo; **p. 461** (bottom), courtesy of NORML, the National Organization for the Reform of Marijuana Laws, 237 M Street NW, Washington, D.C. 20037; **p. 463,** Daniel S. Brody, Editorial Photocolor Archive; **p. 463,** Danny Lyon, © 1970 Magnum; **p. 465,** Leonard Freed, Magnum; **p. 466,** Culver Pictures; Table 16.3, **p. 470,** U.S. Department of Justice, FBI Uniform Crime Reports (Washington, 1978). Table 16.4, **p. 471,** *Criminal Victimization in the U.S., 1976,* No. SD-NCS-N-7, National Criminal Justice Reference Service, p. 73; **p. 472,** UPI, **p. 477,** © Rhoda Galyn; **p. 479,** UPI.

**Chapter 17**
**p. 486,** UPI; **p. 487,** Wide World; **p. 489,** UPI; **p. 490,** UPI; **p. 492,** UPI; **p. 493,** Wide World; **p. 495,** UPI; **p. 496,** UPI; **p. 499,** © 1970, Eliot Landy, Magnum; **p. 500,** UPI; **p. 501,** UPI; **p. 504,** UPI.

**Chapter 18**
**p. 508,** from Sears Catalogue, 1902; **p. 511** (top), The Coca-Cola Company; **p. 508** (bottom), McDonald's International Division—McDonald's, Japan; **p. 512,** Wide World; **p. 513,** Culver Pictures; **p. 514,** Newspaper Enterprise Association; Figure 18.1, **p. 515,** based on data in U.S. Bureau of the Census, Population Characteristics, Series P-20, No. 233 (Washington, D.C., 1972); **p. 516** (Box), article appearing in New York Times, June 30, 1979. © 1979 by The New York Times Company. Reprinted by permission. **p. 518,** UPI; **p. 519,** U.S. Department of Agriculture; **p. 520,** based on data from the U.S. Bureau of the Census, prepared by the New York Times Service, San Francisco Chronicle, March 3, 1973, p. 4. Reprinted by permission. **p. 521,** Jim Pickerell, courtesy of ACTION Peace Corps; **p. 523** (top), reproduced from the collection of the Library of Congress; **p. 523** (bottom), Donald Dietz, Stock, Boston; **p. 524,** courtesy of U. S. Army; **p. 528,** British Airways; **p. 531,** U.S. Environmental Protection Agency, EPA Documerica, Gene Daniels; **p. 532,** UPI.

**Chapter 19**
**p. 540,** UPI; **p. 542,** Charles Gatewood, Magnum; **p. 545,** UPI; **p. 548,** T. Schwartz/Margaret Mead and the American Museums of Natural History; Figure 19.2, **p. 549,** General Social Survey, 1973. National Opinion Research Center, University of Chicago. From Roper Organization, Roper Study 524, October 1971; Figure 19.3, **p. 549,** courtesy of Congressman Tim Hall; Figure 19.4, **p. 550,** Bonnie Bullough, "Poverty, Ethnic Identity, and Preventive Health Care," *Journal of Health and Social Behavior* 13 (December 1972), 353; **p. 552,** UPI; **p. 555,** © 1977 Yan Lukas, Photo Researchers.

# Name Index

# Subject Index